"TO GIVE THE NEWS IMPARTIALLY,
WITHOVT FEAR OR FAVOR,
REGARDLESS OF ANY PARTY,
SECT OR INTEREST INVOLVED"

THE CREDO OF THE NEW YORK TIMES

*Taken from the salutatory of Adolph S. Ochs, publisher from 1896 to 1935. The bust,
which stands in the lobby of the Times building, is the work of Vincenzo Miserendino.*

THE STORY OF

The New York Times

1851-1951

BY

MEYER BERGER

SIMON AND SCHUSTER

NEW YORK

First Printing

PN
4899
N42
T53

MANUFACTURED IN THE UNITED STATES OF AMERICA
ILLUSTRATIONS BY LIVERMORE AND KNIGHT CO., PROVIDENCE, R.I.
TEXT AND BINDING BY H. WOLFF BOOK MFG. CO., NEW YORK, N.Y.

Foreword

As a man grows older he is less and less inclined to celebrate the anniversary of his birth. He knows that each year passed means one less to be lived in the span that has been allotted to him. But an institution records its advancing years with all the pride of a child counting candles on a birthday cake, and when it reaches its hundredth year as we do today, it seems only natural that it should regard itself as "the grandest Tiger in the Jungle."

Years have not sapped our vigor nor has their passage limited our future. Quite the contrary. We have gathered strength and momentum and we offer this centennial history as an evidence of why we contemplate the future with assurance as to our ability to serve our city and our nation.

Adolph S. Ochs, whose genius recreated this property, died in 1935. Since then, I have served as chairman of its Board of Directors, President of the Company and Publisher of The New York Times. That represents, in time, one-sixth of its one hundred years. In effect, it represents far more, however—for during that period The Times ceased to be solely a newspaper and took on the atmosphere of an institution.

I fell heir to the posts just referred to by virtue of the fact that during the eighteen years prior to Mr. Ochs' death I had won his confidence and I was in a position to win it because in 1917 I had married his only child. When Mr. Ochs died, he was both a loved and a legendary figure. His word was law. He exercised no arbitrary power but he was very much of a paternalist in his approach

v

to those who labored to make the great newspaper that he pub-
lished.

As I have said, I fell heir to the posts that Mr. Ochs had filled.
I could not aspire to the position that he occupied in the heart and
mind of his fellow workers. It became my task therefore to build
a machine, to make an institution, and to that end I have labored.
We present this volume not only as a record of the past, but also
as evidence that the transition from paternalistic management to
team play has been successful.

In this history, we review the life of our community for one
hundred fateful years. In doing so, we must, of course, talk about
the present management as well as that of the past. But can the
present be called history? And if not, how far must one go back
to make such a claim valid? Can history be written by one like
Meyer Berger, whose every fiber is a part of The New York Times?
(Meyer Berger, by the way, who has modestly mentioned himself
only once in this account but who should rightfully have a promi-
nent place in its latter pages.) I had thought that if an episode were
closed, it could be treated historically and that therefore episodes
might determine the historical approach. When a war was in prog-
ress it was news; when it ended it was history. But what war has
ended?

The death of Mr. Ochs might be said to have made a definite
break in The Times' story, so that the historical label might fittingly
be applied to all that went before; and yet, in this volume, we are
striving to prove that April 8, 1935, was but of sentimental im-
portance to this institution and that, on that day, we merely closed
our ranks with sadness and with reverence, and, with certain
changes to which I have referred, continued the life and the
growth that he had inspired.

One thing is certain—we can talk about The Times under the
management of Mr. Ochs in different terms from those we use to
speak about ourselves in these later years and if, at that point in
the narrative, the reader notices some change in pace, he has this
explanatory word to account for it.

We present our past with pride, our present with satisfaction.
We look to the future with courage and with confidence.

September 18, 1951   ARTHUR HAYS SULZBERGER

Table of Contents

List of Illustrations

xiii

THE STORY OF
The New York Times

CHAPTER

1

IN EACH FRESH DAWN in 1951 heavily laden motor trucks fan out from The New York Times plant west of Times Square. Their cargoes of throbbing current history are marked for the farthest corners of the earth, as for the nearest corner newsstand. They soar from metropolitan airfields to cross oceans and wide-spreading continents, and they move by train and by other common carriers to more than 12,000 towns in the United States. Kings and presidents will scan them, rich and poor will discover in their pages the freshest track made by mankind on the road to eternity.

Readers in most cases will know little about the great institution that gathers, winnows and redistributes the news from the plant west of the Square, but it is an amazing creation. It spends more than $36,000,000 a year for payroll and paper alone, and sends its news-gatherers to seek out even the most remote places on the globe to observe man's endless endeavor. Every day of the year its reporters and the news agencies to which it subscribes pour in more than 1,000,000 words to be processed for entry into mankind's daybook—tomorrow's New York Times. It prints approximately 145,000 words of news in average daily editions, exclusive of several pages of financial and business tables. Eight to ten times that volume on Sunday. No other daily publication in mid-Twentieth Century keeps the mortal record so completely.

But the institution did not spring full-fruited into its current pro-

1

portions. It was 100 years a-forming, and the original seed was small, sown in another century in a grubby New York side street.

Late wayfarers stumbling through ill-paved Nassau Street between Ann and Beekman Streets in lower New York late in the night of Sept. 17, 1851, were a little astonished at the extraordinary activity in the unfinished office building at No. 113.

The structure had no glass in its windows, but from street to roof, whiskered and heavily mustached men were bent over copy paper or printers' forms. They worked by candlelight and the scene had a Dantesque cast.

Most of the candles were stuck on nails jutting from pine blocks, leftovers from recent building carpentry. The blocks rested on books or small boxes set a little higher than the copy paper on which reporters scribbled with pencil, or with pen and ink. The printers had fastened their candles on the type cases. Under the writing desks and around the cases fresh sawdust and carpenters' litter sent up heady pine aroma.

In this weirdly lighted setting the first issue of The New-York Daily Times was being born.

The city outside the unglassed windows was a vest-pocket edition of grubby nineteenth century London. It lay squat and ugly with most of its 500,000 island residents packed into the area between the Battery and Fourteenth Street. Hardly a building, except for an occasional church spire, was more than three or four stories high. It was muddy, ill-paved and ill-lighted.

Between Fourteenth and Forty-second Streets houses were widely spaced. Miniature farms still yielded family crops in parts of that area. North of Forty-second Street lay more or less open country and woods, where cows and swine strayed.

From City Hall cupola, watchmen had a clear view for miles in all directions. They sounded fire alarms by pounding a five-ton bell with a great hammer. Sailing vessels tacked tranquilly in the marginal rivers. Downtown side streets, and even lower Broadway, still had friendly shade trees.

When fire alarms sounded, volunteers with alcohol breaths ran their apparatus by hand down Broadway and raced for pump positions. They often went in for a bit of house-looting. The Bowery teemed with homicidal toughs, bloated drabs and whisky-soaked

slatterns. Hoodlums kept the lower city in terror. Walks after sundown in the ill-lighted streets were dangerous adventures.

The town was at political boil. Barnburners and Hunkers fought
to dominate the local Democratic Party. Foul holds of European
sailing vessels kept dumping fresh loads of bewildered greenhorns
onto the island, and competing ward-heelers scrambled unashamedly for their votes.

The nation was writhing with growing pains, New York worst of
all, on the September night that The Times was born.

Grimy printers' devils clumped on the wooden stairs from the
fifth-floor composing room, bumping one another on the way, and
burst onto the news floor bawling "Copy." Calls from the city desk
across the untidy news room, the clank of the new Hoe press,
warming in the basement, betrayed the general excitement.

Henry Jarvis Raymond, the wiry 31-year-old darkly whiskered
Times chief, bent over his own copy. His face, etched in candle
shadow, changed expression with each flare-up, each drop of the
light. This made weird setting for the start of a great newspaper,
but Raymond could wait no longer for the contractors. He had
promised all summer long that the 1-cent Times would come out
on Sept. 16, and the first issue was already late.

Raymond knew what he might expect from the 2-cent papers—
from James Gordon Bennett's raucous Herald and from Horace
Greeley's Tribune—if The Times did not come out the night of Sept.
17 bearing the next day's date. The name The Times had been ill-
starred in New York's early journalistic history, anyway. Seven
other publishers before Raymond had launched dailies with that
name. Most of these ventures had gasped only briefly before they
died.

The first New York Times, published by a David Longworth and
printed by Nicholas Van Riper, was put out in 1813. It died almost
a-borning. The only known copy is in the British Museum. There
was a New York Times and Weekly Register in 1822. The third
Times was edited in 1826 by Gold S. Silliman at 45 Pine Street and
was printed by Edward Bellamy. It ran four dull pages daily, chiefly
"marine intelligence," and reprints, mostly on the literary side,
clipped from London newspapers. It lasted less than a year.

Another New York Times panted along from May 12, 1834, to

October, 1837, with daily and semi-weekly editions. The publishers were William Holland and Edward Sanford. It was quite undistinguished, even for its day, when standards were low. Then The Times and Commercial Intelligencer was tried. It limped along from 1838 to 1841. Though Democratic, it supported Henry Clay, the Whig, for President. It was changed to The New-York Times and Evening Star, but still was no great shakes. William G. King published a Daily Times at 47 William Street from Jan. 5, 1846, to Feb. 16 of the same year. This was newsier than most of its predecessors, but King was a narrow man, violently anti-Catholic. When he set forth among his journalistic principles that his sheet would be "devoted to native American principles and the news of the day" he actually meant that he would campaign against the growing Irish population in the city—and did, with rabid vehemence.

The tempestuous New York publisher Mordecai Manasseh Noah, too, put out a Sunday Times in 1846, after King's venture had gone under. He did no better. Then, five years later, Raymond's Times was started.

It was tradition one hundred years ago for established newspapers to meet fresh rivals with hostility, as bullies greet new boys at school. In his twenty-first year Raymond had helped Greeley put out the first Tribune. Then in 1843 when he worked for Col. (later General) James Watson Webb's Courier and Enquirer he had written poisonously about crusty Horace Greeley. He had broken a few lances against Bennett's Herald for its brash news policies. He realized that now he could not look to Greeley, Bennett or Webb for kindly indulgence.

Not that the first Herald, or first Tribune, had been perfect. Raymond's initial copy of The Times, it turned out, was a masterpiece compared with theirs, but it was convenient for Bennett and for Greeley to forget the days of their journalistic swaddling-clothes. Bennett had launched his first Herald in a dark basement at 10 Wall Street in 1835. His only office equipment there had been two boards laid across two flour barrels. Myopic Greeley had put out the first Tribune on April 10, 1841, in a cramped, ill-lighted attic in a two-story tumble-down shack in the rear of 30 Ann Street. Raymond had worked with him there at $8 a week. Indeed, The Tribune's first editorial page had publicly acknowledged that it was prepared by Greeley, "assisted by Henry J. Raymond."

The Times of Sept. 18, 1851, despite all the rush and bustle, was late reaching the street. Eighteen printers led by Monroe F. Gale, composing room foreman, who had climbed the stairs early on the afternoon of Sept. 17, with high silk hats set at cocky angles, were red-eyed and thirsty when the last form was locked early next morning. Like the reporters and editors, they had worked by uncertain light. Occasional passers-by had watched them at their cases, heads bent low over the copy, setting the type by hand.

Night retreated from downtown Manhattan's low, soot-blackened roofs when Raymond and his chief editorial lieutenants, Louis J. Jennings and George Sheppard, and George Jones, The Times publisher, looked on their finished handiwork—four pages of six columns each. They found it good, though the new press, as had been anticipated, printed unevenly.

"The New-York Daily Times," said a slightly apologetic notice in the first issue, "is printed on one of Hoe's celebrated Lightning presses, built expressly for this establishment, and just put up in the basement of 113 Nassau Street. The Press is one of the finest ever built, but as it is perfectly new . . . its work is not as good as it will be after a while. The greater part of the imprint this morning was imperfectly printed—part being clear and more distinct than the rest. This is unavoidable from the operation of a new press, but a few days will effectually remedy it."

The first issue stood up well in comparison with the 2-cent sheets, though it was weak in a few departments. It reported a little too blithely that fire alarms had rung in from the Sixth District but that "our item gatherer failed to discover the first spark of a fire." Item gatherers for The Herald and The Tribune found the fires with Greeley's men gathering more detail than Bennett's. The fire was in James O'Donnell's iron foundry in an old frame shanty at 288 Stanton Street.

The lead city paragraph on the front page said: "The weather was the theme upon which we hinged an item for this morning's edition, but we have been forced to forgo the infliction of it upon the public by the proceedings of the Boston Jubilee, which our special correspondent has forwarded us. Never mind, the President cannot always be lionizing through the country, and as soon as he returns home, we shall endeavor to do this important subject full justice."

How Raymond's item gatherers managed to miss the foundry fire with literally the whole low-roofed town within range of vision through the open windows in Nassau Street, is hard to figure—but they got almost everything else that the older papers had turned up.

They reported a forest fire in remote Flatbush, a furor in Sixth Avenue over a couple of daring ladies' startling new bloomer outfits; a two-pound tomato grown in rural Hempstead, L.I. There was a cheerful piece about boats and carriages bringing New Yorkers back from the country. Though there was no weather story, as such, the vacation item told that "Summer is on the heel," and that a thirty-degree temperature drop had brought out beavers and furs.

A good part of The Times was fashioned out of items culled from European newspapers, and from journals all over the United States, chiefly from California, where the great gold rush was on. The telegraph was working, but rates were high and links were widely separated. The Atlantic cable had not been laid. Pony riders, ships, stage coaches and infant railroads still brought in the bulk of domestic news, days and weeks behind actual happenings.

On its third publication day, The Times continued to apologize to its readers for leaving out certain stories. "About two columns of New York and Brooklyn items," it confided editorially, "are driven out this morning by the speech of Senator Douglas at the State Fair (in Rochester) on account of the Boston Jubilee, and the news from California. They will appear in The Evening Times this afternoon."

The Evening Times was not much different from the morning edition except in a few columns of "late" news that was a day, a week, or a month, old. There was a separate Sunday paper, too, and a special edition for California, Oregon and the Sandwich Islands. The West Coast edition went out whenever a ship sailed. The Times for Europe, sold in London and Paris for 6 cents, ran from May 24, 1856, to Feb. 20, 1857.

Greeley's Tribune of Sept. 18 found plenty of room for its Boston Jubilee story—much more of it than Raymond's special correspondent sent—and for a weather piece, too. But Greeley was in a

Christian mood about Raymond's little paper. After he had studied the first issue he wrote in his Sept. 19 edition, under "City Items":

"The New-York Daily Times made its appearance yesterday in a sheet handsomely printed, considering the difficulties attendant upon the first working of an untried cylinder press. Its columns bear the marks of the ability belonging to the accomplished editor and his assistants. It is by far the best paper published in New York for *ONE* cent a copy, and cannot fail to attain wide circulation and correspondent influence."

Bennett, biding his time, ignored the newcomer.

Conservative townsfolk took to Raymond's paper. They liked the dignity with which it handled the news. Bennett's 2-cent Herald was a lively sheet—but it leaned more than a little to the sensational, and conservatives shunned it. It gave crime news and town scandal in extra measure and was quick to pick quarrels and to sneer at whatever Bennett happened, at the moment, to dislike— and he was a man of many aversions.

Greeley's paper was an excellent news sheet, but it alienated the upper and middle class market because it advocated radical social reforms. Greeley was forever thumping his editorial tub for some ism. He felt deeply for the common man, and in idealistic fervor backed Socialist movements. He had courage, but his white shield was always up, and contemporaries fattened their circulation by constantly tilting at him. Readers had to buy the sheets on both sides to enjoy these literary Donnybrooks to the full.

Raymond had promised a 1-cent newspaper that would give all the news free from the morbid and the scandalous; that would try to avoid the common fault of mid-Nineteenth Century editors scratching at one another with their pens in bitter personal feuds. The Times, he assured potential readers, would, "seek to allay, rather than excite, agitation . . . and substitute reason for prejudice, a cool and intelligent judgment for passion, in all public action, and in all discussion of public affairs."

This was journalistic heresy. Publishers and editors of the period, were, by tradition, likely to carry their editorial arguments into Broadway and to take whip or pistol to one another. Benjamin Day of The Sun, for example, got into an editorial feud with Bennett over circulation and wrote in his paper:

"Bennett, whose only chance of dying an upright man will be that of hanging perpendicularly upon a rope, falsely charges the proprietor of this paper with being an infidel, the natural effect of which calumny will be that every reader will believe him to be a good Christian."

A little later Colonel Webb of The Courier and Enquirer horse-whipped The Herald's publisher in Wall Street while bootblacks, cartmen and brokers looked on with open delight. Day reported for his readers with relish how the colonel had laid it into "the notorious vagabond, Bennett." "The Colonel met the brawling coward in Wall Street," The Sun said, "took him by the throat, and with a cowhide striped the human parody from head to foot."

Bennett, never one to pass up a news item, ran a little piece on it in his own sheet. "Horse-whipped Again," he captioned it cheerfully.

Yet two days later Day's Sun, with lively impartiality, was out for the colonel's hide. The colonel had charged that The Sun crew had waylaid his copy of President Andrew Jackson's message to Congress and had rewritten, and used it. When he got indignant about it, he was told in The Sun's columns, "He will find each of the three editors of The Sun always provided with a brace of 'mahogany stock' pistols, to accommodate him in any way he likes."

Even Raymond, for all his announcement that his newspaper would seek to allay rather than excite agitation, had turned a fair share of cultured invective against Horace Greeley in The Courier and Enquirer's dispute with The Tribune over Charles Fourier's socialistic design for living, which Greeley championed. This exchange had run through 1846-47 when Raymond worked for Colonel Webb, and Greeley's kind words for the first issue of The Times must have surprised Raymond.

There was reason to suspect that Greeley might not have been altogether sincere in his flattery in City Items. A few days before The Times hit the sidewalks, he had threatened to drop any Tribune carrier who dared to handle it. In a "Notice to Carriers," he had written: "A new daily paper is to be issued in a few days, and any carrier of The Tribune who interests himself in said paper will forfeit his rights of property in The Tribune."

Carriers took on The Times just the same. To make matters a little worse, some fifteen or sixteen other Tribune workers—three editors, a dozen printers and key men from The Tribune pressroom and composing room—deserted Greeley to work in the breezy new shop at 113 Nassau Street.

On Jan. 24, 1820, when New York was a cluster of old shacks on lower Manhattan, Henry Raymond was born on a lonely farm in Lima in Livingston County in western New York, then on the edge of a wilderness. Young Henry was something of a prodigy. He could read at 3. He was an elocutionist at 5. He devoured knowledge. He was a country teacher in Wheatland, in Genesee County, at 16, and at 17 turned out the stuffy, bombastic verse so admired in the early Nineteenth Century. "Hail, Bold Truth: Hail! Sacred Right, Whom Heaven gave birth ere dawned the light!" That sort of thing.

One stifling August day in 1839 he strode chestily to a platform at the University of Vermont's Junior Exhibition and delivered a resounding and lengthy oration he had written. Perspiring farmers stood open-mouthed at the dark young man's eloquence and adult earnestness. Even the baldish guest of honor, stiff in voluminous black frock coat, leaning on his cane, with his great beaver hat between his legs, was impressed by Henry Raymond's stentorian phrases. When the young orator, a-sweat with heat and fervor, bowed out, the beetle-browed visitor turned to a platform neighbor. He said, "That young man will make his mark." The visitor was Henry Clay.

A year later Raymond was in New York. He came as Horace Greeley had come, with only the clothes on his back. He asked Greeley for a job on The New Yorker, which the New Englander ran on a threadbare shoestring in dirty, crowded Ann Street. Greeley had no money for an assistant. He was barely able to eat and pay his board on the money he made out of The New Yorker and from job printing—mostly lottery tickets, incidentally—but he gave Raymond desk room.

In exchange for the desk room young Raymond added election returns, culled stuff from out-of-town newspapers, reviewed books and read proof. After three weeks, squeaky-voiced Horace realized his tenant's potential journalistic value. When Raymond was tempted by a teaching job in North Carolina at $8 a week, Greeley got nervous. That afternoon he asked Raymond to walk to the post office with him.

With characteristic New England caution he said, "What will the school job pay?"

Raymond said, "Four hundred a year." That sounded better than $8 a week. Greeley squinted across Printing House Square at the crowding drays and at ladies and gentlemen picking their way through muddy Broadway. He thought deeply. Finally he said, not too eagerly, "I'd give you that if you'd stay here."

Raymond's destiny was decided at that moment. He was on The New Yorker six months. He kept alive by writing for newspapers in Philadelphia, Bangor, Cincinnati and Buffalo, and taught Latin in an obscure girl's seminary, read law and wrote patent medicine ads for 50 cents a day. When The New Yorker died he helped put out the first Tribune.

When he ended his daytime chores in the gloomy attic in 30 Ann Street—an old, unpainted frame shack on a muddy, sunken-stoned street where pigs at odd times tried to root for tidbits—he snatched a sandwich, gulped hot coffee and hustled to the old Tabernacle Church on night assignments, mostly dull pseudo-scientific lectures. One night he trudged back from one of these sessions in a cold drizzling rain and sat in the draughty office. He wrote, in wet clothes, until almost daybreak. Next day he lay in a scrubby little room in his boarding house at Church and Vesey Street, delirious with fever.

There was an even chance, then, that The New-York Times might not be born, but after eight miserable weeks, even without medical aid, without decent food and without pay, Raymond somehow survived. Greeley had cut him from The Tribune payroll the morning he fell ill. The Vermonter had sorely missed him, but was so deeply tied up in his own multitudinous tasks that days had gone by before he could visit Raymond.

He wondered then when Raymond might be ready to get back to work. Wasted and still feverish, Raymond exploded. He told the startled Greeley, "I am never coming back, not for what you pay me." His salary, just before he took to his bed, had risen to $15 a week, but only because he was doing the work of three ordinary reporters. Now, he insisted with the firmness of utter desperation that he wanted $20 a week. Greeley was honestly shocked; he drew barely that much himself. He finally gave in, though; he had to.

This experience affected Raymond's policy when he became part-owner of The Times. "I made up my mind," he once told Jones, "to leave, at the first opportunity, the journal that had used me so cruelly, and I determined that no man who might ever work for me would have to suffer as I did during those hideous weeks." He lived up to that. No Times man's salary was ever held up when he became sick. That became Jones' policy, too, and remains Times policy to this day.

Raymond had become Greeley's strong right arm, and The Tribune was making ground against The Sun and The Herald. Much of The Tribune's popularity was due to Raymond's writing. His classic report of the sensational Colt murder cases added thousands of new Tribune readers.

In 1843, after he had been with Greeley three years, Raymond quit The Tribune for a job with Colonel Webb's Courier and Enquirer. Greeley hated to have him go, but Raymond, then 23, and sternly set in matters of principle, could not abide Greeley's weakness for social experiment.

Raymond had worked hard for The Tribune and had put over some notable beats. In that day the telegraph had not come into general use. There were no telephones. Even Presidential speeches were not sent out in advance. The richer newspapers—and this is where Bennett's enterprise outstripped competition—hired locomotives and private pony express to hurry stuff into the office, but this cost heavily. One day in 1843, before they parted, Greeley sent Raymond to cover an important afternoon speech by Daniel Webster in Boston. All the other newspapers sent their best men, too. They left Boston on the night boat for New York. At the restaurant and in the ship's bar, the other men missed Raymond. They wondered about it and got a little uneasy. Finally they found him in one of the ship's cabins, writing furiously. A printer stood beside him setting his words in type as fast as they came from the pen. When the boat reached the dock in New York at 5 A.M. the story was all set. The Tribune was on the street with it inside of an hour. The beat made journalistic history.

By 1850 Raymond was giving some thought to the chances a

new paper might have. The cumbersome blanket sheets were all but dead on their feet. Their circulation was going down the maws of The Herald, The Sun and The Tribune much as smaller monsters destroyed bogged mastodons. Yet The Herald offended the sensitive, The Sun was pretty much a backstairs sheet and Raymond himself had badly wounded The Tribune with his coldly logical attacks on Greeley's Socialist beliefs. He thought more and more of a newspaper that would, in a manner of speaking, circle these journals around right end and appeal chiefly to New York's intelligent conservatives.

The birth of The New-York Times was delayed when Raymond went to Albany in 1849 as Whig Assemblyman from the Ninth Ward. He was re-elected in 1850. In January, 1851, he was made Speaker of the House. General Webb (he rose in rank in 1849) had gone to Europe the year before for a long vacation. While he was away, Raymond dressed up and enlivened The Courier and Enquirer. But Webb never kept on peaceful terms very long with any man. He had senatorial ambitions, and tried to persuade Raymond to get Whig support for him. Raymond didn't like the idea. He left Webb's payroll in the spring of 1851.

It was during this vacation, while Raymond was in Europe, that he first put on paper the idea that had grown larger in his thinking. He wrote from London to his brother, Samuel B. Raymond, in June: "You will probably have seen that I am no longer in The Courier and Enquirer. Two gentlemen in Albany propose to start a new paper in New York early in September, and I shall probably edit it."

During his two terms at Albany Raymond had talked a lot about his idea and George Jones, a banker in Albany, who had once worked for Greeley, was interested. One day, during the Legislature's winter session in 1850, Raymond left the capital to meet his father, due from Lima at Greenbush station opposite Albany. He stopped at Jones' house, and the banker walked with him to the station. The Hudson was frozen solid that year. They crossed on the ice.

Jones said: "I hear Greeley's Tribune cleared over $60,000 last year." That was handsome profit 100 years ago. Raymond was certain the sheet he planned could do as well, or better.

Jones said: "If the Legislature should pass the bill to reduce the redemption rate on country money, I think I might quit banking and start that paper. If that bill goes through we stand to lose a good part of our business." The bill passed.

Jones had desk space at this time in Albany offices owned by Edward B. Wesley, another banker. Wesley knew nothing about newspapers, but the project caught his fancy and he got Jones to introduce him to Raymond. Oddly enough, Jones had first told him of Raymond's plan when he and Jones were crossing the frozen Hudson one morning to pick up the New York papers on the far side of the river.

After two talks with Raymond, Wesley became even more enthusiastic over the project than Jones had become. With Raymond's consent he rode down to New York to try to get some Wall Street friends interested. They were cold to the plan. So were the brothers Harper, then a new major force in the magazine field.

Undiscouraged, Wesley told Raymond to write up a prospectus, and assured him that the capital would come from one source or another. Raymond wrote the prospectus on his way to Europe for a vacation. It reached Wesley on July 3, 1851, and next day, when the hot sun beat down on the ruins of old Fort Putnam at West Point, he read it aloud there to Jones and to his friend Capt. Stephen R. Rowe, an army officer. They liked it.

Wesley had the prospectus printed in Albany. He figured at that time that he would merely raise the capital for The Times, but take no further active part. It developed, though, that Jones got sick in October, 1851, and Wesley came down from Albany to run the business end of the venture in his place. He was to be financial chief until 1856, when Jones took hold again.

Raymond's proposed new sheet was excitedly discussed in and around Printing House Square all through the summer of 1851. He was in Europe on vacation, but Jones, who was named publisher and head of Raymond, Jones & Co., kept him informed of the gossip. Some of it was malicious. Competitors hinted that The Times would be a political tool for abolitionists and radicals.

The Raymond prospectus hushed most of that talk. It said flatly that "in its political and social discussions, The Times will seek to be CONSERVATIVE, in such a way as shall best promote needful

REFORM"; that "its main reliance for all improvement, personal, social, and political, will be upon Christianity and Republicanism . . . and that the publishers would make The Times at once the best and the cheapest daily family newspaper in The United States."

The statement was bluntly aimed at both The Herald and The Tribune. Men who bought The Herald for its lively news coverage did not take it home because its crime news was a little strong for Nineteenth Century family diet. The accent on conservatism was a direct challenge to The Tribune as well as The Herald—to Greeley's newspaper chiefly because of its (then) extreme socialistic leanings.

The brownstone taken over for The Times was to have been a store and loft building, but the builder went broke before he finished it. The new paper hoped to have it completed in early September. The whole city, bursting its municipal britches as immigrants flooded in on every vessel from Europe, was almost hysterically tearing down its older shacks and putting up new ones. It was difficult to get enough skilled workers to make needed changes.

The brownstone not only was without windows in mid-September, but had no gas for lighting and no dumbwaiters to carry type and copy, and lacked the speaking tubes generally used in New York 100 years ago for inter-floor communication. With all these handicaps, though, Raymond and his staff got out the daily editions, the afternoon paper and the weekly and California editions more or less on time after the first number hit the streets.

Within a week, The Times circulation exceeded anything even the optimistic Raymond had expected. Advertising came with a rush, too. Four days after the first issue Times newsboys started leaving copies of the paper in residential districts all over town. Raymond meant to reach as many of New York's 500,000 residents as possible with samples of his handiwork. With the samples went a small handbill that said:

"The carrier of The New-York Daily Times proposes to leave it at this house every morning for a week, for the perusal of the family, and to enable them, if they desire it, to receive it regularly. The Times is a very cheap paper, costing the subscriber only

SIXPENCE a week, and contains an immense amount of reading matter for that price.

"The proprietors have abundant capital, able assistants and every facility for making it as good a paper as there is in the City of New York. It will contain regularly all the news of the day, full telegraphic reports from all quarters of the country, full city news, correspondence, editorials, etc., etc.

"At the end of the week the carrier will call for his pay; and a continuance of subscription is very respectfully solicited.

"New York, Sept. 21, 1851."

On Sept. 27 The Times told its readers—and its competitors—a little loftily: "This is the ninth number of The New-York Daily Times, and it has now a regular paying circulation of over TEN THOUSAND copies. If any other newspaper in this or in any other part of the world ever reached so large a circulation in so short a time, we should be glad to be informed of the fact. It is taken by business men at their stores, and by the most respectable families in town."

Though response to this promotion stunt was astonishingly fruitful, the capital pooled by Jones and the other up-State investors was all but gone before The Times showed substantial profit. Somewhere near $70,000 of the nominal capital of $100,000 had been put up. In the first year, $13,000 was paid in wages to the editorial staff, including Raymond, who then drew $50 a week. Eventually his pay came to $10,000 a year. The first year about $40,000 went for paper—good rag paper, in those days—and more than $20,000 to the mechanical departments. But The Times was already solidly on its feet, and a little heady about it, too.

The paper led on Sept. 17, 1852, with a notice that would startle Twentieth Century readers of any conservative journal, but which was mild for its time:

"This day's issue closes the first volume of The New-York Daily Times. The year's experience has disappointed alike the expectations of its friends, and the predictions of its foes. At the outset, owing mainly to personal causes, it was compelled to encounter as fierce hostility as any new enterprise ever met. Advantage was taken, by men whose personal resentments uniformly overbear all considerations of justice and fair play, of the absence from the country of the principal editor, to defame his character, belie his motives, misrepresent in the most shameful manner the objects and scope of the enterprise, and to prejudice, by all arts of unscrupulous cunning, the public mind against The Daily Times. These efforts were continued with relentless and unrebuked mendacity, for some months previous to the commencement of the paper; and were seconded in various quarters by those who became innocently their dupes, as well as by those whom selfish fear of rivalry prompted them to a similar course."

How cocky little Raymond did lay about him! Though he had promised to substitute "cool and intelligent judgment, for passion," he worked up quite a glow over his paper's showing.

"The strongest possible proof that the public confidence in The Times has not been in the least touched by these assaults," he wrote gloatingly, " is found in the success by which it has been crowned. It has been immeasurably more successful, in all respects, than any new paper of a similar character ever before published in the United States. There is not one of the established and powerful journals by which it is now surrounded, in this or in any other city, which closed the first year of its existence with an experience at all comparable to that of The Daily Times."

In the same article captioned, "The Year One," the public was told that The Times had printed 7,550,000 copies for an average circulation of more than 24,000 a day, and that this circulation represented "the best portion of our citizens," who liked the new paper because it did not "pander to any special taste, least of all to any low or degrading appetite." Bennett, down the street, had no trouble figuring out where that one was aimed.

Next day, the paper ran a modest paragraph that said: "In consequence of our limited space we have been compelled to keep advertising down by fixing so high a price upon it, that we could reserve a reasonable portion of room for reading matter." This was extraordinary for a one-year-old newspaper, but the advertising grew and Raymond's paper waxed fat on it. The price of the paper went to 2 cents.

A few days later, Bennett openly questioned The Times circulation figures. Raymond ran a challenging editorial. It said: "We doubled our paper and price to 2 cents on Saturday, and have an experience of three days from which to judge of its effect upon our circulation. If our neighbor will step in and examine our books—." Bennett didn't bother.

And at the end of that first year, The Times was cramped in the Nassau Street brownstone. "Have suffered . . . from lack of room," it said, a little loftily. "Owing to the limited size of the sheet, we could neither give as much reading matter daily as we desired, nor afford to take advertisements at so low a price as other papers. We shall endeavor, during the coming year, to obviate these difficulties, so far as possible."

The New York Times was on its way. Except for a few faltering steps, it was to march steadily from one building to another, expanding to meet advertiser demand for more and more space. Within the century it was to grow from the windowless little brownstone in Nassau Street to the largest and best-equipped newspaper plant in the world; to the point where the $70,000 that went into the first year's operation would barely pay for twelve hours' expenses in 1951.

Early in 1854 The Times owners took a new building at the southeast corner of Beekman and Nassau Streets, thinking this would house them for many years to come, but within three years they were to find themselves straining the walls again, and under compulsion to seek a much larger plant.

CHAPTER
2

ON SEPT. 27, 1854, not long after The Times had moved into its second home, the passenger steamer Arctic with 300 men and women aboard was passing Cape Race inbound from Liverpool when the French ship Vesta collided with her in a fog. There was no wireless to flash the news to the world, and it was not until the night of Oct. 10 that New York newspapers began to hear vague rumors of the collision. These established that the bark Huron, which picked up some of the survivors, was off Sandy Hook.

The Times was all but made up for the press when these reports came. E. M. Bacon, night editor, sent the staff scurrying to the waterfront and to sailors' dives around Cherry Hill in a desperate attempt to find someone who might have enough information to build up a front-page story. It was much too late to try to get a man out to Sandy Hook, or to Quarantine, and there was no direct wire communication with the Government stations at those points.

Bacon told a reporter to pencil a covering paragraph to relieve the sting of a possible beat by The Sun or The Herald. This paragraph, heavily leaded—that is, with much spacing between the lines, went on the front page next morning. It said:

"At a late hour last night we received terrible news of the steamship Arctic. We hope it is unfounded, but still the reports that reached us were so straightforward as to justify the most serious apprehensions."

18

This carried a heavy-type headline: "Loss of the Arctic."

The skimpy paragraph was poor substitute for fact, but there was nothing else to do. Bacon studied the thin proof with disappointment when it came down, shrugged into his long coat, clapped on his beaver hat and started for home. It was early morning. Nothing moved in the wind-swept and dimly lighted cobbled streets. By and by, a Broadway stage, bound uptown, loomed out of the dark with swaying lantern headlights. The horses' hoofs struck sparks from the paving blocks. The editor hopped aboard and sank gloomily into a seat, his legs thrust into the floor straw.

A half-mile beyond The Times office, the clopping horses were jerked to an abrupt stop and a bearded passenger lurched tipsily aboard. Thick-tonguedly talkative, he kept pressing the stage driver with incoherent details about a shipwreck. At first neither the driver nor The Times man could make anything of the narrative but The Times man came suddenly upright when he heard the drunken passenger mention the Arctic.

It turned out that the tipsy fare was George H. Burns, a messenger for the Adams Express Company, one of the Arctic survivors. He had come in on the Huron. One of James Gordon Bennett's men had found him on the waterfront in early evening and had brought him to The Herald offices. Even after he had been sucked dry of all the information he had on the wreck and the rescue, The Herald reporters had detained him. They had supplied him with whisky and then, to get him safely past the other newspaper offices downtown, had walked him part way to his hotel, the St. Nicholas.

The stage driver and the drunken messenger were a little startled when, having picked up these details, the dignified gentleman with the beaver hat leaped recklessly into gloomy Broadway. They saw him go pounding south in the dark, hat in hand, coat tails flapping in the strong October wind.

Bacon raced up the stairs in Nassau Street, his breath all but gone. The city room was deserted. He pushed into the pressroom and shouted to the astonished foreman to stop the morning run. "The Herald," he panted, "has put one over. It has a complete exclusive on the Arctic story. Hold your men. See if we can't round up some of my staff."

The printers scattered to the nearby groggeries to recall co-workers. A few late-drinking reporters came in with them. Bacon meanwhile had learned from the pressroom foreman that John Long of the pressroom gang had once worked for Bennett. The foreman figured Long might, in some way, get a copy of The Herald with Burns' account of the sinking, before The Herald got to the street.

Bacon explained to Long how important it was for The Times to get the Arctic story to replace the skimpy paragraph that was already set. He told the pressman, "It would be worth $50 to us to get that story for the first edition." Long liked that idea. He said, "I'll see what I can do," and went into the street.

The city room clock ticked off some twenty minutes while the staff stood at the windows staring out over the sleeping city. Bacon drummed nervously at his desk. A little after 4 o'clock, the press-man came back with The Herald's Arctic extra.

Long told how difficult it had been to snatch a copy. He had found The Herald's pressroom doors locked. Even the newsboys, usually allowed in out of the cold before edition time, had found entry barred. They had been told that the edition was to be held up till 9 A.M. They had not been told why, but the cause was ob-vious. The Herald meant to hold up distribution until every other newspaper office in the city had sent its staff and its printers home. How Long had managed to get past the doors no one ever knew.

Bacon cut The Herald's Arctic story into four-line takes, and had copy editors make some changes. The takes were distributed around the composing room and the printers, standing in sickly yellow light at their type cases, dropped the type into place with nimble fingers in record time. The last piece set was a new lead for the story, rewritten from The Herald version by one of The Times staff. It took almost three hours to tear down the original Times front page, and to set up the new one, but The Times was on the street by 8 o'clock. It was sold out before The Herald, smugly sure it had the Burns story exclusively, turned its extra loose, an hour later. The demand for The Times that day was so great that the presses kept running until 11 A.M. It was a crusher for The Herald.

Fletcher Harper Jr., then publisher of The Times, gave pressman Long his $50 bonus next day. Bacon drew a $5 increase. It was dog eat dog along newspaper row then. The trade has acquired some ethics since.

Times men could—and probably did—gloat over the way they had beaten Bennett on his own story, but one hundred years ago the journalistic code was a little crude and raw, and almost anything went. Property rights in news have been established through the years that have passed between, and, instead of a reward for a stolen story, a Times man today would probably wind up with a reprimand, if not dismissal; the code has changed that much.

On Oct. 12, when Arctic survivors and their rescuers came into New York on the Huron, the whole Times staff, including Henry Raymond, turned out to work on the story. The larcenous Arctic beat was to remain the favorite office legend for more than thirty years, when it was replaced by another wreck scoop on the sinking of the Cunarder Oregon, in 1886.

All through those early years Henry Raymond was The Times. His name carried weight all over the country, and the solid straight-news job the paper did under his direction—aside from journalistic joustings with Webb, Greeley and Bennett—was new enough to command healthy circulation. His personal courage, reflected in The Times, had as much to do with it as anything else.

In 1856, Raymond got credit—not universally, but in most places —for defining and outlining the purposes and principles of the Republican Party at the Pittsburgh convention. Raymond's speech was the keynote. He called for the new party to resist slavery, to back Kansas' admission to the Union and to oppose the Kansas invasion by Southern slavery advocates. It was a powerful speech, one of the early rumblings that warned of the approaching Civil War. It earned him the title "Godfather of the Republican party."

In 1857 Times circulation had boomed to the point where the old brownstone at the corner of Beekman and Nassau Streets had become hopelessly inadequate. Raymond, Jones & Co., (later H. J. Raymond & Co.), which owned The New-York Daily Times, bought the Old Brick Presbyterian Church and graveyard at the northern apex of the triangle formed by Park Row and Nassau and Beekman Streets. Workmen broke ground for The Times Block, as it was called then, on May 1, 1857. On Sept. 14 Raymond shortened the paper's name to The New-York Times. The hyphen in the title was not dropped until Dec. 1, 1896. The cornerstone was put down on May 12.

On May 1, 1858, the staff moved into the new building. Handsome new Hoe cylinder presses and other new machinery had been installed. The building, five stories (eighty feet) high, was the handsomest newspaper structure of its day. Tradition had called for dull, faded, wheezy housing for daily journals, but The Times was arrogantly rich in glittering new plate glass, marble floors, handsome paneling and frescoes. It was one of Gotham's show places. Other publishers thought Jones and Raymond slightly mad and figured that the building's cost might ruin them. It worked out quite the other way. It was excellent promotion and started a new trend in newspaper-building architecture.

Raymond's office suite overlooked Printing House Square, the City Hall and City Hall Park. It was handsomely furnished. His desk, a warm-colored reddish wood, probably cherry or red mahogany, was set against the wall opposite the main window to keep the view clear. The floor was rich in Kidderminster, and handsome paintings covered the walls. In this lush setting he wrote his powerful pre-war editorials.

Raymond's success with The Times bit deeply into Bennett's Scottish pride. In mid-December, 1861, The Herald questioned The Times' circulation figures and joyfully leaped to old-fashioned frontal assault on the issue. Before Raymond knew it, and in spite of his original intention to keep editorially calm, he found himself in a roaring shindig.

On Dec. 11, 1861, he devoted two full front-page columns to The Herald's challenge. Words failed to convey the full extent of The Times' injured pride, so it printed two cartoons in which Bennett appeared as Satan, with oversize horns, blowing up a bladder.

"Brother Bennett (profanely styled The Satanic)," said the cartoon caption, "Inflating his well known First Class, A No. 1 Windbag, Herald."

"Our neighbor of The Herald," The Times said scornfully, "fights like a man whose wind has gone, and whose 'peepers' are closed. He hits wild and very low. His profession of religious scruples against betting speaks volumes concerning the condition to which he has been reduced . . . We have already offered a wager of

$2,500 for families of volunteers, that, deducting those Wards in which the number of grog shops, gambling houses and houses of prostitution exceeds the number of respectable dwellings, our circulation in the City exceeds that of The Herald."

Raymond, in his fight on the slavery issue, seemed to sense, better than his contemporaries, that there was great danger of blood-letting over it. In 1859 he had written: "All great movements of great communities are movements of passion. States and nations seldom, or never, stop to count the cost . . . If our fathers had foreseen the cost of independence . . . they would scarcely have plunged, as they did . . . into the long and bloody war of the Revolution."

Raymond had counted the potential cost of the slavery issue clearly. When the thunder broke over Fort Sumter in 1861, he stuck by avowed principles. Other New York newspapers, as the toll in lives mounted, started murmuring for compromise.

In June, 1863, Horace Greeley pleaded in The Tribune: "If the rebels are indeed our masters, let them show it, and let us own it. If the rebels beat Grant and water their horses in the Delaware, routing all the forces we can bring against them, we shall be underfoot, and may as well own it."

Raymond knew no such weakening. In July, 1863, when the Draft Riots loosed blood-thirsty, looting mobs in New York's streets with incendiary torches and with guns, cobblestones and pikes, he reaffirmed his beliefs.

On Monday, July 13, the larrikins from the Five Points, and roving bands of plunderers from Philadelphia and Baltimore, put the torch to the draft registration office at Third Avenue and Forty-sixth Street. They set fire to station houses and beat and burned innocent Negroes. They hanged several Negroes to trees in that neighborhood and elsewhere. They charged the police with stones, guns and cart-rungs and left them senseless. All day long they ranged the city in packs of from 200 to 5,000, and none could withstand them. The Times devoted all its front page and a lot of inside space to the running story.

Leonard Walter Jerome, grandfather of Winston Churchill, Prime Minister of Britain in World War II, held a substantial amount of the newspaper's stock, then listed as shares of The New-

York Times Newspaper Establishment. Jerome had maintained a
financial interest in the newspaper since 1858 and his holding during the Civil War period ran to around fifteen to twenty of the
100 shares, each of $1,000 par value.

He was rather a gay blade, especially fond of horse-racing and
horse-breeding, and the last man to look the other way when a
shindig was on. He took fire from Raymond's impassioned pieces,
and decided that as a major stockholder his place was at The
Times. He drove down one night during the riots and offered his
services.

The Army had given Raymond two mitrailleuses, the then new-
fangled breech-loading machine gun with a number of barrels.
These had been set up in The Times' north windows to sweep the
approaches most likely to be used by the Bowery bully-raggers.
Jerome joyfully manned one and Raymond the other.

The editor and the financier eagerly scanned the lengths of
Centre and Chatham streets, hoping the rioters would charge their
plant. Nothing happened. The hoodlums somehow got word of
the new guns and instead of attacking The Times decided to go
for The Tribune.

At 7 P.M. the mob charged into Printing House Square out of
City Hall Park, roaring against the newspapers. The Times was
brilliant with gaslight, and the staff, armed with rifles, stood by
the windows, with ground-floor offices locked. The mob tried to
burn down The Tribune first.

The hooligans chanted, "We'll hang old Horace Greeley to a
sour-apple tree," and, with brawlers from the Bowery and Cow Bay
at their head, smashed The Tribune's windows. Raymond sent sixteen Times men with Minie rifles across the Square by way of back
streets, to help The Tribune's printers and reporters stand the mob
off. The mob fought its way into The Tribune's publication offices,
smashed windows and put the torch to the walls and to piles of
paper.

Two hundred policemen, from all parts of the city, and from
Brooklyn, marched into the Square. They plunged into the mob
with flailing nightsticks and with their revolvers cocked. They left
three-score of the tough boys lying in Printing House Square with
cracked heads, and sent the rest in flight across the Park, crying

hoarsely, their hands to their heads and faces. That night the sky was red. Reporters, watching from The Times' windows, saw private homes and public buildings burning at every point of the compass. The more timid residents thought the city was doomed. Raymond let up on Greeley in that dramatic hour. He wrote: "We have not always agreed with our neighbor on political policies, but . . . when such an issue is forced upon us journalists, they must make it their common cause. They had the aid of some of our employes in protection of their property and shall have it again whenever the invidious favor of the mob shall again release us from the necessity of defending our own."

Raymond showed his courage in an editorial in The Times of July 14 titled "Crush the Mob."

"No man, whatever his calling or condition in life, can afford to live in a city where the law is powerless," he wrote.

"This mob must be crushed at once. Every day's, every hour's delay is big with evil: Let every citizen come promptly forward and give his personal aid to so good and indispensable a work."

The rioters burned down the huge Orphan Asylum for Colored Children at Fifth Avenue and Forty-third Street.

On the second day of the riot the local toughs and their out-of-town reinforcement—the Plug Uglies and the Blood Tubs of Baltimore, the Schuylkill Rangers from Philadelphia—scourged the city again. The Dead Rabbits from the Bowery, Roaches Guards and the Cow Bay gangs, smashed the windows in Brooks Brothers' clothing shop at Catherine and Cherry Streets and came staggering out, arms filled with suits, shoes, hats.

Three hundred policemen converged on the shop, shooting and lashing out with their nightsticks. They piled the trapped toughs on the floors. One giant was shot as he charged down the stairs at the police. The night was filled with cursing and groaning, and the policemen—with the firemen who fought at their side—reeled under showers of stones, and rifle fire. Finally the mob broke and ran, smashing windows as it fled.

On July 15, The Times' front page carried the headline "The Reign of the Rabble." It told how regiments had been rushed by train from Washington to put down the riots, and how:

"Last night The Times office again presented itself in a state of the most formidable defense. It appeared able to withstand a long siege before it would surrender to the mob."

Lieut. Charles E. Smith of the Regular Army, sent from Governors Island with thirty regular troops and 150 volunteer soldiers, had established bivouac in The Times. One cannon was trained on Nassau and Spruce Streets, a second pointed toward Park Place. The Times said: "Last night (July 15), for the special benefit of the mobocracy, the illumination (at The Times) was repeated, but on a more extensive and splendid scale." The mob didn't show up, though. Policemen were all around the Square and batteries had been set up in City Hall Park.

Raymond was impatient with Governor Seymour, who had come from Albany and had tried to quiet the crowd with speeches. "This monster," Raymond wrote flamingly of the mob, "is to be met with a sword, and that only . . . It is to be defied, confronted, grappled with, prostrated, crushed. It is true, that there are public journals who try to dignify this mob . . . The Herald characterizes it as the PEOPLE, and The World as the LABORING MEN of the city. These are libels that ought to paralyze the fingers that penned them . . . The people of New York and the laboring men of New York are not incendiaries, nor robbers, nor assassins."

On July 17 Raymond trained his wrath on The New York Express. "The Express," he wrote, with fine contempt, "is a very curious journal. It 'begs' and 'implores' us to 'hush up' the statement that the President has not ordered the draft suspended . . . We prefer, for our own part, to tell the truth and shame The Express.

"The draft itself ought *not* and must not be abandoned."

Raymond said that though the mob had originally cried out against being drafted, the vast majority of its members were thieves and killers, under draft age.

"Justice and mercy, this time, unite in the same behest," he argued at the close of this fearless editorial. "Give them grape, and plenty of it."

That's what the police and the militia did. It cost lives, as Raymond had known it would, but it restored the rule of law.

The Times' Civil War coverage under Raymond's direction added tremendously to its prestige as a straight news purveyor.

Raymond himself and James B. Swain, the newspaper's Washington correspondent, turned in magnificent running stories of the first Battle of Bull Run. William Swinton wrote dramatic and colorful copy on the moves of the Army of the Potomac, and so did Lorenzo L. Crounse. He did the series on the seven days' fighting around Richmond and was right in the fighting at Chancellorsville. He covered Antietam and Gettysburg and in the Fall of 1863 did a remarkable piece on the Battle of Lookout Mountain in Chattanooga.

The Times' star man in the field, though, was Ben C. Truman who came through with a series of spectacular exclusive battle stories, somewhat to the annoyance of Secretary of War Stanton who was chagrined to find repeatedly that he could get battle results days sooner through The Times than he could through official sources. Truman had the story of the Battle of Franklin in The Times four days before the news reached Stanton, and had a fortnight's headway on the plans for General Sherman's historic march to the sea.

One Times man got a little too close to the action at Harpers Ferry and almost got himself hanged as a spy. Mosby's guerrillas captured Crounse, but let him go after they had taken his notes and credentials. Thirty-four Times men, incidentally, saw Civil War service, thirty-two on the Union side, two with the Confederates. George F. Williams, a Times printer, got a chance as war correspondent and did so well at it that he eventually wound up as general news editor.

Truman was probably the most colorful reporter on The Times during the Raymond period. He had a particular weakness for the ale at Pfaff's in lower Broadway and often, after work at night, sauntered, frock-coated and silk-hatted, to another old saloon in Chrystie Street where Stephen Foster, the songwriter, was slowly drinking himself to death. There the brawny Benicia Boy, the heavyweight John C. Heenan, was a hanger-on too. Truman died in Los Angeles on July 18, 1916, in his eighty-first year.

One story from Gettysburg (then spelled with an "h") that deeply moved Times readers the morning of July 6, 1863, has long been forgotten, but it was talked of almost everywhere when it happened.

It was a dispatch datelined, "Gettysburgh, Headquarters Army of the Potomac, Saturday Night, July 4."

"Who," it said, "can write the history of a battle whose eyes are immovably fastened upon a central figure of transcendingly important interest—the body of an oldest born, crushed by a shell?"

This was followed by a description of the last day's fighting at Gettysburgh that began:

"For such details as I have the heart for, the battle commenced at daylight on the side of the horseshoe position, exactly opposite to that which Ewell had sworn to crush."

The story closed on the note:

"My pen is heavy . . . O, you dead, who died at Gettysburgh have baptized with your blood the second birth of Freedom in America, how you are to be envied! I rise from a grave whose wet clay I have passionately kissed, and I look up to see Christ spanning this battlefield . . ."

The story carried, at its end, the byline of Samuel Wilkeson of The Times. He had been sent from The Times Washington bureau to help Crounse. On Saturday morning he had come upon the shattered body of a 19-year-old lieutenant, dead with all the men of his command, Battery G of the Fourth United States Artillery. It was his own son, Bayard Wilkeson.

It is generally said that when the Gettysburg battlefield was dedicated by President Lincoln the press gave short shrift to his address. The Times ran it in full on Nov. 20, 1863, the day after it was delivered. It indicated six applause breaks and closed with "(Long continued applause)."

It is true, though, that apparently no newspaper thought the President's brief remarks stacked up against the long address (a solid page in The Times) delivered by the statesman Edward Everett.

A Times editorial on Nov. 21 said of Everett's remarks, "His exordium is of great beauty; and his peroration is splendid." The editorial predicted that Everett's words would "command the attention of the day, and not of this day only." It did not mention the Lincoln address.

On April 15, 1865, The Times front page had an extraordinary make-up. All its column rules were turned upside down to make black borders. The headline, contained within a single column at the extreme left, merely said:

AWFUL EVENT

It was the story of the shooting of President Lincoln in the Ford Theatre. The black borders are puzzling. Lincoln still lived as the paper reached the street that morning. It may be that the heavy black rules were intended to call reader attention to an extra.

The Times of April 16 again was black-bordered and the headline told of the President's passing with the words:

OUR GREAT LOSS

The line that actually told of Lincoln's death occurred in the second paragraph, in the story written under an April 15 Washington dateline:

"Abraham Lincoln died this morning at twenty-two minutes after 7 o'clock."

The only other occasion on which The Times had used black borders was on the morning of Oct. 25, 1852, when it reported the death of Daniel Webster. In that case only the outside rules were inverted to make a black frame. There was an office legend, years afterward, that Raymond wrote steadily all that day and far into the night, to turn out the Webster obituary. It ran to four solid pages and two columns over. He did it all with pen and ink.

Raymond, a power in Republican politics in the Sixties, helped get the Vice-Presidency for Andrew Johnson. During Abraham Lincoln's second term Raymond was elected to Congress. He worked hard there and in The Times to help reconstruct the South.

"If we are to have peace at all, we must seek it in the ways of peace," he argued, "not in the ways of malice, hatred and uncharitableness. We must be willing to let the dead past bury its dead, and to live for the present and future generations."

He said this years later in a speech at Cooper Union after Johnson, then President, had vetoed the Freedman's Bureau Bill. He had helped put Johnson in the White House, but had come to regret it. Once he realized the error, he and The Times did all they could to redeem it.

At the close of the Thirty-ninth Congress, Raymond finally gave up politics. The double burden of running the paper and performing his congressional duties had told. Partial paralysis had weakened his hands, but he went back to his desk off Printing House Square. When Charles Dickens ended his second visit to the United States in April, 1868, it was Raymond who delivered the press' farewell. Curiously enough, the president of the Press of New York at the time was Greeley, from down the street. Kindly, half-blinded, he beamed through his spectacles when Raymond, his former employe and journalistic foe, called him that night "the honorable, the distinguished, the honored President."

Then Raymond said: "We are all laboring in a common cause. I think it may be truly said that the press, the free press all over the world, has but one common mission—to elevate humanity."

This was his last major public appearance. On June 18, the following year, he journeyed out to Green-Wood Cemetery to the grave where his 15-year-old son, Walter, had been buried only five months before. At midnight he was found unconscious in his own hallway at 12 West Ninth Street. He died before dawn. He was in his fiftieth year.

Augustus Maverick, one of Raymond's assistants on The Times, and later Raymond's biographer, conjectured that Raymond got sick as he approached the house, but locked the front and inner vestibule doors before he fell in an apoplectic stroke.

John Bigelow, who was to succeed Raymond as editor in chief of The Times, though only for a short while, had a somewhat different version. On June 22, 1869, he wrote in his diary:

"At a late hour last Friday night (June 19) the body of Henry J. Raymond was brought home in a carriage and thrown on the hall floor of his residence by two men who immediately disappeared. The servant who opened the door, being in her night clothes, escaped as soon as she had turned the key of the door (to admit the party) so that what happened thereafter was not discovered until early morning, when Raymond's stertorous breathing was heard by his daughter, Mary. I attended his funeral yesterday. I called upon Mrs. Raymond this afternoon. She told me that Raymond's relatives, that is, his mother, and her father and an uncle on the mother's side, had died in the same way."

In a later diary entry, Bigelow told how he discussed Raymond's death with the Rev. Henry Ward Beecher, on the way home from the funeral.

". . . he told me," Bigelow wrote, "that Raymond was returning from the residence of a somewhat popular actress, Rose Eytinge, where he had had a very stormy time, and since his wife's return from Europe where she had been residing with the children for a considerable time, he had been trying to extricate himself from the toils of this woman, who determined, however, to make him pay for his emancipation.

"Raymond had left home, so the papers had it, to go to a political meeting but in fact he went to Miss Eytinge's apartment in reply to a summons from her that he must come or she would go to his house. His letters in her hands were her instruments of torture . . . Raymond was now trying, I presume, to lead a more exemplary life, but the devils by which he was obsessed are not exorcised by prayer and I fear Raymond had but imperfect notion of the efficacy of prayer."

Rose Etynge was something more than the "somewhat popular actress" described by John Bigelow. She was a dark-eyed beauty of 34 years when she knew Raymond. She was the toast of the town then and later was the toast of London, Cairo and Philadelphia, too, and a friend of Charles Dickens, the Prince of Wales (later Edward VII), Abraham Lincoln, Augustin Daly, Edwin Booth and Lester Wallack. Brigham Young, with twenty-one wives in his Salt Lake City household, put in a bid—as she described it later—"that I be sealed with him." Lincoln had her as a White House guest when she played with Booth in Washington. She died in a home for indigent actors in Amityville, L.I., a week before Christmas in 1911 in her seventy-sixth year. She had outlived Raymond by more than forty years.

The day after Raymond died The Times sorrowfully ran his obituary. In its editorial it said, "As a journalist no man ever dared approach him with a corrupt or dishonest proposition." The publishers into whom he had dug his pen again and again were kindly in their final estimates of Raymond the newspaper man. Greeley's Tribune said: "We doubt whether this country has known a journalist superior to Henry Raymond . . . There was nothing in the whole range of newspaper work that he could not do well, and (what is of equal importance) with unhesitating promptness."

Bennett did not go quite that far. He called Raymond "a brilliant speaker, and able and accomplished writer, a good, experienced and successful journalist." The Herald editorial said that Raymond established The Times "on The Herald idea of the latest news." It predicted that "The Times will go on as before." Not only Greeley, who had named Raymond "Little Villain," but even old Brimstone Webb, acted as pallbearers at the burial on June 21 in Green-Wood.

George Jones took over the editorial end of The Times after Raymond's death, as well as the financial end. The paper's stock, in Raymond's lifetime, had gone from $1,000 a share to $11,000. Offers as high as $1,000,000 were made for the paper but Jones turned them down. The Times was still expanding, still gaining power.

CHAPTER
3

WHEN The Times fell abruptly into George Jones' hands in 1869 he was not equipped to carry on the scribbling-publisher tradition. He had no literary fire, but he did have common sense and high moral courage.

Perhaps it was just as well that Jones was no writer. Fire-eating newspaper owners with a flair for inky invective, who attracted circulation through personal controversy, were on the way out. Webb, Bennett, Greeley and Raymond were almost the last of the breed.

When Raymond died, newspapers were drawing readers chiefly by straight news content. The editorial, which had been the journalistic heart worn on the publisher's sleeve, thumped less violently now behind the news, where it belonged. So George Jones set up as the first great businessman publisher, a type that was destined to take over, almost everywhere.

It was curious that almost all New York newspaper publishers of the period had come out of tiny hamlets and obscure byroads—Raymond out of backwoods Lima, Greeley from Amherst in rural New Hampshire, Jones from remote Poultney in Vermont. They had reached high places out of comparative poverty. They had taken their basic education in primitive country schools and all had known farm toil in their nonage.

Jones, the son of Welsh Baptists—he joined the Episcopalian Church later—was born in a farmhouse in Poultney on Aug. 16, 1811. He had known Horace Greeley when Greeley was a printer's devil on East Poultney's Northern Spectator, and had called him "Ghost," as other boyhood playmates had. When Jones came down to New York in 1841, a greeny of 30 years, Ghost offered him a partnership in The Tribune, which was founded in that year.

Lacking even the few meager dollars needed for the partnership, Jones settled for a job in The Tribune business office. It was there that he first met Raymond. In the little free time they had away from Greeley's scrubby newspaper plant, they walked Manhattan's cobbled streets, avoiding the grunting porkers that were the city's street-cleaning department. They talked, sometimes, of starting a newspaper of their own, but neither had the capital, and nothing came of it—not for another full decade.

Henry Warren Raymond was at Yale when his father died. The family held, at that time, thirty-four of the existing 100 shares of New-York Times stock and Jones held thirty. George Jones realized, when he took over, that he could not expect young Raymond to replace his father, even if Jones should hold The Times as a kind of regency for a few years.

Young Raymond had not inherited his sire's talent for crisp journalistic prose. He inclined more toward the purple side—toward the tender arts. He had worked around The Times office during college vacations, but it was the work of the dilettante. His father had tried to nurture the boy's talents—even bought for him from The Times, for $15, a description of the fall of Fort Sumter—but the spark was feeble.

After young Raymond got out of Yale in 1869, he took his A.M. (1872) and then studied law at Columbia. He tried publishing books in Chicago, but much of his share of the money his father had accumulated on The Times was lost in that venture. Later he worked on The Chicago Tribune as literary editor and as music critic until 1883 when he took over the Germantown Telegraph, a Pennsylvania agricultural and family sheet. Thereafter, he settled down to a calm, bucolic existence. He was still in Germantown when he died in February, 1925.

Jones had barely taken over as Henry Raymond's successor, before he had on his hands the toughest fight in New York's journal-

istic annals. Tammany Boss William Marcy Tweed and a swarm
of free-swinging Democratic grafters had been busily and unashamedly looting everything in the municipal coffers, and no one
had the courage to try to stop them.

Jones knew what it would mean if he should start swinging at
Boss Tweed and the Ring—and miss. He did not own a controlling
interest in The Times. He didn't know into whose hands the Raymond stock might eventually fall. To complicate things just a little
more, one of The Times directors, James B. Taylor, was a business
partner of Tweed's in the New York Printing Company.

Fate stepped in. James Taylor died in early September in 1870.

Before the month was out, though he stood to lose everything
if his crusade failed, George Jones ordered his staff to get Boss
Tweed. It was a tremendous and dangerous order. Louis J. Jennings, a Briton who had worked in India and in London, manned
the editorial guns. John Foord, a Perthshire Scot, with newspaper
experience in London and on sheets in northern England, handled
the reporting end.

Every newspaper in town knew the Tweed Ring was up to its
hairy elbows in municipal thievery. Wall Street knew it, too. Big
figures, like Jay Gould and James Fisk Jr., had fattened their own
bulging purses in outrageous railroad deals with Bill Tweed as
partner.

Yet the Tammany Tiger stalked unchallenged. The Tiger concept, incidentally, was just then a-borning in the mind of Thomas
Nast, cartoonist for Harper's Weekly. He drew it for the first time
for Harper's issue of Nov. 11, 1871. The idea stemmed from the
tiger's head that decorated the fire engine of Volunteer Company
Big Six, called Americus, a collection of big-throated larrikins,
whose foreman was Bill Tweed, the chairmaker.

Jones looked like anything but a tiger-tamer. He was a grave,
lush-bearded, ponderous man close to 60, who peered through
thick-lensed gold-rimmed spectacles. He inclined to the extreme
auditorial mold—hardly the type to go on a safari against political
man-eaters. It was not strange that Tweed underestimated him.

When the first Times editorials on Tweed started in September
1870, the Boss and his gang shrugged them off as partisan Republican effusions. They spread the idea that The Times howled be-

cause the City was holding up payment of a bill for $13,764 for municipal advertising. Actually, The Times had abruptly rejected ring-distributed city advertising, though most New York sheets kept taking it as the price of silence.

New York Democrats were assembled in convention in Rochester when The Times opened up against Tweed. On Sept. 20 it ran a long editorial on "The Democratic Millenium" in which Louis Jennings applied the needles.

"We should like to have a treatise from Mr. Tweed," he wrote, "in the art of growing rich in as many years as can be counted on the fingers of one hand . . . You might begin with nothing and in five or six years you can boast of your ten millions. How was it done? We wish Mr. Tweed or Mr. Sweeney, or some of their friends, would tell us. The general public say there is foul play somewhere. They are under the impression that monstrous abuses of their funds, corrupt bargains with railroad sharpers, outrageous plots to swindle the general community, account for the vast fortunes heaped up by men who sprang up like mushrooms."

Boss Tweed, Mayor A. Oakey Hall, Controller Richard B. (Slippery Dick) Connolly and Peter B. Sweeney of Tweed's City Park Board were mildly startled. Though everyone in town knew that Tweed and his train-bearers were wallowing in Neroesque luxury, no one had previously dared to ask publicly how they had come by their wealth. Tweed, bankrupt in 1865, now owned a magnificent mansion at Madison Avenue and Fifty-ninth Street. He had acquired a glittering yacht. He wore enormous diamonds on his shirtfront, on his fingers and on his watch chain. He and his family had elegant custom-built carriages and stylish horses. It was only fussy Mr. Jones who asked, "How come?"

He was to cry out alone, or almost alone, for fourteen months. In all the great city, then grown to almost 1,000,000 population and swelling rapidly, the only help The Times had in its crusade came from Thomas Nast's biting pen. Other publications not only wore editorial blinders throughout this period; some even tried to trample The Times' crusade as harmful to New York's credit. The World and The Sun scolded most sharply of all.

Tweed power was brought heavily to bear from all quarters in an attempt to frighten Jones. Big advertisers—and many small ones —pulled out in fear of the Tiger's claws. Tweed's Wall Street henchmen brought financial pressure. Jones' one fear at this time was that with big-name fronts Tweed might somehow get his hands on the Raymond estate's interest in The Times, and weaken him at his own council table. Tweed had city attorneys attempt to prove that The Times' title to the Brick Church property was defective, but this suit fell flat. Jones took his advertising losses grimly, ignored the Wall Street men's displeasure—and kept to his course. When other city newspapers sniped at The Times he told Jennings to strike back. Jennings did. He loved a fight, too.

On Sept. 25 he wrote: "The World once more makes its appearance in the ring as the defender of Tammany. After many dismal experiences it has returned humbly to the fold, and now nibbles its grass as if it had never been a rover."

The World, then owned by Manton Marble, had carried an editorial that asked: "Why does that journal (The Times) so stultify itself? We could easily state the reason, and may do so at no distant day . . . The Times seems demented by its hidden grievances." What The World probably had in mind was The Times' failure to collect the $13,764 owed to it by the City.

Jennings' answer was: "Here is a fearful menace, and a most alarming situation. Now to what does The World allude? Will it have the kindness to explain? We are sorry to see it get into a passion and utter threats, for that is an undignified course; and, therefore, we should be glad if it would make a clean breast of it, and tell all it knows.

"It will then have to state, if it speaks the truth, that The Times has waged no mock war against Tweed and his Ring, but an earnest, steady, relentless war; that we have been threatened over and over again for daring to protest on behalf of the public against the robbery practiced in the cliques; that vexatious actions for libel have been brought against us; and that while The World has quickly gone back to its place in the Ring, we are prepared to fight that Ring until we have brought it to the ruin and disgrace which are quite sure to overtake it, some day or other."

Next morning, Jennings jabbed Tweed again.

"No Caliph, Khan or Caesar," he wrote, "has risen to power or opulence more rapidly than Tweed I. Ten years ago this monarch was pursuing the humble occupation of a chairmaker in an obscure street in this city. He now rules the State as Napoleon ruled France, or as the Medici ruled Florence . . . His immediate personal followers are a more despicable and unclean herd than has ever surrounded the paltriest Asiatic despot . . . And there he sits today, pocketing our money and laughing at us."

In a column hard by, John Foord had a piece about Tweed payroll padding. It told how Tweed had put 1,300 new names on the city books within six weeks. It told how Tweed bred a peculiar type of adherent on a diet of whisky and black cigars, how park lamps were painted on rainy days so that the paint immediately ran off to make more work—and more pay—for Tweed hoodlums. Foord called these Ring followers "rowdies, vagabonds, sneak thieves, gamblers and shoulder-hitters."

Foord said: "Taxpayers must pay the bill and work hard to support in idleness and debauchery that portion of our criminal population who hesitates at no crime—not even excepting murder, and who, by physical force and brutal conduct, make our city elections the burlesque it has been for years."

This was no exaggerated picture. Tammany had built, within a few years, the greatest army of toughs and homicidal buckos in New York's history.

When The World was not back-biting, The Sun was. In an editorial it got after Jennings:

"The decline of The New York Times in everything that entitles a newspaper to respect and confidence, has been rapid and complete. Its present editor, who was dismissed from The London Times for improper conduct and untruthful writing, has sunk into a tedious monotony of slander and disregard of truth, and black-guard vituperation . . . Let The Times change its course, send off Jennings, and get some gentleman and scholar in his place, and become again an able and high-toned paper. Thus it may escape from ruin. Otherwise it is doomed."

Actually, Louis Jennings' journalistic career was unblemished. He left The Times in 1874 for London and won added honor and respect as a Member of Parliament. He was through with The Times, though. Instead he wrote a weekly London letter for Bennett's Herald, signed "Louis Jennings, M.P." Jones and The Times were yet to see their brightest day.

For a long time, though, storm clouds piled up. In October, 1870, after The Times had called repeatedly but in vain for the City accounts to be opened for public scanning, Controller Connolly figured out a neat trick. He opened one set of city accounts for a group of leading New York businessmen, including John Jacob Astor, Moses Taylor and George K. Sistare. Marshall O. Roberts, one of the owners of The Sun, was on the Committee, too. The timing was shrewd. Just before election, when The Times was hammering hardest at Tweed and Tammany, the businessmen reported that "the account books . . . are faithfully kept. . . . We have come to the conclusion and certify that the financial affairs of the city, under the charge of the Controller, are administered in a correct and faithful manner."

This report hurt. It indicated that the ledgers held nothing to back up the newspapers' charges against the Ring. It developed later that the committee had spent only six hours in its survey of the Controller's accounts, and that what it had seen was only a screen for the record of unprecedented municipal thievery.

Tammany swept the city in the 1870 election.

The Times was accused of indulging in personalities in scolding Astor, Taylor, Roberts and the rest of the businessmen who had signed the report that white-washed Tammany. Jennings wrote in answer:

"Forbearance has no place in a fight like this. We are battling with a band of thugs supported by the freebooters of the press. It would be worse than useless to go into such a fight armed only with rose water."

When the "indulging in personalities" charge was made again by David Dudley Field, a lawyer, The Times replied:

"We demanded the production of the official reports which the Controller is bound by law to issue every year. At this stage, Mr. Astor, Mr. Taylor and Mr. Roberts . . . made superficial examination of a few city accounts and roundly certified that they were all faithfully and properly kept. Accountants assure us that such an investigation, to be of any value, would have occupied fully three months, even if assisted by a staff of clerks . . . We hold still that

Mr. Astor and his friends were guilty of a breach of faith toward the public, and that it was our bounden duty to say so . . ."

Astor and Taylor were hardly less formidable targets than the Tiger, but Jones never backed away from them.

Tweed's charges that The Times' attacks were merely Republican partisanship were answered when Jennings lashed at the Ring's Republican trough-sharers. He openly named influential Republicans. He wrote bitterly that Henry Smith, the Police Commissioner, a Republican, had accepted $10,000 in silver plate from Tweed for a favor never explained. All this cost The Times heavily. George Jones, who liked to spend some of his leisure time in the better city clubs, found himself running into chilly zones. He didn't seem to mind.

The editorial ink might have been splashed in vain at Boss Tweed, the Ring and affiliated Republicans, if fate had not stepped in again. With her first helping hand she had removed The Times director, James Taylor. Now she provided another death, in a bitter snowstorm.

On Jan. 21, 1871, the day that The Times defended its stand on the Astor Committee report, heavy snow sifted down on New York. It was soft and gentle, at first. Then a strong, biting wind got behind it and the city gasped and groped through it. Stages drawn by pitifully winded horses, coated with ice and snow, skidded in the ruts. Clumsy drays were marooned in drifts. Broadway was clogged with abandoned rigs. By Monday everything was at a frozen standstill. The Times, as well as other local dailies, ran columns on it.

Four days after the storm struck, an insignificant item appeared near the bottom of The Times' front page. It was headed:

"Probably Fatal Accident in Harlem Lane."

No one suspected it then, but this was fate's frosty joke on the Tweed Ring—and the answer to Jones' prayers. The item said:

"Mr. James Watson, the County Auditor, was nearly killed yesterday afternoon in Harlem Lane by a collision. While driving down the Lane . . . at 138th Street, a German, who was going up at a rapid rate in another sleigh, suddenly turned his horse 'round in such a manner that Mr. Watson's team became entangled and he received a kick on the left temple from one of the three animals. The wound proved to be a terrible one . . . A mare of Mr. Watson's, valued at $10,000, was killed in the collision."

James Watson was Tweed's paymaster. He died a week after the sleighing accident. Mention of his $10,000 mare caused some eyebrows to lift, but the populace had come to know that anyone who worked with the Boss could own blooded stock and a mansion, as Watson had, on a city job that paid only a few thousand a year. That was Tweed magic.

In March, a few weeks after Watson's death, word got around that Boss Tweed and his crew were hinting that they were ready to spend $5,000,000 to buy The Times. Jones wrote on the editorial page that *"No money"*—he italicized these words—could induce him to sell a single share of his Times stock to Tammany "or to any man associated with it or indeed to any person or party whatever until this struggle is fought out."

He announced at the same time that if he were forced out of The Times he would "immediately start another journal to denounce these frauds which are so great a scandal to the City," and that he would take Jennings and Foord with him to keep up the crusade.

Boss Tweed and his lieutenants were careless in replacing Watson with Stephen C. Lynes Jr., a city bookkeeper. He held on only a little while before the job was given to Matthew J. O'Rourke, an auditor. This was the Ring's fatal slip. O'Rourke, though probably none of the Tweed men knew it at the time, was working secretly for a Tammany insurgent, former Sheriff James O'Brien, head of the Young Democrats, who wanted Tweed's post as Grand Sachem. O'Brien had caught some of the Tweed Ring's rich drippings but wanted no more. He had put in a bill for $350,000 as his share of the general loot, but the Boss had turned him down. Now he was out for blood. Through O'Rourke, O'Brien got a tax accountant into City Hall to copy some of the most incriminating entries in the Tweed Ring's books. The accountant was William Copeland, another O'Brien adherent.

The spying was slow and dangerous. Only a few entries could be copied at a time. Copeland did not know it, but when he had chosen a few items, O'Rourke noted which he had fixed upon.

When Copeland left, O'Rourke made copies for himself. Apparently neither O'Rourke nor O'Brien was aware of it, but each was to compete with the other eventually in attempts to unload this auditorial dynamite. Both were probably hurt and astonished when there were no immediate takers.

O'Brien tried The Sun, first. That newspaper wanted no part of it. How many other newspapers got the offer no one will ever know now. There were rumors at the time that reports of these offers leaked through to the Boss. O'Brien said later, without going into detail, "Tweed tried to murder me to get those papers."

One torrid night in early July, 1871, some months after he first got the copied evidence against the Ring, O'Brien dropped into The Times. Out in Printing House Square, and in City Hall Park, loafers gasped for air. In the stifling news room, bearded staff men in shirtsleeves, collars open at the throat, perspired over their copy. Jennings' editorial office was open to catch any vagrant breeze when O'Brien panted in.

"Hot night," O'Brien said, vaguely. He mopped his balding forehead.

"Warm," Jennings conceded.

O'Brien sat on the edge of a chair, nervously fingering a large paper envelope. It was the one he had offered elsewhere. Only desperation had forced him to bring it to a Republican shop.

There were a few seconds of awkward silence. The ex-Sheriff did not quite know how to dispose of his burden.

He said, "You and Tom Nast have had a tough fight."

Jennings nodded. "Still have," he said.

"I said, 'had.' " O'Brien laid the envelope on Jennings' desk. He thumped it with a damp, bediamonded fist. "Here's the proof to back up all The Times has charged," he said. "They're copied right out of the city ledgers."

He was red-faced. Sweat poured down his jowls.

Jennings lifted cautious eyebrows. He left the envelope untouched, though his long fingers itched to get at it. He had carried the fight a long way on very little. If the former Sheriff's words were true, here at last was deadly ammunition.

O'Brien got up heavily. He clumped back into Printing House Square. Jennings pounced on the envelope, scanned it—and bore it excitedly to Foord and to Jones. When it was spread before them, they were ecstatic. It was more than they had ever hoped to lay eyes on.

A sleighing accident in January had opened the way for hot news in July. The Times was equipped now to break the most startling graft story in New York's history.

CHAPTER
4

ON JULY 8, 1871, Times readers got a nibble of the fruits of O'Brien's and O'Rourke's spying. O'Rourke had come in just behind O'Brien with his own copies from the Ring books, and with some items that were not in the O'Brien collection.

"We lay before our readers this morning," Jennings quietly gloated on the editorial page, "a chapter of municipal rascality which in any other city but New York would bring down upon the heads of its authors such a storm of public indignation as would force them to a speedy accountability before the bar of a criminal court, or compel them to take refuge in flight and perpetual exile.

"We apprehend that no one will complain of a lack of facts and specifications in the articles to which we now call the reader's attention; and that not even The Tribune or any other of the eighteen daily and weekly papers that have been gagged by Ring patronage will be able to find an excuse for ignoring the startling record presented here, on the ground that it is not sufficiently definite."

A few columns away Foord had a long news piece headed:

"More Ring Villainy." It told of "Gigantic Frauds in the Rental of Armories," and made the flat statement: "Eighty Per Cent of the Money Stolen."

Foord's article listed the places for which the Tweed Ring was charging the city staggering rentals under the pretense that the premises were used as city armories. The list included five grog shops, dark and small, and eight dark, little rooms over shabby stables. In most cases, the alleged rentals were many times the value of these miserable properties. Charges for "repairs" and furnishings for the groggery armories and stable drill floors made even headier reading. Foord had evidence, too, that an arms company, owned by Tweed and by James H. Ingersoll, his partner in the chair business, was supplying weapons to the National Guard at breath-taking prices.

At the end of this piece, Foord wrote in editorial vein:

"Who are responsible for these frauds? First, Mayor Hall and Controller Connolly, who pass upon these claims and sign checks for their payment—knowing them to be fraudulent. Second, William M. Tweed and Peter B. Sweeney, who pocket their share of the proceeds—knowing them to have been fraudulently obtained. Third, James H. Ingersoll, Joseph B. Young, clerk to the Board of Supervisors, and Stephen C. Lynes Jr., present county auditor, whose agency in these matters is as palpable as it is shameful."

Waves of rioting and skull-cracking, which started in a dispute between Orangemen and men from the South of Ireland, held the news and editorial pages for more than a week, and it was not until July 19 that The Times released more about the armories.

Jennings wrote for that morning's issue:

"Tomorrow morning we shall publish a still more important document, also compiled from Connolly's books. We shall prove . . . that not less than ninety millions a year pass through the hands of Hall and Connolly, and that they had their fellow conspirators steal a large part of the money.

"Our article tomorrow, though of the greatest importance, will be exceeded in interest by a *true copy*, which we shall shortly publish, of the money paid on warrants during 1869 and 1870 for the new County Court House. These figures will convince any man beyond a doubt, that Hall and Connolly, who signed the warrants, are swindlers, and as such we once more arraign them before the bar of public opinion."

His head for this piece was brutally blunt. It simply said: "Two Thieves."

Early in 1871 Henry Raymond's widow, who held thirty-four

shares of The Times' capital stock, asked Jones for a general accounting of the newspaper's holdings, including an inventory of supplies and a list of salaries paid to editors and to reporters. Jones gave her a complete inventory.

Soon after this information had been turned over to Mrs. Raymond, Robert Griffin Morris, The Times city editor, was in City Hall just strolling after his midday meal when he happened to hear Mayor Oakey Hall tell Comptroller Connolly:

"I think that deal with Mrs. Raymond will go through."

Morris was startled. He guessed that this could only mean that Mrs. Raymond was preparing to turn her Times holdings over to the Tweed crowd. There had been rumors that the Ring, with the help of Cyrus W. Field and Jay Gould, was trying to get control of The Times by clandestine purchase of shares through proxies. Morris hurried back across the park and passed the information to Jones.

Jones immediately wired to Col. E. D. Morgan, one of the original investors in The Times, who had also been one of the founders of Wells-Fargo Express. The colonel, now a multi-millionaire, came out of rural retirement to block the Tweed move. "The old colonel," according to John A. Hennessy who was Jennings' office boy at the time, "was angry right down to his woolen socks." He visited Mrs. Raymond next day, checkbook in hand.

On the day that the piece about the "Two Thieves" ran, there was a triumphant announcement by George Jones, just above it. This said:

"It has been repeatedly asserted that the Raymond shares were likely to fall into the possession of the New York Ring, and it is in order to assure our friends of the groundlessness of all such statements that we make known the actual facts.

"The price paid in ready money for the shares in question was $375,000. Down to the time of Mr. Raymond's death the shares had never sold for more than $6,000 each. Mr. Morgan has now paid upward of $11,000 each for thirty-four of them, and this transaction is the most conclusive answer which could be furnished to the absurd rumors sometimes circulated to the effect that the course taken by The New York Times toward the Tammany leaders had depreciated the value of the property."

On July 20, under the headline "Proofs of Theft"—still on an inside page—John Foord had a story that told how the Ring had made out fraudulent bills to the city for phantom repairs to the phantom armories. This little item came to almost $1,000,000. Foord had exact figures from Slippery Dick Connolly's books to back him up. They included $431,164 for carpentry, $197,330.24 for plastering, $142,329 for plumbing and $170,729 for chairs. Chairs, curiously, kept turning up all through the doctored accounts, probably because Boss Tweed had been apprenticed in the trade, and had an inordinate fondness for chairs.

The stolen money, Jennings pointed out in the July 20 editorial, went "to meet the expense of the Ring in the matter of fast horses, conservatories, handsome houses and newspaper editors." This was no way to endear himself with fellow craftsmen, but Jennings couldn't resist. Nor could he withhold another jab at the gullible money masters of the town who had looked on Slippery Dick's accounts before the 1870 election, and found them good. He wrote: "We ask the public to look well into the figures we place before them today, and into those we shall publish hereafter . . . and then decide whether Astor, Taylor and Roberts were justified in testifying to the accuracy and good faith of the city accounts."

Tweed and Connolly were grimly desperate now. They tried in vain to reach Jones. The publisher ignored all overtures—and they came from many quarters. Tweed used some of the most influential men in New York to try to arrange a meeting. Jones was stubborn as flint.

One afternoon, after The Times had released the Foord stories on the armory deals, a lawyer who had offices in The Times Building asked Mr. Jones if he would drop in for a few minutes. He did not indicate what he had in mind.

As Jones entered, Slippery Dick Connolly stepped from an inside door. Jones stiffened and his blue eyes stared coldly at the Controller. He told the lawyer, "I do not care to see this man."

Connolly whitened and said, "For God's sake, Mr. Jones, let me say a word or two. Listen for just a moment. Wouldn't it be worth, say, five million dollars, Mr. Jones, to let up on this thing? Five million dollars, sir!"

Jones confessed later that his breath was taken away by the offer. When he spoke, though, his answer was: "I don't think the devil will ever make a higher bid for me. My answer still stands."

The Controller clutched at the publisher's sleeves. His pleading words tumbled over one another. "With that money, Mr. Jones, you could go to Europe—anywhere—You could live like a prince . . . You could—"

Jones bristled.

"True, sir," he interrupted. "All true. But I should know while I lived like a prince, that I was a rascal. I cannot consider your offer —or any offer. The Times will continue to publish the facts."

The Tweed Ring had found someone money could not buy.

The Times of July 22, 1871, threw the town into an uproar. Foord's earlier pieces about grog-shop armories and stable drill floors had been played up, with astonishing modesty, inside the paper, opposite the editorial page, but the July 22 edition carried the front page headline three columns wide: "The Secret Accounts" with the subheads, "Proofs of Undoubted Frauds Brought to Light" and "Warrants Signed by Hall and Connolly Under False Pretenses." This was the first time in the twenty years of its existence that the newspaper had printed any headline more than a column wide. Even the Civil War's end and the assassination of Lincoln had not caused The Times headline type to spread.

"The following accounts, copied with scrupulous fidelity from Controller Connolly's books require little explanation," Foord had written under the headlines. "On the face of these accounts . . . it it clear that the bulk of the money somehow or other got back into the Ring . . . They purport to show the amount paid during 1869 and 1870 for repairs and furniture for the new [County] courthouse." The total came to $5,663,646.83.

High-hatted and be-spatted gentry, as well as ragtag and bobtail in Five Points drammeries, gagged on the gigantic dimensions of the Ring's thievery. Men discussed the scandal on street corners in excited groups. The articles were cunningly played. Foord's story and Jennings' editorials made the most of the fact that G. S. Miller, an obscure carpenter, had—at least on the record—been paid $360,751.61 for one month's work. Men whistled over this figure.

On the editorial page, Jennings sounded the cry for Tammany's hide.

"Let us ask," he wrote, "is there no body of citizens with sufficient respect left for the good name of the City (to say nothing of their own pockets) to institute proceedings against Hall and Connolly for signing these warrants?"

Readers were left to simmer over the week-end on what had become of the millions the Ring had collected for work never done, for furnishings never bought, for repairs to armories that never existed. And simmer they did. The Boss and his braves tried to be defiant, but the communal muttering reached their ears. They were worried.

On Monday, July 24, The Times again ran the "Secret Accounts" headline in three-column width, and labeled it, "Second Series." Foord's lead said:

"The following accounts are copied *verbatim* from the Controller's books, the book entitled 'The Register of Warrants,' and the 'Book of Vouchers.' We print them precisely as they appear in these books . . . We must once more explain that these are County accounts; and we repeat our statement that if the Controller can be made to produce the City accounts, still greater frauds will appear."

The new set of figures showed payment of $2,870,464.06 in 1869 and 1870 for plastering work, chiefly in the new courthouse, some of it on the armories that had never known a coat of plaster. The plasterer was Andrew J. Garvey.

"As C. S. Miller is the luckiest of carpenters," Jennings wrote, "so Andrew J. Garvey is clearly the Prince of Plasterers. His good fortune surpasses anything in the Arabian Nights."

This was no exaggeration. The figures showed that Garvey collected $45,966.99 for one day's plastering—on July 2, 1869; that in one month his plastering bill came to $153,755.14 and for two months, May and June, to almost $1,000,000—$945,715.11, to be exact.

On Wednesday, under another three-column headline The Times printed the last of the figures that O'Brien's spies had copied. These showed payment of $1,231,817.76 for plumbing and gas fitting in the new courthouse. The total figures for the plastering, carpentry and plumbing came to $9,789,482 and more than 85 per cent of it went directly to the Ring caliphate.

On Saturday of that week, Jones put out a four-page "Supplement To The New York Times," devoted entirely to "Connolly's Secret Accounts," the "Gigantic Fraud of The Ring Exposed." The supplement carried all the figures in bold face type, with a recapitulation of the "Astounding Bills of a Furniture Dealer, a Carpenter, a Plasterer and a Plumber." A cross bar of the headline asked, in heavier letters: "Are The Tammany Leaders Honest Men Or Thieves?"

Jones put out 500,000 copies of this supplement—one for every two persons in the city. They melted from the stands as fast as they came from the pressroom. The publisher had decided originally to keep this special edition down to 200,000, but the clamor for it was so insistent that he kept the press gang going in the July heat until the demand died. Half the supplement exposed Tammany's incredible roguery in English, and half told the same story in German because the German population in New York had swelled tremendously and the newcomers got most of their news from the German Staats Zeitung.

Neither Jones nor Jennings let up on the Ring after their figures ran out. They sent John Foord and other reporters to interview the princely plasterer, the fabulous carpenter and the king of plumbers. These were real characters, though the money they were supposed to have drawn actually went to Tweed, Hall, Connolly, Sweeny and the lesser, or pin-feather, braves in the Wigwam. The Croeses of the saw, the hod and the plumbing kit were not around when the reporters called. Tweed had sent them scattering—some to Europe, some to Canada—to keep them beyond reach of journalistic and reform-committee investigators.

Newspapers all over the United States came out editorially with column after column of praise for The Times and for Jones. Many wrote scornfully of other New York publications that had kept silent about Ring skulduggery. The Times was not bashful about this acclaim. It ran pages of it to show that it had made the Tweed Ring a household word for corruption. It must have come a little hard for the Bennetts when Jennings asked The Herald to disprove the report that Tweed had paid $80,000 a year to some of its staff.

It must have been almost as difficult for Greeley to concede editorially:

"We do not endorse it [the crusade]; neither do we discredit it. We are not in possession of facts that would warrant us in making charges. If it be justified by facts, Messrs. Hall and Connolly ought now to be cutting stone in a State prison. The Times deserves the thanks of the community."

George Jones had skinned the Tiger.

In the city elections of 1871 Tammany candidates were trodden underfoot—all, oddly enough, but the Boss. In his home district, where affection for the Old Man never ebbed and where he had been kind to neighbors with his stolen money, he was re-elected to the State Senate.

This was an empty victory for Tweed. A citizens' committee probed into the tangled city accounts, or what was left of them after Connolly had sabotaged his own records, and dredged up enough evidence to have Tweed indicted on multitudinous counts. At noon on Dec. 16, 1871, Sheriff Matt Brennan, one of his own appointees, came into Tweed's lushly carpeted office, hat in hand, and apologetically served the arrest warrant. "I guess you're the man I'm after, Boss," he mumbled awkwardly, and timorously extended the paper. Tweed accepted the paper quietly.

It was around this time that the Boss' emotion got the best of him. He is supposed to have told friends publicly, "If I were twenty to thirty years younger I would kill George Jones with my own bare hands."

Instead of going to the Tombs on the night he was arrested, as any other prisoner would have had to do, Tweed (and the Sheriff) went to the Boss' magnificent suite in the Metropolitan Hotel, one of his nicer city properties. They had a good dinner with the Tweed family and then a good night's rest. Next morning Tweed shopped around until he found a judge who would release him in $5,000 bail.

Tweed came to trial in 1873 in the county courthouse he had built. He was sentenced, eventually, to serve twelve years in prison and fined $12,500. He served only twelve months in the Tombs and on Blackwells Island, and had to pay only $250 of his fine by the time his eight lawyers—one of them young Elihu Root—got through with legalistic maneuvering. This saving was dwarfed by counsel fees that exceeded $500,000.

The other members of the Ring and the princely carpenter and his fellow artificers stayed out of the jurisdiction until they obtained immunity by promising to restore to the city some of the staggering sums they had pilfered. The total amount returned to the city, though, came to only $876,241—a mere fraction of the loot. No one has ever figured out how much had been stolen. It has been variously estimated between $50,000,000 and $200,000,000.

When Tweed came through Blackwells Island gate after having served his shortened term, papers in a $6,000,000 civil suit were served on him. He was rearrested and taken to Ludlow Street Jail, one of the municipal construction jobs that had lined his pockets.

He tired, at last, of the battering he was taking when all his fellow-conspirators stayed out of reach. One day in December, 1875, when the warden and a turnkey had him out for a carriage ride and for dinner in his Madison Avenue mansion, he slipped away. The newspapers set up hue and cry, and $10,000 was posted for information as to his whereabouts.

It was curious that Thomas Nast, who had done so much to stir the populace against Tweed, should have been the indirect cause of his capture. Tweed was in Vigo, Spain, when a Nast cartoon brought over from London, identified him. Ten months after his escape he was escorted aboard the United States cruiser Franklin and returned to New York. He stepped onto Pier 46, a tired, untidy old man stripped of his diamonds and finery and crushed in spirit.

William Tweed was not the gross illiterate portrayed in some accounts. He was well-read, a good conversationalist, at ease in intellectual society. In December, 1876, he wrote dejectedly to Prosecutor Charles O'Conor:

"I am an old man, greatly broken down in health, cast down in spirit, and can no longer bear my burden. Viewing the fact of my return to the wards of this prison . . . I am indeed overwhelmed. All further resistance being hopeless, I have none now to make and only seek the shortest and most efficient manner in which I can yield an unqualified surrender."

He submitted to all manner of investigation and answered freely all questions that were asked, to the point where even prosecuting groups were a little saddened. "We are not sitting as a court," one of the inquisitors muttered. "This is an inquest."

On the morning of April 12, Tweed's family came to his cell. The Boss was sinking. He had said over and over again that he wanted to die. He murmured to Mary Fitzsimmons, a jail matron: "Mary, I have tried to do good by everyone. I know God will receive me."

It was a drowsy day in early spring. Church bells and the City Hall bell tolled noon. A few minutes later the Boss was dead.

CHAPTER
5

THE TIMES started a second national crusade in 1881 that kicked up almost as much editorial dust as Tweed's local corruption had. This time it went after the contractors and sub-contractors who, with the influence of Senators and former Senators, were—and had been—robbing the United States Treasury of millions in what came to be called the Star Route mail frauds.

Star Routes, in post office terminology, were those that reached hamlets and settlements remote from railroads and steamboat lines, where bulk mail was dropped. Deliveries were made by carriers on horseback or in buggies. The routes were designated in postal records with three asterisks symbolizing "celerity, certainty and security," the basis on which delivery contracts were let.

First hints of the mail frauds came to The Times from someone in Washington. The tip was offered to other newspapers first, as the Tammany boodle records were, but it went begging until it came to George Jones. If other publishers thought it was too hot to handle, as they had in the Tweed case, Jones welcomed it.

In Washington for The Times then was Frank D. Root, only nine years out of Yale and on the paper only three years. He devoted full time to digging out the facts from reluctant underlings and subordinates in and around the Post Office Department. They were frightened of the consequences, as Tweed underlings had been, but finally Root had enough to begin his exposé.

In the spring of 1881, the Star Route scandal exploded on The

Times' front pages. Newspapers all over the United States took it up. The accused contractors issued blustering statements and counter-statements. They were careful, though, to hire the best legal talent, including silver-tongued Col. Robert G. Ingersoll.

Root showed that for service on one small Star Route, contractors had persuaded Congress to appropriate $50,000 a year. "Increase" in mail and "expediency" were urged for a community of fewer than 100 persons, though the route yielded only $761 a year in revenue. Root was able to prove that despite the "expediency" plea, no mail had been delivered on that particular route for thirty-nine days.

Root had learned that the contractors had used padded petitions as a lever for the appropriations; that in many cases there were more petitioners' names than the total route population. It was thorough reporting, and the consensus—as in the Tweed case—was that the racketeers would end up in the penitentiary. The frauds totalled from $4,000,000 to $10,000,000.

Indictments came easily in the District of Columbia. They covered frauds on ninety-three mail routes. Colonel Ingersoll and the other pleaders for the racketeers, in delaying tactics, piled writ on writ, using every legal trick to postpone trial. The contractors were finally put to the bar in 1882 and 1883 with astonishing results.

After Colonel Ingersoll had all but hypnotized the wide-eyed jurors, they retired for lengthy deliberation. On the morning of June 14, 1883, they came in with the verdict, "Not guilty as indicted." Colonel Ingersoll, quick to emotionalism, wept in open court. So did the defendants and their wives before they went out into Pennsylvania Avenue to set up drinks for their friends.

The mail route frauds were ended, though, even if there was not a single conviction. The Government, the final accounting showed, had spent more than $500,000 in the futile effort to put the contractors and their Senator friends in prison.

The Times and other papers fumed editorially against this miscarriage of justice. Public interest switched to stories of General Crook's forays against Apaches and other warring tribes in the Sierra Madres. But The Times had scored again and added to its circulation and prestige.

While Colonel Ingersoll was summing up for the defense in the

Star Route frauds, The Times ran on its back page on Sept. 5, 1882, under the heading "Miscellaneous News," an item on Thomas A. Edison's electric light service.

Though this was probably one of the greatest scientific advances of the period, The Times did not seem unduly excited about it. It had carried earlier pieces about Edison's experiments, but the September story marked the beginning of commercial lighting.

The first area to benefit by the Edison service was bounded by Spruce, Wall, Nassau and Pearl Streets, so that The Times just squeezed in on it. The lights blinked on at 41 Park Row at 7 P.M. on Sept. 4. The story was headed:

EDISON ELECTRIC LIGHT

"THE TIMES" BUILDING ILLUMINATED
BY ELECTRICITY

"Edison's central station, at 257 Pearl Street," the story said, "was yesterday one of the busiest places in town, and Mr. Edison was by far the busiest man in the station . . . The giant dynamos were started at 3 o'clock in the afternoon, and according to Mr. Edison, they will go on forever unless stopped by an earthquake . . .

"Yesterday for the first time The Times Building was illuminated by electricity . . . To each of the gas fixtures in the establishment a bronze arm was attached, and the electric lamps were suspended from the ends of these arms . . . The light was more brilliant than gas, and a hundred times steadier. To turn on the light nothing is required but to turn on the thumbscrew . . . As soon as it is dark enough to need artificial light you turn the thumbscrew and the light is there, with no nauseous smell, no flicker and no glare."

The Sept. 5 story explained that twenty-seven of the new-fangled lamps (minutely described) were wired to the gas fixtures in the editorial rooms and "twenty-five in the counting rooms," which included the advertising department. "It was so light," wrote the reporter, "a man could sit under it for hours without consciousness of having any artificial light about him." The composing room and the pressroom got the new lighting a few months later.

There was a highly significant editorial that same day on the

Labor Parade that was to start in Mail Street at City Hall next morning and wind up in Elm Park at Ninth Avenue and Ninety-second Street. The Times editorial writer seemed somewhat puzzled at this curious manifestation and wrote rather testily of the banners the marchers were to carry—absurd things calling for an eight-hour working day, among other things.

The Times gave liberal space to the march of the 10,000 working men next day and John Swinton, a former Times editorial writer, was one of the reviewing officers in the little cottage in Union Square past which the procession tramped.

"Nearly all [the marchers] were well clothed," The Times reporter noticed, "and some wore attire of fashionable cut . . . The great majority smoked cigars." He listed, at great length, the slogans carried by the marchers. If anyone of the paper then realized the role labor would eventually assume in government, it did not show in the writing of the period.

Jones hired John Bigelow to replace Henry Raymond in August, 1869. Bigelow was stuffy, even for the age, and something of a literary snob. He leaned toward Europe's men of letters rather than toward American writers. He hobnobbed with European literati—with Dickens, Wilkie Collins and with famous French and German writers.

In his youth, Bigelow had worked for William Cullen Bryant on The Post. As a literary journalist, he did not hit it off with practical George Jones. It was fairly evident from the start that Bigelow was not to stay with the paper long. In early October, 1869, a few days after he had left 41 Park Row in a huff, he wrote to a friend:

"I may say that everything about The Times, inside and out, disappointed me from the day I entered my editorial chamber and found neither pen nor paper nor any provision for my *avenement*. The *milieu*, morally and intellectually, was uncongenial." John Bigelow dearly loved to show his Continental polish.

In the eight weeks he was with The Times, Bigelow tried to fill the staff with fancy literary talent, rather than with foot-slogging reporters. When Jones murmured about this, Bigelow was hurt. There were thirty-six men on the staff at the time, not counting foreign and domestic correspondents. Their pay averaged around $30 a week, though some of the younger and newer men got from $8 to $15.

"Mr. Jones began to complain that I was running up expenses of the office and I was elevating the standard of the paper too high," Bigelow confided in another of his endless letters. "He complained that I had abolished the title 'Minor Topics,' [which became Topics of The Times on Sept. 8, 1896] which he regarded only as less profane than dancing on Raymond's grave."

On Aug. 6 and 7, 1869, The Times ran two editorials based on a talk Bigelow had had with President Grant on the nation's financial condition. On Aug. 19 President Grant returned through New York, and again Bigelow talked with him.

Jay Gould learned of the second interview and figured out a scheme for using it to advantage in his plan to increase the price of gold. His partners in the move were James Fisk Jr., and A. Rathbone Corbin, President Grant's brother-in-law.

Corbin prepared an article titled "Grant's Financial Policy." Gould persuaded James McHenry, a British capitalist and close friend of Bigelow's, to offer it at The Times as a lead editorial accurately reflecting the President's attitude on gold.

The plot almost worked. Bigelow had the editorial set and was prepared to run it exactly as it had been written. Before it got into the paper, though, Caleb C. Norvel, The Times financial editor, scanned it. He was horrified. He read copy on it and cut out the last paragraph, the one on which Gould had counted most heavily for public effect.

This was lucky for The Times. When Black Friday darkened the country on Sept. 24, 1869, The Times was guiltless of any responsibility for it, though not because of the sharpness of its new chief editor. Bigelow had let the piece go through in all innocence. But the near-blunder was his undoing. Jones replaced him with 50-year-old George Sheppard, who had been with Raymond as an editorial writer for six years.

Before Bigelow left The Times he hired the city staff's first woman reporter. One September day, in 1869, the city room boards creaked under the weight of a giant female in men's brogues, whose stride caused the staff to look up. They saw her vanish into Bigelow's sanctum and she was there a half-hour or so. Next morning, to the staff's astonishment, they heard the same heavy clump-clump on the boards, and the oversized lady was gallantly escorted to an empty desk by Bigelow himself.

One by one, the editors, and then the men on the staff, were called over to "meet Miss Maria Morgan, who is to handle live-stock news, horse shows and dog shows and racing for The Times." Miss Morgan grasped each man by the hand, leaving his fingers semi-liquid. Her voice, rumbling from a cavernous chest, was brusque and impressive. So was her hair high-piled, with a grim straw bonnet perched at the summit. She preferred men's serge and mannish tweeds to wispy stuffs and her shoes trailed aromas of stable and cattle pen. She was the first woman hired exclusively for the city staff.

Midy Morgan, born of Irish landed gentry, became a legend along newspaper row. There was a little snickering at first over the idea of having a woman—and a woman past 40 at that—cover livestock, but her extraordinary energy wore out competition. She helped pick racing stables for President Grant, King Victor Emmanuel II, Commodore Vanderbilt, Roscoe Conkling, former President Chester Arthur and Leonard Jerome, all of whom highly respected her knowledge of horseflesh. All the trousered livestock reporters came to look upon Midy with some awe.

Tireless, Miss Morgan stormed into piggeries as more delicate females might assail a Fifth Avenue shop for a sale of something exotic by Chanel. On rainy days she climbed into hip boots and sloshed around the Jersey City cattle yards. If a downpour beat her wide-brimmed bonnet down around her ears, she paid no attention.

Midy, who died in 1892, stayed with The Times for twenty-three years. In that time the men came to have a warm affection for her.

Though Miss Morgan was the first woman admitted to The Times city room as a reporter, she was actually the second woman reporter on the newspaper's payroll. The first was Sara Jane Clarke, a friend of John Greenleaf Whittier's, who wrote under the pen name "Grace Greenwood."

She was the daughter of Dr. Thaddeus Clarke, a physician in Pompey near Syracuse, N.Y., where she was born in 1823. She was a militant abolitionist—read proof on "Uncle Tom's Cabin" when she worked for The National Era in 1852—and was something of a traipsing woman for her time.

She did endless travel pieces from the West for The Times in the late Fifties and afterward from Europe. She was Washington correspondent, too, for a time, and was a friend of President Lincoln's. She died in New York on April 20, 1904.

CHAPTER
6

THE NEW YORK PICTURE was swiftly changing. The city was losing its Dickensian flavor. The Machine Age roared in. Edison's
light was only one of multiple new wonders. Mechanical advances
came on so rapidly that men were bewildered. In Henry Raymond's
day a man and his newspaper were easily heard above horses' clop-
clop and the sleepy rumble of drays and coaches, but the Machine
Age called for a voice with greater range.

Day by day, The Times recorded this story of change in a city
about to burst its seams with swelling population, and told it in
dignified, newsy fashion without trimmings. Under Jones it pursued a consistently even way. Its editorial page had quietly
dropped behind the news and under the influence of Associate
Editor Edward Cary, an up-Stater born of Quaker stock, took on a
mellower and gentler tone, fairly free from petty personal bickering, and from journalistic back-biting generally.

The Times told the story of the new-fangled Brush arc lamps
that replaced gaslight in Broadway; of how rustics came from
Brooklyn and from Queens and from far-off Bronx to gape at them;
of the new elevated railroad that coughed black smoke on the high
trestles on Third Avenue; of the new cable cars in Broadway over
the route that the clattering stage had run; of the stripping of overhead telegraph wires from street poles, and their burial under pavement; of Edison's application for a patent for the kinetographic
camera, sire of motion pictures; of Ward McAllister's list of the

Four Hundred (actually less than 300) for Mrs. William Waldorf
Astor's party in her mansion at Fifth Avenue and Thirty-fourth
Street; of a mastodon's tooth found in Broadway in an excavation
for the approach to the Harlem River Ship Canal; of the new world
wonder, Brooklyn Bridge.

There was, too, an occasional spectacular scoop.

On Sunday, March 14, 1886, news was dull and scant—a few
cheap fires, a few flat meetings, but nothing worth while for Monday's front page. City Editor William J. Kenny stared gloomily
through rain-lashed windows into Printing House Square and into
deserted City Hall Park.

Most of the news staff were downstairs at dinner. A few worked
at inconsequential items far down the city room. Dispirited telegraph keys chattered every now and then and lapsed into Sabbath
quiet. Twilight was early. Lamplighters on bicycles touched off
blobs of illumination and the gaslight wriggled on wet sidewalks
and cobbled streets.

A man from the waterfront beat pounded breathlessly up the
stairs. Rain had beaded his face. He said: "There's a rumor down
at the waterfront that the Cunarder Oregon collided with some
other ship and went down in twenty fathoms off Fire Island this
morning. She's supposed to have 1,000 on board, counting crew,
and the German liner Fulda is supposed to have picked all, or
most of them, up."

Kenny wheeled. He called Charles Tracy Bronson and Thomas
B. Fielders, staff men, from routine tasks. At his desk they figured
from tide tables that the Fulda, which drew twenty-seven feet of
water, could not cross Sandy Hook bar before high tide at midnight. It would be 3 o'clock in the morning before survivors reached
Quarantine for interviewing—too late for a Monday story.

There were no telephones in newspaper offices then. A man
could not sit at a desk and order a tugboat. He had to go out on foot
or with horse and buggy to search for one. Kenny remembered,
though, that the Luckenbach tugboat Ocean King had left harbor
early that morning with a load of rich young bloods, who had put
up a $1,500 purse for a championship fight at Larchmont in West-
chester. It was to have been an afternoon bout and the tug was
due at her Erie Basin dock in Brooklyn around 8 P.M.

Kenny had one of the older staff men sit in for him on the city desk. Then he, Bronson, Fielders and George Holbrook, a Times telegraph operator, set out in the lashing storm to find a tug to take them to the German ship, beyond Sandy Hook bar. Holbrook carried a telegraph key and a heavy coil of wire, to tap out the story. That way they might still make the first edition.

The Hudnut Pharmacy thermometer at 230 Broadway showed 36 degrees when The Times sea-going expedition passed it, heads bent, topcoats bellying like filled sail. It was to drop to freezing within three hours. On the ferryboat, the northwester chipped at the men's faces, and the craft itself creaked and shuddered. It was a mean night for a sea jaunt, but competition was fierce in those days.

The men found that the Ocean King had already debarked the sporting gentry—"clubmen who delight in seeing two men disfigure each other," The Times was to call them in the fight story next day. Of the tug's crew only a steward and the skipper were aboard. They were tired and disinclined to put out again, but Kenny hired a rig, drove to the Lewis Luckenbach home in Union Street, not far off, and got a written order to the skipper to take The Times crew to Sandy Hook bar. The contract stipulated that Kenny, Bronson, Fielders and Holbrook were to double as crew—to fire the boilers and to obey the captain's commands.

Full night had settled over the inner harbor when the Ocean King pulled away from Brooklyn. Shore lights vanished behind the rain curtain as the tug met crashing seas. With The Times men taking turns at the boilers, the Ocean King churned on.

Halfway to Sandy Hook she overtook a smaller tugboat in distress in the heavy seas. The Ocean King got a line aboard and took her in tow.

The skipper of the smaller craft bawled: "Ocean King, where ya bound?"

"Headed for the North German Lloyd liner Fulda anchored off Scotland Light."

There was a pause. Then the small-tug man hollered, "We have a ship news reporter for The Sun aboard. He wants to make the Fulda. Can you take him aboard?"

Kenny grabbed the Ocean King captain. He explained that The

Times had chartered his vessel to get an exclusive story, and that The Sun was a competitor. He said, "We saved them, and we've lived up to the laws of the sea, but we're not taking The Sun man to the Fulda."

It turned out that The Sun man was John R. Spears. He pleaded across the angry black water, but he pleaded in vain. The Ocean King dropped the rival tug in a cove at Sandy Hook and plowed on toward Scotland Light.

At 11 o'clock the Ocean King came under the Fulda's starboard rail. The rain had left off, and the liner's mountainous bulk was outlined in lights. Captain Sam of the Ocean King—he was never otherwise identified to The Times crew—was worried about putting Kenny and his men aboard.

"It's illegal," he pointed out. "By rights no man can board an incoming vessel until the Government doctor has cleared her."

"You give her the doctor's signal," Kenny urged. "We'll take care of anything that may develop."

Captain Sam shrugged. He gave the Government doctor's toot, or, as The Times itself slyly told it in the paper two days later, "There was a strong dash of Health Officer in the tug's whistle."

The Fulda dropped a boarding ladder and Kenny, Bronson and Fielders made the ascent, leaving Holbrook, the steward, and Captain Sam to man the Ocean King. Kenny had arranged a set of signals to bring the tug back to the starboard rail when he and his men had finished their interviewing.

The Times, in its account of the boarding, said: "The extremely courteous [Fulda] officers tipped their caps to the reporters who were amused, though rather mortified, to discover that they were mistaken for health officers. Being in a hurry, they decided to defer explanations. They went into the smoking cabin."

The Fulda skipper had lined his crew in the traditional formation for receiving an official boarding party. When he learned that the boarders were reporters instead of the health officer, he exploded with Teutonic rage. Kenny, Bronson and Fielders were ordered put under arrest, but at a quick signal from Kenny all three broke in different directions. They lost the crew on deck in the dark. By prearrangement they met in the smoking cabin.

Kenny interviewed Captain Philip Cottier, the Oregon's skipper, with a group of survivors shielding him from the Fulda's searchers. Captain Cottier told how an unidentified schooner had rammed his ship at 4:30 A.M. Sunday as she neared New York under a full head of steam; how he got all his passengers and crew off in lifeboats, and how the Fulda had picked them up as the Oregon sank in twenty-two fathoms at noon, eight hours after the collision.

The Times men got not only the Oregon skipper's story, but also the passenger lists, other survivors' stories and a history of the Oregon. Then they separated to write behind a shield of friendly passengers who were eager to get the story before friends and relatives. It was after midnight when the stories were finished. They were rough, with many omissions, but in such shape that a copy editor could complete and smooth them.

Kenny had a passenger bring some heavy-handled cutlery from the dining room. He weighted each batch of copy with a knife, a fork or a spoon. It was his plan to have one man make the Ocean King, with or without a Jacob's ladder, and for the others to throw their copy down to him.

The wind had died down when The Times men made it to the upper deck with their copy. The Fulda had hoisted anchor, and was under way for Quarantine. The boarding ladder had been pulled up.

Just then the Fulda's crew sighted Kenny and his men and converged on them. Kenny tried to persuade the skipper that no one had been harmed and that New York was waiting for the story of the Fulda's heroic rescue. Passengers added their pleas, but their breath was wasted.

The Fulda's master roared: "No one leaves this vessel until we reach Quarantine. You newspaper fellows will be turned over to the Government for breaking the law." He ordered his men to take the three below.

A seaman grabbed Fielders. This was a mistake. Fielders was a college athlete with a short temper. He knocked the man flat and climbed the starboard rail. The Ocean King was then racing alongside the Fulda.

Fielders shouted, "Ocean King, ahoy," and Captain Sam brought his snubby craft dangerously close under the rail. The tug's deck was fifty feet below, but Fielders leaped into the dark. He hit one of the thick steel cables that guyed the Ocean King's stack. He caught the cable with his hands, which were torn, but he made the deck.

Meanwhile, a free-for-all went on at the Fulda's rail. Billy Kenny's collar, shirt and undershirt were torn away by the Fulda's skipper. Bronson lost his hat and his storm coat in a tussle with the crew. Both got clear long enough, though, to drop their cutlery-weighted copy to Holbrook and Fielders. Then, panting, they submitted to arrest.

The Ocean King hooted that all the copy was safe—another Kenny signal arranged before boarding—and foamed toward Manhattan. All the way in Fielders labored at editing the copy in the skipper's cabin with handkerchiefs over his palm wounds.

Ten minutes after the tugboat had nosed into a South Street pier, he was at 41 Park Row. The whole composing room night shift worked feverishly at setting the Oregon wreck story in type.

The Times scored a clean beat. It gave five of its seven front-page columns of March 15 to the Oregon story. No other newspaper in town had a line.

When the Fulda reached Quarantine at 3 A.M. the fuming German skipper turned Kenny and Bronson—both disheveled and bruised, but grinning and triumphant—over to the custom authorities.

Frustrated reporters from other morning newspapers had tried desperately to make the Monday morning editions. Captain Coffin, The New York World man, had kept the lone Quarantine telegraph wire open by having two Western Union men copy column after column of stale stuff from The Sunday World.

Spears, the Sun man, had reached Quarantine by buggy. Enraged at having been dumped on a sand bar by The Times crew he clamored for Kenny's and Bronson's detention. Neither he nor any of the other ship news men knew, until later, that Fielders had reached The Times with the wreck story.

This beat remained a favorite Times legend for many years. John C. Reid, managing editor, kind and not ordinarily given to editorial sniping, could not resist a mild paragraph about the scoop in Tuesday's paper. One of his men wrote:

"It was rumored that The Sun and The Herald had chartered tugs, but the rumor could not be traced to a reliable source. The Tribune, of course, did not make any effort to get the news, and, like the other dailies, will, presumably, reprint in their issues today what was in The Times columns yesterday."

The men who figured in the Oregon story eventually scattered far and wide. Bill Kenny became head of a securities advertising company. Fielders went to Europe to edit the Pall Mall Gazette. Bronson died in New Haven, Conn., on Oct. 4, 1925, in his seventy-fourth year. Holbrook ended his days as a telegraph operator on the Great Northern Railroad in the Dakotas.

The Oregon scoop was one of the last in the Jones regime. Jones was not to see the metallic fruits of Ford's genius, nor the swelling of the city's population to O. Henry's "The Four Million," nor the rise of the skyscrapers, as the century groaned and pivoted. He had come to the office every day through the Eighties until he left in June for the summer vacation of 1891. On the morning of Aug. 12, 1891, he died in his summer home in Poland, Me. Next day The Times' front-page rules were turned to make mourning borders, and the editorial page told again the fabulous story of how Jones and Horace the Ghost had worked as boys for Amos Bliss in Poultney, Jones in the Bliss general store, Greeley as printer's devil on The Northern Spectator.

When George Jones died, the magic touch of the original dynasty was gone. The Jones heirs were not journalistically minded. Though their father had asked in his will that they hold onto the paper, they were prepared, within a year of his death, to dispose of it to almost any bidder. They had good reason, too. The Times had passed from mere limping into blind staggers. It seemed as though the paper must surely die. Politics had helped bring it to this condition.

Ever since Raymond had helped shape the Republican party, The Times had remained steadfastly conservative Republican. In 1884, when it seemed certain that James G. Blaine would be the party's choice for President, there was an editorial council on the issue.

Charles Ransom Miller was editor in chief. He felt that corruption had changed the party. Most of his assistants agreed. Only

Reid, who had been managing editor since 1872, held out against The Times' turning its back on Blaine; he was a die-hard Republican.

Jones finally made the decision—The Times would fight a Blaine nomination, and if Blaine were nominated the newspaper would support another candidate. With this official go-ahead, Miller opened fire on Blaine.

"If the nominee of the Chicago Republican Convention," The Times said on May 29, 1884, "is a man worthy to be President of the United States, The New-York Times will give him hearty and vigorous support. If he shall be a man unworthy to hold that high office, a man who personally and politically, in office or out, represents principles and practices which The Times abhors and has counseled the party to shun, we shall watch with great interest the efforts of those responsible for such a nomination to elect the candidate, but we shall give them no help."

Blaine was nominated. The Times headed the Mugwump movement and helped elect Grover Cleveland.

It was a bitterly costly moral victory for The Times. Indignant Republicans fled from it en masse, and many took their advertising with them. The paper's profits fell from $188,000 in 1883 to $56,000 in 1884. This did not prevent it from supporting Cleveland again in 1888, when he was defeated, and once more in 1892 when he was re-elected, but at the end of his second Administration the paper was gasping for sustenance. Cleveland had justified The Times' faith in him, but newspapers do not survive on vindication alone. By 1890 profits were down to $15,000 and still falling.

The swing to Grover Cleveland, the crushing cost of the new building, the panic and depression that were stirred by the free silver bogey in 1893 seemed to be death blows. The Jones heirs who might have had more for their father's majority holdings, let them go for less than $1,000,000 to a group of Times men headed by Edward Cary and Miller, the chief editor. The heirs had made one futile stab at saving the paper. They had raised its price to 3 cents four months after their father died. A unique printing device was conceived by Gilbert Jones, the publisher's son, for calling public attention to the price rise. Head of the newspaper's mechanical department at the time, he had the front-page borders printed in color

—red, blue, and green. It was the only occasion in Times history when the news section carried color. Yet the price increase was futile. It merely served to weaken further an already exhausted sheet. The mourners waited in the wings.

Miller, a farm boy from New Hampshire, who had come out of Dartmouth to The Springfield Republican, and eventually to the telegraph desk of The New-York Times, had been named editor in chief of the paper by Jones on April 13, 1883. He was a scholar, brilliant in understanding of the classics and in international affairs, but was a clumsy hand at running a business. Kindly Edward Cary, who had been on the editorial staff since 1871 and was to keep writing until his death in 1917, was no ledger-and-journal man, either. They soon found that they had bought a ghost—a mighty sick ghost, at that.

When they came to look at what their money had brought them they found that they had merely rented a building at $40,000—the structure at 41 Park Row was not included, of course, in the sale price—and that they could expect no working capital from payments owed to The Times, since the contract stipulated these were to go to the Jones estate. To make matters worse pressroom equipment had somehow been overlooked in the rebuilding by Jones. The presses were a bit wobbly and needed frequent repair. There was no cash on hand with which to bolster the news service, either, and down the street William Randolph Hearst and Joseph Pulitzer were running plants that had the town by the ears. They were slugging it out in a wastrel conflict to decide which could turn out the more sensational penny sheet—and both had money to burn.

The Times grew feebler and feebler. The word in Printing House Square and in Park Row was that the undertaker would be in any minute, now. Some of the printers pulled out, and reporters looked around for something a little more secure. The Times seemed past all saving.

CHAPTER

7

O NE OCTOBER DAY in 1872, about three years after Henry
Raymond died, Capt. William Rule looked up from his writing in The Knoxville Chronicle's untidy editorial room dreamily
aware that someone had stepped in from Market Square, and
quietly awaited his attention. A rather undersized urchin about 14
years old, with moist flat curls tight against his high forehead,
stood by the worn desk and stared at him out of steady blue eyes.
The boy wore hand-me-downs, the universal garb for small fry in
post-bellum Tennessee, but what he had was neat, if a little off-
size. The child's gravity intrigued the editor. Something about him,
peculiarly tense and adult, betrayed that here was a boy destined
to move soberly among impish contemporaries, one marked to
know grownups' responsibility in childhood.

The boy wanted work. Captain Rule, at first inclined to get on
with his writing, found himself, instead, further intrigued by the
softness of the voice, and its extreme politeness. Through The
Chronicle's dusty windows came outdoor sounds—the complaints
of overloaded carts, the clop-clop of spirited mounts on the cobblestones, the hoarse urging of weary teams and the snapping of bull-
whips. Knoxville was struggling out of post-war poverty, and
traffic was heavy.

Finally the captain said, "The only opening here, bub, is for a
chore boy and printer's devil. We need someone to clean this

place, do the sweeping, run galleys and sort type—if you know what that means."

The boy nodded and his curls shook. He said, "I know what that is, sir. I'd like that." The lad's eagerness amused the captain. He said, "All right, bub. You can start now."

The boy put his little pork pie hat on a shelf. He looked around the room and decided to tackle Captain Rule's desk lamp, which, Heaven knows, needed attention. Housekeeping was a neglected function in the shabby, ink-and-tobacco-scented newspaper plants in the South in those days. The boy lifted the lamp from the editor's desk. He polished a smooth gleam on the smoky chimney with newsprint. He scrubbed the lamp proper, and when that shone to his satisfaction, trued the blackened wick with editorial scissors. He borrowed a match to test his handiwork. The wick burned evenly, with steady flame. The boy blew out the light, and went to fresher chores.

Getting out next day's editorial with scratchy pen, the captain paused briefly at irregular intervals to watch. The boy picked up grimy, boot-marked Chronicles from the splintered floor and gathered inky scrap paper, tobacco-ends and burnt matches. With a stubby broom fetched from the composing room at the back of the office—The Chronicle plant was housed on a single floor in a faded red-brick building—the boy stirred ancient dust until it turned, almost solid, in shafted October sunlight. He worked silently and with odd concentration, as if these were the most vital chores a boy had ever undertaken.

By late afternoon the captain's sanctum was almost distressingly neat. Never had a Chronicle office boy done so much, so thoroughly, in so short a time. The urchin's forehead gleamed faintly with perspiration and his breath came a little hard. He had cleaned the press rollers with cotton waste, had picked up type dropped by harried printers and had emptied and refilled the printers' spitboxes, the blunt name for office cuspidors. The refill was sweet-scented sawdust. The captain looked on the work and found it good. He said, gently, "Don't overdo it, bub. You've put in a full day." The boy knew from the inflection that this was an accolade. He looked at the results of his labors, took up the worn hat and went into Market Square, a little heady with exultation.

He hurried toward home, a two-story unpainted shack in Water Street near the East Knoxville line. Even his walk somehow belied his years. It was a little chesty, in the adult manner. At the northern end of the Square, through vacant lots, the boy saw the distant fields, and all about him the purpling Cumberlands and the Blue Ridge. The Tennessee, calm, peaceful and broad, was gelid silver in the twilight, with dancing patches of liquid gold. On College Hill, cows turned barnward, and war-scarred school buildings were clear silhouettes against the sky.

In mountain meadows and under browning trees, just outside the town, boys called shrilly at play. A group of lads, barefoot and begrimed with romping, sighted Captain Rule's lamp-polisher. They cried, "Mooley—Hey, Mooley," and The Chronicle's new office boy turned to the greeting. "Mooley" was a common term among farm boys then, for any hornless steer or cow, and they had given him that nickname in juvenile glee because they thought it fitted so well with his last name. No one watching Captain Rule's new boy making down the street in the twilight could have guessed it then, but blue-eyed Adolph Simon Ochs had put a firm foot on journalism's ladder. One day he was to take over The New York Times, and lift it to such prominence in international journalism as Henry Raymond and George Jones, in their highest optimism, could never have dreamed.

Mooley Ochs broke over the threshold of the house in Water Street, bursting to tell the family the story of his job, and what he had done all day. He was the oldest child, born March 12, 1858. Nannie, his 9-year-old sister, hugged him affectionately. George Washington, who was 8, clamored for permission to get a job too, and so did Milton Barlow, wide-eyed 5-year-old. He did not quite understand what it was all about, but the excitement made it seem desirable. Ada, 3 years old, stared up at the group silently and Mattie, the 1-year-old baby, gurgled in her crib.

Capt. Julius Ochs, a bearded esthete, seemed a little saddened. He and Bertha, his wife, had wanted their sons to be scholars but it was the age of the Horatio Alger pattern when many children found work long before they got into their teens. Besides, Captain Ochs' earnings were thin and uncertain. His fees as United States Commissioner for Knoxville came to about $2 on good days but were apt to be $1 or less on leaner ones. He had been a Magistrate in Knoxville but had lost that office by twelve votes at the election a few months before. The 25 cents a day that Mooley was to get at The Chronicle would buy a lot of food. Eggs were only 10 cents a dozen at the time, and a bushel of corn sold for as little as 15 cents.

Captain Ochs, born in Germany to parents of Jewish faith, who had come to the United States in 1845, was well-meaning and kindly but more visionary than practical—a sort of wistful Micawber. He had been a good soldier in volunteer units in both the Mexican and Civil Wars, but when he turned his hand to trade, money faded from his fingers. He had had one brief spell of opulence since the day in 1865 when he had driven his family in a covered wagon to Knoxville, from Cincinnati, Adolph's birthplace. While he was with the Army, his investment in a draper's shop in Knoxville had grown to around $25,000, a fortune in that period. The family had owned a house in Cumberland Street, then, and Ochsenburg, a small estate four miles out in the country. They had two servants, a carriage with two horses, and Captain Ochs had presided over joyful house parties and picnics. He had entertained intellectual friends over week-ends with lengthy and earnest discussions on the arts. He had played sweetly for them on his guitar and had been generous with good foods and wines. This happy bubble burst in 1867, a year of panic in the South. The draper's shop was loaded with goods bought at inflated wartime prices when the bottom dropped out of the textile market. Captain Ochs was left penniless. Ochsenburg, the servants, the carriage, the lively parties, and the house in Cumberland Street faded as in a mirage.

Adolph Ochs showed extraordinary devotion to his family to the day he died. Somehow he had known since childhood that he, and not his dreamy father, would carry the family burden. Actually he had no childhood. When classmates picked berries and whooped and hollered on College Hill, or played in Fort Sanders' ruins, he was at work.

In 1870 he had worked briefly as cash boy in an uncle's grocery in Providence, R. I., and had gone to a business school there at night. In 1871 he was back in Knoxville, apprenticed to a druggist, but had no heart for it and returned to school for another year.

Early examples of Ochs' prose show no rare writing talent. One afternoon in November 1862, when he was in his fourteenth year, the boy wrote a school composition on his father's Justice of the Peace letterheads. It was titled, "A Glimpse of everyday life at the E.T.U.," and carried his byline in his own flourishing hand.

"The E.T.U.," the composition said, "is situated at knoxville east tenn, it is situated on a hill in the north eastern part of knoxville, The government made an appropation to the University, & sent a U.S. Army Officer there; since then it has become a miliatry school, Now to go back to my subject, At six o'clock the bell rings to rise, at ½ past eight the bell rings again for school to take up, I will take the room I go in for my subject, The last boys in have a way of singing out 'here', before even the roll is called. (jist forr the fun of it) the first thing the roll is called & then prayers & then comes grammar, in this rescitation. . . . . . ."

The whole long screed has the same Tom Sawyer quality. There was nothing about the piece to betray the promising newspaper publisher.

Ochs quit school forever in 1873 when he was at The Chronicle. He left the academy with the headmaster's special recommendation for "application to study, and general demeanor." The boy's lack of college education, though, colored his later existence. He stood ever in awe of the learned, and looked with wistful respect on his own editors' scholarship.

Three years before he became Captain Rule's chore boy, Mooley Ochs had been a newspaper carrier. He would wake in darkness to get Chronicles as they came from the press around 4 A.M. He folded them by hand, and started on a house-to-house route that took in some four square miles of East Knoxville. In spring and in summer he went barefoot. Later his brothers, George Washington and Milton Barlow, were Chronicle carriers, too. Captain Ochs would wake when the boys did and walk with them to the plant. This was a kind of humble apology, his way of letting them know that he shared the discomforts that resulted from his misfortunes. He kept trying new business ventures in the hope of restoring the happy days of Ochsenburg, but he lacked the golden touch. Every venture failed.

Two years after Captain Rule took him on, young Mooley became a full-fledged "devil" on The Chronicle. On cold days he started the fire in the pot-bellied stove, carried the ashes into the alley, cleaned and trimmed the lamps, scoured the printing rollers, pulled proofs, hustled down to the Western Union for dispatches, legged it to the post office for Chronicle mail. His gravity, his eagerness for learning the fine points of printing, his zest for work, astonished happy-go-lucky journeymen who kept wandering in and out of Chronicle office jobs as whim, or alcoholic fancy, dictated. He was the butt of crude jokes, but that was any "devil's" lot, and he took it good-naturedly.

From 1873 to 1875 he was a printer's apprentice. He completed this phase of his learning in half the average time under Henry C. Collins, the baldish, walrus-mustached, myopic foreman at The Chronicle. He worked at night under flaring gas lamps until printer's ink was ingrained not only in his finger-whorls, but in his soul. Many years later, when he owned The New York Times and sat with other publishers to negotiate with union printers, he was to say, wistfully, "I still feel I am on the wrong side of this table. I belong with the boys from the composing room." He was a good printer. When other journeymen fumbled at the type with unsteady fingers, during or after a spree, or slept on the composing room floor, Mooley Ochs stuck grimly at his case by The Chronicle window, his nimble fingers assembling type at astonishing speed.

One night in October 1875, when he knew he had no more to learn from Collins, Ochs decided to take to the road as a tramp printer. There was a party after the paper had been put to bed. Galley boys brought steaming oysters, beer and crackers from Mick's upstreet. They set banquet boards on wooden horses between the type cases. There were elaborate speeches, and the journeymen roared choruses of bawdy and sentimental ballads. Just before sun-up the foreman gave his earnest pupil the parting gift—a volume of Thomas Hood's poems, with each printer's name written waveringly on the flyleaf.

Captain Rule wrote a little piece about the party for the Oct. 13 issue of The Chronicle. It said: "Mr. Adolph Ochs, for some years past an attaché of The Chronicle office, leaves on the westbound train today, on a protracted visit to Louisville, Ky. and other points.

"Mr. Ochs carries with him the well wishes of all connected with this office, and we would recommend him to all with whom he may come in contact, as a young man well worthy of their confidence and esteem."

No one quite knew the dreams that Ochs carried with him. Captain Rule conceded later, that even he had not appreciated the extent of the genius that lay under the black curls and behind the steady blue eyes of the diffident urchin who had come into his dusty office, six years before, to be chore boy, carrier and devil.

About this time, Mooley Ochs thought he might try to work his way as journeyman printer to California where gold fever continued high. He got no farther than Louisville. There he worked on Marse Henry Watterson's Courier-Journal. He set type at first, became assistant composing room foreman, and did some reporting. His first big assignment was the burial of Andrew Johnson. God had never intended him for authorship, though. His writing was a little of the rigid, or maxim-book style. During the Louisville period he sent home whatever money he could save by boarding with the Francks, his cousins, and by stinting on entertainment.

One day when young Ochs was walking with Lucien Franck, his cousin asked him how much savings he had at the bank. Ochs was silent a moment.

He said, "I don't have any, Lu."

He took a letter from his pocket. It was from his mother. One paragraph in it said: "I am ashamed to send the children to school, now. They have no decent shoes and no stockings, and their clothes are almost past mending."

An hour after Ochs had received the letter he had withdrawn his total savings, $56—and sent them home. Besides, he was homesick; his nightly letters betrayed that. He missed the family. Within six months he was back in Knoxville.

In the spring of 1876 about six months before his eighteenth year, Ochs labored over the type cases on The Knoxville Tribune. Here, too, he was marked by extraordinary concentration. Perched on his stool by the window, his curly head bent over the printer's stick, he plucked type from his case and dropped it into place with dogged rhythm. The jokes, horseplay and off-line stories of fellow printers amused him but his work stride never faltered. When tipsy journeymen broke into song—hymns, often as not, or plantation melodies—he joined in. He always loved popular music.

One day Col. John Fleming, The Tribune's editor in chief, wrote sulkily of a rainy-day Republican caucus at the county courthouse, "It was damp, dry drivel." Ochs the printer got it into type as, "It was a damn dry fizzle." This delighted fellow-journeymen who knew his pride in craftsmanship. Colonel Fleming let it pass without reproach, but young Ochs was mortified. All through his career as publisher he had a printer's eye for a typographical error but was apt to be irritated, rather than amused by it.

His journalistic idols then were the great Horace Greeley, the New Hampshire farm boy who had struggled from the type cases and poverty to ownership of the influential New York Tribune, and kindly Captain Rule. Herein lay his dream. He talked of it, sometimes, with scholarly Col. John Encil MacGowan, long-bearded editor on The Knoxville Tribune, and with Franc M. Paul, the paper's business manager, but the Ochs family's low-ebb finances made it seem unlikely that he could launch into publishing in the near future if ever.

Actually, the dream was near realization. Franc Paul had a few hundred dollars. He wheedled Colonel MacGowan and young Ochs, whose grim application to business he recognized as genius, into helping him start a newspaper in Chattanooga, which then was pretty much like a frontier town. There were no sidewalks. Spring and autumn rains ran yellow torrents through the unpaved streets. Stones were set in the mud before ramshackle one-story shops to keep the customers' feet dry. During the siege of Chickamauga, Union soldiers had burned all the trees for fuel, which added to the drabness. Boisterous veterans, both native and from the North, swashbuckled from saloon to saloon boldly equipped with derringers and with hip artillery. Shootings were so frequent they rarely got more than a paragraph or two in the local sheets. On ill-lit Saturday nights the rivermen—this was a kind of tradition—came up from the landing to "likker up," commandeer the local horse-drawn stages and, in pre-Sabbath hilarity, first ride the roof, then tip the vehicles, passengers and all, into the mud. In this raw and melancholy setting, late in 1877, Franc Paul launched

The Chattanooga Dispatch, with Colonel MacGowan editor in chief and Adolph S. Ochs as business solicitor.

During Reconstruction in the South, newspapers grew like weeds, but were nowhere near so hardy. The Dispatch lasted only a few months. Ochs, idle, had an interest in the newspaper's job-printing plant, a decrepit old Gordon hand press, and to hang onto it, got the idea of publishing a "Chattanooga City Directory and Business Gazetteer." For weeks he worked tirelessly. He tramped Chattanooga's rutted streets in rain and in fair weather visiting banks and stores, mansions and converted Civil War sutler's shacks along the river, getting his copy firsthand. He did all the work on it except the binding. The wheezy Gordon press sighed, and gave up, halfway through the printing and the final pages were printed on Harry Griscom's somewhat less rickety press in the office of The Chattanooga Commercial.

Before his little book was out, Ochs had gone to every influential man in town, as well as every corner loafer and roustabout. The bankers and merchants, in turn, came to trust and respect Ochs, which was to work to his advantage later. He was only 19 years old then and had grown a mustache with the thought that it invested him with greater adult dignity. Results indicated that it probably had this effect, yet old tintypes show him looking, at the time, not unlike young Charlie Chaplin—with something of the same general coloring, the same grave demeanor touched, somehow, with a kind of sadness.

The directory ran to 126 pages. It yielded barely enough to provide six months' pocket money for Ochs and his partner, Dave Harris, another journeyman left jobless by The Dispatch demise. It carried on one of its pages the simple line, in lower case type, "Ochs, Adolph S., manager Chattanooga Dispatch Job Office, bds S. Bissinger, 207 Market Street." (Samuel Bissinger was an uncle and the boy publisher lived with him for more than a year). Another entry in the directory, "MAC GOWAN, J. E., EDITOR DAILY DISPATCH" was in bold upper case—upper case for the editor of a publication that no longer existed. There was something touching about this boyish tribute to a scholar whom Ochs came to love. The directory venture marked the passing of Mooley Ochs, the boy, and introduced "Adolph S. Ochs, publisher."

Captain Rule's chore boy had an insecure footing on the second rung of journalism's ladder.

Job printing kept Ochs in barely enough money to meet rooming-house expenses. He sent about $2 a week to Knoxville whenever he had it. His slender figure, not too fashionably clad—though he was something of a dandy by nature—was a familiar sight in Chattanooga's streets as he moved about soliciting work for his ancient press, which he had restored to running order. People liked him and were impressed by his honesty. He never backed down on a promise and never contracted a debt he could not pay. It was not uncommon for losers in business ventures in that precarious era to fall back on the law for relief. He never did. He even liquidated every cent of debt incurred by the short-lived Dispatch.

In the spring of 1878, Chattanooga's streets were at last free of seasonal mud, and the Cumberland foothills were decked in fresh green and rich in bloom. S. A. Cunningham, editor and owner of the wobbly Chattanooga Times, was in despair. His paper was selling barely 250 copies a day and subscribers were slow with payment. He had bought in the remains of The Dispatch, but this was an added burden rather than a help. Ochs knew this situation, and talked it over with Colonel MacGowan, who was out of a job. It was Ochs' idea to raise some money. He thought he might do it on his reputation for hard work and integrity. He had no collateral. He wondered if Colonel MacGowan would cast in with him on a shoestring and try to take over The Times.

The colonel's outright acceptance of the idea illustrates a peculiar Ochs characteristic—the quality that led older men to trust his business judgment. Ochs was barely past his twentieth birthday then. MacGowan, at 47, was a Union veteran who had been breveted brigadier general. He was a lawyer and a scholar and accustomed to command, yet he sensed in Ochs a genius that might save The Times. He agreed to work as editor in chief for $1.50 a day until the venture might pay more. Four journeymen printers, stranded by the Dispatch failure, were in on the meeting too. Like Ochs and MacGowan, they were penniless—not $3 cash among all six. They said they would work for short wages until things got better.

With these assurances negotiations were started. At first Cunningham insisted on $800 cash for The Times. Eventually Ochs got a half-interest in it for $250 cash, with the right to buy the second half after two years, arbitrators to decide then what that half was worth. (Eb James, a struggling businessman in Chattanooga who had some political ambition, endorsed Ochs' note for $300 at the First National Bank, so James acted purely on faith in a youth he had known only a few months.) He was one of the influential men Ochs had met while compiling the directory. Cunningham got his first payment, and Captain Rule's chore boy had advanced from printer's devil to newspaper owner, within eight years. It was written into The Chattanooga Times masthead on July 2, 1878: "Adolph S. Ochs, Publisher."

It was a tottering sort of miracle. Not one man in 100,000 would have plunged into publishing a daily on the capital that remained to Ochs after the cash down payment on The Times—not to speak of the debts he had acquired with his purchase. A curious fact about the transaction was that Ochs was not of age, and could not have been held legally responsible for the contracts he had assumed. His father signed all papers until Adolph passed his twenty-first year.

Ochs' working capital when he started publication of The Chattanooga Times was $37.50—what was left of the $300 bank loan. His printing equipment was worn—type all but gone, presses none too sturdy—and the paper supply was short. The unlovely little one-story brick building at Eighth and Cherry Streets, off a weed-grown alley, was rented at $24 a month. Its floors were splintery and creaky, its walls were unpainted and smeared with ink. Only someone with extraordinary courage and vision would have gone into debt to acquire this wreck.

On July 3, the day after he took over, he spread his thin cash for the barest necessaries—one lamp chimney, 5 cents; man to carry oil, 5 cents; lead pencils, 10 cents. For the first few months he gave his staff due bills, good at the grocer, the druggist and the shoe store. Each night, as the printers and the rest of The Times crew straggled by the counter, he portioned out from 25 cents to $1.50 (for Colonel MacGowan) toward salaries—when he had it. Eventually, though, he paid every last cent, and could honestly boast he owed no man. That day, though, was a few years off.

The Chattanooga Times published four pages daily, six columns to the page. It was set in long primer, or ten-point type, and brevier, eight-point. Printers drew 25 cents a day per 1,000 ems—linear measures of type. The slower journeymen were lucky to set $7 worth in a six-day week and the faster seldom made more than $10. Ochs had six men in his composing room when he took over on July 2, 1878.

He not only had no money for his printers half the time, but was hard-pushed to get together enough for his four delivery boys, for Will Kennedy, his one reporter, and for his two pressmen. Colonel MacGowan, like the rest, frequently took due bills in lieu of cash. The entire staff knew The Times was operating on something less than a shoestring, but, again, the loyalty that Ochs, even as a boy, could command from other men, was astonishingly demonstrated.

This was due, mostly, to the fact that Ochs worked harder and lived no better than his help. He traded advertising space for life's necessaries, even as they lived on due bills. He stood side by side with his men—got stories, worked at the type press, took ads over the counter, solicited business and acted as business manager and bill collector. If he had shown incredible energy as a directory publisher, he now outdid himself. He got by on little sleep.

Two powerful Negroes on the staff, Randolph Miller and Albert Williams, turned the wheel that powered the ancient press, and The Times came slowly off the machine one sheet at a time. Miller, incidentally, later became an editor in his own right. He put out The Chattanooga Blade, a Negro weekly of uncertain typography and even less certain sentence construction. Ochs' cash contributions saved The Blade from perpetually imminent bankruptcy for many years, and Randy Miller's paper always referred reverently to Ochs as "The Grand Chief."

The first three Chattanooga years were bitter years. Ochs sometimes kept his Times plant going on sheer will power. He borrowed money on one-day and two-day notes to meet the most pressing bills, and a diary he kept during this period is sprinkled with notations of this feverish borrowing and repayment. On New Year's day in 1881, for example, despair crept into the diary:

"Dismal day. Seems as if the new year is not to be a good one for me. How to wash out of financial troubles bothers me. Prospects gloomy. I have thought of many plans, but the next few days must tell what I shall do . . . My entire indebtedness . . . will be no less than $9,000, all of it due within the next two years."

Below this: "Jan. 3 borrowed $300 from First National."

"Jan. 4: H. H. Souder paid me $108. A Godsend. Borrowed from Ewing Brothers $125 for a few days. Asked Mr. Z. C. Patten for the loan of $200 for a few days, but he could not do it. He was going to the bank to try to get some for himself."

"Jan. 6: Borrowed of Moon and McMillin, to be returned Monday, $100.00."

"Jan. 14: Father overdrew $192 at bank, but had deposited $150 he had borrowed from D.B.L. and Company to be returned today . . . I endorsed a renewal of $100 for sixty days for Colonel MacGowan."

Fate did nothing to lighten Ochs' progress toward success with The Times. Early in September, 1878, while he was in Cincinnati, Knoxville and Louisville, putting in eighteen hours a day seeking additional loans, arranging credit for newsprint and new press equipment, dread yellow fever spread northward through the Mississippi Valley, and all but depopulated Chattanooga. Families pulled out in carts and wagons, or fled along the hot and dust-choked roads on foot. The river boats R.M. Bishop and J.T. Wilder carried away additional hundreds with all their portable belongings. Shopkeepers fled with the rest, and The Times lost its advertising income.

Randy Miller and Albert Williams sweated at the press wheel, but the paper was down to a single page. Tough old Colonel Mac-Gowan wrote daily editorials calling for more help for the afflicted, and small, red-bearded Will Kennedy, the Times' sole reporter, moved recklessly among dead and dying in the deserted town, making up grim lists for publication, writing lightly of the curse that had overtaken the community. "The hospital's awful handy to the graveyard," he wrote cheerfully, and, "Eleven deaths yesterday, and more coming. Trot out your next funeral." It looked then as though the plague might end Adolph Ochs' dream, but the plague passed with the first November frost. Refugee Chattanoogans trekked back, and The Times returned to four pages.

What instinct inspired Ochs to establish a policy of utter independence, political, social, religious in his handling of news and advertising, no man can say. It was startlingly original and courageous, especially in his time. Other newspapermen admired it, but thought it suicidal.

"We shall give the people a chance," he wrote in his initial declaration of policy, "to support that which they have been asking for, a paper primarily devoted to the material, educational and moral growth of our progressive city and its surrounding territory."

Behind their mastheads other publishers snickered at this bold statement from a stripling, not yet of age. They truly believed that a newspaper had to do a certain amount of pandering for patronage. They figured, "This ink-smeared David will not live up to this challenge." They were wrong.

In 1879 The Times stoutly fought for a nonpartisan city government for Chattanooga—and won. It advocated revival of Tennessee River improvement, called on the city fathers to build a modern sewer system, cried up Chattanooga's natural advantages —and attracted new business. Later it led movements for new schools, for new parks, for theatres, for establishment of Chattanooga University, among other things. Ochs, with his Scottish editor in chief putting his progressive ideas into convincing words, was to be recognized, eventually, as an outstanding leader in the South's Reconstruction.

Other newspapermen gasped at the chances he took. He spent $25 of his $37.50 on the day he took over The Times, to save the paper's credit with The New York Associated Press, his chief general news source. A few months later he moved his plant downstreet to roomier quarters over McCorkle's Saloon and Bowling Alley. He started new publications—The Tradesman and later a religious newspaper and an agricultural journal. He went way over his depth for new presses and took on additional correspondents all over the South to increase his news coverage. Even then his fetish was for "all the news," instead of the traditional wordy fillers and vituperative editorial attacks on competitors. He took the personal slant out of journalism.

He worked almost to exhaustion. "Left the office at 5:30 this morning; up all night," reads a diary entry for Feb. 17, 1881. This became a familiar notation. On June 23, he wrote, wearily: "Got a note three months after date for $2,000 discounted at Cumberland National Bank, C. E. James and D. B. Loveman, endorsers. C. E. James was an iron monger, and Loveman ran the dry goods and shoe store across the street.] Gave James $7,500 stock of Tradesman as collateral and D. B. Loveman deed of trust on a lot on Caroline Street. [He got the lot as payment for advertising space.] The work necessary to get this loan was very hard, and many unpleasant things had to be overlooked."

By 1882 Ochs could take an occasional breather. He had paid S. A. Cunningham $5,500 for the second half of The Times—the price fixed by the arbitrators, with the paper prospering—and his staff was drawing steady and increased wages in cash. He was one of Chattanooga's most important men, and was taking more and more time out for entertainment. His family was with him, too, Captain Ochs in the counting room, George and Milton on the editorial payroll.

In January, 1882, Ochs bought a roomy two-story brick house at Cedar and Fifth Streets from John Bell, deputy county clerk, for $5,000. He paid $1,000 down. The Ochs family moved in that May, with Mother Ochs in absolute control, as at Knoxville.

One night in 1882 Adolph Ochs called on Leo Wise, son of Rabbi Isaac M. Wise, in Cincinnati to talk over a new Times venture. A dark-haired, lively eyed girl walked into the parlor and said: "Who are you? I'm Effie Miriam Wise." The curly-haired publisher with the new mustache introduced himself a little stumblingly. She seemed to delight in his embarrassment but listened when he started desperately to describe a race between Longfellow and Harry Bassett, two great race horses that he had seen a few days before. He told her he owned a shoe that Harry Bassett had cast in the contest, and childishly offered to send it to her as a gift.

This awkward beginning launched a fervent courtship. Ochs' trips to Cincinnati all but wore out his free railroad pass. Iphigene Wise visited Chattanooga at his eager request, and he showed her his plant and the town. She was a short, pert figure with glossy bangs and was not inclined to talk much. She listened with great amusement to his enthusiastic chatter—to his dreams for the future.

They were married on Feb. 28, 1883, in Plum Street synagogue in Cincinnati before an altar ablaze with gas-lit candelabra, the ark covered with brocaded white silk, and to the sonorous roll of "Resound, Ye Domes" from the great organ. Chattanooga's leading citizens came up for the ceremony by special train, and Colonel MacGowan and his daughters had a place in a front pew.

When the wedding trip was ended, Ochs brought his bride to the house he had bought from Bell. She submitted meekly to matriarchal law, as did Captain Ochs and his children. They came under the spell of her charm. He liked to bring her gifts—flowers and trinkets, mostly. She spent nights at The Times plant with her husband, became his book reviewer because she loved reading, probably more than anything else in life, after her family. She tended, though, to live pretty much in a world of her own.

Real estate fever had caught the young publisher—24 then—as it had most Chattanooga businessmen. Lots and virgin acres far outside town limits changed hands over and over again, in increasing price spirals until 1886, when the land-trading reached hysterical proportion. The Times, already famous as "The Builder of Chattanooga" was more or less responsible for this period of madness. In his heady enthusiasm about Chattanooga's future, Ochs had over-sold it—even to himself.

In 1882, though, the dreams seemed justified. Everything looked rosy. The publisher raised Captain Ochs' salary to $1,000 a year and gave increases freely all round. He was endorsing sizable notes for others now instead of scrabbling for endorsements on his own. An entry in February, 1882, shows, for example, that he "Endorsed for J. E. MacGowan two notes . . . for $5,405." This was only one of dozens of similar diary entries. Ochs had come a long way from the nights four years before when he had doled his scant fund of dimes and quarters to editor and printers. The Times moved forward under a full head of steam.

There were physical hazards in publishing in the Chattanooga Times' early days. One day in the mid-Nineties E. Y. Chapin, a lawyer just come from Petersburg, Ky., stormed up to Ochs in the office, pale, and shaking with anger. He held a pistol in one hand, a Times editorial in the other. The Times, it seems, had called him "a jackleg lawyer." Ochs stared up, steady-eyed, and quietly reached for the clipping. Inwardly he quaked, but he said, "I'd like to see what this is all about. I've been in Cincinnati on business a few days; just got off the train"—which he had. It turned out that long-bearded MacGowan, a sound-money advocate, thought that Chapin had written an Evening News editorial attacking J. L. Laughlin, a sound-money authority. The colonel had, on that basis, applied the "jackleg" epithet. When it developed that he was mistaken, he apologized orally and, later, in The Times. Chapin and Ochs became friends, and Chapin always said of the publisher: "He made Chattanooga a subject of national interest in the early Eighties, a symbol of the resurrection of the South."

Threats of shooting and horsewhipping, incidentally, were not infrequent, but they never swerved Adolph Ochs from fixed policy. George Washington Ochs was a little more fiery. He had come on the paper as reporter in 1879 at $9 a week. While he was city editor, in 1883, a nephew of the Chief of Police, angered by a Times divorce story, attacked him with a heavy cane. George Ochs shot him in the hip. A week later the wounded man's brother, Sheriff in the next county, spread word that he meant to shoot George Ochs on sight. They met in Market Street. George Ochs whipped out two derringers. He told the Sheriff, a giant: "I shot your brother in self-defense. If you reach for a gun now, I'll kill you." The Sheriff backed down and was led away by friends. Newspaper life was like that in early Tennessee.

CHAPTER
8

DISASTER, which had begun to stalk The New York Times in the late Eighties, stuck its head inside Adolph Ochs' door a few years later.

Although Ochs had earned healthy profits from his various publications he kept plowing them back into the business, a principle he followed all through his publishing career. During the Eighties he printed a weekly Chattanooga Times as well as the daily edition; ran The Tradesman, which was compulsory reading for Southern industrialists; The Rural Record, an agricultural journal; and The Baptist Union. His job printing plant did exceedingly well.

If his venture in Chattanooga real estate had not tripped him he would have been, by local standards at least, a rich man. But paying off the real estate debts, and plowing profits back into The Chattanooga Times left him short of cash, a fact he kept from common gossip by going back to the same borrowing system he had employed to get started.

In 1892, with characteristic business daring, Ochs completed the handsomest newpaper plant in the South and filled it with the newest machinery at a total cost of around $150,000, almost all of it bank-borrowed money. Chattanooga was inordinately proud of the lovely gold-domed edifice. When the plant was opened on the night of Dec. 7, 1892, more than 10,000 persons rode in to gasp at it. Chattanooga's foremost clergymen, bankers and merchant leaders talked for hours of Ochs' tremendous contribution to the community, and gave him a handsome grandfather's clock, suitably inscribed. David M. Key, a Chattanoogan who had been United States Postmaster General, spoke in glowing praise of the poor lad from Knoxville who had brought fame and honor to the city. The clock, incidentally, still ticks away, almost sixty years later, in a corridor on the publisher's floor at The New York Times today.

The Chattanooga Times had become one of the richest newspaper properties in the South. It was earning around $25,000 a year—a large sum for any enterprise in a small city in those days— but a good part of the profits were draining off to satisfy personal notes that Ochs had assumed in the Chattanooga land madness.

One shrewd Tennessean had refused to sell his property to the Chattanooga Land, Iron and Coal Company, as a syndicate, but had transferred it to Ochs on the latter's personal note. He held the publisher to the letter of their contract. Ochs had actually bought the property for the syndicate, but after some legalistic bickering, gave his personal check for $103,000 to satisfy the debt. This was only one of many that pressed. He made good on all, in time, but in the late Eighties and early Nineties it seemed as if he and his newspaper must be swept away.

Business burdens were only part of Ochs' overwhelming responsibilities. Effie had had two unfortunate childbearing experiences —the first baby had died at birth, the second when it was only a few months old. Ochs was tortured with fear that the death of the second baby might have crippled Effie forever. Finally, after several anxious weeks, she was able to move feebly about the house for brief periods. Her legs had been affected.

There was another yellow fever scare in Chattanooga in mid-1888, but Ochs continued to spend day after day at the county courthouse in the land-deal litigation, and all his nights in the newspaper office. He warned his wife not to listen to wild rumor about the yellow fever spread.

"Do not believe any stories from here that I do not confirm," he pleaded in one letter in late September, 1888. "I will take good care of my hide. You can rest safe under that assurance."

Just before Christmas in 1890 when his wife was in Cincinnati, still weak, the publisher gave some hint of how hard pressed he was. "Money matters here," he admitted, "are very bad. The banks have exhausted themselves. We must move along on our cash resources and I am consequently curtailing every expense. I am in fairly good shape to stand a long siege of depression, but I do not want to fritter away my resources. The Times has little or no debt, and I am in better shape than any business house or bank in this city." That was true enough, but the hard fact was that all Chattanooga's banks and stores had been gasping since the gas had hissed out of the land bubble. Ochs spent more and more of his time doing exactly what he had done when he started publishing on a shoestring. He borrowed desperately, though on a greater scale, to keep the world generally from knowing how bad matters really stood.

He spent more and more time in New York, arranging loans. During these New York visits he was the wide-eyed country innocent, despite his Chattanooga prestige. The greenhorn touch showed through his personal correspondence. He was awed by big names, and looked upon metropolitan publishers as a breed apart. In 1891, a few months before George Jones died, the Chattanooga publisher told his wife of the big men he had met at a press dinner—Alex McClure, Joseph Howard of The Brooklyn Eagle; the owner of The Chicago Daily News, "and other bright lights," as he put it. "I was introduced as one of the most successful newspaper publishers in the South," he naïvely told Effie. "I spoke for a few minutes at the dinner. I don't quite remember what I said, but I was frequently applauded."

Between 1890 and 1895, Ochs' letters to Effie were filled with Micawberesque optimism. The 1893 panic and the hungry land debts were pushing him to the wall, though he never openly admitted it. In May, 1891, he wrote from New York: "My object in coming here was to get money, and I am glad to say I have good prospects in that line. I can't write to you understandingly about it, so I will defer my explanation until I return." In September of the same year he was still writing in that vein.

Ochs knew that The Chattanooga Times could not, prosperous as it was, lift him out of the financial slough into which he had fallen when the land bubble collapsed. He looked around for some new income source. He had decided by that time that he knew the newspaper field better than any other, and that he must never venture too far outside it. He thought that if he could buy some wobbling sheet in the South, he might build it into another Chattanooga Times, and get out that way.

In late September, 1891, the financial load was heavier. "It is a very disagreeable business, this borrowing money," the publisher conceded in a weary letter home, "but I will get through with it some day, I hope." Next day he was cheerful again. Watching his new plant rise in Chattanooga, he wrote, "The new office building is simply immense. My bosom swells with pride as I behold the structure."

That fall Ochs tramped from one New York bank to another seeking new loans. He knew that sooner or later he would have to pledge the new Chattanooga Times plant, but he kept putting it off in the hope that some turn of luck might save him this heart wrench. He wanted it, above all else, to stay free and unencumbered. Most of all he did not want Chattanoogans, who pointed to him with civic pride, as they did to Lookout Mountain, to know his true plight. "I am borrowing money on the building," he finally wrote to Effie from New York on Oct. 24, in 1891. "It is the meanest business a man ever undertook."

On the loan expedition to New York Ochs tramped the streets to save carfare, stayed at second-rate hotels because he could not afford the better ones, and did most of his railroad traveling on passes, as did most publishers of the period. He got a few thousand dollars in one place and a few more in another, but never enough.

He wrote, early in 1892, of meeting Charles Dana of The Sun at a press dinner. "I was one of six speakers there," he told Effie. "I replied to some of Mr. Dana's criticisms of weekly newspapers, and had a good reception. Dana applauded my remarks and was otherwise very attentive to me." Dana and Raymond had been his boyhood journalistic gods. He had never dreamed that one day he would sit with one of them to exchange trade views. He was still the country editor, awed by big-city names.

Later in life Ochs was subject to periods of melancholia, but never when the going was rough. When he tramped the New York pavements, during the early Nineties, far from home and friends, begging loan upon loan, he still found time to amuse himself at the theatre and in congenial company and remained in generally good spirits.

He was loan-seeking again in February, 1892, and doing pretty well. He told Effie, "I applied to New York Life for $75,000 on the [Chattanooga Times] building. They decided to make the loan provided the value of the building, upon investigation, proves to be as represented by me . . . I am quite sure it is all right. De Lamos and Cordes have issued a statement that the building alone is worth at least $150,000." On the basis of this loan promise the publisher's spirit soared. He wired his wife to prepare a celebration. "Put three quarts of Mumm's Extra Dry on ice," he wrote. "Ask Aunt Julia and the girls. Get up a swell dinner."

Ochs was sentimental, but was never emotional in public. He was kindly in a stiff Victorian manner, and at odd moments admitted that he had deliberately molded his life and habits in the Victorian pattern. "There was nothing wrong with the Victorian Era," he would argue. "It brought great advancement to the world culturally and its moral code was good."

Ochs was given to writing—perhaps a little stuffily, in sampler motto style—his philosophy of life, even in his boyhood. He never changed.

Two days after his third child, Iphigene, was born on Sept. 19, 1892 in Cincinnati, he wrote to his mother: "God in his infinite wisdom, has seen fit to bless us with success and good health. What more could we wish for? To be loved by your friends, feared by your enemies, and to enjoy respect of both is truly a satisfactory condition of affairs.

"I realize I have prospered beyond my desserts and my merits, and can account for it only by my good luck . . . These reflections arise because of an overflowing heart of gratitude to you, for the many messages of love and affection sent to Effie and to me, and to that precious lump of humanity, our daughter.

"The child is a great big baby with much dark hair, eyes between blue and gray, a nose that seems inclined to be puggy. She has a double chin, the cutest of hands and nails. I bought the kid a handsome cloak and two pairs of infants' shoes."

News of Iphigene's birth had caught the publisher at a hot and bitter Associated Press meeting in New York. It came a few minutes after the last train for Cincinnati had left. He got off a few excitable wires, then tried to sleep, but he was restless, and anxious to share his excitement. He told the hotel clerk about his daughter, then told the telegraph operator, the maids and the bellboys. Finally, he drifted out to the bar. He set up the drinks and shared with congenial strangers the telegrams announcing Iphigene's arrival. Before he left New York at noon, still without sleep, there was a final champagne toast to the mother and the baby.

At Cincinnati's Hotel Alms, where the child was born—it was his jest forever after to remind her that she was born in an Alms house —he wrote frenziedly to friends and kin, and quaffed endless toasts. He told his mother four days after Iphigene's birth: "I have drunk enough to the health of the mother and the baby in the past few days to drown the whole family." In the same letter he wrote: "Permit me, ladies and gentlemen, to introduce Miss Iphigene Bertha Ochs, named for her mother and her grandmother, and to be known as Gene [which she never was] for short. Long may she live, and ever happy be."

When the baby was 3 years old, Ochs was still on the hunt for a second newspaper, still borrowing from Peter to pay Paul. He had weathered the 1893 panic but was still deep in financial bog. He had all but abandoned, by that time, the idea of trying to build up another Southern sheet. A deal for The Nashville American was still being discussed, but was slowly fading.

Ochs had his eyes fixed on New York now. Although confident when he discussed the New York possibilities with bankers and big town editors, he was never inwardly sure he could swing a large New York daily. Over and over again, during this period, he confided to Effie that maybe he was getting a little beyond his depth for, as he put it, "a country newspaperman burdened with debt."

This did not keep him from trying. In May, 1895, it seemed likely that he might buy a half interest in the fast-dying New York Mercury, a Democratic free-silver organ. He never made an important business move, though, without first talking it over with his wife. Though he liked to think of her as elfin because she was always languid and inclined to whimsy—Peter Pan was his favorite name for her—she was bound to come through with sound practical suggestions that straightened the kinks in his troubled mind.

"I believe," he wrote to her that May, "that if I take hold of The Mercury and conduct it as the organ of the Silver Democrats that within two years I could pay every dollar of my indebtedness and have the controlling interest in a valuable newspaper property in New York.

"With the lights before me at present I am conscientiously opposed to the free coinage of silver, but I must admit also that this opinion is not the result of a thorough understanding of the question.

"I will admit that the science of the use of silver and gold as money is beyond my comprehension. You can appreciate the dilemma I am in. I shall do nothing until I return home."

He went back to Chattanooga, and they mulled over the question. He had religiously fought free silver in The Chattanooga Times, with gray-bearded MacGowan writing strong editorials on the subject through the long years. He finally decided to keep trying for The Mercury, but only if he could have complete control of its business affairs, and its editorial stand.

The dickering kept on all summer. In the fall of 1895 it seemed fairly certain that he could have The Mercury pretty much on his terms.

He told Effie in late September: "At first they [The Mercury owners] scorned the idea, but finally proposed to sell me half interest for $75,000, giving me control and a reasonable salary before division of the profits. I think they will eventually take $25,000 cash, provided another $25,000 goes into the treasury as working capital. Mr. Noble of The Mercury pretends to be greatly impressed with my ability to make a success."

Ochs was never one to go after a deal blindly. Before he entered into serious conversation with The Mercury's owners, he knew their plant and their personnel probably better than they did. He learned that The Mercury was dropping close to $2,000 a week; that the paper's business manager was a blockhead. He had found, for example, that instead of hiring trained linotype operators for newly installed machinery, the composing room foreman was trying to break in old printers who knew only hand composition. He said, "Six expert operators can do as much as the nine novices and twenty hand compositors." He knew. He had installed the first linotype machines in the South in his own plant and had carefully studied their output.

Finally The Mercury deal broke down entirely. The owners insisted on putting into the contract a clause that would have compelled Ochs to vacate the plant within sixty days should they see fit to ask it. Much more important was Ochs' discovery that The Mercury owners were not in a position to transfer their United Press connection to any new publisher. The negotiations blew up at the end of March in 1896.

Ochs was not too disappointed. He had a fresher and higher ambition now. He had been told on his thirty-eighth birthday, in a wire from Harry Alloway, a Wall Street reporter for The New-York Times, that the old Raymond-Jones property was headed for the graveyard unless someone could save it. The barefoot boy from Knoxville was beside himself with excitement. When he heard that there was a possibility of The Times' going on the block, he turned his back on The Mercury, leaving it to die—which it did, soon after.

On March 27 in 1896 he sent a breathless kind of letter to "My Darling Wife and Baby." It was in his warmest Micawber mood, written in the Fifth Avenue Hotel.

"I doubt," he began excitedly, "if there are many men in these United States who are as subject to the caprices of circumstances as I am. Here I am in New York less than twenty-four hours ready to negotiate for the leading and most influential newspaper in America. I could write an interesting book of no small dimensions of my experiences of yesterday and today."

It was a long letter, even for him—and he wrote freely. He described his talk with Alloway, whom he had first met in Chattanooga when the reporter stopped off there one day on a New-York Times assignment.

"Now for the supreme gall of a country newspaperman burdened with debt," he scribbled, heedless of the muffled traffic that streamed up and down Fifth Avenue on a thin, hard snow. Smart horse-drawn carriages with dull yellow lamps crunched past the writing room window. "Alloway thinks I am the man—the ideal man—for The Times. He hopes to get a good job on the paper and some financial reward in case of my success, of which he has no doubt."

Alloway had talked with Gen. Sam Thomas, a Wall Street man, who held $25,000 in Times stock, and with Charles R. Flint, a close friend of President Grover Cleveland, who held the controlling stock. When he told them the miracles Ochs had achieved on a $250 shoestring in Chattanooga, they were impressed. Alloway assured Ochs that Flint's $550,000 control could be bought for one-fourth its paper value.

"Alloway's plan is," Ochs told Effie, "that I get an option to purchase for a year or more if I will undertake the management and guarantee to run the paper without incurring additional debt. He says the paper is now losing about $1,500 a week. He believes sensible management can quickly remedy that. The Times circulation has fallen very low [the figure turned out to be 9,000 a day], but its advertising business is still good. Prices well maintained."

Leopold Wallach, a friend of Ochs', heard Alloway's outline of how things stood at The Times, and how he had convinced General Thomas and the powerful Flint that The Chattanooga Times' owner was the man to pull The New-York Times back from the grave. Wallach had intended to return to his office after the talk, but he became as excited as Ochs did. He arranged immediately to have Ochs meet the General, whom he knew, and persuaded Ochs to have John Inman fix up an interview with Flint. Inman, an associate of Flint's, had lent the Chattanooga man substantial sums in the past, and admired his business judgment.

"Alloway took dinner with me tonight," Ochs wrote to Effie, almost bubbling over in the writing. "He is a schemer from 'way back yonder, but he is very much in earnest. He sincerely believes that I can get The Times. Tonight I am going to write to Grover Cleveland to grant me an interview for Sunday, and I am going to ask a letter from him to Flint, also one from Lamont. How's that for cheek?"

Wallach was so caught up with the idea of the deal at this point that he assured Ochs that he could certainly borrow enough capital backing, once he had an option on The Times.

As Alloway and Wallach bucked their way across Fifth Avenue in the wind-driven storm, Ochs wandered dreamy-eyed to the writing desk again.

"Wallach says I can handle anything," he told Effie, "and I am vain enough to believe it. I do not wish you to build up any great hopes on the scheme, but it is well worth trying for, and stranger things have happened. I shall remain here until I know exactly what can be done."

He left off writing. He was exhausted. Words on paper were not enough to convey his excitement. The grave-eyed boy who had rubbed Captain Rule's editorial lamp in Knoxville, only a little over twenty-five years before, felt now that he might really own the great newspaper that had been started by one of his heroes, Henry Raymond of The Times. He was all but overcome with the thought. It really had been a magic lamp.

CHAPTER
9

TIMES FEVER burned almost to searing after the dinner with Alloway. When Ochs had finished his excitable screed to Effie, he stayed up past dawn writing to some fifty influential men in different parts of the country to ask for letters that would recommend him to Charles R. Flint.

His list included ministers, publishers, editors, bankers, railroad men, merchants, Representatives and Senators.

"I am negotiating for a controlling interest in The New-York Times," he explained, "and have fair prospects of success. I write to respectfully ask that you address by return mail a letter to Mr. Spencer Trask, chairman of The New-York Times Publishing Company, giving your opinion on my qualifications as a newspaper publisher, general personal character, and my views on public questions, judged by the course of The Chattanooga Times, especially on the money question. In other words, say what you can of me as an honest, industrious man and capable newspaper publisher. I wish to assure you that the enterprise I contemplate is not too large for me. I am able to handle it financially and otherwise."

One letter, addressed to Henry T. Thurber, secretary to President Cleveland, sought an interview with the Chief Executive. Ochs had met the President several times, once in Chattanooga back in the early Eighties.

The scribbling publisher probably forgot some of the details of that Chattanooga meeting. He had owned only one suit then. He had borrowed a frock coat from his cousin Ben Franck, and had ridden in the Presidential procession in a borrowed barouche lined with tufted scarlet brocade. He felt that the town's leading newspaper owner could do no less.

Before the parade ended a drenching rain drummed on the procession. The red brocade was something less than color-fast and when young Ochs left the barouche with characteristic dignity, hilarity broke out behind him. Franck's frock coat was ruined in the most obvious places.

"I wish," the letter to the White House explained, "to secure from the President a few words of commendation . . . on my conduct of The Chattanooga Times and on the general character of The Times, its adherence to sound and honest Democracy, and in a general way his estimate of my qualifications as a newspaper publisher."

President Cleveland responded within thirty-six hours:

"In your management of The Chattanooga Times you have demonstrated such a faithful adherence to Democratic principles, and have so bravely supported the ideas and policies which tend to the safety of our country as well as our party, that I should be glad to see you in a larger sphere of usefulness.

"If your plans are carried out, and if through them you are transferred to metropolitan journalism, I wish you the greatest measure of success possible."

Every endorsement Ochs had asked for came through. The extraordinary success of The Chattanooga Times had spread his name and his reputation throughout the East—farther than even he knew.

Harry Alloway was busy, too. After he had left Ochs dreaming of what he could do for and with The New-York Times, he persuaded Charles Miller, then president and editor, to listen to the Chattanoogan's ideas for saving the paper.

Miller was depressed. He had kept The Times barely alive for three years. A $250,000 debenture plan had helped tide it over the 1893 depression when its financial advertising—a chief source of revenue—had all but ebbed out. Now it was gasping again. Its news staff was depleted for lack of payroll money. Since it had no funds with which to go after the news, it was curiously transparent on the news side. Strong editorial backbone helped to hold it up.

The Millers had given up their handsome home in Brooklyn. They lived, with their two children, in West Fifty-fifth Street, and around the time that Ochs came into the picture were so reduced in funds that they rented their lower-floor rooms to lodgers. Mrs. Miller's mother, who had already put a substantial amount of her money into Times stock, had to come to their aid again. Miller was at the end of his rope when Ochs called at his home. Secretly, he saw no real hope in the little publisher from the South but decided to hear him, then go to the theatre with his family. He had the tickets.

It did not work out that way. A spark of Ochs fire caught immediately. When Mrs. Miller and the children were dressed and ready to leave, the murmur of animated conversation still drifted from the parlor. Mrs. Miller thought that perhaps her husband needed rescue from the dark-haired stranger. She pointed at the clock. She said, "We'll miss the opening, dear."

Miller could barely take his eyes from Ochs, but he looked up briefly. He said: "You go on with the children. We have a few more things to discuss; I'll come along soon."

He was not in the theatre at curtain's rise, nor at curtain's fall. When Mrs. Miller and the children got back to Fifty-fifth Street before midnight the two men were still in the parlor. Mrs. Miller sensed that a minor miracle had happened. Her husband's melancholy had dropped from him. He wore the militant look she had known when he first joined The Times as telegraph editor, almost twenty-five years before. The family went quietly to bed. The parlor conference continued into morning.

Miller brought Ochs before Charles Flint and Spencer Trask who had backed several Thomas A. Edison enterprises. They suggested that the man from Chattanooga buy a large block of the proposed new stock, and undertake to restore the paper at a salary of $50,000 a year. A $50,000 salary was more than any Southern newspaperman had ever earned, but Ochs did not want that.

He bluntly told the bankers that he knew that The New-York Times was bankrupt, that its circulation was only 9,000, not 21,000, as publicly announced, that it was more than $300,000 in debt and that it had been losing money steadily since George Jones' death. He had learned that between 1893 and 1896 the weekly deficit had run to $2,500, and still hung at that figure.

"I know," he told the bankers, "that I can manage The Times as a decent, dignified and independent newspaper and still wipe out the deficit. I'm sure that I can make it pay 5 per cent a year interest. I could change your $100,000-a-year loss into at least a $40,000-a-year surplus."

"We're prepared to pay you $50,000 a year to do just that," the bankers countered.

Ochs shook his head. He said: "I simply will not take the job for merely a fixed salary, not even though you should offer $150,000 a year. [Brave words, but he must have gulped a little when he uttered them.] I am not looking for employment. Unless you offer me eventual control of the property—based, of course, on my making good—there is no sense in keeping on with these negotiations. I am merely trying to say, Mr. Flint, that if I can bring about the results I have outlined, I am entitled to something more than a fixed salary."

The bankers wanted time to talk this over with the other stockholders.

Meanwhile, another group of Times stockholders, opposed to Trask and Flint, wanted to start a Times-Recorder syndicate. The failing New York Recorder was another metropolitan daily that was weak and spent from wild punches thrown by Joseph Pulitzer of The World and William Randolph Hearst of The Journal, whose new-type "yellows," so-called, had worked up the town's blood pressure. Pulitzer and Hearst were trying to slug each other to death with heavy money bags. In their fierce combat they left journalistic corpses all about them. Uneasy advocates of conservative news presentation thought their own day was ending. But they counted without Captain Rule's "devil."

Edward Cary and Charles Miller blocked the Times-Recorder group by putting The Times into receivership. Then they introduced Ochs to Alfred Ely, the receiver. Ely had talked with other newspapermen who had distinguished records in metropolitan journalism, but they had shied away from any suggestion that they try to revive the Raymond-Jones sheet. They thought that there was not enough capital around to stand off Hearst, Pulitzer and the Younger Bennett. The Tribune and The Sun were not doing too well, either. A few hours with Ochs, though, and Ely's hope was restored. The Southerner's common sense and confidence were infectious.

Printing House Square, meantime, buzzed with fantastic rumor about this little man from the South. The most persistent barroom stories were that Wall Street was to control The Times with Ochs as figurehead. This was based on the fact that August Belmont and J. P. Morgan each owned $25,000 of the old Times debentures. The rumor hung on long after Ochs had retired the Morgan and Belmont holdings.

In mid-June, Ochs' own plan for rebuilding The Times was accepted.

A new company was formed with a capital of 10,000 shares of par value of $100. Two thousand shares were traded in for the 10,000 of the old company, then represented by a group of bankers headed by Spencer Trask. Holders of the outstanding obligations of The Times, amounting to some $300,000, received in exchange an equal amount of 5 per cent bonds of the new company, and perhaps the most exacting part of the financing of the reorganization was accomplished when $400,000 more of these bonds were sold at par. This was to provide the operating capital, lack of which had been so severely felt in past years.

As a persuasive, fifteen shares of stock were offered to each purchaser of a $1,000 bond. Ochs himself scraped together all the money he had or could borrow, bought $75,000 worth of these bonds and automatically received with them 1,125 shares of stock. Of the remaining capital stock of the company, 3,876 shares were put into escrow to be delivered to Ochs whenever the paper had earned and paid expenses for a period of three consecutive years. Thus, he would have, and within less than four years did have, 5,001 of the 10,000 shares. The bonds referred to have long since been repaid and much later, against each share of common stock, there was declared over a period of years a dividend of twenty shares of 8 per cent preferred stock.

Through spring and early summer in 1896, Ochs put in hours that might have burst another man's heart. Every night he made an arduous schedule and the next day grimly carried it through. In mid-June, when other men had slowed down in the heat, he never slackened, pumping down Broadway, around Wall Street, and to and from the Madison Hotel, all day and into the night. After Trask and Flint had signed the contract he had worked out, and had obtained the signatures of other stockholders and of Ely, Ochs went from creditor to creditor, to sell them the idea of accepting new Times bonds in lieu of cash.

On June 15, for example, his schedule allowed him a quarter-hour with Flint in Pine Street, a half-hour with Wallach, who was looking after the legal end for him, an hour with August Belmont, forty-five minutes with lawyers for a paper company that was a principal creditor, an hour with the Western Union to which the paper was heavily in debt. He gave himself forty-five minutes for luncheon, then went back to Western Union for another half-hour. Between 2:30 and 5:30 that afternoon he got around to Wallach's office again, to the Glens Falls Paper Company and to The New York Sun, and kept four other appointments, most of them with creditors. At 5:30 he was back in Flint's Pine Street office to report on the day's progress.

Things were going his way, but only because he worked fiercely for them. He was tired and a little homesick—he was to spend a full three months away from Effie and the baby during this ordeal, the longest absence since his marriage—but his extraordinary drive never slackened. When he got back to the hotel every night he did not sleep until he had written a good-sized letter to Effie, telling the day's achievements. These letters were proud and a little boastful. Like a child, he was always bidding for her praise.

He took no breathers. On June 16 he covered as much ground as he had the day before, if not more. "It took me just fifteen minutes," he told Effie happily, "to get J. P. Morgan's signature on the agreement to exchange his old stock for new. The United Press signed." He mentioned nine others whose signatures were added after he had explained his plans for hauling The New-York Times to its feet. Wherever he went the Ochs magic and fervor caught. He was extraordinarily persuasive, even with men whom, inwardly, he looked upon with awe.

He told how Jacob Schiff, the financier, had taken to him. He said: "It is a great story. Mr. Schiff has $25,000 in old Times stock that cost him $25,000 cash, but he told me to come again tomorrow and he would give me the certificate, and I could do with it as I pleased. He said this was merely a personal endorsement for me. He said he wanted no interest, and could give no encouragement to a newspaper with Democratic leanings. He said he had been a Mugwump, but henceforth he would be Republican. He made me a present of the stock. Of course, he thinks it has no value but it will get $5,000 of new stock, and I hope to make that worth par in less than three years."

At this stage, though months were to pass before he actually took over The Times, Ochs was overwhelmed with letters from men who wanted to work for him. Some were old newspapermen from Knoxville and Chattanooga. Even old Captain Rule, still on The Chronicle, put in a jesting bid. He warmly wished his old chore boy luck.

Another job-seeker showed up that June, a gnomish man with astonishing bounce and eagerness, who came to the Chattanoogan's room at the Hotel Madison one night. It turned out that he worked with Laffan of The Sun, and that he had heard Laffan and other important men in journalism predict that the publisher from the South might perform miracles at The Times. The effervescent little stranger had a gift for gab and flattery, and Ochs found himself liking it. He told Effie later: "He said I had won the confidence and admiration of everyone, and that they were amazed at my determination and hopefulness. This young man said that was why he had hurried over to offer his services. He said he would like to be my business manager on The New-York Times." Later the man from Chattanooga was to express a little irritation at what he called The Sun man's "excessive persistence." In the end, though, the little man got the job. He was Louis Wiley, who was to be Times business manager and Ochs' close friend for decades.

The court procedure necessary for ending the career of the old Times to clear the way for the new dragged through torrid summer days. Ochs chafed over this. He blamed Ely, the receiver, for the delay. He felt sure that Ely's dallying was motivated by a desire to enlarge his fee. "He will certainly not be on my Board of

Directors," Ochs told Effie, bitterly. "He has cooked his goose with me. He has given me entirely too much anxiety to enlist my future friendship."

During the waiting period, Ochs studied New York closely—its shops, its industries, its streets, its amusement places. He kept a sharp eye on the Hearst-Pulitzer feud, and on the metropolitan dailies' promotion methods. During the Democratic convention he studied the Hearst blackboard, framed in electric lights, on which a chalk artist wrote bulletins for the passing throngs. He thought this better than Pulitzer's "indifferent show" with mere bulletin sheets. He noted that The Sun and The Times were broodingly dark and wrote home: "I stood there regretting I was not in a position to teach these papers something. I walked up to Herald Square, and the display at The Herald was extremely poor." He walked to his hotel meditating on this, and ideas boiled and bubbled in his active mind.

Before he turned in at midnight he wired Colonel MacGowan in Chattanooga to write an editorial blasting William Jennings Bryan and the Democrats for their sixteen-to-one platform. Bryan had made his classic "Cross of Gold" speech in Chicago the week before and the party had nominated him for President. Brown-derbied New Yorkers in the still ill-lighted city snarled at one another over their schooner-sized 5-cent beers or their canvasback duck and terrapin, each according to his station and political belief. Ochs had seen 150 fanatic Wall Street Democrats tramping in parade on the Stock Exchange floor that day, wearing McKinley buttons under bobbing flags and under signs that cried, "Down with the Red Flag [anarchy] and up with the Stars and Stripes."

Court action on The Times was due on July 14. Two days before, on a Sunday, Ochs was restless and in mental turmoil. He had gone through all the Sunday papers. They lay in a neat heap beside him on the desk in his hotel room. He sat down to write the day's usual volume of letters, then studied (though he knew every punctuation mark by heart) the contract that was to make him publisher of The Times.

At 4 o'clock the heat was oppressive. He put on the bicycle suit he had bought for $5 the week before, hired a wheel in Central Park and, as New York panted in mid-summer heat, became one with the hosts of cobble-jarred bikes that moved like swarming fireflies through a humid dusk. He rode his bike down the West Side, over the Brooklyn Bridge and out Ocean Parkway to Manhattan Beach. It was midnight when he got back to his room, muscle-weary and wet through with perspiration. He bathed, then fell a hundred fathoms deep, into slumber.

Next day court action on The Times was postponed. It was July 20, after more irksome delays, before Judge Stover fixed the date of sale of The Times for Aug. 13. Fresh anxieties crowded Ochs' mind, then. Rumor washed around him like surf. There was talk of "some Monte Cristo," as he put it, who was to bob up at the sale to take The Times from him at a fabulous price. He told Effie, "Arkell of Judge Magazine is said to be itching for it. There is a rich man from Troy said to be quietly in the field. The Recorder consolidation group is supposed to have something up its sleeve. There's another rumor about some rich Chicago banker—a very rich man named Torrence, with money to burn. They say he wants to buy The Times to out-Hearst Hearst. The air is full of such stories. They do not really disturb me. I believe I am master of the situation. I don't believe anyone will compete after they learn my true strength. To defeat me at the sale they will have to have more money than sense. *I will win;* [he underlined the words] put that down."

Brave front again. The truth was that Ochs had arranged through Chattanooga bankers who had unquestioning faith in him to have $25,000 put in his check account. He had pledged $25,000 in Chattanooga Times bonds as collateral and he was prepared to surrender more—all his Chattanooga Times holdings—to get The New-York Times. Even in this crucial hour, with only borrowed backing, he had to expand his chest to Effie. He wrote her: "I find I do not feel any way stuck up because I can draw my check for $25,000. I hope I can soon draw ten times that for disbursement among my acquaintances."

On Aug. 13 the sale came off quietly. No Monte Cristo turned up, no Torrence, no Arkell, no nabob from Troy. Spencer Trask bid—this was mere formality—$75,000 for the old Times, and it was knocked down to him. There were no other bids. Ochs' reaction, after months of incredible strain, was a little astonishing. He told Effie, who had come up to Atlantic City to stand by: "I went to bed the night before the sale, totally unconcerned. I was the least excited of all before the bid was put in."

Five days later, Ochs moved into his office at 71 Park Row. On Times stationery he wrote: "My Darling Wife and Baby . . . The first New-York Times letter sheet I use carries my love to those who are dearer to me than the great prize I have won. I was formally installed at 3:30 P.M. today, and an army of men stands ready to carry out my wishes. I have succeeded 'way beyond my fondest hopes, and with God's help will maintain the position with credit. I am a lucky fellow . . . I will move from the Madison Avenue Hotel to the Astor House tomorrow. I will reside there until you come. Address your mail care of The New-York Times."

Nowhere was there even faint indication that Ochs ever dreamed he might fail. The curly-haired child who had walked into Captain Rule's splintery-floored office a little more than twenty-five years earlier, had had his eyes steadily fixed on a star. Now the star was in his hands. He was not blinded by it.

CHAPTER
10

O<small>N</small> A<small>UG.</small> 19, 1896, The New-York Times (the hyphen in the title was retained till December) carried the new owner's declaration of principle. Effie, still at Atlantic City with the baby, had helped him smooth the first draft, which had what he called "a lot of pyrotechnics." He cut these out. The declaration over the new publisher's signature appeared on the editorial page under the heading: "Business Announcement." It said:

"To undertake the management of The New-York Times, with its great history for right-doing, and to attempt to keep bright the lustre which Henry J. Raymond and George Jones have given it, is an extraordinary task. But if a sincere desire to conduct a high-standard newspaper, clean, dignified and trustworthy, requires honesty, watchfulness, earnestness, industry and practical knowledge applied with common sense, I entertain the hope that I can succeed in maintaining the high estimate that thoughtful, pure-minded people have ever had of The New-York Times.

"It will be my earnest aim that The New-York Times give the news, all the news, in concise and attractive form, in language that is parliamentary in good society, and give it as early, if not earlier, than it can be learned through any other reliable medium; to give the news impartially, without fear or favor, regardless of any party, sect or interest involved; to make the columns of The New-York Times a forum for the consideration of all questions of public importance, and to that end to invite intelligent discussion from all shades of opinion.

"There will be no radical changes in the personnel of the present efficient staff. Mr. Charles R. Miller, who has so ably for many years presided over the editorial page, will continue to be the editor; nor will there be a departure from the general tone and character and policies pursued with relation to public questions that have distinguished The New-York Times as a nonpartisan newspaper—unless it be, if possible, to intensify its devotion to the cause of sound money and tariff reform, opposition to wastefulness and peculation in administering the public affairs and in its advocacy of the lowest tax consistent with good government, and no more government than is absolutely necessary to protect society, maintain individual vested rights and assure the free exercise of a sound conscience."

Newspapers all over the country reprinted this statement.

One by one Ochs came to know the members of his staff. Though he never put it in words, he was looking for someone, preferably a man with business sense, with whom he could discuss The Times' ills. Reporters were apt to be starry-eyed, and devoid of commercial acumen, but finally Ochs found the talent he desired in Henry Loewenthal, the city editor.

Loewenthal was rather grave and only five years older than Ochs. He had been on The Times twenty-one of his forty-three years, and had served on The Tribune before that. He had worked under George Jones, and he had seen The Times decay after Jones died. He knew that poor business administration had reduced The Times to its beggarly state; he had devised remedies, but he had not had Miller's ear.

Loewenthal thought that expansion of financial and business news generally would bring old subscribers back. Ochs soaked up all this sound talk, and added his own ideas along the same lines. When Loewenthal suggested a daily column listing buyers newly come to the city, Ochs seized on it. Between them they worked out a complete plan for giving The Times the best financial and business section in New York.

Night after night, when they had put away a light dinner at Hitchcock's, Childs or Dennett's—sometimes at Perry's—they walked the gas-lit sidewalks and talked endlessly of changes that might benefit The Times. They saw eye to eye and they talked a common language. If ever two men were well met, they were.

On Nov. 8, 1897, Loewenthal got up a weekly financial review. It ran every Monday morning and eventually became The Annalist, a separate Times publication.

Ochs made Loewenthal managing editor and kept him in that post until February, 1904. The list of buyers began running in The Times on Sept. 30, 1896, as "Buyers In Town" but next day was changed to "Arrival of Buyers." The idea caught on swiftly, though some newspaper men scoffed at it. It kept expanding with the years and a half century later it sometimes contained more than 2,000 listings a day. It was one of the columns that helped make The Times the merchant's and financier's newspaper.

Ochs himself performed wonders with type on the financial pages and throughout the paper generally. The Times lost its downcast look and brightened as a woman might after judicious application of cosmetics. Loewenthal, stern but kindly, injected new life into his Wall Street reporters, goading them to greater output. Eventually (1914) Loewenthal was to become director of business news, and father of a column titled "The Merchant's Point of View." He died on Nov. 5, 1927, an intimate of Ochs' to the end.

General news reporters on The Times, and on other sheets, at first sneered at Ochs' drive for financial and business matter; they thought it would make The Times duller than it had been under Miller. To their astonishment the Ochs innovations brought thousands of new, substantial readers and a brisk flow of advertising, far beyond anything Miller had been able to attract. Men of affairs soon learned that no other newspaper gave them coverage so complete on subjects related to their daily enterprise. "Business Bible" they called it.

Quite beyond explanation is the fact that other New York publishers looked helplessly on while Ochs made his changes. They took no serious step toward competing with him in business and financial coverage—not for a long time, at least, and then they were too late. He had the field all to himself.

"The neglected non-sensational departments of news," he related a quarter century afterward, "were quietly and unostentatiously improved in The New York Times and made as far as possible complete—such as financial news, market reports, real estate transactions, court records, commercial and educational news; the news of books, routine affairs of the National, State and City Governments . . . Altogether the task undertaken in this direction was to tell promptly and accurately the happenings and occurrences that were not sensational but were of real importance in people's routine affairs."

Another angle that newspapers generally had overlooked was the open forum for subscribers, the Letters-to-the-Editor columns. Ochs was the first New York publisher to expand this department. Unlike other publishers, he ran letters whether they conformed or disagreed with The Times' outlook on affairs. He let both sides have their innings, which was something of a wonder in his time. He demanded only that writers identify themselves, whether their real names were published, or not. He cast aside anonymous offerings, for obvious reasons.

Among the men Ochs came to know when he took over The Times was a Down-Easterner, Frederick Craig Mortimer, a sandy-haired, blue-eyed man who might have stood six feet tall if he had not been severely crippled. He had come to The Times in 1886.

Mortimer thought he would like to start an editorial-page column of paragraphs on light subjects, on anything new that sprang into the news, from science to poetry. There had been something like it in The Times in the 1860's, done by William Livingston Alden, a lineal descendant of John and Priscilla Alden. That feature had run under the heading, "Minor Topics," and was known in the office as "The Sixth Column." Bigelow dropped it. Ochs had enormous respect for Mortimer's knowledge and thought The Times could stand a bit of leavening.

Mortimer started "Topics of The Times" on Sept. 8, 1896. He retired thirty years later and was succeeded by Simeon Strunsky. In recent years many Times men have contributed to "Topics." It is no longer the product of any one man's pen.

Ochs liked to sit and talk with Mortimer. Mortimer would roll his Bull Durham cigarettes and expatiate endlessly on vital subjects. He kept up with everything new in science, and in social change. He helped scores of young American poets to success by printing their contributions in The Times.

Among the poets who benefited from his counsel were Barbara Young, Edith M. Thomas, Violet Alleyn Storey, Roselle Mercier. Other poetry contributors were Rudyard Kipling, Alice Duer Miller, Elias Lieberman, Henry van Dyke and Arthur Guiterman.

Because of his deformity Mortimer disliked visitors. The young poets, and hundreds of others who admired his extensive knowledge and lovely writing style asked in vain for interviews. On one of the few occasions when he did break this rule he created office legend.

The visitor was the electrical genius Charles P. Steinmetz. He knew nothing of Mortimer's physical handicap; he merely wanted to pay tribute to a man who, in his estimate, anonymously did the best pieces on advances in electrical science.

The spectacle of these two come face to face beside the battered old desk where Mortimer turned out his "Topics" in wavering, crabbed script, tightened the throats of the few persons who witnessed it—Mortimer, balanced on crutches and grotesquely bent, Steinmetz hunchbacked and feeble. It was as if one or the other had stepped before a distortion mirror.

The Times, in an editorial after Mortimer died, said "Into 'Topics of The Times' he freely poured the precious life-blood of a master spirit . . . There was an austere and heroic quality in Mr. Mortimer."

Ochs did not change basic Times policy. He merely did what Raymond had done nearly a half century before: stepped into the picture when New York was beginning to sicken of sensationalism —Hearst's and Pulitzer's in the Nineties as against Bennett's and the old Sun's in 1851—and promised to give straight news as fast as any other sheet or faster. His principles were Raymond's principles. The two thought alike. The time had come again for a straight news sheet to lead the way.

Dana's Sun was beautifully written but inclined to features rather than to full coverage of the news. The Mercury, The Recorder and The Commercial Advertiser were walking their last mile. Again, as in Raymond's time, there was need for a newspaper that was a newspaper, not more or less. Curious as it may seem, no one else in New York—at least no one who had taken hold at The Times —had realized this, until the man from Chattanooga showed up.

The Tribune in 1896 was shaky. The management's attempts to bolster it were on the hysterical side. In a desperate effort later to catch up with the yellows, for example, it took over The Recorder, which Duke, the tobacco man, had owned. The Recorder had specialized for a while in giving away highly colored lithographs of actresses. Tribune readers picked up their papers one Sunday morning and out fell a lithograph of a basket of strawberries and a bottle of champagne. Chromo berries and wines apparently were not to their taste. The Tribune hastily dropped the idea.

As Ochs came into the fight, city circulation figures stood about; The Evening World, 400,000; The Evening Journal, 130,000; The News, 145,000; The Evening Post, 19,000; The Evening Sun, 60,-000; The Mail and Express, 3,000; The Commercial Advertiser, 2,500. The Morning Journal, 300,000; The (Morning) World, 200,-000; The Herald, 140,000; The (Morning) Sun, 70,000; The Press, 18,000; The Tribune, 16,000; The Advertiser, 12,000; The Times, 9,000. No one could have predicted then that Ochs would live to see the day when all but The Times had died or had been absorbed in mergers, while his paper stood pre-eminent throughout the world.

Dana touched off a city-wide feud some weeks after Ochs took over at The Times. He said in his paper one morning: "Our next-door neighbor, The Tribune, which has taken into its house the remains of the defunct Recorder, dead of vulgarity, announces its intention of producing, evolving or disgorging a serio-comic supplement 'as a regular feature henceforth, of the Sunday edition.' " In the same piece he dug editorial needles deeply into Hearst's Journal and Pulitzer's World.

He was poking tigers. The yellows leaped on Dana and while they were at it they went for the newcomer down the street at The Times. The World ran a long series on what it called "Journalism's Poverty Row," which was Park Row. It made amusing maps to illustrate its point. It accused The Times—without evidence—of pandering to Wall Street. It called Ochs "the conductor and caretaker of the deficit," and ran what it called "the record of the dying and the dead." The Times was prominently included. Joseph Pulitzer could be vitriolic in such campaigns, and this was an all-out effort.

During Ochs' first sweltering August days at 41 Park Row he dug into the office records that told in detail the true story of The Times' plight. Telegrams and letters from old Times readers and from newspapermen all over the United States who had read his declaration of principles poured in to wish him luck. Interviewers for trade journals took a lot of his time. He was patient. He knew the value of promotion. Within a week the trade journals and newspapers spread his name everywhere in the journalistic world.

He told Effie, "I have an endless task ahead of me, but I find it pleasant, even in this steaming climate." When the paper work piled up so that he could not keep abreast of it, he hastily wired Miss Kate Stone, his secretary in Chattanooga, to hurry North. She was to stay with him for many years. He passed the reins of The Chattanooga Times to his brothers.

The advertising, news and composing room staffs at 41 Park Row, a depressed and melancholy group, waited uneasily for the traditional axe to fall. They felt that The Times was doomed and that no unknown from the South could save it.

Ochs immediately ordered a number of seemingly small changes that helped brighten the paper. He threw out the cheap backstair fiction that Miller had run on the bottom of the first page. He banished most of the agate type—fine, small letters—from news stories, widened the space between lines of type and shortened column rules to lessen the strain on the old presses. He bought better newsprint and ink to obtain sharper reproduction, threw out standing ads that returned next to no revenue and were eyesores, and started using datelines on important stories originating outside New York. Actually, The Times was not getting more news; Ochs was pointing it up better and simplifying locale identification. The trade journals and other New York publications recognized in these changes the hand of a master.

The John Rogers spaceband, or automatic space-equalizer, a device that Mergenthaler had introduced in 1892, had greatly speeded newspaper printing and Ochs was quick to see its advantages. He kept his linotype batteries up to date, replacing the original Rogers spaceband with improved ones as rapidly as they became available. His heart remained in the composing room, even as wealth and power came to him in increasing proportions. He roamed through that part of the plant, with a sharp eye to waste, and sternly enforced his order that it be kept scrupulously neat and clean.

One night, soon after he took over, he turned up in the composing room, and assembled the foreman, and all the printers. He told them: "I'm a printer, as you are. I've done my turn at the case with handset type. I want to make The Times the best example of the printing art in the whole newspaper field, and I know that with your help I can do it." He shook hands with all the men, learned all their names, though he rarely called any man by his first name, even after he had known him for years. A printer was "Mister" to him, just as Charles Miller, his chief editor, was. He was a little stiff in such matters, and he never changed.

Leaving the composing room that Wednesday night, he said: "I'll keep my office door open to any Times man, at any time. That goes for the chief editor and it goes for the printers and the boy who sweeps the composing room floor." The talk established a warm relationship. One printer could always understand another, and printer's ink, like blood, was thicker than water. The Times printers' next chapel notes—the union was divided into chapels, and still is—gave supreme accolade to the new boss. They said, "He is a practical printer who worked up from office boy." This was all the biography they cared about.

The Newspapermaker, Fourth Estate, Newspaperdom, dailies in almost every state and even in Canada, printed long pieces about the new publisher at 41 Park Row, and about the astonishing things he was doing there. They ran his picture. It showed a strong-faced, wide-eyed young man trying hard to look stern, strong jaw set above a gates-ajar collar, with a huge-knotted cravat ornamented by a small diamond crescent scarfpin.

Nine days after Ochs had first stepped into 41 Park Row as boss, The Newspapermaker said: "A glance at The New York Times since it has been in the hands of Adolph S. Ochs is like a gleam of sunlight on a cloudy day. The professional sees at once the handiwork of a fellow artist. With the reputation of printing on the worst presses in the city, The New York Times now appears a typographical beauty."

Notices in other publications were in that vein. Downstreet, the bundle of nerves that was Joseph Pulitzer did not like the fuss over this new competitor. He snarled at him in The World:

"No newspaper can long stand inspection which has for its owners bond syndicates, sugar trusts, leather trusts and other corporate interests so repulsive to the readers of American newspapers. The Times has lost $1,750,000 and is still losing. From having been a foe of trusts and aggressive combinations of capital in the days of George Jones, it has become their apologist and friend. It is muzzled and no longer represents honest conviction in the treatment of public questions. Deficit is doing the business. The shadow of death is settling slowly, but surely, down upon it."

A few years later Pulitzer, then blind, was to sit down with Ochs in a room in Paris, where the walls were insulated against footfalls because he was so sensitive to noise, and concede that he had been out-mastered, by the man from Tennessee.

Ochs meanwhile shuttled between 41 Park Row and his room at the Astor House on Broadway at Barclay Street, just across the park. He slept only five or six hours a night and snatched his food in inexpensive restaurants.

Henry B. Hyde, founder and head of the Equitable Life Assurance Society of the United States had become interested in the revival at The Times. He told Ochs that he felt the paper eventually would be to the United States what The Times of London was to Britain. This encouragement drove Ochs even harder. He said: "I don't see how I can fall down, with men like that behind me. The problem is simply to get started; the future is certain." Hyde saw The Times when it was starting upward. He died in 1899 and his interest was taken over by his son, James Hazen Hyde.

Miller had used the ivory-tower technique in his attempts to revive the ailing Times. Ely had lacked the journalistic background needed for the task. Ochs went at it in the manner of the thoroughly practical newspaperman who knew from the outset what had to be done. He hitched Vision and Work to the load, and handled the team smoothly. It would take a lot of straining, but this pair would haul The Times clear.

Ochs talked with newsboys to get first-hand reports on Times sales, observed reader reaction wherever he went, watched the trade journals and his competitors, and studied every Times department to remedy any frailties. Reporters, advertising men, printers, sensed at once that this man knew the business. Within a fortnight they were putting everything they had into the job, and The Times showed it. It was journalistic resurrection.

Three weeks after Ochs took over he had cut weekly expenses by $400. At the end of seven weeks it was $2,000 less than it had been a year before. Ochs made staff cuts in every branch except the news department. In many cases he reduced two jobs to one. By the end of October he was getting out a far better newspaper, with much less money, than either Miller or Ely had, and advertising volume was booming. He had added an illustrated half-tone Sunday supplement and a Saturday book review section with his smaller force. Both were instantly popular, and drew fresh revenue.

Dealers and circulation canvassers reported incredible things. The Times was selling out early each day in places where it had hardly moved at all. "Boy on Brooklyn side of the Bridge told me this morning that he very nearly had a fit one day this week," a circulation canvasser wrote. "He sold all his Times, something he'd never done before, and not only that one day, but every day since." It was the same story all over town.

Owners of Manhattan's largest department stores, who had reduced their advertising space in The Times to a few lines, started inviting Ochs to their offices or to dinner. Almost every letter to Chattanooga recorded some fresh advertising account. "There is no doubt," Ochs wrote home, "that I have got the chance that occurs only once in a century."

The Sunday supplement, first issued on Sept. 6, 1896, was run along the same lines as the daily paper. While other publications still stuffed their Sabbath editions with vapid chromos and with dead material, Ochs kept his hinged on current events. When the horse show was on, he had a horse show feature. When the opera opened, the main piece was on the opera. The weekly illustrated newspapers had something to worry about. It turned out that the circulation they were dropping was going to The Times.

The Fourth Estate was only one of several trade publications that mentioned The Times' quick surge in Sunday circulation. It said:

"The New York Times Sunday supplement is the realization of the newspaper magazine, clean, clever and excellently printed. The half-tones come out with clearness due to artistic printing. The timeliness of the topics makes it what it is meant to be."

Clergymen, educators, newspapermen outside New York and prominent public officials, including droves of Republicans who had frowned on The Times for almost twelve years, became highly vocal over the paper's fresh, clean appearance and its news treatment. In the pulpit, clergymen who had thundered against the yellows, spoke in praise of The New York Times as "a decent, readable newspaper, fit for any home." The response to the Ochs-wrought changes was almost universal acclaim.

In October, Ochs thought it might be a good idea to reduce to slogan form the praises that poured in on The Times for the straightforward news policy he had reaffirmed. He and his own editors tentatively chose as the slogan, "All the News That's Fit to Print," but he offered a $100 prize for a better slogan of not more than ten words. Richard Watson Gilder, editor of the dignified Century Magazine, consented to judge the contest.

The reponse was astonishing and Ochs shrewdly made the most of it. Every day for weeks he printed from a column to a column and a half of entries for the prize. Newspapers as far west as San Francisco discussed it and the revivified Times at great length. The editor of the San Francisco Argonaut, for example, wrote in one such piece: "Realizing that the sewer and morgue fields were fully occupied by The World and The Journal, Ochs determined to issue a clean paper for a change. Very much to the surprise of himself and New York, he is making a success of it." Such advertising could not have been bought.

There were thousands of entries in the contest, mostly in the vein of "All The News That's Fit To Read," "All the News Worth Telling," "Free from Filth, Full of News," "News for the Million, Scandal for None." The $100 prize went to D. M. Redfield of New Haven, Conn., for "All the World News, but not a School for Scandal." But Ochs and his editors decided to cling to their own slogan. It became a household saying, and still is. It was first printed on the editorial page of Oct. 25, 1896. On the following Feb. 10, it was put on the front page in the spot it still occupies.

Before the slogan ever appeared in The Times, it glowed in electric lights on the north end of the Cumberland Hotel at Twenty-
second Street between Broadway and Fifth Avenue, overlooking
Madison Square.

At the end of October the Saturday Book Review broke The
Times record for book advertising. General advertising, especially
from department stores and from financial houses, kept pouring in.
On some days, even within two months of Ochs' taking over, the
volume ran ahead of that of The World and The Journal.

Meanwhile, Miller used his pen against the Bryanites and free
silver, and whooped it up—in the most dignified and scholarly
style, of course—for sound money. Ochs sat in at every editorial
council. He saw improvements in the editorial page, but he kept
after Miller for more. Incidentally, he regarded Miller, as he did
other learned men, with genuine awe. He never got over the feeling, even when his ship was in, that he had lost a lot in life through
lack of a college education. He often was wistful about it.

In late October, 1896, Ochs marched in a Sound Money Parade
with fifty of his staff, carrying silken banners that simply said,
"The New-York Times." It rained that day, but more than 100,000
men, women and children lined the route from lower Manhattan past a reviewing stand in Madison Square. Ochs led The
Times delegation and was elated when thousands called him by
name. The Times group trudged happily through lanes of New
Yorkers hoarsely shouting, "All the News That's Fit to Print!"
though the legend was not borne on the march. Hundreds of times
during the two-hour swing uptown, throngs lustily shouted, "Hur-
rah for The New-York Times!"

There was a glow of triumph, too, in Ochs' heart that night,
though by nature's strange chemistry, it did not extinguish a natural
sense of humility. Footsore from the long march, and with New
York's thunderous cheers still vibrating in his ears, he went to the
Fifth Avenue Temple to bow his head in prayer. His father, whom
he always revered, had died on Oct. 26, eight years before, and
every year on the anniversary date Ochs honored his memory with
prayer. The strongest belief the publisher held from boyhood until his own death was, "Honor thy father and thy mother."

CHAPTER
11

THE ROUTINE of putting The Times back on its feet became crushing, even for Adolph Ochs. From Chattanooga, he summoned Ben Franck, the cousin whose frock coat he had ruined in the welcome to Cleveland. Franck took some weight off his back, but every day Ochs, in addition to visiting prospective advertisers, checked on every department in the paper and kept careful eye on expense and income. In mid-October he came wearily back to his desk one day and found a jingle Franck had written about him:

> I am the Boss
> The Editor bold
> And the Chief of
> The New York Times,
> The Big Ad Man,
> The Office Boy
> And he Who handles
> The Dimes.

He was all those things and more. He kept dreaming up new ideas for the paper. On Oct. 18, 1896, the left-hand column on the front page blossomed with an index, "The News Condensed," the grandsire of the current "World News Summarized." He kept improving the Sunday supplement and the Saturday Book Review. He was a little hurt when the comic magazine Life printed a cartoon showing loose pages of the Book Review piled in heaps on a trolley car floor. The caption was, "The Times Litter'y Section." He profited

119

by the cartoon. Thereafter the supplement was bound and there were no loose leaves to clutter public conveyances.

Ochs found his new position filled with social complications. The man who had come into New York only a few months before to live in inexpensive hotels and to roam from one bank to another seeking loans to cover his unfortunate Chattanooga real estate investments found himself sought for dinner at the homes of New York's most prominent men. He was deluged with offers of membership in exclusive clubs and with requests to serve on committees. These came from persons with whom he had to maintain warm relationships, but the social demands cut too heavily into his time. He needed every possible hour to bring The Times round to his ideal of a newspaper.

He was finally compelled to delegate someone to represent him socially. Most of the burden was borne by Louis Wiley, the "persistent fellow" from The Sun. He was to be Ochs' social alter ego for decades, and he loved it. He was always quick to defend his chief from criticism. It got so, in later years, that Wiley was frequently mistaken for the owner of The Times.

Ochs' concentration on rebuilding The Times was not his sole reason for avoiding social engagements when he could. He was still at heart the "Southern greenhorn" he had called himself when he first came to New York, and was inclined to shy from the company of the wealthy and the great.

Ochs staked a lot on the first election coverage by The Times under his ownership. The cost was only $2,000, but this represented a daring splurge for a man whose capital was so limited.

The night before the balloting he walked from lower Manhattan to Herald Square, a little man in the throng of bustled women in gigantic hats escorted by brown-derbied and mustachioed gallants in fawn-colored topcoats. He saw that Hearst's Journal had built a bandstand in front of its main office for musicians to blow brassy serenade for returns watchers in front of The Journal bulletin board and had hired chalk artists to entertain the throng during intermissions. The World, he noticed, had put up an eighty-foot screen on the Franklin Street side of the gold-domed tower.

He was not prosperous enough to compete with such displays. He had five modest bulletin boards set in as many windows on the second floor at 41 Park Row, three facing on Printing House Square, two on City Hall Park. At the southern end of Madison Square he had a twenty-foot screen under the electric slogan "All the News That's Fit to Print." He had worked out something new in stereopticon slides—a gelatine sheet that took ink without blurring, as other slides did. "I suggested that to one of the stereopticon operators when we discussed our display," he told Effie bitterly, "and he spread the idea all over town. All the newspapers copied it."

On Election Night Ochs stood at his window in The Times awed at a sea of upturned faces in City Hall Park, where 50,000 persons were jammed watching the returns. His display, he had to concede, was surpassed by The World's, but it exceeded any his scholarly predecessor had achieved. Around 10 o'clock helmeted policemen helped him through the crowds when he left the office to see how his Madison Square screen had drawn.

The turnout in Madison Square was larger than downtown's and Ochs' heart beat fast when the crowd roared, "Hoorah for The New-York Times!" The election went as he had wished. McKinley and sound money had beaten the Golden Voice and free silver. He knew that the election results would bolster Times prestige. One clubman had pledged himself, he recalled, to buy $5,000 of Times bonds if McKinley should win.

He told Effie: "I could not help thinking as I watched our display on Twenty-third Street how deeply interested I was in the outcome, and how it would effect a great many of my plans. Yet, I must be peculiarly constituted. The closer quarters I get into, the calmer and cooler I get. I do not think that is usually the case with men of large affairs. I am not seeking the bauble of fame or honor, power, glory or anything of that kind. I have only one fixed purpose —to be freed from the thraldom of my creditors."

A few days after he had told Effie of the thoughts that had raced through his mind on Election Night, he turned down $33,600 in city advertising, The Times' share of $200,000 the Board of Aldermen had voted for having six New York newspapers print a complete canvass of the New York vote. On Nov. 12, he had Miller write a strong editorial attacking the $200,000 expenditure as an outright waste of public funds. The Aldermen hastily issued a statement that they were not aware that the advertising bill could run so high.

One of his editors told Ochs, "That's probably the first time in the history of New York journalism that a newspaper threw its own fat in the fire." The staff and the readers applauded the publisher's courage. Money could not have bought the prestige it gained for him.

Tammany made another bid for Ochs' favor early in August, 1898. Richard Croker, its Chief Sachem, sent Samuel Untermyer, the attorney, to offer The Times a preference on all city advertising if he would hire " a certain millionaire newspaperman," not otherwise identified, at a salary of $10,000 a year. Ochs told his wife, "Untermyer kept urging me to accept the offer, but I held to my decision. He thinks I am supersensitive and that I lean backwards in these matters, but in his heart he must believe that I am right. I will enter into no understanding with Tammany." He never did, though the pressure never left off.

Prodigious problems kept Ochs' mind at work eighteen to twenty hours a day. He would drop into bed at the Astor House, physically and mentally exhausted. He was lonesome in New York and yearned for the companionship of his wife and his daughter. Late in November in 1896 he asked Effie to come North with the child, and to put up at a hotel until they could find a home. He told her: "You run around and see what is offered. You will be spending more time in it than I will and I want you to be pleased. I believe it would be quite jolly to have an apartment—our own little home. I am going to make it your responsibility. You exercise your wish and your taste."

Mrs. Ochs came North with Iphigene, and rented a comfortable apartment from the Rhinelanders in a small brick house in East Thirty-ninth Street, off Lexington Avenue.

He felt then that The Times was definitely lumbering upgrade. On Nov. 28 it passed The Tribune in advertising, and circulation was still soaring. The trend to success was so obvious that trade journals and daily newspapers started running stories, all based on false rumor, that this or that rich man was about to take over.

The Minneapolis Sunday Times came out with a rumor that William Waldorf Astor of Cliveden was bidding for The Times.

Ochs wired the editor: "The whole story has not a scintilla of excuse for publication. I am confident you will make a satisfactory denial." The editor did. He wrote:

"The truth is, and we take sincere pleasure in declaring it, that The New York Times is not only managed with unusual ability in its business department but editorially is without a superior in the United States . . . There is no other journal in the country that approaches more nearly the ideal daily newspaper."

At the end of the first year of his management, Ochs received congratulatory messages from high places and humble—from the White House down. In a short twelve months the harried man who had come to New York from the South, with disaster hot on his neck, had not only saved the handsome Chattanooga Times plant, which he had pyramided out of an original investment of $250 in 1878, but had lifted a dying metropolitan journalistic giant to its feet on borrowed capital. Its advertising and circulation were higher than they had been for fifteen years.

"Mr. Adolph S. Ochs," said The Journalist, "celebrated the first anniversary of his connection with The New York Times last Wednesday by doing a double day's work and putting on extra hustle. He has been remarkably successful in his efforts at reviving The Times, and is a decided addition to the brightest newspapermen of the metropolis."

Ochs brought this and a load of similar clippings to dump into Effie's lap. Since she was with him, he felt stronger and his dreams expanded.

In the fall of 1897 the publisher moved his family to 14 West Seventy-second Street where they boarded with the family of Thomas Read, a teataster. Ochs felt that Iphigene needed the company of other children, and the Reads had six lively offspring, one a boy about his daughter's age. The move worked out well. Iphigene and the Read boy hit it off together, and Ochs frequently took the lad along on short trips to keep the little girl company. They were to live with the Reads until the fall of 1899, when they moved to 2030 Broadway, near Seventieth Street.

Early in 1898, though The Times was still picking up circulation and advertising, chiefly because of typographical changes and a livelier straight-news policy, Ochs' fertile mind kept thinking up fresh ideas for the paper. He was the first publisher, for example, to solicit circulation by telephone. Then he ran a subscription contest offering a trans-Atlantic voyage and a bicycle tour of France and England to the 100 persons getting the most new subscribers.

This was not an indiscriminate bid for any kind of circulation. The contest notice was aimed principally at school and college teachers, and among them it found rich response. It characterized The Times as a "dignified, enterprising newspaper," and said, "To be seen reading The New York Times is a stamp of respectability." The contest brought thousands of new readers.

But trouble was in the offing. The Spanish-American War came on, and The Times and other newspapers lacked the resources to report it as Hearst and Pulitzer did. These giants hired dispatch boats without thought to cost, sent correspondents to every front and extra men with New York regiments to clutter their columns with sensational war features. Only Bennett the Younger came anywhere near meeting this competition.

Ochs and other publishers saw their circulation and advertising slipping. The Times gave prominent display to Associated Press dispatches, which told the story of the war in adequate detail, but the coverage looked pale beside the offerings of The World, The Journal and The Herald.

Around this time rumors were renewed that The Times was again in a bad way. The New York correspondent of The Minneapolis Sunday Times relayed to his office: "Something is going to be done with The New York Times. It is running behind in its finances and its Wall Street backers are said to be getting tired of meeting deficiencies."

Things did get gloomy at 41 Park Row. The Times had slowed in its astonishing forward surge because of the war. Ochs entered into a news combination with The Mail and Express and The Commercial Advertiser, in the hope that by pooling material they might make a better showing, but the results were feeble. This was a desperate hour. The Southerner saw his gains vanishing. He was in the position of the frog in the well. He had leaped high, but had fallen back. He saw need for some radical move and mulled over it for weeks.

He had made up his mind by early October. He figured that if he could not fight Hearst and Pulitzer in war coverage, he might make some headway against them on the home front by dropping the price of The Times from 3 cents to 1 cent. The World and The Journal were selling at the time for 2 cents.

His announcement of the reduced price exploded on the journalistic world with extraordinary detonations.

Newspapers all over the United States played Ochs' decision as straight news and it gave The Times tremendous advertising, not all of it good. His own staff interpreted the move as a descent into sensational journalism. Several reporters immediately began whooping up their copy in Hearst style. These offerings were coldly rejected. Ochs said there would be no change in news policy.

For every newspaper that defended the decision, five sneered at it. The Journalist argued: "Men who want The Times would pay 3 cents as soon as 1. The circulation won't increase one little bit." The Buffalo Express said, "The spectacle of the staid and respectable old Times trying to compete with The World and Journal is enough to make the ghosts of Henry J. Raymond and George Jones go tearing down Broadway in their war chariots." The Philadelphia Ledger remarked on how Ochs' move had "startled his contemporaries," and said, "The entrance of such a paper into the 1-cent field could not fail to evoke criticism and renewed discussion of the old question whether it is possible to publish on sound business principles a paper of the highest quality and character for 1 cent."

Unfriendly sheets openly published their belief that the Ochs move was financed by Richard Croker, that the Tammany boss, through a promise of increased city advertising, had persuaded the Tennessean to drop the price of The Times so that the paper might reach more prospective Democratic voters in the weeks leading to the November elections. This slant was based on the fact that Ochs had not immediately dropped the price of The Times outside of New York. He did that a fortnight later. The Cambridge Post, an up-state Republican publication, asked slyly: "Will the price be raised to the old figure after Nov. 8? And who makes up the deficit while the 1-cent issue continues?"

Ochs stood firm. He had announced:

"It is the price of the paper, not its character, that will change.

In appealing to a larger audience The Times by no means proposes to offend the taste or forfeit the confidence of the audience it now has, already large, discriminating and precious to it as lifelong friends.

"It seemed to the management of The Times that, while the growth of its sales was steady and substantial, it was too slow . . . It puts before the people of New York a clean newspaper of high and honorable aims, which prints all the news that is fit to print, and expresses its editorial opinions with sincere conviction and independence."

A subsequent announcement said that as fast as The Times could arrange for increased circulation its price would be dropped everywhere to 1 cent—and it was.

Within a month of the daring price decrease, all who had cried out against it, were retracting their words. The San Francisco Argonaut, which ran a weekly feature on the press of the nation, said on Nov. 14, 1898: "It is nearly a month ago that The Times reduced its price to 1 cent, and the expected has not happened yet. Neither has it gone to the 'demnition bow-wows,' nor has it betrayed the cloven hoof of Tammany. The wiseacres have failed in their predictions. The cynics have been abashed."

Circulation leaped. Dealers reported orders multiplied five to eight times in certain districts. Some critics held that cheapening the price of The Times had also cheapened it as a high-class advertising medium. The magazine Fame deplored the drop as an indication that The Times intended to compete with papers that bid for "cheap public favor."

Fame opened its columns to Ochs for a defense of his policy. In his two-column answer he argued that having the presses, the pressmen and the stereotypers, it cost him much less per copy to print 100,000 copies than 40,000. "After the first copy is struck off, the cost of production that varies with the number of copies issued, includes only white paper and ink," he said.

He challenged anyone to show where The Times had lost caste by the price drop. He said it was not true that a reader placed the highest value on the newspaper that cost the most. "A man values most the newspaper which presents him the most matter that is of most interest to him," he said. "The theory that a 1-cent newspaper cannot maintain the character of its advertising is baseless. The Times is now carrying more of the advertising of the best houses than ever before in its history. It is maintaining its advertising rates. I have refused during the month of December [1898] nearly $50,000 worth of business offered at less than its rates."

He also pointed out that book advertisers had spent more in The Times since he had taken over the management than they ever had spent in any other newspaper. He added: "People who buy books are the best class of newspaper readers. In a recent issue of The Times there were nearly 20,000 lines of book advertising."

There was no rebuttal.

Circulation went from 25,726 on Oct. 10, 1898, to 76,260 within one year and advertising grew in proportion. The drop to 1 cent paradoxically lifted Ochs and The Times over the final hurdle to success.

Effie Wise Ochs and the child, Iphigene, were in New York and had begun to like it. Iphigene had a French governess. Mrs. Ochs made no attempt to accelerate her own languid pace or manners to match the brisker nervous tempo of the metropolis. She was calm in all her husband's business crises and managed by her own peculiar magic to soothe and comfort him when he was most deeply troubled. She could always do that when no one else could.

Once he had The Times well on its feet, Ochs slowed down just a little. He hired John Norris, who had been Joseph Pulitzer's general manager, as his assistant. Norris assumed a large part of the publisher's work burden. Ochs began to enjoy his clubs and gave more dinners in his own home and was a frequent dinner guest in the homes of leading merchants, bankers and intellectuals. He took his daughter to museums and musicales. He shielded her from being spoiled by his new fame and riches; he could not have tolerated any tendency toward childish snobbishness.

Four years from the day he took over, Ochs' greatest dream came true. He had brought The New York Times to the forefront in New York and he had pulled The Chattanooga Times out of debt. The dusty Park Row wreck into which he had stepped on Aug. 14, 1896, was a throbbing, humming plant. The personnel, considerably increased, had the highest morale in town. Times circulation had gone from 9,000 a day in August, 1896, to 82,000 in 1900. Advertising had soared to 3,978,000 agate lines. In another year circulation was to go to 102,000 and advertising linage to almost 5,000,000.

On Aug. 14, 1900, the reorganization group turned over to Ochs the certificates that legally established his control over The New York Times.

"The deed is done," he gloatingly announced to his wife that night. "The contract I made in 1896 is ended. My title is perfect. Now I am monarch of all I survey, and none my right to dispute."

But Ochs was not the type to dwell on old dreams. Effie saw the blue eyes fix on greater visions. She knew all the signs. She listened patiently and with quiet pride.

"You and baby will share all this and my happiness in having achieved it," he said. "We can now consider ourselves rich as we ever expected to be. Better than that, Effie, we have the consciousness of knowing that it has all been secured by honorable and ennobling work. I hope we may enjoy its fruits for many years yet to come."

CHAPTER
12

In 1900 New York was growing upward and downward, as well as spreading out. Armies of laborers dug the first subways, laid the foundations for the first skyscrapers and rooted up out-moded cobblestones in preparation for smoother paving. The city launched a tremendous dock-building program. Concrete and steel superseded brick and frame. Great corporations all over the country opened New York headquarters. The whole nation boomed, but nowhere at such pace as in New York—and Adolph Ochs' revitalized Times boomed with it.

In the month of January, 1900, the newspaper's revenue came to more than $100,000, its Jan. 7 Financial Review alone carrying $10,000 worth of linage. The annual advertising revenue was to exceed $1,000,000 in 1900. Bids for The Times increased in size and in number. That year there were several offers of $2,000,000 and more for the Ochs' majority holdings. He was not tempted.

He liked to talk now and then about retiring at the age of 50, a decade in the future. When he discussed it with his wife she listened sympathetically, but she knew that in his heart he did not mean it. He told her, "I would not sell now for $10,000,000. I want to prove that what I have done here is only the bare start. When I have completed my work $10,000,000 will seem trifling."

Early in January, 1900, Adolph Ochs sent for his brother, George, who was then general manager of The Chattanooga Times, to outline a plan for printing The New York Times at the Paris Exposition that year. He had already arranged for 1,500 square feet of space in the American Pavilion Annex at the fair and had put $50,000 into six linotype machines, an octuple Goss press, and a stereotyping plant.

He told George: "The New York Times is already well known in Europe, but this promotion shall make it better known. The Times will be the only newspaper printed at the Exposition. People from all corners of the world will visit the fair grounds. When they leave they will have a better idea of how we work here in New York."

The exposition plant was ready in March. With matrices for some pages sent from 41 Park Row, and with news assembled, written and printed on the spot, before exposition strollers' eyes, George Washington Ochs put out a daily edition of some 20,000 copies, six days a week for eight months. The issue ran from ten to fourteen eight-column pages, exactly like the parent sheet.

The $50,000 was well spent. Every day at 4 P.M., when the press rolled, exposition visitors gaped through the great plate glass windows and excitedly discussed this American marvel. Georges Clemenceau, white-bearded King Leopold of Belgium, Prince Henri, Bourbon pretender to the French throne, and countless dukes, lords, earls and ministers came to inspect the plant. King Leopold was fascinated. He stepped dangerously close to the whirling press, making aides and courtiers nervous. When he left he shook hands with George Ochs, and wrote the royal signature in The Times guest book with a regal flourish.

Back in New York that year, Adolph Ochs slowly rearranged his design for living. He gave Mrs. Ochs $100 a week to run the household. This was not to cover the cost of wines, schooling, doctor bills. The publisher also decided to set aside $1,000 a month to cover his own end of household and personal expenses. He spent freely for gifts. Often he came home with loads of toys and books. He loved to get on his hands and knees with Iphigene and other small fry as they squealed happily over the gifts. His favorite game with children was guessing the date of a coin. He would hold a coin tight in his fist, and the child who came nearest the date, with sly leads from him—"hot" when close, "cold" when not—would win. He kept up this game with his grandchildren to the end of his life.

From the time that the real estate bubble broke in Chattanooga, the publisher had denied himself the services of a tailor. It was a real sacrifice, because he was something of a dandy. In 1900 he was able to order tailor-made clothes. He bought his first custom-fitted suits at Rock's in Fifth Avenue, and was so pleased he could not help boasting to his mother: "Paid $75 at Rock's for a new suit. Not bad for a country greenie from Tennessee, eh?"

One day in May, 1900, a pretty woman, then a little faded, sent her card into the publisher's office. It bore a Knoxville address. He was always eager to meet folk from the town he had roamed in his childhood. He had her in. When she had gone, he took from his office desk a worn, well-thumbed brown leather book bravely marked "autographs," and read in it a copper-plate inscription dated "Oct. 7, 1876."

It was one of the recommendations he had borne with him when he had turned his back, at last, on the dusty little newspaper shop where he had swept the floors and collected Chronicles for pre-dawn delivery. It said:

"Adolph Ochs was until the summer of 1873, a pupil in the Preparatory Department of this institution [Eastern Tennessee University] for several years. His application to study, and his general demeanor, during that time, were very satisfactory and creditable to him . . . I cordially recommend him to the kind regard and friendly attention of all persons of worth and influence, wherever he may go." It was signed: "Thomas W. Humes, President, Eastern Tennessee University."

Ochs stared across the green of City Hall Park, and his eyes misted as his mind cast back over the long years.

"My visitor," he told his mother in a letter that night, "was Miss Frances Humes, daughter of the late Dr. Thomas W. Humes of Knoxville. She is eking out an existence as a fashionable modiste. She contemplates a trip to Paris, and wishes to write a few fashion letters for The Times. I told her we would be overjoyed to have them."

Then he wrote:

The world goes 'round and 'round
Some goes up, and some goes down.

He returned the old school autograph book to a far corner of his desk. The incident had saddened him. He was often swept emotionally by memories of his remote past, and not all the stern dignity he could muster successfully concealed the sentimentalist in him.

During this period the publisher's editorial columns were raking Tom Platt, Republican up-State boss, and not at all gently. Under Ochs The Times had come to surpass the political influence it wielded in Raymond's day, and Tom Platt winced. He took the matter up with President Hyde of the Equitable Life, and Hyde tried to persuade the Southerner to go a bit light. Ochs had always stood in awe of the financier, and in turn had won Hyde's admiration, but he bristled at this attempt to influence Times editorial policy. It was not the most comfortable moment for bristling. Hyde held the publisher's note for a personal loan of $100,000.

The interview was polite, but with a dangerous undercurrent. Hyde was inclined to think the publisher owed him a certain obligation; Ochs held grimly to the tenet that no personal obligation was great enough to change a newspaper's honest opinion on any man or issue. Ochs left the Equitable offices determined to sever his business relationship with Hyde.

In the fall of 1900 Ochs was deep in plans for a new Times building. He had his eye on the present site of the Woolworth Building, and the dream was of a white skyscraper that would, as he put it, "wake up the natives." Brokers quietly took options on most of the lots needed, but several lot-holders learned what was up, and put their prices out of reach. Ochs dropped the plan to build, but only briefly.

The family was a little worried about the publisher at this time. They knew how his visions sometimes swept him off his feet, as they had in the Chattanooga real estate disaster. Their uneasiness only amused him. He told his mother: "George is charging me with vaulting ambition that may bring me to grief because of my negotiations for a Times building and tentative negotiations for a news alliance with The Times of London. He thinks I am trying to do too much, and that I am given too much to big schemes and to new enterprises."

George tried to persuade Effie to talk her husband into a tour of Europe to keep him from temptation. These family intrigues did not remain secret. Adolph laughed at them. He told his mother:

"George is afraid that after all my newspaper schemes are exhausted I will start to plan a road to the moon, or some such visionary enterprise. I find this amusing. I pass it along in anticipation of what he may say when he gets back to Chattanooga."

An alliance with The Times of London was indeed seriously discussed, and fairly complete plans for it were made. W. Moberly Bell, brilliant manager of The Times of London, had a skeleton draft of the plan ready by Oct. 6 in 1900. It called for:

1. The New York Times to have the exclusive use of London Times news in the United States.

2. The New York Times to pay The London Times $10,000 a year and all expenses (including rent of offices in London Times Building, editing the news and transmission charges to New York) and 25 per cent of the gross income from the sale of the news to other newspapers in America. The London Times to have free of rent an office in The New York Times Building and to have duplicate proofs of New York Times news matter.

This was only one phase of the tentative plan. A second concerned organization of an International Times, to be owned and put out jointly by The New York Times and The London Times. Moberly Bell's memorandum called for:

1. A limited liability company to be formed.

2. The newspaper to be a daily morning newspaper.

3. The name: Paris Edition London-New York Times, or The European Times, or International Times.

4. The London and The New York Times to supply equally the cash capital, limited to $50,000 each, and jointly control publication.

5. The news service to form the nucleus for a news distributing agency.

Ochs' journal had by that time become probably the greatest news gathering agency in the United States, at least in the straight news, or conservative field. The Times of London stood pre-eminent in the same field abroad. The combined services might well have produced an International Times that could have spelled doom for James Gordon Bennett's Paris Herald, but nothing came of it. The reasons now are obscure, but at least one factor that decided Ochs against it, in the end, was fear of being labeled Anglophile. That charge kept coming up, anyhow, and was to be played to crescendo by the Kaiser's propagandists when the first World War broke.

With Louis Wiley and John Norris carrying part of his burden, Ochs widened his acquaintanceship. He met the most important persons of the era, but he was still a little uneasy in such company; he kept saying, "I am embarrassed by the attention they give me."

He felt that he wanted more room for his family. They were content in their snug and convenient apartment, but it was hardly large enough, especially when friends came. Mrs. Ochs was not too happy about large dinners or large-scale home entertainment, but she agreed that it might be better if they took a whole house for themselves. Iphigene was doing well at school. Her father spent a lot of time with her, and liked to repeat bright remarks she made, or strange questions she asked. He took her to The Times office frequently, and delighted in showing her how the plant was run.

After dinner at home on Dec. 31, 1900, Ochs bundled his daughter into warm clothes, and he drove her through a damp, freezing night to his offices at 41 Park Row. She was aware of unusual activity in the plant. This was her first night visit, a special occasion.

At 10 o'clock her father took her to the office window. He pointed down into City Hall Park. Thousands of men and women had gathered there. They blew tin horns and trumpets and jangled cow bells. The din came up to the child in waves.

City Hall itself was outlined in red, white and blue electric lights. It made a colorful sight. The publisher caught the child's puzzled expression. He sat her down and explained:

"Every hundred years make a century. Tonight the people of this city, and in cities all over the world, will assemble in crowds as they have here in City Hall Park. They will say farewell to the nineteenth century, and they will welcome in the twentieth century. It is an unusual event. No person shall ever see two such cele-

brations. I brought you here tonight to watch. It is something you
will always remember."

The night filled with wondrous sound, new to the child's ears.
From the southern tip of the city, Trinity's chimes sent hymns
quivering on the cold air. Sousa's Band, the players heavily muffled,
sent brassy overtures up to The Times windows. The German singing societies, a chorus of more than 500 voices, sang old German
lieder, and the People's Choral Union sang alternate numbers.

At 11:55 o'clock there was great stir in the building. Singing
printers tramped up the stairs toward the tower, bearing Roman
candles and skyrockets. One minute before midnight a hush fell
on the throng in the park. The City Hall lights went dark. The
silence had dimension.

Then midnight. Trinity's bells broke into wild, joyous clangor.
River craft roared and hooted. Men and women blew madly on
their horns and rang their bells. The City Hall outline again broke
out suddenly in red, white and blue incandescents, and a new sign,
"Welcome Twentieth Century" leaped into life in huge electric
letters across the Hall's wide front.

On The Times roof, in a cutting wind, the printers lighted their
Roman candles and skyrockets. Fire soared to the sky, and sparks
cascaded in golden Niagara past the publisher's windows. All over
the city fireworks flowered against the night and Lyddite bombs
broke and thundered. The child at the publisher's window had
never been up so late. She was wide-eyed with the wonder of it.

Down in the basement The Times presses got under way with
rumble and roar. Newspapers coming fresh from the mechanical
carriers bore the headline: "Twentieth Century's Triumphal Entry.
Welcomed By New York With Tumultuous Rejoicing."

Ochs sat at his desk turning out an eight-page letter to his mother
in Chattanooga. He asked: "How do you like the new century? It
certainly opens auspiciously for us. We have so much to be thank-
ful for."

CHAPTER
13

IN THE SPRING OF 1901 the country witnessed a battle of Wall Street giants—J. P. Morgan, Edward H. Harriman, James J. Hill —over the merger of the Northern Pacific, Great Northern and Burlington railroads. The maneuvering shot stock prices alarmingly high. Fortunes were won and lost.

One May night when The Times was preparing a story on the struggle between the railroad titans, Ochs left the office with Lucien Franck to have dinner somewhere along Park Row. It had just been announced that the stock in Northern Pacific had gone to $1,000 a share.

"You know, Lu," Ochs told his cousin, musingly, "I could have made over a million dollars this week on that railroad deal. I was tipped off to what was going to happen."

"Why in the devil didn't you?" Franck blurted out.

"When I came to New York, Lu, I pledged myself never to dabble in Wall Street. I knew I would have to give all my time to making a success of The Times. I swore I'd concentrate on that."

Actually, Ochs could not forget what had happened five years before in Chattanooga when he had stepped outside the newspaper field to dabble in the land boom; he did not want to make the same mistake twice. He adhered sternly, ever afterward, to a policy of limiting his investments of his own money and Times corporate funds to Government bonds. His successors, many years later, were to adhere to the same investment principle.

In the summer of 1901 The New York Times was handling more than $100,000 in advertising a month. Its news service, especially its foreign news, exceeded any in its previous history. Its coverage of Queen Victoria's death in January had drawn comment wherever newspapermen met. So had its reporting of the assassination of President McKinley. The stories were factual, without lace trimming; the editorial comment was sober.

A few weeks before the President was shot, Ochs was a White House visitor. As he waited for President McKinley he noticed a copy of The New York Times open on the Chief Executive's desk. He said to the President's secretary, "I guess this would be the equivalent of putting out the visiting relative's own picture when the relative is expected." The secretary assured him the open Times was no social prop. He said: "It is the first newspaper Mr. McKinley reads each morning. It would have been there whether you had come or not."

Around this time Fifth Avenue began its career as a street of rich shops. The Flatiron building was going up at Madison Square as the first of the uptown skyscrapers. Down in Beaumont, Texas, the first great oil gusher blew in with fuel for the gasoline buggies that soon would be noisily nudging horses off the streets. Three more East River bridges were under way or on drawing boards as floods of immigrants strained available housing facilities in downtown Manhattan, waiting to spill into Brooklyn and Queens.

All this growth was reflected in Times circulation and advertising. Times men who had wearied of fellow-craftsmen's gibes in Park Row bars and beaneries now luxuriated in the new strength and prestige their sheet had acquired. The man from Chattanooga was on sure ground.

The trade journal The Newspapermaker, analyzing the formula that had made The Times so successful within a few years, said in its issue of Feb. 21, 1901:

"The success of The New York Times has astonished and pleased those publishers who feared the 'yellow peril' . . . The answer is found in 'All the News That's Fit to Print.' It has modestly attempted to reflect, not to make public opinion. It has aimed to be a complete daily newspaper, edited for the self-respecting man, his wife, son and daughter. It does not print pictures, neither does it indulge in freak typography. It has avoided sensationalism and fakes of every description. It has not attempted to do stunts in the name of public service. It has cultivated impartiality and independence. It does not print any advertisement in the ordinary news type of the paper, and it prints 'readers' in agate type only, with 'Adv.' after them."

The article gravely listed Ochs' index expurgatorius in advertising including, "word contests, prize puzzles, immoral books, diseases of men, female pills, fortunetellers, clairvoyants, palmists, massage, offers of large salaries, offers of something for nothing, guaranteed cures, large guaranteed dividends."

Ochs, said the article, had taught other New York publishers nothing new; he had simply "reminded them of that which they had forgotten . . . that a newspaper fit for the home is the best sort of newspaper."

Time and changing conceptions, which must come even to the most conservative journals, eventually compelled The Chattanooga Times to yield to the demand for comics. It began with black-and-white strips in its daily issues early in the 1920's, and in the spring of 1928 launched its first colored Sunday comic supplement. Ochs was a little shamefaced over this compromise, though the move was dictated by circulation pressure, and was entirely practical. He fed his conscience one tidbit when he made the move; he refused to permit any promotion hullabaloo over the colored Sunday supplement. There was to come a distant day, after he had passed from the scene, when even his New York Times would print first Sunday, then daily, crossword puzzles and—astonishingly—find its readers cheerfully accepting them.

Ochs had earned a rest, and early in August of 1901 he took Effie and his daughter to Europe. All through his tour across the Continent he was the wide-eyed country boy seeing story-book scenes come true.

The Times office had been a sorry and dusty place when Ochs took command. Miller, confused and worried, had seldom left the ivory tower. Maintenance had fallen to a bare minimum. The wooden floors were splintery and mice romped and scampered in the city room when it was quiet. Wanamaker, the Negro man-of-all-work, never quite caught up with his multitudinous chores. His mops and brooms were worn, and Ben Franck bought washing soda by the pound rather than by the barrel, until Ochs heard of it. The Southerner knew the need for skimping, but did not want to draw the line that tight.

There were only two telephones in the whole Times plant, one connecting the city desk with the man at Police Headquarters, one for the advertising department. There were a few typewriters in the city room, but these were not Times property; they were owned by the newest and youngest reporters. The older staff men who wrote by hand at sloping desks hated them; said they disrupted thought. Wanamaker finally dug up an old table, covered it with linoleum and felt and moved it to a far corner where typewriter-users could hammer away without bothering pen-and-pencil crusties.

Reporters were perhaps a little more inclined to the convivial in those days than they are now. They spent a lot of their time at the Astor House bar, at Perry's in the World Building or in Lipton's bar on the ground floor in The Times Building. They ate in Hitchcock's at Park Row and Ann Street, or went down street for Dolan's beef-and-beans. When they had the time and the money they walked to the waterfront for an eight-course feast at Smith McNell's in Washington Market, or splurged on fried chicken, the specialty at Katy's in William Street.

Most mornings the last reporter was out of the building right after 2 o'clock. There had been a nightly poker game for years that had kept the staff around until dawn splashed on City Hall dome across the street, but Loewenthal had broken that up early in 1901. Moral scruples were not involved. A visiting delegation of poker players from The Herald had cleaned Loewenthal's men out one night and The Times men's wives had complained.

At 2 o'clock on Friday morning, Sept. 13, 1901, the news staff left after having worked a good part of the night making changes in the story of the shooting of President McKinley. Early in the evening the President, wounded by an assassin in Buffalo, N.Y., was sinking. Later he had rallied and seemed safe for the night. When the story had been rewritten along these lines, Loewenthal, his immediate aides and all the staff went home.

Tommy Bracken, night office boy in the news room who sometimes doubled as Loewenthal's secretary, was alone in the shop. He often stayed after all the reporters had gone because his head was filled with romantic notions about newspaper work. This morning he was typing a Sunday story. The hammering keys set up echoes, but in brief silences between lines the mice came out for their nocturnal pastimes. Horse-drawn news wagons and mail trucks occasionally passed outside, but mostly there was stillness.

At 3 o'clock young Bracken was startled by the sudden impact of an Associated Press pneumatic-tube carrier bumping its leather head against the bin wall nearby. Ordinarily, the A. P. message would have rested in the bin undisturbed until the day men came in, but Bracken was curious. It was unusual for A. P. to be sending copy to a morning paper at that hour.

It was an A. P. bulletin from Buffalo. It said that President McKinley's condition had suddenly grown worse.

The second edition, Tommy noticed had carried a headline that McKinley was having a restful night; that at midnight his physicians had said he was considerably better.

Tommy wavered. Instinctively he knew the bulletin was important, but he was a timid fellow, not given to rash impulse. As he stood in the quiet with the bulletin in his fingers, the pneumatic tube hissed again, and a second late bulletin clunked head on against the bin.

"President McKinley is sinking," it said.

Tommy raced to the composing room, where a few men were cleaning up the forms. The subforeman in charge was slow to catch Tommy's enthusiasm for an extra.

"The other morning papers will have this," Tommy pleaded. "They'll beat us. The Times will look silly. It'll be a disgrace."

Finally the subforeman shrugged. He walked to the talking tube, and had the presses stopped. Tommy found more A. P. bulletins in the bin when he got back to the news room. He scanned them excitedly, and sat down to write a headline for the extra.

It was not a masterful job. It was the first headline Tommy had ever written. Still, it told the story:

MR. M'KINLEY HAS
SINKING SPELL

Under the headline Tommy ran all the bulletins the A. P. had kept pouring in. They told in hasty snatches how the President's sinking spell had set in at 2:15 A.M., how more physicians had been summoned to the bedside; how a hasty call had gone out for Cabinet members and the President's closest advisers.

The hodgepodge Tommy threw together in his inexperienced way made more exciting reading, somehow, than a smoothly written piece. It gave a greater sense of urgency. The skeleton printers' crew helped shave the headlines and the subheads to fit column rule, got all the stuff into print, and the extras went into the wagons. Tommy and the composing room and the pressroom crews worked until daylight, adding A. P. matter as fast as it came in. They put out three editions, all told, before sunup. It was daylight when Tommy rode the horse cars uptown to the Astoria ferry, on the way home. He thrilled to the newsboys' cries, "President McKinley Dying!"

Back at The Times at 1 o'clock that afternoon, his tow head was barely inside the city room door when Loewenthal called him. Tommy stood beside the editor's desk.

"Who wrote this headline?" Loewenthal demanded. He seemed a little angry. His finger stabbed at Tommy's handiwork.

"Well, Mr. Loewenthal, I wrote it. I—"

"Why did *you* write it? Where was everybody?"

Falteringly, Tommy told the whole story. Loewenthal heard him out, then gruffly muttered something about watching his verbs next time he wrote a headline. He dismissed Tommy. That afternoon, though, the editor posted a notice on the bulletin board:

"I take this opportunity publicly to express my appreciation of the work of Mr. [everybody was 'Mr.' on Ochs' Times] Thomas Bracken who, alone and unaided, this morning got out the third, fourth and fifth editions."

There was more, but that conveys the theme. Next day Tommy got a $20 goldpiece from the publisher. Tommy had created Times legend.

In the fifty-five years that Tommy Bracken put in on The Times (he retired, eventually, in April, 1947) he got out two more extras after the regular news staff had left for the night—one on the morning that Gov. William Sulzer was impeached in August, 1913, another when Senator Huey Long died, Sept. 10, 1935, of an assassin's bullet. He was keeper of The Times morgue then.

Less than five years after he took over The New York Times, Ochs bought the sagging Philadelphia Times. The contracts were signed May 7, 1901. Fourteen months later, on July 21, 1902, he acquired The Philadelphia Public Ledger. He combined them under the title, The Public Ledger and The Philadelphia Times, and put his brother, George, in charge, but kept his own sharp eye on the new project, and frequently rode down to Philadelphia to make changes.

There was talk, then, that Ochs had soaring dreams of a national and possibly an international chain of Times papers with The New York Times as principal link. There were rumors that he had put $5,000,000 of Wall Street money into the merged papers. Like most rumors these were utterly unfounded. He got The Philadelphia Times, including the entire physical plant, for $100,000 in cash and by assuming $200,000 of bonded debt. He bought The Public Ledger for $150,000 cash and by assuming a bonded debt of $1,500,000. Instead of using Wall Street money he did all this on personal credit. He kept the combined paper less than eleven years. He sold it on Jan. 1, 1913, to Cyrus H. K. Curtis.

He was glad to be rid of it, too. The New York Times was all one man could handle properly. He conceded that in talks with friends.

In February of 1902 fire destroyed The Baltimore News plant. The Washington Post let The News share offices and presses temporarily, but Charles Grasty, The Baltimore News president, cast about frantically for something permanent. One night the telephone rang in the Ochs home, and when The New York Times publisher answered it, the voice said, "Hello, Mr. Ochs? This is Grasty of The Baltimore News. I'm in New York." Ochs said how sorry he had been to hear of the fire.

Grasty said: "Everything was destroyed down there. How about your Philadelphia Times plant?"

Ochs said promptly, "It's at your service."

"At what price, Mr. Ochs?"

"Just take it. It's yours. Take it to Baltimore. If we can't agree on a price later we'll leave it up to some third party. Don't let the details worry you."

Grasty was overwhelmed. He poured out profuse thanks. When word of this informal transaction got around, other newspapers printed all the details. The Minneapolis Tribune remarked on the wonder of one publisher turning over a complete newspaper plant to another for the mere asking. Things had come to that pass. The man who had entered New York journalism virtually bankrupt now had newspapers to give away.

During this period Iphigene Ochs spent considerable time with her cousin, Julius Ochs Adler, nicknamed "Son" and the child of Ada Ochs, the publisher's sister. Her husband, Harry Adler, was on The Chattanooga Times. Both children had vivid memories, in later years, of hot days at family parties and at weddings, when they twisted and squirmed uncomfortably in upholstered chairs between numerous aunts and uncles. Iphigene's mother managed, somehow, to stay out of these gatherings.

In the spring of 1902, when Iphigene had begun to resent being called "Baby" by her father, she developed violent headaches. The family physician advised that she wear glasses, particularly while she studied. Effie Ochs would not have it. "She has taken Baby out of school," the publisher wrote desperately to his mother, "and Baby is growing fat and lazy at home—probably not lazy. Effie says there is no need of Baby going to school until she is 12 years old; that she can learn enough at home. I don't agree, but as school will be out in a few days anyway, I will make no vigorous protest."

Ochs tried to cram the child full of general knowledge. When there were lectures, Iphigene had to attend them, and then had to listen to her father interpret their meanings. Both in New York and on the Continent he took her to towers, ruins, museums and to the wax works, of which he seemed inordinately fond. For years afterward, Iphigene's dreams were nightmare—ridden by scenes she had encountered in various chambers of horrors. Her father thought of them only as an easy way for her to learn history without straining her eyes.

Iphigene's imagination developed swiftly. As early as her fourth or fifth year she had been quick to identify herself, or her dolls, with figures out of fiction or mythology. Margaret Redmond, a character in a story told by one of her early governesses, became a kind of alter ego for the child. When Iphigene was guilty of some juvenile transgression she was apt to try to convince her parents, or the governess, that the act was Margaret's, not her own.

In another phase of the curriculum he had worked out for his daughter, the publisher took her to homes for the aged. He tried to get her to understand that one day she, too, would be old, as these men and women were, and that she must treat the aged with respect. He preached practical democracy, and emphasized it with living example. He tried to instill the basic ideas of philanthropy in the child's mind before she was 10. It was more than any little girl could sop up, but he kept at it. In addition to all this, he took her frequently to his office, and onto the news floor, trying to get her to understand how the world news was gathered, assembled and served up in print. He imparted to her his own great love of public parks, and they became a major interest of her adult life. She was to work tirelessly for more and better park space in overcrowded New York.

Early in August of 1902 President Theodore Roosevelt sent Iphigene Ochs an autographed photograph. He had asked her name when her father had visited him at Oyster Bay. The publisher was ecstatic. He told his wife: "Perhaps this incident may impress you with the importance of the training Iphigene should have. She will be much courted. Her good will shall be placed at a high value. There is nothing beyond her reach if I live ten years longer and meet with no mishap."

Into his writings around this time there was apt to creep a little melancholy, every now and then. The thought of death kept cropping up. He bought a family plot in the cemetery at Chattanooga. "On nice, high ground," he wrote chaffingly to Effie. "Very desirable. No malaria."

On July 1, 1902, before the family left for Europe, the publisher closed a deal for the ground on which to build The Times Tower at Forty-second Street. He was glad, then, that negotiations for the land that became the site of the Woolworth Building had fallen through. The trend was strongly northward, and he realized that Park Row was slowly dying, just as old persons die. The uptown site he had chosen was the triangular plot between Broadway and Seventh Avenue, from Forty-second to Forty-third Street, on which the Pabst Building stood. Mid-town then was given over mainly to two and three-story brownstones, but theatres were slowly creeping in. The Astor Hotel was near completion, and the first of the white lights were glowing between Thirty-fourth and Forty-second Streets. The Great White Way and Times Square were about to come into existence together.

Two blocks east of the Tower site laborers at this time were laying the cornerstone for the New York Library in Fifth Avenue. Final plans for extending the subway under the East River to Brooklyn were complete. Within a few months workmen were to begin excavating for it at State and Pearl Streets. The New York Times and other newspapers were excited over a "long distance" telephone connecting New York and Newark by direct cable. Ochs' keen eye picked out still another news item of this period that set him dreaming new dreams for The Times. The story related how Guglielmo Marconi had managed to send three messages from Cape Breton across the Atlantic to Britain by wireless.

Puzzled publishers of other sheets were slow to figure how Ochs had wrought his journalistic miracle. The answer was astonishingly simple. He kept unswervingly to his straight-news formula, and held firmly to printing only honest advertising. He ruled out everything questionable. Men who honestly thought that the public preferred its news spiced or slanted had something to think about. Ochs simply said: "I do not understand the tributes that come my way. I merely proved that, given the chance, the reading public would choose a newspaper that served up the news without coloring. I knew it would work out that way."

Ochs' common sense helped him keep his feet during this period when rich and powerful men and great institutions were bidding for his friendship. He was flattered by their attention but wisely decided to keep out of the public eye as much as possible. His lack of formal education probably was a factor in this.

Early in 1903, for example, when he was invited to be one of the judges at a Yale-Harvard debate, he politely declined, pleading business pressure, but could not keep from letting the family know the position he had attained as publisher of The Times.

"I turned down the debate bid," he wrote to his sister Nannie on March 19, "on the theory that the higher a monkey climbs the more he shows his tail."

Early in July in 1903 the family was off to Europe again and little Iphigene was whirled along for an educational tour. While Mrs. Ochs was sleeping peacefully at 7 A.M., as at Carlsbad, Ochs would wake the little girl and have her walk with him some two or three miles to the gardens there, even before breakfast. On the way back he would have her try out her French and German at the baker's shop. She would negotiate for the breakfast rolls. When he encountered friends or acquaintances along the route—as he often did—they were bound to draw him into discussions on political and international affairs. She would stand by silently, clutching the bag of rolls, until these weighty adult conversations ended.

He delighted in putting the child's French to the test at every opportunity. "Iphigene," he told his mother, "is quite at home talking French. She attracts much attention." She was going on 10 then, a shy, soft-spoken little girl with smoky brown eyes and glossy jet-black curls. Her father did not seem to realize during the European journeys that he was concentrating on her the tremendous energy that customarily went into handling his expanding publishing ventures. He wrote to his mother: "I have not given a moment's serious thought to my affairs at home. I have entirely dismissed them from my mind."

Ochs spared his daughter one great trial. He did not take her on the long Alpine walks. His companion on these was Miss Christine Hegi, who had been the child's governess since 1901. One Saturday morning late in July of 1903 the publisher and his family left Chamonix in two carts for the eight-hour pull over rugged mountain roads, into Martigny in the Rhone Valley. Miss Nannie Ochs, the publisher's gentle sister, was with them. During a stopover at Tête-Noir they changed equipage and drivers. They had gone only a little way when Ochs paled with fright. The little cart in which Effie and Miss Nannie rode with some of the baggage, was teetering dangerously close to the edge of an awesome precipice. The road was narrow and winding, and they were thousands of feet above sparkling lakes and rivers.

The publisher called a halt. He ran up ahead and stopped the forward cart. The guide, who was driving, had had too much wine. Ochs transferred his wife and sister to the second cart and they proceeded slowly that way. Edward Hegi, the governess' 18-year-old brother, an earnest youth clad in Tyrolean leather breeches, who had come out from Lausanne to meet his sister, took over. The governess' fiancé, who had also walked up from Lausanne, took the second cart. The original hired drivers were dismissed and the party descended into the lovely valley, the Swiss boys leading the little horses. Ochs walked with them, all the way, animatedly discussing the scenery. Iphigene got out and walked, too. Even her mother, customarily cold to any suggestion of exercise, made some of the long journey on foot.

This adventure high in the Alps worked out in Horatio Alger pattern for young Hegi. The publisher liked the lad's frank, gentlemanly bearing, and during the long descent gathered that Hegi intended to go to London to learn English. Ochs talked the boy out of the notion. He pictured the great opportunities that democratic America held for a young man. "You could come to work for The New York Times, if you think you'd like that," he offered. On the wintry morning of Feb. 29, 1904, Hegi did show up at 41 Park Row. He became, as his sister had before him, a kind of family pet. He worked diligently in The Times accounting office, wrote place cards for the Ochs family in a fine copper-plate script when there were formal parties and kept moving up in his office job. Eventually he became cashier of The Times. He still holds that job.

Back in New York, Ochs found the nation's tempo rapidly increasing. A Packard automobile called "Old Pacific" had crossed from San Francisco to New York in fifty-two days over roads laid out originally for horses and wagons. The Police Department in Boston had converted from horse and buggy to motor cars for suburban patrol. Orville and Wilbur Wright were ready to try their first motored plane at Kill Devil Hill.

The Pennsylvania Railroad had started work on East River and Hudson River tunnels. New York's surface and rickety elevated lines were carrying greater passenger loads than the combined railroads of the North and South American Continents. Morning and evening rush hours had attained proportions capable of producing a raw edge on nervous systems and reducing the urban dweller's life span. To make matters worse, the immigrant tide was still at full flood; more than 857,046 Europeans were to swarm through Ellis Island gates in this year.

Williamsburg Bridge was to open shortly, and not long afterward, Manhattan Bridge, but even with these and with the subway then a-building, transportation was far short of decent accommodation. It did not help much that in October of 1903 the self-appointed Elijah The Restorer, John Alexander Dowie of Zion City, led his "Salvation Host" of fanatic followers into the city for noisy revival, to be hissed and booed in Madison Square Garden, while perspiring gray-helmeted cops fought to break up near-riots.

Though transportation engineers and housing authorities were breathlessly trying to keep up with the swelling population, The Times prospered mightily. Ochs had sensed that pretty soon lower Manhattan Island would be overwhelmed with traffic problems. He had realized that the island's center of gravity would shift northward and that is why he had turned in that direction for a new site for his newspaper.

CHAPTER
14

B Y SEPTEMBER, 1903, Ochs' dream of the finest newspaper plant in the world was taking shape. Laborers on the foundation sloshed around as hidden midtown streams flooded the deep excavation. Alongside them contractors' crews toiled on the Times Square station, which was built above The Times pressroom. The extra depth for the press beds made it, as several contemporaries called it, "The deepest hole in town." Ochs' fine sense of publicity values showed up sharply in this project. British, German, French and Scandinavian newspapers and magazines did breathless illustrated pieces about The Times skyscraper. "Wolkenkratzer," Teutonic sheets called it. Even his competitors, The World, The Herald and The Tribune could not ignore the change his tower was to bring in Longacre Square.

James Gordon Bennett's Herald swallowed hard before it gave its readers a few columns about the building operations with pictures that ran a half-page deep. The Herald writer managed to avoid mentioning that the excavation was The Times' site. Under the heading, "Deepest Hole in New York a Broadway Spectacle," it described what the lead called, "perhaps the most interesting engineering feat to be seen anywhere on Manhattan Island."

"Never before, doubtless, has a similar undertaking been watched by so great an audience," the writer continued. "The excavation is highly interesting by night. The brilliant illumination of Broadway scarcely reaches to the well-like depths of the great shaft. The jagged rocks stand out in striking relief against the shadows. The great throng which surges along the brightly illuminated sidewalks of Broadway looks down at an abrupt angle into what appears to be a bottomless abyss."

Every charge of dynamite that sent giant rock slabs thundering into the great street gap was a salute to the man from Chattanooga.

All that fall and winter, especially when Effie and Iphigene were visiting in the South or in Ohio, Ochs kept an eager eye on the handsome modern version of Giotto's Florentine Tower that went up, floor by floor, first in skeletal steel, and then in brick, terra cotta and limestone. He frequently took a room in the Cadillac Hotel at the northeast corner of Forty-third Street and Broadway, where he could look down on the operation. Around this time he was under strong pressure to succeed Whitelaw Reid as a director of The Associated Press, but he had so many other responsibilities that he declined the honor.

Sometimes Ochs seemed a little frightened by his success. Late in September, 1903, as the Tower rose against the midtown skyline, he wrote humbly to his mother:

"We should from the bottom of our hearts thank the Lord for the blessings we have and do enjoy, and with all our love sing His praises. Whenever I contemplate our lives I drift to the conclusion that there is a Destiny that controls. Our cup of good things is running over. We have more than we can, perhaps, appreciate."

The Ochses had moved from Broadway and Seventieth Street in 1903 to a furnished house at 481 West End Avenue. They were to occupy it until 1909 when the publisher bought 308 West Seventy-fifth Street. His wife decorated the Seventy-fifth Street house to her somewhat melancholy taste—filled it with pallid busts and heavy draperies, luxurious carpets and knickknacks picked up in the family's extensive travels. Iphigene was 11 years old when they moved into it. She was to be the mother of four children before the family moved out of it.

At 3 o'clock on Jan. 18, 1904, the Tower's cornerstone was swung into place. Bishop Henry C. Potter opened the simple exercises with a prayer. Charles Miller, head bared to the crisp winter wind, spoke of the Tower's significance. When the editor had finished, Ochs nudged Iphigene, muffled in winter wraps, and she advanced to the great cornerstone with a silver trowel. She smoothed the mortar, then in a clear voice said:

"I dedicate this building to the uses of The New York Times. May those who labor herein see the right and serve it with courage and intelligence for the welfare of mankind, the best interests of the United States and its people, and for decent and dignified journalism, and may the blessing of God ever rest upon them."

Into the cornerstone went The New York Times' fiftieth anniversary edition of Sept. 18, 1901; the annual financial review printed on Jan. 3, 1904; The Chattanooga Times' twenty-fifth anniversary edition of July 1, 1903; photographs of C. L. W. Eidlitz and Andrew McKenzie, the architects; a copy of The New York Times of June 23, 1903, describing the new Tower; a complete roster of employes; Who's Who for 1904; The World Almanac for that year, and copies of all the New York newspapers of that day.

When the stone was lowered the little girl patted it three times with the silver trowel. She murmured, "I declare this stone to be laid plumb, level and square."

Ochs made no front-page splash over the ceremony. The story ran quietly for one and a half columns on Page 9, alongside social notes. In his heart, though, triumph surged. He showed his pride only to his family. A few months later, when he set off for Europe again with his family, he wrote to his mother from the Deutschland, at sea:

"The new building loomed up in all its beautiful and grand proportions, out of mid-New York, as we sailed away, and my heart swelled as I thought of association with its erection. Then it stood foremost and most conspicuous among the best buildings in the Metropolis of the World—and I really grew sentimental.

"It is a beauty, and even though the $2,500,000 that went into it cost some anxieties, it is there and it will be a monument to one man's daring."

Magnificent as his tower was, Ochs was still under tremendous strain trying to get enough capital to assure The Times' renaissance. He had plunged on the skyscraper and knew it would pay great dividends, but he was strapped for working cash.

A group of creditors delegated Richard Delafield of the National Park Bank to sound out Ochs as to where he stood financially. When the publisher and Delafield met in the banker's offices, Delafield said:

"We would like to know how much you owe, and to whom, so that we may work out a complete new financial program for you. Some of your creditors think you may already have gone beyond your depth."

It was a bad moment for Ochs. Any sign of weakness might have destroyed his dream, even at this stage. He did not weaken.

He said: "Mr. Delafield, I am not going to give you the statement you request because I think there are only two times in a man's life when he should do this—one is when he is about to go into bankruptcy and the receiver lists his assets and liabilities to distribute the assets pro rata to his creditors; the second is when he dies and his administrator appraises his estate. I am neither broke nor dead. I am not going to give you those figures."

Delafield had admired Ochs from the moment when they had first met, about six years before. He liked this blunt answer too. He said, "Ochs, I think you're quite right." The Southerner left with an additional $200,000 loan from Delafield's own bank. This was Ochs' last major financial crisis. He told friends much later that he could never forget Delafield's kindness and that as long as he lived The Times' account would remain with the National Park Bank, which it did.

The Tower did become a monument. Tourists, as well as New Yorkers, came to gape at it. Its height above ground of 375 feet was second only to the Park Row Building, which rose 392 feet. The over-all top-to-bottom size of Ochs' new plant was greater. Its basements and sub-basements, where the presses were seated in bedrock, went 55 feet below street level.

On April 9, 1904, The Times ran a map on Page 2 of the area from Forty-second to Forty-seventh Street between Broadway and Seventh Avenue with the caption: "Times Square is the Name of City's New Centre"

The legend beneath the map said:

"Mayor McClellan yesterday signed the resolution adopted by the Board of Aldermen on Tuesday last changing the name of Longacre Square to that of Times Square . . . Times Square takes in the triangle on which the new building of The New York

Times is situated and the name applies to the entire section . . ."

The Square was to become an international crossroads, and the newspaper from which it took its name was to set new high standards in international news coverage.

Sailing away, the publisher thought that he had built a home for The Times that would meet all the newspaper's needs in his lifetime. He was wrong. In less than a decade business volume was to compel expansion to an annex in Forty-third Street—and even that was, in just a few years, to prove inadequate and require enlargement. The barefoot boy from Knoxville had parlayed his crude one-story Chattanooga newspaper shack with hand-operated press into the most magnificent newspaper structure in the world—all in a little more than twenty-five years.

In the first week of June in 1904, the publisher spent some time at Carlsbad with Joseph Pulitzer. Ochs bore no resentment against the acid-tongued Pulitzer for the sharp and harsh things The World had published about The Times and its "keeper of the deficit," as Pulitzer had sneeringly called him. In Carlsbad, when the weather was right, they rode out together and talked without cease of newspapers and of national and international politics. The Southerner really came to know Pulitzer in those sunlit hours together.

"He is a remarkable man," Ochs wrote later, "a man of great strength and great intellectual power, and of education and culture. His success has not been accidental. He is a man among thousands. He is positive, well informed on current topics, truly a philosopher. It is a great and tragic misfortune that he is virtually blind. If he had not that affliction he would be a tremendous figure in national affairs. He told me that he is an invalid, that he suffers continually from severe headaches, and that he is extremely nervous. He is so nervous that he objected to the scraping of the brakes of the carriage wheels. He has to have such quiet that he takes a whole villa for himself. He was very cordial, and very complimentary to The New York Times. He spoke disparagingly of his own New York World."

In a subsequent letter from the Hotel Splendide at Aix-les-Bains, The World's publisher entreated Ochs to visit him at Bar Harbor in Maine. He said: "Do give me the pleasure of seeing you again if you come to Bar Harbor, and let me congratulate you upon the splendid growth and success of The Times. You may not know that I have The Times sent to me abroad when The World is forbidden, and that most of my news I really receive from your paper. You have a very, very able editorial page."

There was no doubt now that the bitterness that had bubbled up when the two men first met in New York's journalistic arena had completely vanished. In its place there was mutual admiration and respect. Ochs was pleased and happy that it had turned out so.

The family got back to New York early in August. Now the publisher handled only the major Times transactions. He left the detailed work to Louis Wiley and to John Norris. He had no fear now of leaving his desk for hours or for months. He frequently joined his wife and daughter at the Jersey shore, and spent more time with his friends.

Ochs was back in New York when the builders put the last touches to the Tower. It was a structure of extraordinary beauty. Morning sun flushed its eastern wall, and sparkled on the cream-colored brick. Descending sun suffused the west wall with a delicate crimson, and laid golden shafts across the publisher's desk on the twentieth floor. It flooded the news room on the seventeenth and made the composing room, on the sixteenth, a great hall of hulking shadows, spaced with gold.

Incidentally, there is a stone in the building's east wall, at the south corner, high above the sidewalk, that puzzled New Yorkers when the Tower was finished and brings up questions even now. It bears, in Old English letters, the name "Charles Thorley"—nothing more. It is one of those monuments to whimsy that keep turning up in buildings. Charles Thorley was a poor boy, born and brought up around Washington Market, who became a real estate operator, a Fifth Avenue florist and a power in Tammany. He had leased the Tower site from a Henry Dolan in the Nineties when it was a scrubby lot with a tumble-down shack on it, when the Rialto site was an unpainted horse stable and the Knickerbocker Hotel site, now The Newsweek Building, was honeycombed with dusty rookeries. Thorley leased the spot for 105 years at $4,000 a year. When he rented it to The Times on Sept. 1, 1902 at $27,000 a year he stipulated that his name be set in The Tower and into the wall of any structure that might come after it. Thorley died in 1923, and four years later The Times bought the leasehold from his widow.

On New Year's Eve in 1904, Times Square was crowded with hundreds of thousands of horn-blasting, bell-ringing celebrants, come to witness a brilliant fireworks display touched off in the Tower. Midtown skies reverberated with the thunderous bursting of flights of bombs. Skyrockets and flares streaked against the midnight sky in the first Times Square New Year's Eve show, centered around the Tower. These assemblages became traditional with Times electricians controlling incandescent figures that spelled out the dying year, and spelled in the new. The signal for the old year's passing was a massive illuminated globe that slid down the Tower pole while the crowds far below on the sidewalk cut loose with ear-splitting din. A final burst of fireworks wrote "1905" in flame against the heavens, and the throngs screamed and shouted themselves hoarse. It was one of the greatest promotion projects of the age. The idea was Ochs'. He knew the value of such advertising.

The last issue of The New York Times printed in the old Jones building at 41 Park Row rumbled from the presses early Sunday morning, Jan. 1, 1905. The machines had barely rolled to a stop when swarms of Mergenthaler Linotype men took over, followed by an army of Hoe Press Company mechanics, and hundreds of other artisans. These men toiled all through Sunday, stripping what was usable, loading it all on great horse-drawn drays, which bore it uptown to the Tower.

By noon that Sunday almost everything was in place in the new building. Down in sub-basement bedrock under Times Square, the new Hoe presses, geared to throw off, fold and count 144,000 six-teen-page papers an hour, were warming for their initial full run. Rehearsing mailers and pressmen had to get used to their new quarters. As they labored at their tasks, subway trains rumbled heavily overhead in the new Times Square station.

Ochs had bought eleven new Mergenthaler Linotype machines for the Tower composing room. The twenty-seven that had functioned at 41 Park Row were dismantled at 3 A.M., and were set up beside the new ones before 4 P.M. that Sunday. At 5 P.M., they were going full-speed, setting Monday's paper. Though each machine had from 4,000 to 5,000 parts, not one was lost in the three-and-one-

half-mile haul. The last items to pull up at noon on Sunday were
the reporters' typewriters.

The first New York Times turned out in the new building on Monday, Jan. 2, 1905, was Vol. LIV, No. 17160. The lead story told how
the Russians seemed prepared to yield Port Arthur to the Japanese.
In column one, on the left side of the front page, was a modest account of the Tower opening. The make-up that morning was what
printers called "Tombstone Make-up"—single column heads, side
by side, like so many stones in a churchyard—typical Ochs make-
up, a model of conservative neatness.

The headline on the Tower story said: "Today's Times Issued
from Its New Home," and the banks continued: "Delicate Task of
Removal Well Completed. Big Machines Transferred. Subway
Helps Distribute This Morning's Issue."

"Under the most auspicious circumstances," said the story, "The
New York Times this morning begins publication from its new home
at Times Square. The lights in its Park Row Building went out for
good, so far as The Times is concerned, after the last edition of Sunday's paper had gone to press."

Handlers cheered when they threw the first bundles from the
presses onto shiny new subway trains bound downtown. They
dropped papers off for dealers who waited at stations along the
route. At Park Row they unloaded the rest. There bundles were
hustled to waiting wagons, drivers laid on with the whip and the
first Tower issue went tearing across skiddy Brooklyn Bridge in
crisp winter starlight. Publishers who had shaken their heads over
the idea of printing a newspaper in midtown had not counted on
Ochs' use of the new subway. They had figured his wagons would
lose time between Forty-second Street and Brooklyn Bridge.

In the spring of 1905 the publisher showed his new Tower to
twelve directors of the powerful National Park Bank, among them
John Jacob Astor and Richard Delafield. Miller, Edward Cary
and the rest of The Times editorial board, with Ochs' business aides
and his news chiefs, sat down to a magnificent spread on the building's twenty-third floor, then toured the plant and later went to a
show.

The picture had changed astonishingly. When Ochs had come to
New York less than nine years earlier he had been worried over

whether he might safely invest in a new suit before calling on bankers. Now he moved at ease among those same men who marveled at his success and enjoyed his rich hospitality.

James Hazen Hyde, son of Henry B. Hyde of Equitable Life who had tried to swerve Ochs from his editorial attacks on Tom Platt, was now in a jam over a pending insurance investigation. He and the publisher had resumed friendly relations after the elder Hyde died, and young Hyde had come to admire the Southerner's courage. He asked Ochs to dine at his home and for two hours, as Ochs told it later, "unburdened himself to me." He disclosed that his father had always regretted the Platt incident. The son, a bearded playboy, and a fanatic Francophile, had filled his chateau on Long Island with French servants, spent vacations in France, and had startled New York with a $100,000 French costume party at Sherry's only a few months before, but he had his strong side, too. He was a stout-hearted scrapper. "He aroused my admiration," Ochs confided to Effie. "I think he will win out."

Though Ochs had borrowed a large sum from Hyde's Equitable Life Assurance Society for the building of his Tower, The Times pulled no punches during the insurance investigation by a legislative committee, which had Charles Evans Hughes as counsel. When Hyde, E. H. Harriman, Benjamin Odell and Henry Clay Frick came under Hughes' caustic fire that fall, The Times printed as much about the proceedings as any other newspaper in the city, if not more.

One night during the investigation, Percy Bullock of the city staff paused in his rush to get out the insurance story to listen to a little man in a Panama hat, who kept putting questions to him about it. Down the long city room a new night city editor drummed nervously on his desk, and glared at Bullock and the stranger. The new night editor was Frederick T. Birchall, a myopic little Lancashireman with a neat Vandyke beard. He stood the talk between Bullock and the intruder about as long as he could. Suddenly he bounced out of his chair, tapped briskly down the room to the reporter's desk and coldly told him: "Mr. Bullock, you may entertain your friend some other time. I want that insurance piece right away."

Flustered, Bullock got to his feet. He mumbled: "I'm sorry, Mr.

Birchall." He turned to the man in the Panama hat. He said, "Let me introduce you to Mr. Ochs." The publisher and his new night editor had never met. The little Briton put out his hand, but at the same time told Bullock, "Finish that story, laddie. Get along with it." Ochs apologized for the interruption. He told Birchall: "You were perfectly right in breaking it up. I didn't realize you were close to deadline. You were looking after my business. It was the thing to do." He left the floor.

Ochs was uneasy lest the insurance investigation disclose that he was an Equitable debtor. He knew what Hearst and other former neighbors on Printing House Square might do with such material. He decided finally to call on Marcellus Hartley Dodge, grandson of the arms manufacturer Marcellus Hartley, who had lent him $100,000 in 1896 to be used as working capital for the reorganized Times. He explained frankly to young Dodge, whom he had come to know through his grandfather, what harm might come to The Times should the insurance investigation turn up the information that the newspaper was one of the Equitable debtors. He told Dodge, "I want to take up the loan from Equitable, and I'd like to borrow an additional $300,000." He offered to put up 51 per cent of The Times' stock as collateral.

Ochs said he had come to Dodge because he was anxious to keep away from Wall Street corporations with political ties. Dodge discussed the project that night with George W. Hebard, a vice president of Westinghouse Electric and Manufacturing Company, who was executor of the Marcellus Hartley estate. Hebard told Dodge, "I see no obstacle to such a loan."

Next day Ochs surrendered his precious majority of Times stock, and got the money. With part of the money he cleared the Equitable loan. Young Dodge put the stock certificates in his personal safety deposit box. We move a little ahead of our story here to 1916. The Remington Arms Company, in which Marcellus Dodge had a considerable interest, was squeezed then for ready funds. The Russians, who had placed tremendous orders with the company, had collapsed and Remington's situation was awkward. Mrs. Dodge happened to mention this to Ochs during a social visit. The publisher immediately paid off the $300,000 loan.

The Dodges and Ochses remained close friends during the publisher's lifetime. "Adolph Ochs," Dodge liked to remember, "gave me generously of his advice and counsel. I was only in my teens when I first met him at The Times in Park Row. In fine weather grandfather and I usually walked to church. We would stop in before service of a Sunday morning to call on Mr. Ochs. I remember how, in his early days on The Times in the Nineties, Mr. Ochs would turn to a lower drawer in his desk and bring out quite regularly, for them to discuss, the current financial reports of the paper. One could not be brought in contact with Adolph Ochs without feeling his great power of leadership, and his sound judgment."

During the eleven years that The Times stock lay in Marcellus Dodge's deposit vault, no one knew of it except Ochs, the Dodges and Hebard. Dodge kept the secret until long after the publisher's death.

CHAPTER
15

ADOLPH OCHS had a genius for picking men of stature as aides, and he gave their talents free rein, in the news room or in the counting room. His wisest choice was Carr Vattel Van Anda, born on Dec. 2, 1864, in Georgetown, Ohio. Van Anda had an extraordinary flair for extending news-gathering techniques into fields previously held too deep for the reading masses. Van Anda had been with The Sun for sixteen of its brightest years. He was 40 years old when he left it at Ochs' beckoning in February, 1904. In the next twenty-five years he helped carry The Times to new peaks. He became one of the greatest newspaper legends.

The Ochs pattern was already firmly established when Van Anda —"V.A." or "Boss" on the news floor—came to 41 Park Row, eleven months before the move to midtown. Ochs had declared for "All the News That's Fit to Print" and had grimly abided by it, even at the cost of valuable advertising. Van Anda was of the same mind.

There may have been somewhere in newspaper history a more perfect publisher-managing editor team than the Ochs-Van Anda set-up, but none comes to mind. The Tennessean had the same eager curiosity for news about the unknown in the sciences and about the remote unexplored corners of the world that Van Anda had. His natural keen news sense told him that intelligent readers shared this eagerness, and that The Times might perform enormous public service by providing the answers to these mysteries. Without Ochs' willingness to pay almost any sum for exclusive rights to stories on modern exploration, on the advancement of science, and on the development of aviation and of transportation generally, Van Anda could never have made The Times a leader in that kind of journalism, but Ochs gave Van Anda his head. Between them they won for The Times a leadership in the field that was never overtaken.

Sometimes other Times executives showed a little fright at the new managing editor's free expenditure of corporate funds when he went after important stories, but Ochs soothed them. If it was necessary to resow a goodly portion of the profits to improve The Times, Ochs was for it. He wisely persisted in his policy.

Like the publisher, V.A. scorned the sensational, cheap or tawdry appeal. The Times under Jones had enriched journalistic annals with its Tweed Ring and Star Route crusades, but was never again to bid for a crusading record. It was to make fresh newspaper history by the simple, yet somehow extremely difficult, method of serving up the news as swiftly and as accurately as human ingenuity and mechanical progress allowed, and in greater volume than any other daily. Under Van Anda, Times prestige in news-gathering and news-presentation was built on day-by-day efficiency rather than on the Hollywood type of "scoop."

There were many in the trade, and out of it, who preferred garnished fact and the literary touch—the journalistic cocktail—to the news that Van Anda served straight. They found The Times stuffy and elephantine in pace, even if it was complete, and completely honest. They jeeringly compared it with the much more colorful Press, Sun, World, American and Herald. These scoffers lived to see the more sparkling sheets fade and die while The Times, putting on more weight with the straight-news diet, pushed past their tombstones. The years were to prove that the Ochs and Van Anda formula was best for the long haul, that an intelligent reading public bought newspapers—strange as it seemed to some—to read the news.

Ochs' newspaper had bought exclusive use in the United States of stories of The Times of London after the news-exchange plan fell through in 1900, and from time to time both newspapers shared expenses on special stories. Between them in 1904-1905 they had such an arrangement for coverage of the Russian-Japanese War.

Van Anda was in the office on the morning of April 14, 1904, when a copy boy came to the desk with a war dispatch from Lionel James of The Times of London. It had been sent from Port Arthur by wireless to Pe-Chi-Li, thence to London and from London to New York by cable. Van Anda was ecstatic. It was the first wireless report in history of a major naval engagement. He knew no other American newspaper would have it.

Eagerly he read the full dispatch. In it Lionel James told how the Japanese had steamed boldly into Port Arthur and had all but wiped out the Russian fleet, sinking among other men-of-war, the Czar's mighty Petropavlovsk, Admiral Makaroff's flagship. This was the moment all editors had awaited—the showdown between the Japanese and Russian sea forces.

Van Anda feverishly wrote the headline, took the copy to the composing room himself, and stood over the printers as they put the type in that morning's Page 1 form:

TORPEDO ATTACK YESTERDAY

FOLLOWED BY BOMBARDMENT
OF PORT ARTHUR BY JAPANESE

The credit was a bit top-heavy:

London Times-The New York Times
Special Cablegram
Copyright 1904 The New York Times
By De Forest Wireless Telegraphy
to The New York Times

The story carried the historic dateline "OFF PORT ARTHUR, On Board The Times Steamship Haimun, April 13."

"The Japanese torpedo craft attacked Port Arthur early this morning and the fleet shelled the port. The bombardment began at 9:45 o'clock." Then the story went into dramatic detail.

Other newspapers in New York leaped on the Port Arthur extra and rewrote the wireless story. On April 15 a stern editorial in The Times under the heading, "A Warning," rebuked them. A second editorial, just below it, with the single-word caption, "Wireless," pointed out the wonder of the new communication device.

". . . Consider such a piece of news as The Times had the pleasure of presenting to its readers yesterday about the attack on Port

Arthur. This news is dated simply 'Off Port Arthur' . . . It is absolutely from out at sea that The Times' steamship Haimun is able to relieve the anxiety of a waiting world by sending the results of ocular observation of a sea fight between Russia and Japan."

This episode, which opened the way for on-the-spot wireless war dispatches, threw the Czar's military advisers into agonized uproar. They talked of seizing the Haimun, even of sinking her, and of arresting Lionel James as a spy. The State Department, the British Foreign Office and Russian diplomats hotly argued the point. Military men generally muttered against this new menace to important war strategy; some even thought they could condone the correspondent's arrest as a spy. The Times ran long editorials on the subject. In the end, though, nothing came of it.

On Saturday morning, May 27, 1905, Van Anda gave lead position to the story: "Tokio Sends Rumor That Sea Fight Is On."

He prepared seven columns of copy on the relative strengths of the two fleets, giving each vessel's size, tonnage and crew. With his chess-player's eyes he studied maps of the Sea of Japan and tried to figure out where the two fleets might meet. He had his staff write biographies of the Russian and Japanese fleet commanders—and then nervously waited.

Sunday's Times had little important war news. Japanese censors were holding back most correspondents' copy.

CZAR'S SHIPS NEAR;
TOKIO REFUSES NEWS

Van Anda wrote that headline for the Sunday paper, and again he waited. Each morning he kept a skeleton staff about him until the sun was on Manhattan's roof tops. Soon, now, he knew, he would have the biggest story of the war. His eyes had the faraway look of the fanatic news hunter.

At 4:31 A.M. on Monday, May 29, 1905, a telegraph key in the Times Tower's eighteenth floor broke into insistent metallic yapping. The Times operator rapidly transcribed:

TOKIO, May 29, 2:15 P.M.—It is officially announced that Admiral Rojestvensky s fleet has been practically annihilated. Twelve warships have been sunk or captured, and—

The managing editor's thin, nervous fingers raced over copy paper as he fashioned the multi-banked headline for a story that ran three columns on the front page. His advance material filled most of the second page.

TOGO SMASHES
RUSSIAN FLEET

TOKIO ANNOUNCES 12 SHIPS
SUNK OR CAPTURED

2 TRANSPORTS DESTROYED

2 TORPEDO BOAT DESTROY-
ERS SENT TO BOTTOM

JAPANESE CRUISER LOST

TEN TORPEDO BOATS ARE
ALSO SAID TO BE GONE

FIGHT BEGAN SATURDAY

BETWEEN 2 AND 3 O'CLOCK IN
AFTERNOON FOG LIFTED AND
TOGO FOUND HIS FOE

Van Anda wrote a one-column box for the top of the front page, and marked it for boldface type to call reader attention to the extra:

POSTSCRIPTS—5 A.M.

The official announcement from the Japanese capital was timed 2:15 P.M. It came across the world, through Manila and San Francisco, before it reached The Times.

Nineteen minutes after the story had come off the wires, Van Anda had his extra on The Times presses. All regular Times deliveries had been completed by then, but he had ordered a few delivery wagons—motor car delivery lay a few years ahead—to wait at The Times Tower curb.

Forty thousand copies of the battle extra were run off. When they

had been thrown into the wagons, Van Anda climbed beside one
of the drivers and in the spring pre-dawn, headed the delivery fleet
on its route. The drivers pulled back earlier editions from news-
stands in and around Times Square, left fresh bundles at the leading hotels, and got rid of the last of their loads in the Wall Street
area and at Brooklyn Bridge.

Dawn spilled thin gold on City Hall and on Pulitzer's already
gilded dome when the chore was done, and Van Anda, nocturnal
creature, headed home. This was the first of a series of brilliant
journalistic achievements that were to compel other newspapermen's awe. Ochs was delighted.

There was no whoop-de-doo, no inky caper-cutting during Van
Anda's reign. Genius does not always throw blinding sparks. Men
like Ochs and Van Anda could dream, yet escape fantasy; they
could see the heights but approached them with sure-fire tread.

In his freshman year at Ohio University Van Anda had fixed on a
career as a mathematician. Then printer's ink got into his blood and
he turned printer, as Ochs had, and ended up in the editorial chair.
When Van Anda was not concentrating on digging out an elusive
news item or when he was not in the composing room breathing
down the necks of printers he went in for such mental exercise as
higher mathematics. He excelled as an editor because the more
challenging the news problem the harder he went after it—and he
could not abide frustration.

Van Anda, like Ochs, was fanatically interested in any device to
speed news transmission. Between them they contrived to have the
first wireless press message from Europe addressed to The Times.
It was printed on the front page on Oct. 18, 1907.

The story's one-column headline said:

WIRELESS JOINS
TWO WORLDS

MARCONI TRANSATLANTIC SERVICE
OPENED WITH A DISPATCH TO
THE NEW YORK TIMES

Actually there were many dispatches—some in the form of greetings to The Times from Marconi, the Duke of Argyll, Georges

Clemenceau, and a message from Lord Avebury, Privy Councilor, reproduced in three-column width from the special Western Union stationery printed for the occasion.

The newspaper thereafter ran infrequent wireless dispatches from time to time, mostly on Sundays, but it was a full five years before it carried them in any bulk—two to three pages from Europe every Sunday, each item under the line, "By Marconi Wireless Telegraph." From late January, 1912, until war interfered, the Marconi service worked out so well that skeptics figured it was some sort of hoax. When German cable officials expressed this doubt in Berlin, Van Anda ran their remarks in next day's paper under the taunting line, "By Marconi Wireless to The New York Times."

At 10 o'clock on Monday night, Feb. 3, 1908, David P. Mac-Gowan, a Chicago Tribune staff reporter, flashed word from the Cunarder Cymric 500 miles from New York that he had witnessed an exciting rescue by the Cymric's crew in a storm off Cape Sable. MacGowan was a passenger on the Cymric.

The Times then—as now—had a news-exchange arrangement with The Chicago Tribune. When the message, relayed through the Marconi station at Cape Sable, reached Van Anda's hands, he reacted with characteristic speed. He had Cape Sable ask Mac-Gowan for all possible details.

It was the first time a reporter at sea had ever received such an assignment. MacGowan gathered the rescue facts from the Cymric's skipper and crew and as the liner plunged and rolled in the tempest, filed the longest wireless dispatch, as a Times editorial later put it, ever sent "landward from a ship at sea."

Both The Times and The Chicago Tribune ran every word of it. Details were still coming in when The Times' last edition went to press at 3:50 A.M. Tuesday with more than two and one-half columns of the story under the one-column headline:

15 LOST FROM
BURNING SHIP

THE CYMRIC SAVES CAPT. LEWIS
AND 36 MEN FROM THE ST.
CUTHBERT OFF CAPE SABLE

It carried the impressive dateline "ON BOARD WHITE STAR STEAM-SHIP CYMRIC, Off Cape Sable, N.S. Feb. 3," and the credit line "By Wireless Telegraph To The New York Times."

MacGowan sent a follow-up story for next day's paper when the Cymric was inbound, and off South Wellfleet, Mass. This took three columns with a complete list of the dead and the rescued. Only The Times and The Chicago Tribune had the service that day, and The Times did a bit of chest-pounding over it.

An editorial on Feb. 5 headed "By Wireless From Midocean" set down for the record that MacGowan's dispatches were "the first account of an ocean disaster reported from mid-ocean through the Marconi system of wireless telegraphy." "It was no formless statement," the editorial writer exulted, "but a spirited and well-written account of an ocean disaster as thrilling as a chapter by Marryat."

It was a good week for The Times on the air waves. On Sunday, Feb. 2, the lead story was from Lisbon, Portugal, by Marconi service. It was a five-column account of the assassination the day before of King Carlos of Portugal and the Crown Prince Luiz Philippe. Van Anda ran a three-column headline over it, and used front-page pictures of the King and the Crown Prince to illustrate the piece.

The next great achievement under Van Anda was Commander (later Rear Admiral) Robert E. Peary's own story of his discovery of the North Pole.

This was only the first of a long series of Times exclusives on exploration and on scientific pioneering. Ochs had a kind of boyish curiosity about remote places that nature had stubbornly locked against man and he eagerly sought exclusive accounts of the daring souls who ventured into them. The new managing editor was just as avid on the subject. Their teamwork was perfect and it made exciting history.

Only once before had the journal bought story rights in an exploring expedition. In 1886 Lieut. Frederick Schwatka, a West Point graduate, sent the newspaper a series on his discoveries in Alaska. The copy was, by current standards, on the dull side, but it was front-paged intermittently from June 21 through mid-November under frankly promotional headlines: "Work of 'The

Times' Alaska Expedition," "Perilous Landing of 'The Times' Alaska Expedition."

The Schwatka stories were somewhat feeble compared with the adventure series so successfully promoted by the younger Bennett of the Herald, the Stanley-Livingstone expedition, and with the Arctic journey of the Jeanette's three-year search for the Sir John Franklin Expedition in the late Eighties. The Jeanette venture had cost Bennett more than $340,000 and had kept his reporter Jerome J. Collins out of the office for more than three years, probably the longest assignment of its kind in journalistic annals.

Schwatka discovered and ascended Mount St. Elias in Alaska to a height of 7,500 feet and wrote at great length of giant bears and of the Sitka Indians who were his guides. His proudest discovery was the Jones River, named after George Jones of The Times, but some of the newspaper's competitors scoffed at this feat. The Sun, in particular, intimated editorially that the find did not amount to much, and said a couple of Frenchmen had stumbled across the same stream a long time before.

Jones' editors blew fire through their whiskers and tore at The Sun in defense of the boss.

"Will the editor of The Sun," they demanded on Oct. 3, 1886, "retract his misstatements concerning Lieutenant Schwatka's work and apologize to him and to The Times, or does he prefer by refusing to take this honorable course, to have these lies crammed down his throat by The Times?"

The Sun coolly ignored the challenge. The horsewhip and derringer days of newspaper editing were definitely over.

Curiously enough, The Times got the Peary story by accident. The explorer had tried several times to reach the North Pole, and the younger Bennett had bought the newspaper rights to those Peary expeditions. In 1908 the shaggy commander clumped again into The Herald office to talk with the executives who had bought the early expedition rights. He asked for William Reick, who, as financial manager of The Herald, had arranged the previous contract. On that expedition Peary had written gripping accounts of his struggles to 89 degrees North Latitude, the nearest man had ever come to the pole.

"Mr. Reick is no longer with The Herald," the commander was

told. "He's over at The New York Times." William Reick had been
with Bennett for many years, but had become an aide to Ochs on
both The Times and The Philadelphia Ledger on Jan. 1, 1907.

Commander Peary was baffled for a moment. He asked, "May I
talk with Mr. Lincoln?" Charles M. Lincoln, as city editor of The
Herald, had been in on the earlier Peary negotiations.

"Mr. Lincoln isn't with The Herald any more, either," the commander heard. "He's over on The Times, too."

The explorer must have felt like Rip Van Winkle just down from
the mountains. He said, "Who *is* in charge here? May I see him?"

The new city editor came out. Peary had never met him before.
The commander explained that he had raised almost enough
money for his next attempt to reach the pole and he would like to
sell the story rights to The Herald, as he had when Reick and
Lincoln were there.

The Herald's city editor was kind, but he felt that Herald readers
were probably a little tired of Arctic adventures that always fell
short of the pole.

He said: "I just don't think we want to be in on this trip, commander, at least not for exclusive rights. If you make the pole, we'll
get the information through routine channels. Thanks, just the
same."

The explorer was hurt. He walked slowly uptown to the Times
Tower. On the seventeenth floor he asked the newsroom reception-
ist if he might see Lincoln, who was Sunday editor.

Peary's reception at The Times was in sharp contrast with that
at The Herald. Lincoln was genuinely glad to see him and introduced him to Van Anda.

A few minutes later Peary, Van Anda, Lincoln, Reick and Ochs
were listening to the commander's plans. They sounded good. It
was an hour's task to draw a contract.

The Times had decided to pay Peary $4,000 for New York rights
to his story. It was also to act as Peary's agents for the story elsewhere, and to handle distribution. It would turn over to him every
penny of profits from syndication.

Walter Scott Meriwether of the city staff was assigned to do a
series on Peary's preparations. He described the Roosevelt, the expedition's ship, and the food and equipment for the journey over

ice. He was kept on the story until Peary pulled out of New York. Meriwether was another former Bennett man. He had come to The Times with Reick.

Ochs' original idea of cash prizes, to stimulate progress in aviation, was abandoned. It might be well to explain, here, that after 1920 he and Arthur Hays Sulzberger, who succeeded him many years later, sternly held to the principle that they would not capitalize on another man's daring. They ran up, between them, a series of impressive beats in pioneer aviation and in exploration, but after the early prize ventures they never sent an explorer, a scientist or flier to risk his life for mere benefit of newspaper circulation.

They bought rights to such adventure stories only from men who were already committed. They signed only after funds had been subscribed from other sources, and then only for such projects as were intended to extend man's knowledge of the world.

This, incidentally, produced a curious tradition that amounted almost to a superstition. Airmen, scientists and explorers came to think of a Times hook-up as a guarantee of good luck. In almost all cases, fortunately, it worked out that way.

When Commander Peary left New York Harbor on July 6, 1908, a blistering day, he vanished into northern silence. There was no shipboard wireless then with which to send day-by-day progress reports. Occasional letters were dropped off at remote points in Newfoundland and Labrador. After that, nothing.

CHAPTER
16

O N SEPT. 1, 1909, when Ochs was at Lake Louise in Canada on vacation, the world was thrilled by word from the Shetland Islands that Dr. Frederick A. Cook of Brooklyn had reached the North Pole on April 21, 1908. Previously no one had paid much attention to Cook. He had been surgeon on two Peary expeditions, in 1891 and in 1902, and had gone north another time with the Belgian expedition in 1897-98. The public knew little more than that about him.

The New York Herald, it turned out, had bought the Cook story rights for $25,000. The Times, like other United States newspapers, had to pick up the bare facts from London and Danish newspapers.

"After a prolonged fight with famine and frost," Dr. Cook's first story said, "we have at last succeeded in reaching the North Pole. A new highway with an interesting strip of animated nature, has been explored, and big-game haunts located, which will delight sportsmen and extend the Eskimo horizon.

"Land has been discovered on which rests the earth's most northernmost rocks. A triangle of 30,000 square miles has been cut out of the terrestrial unknown."

It was bitter medicine for The Times to take, but it gave three full pages to Dr. Cook's achievement, running down every possible scrap of information in London, Paris, Brooklyn, New York and Copenhagen. Van Anda was too good a newspaperman not to play up the story of Peary's rival.

At the same time, he was too sharp to accept the surgeon's claims without close scrutiny. He ran the facts as they came in, but The Times editorial page cautiously asked, "Has Man Reached The Pole?" At least 577 expeditions had tried in vain to attain that goal; scores had been lost in the ice since 1800. Van Anda wanted positive proof.

It was not readily forthcoming. Some of the London journals, too, were frankly skeptical of Cook's story. They questioned that he could have crossed from Cape Columbus to the pole within thirty-five days, as the story said he had. Admiral G. W. Melville, U.S.N., reached by The Times correspondent in Philadelphia, bluntly called Dr. Cook's story "a fake." The admiral had been out with the Jeanette expedition. He said there was no smooth ice that far north, and that the march had to be made in endless night.

When Dr. Cook reached Copenhagen in the steamer Hans Egede on Sept. 4 that city roared tremendous welcome. The King honored him. Members of the Danish learned bodies were eager to hear his story in detail. Only here and there did doubters attempt to question the surgeon's claim.

Philip Gibbs—later knighted for his outstanding correspondence in World War I—was sent posthaste to Copenhagen by The London Daily Chronicle to ask Dr. Cook certain specific questions posed by members of geological and explorers' groups in Britain.

The Gibbs interview tended to support the doubters' stand. Dr. Cook blandly said he had no written records with him; that he had sent these on to the United States from Greenland with one of his party. He was forced to admit that the only persons with him in the icy wastes on the last leg of his journey were Eskimos with no knowledge of scientific observation.

The Gibbs story, printed in The New York Times in full, politely but firmly labeled Cook's claims "inconclusive." The between-the-lines imputations were obvious.

Meriwether had been shifted from the city staff to the Sunday Department. He was at work there one sweltering night—Sept. 6, 1909, more than a year after Peary's sailing—when, as he told it later, Boss Reick "erupted into the room," waving a telegraph blank.

It was a message from Peary who had just put in to Indian Harbor in Labrador. It had come by Marconi wireless to Cape Ray in

Newfoundland, had been retransmitted to Portmun Basque by
land line, then to Canso in Nova Scotia, and by Commercial Cable
from that spot to the Times Tower.

The message simply stated, "Got O.P." the cipher prearranged
before Peary left New York. It meant that he had reached the pole.
The newsroom was in a dither.

Ochs was on his way home from Atlantic City by motor car when
the message arrived. Van Anda stalked about crisply ordering special side-bar stories to go with Peary's startling message. He sensed
the volcanic controversy it would start. Cook was still warming his
spirit in public adulation abroad.

Meriwether was dressed for Manhattan's tropical heat wave. He
wore a straw hat and a palm beach suit, both somewhat wilted, but
Reick thrust a wad of cash at him. He said, "There's barely time to
get a train. Grab a cab to the station. Hurry. We'll telephone to
your wife." Meriwether left his unfinished Sunday piece, ran for
the elevator, and was plummeted to the street.

On the basis of that brief Peary message out of remote Indian
Harbor, and from subsequent bits that came through that night,
The Times put out five pages on Peary's discovery, led by a three-
column story on the front page. Peary's messages to the newspaper,
to his wife and to explorer friends were nested in a front-page box,
a half column deep. The three-column headline announced:

PEARY DISCOVERS THE NORTH POLE
AFTER EIGHT TRIALS IN 23 YEARS

"I have the pole, April 6 [1909]. Expect to arrive Chateau Bay
Sept. 7," Peary had flashed. "Secure control wire for me there, and
arrange transmission big story."

Nudging this front-page splash was a story out of Copenhagen.
It told how Dr. Cook, wearing a lei made of pink roses, heard the
news of Peary's message at a banquet in the Tivoli Casino. He was
startled, but he congratulated his former expedition master. He
even sent a cablegram to The New York Times, which Van Anda
put into the box under the Peary messages. It said: "Glad Peary
did it. Two records are better than one and more work over an
easterly route has added value."

That brought the pot of dispute to explosive boiling point. Leading scientists and explorers took sides, and rival newspapers went at it with hot ink. It developed into the controversy of the age.

In Copenhagen, Philip Gibbs relentlessly—if with utter journalistic politeness—returned to putting sharp questions to Cook. He bearded the surgeon at a lecture where Cook was to speak before the King and Danish academicians. He came away to report that Cook "flushed and perspired under the stabbing queries"; that his answers "prove conclusively that his claims to have reached the North Pole belong to the realm of fairy tales." He described as "delirious dreams" the Cook effusions of sighting big game and of opening 30,000 square miles of previously unpenetrated territory.

Bad weather held up Peary's own account of his adventure. On Sept. 8, The Times ran another front-page box, headed: "Peary Report Delayed." It said: "Commander Peary having been delayed yesterday at Indian Harbor, Labrador, did not reach Chateau Bay, whence he had intended to telegraph to The New York Times his account of the discovery of the North Pole. In a brief message to The Times last night the explorer said that he expected to reach Battle Harbor, Labrador [his crew awaited him there on the Roosevelt], today, and that he would send from there a 'great story.'"

There were pages of side stories, columns of pictures on Peary and his preparations for the voyage, and many columns of comment from experts on both the Cook and Peary claims.

Meriwether meanwhile had landed in Sydney, Nova Scotia, a harried man strangely garbed for that climate. He found the town alive with a hundred other newspapermen, all frantically searching for a ship to take them to the Roosevelt at Battle Harbor. Finally, a fishing boat turned up, and the newspapermen, Meriwether included, paid shares to charter it. Meriwether wired Boss Reick that he was on his way.

To Meriwether's complete shock, while the reporters were hustling their baggage onto the chartered craft, he got a stern message from Reick ordering him to withdraw immediately from his share in the chartered-ship venture. Reick explained that any unauthorized act by The Times—such as sending a man north to take the story from Peary—might jeopardize the whole contract. Reick peremptorily ordered Meriwether to confine his activities to arranging wire clearance for the explorer's copy.

Meriwether disconsolately watched the chartered ship pull out. He wandered unhappily around Sydney until the vessel returned with his eager contemporaries. They had had a two-hour interview with Peary. Their voyage might have been useless, if it had not been for the Dr. Cook angle. When Peary heard of the surgeon's claims, and of the stir they had created all over the world, he talked, and he spoke in anger. He said he had seen no trace of Dr. Cook at the pole. It made good copy, but no Times man was there to take it.

Late Wednesday afternoon, after the reporters had scrambled back to their chartered craft with the interview, Peary wired The New York Times:

"Cook's story should not be taken too seriously. The Eskimos that accompanied him say he went no distance north. He did not get out of sight of land." The Times also got—and ran—a message he sent at the same time to Mrs. Peary at Portland, Me. This said: "Delayed by gale. Don't let Cook story worry you. I have him nailed . . . Bert."

The first part of Peary's story was barely more than a summary of his dash for the pole from Cape Sheridan, but it ran on the front page on Sept. 8, beside a quarter-page map showing how he had progressed from point to dangerous point.

It told how Ross Gillmore Marvin of Cornell University faculty, an engineer, had died on the ice on April 10, 1909. The story was a teaser for what was to follow—the most exciting and most important story of its kind ever carried by a newspaper up to that time.

Ochs had returned to New York from his vacation travels. His brother, in from Philadelphia, and Ben Franck, his office aide, were waiting for him, bursting with details of the Peary story. When he was brought up to date on it, the publisher sat down in his office to scribble a hasty, exultant letter to his wife and daughter:

"I find all well, and the office in the greatest excitement about our marvelous and overwhelming good luck in regard to the Peary story. We are the exclusive publishers of Peary's story, and only through us can newspapers get the right to print it. Every newspaper in New York is in a panic about our tremendous scoop, and they are moving heaven and earth and offering all kinds of money to us and to our employes to get hold of it. Nothing in American journalism equals this achievement of The New York Times.

"We are flooded with telegrams from newspapers all over the world asking to buy the story. Our orders exceed ten thousand dollars—all of which we shall give Peary. There is little doubt now that Cook is a faker."

This letter was rounded off with an amusing little practical touch in the postscript: "Write me at once what you wish done in painting and papering at the house."

The Times wire room sold more than 350,000 words on Peary all over the world. The final payment to the explorer, from this syndication, came to around $12,000.

Several newspapers, though, lost their restraint at sight of The Times' Peary monopoly, and tried a trick to get the story without payment. The Times had sold the Peary account in London, among other places, and frustrated sheets—The World and The Sun in New York; The Inter-Ocean, The Record-Herald, The Examiner and The American in Chicago; and several Canadian publications —had their London correspondents cable the story as run in London.

The New York Times enjoined all these newspapers by court order and printed that fact in bold type in a front-page box. That was a characteristic Van Anda maneuver. He shrewdly figured that it would serve to drive home to the reading public the fact that The Times was first with great stories.

Peary's vivid account of his journey on the ice to the pole ran for four days—Sept. 8 to Sept. 11. On Sept. 10 the explorer wired Reick from Battle Harbor:

"Hope my story went through without too many errors creeping in during transmission. Roosevelt's to remain here three or four days coaling and overhauling. Expect arrive Sydney about Sept. 15.

"Do not trouble about Cook's story, nor attempt to explain any discrepancies in his statements. If he has not yet published a full statement he will make use of the information in my story to render his more plausible. The affair will settle itself. He has not been at the pole April 21, 1908, or at any other time. He has simply handed the public a gold brick.

"These statements are made advisedly. I have proof of it. When he makes a full statement of his journey over his signature to some geographical society or other reputable party, if that statement contains the claim that he has reached the pole, I shall be in position to furnish material that may prove distinctly interesting reading for the public."

The Times did not run this message. There was no need. The controversy was long-drawn and covered acres of newsprint, but in the end Peary's feat was recognized by Congress and by scientific bodies the world over. The surgeon eventually got into a legal tangle in a mail fraud case and went to Federal prison—but that is another story. The Times and Peary were triumphant and Times circulation zoomed.

Seventeen years later The Times broke an exclusive copyrighted story out of the sub-Arctic that stirred the wraiths and sent reporters scurrying back to the morgue for the details of the 1909 Peary expedition.

The story, written by George Palmer Putnam on board the Arctic schooner Effie Morrissey at Sydney on Cape Breton Island, told of the "farthest north" murder. It disclosed that Ross G. Marvin, the Cornell man who had been Peary's second in command on the 1909 dash across the polar ice had not been drowned, as originally reported by Peary. He had been killed by Eskimo companions.

Putnam had run into the murder story on his way back from a polar trip for the American Museum of Natural History. His skipper on the Morrissey was the same Capt. Bob Bartlett who had commanded the Roosevelt in 1909, and Peary's son, Robert, was in his crew. The Putnam story ran on the front page on Sept. 25, 1926.

On Jan. 31, 1908, while Ochs was engaged in negotiations with Peary and with other pressing business his mother died in his home at 481 West End Avenue. She was in her seventy-fifth year, and he was six weeks short of his fiftieth.

Her body was borne back to Chattanooga for burial on the knoll overlooking the town. Her husband had been a Union Army officer and had been buried by his comrades with the Stars and Stripes. She had been loyal to the South and was buried with the Stars and Bars. Eighteen years later, in 1926, Ochs gave $400,000 to the Mizpah Congregation of Chattanooga for construction of a temple and community house as a memorial to his father and mother.

In June, 1908, when the Republican Party was torn over platform issues, just before the convention in Chicago, Van Anda let word get out to his staff that he would prize no story above an advance copy—exclusive to The Times—of that controversial platform.

His men opened every available door in attempts to get it. They met with discouragingly frigid reception at all points—all except Oscar King (called O. K.) Davis, The Times Washington man.

When all other sources failed, Davis approached Senator William E. Borah of Idaho, whom he knew well. The Senator never said he would give Davis the document; nor did he refuse it, but with masterful indirection somehow indicated there was at least hope.

On Sunday night, June 14, Davis was invited to the Senator's hotel suite in Chicago. They talked of many things, but not of the platform. Presently the Senator fetched a brief case. He fished around in it, pulled out some papers, left them on top of the case —and went into the washroom.

He had not uttered a syllable. He had not gestured toward the document. But Davis clearly understood that the prize lay before him. He took it up without stopping to read it, got into Michigan Boulevard and raced for The Times suite. It was a little before midnight.

Monday's first edition was already on the presses in New York when Davis thrust the papers at Arthur Greaves, Van Anda's convention staff chief in Chicago.

"What's this?" Greaves asked gruffly.

"Taft's platform," Davis told him.

Greaves never asked how, or from whom, Davis had got the document; he just exploded in characteristic Greavesean oaths and let his eyes race over it.

"Boy!" he bawled.

A sleepy boy, hired to run errands, came before him.

"Get a typewriter," Greaves ordered.

When the machine was brought in, Greaves started dictating:

Special to The New York Times

CHICAGO, Ill., June 15—Below is the platform which the Republican National Convention will adopt with little, if any, change. It is a verbatim copy, even to every punctuation mark, of the draft prepared by the Administration powers who so absolutely dominate the party situation here . . .

He dictated a few more paragraphs, and stood over the Western Union operator who sent them direct to The Times in New York. Sheet by sheet, as the operator finished, he reassembled the platform and stuffed it into his pocket. He did not want it out of his hands.

Van Anda fairly wriggled with delight as he read the copy in the Tower. Like Greaves, he did not ask how the platform had been obtained. He held the story for Tuesday's paper. When it reached the street the Republicans howled with anguish, no one louder than the White House. They denounced the Times platform version as spurious. The Associated Press picked up the platform from The Times just the same and sent it out, with cautious credit.

Ochs ordered the platform run again on Friday, June 19, when it had been officially released in Chicago. He gave a full page to it with the banner head: "Platform the One The Times Printed."

He marked where minor changes had been made in the document, and editorially demanded that Administration spokesmen admit they had falsely accused The Times of running an untrue version.

He even stepped back in journalistic time, to the Raymond-Jones era, to poke a little at both the Administration's and his competitors' wounds.

"We Make Acknowledgements," was the caption of an editorial on Friday.

"Our salutations to the young men whom it was our privilege to send to Chicago to report for the readers of The Times the proceedings and incidents of the Republican National Convention. Their portraits and biographies have not been printed in this newspaper, nor, so far as we know, in any other. But a very large part of their work has appeared in nearly all the other newspapers, a day after its publication in The Times, with that degree of courteous acknowledgement which is one of the chief charms of an urbane and generous profession."

Van Anda and Ochs licked their chops over that one. They wired to O. K. Davis to come to New York as soon as the convention was ended. Van Anda, whom Davis saw first, warmed astonishingly as he congratulated him.

Ochs sat back quietly as Davis told him how he had obtained the platform. The publisher got up, shook Davis by the hand, and left a little gift box in his palm. A few seconds later, in the hall, the Washington correspondent opened the box. It contained a handsome gold Tiffany watch. Inside was engraved:

"Presented by The New York Times for services of exceptional merit."

CHAPTER
17

F ORTY YEARS AGO man was just beginning to get the feel of new-
 fangled mechanical wings, but he did not then know the ultimate potentialities or the contraptions he was putting together in
barns and other primitive workshops. The Wrights were showing
the astonished Germans at Tempelhof what they could do with
their little pushers. The first Zeppelins were maneuvering clumsily
over Berlin.

Newspapers of the period, to put it bluntly, were not keen on
science and aviation. There is a legend that on the afternoon of
Dec. 17, 1903, a Coast Guard officer stationed somewhere on the
North Carolina Coast asked The Times by telegraph if it would
like a little story about an airplane flight he had seen. His bid was
turned down.

Eight days later, on Christmas, news was light along Park Row,
and the bored telegraph editor grudgingly sent to the composing
room a short piece with the one-column headline:

AIRSHIP AFTER BUYER

INVENTORS OF NORTH CAROLINA BOX KITE
MACHINE WANT GOVERNMENT TO
PURCHASE IT

The story was printed on Page 1:

Special to The New York Times

WASHINGTON, Dec. 25—The inventors of the airship which is said to have made several successful flights in North Carolina near Kitty Hawk are anxious to sell the use of their device to the Government. They claim that they have solved the problem of aerial navigation and have never made a failure of any attempt to fly.

Their machine is an adaption of the box-kite idea . . . The use to which the Government would put it would be in scouting and signal work and possibly in torpedo warfare.

This cautious and cynical item was the first Times account of the Wright brothers' revolutionary experiment at Kitty Hawk. Their "device" was to revolutionize war and human transportation.

One of the most important aviation stories in The Times after the Wrights' flight ran on Jan. 14, 1908, under a Paris dateline of the previous day. It told how the French aeronaut Henry Farman had won the $10,000 Deutsch-Archdeacon award that had been promised to the first man to fly a circular kilometer in a heavier-than-air machine. Farman had flown 1,630 yards all told at an altitude of twenty-five feet and at a speed of thirty-four miles an hour above a meadow at Issy, five miles southwest of Paris. He was the first man to return to his starting point after a ground take-off. The Times had him write a half-page Sunday piece on it for Feb. 2, 1908.

Just before the Cook-Peary controversy, The New York World offered $10,000 to the first person to fly from Albany to New York in a single day. There had been no long cross-country flights up to that time. Even motor cars of the period were still followed by boys hooting, "Get a horse!"

New York then was still spreading like Alice when she ate magic cake. Flatbush, the Bronx and Queens were just opening to fresh clusters of population. Grand Central Station was only half finished. New York Aldermen were thinking up new ways to spend municipal funds on the Hudson-Fulton celebration. George Bernard Shaw was a peppery chap barely in his middle years and his "Arms and the Man" had just reached Broadway as the musical play "The Chocolate Soldier." Dr. Eliot was choosing the Five Foot Shelf of Classics. Christy (Bix Six) Mathewson was McGraw's Giant pitching ace, Hal Chase was at first base for the Yanks and Hans Wagner was at short for the Pirates. The favored novelists were Rex Beach, Harold Bell Wright, Jack London, Joseph Lincoln and George Barr McCutcheon.

It was still the derby and ostrich-plume-bonnet period.

Early in 1910, Glenn H. Curtiss began to prepare for The World prize flight, but his tricky, matchbox pusher-biplane was temperamental. Besides, the weather was treacherous. The World, wearied by delays, had gradually paid less and less attention to Curtiss. Its guard was down when the biplane finally took off from Albany at 7:03 A.M. on May 29.

A World reporter who was on hand to watch, heard startling news. Carr Van Anda had quietly hired a special train with which his men were to follow the flight. He had arranged for Mrs. Curtiss to be a passenger on the train, had a cameraman in a baggage car to "shoot" pictures through open doors, and had placed reporters all along the flight route.

The World man tried desperately to hire his own locomotive, but the New York Central firmly refused to operate two high-speed specials. "Too dangerous," it said. The Van Anda special pulled out of the New York Central yard as the Curtiss ship left the ground.

Van Anda's mathematics were apparent at every point of the day's coverage. When the New York Central argued that a locomotive could not race over the roadbed at fifty miles an hour without leaving the rails, he offered to pay for four coaches to be hauled as ballast. The coaches were hooked on.

Curtiss averaged 54.18 miles an hour as he followed the Hudson River southward in a cloudless sky. The Times train averaged 49.6 miles an hour. Neither lost sight of the other during the 150-mile run. Isaac Russell, The Times man in charge of the train, wrote the main story. His aides wrote bulletins to drop at stations, where telegraph operators flashed them to the news room.

Mrs. Curtiss and the newspapermen aboard had some bad moments. The biplane landed on a little farm at Camelot near Poughkeepsie to refuel at 8:25 A.M. The train slowed, and when the little ship took off again at 9:29 A.M. the race was resumed.

Wherever there were station telephones, one of Russell's aides dashed out to keep Van Anda informed. Country correspondents were rushed to get interviews at landing spots.

As they passed Storm King Mountain, Curtiss was rudely bounced by air currents. He made frightening drops of fifty to sixty feet, and shot up again. Mrs. Curtiss held her breath until he had cleared that pass.

A local photographer who had taken a snap of the Curtiss take-off at Albany rushed the plate to a train that pulled out behind the special. The photographer on the special repeatedly risked his life for flight shots from the baggage car. Weighted down with his eight-by-ten plate camera he leaned out the car's door, with train-men clinging to his waist and others behind them, holding on in support. He made dramatic shots at Kingston, Poughkeepsie Bridge, West Point and Iona Island in the Hudson Highlands. Other photographers were planted on the Statue of Liberty to take the final phase.

In The Times office, Van Anda rubbed his hands in energetic dry wash, tne characteristic gesture when something exciting was happening. He sent telephone bulletins of Curtiss' progress to New York hotels and clubs. Bulletins were posted in the Tower building first floor, too.

Hotel roof gardens and apartment house tops were crowded as Curtiss neared the city. Great throngs waited all along Riverside Drive and at the Battery. A red ball atop the Hotel Astor signaled Curtiss approach.

The managing editor had posted reporters in The Times Tower with field glasses to watch for Curtiss' arrival. Visibility was perfect and they shouted notice of the biplane's appearance near Spuyten Duyvil.

At that point when the craft dipped and made for a landing on the old Isham farm at Broadway and 214th Street, Van Anda was on hand to greet Curtiss. He had come from Times Square by car with Leland Speers, a staff man. Minturn P. Collins, son-in-law of William B. Isham, let Curtiss have the farm's available gasoline—which was not too much—to complete the flight.

That last leg was a roaring triumph. River craft held down their whistles. Countless thousands in derbies and picture hats cheered themselves hoarse along the Drive and on West Side piers for which they had started when The Times bulletins indicated Curtiss was due.

Van Anda had brought in all available men for the story. They caught crowd color and reaction. This was summed up in the paper next day.

"Everyone was filled with the sense of something important having taken place in the history of the world's progress," the story said.

The Times had an automobile waiting for Mrs. Curtiss at Grand Central Station, then not quite finished. She sped to the Battery to meet her husband when he crossed over from Governors Island.

Times men had covered every angle of the Curtiss flight—enough to fill almost seven pages in next morning's paper—before Curtiss found time to go to the Pulitzer building to collect the $10,000 prize money from J. Angus Shaw, The World's secretary. Van Anda had beaten The World on its own story.

It was a significant Times victory. Just as Peary had provided the first of many journalistic achievements in exploration and science, the Curtiss flight was the beginning of a string of Times aviation triumphs. The Times was to pre-empt those fields.

Two weeks after the Curtiss Flight, the Ochs newspapers, The New York Times and The Philadelphia Public Ledger, paid $10,-000 to Charles K. Hamilton for completing a New York-Philadelphia round-trip in a single day, June 13, 1910.

Van Anda rode the three-car train that followed—sometimes led—Hamilton over the route. The managing editor had the car roofs painted white so that Hamilton might not mistake some other run for the special.

Pennsylvania Railroad tower men telegraphed word of the plane's passage to The Times in New York. Reporters on the special threw written bulletins to station agents for transmission.

The bulletins were posted in The Times ground-floor windows where throngs swarmed to read them. They were wigwagged from the Tower by Army Signal Corps men relaying to Fort Wood. They were telephoned to fifty-seven United Cigar Stores in the five boroughs, went over the Dow Jones & Co. tickers to Wall Street, were picked up by the New York City News Association for general newspaper distribution, and were telephoned to leading hotels, restaurants and cafes. It was perfect promotion, the like of which the journalistic world had never known.

Another Van Anda touch, unique for 1910 though commonplace

now, was the use of special telephones for coverage. One telephone was set on a platform post beside The Times train in the railroad station in Jersey City. It had direct connection with the take-off spot at Governors Island, and with The Times news room. The phones were the hand-cranked type.

No one paid much attention to it then, but Hamilton carried with him a few copies of that morning's New York Times. This was probably the first shipment of a newspaper by plane. Now The Times flies the oceans every day and is read overseas on publication date.

Hamilton's actual flying time was 3 hours 34 minutes for the 175-mile round trip. Almost twelve hours elapsed before the flight was done, though, because the propeller cracked on the return and the biplane had to land in a South Amboy swamp. Hamilton bounced back onto Governors Island at 6:40 P.M. He had averaged almost 47 miles an hour between New York and Philadelphia, and 51.36 miles an hour on the return.

Of the next day's issue of The Times almost ten of the twenty-two pages were devoted to the Hamilton flight. The three-column front-page headline said: "Hamilton Flies for The Times to Philadelphia and Back in a Day."

Under it was a deep two-column line drawing by Marcus, done from a photograph, and a blurry photo of the take-off from Governors Island. The same lensmen who had snapped the Curtiss flight had done a remarkable job on Hamilton. They were Pictorial News Company photographers. The Times, at that point, had not developed its own photo service.

One Times reporter almost missed getting to his own important assignment that day because he lagged to watch Hamilton take off. He was a specialist hired by Van Anda to go to Reno, Nev., to report the Jim Jeffries-Jack Johnson bout. His coast-bound train out of Penn Station was due to leave around the time Hamilton soared off Governors Island. He made the coast-bound express by a hair. "That Hamilton—he's wonderful," he gasped to the other writers on the train. "I got to see him flying over Jersey City." The Times specialist was the former heavyweight champion John L. Sullivan.

Letters to Hamilton showed that some readers saw the new-fangled airplane as the devil's instrument. "You have defied God," one writer said. "You will be punished for it."

On June 13, 1935, Capt. Eddie Rickenbacker commemorated the twenty-fifth anniversary of the pioneer's flight by a New York-Philadelphia round trip in a Douglas transport in 58 minutes 38 seconds. Charles K. Hamilton was not around to see it. He had died four years after he won the $10,000 Times prize.

Four months after the Hamilton flight, Walter Wellman, who had been a reporter on The Chicago Record-Herald, left Atlantic City, N. J., in the 228-foot dirigible America, equipped with two eighty-horsepower motors and a primitive wireless outfit, in the first attempt to cross the Atlantic.

The Times shared story rights in this astonishing expedition with The Record-Herald, and on Oct. 17, the morning after the dirigible's take-off, ran the headline: "Wellman Now One-Fourth of the Way Across the Atlantic; Engines Stopped Because Equilibrator Makes Trouble."

The equilibrator was an awkward balancing device slung under the gondola. It had been a nuisance on test flights.

A box beside the main front-page story carried two wireless messages signed by Wellman. These had reached The Times by way of the Marconi station at Siasconset, Mass. They said:

Special to The New York Times

WELLMAN AIRSHIP AMERICA, Oct. 16, 10 A.M.—We have shut down the motors and are heading east northeast. We are making twenty-five miles an hour without the engines. We are saving our power for the wireless apparatus. The dynamo is not working. There is a thick fog and no observations are obtainable.

Special to The New York Times

WELLMAN AIRSHIP AMERICA, Oct. 16, 11 A.M.—The equilibrator is jerking on the airship as it leaps from wave to wave, but no damage has been done. The weather is thick. We believe we are south of Nantucket. The outlook is not so favorable, but we are keeping up the flight.

In the Times Tower Van Anda's desk was spread with ocean charts on which he had marked the approximate positions of liners. He sent Wellman a message by way of Siasconset querying a surface ship report that the America had been seen lowering something to the sea surface.

"It's all right," Wellman flashed back. "The bag contained nothing for The Times. Our cat jumped overboard. Irwin [radio man] was fishing for it, and got it."

Van Anda's delight in getting an answer from a craft in flight was almost childish, especially since the exchange had made history. A Times editorial in the Oct. 17 issue said of the flight:

"It is a wonderful undertaking like nothing else that has preceded it in aeronautics. The wireless dispatches from a traveling balloon which The Times has been enabled to put before its readers are without precedent."

Van Anda had maps drawn for Times readers to show the estimated whereabouts of the America, and ran several pages of side-stories and photographs.

On Oct. 18 when The Times went to press at 3 A.M., there had been no word from Wellman. The headline told of "Wireless Search of the Sea for Wellman's Airship America." Next day a four-column headline electrified readers:

WELLMAN AND CREW RESCUED AT SEA, AIRSHIP LOST; VOYAGERS PICKED UP BY TRENT, 400 MILES OFF HATTERAS; LEADER SENDS STORY OF DARING TRIP TO THE TIMES

Wellman's byline rescue story sent by wireless to The Times carried the dateline, "ON BOARD THE ROYAL MAIL S. S. TRENT, AT SEA." It had all the elements of a Mayne-Reid thriller, and Van Anda sucked it dry. He double-leaded the major story and had side-bar stories by the packet master, by J. Murray Simon, who was Wellman's navigator, and a story by Wellman's radio operator, all exclusive to The Times.

In the same edition was another significant story—the trial in London of Hawley Harvey Crippen, the first criminal in history captured at sea by a wireless message from shore. Scotland Yard had reached through the ether for him for the murder of Cora Belle Crippen, his spouse.

In October, 1910, The Times and The Chicago Evening News jointly put up $25,000 for a cross-country flight between Chicago and New York, but this was straining things a bit for the primitive crates of that period. Eugene B. Ely, the only man who tried for the money, took off from Hawthorne Park in Chicago on Oct. 9, and cracked up nineteen miles out in suburban Beverly Hills.

The lead story in The Times of Oct. 12, when Ely had definitely decided he could not take to the air again, told of an impulsive flight by Col. Theodore Roosevelt. He had leaped out of his car at an airfield outside St. Louis and had been taken aloft for four minutes by the aerial daredevil Arch Hoxey.

Another Times-sponsored cross-country flight—Boston to Washington—was won by Harry Atwood, carrying Charles K. Hamilton as passenger. They left Boston on June 30, 1911, and lumbered toward Washington in four jumps. The longest of these was 148 miles from Atlantic City to Baltimore. They ended the venture on July 11.

They were eight miles short of the District of Columbia when they were finally forced down, unable to continue, but Ochs gave them the trophy anyhow. He ran pages on their achievement and proudly pictured the cup they had won under the caption "Conquest of Air."

Probably no two newspapermen in the world were as eager to help aviation advancement as Ochs and Van Anda were. On Oct. 12, 1913, in a magazine piece commemorating the tenth anniversary of the Wrights' flight at Kitty Hawk, they announced $2,500 in awards for contestants in an aerial derby around Manhattan.

The race was spectacular. Five planes took off from Oakwood Heights on Staten Island at 3:30 P.M. on Oct. 13, and bravely struggled up through wintry gusts. Roof tops were crowded all over the city and throngs craned their necks from the sidewalks as contestants lurched out of the mist.

Van Anda had coverage at every conceivable point—on ferryboats in the East and Hudson Rivers, in the Bay, at the Battery, in Times Tower and in the main avenues. Once the ships were in the air it was not too difficult to spot them; the two tallest buildings then were the Woolworth and the Singer.

W. S. Luckey completed the flight of sixty miles in 52 minutes 54 seconds. He got $1,000 as first prize. Frank Niles won second prize, $750; C. Murvin Wood, third, $500. Van Anda had a special telephone line from Oakwood Heights to the city room for take-offs and landings, and posted bulletins of the flight in The Times windows every few minutes.

It was a striking memorial to the Wright flight, and excellent Times promotion.

Because Ochs had never had time for sports in his crowded career he was inclined to give the subject short shrift, even in The Times. Compared with other New York newspapers, his publication was a little backward in developing that department.

Van Anda, on the other hand, was both a racing and boxing enthusiast. When important championship bouts impended, he prepared for their coverage with the same mathematical precision that he used on more significant events.

He preferred to handle championship contests as straight news. He would set up a separate copy desk in the news room, instead of in the sports department and would man it with his own general news reporters and copy editors.

Parsimonious when it came to bylines, he let most Times sports pieces go into print with the author's identity hidden in the same cold anonymity with which he shielded the men who covered routine city beats.

One of the first bylines he printed on a sports story was John L. Sullivan's. It was used over a first-person piece from Reno, Nev., on July 5, 1910, on the Jeffries-Johnson fight, which occupied the lead position on the front page:

BY JOHN L. SULLIVAN
Special to The New York Times

RENO, Nev., July 4—The fight of the century is over and a black man is the undisputed champion of the world.

Sullivan got a second byline on Page 2, where his separate round-by-round account was printed. Van Anda ran four pages on the fight, all told, and posted bulletins in The Times Building windows around which some 30,000 persons were assembled.

To maintain its traditional decorum, The Times counterbalanced its front-page story on the Reno fisticuffs with a rather frigid editorial on the subject the same day:

"Money, indeed, has been the sole object of this brutal and vulgar contest. The result of the fight proves nothing more than that one human being is more alert and stronger than another. No matter which of these pugilists had won, no honor would have fallen upon him."

This attitude from the solemn chamber where Charles Miller presided did not discourage the managing editor. As big fights came up he continued to cover them with gusto.

The Dempsey-Carpentier fight at Boyle's Thirty Acres on July 2, 1921, got a headline clear across the top of the front page next day that startled some Times regulars.

DEMPSEY KNOCKS OUT CARPENTIER IN THE FOURTH ROUND; CHALLENGER BREAKS HIS THUMB AGAINST CHAMPION'S JAW; RECORD CROWD OF 90,000 ORDERLY AND WELL HANDLED

Irvin S. Cobb got a byline on the syndicated fight story he did for the front page. At least ten other Times men were on the assignment, but they got no bylines.

The Dempsey-Carpentier story was spaced over twelve pages. There was even a special story from Paris, signed by Edwin L. James, telling how sad the French were as they learned what had happened to their Georges.

Van Anda sent Elmer Davis, a Rhodes scholar on his news staff, to Shelby, Mont., in 1923 to cover the Jack Dempsey-Tom Gibbons fight, scheduled for July 4. Several regular Times sports writers were also assigned, but they wrote anonymously while Davis got two—sometimes three—bylines in a day on fight preparations. He had three on July 5, the morning after the fight. The story was spread over four pages.

Bulletins on the Shelby bout were supplemented in Times Square by oral descriptions of the fighting. The radio loudspeakers used for the occasion were rather new, and a Times story had to explain to readers how the things worked.

For the Jeffries-Johnson fight in 1910, incidentally, The Times set up an electric bulletin press board, which printed a blow-by-blow description of the fight in letters one and one-half inches high on a roll of paper thirty-three inches wide and seventy inches long. This was the ancestor of the electric sign that girdles Times Tower today.

Even in the early Nineteen-Twenties Van Anda rarely permitted a Times man to have a byline on a sports piece. The first to appear over a baseball story went to James Harrison during the summer of 1924.

Other men on the staff, eager for byline privilege, finally banded together to put their request before the managing editor. Other newspapers, they pointed out, were spraying sports bylines around with abandon.

Van Anda was unmoved by the petition.

"Gentlemen," he told the delegation frostily, "The Times is not running a reporters' directory."

Birchall, who succeeded him, was more liberal. In 1925 sports bylines multiplied like rabbits.

CHAPTER
18

It was Carr Van Anda's habit to come into the office in midafternoon, size up the world news picture, then to go home for dinner and a nap. He returned around 10 o'clock refreshed, to work through the night, often into dawn. These, he liked to think, were perfect hours for what he called "the keepers of St. Peter's daily ledger."

On Sunday night, April 14, 1912, he found the news flow somewhat duller than on most Sabbaths. Only two local stories were candidates for the front page next morning, a Black Hand murder in Brooklyn and a killing in Thompson Street in Greenwich Village. There were two slow-paced political pieces from Washington on the Taft-Roosevelt tug-of-war for Republican leadership, and a long story out of Harrington Park in New Jersey where a church roof had fallen and killed two worshippers.

Sunday's Times had carried a two-column picture of the world's newest and largest luxury ship, the White Star Line's Titanic, which was New York-bound with 2,180 persons including a large crew. She was due in the harbor Tuesday afternoon.

At 1:20 A.M. Monday, the first edition was rumbling off the presses far below the pavement under the Tower. The seventeenth-floor city room was unusually quiet. A rewrite man pawed over sheets of notes. Two copy boys stared listlessly across the floor. The managing editor was restless. Nothing exciting. He retired to his little room and looked through the window at a city falling to sleep after a noisy week-end.

Telegraph and cable copy, in those days, came from the eighteenth-floor wire room to the news floor below in wooden boxes that worked like a dumbwaiter. When extraordinary news broke, the signal from the wire room was a vigorous shaking of the thick rope against the metal dumbwaiter housing.

At 1:20 A.M. the rope flailed madly, startling everyone in the room.

Eddie Stewart, copy boy on the night telegraph desk, hurried to the box, grabbed The Associated Press bulletin that lay in it and rushed it to Jack Paine, acting night telegraph editor, a tall, thin, nervous man. Paine's eyes raced over the words. He leaped from his chair, strode into the managing editor's office and thrust the bulletin at V. A. The bulletin said:

CAPE RACE, N. F., Sunday Night, April 14 (AP)—At 10:25 o'clock tonight the White Star Line steamship Titanic called "CQD" to the Marconi station here, and reported having struck an iceberg. The steamer said that immediate assistance was required.

Van Anda hurried onto the floor, calling sharp orders. The room, which had fallen into somnolent quiet after the first edition had been put to bed, reacted to his electric commands.

John O'Neill, chief of make-up, got orders by telephone in the composing room to tear out the lead story to make place for the A. P. bulletin, and for a brief story of the Titanic's departure from Southampton. It took the headline: "Titanic Sinking in Mid-Ocean; Hit Great Iceberg."

There was barely time to make the mail-edition with just this much, but even as shaggy-browed O'Neill labored at the task in the composing room, V. A. was setting all wheels in motion for details to back up the Cape Race bulletin.

The managing editor's own reaction when Jack Paine had brought him the bulletin had been: "It can't be true. The Titanic's equipped with extra safety compartments." But when his analytical mind had reviewed the few known facts, he concluded that it must be true.

From information he got over the telephone from The Times

correspondent in Halifax, from the man in Montreal and from such White Star officials as his rewrite desk and reporters were able to reach at that hour, he drew definite conclusions:

The Titanic had hit an iceberg. She had sent a message for help. A half hour later her own operator had flashed the SOS and had reported the great ship going down by the head. After that, only silence from the deep Atlantic. White Star executives in New York had had no reassuring word. They were only certain that the Titanic was unsinkable.

Other editors in New York and in London thought they were playing the story safe by printing the bulletins and writing stories that indicated that no great harm could come to the "unsinkable" Titanic.

Not Van Anda. Cold reasoning told him she was gone. Paralyzing as the thought was, he acted on it. His story that first night overshadowed that of every other editor, here and in Britain.

Van Anda was not playing a mere newspaper hunch. He never went on that alone. He was satisfied that there could be but one answer to the Titanic's silence so soon after her SOS.

He sent Tommy Bracken, now morgue keeper as well as managing editor's secretary, to unearth in the morgue every bit of material available on the Titanic. He lifted the two-column cut of the liner out of Sunday's forms and planted it on the front page. The Cunarder Carmania had steered dangerously into New York through floating ice only the day before. Van Anda had a rewrite man expand that story with much of the detail that earlier had been dropped. The French liner Niagara had suffered two hull dents in ice encounters. That too was played up.

Then Van Anda ordered Bracken to get out the morgue folder that dealt with the history of ships that had encountered icebergs in other years. Percy Soule, assistant ship news man, banged out a side-story on that. Early White Star releases had boasted of the notables who had booked passage on the Titanic for her maiden voyage. Van Anda ran the list, and it was impressive. It included Major Archibald Butt, military aide to President Taft, Alfred G. Vanderbilt, F. D. Millet, the French artist; Mr. and Mrs. Harry Widener, Mr. and Mrs. Isidor Straus and Mr. and Mrs. John Jacob Astor.

Birchall, night city editor, sharply ordered copy boys to hasten with "short takes" as fast as they came out of the typewriters. He kept his eyes on the clock and nervously toyed with his little red goatee.

"Five minutes to go," he warned. "Turn it out, lads. Five minutes to make the city edition." As proofs came from the composing room, boys ran them into the managing editor's cubicle and V. A.'s sharp eyes devoured the details.

The managing editor smoked a big cigar. He moved up and down the room, a study in intensity. His nervous fingers interlocked. His restless palms vigorously rubbed together. He figured out from sailing schedules where possible rescue vessels might be in relation to the Titanic's last known position—Lat. 41.46 North, Long. 50.14 West. He had that written into the lead. V. A. was plotting the wreck area.

While editors on other morning sheets were figuring cautious heads about "rumors" of harm to the Titanic, and hedging even on known facts, The Times news chief wrote a bold four-line three-column front-page head:

NEW LINER TITANIC HITS AN ICEBERG;
SINKING BY THE BOW AT MIDNIGHT;
WOMEN PUT OFF IN LIFEBOATS;
LAST WIRELESS AT 12:27 A.M. BLURRED

A heavily leaded two-column front-page box headed: "Latest News from the Sinking Ship," told most of the story as it had come through in bulletin form.

The calls to Halifax and Montreal had brought additional information, and the story appeared under a three-column head. It told, among other things, what capacity for survivors each of the potential rescue ships had. More mathematics.

The last edition, sent to press at 3:30 A.M., reported flatly that the great Titanic had gone down. All day Monday, and even into Monday night, the White Star Line withheld official confirmation of what Van Anda had deduced—only to concede at last, with heavy heart, that he had been right.

No one seemed to notice it that morning, but Page 11 in The

Times had a pathetic two-column ad—"The Largest Steamer in the World, 45,000-Ton Titanic, Sails from New York April 20, 12 Noon."

The Titanic was buried even then, two miles deep in mid-Atlantic.

When Ochs wandered onto the news floor next morning he was astonished to see Birchall, red-eyed from lack of sleep, still at his desk. The night editor had worked out a tentative schedule for Arthur Greaves, day city editor, indicating sources that might be tapped for follow-up stories.

On Tuesday, Wednesday and Thursday mornings, Times coverage of the Titanic disaster was talked of everywhere. London, Paris and Rome cabled praise. Newspapers here and abroad that had timidly held off on the story because they had thought the liner unsinkable had leaned heavily on reprints from The Times.

But they had not yet seen the ultimate in disaster news coverage. On Thursday afternoon Greaves assembled his entire staff—every man except the few on court runs and other routine beats. Among them were veterans and comparatively green hands, like the round-faced boy with the thick-lensed glasses, Alexander Woollcott.

Greaves was characteristically calm. While Van Anda was nervously going into his hand-washing act Greaves told the staff: "The Carpathia, with Titanic survivors, is due tonight around 9 o'clock. She has not answered wireless requests for information. A. P. just sent us this note: 'We have no assurance that we will get any wireless news from the Carpathia as this vessel studiously refuses to answer all queries. Even President Taft's requests for information, addressed to the Carpathia, have been ignored.' "

The day editor explained that each newspaper had been allowed only four pier passes for the Carpathia's arrival, and that no reporters were to be permitted aboard until the last survivor had been debarked, which would be well past first-edition time.

Greaves then disclosed his Carpathia work schedule. On Tuesday V. A. had hired a floor in the Strand Hotel at Fourteenth Street and Eleventh Avenue, a short block from where the Carpathia would dock, and had installed four telephones directly connected with rewrite desks on The Times news room floor uptown.

Greaves said: "I'm sending sixteen of you down to the pier, even though we have only these four passes. Men without passes will have to try to get through to survivors—crew and passengers—on their police cards. If that can't be done they will work as close in as they can and get survivors leaving the pier in cabs."

As soon as a reporter had a story he was to rush to the Strand and be assigned to one of four waiting rewrite men. Tommy Bracken was to act as traffic man in the hotel, posting the list of survivors interviewed on the wall to avoid duplication and waste of time. If two men got the same survivor story, the man with the second version was to go back to try for fresh material.

Greaves turned to the four men who had the pier cards. He told them: "I'm counting on you for the main survivor stories. Get all you can. Get Captain Rostrom of the Carpathia. Get Bruce Ismay of White Star. Get every possible member of the Titanic crew, especially the four officers who were saved. We must get the Titanic wireless man's story, if he's alive, and we want the Carpathia's wireless man." The city editor gave specific assignments to each of the four men with passes.

Then he ticked off other names for specific stories: A man to write a general piece on the Carpathia's arrival. A man to write arrangements for survivor relief. Three men to make rounds of midtown hotels to reach survivors not available at the pier. A man to cover the tugboats sent to escort the Carpathia up the river. A reporter to cover crowds. Another to cover police arrangements.

The imperturbable Greaves re-emphasized the need for copy that would tell how Astor, Straus, Millet, and the Titanic's skipper, had died.

He said: "If our four Strand Hotel wires are jammed, we have three more telephones lined up in Twenty-third Street and Eleventh Avenue, with cars to take you to them. You will recognize our chauffeurs. We have printed Times cards for them to wear in their hats. The Times switchboard has orders to keep every line but one open to Titanic copy only."

The reporters listened tensely. The city editor said, "Any questions, now, before you leave?" There were a few. Greaves answered them. He said: "We will have extra cars for men who happen to pick up pictures, with chauffeurs to get them into the office without time loss. If cars are needed for any other unforeseen reason, they will be there for you to use." There was a pause. Greaves waved his arms. "That's it, men. Go to it." The staff went out in a herd.

Van Anda, meanwhile, had tried to reach Guglielmo Marconi. The inventor lived at the Holland House, but had gone to 254 West 123d Street to talk with John Bottomley, his American manager. The managing editor sent a Times reporter to Bottomley's. Marconi and Bottomley were at dinner. Marconi told the reporter he intended to board the Carpathia to talk with the wireless operators—they were all on the Marconi System payroll in those days—after the ship had been cleared of survivors.

Van Anda was in quiet frenzy. The whole story would have to be gathered, assembled and in type within the three hours between the Carpathia's arrival at 9:30 P.M. and first-edition time at 12:30 A.M., and he was ready to devote almost the entire Friday Times to it. He talked with Marconi, persuaded him to leave for the Carpathia's pier immediately and to do his utmost to take Jim Speers, The Times man, aboard with him. Van Anda and Marconi were friends. William Reick had introduced them when Reick arranged for the first Times wireless service in 1907. Ochs was the inventor's close friend, too. Marconi left his dinner unfinished. At Van Anda's suggestion, he gave up the idea of going to the pier by automobile and went downtown with Speers and Bottomley on the Ninth Avenue Elevated Line. V.A. knew what could happen to a motor car in traffic.

The Times car awaited the inventor, his manager, and The Times reporter as they came down the steps at the Fourteenth Street station. Van Anda had figured out even that detail. The chauffeur drove them to the edge of the great throng as the Carpathia, with more than 700 survivors waving to hysterical kin in the crowd, was warped to her pier. It was 9.35 P.M. Straining policemen were holding back the 30,000 persons who had crowded the pier area. Ten thousand others had waited at the Battery to see the rescue ship pull in.

Red-faced policemen were hostile to Marconi and his companions when they fought their way through the outer throng. The policemen stubbornly repeated: "No one gets through these lines. These are orders. You'll have to stay back." They thrust at Marconi and his escorts. Speers called out: "You'd better get your commanding officer here. Mr. Marconi has official business on the Carpathia. It's important." The policemen reluctantly relayed this message down the line, and an inspector came up.

"All right," the nearest policeman finally conceded. "Mr. Marconi can come, and his manager—but no reporters." The gods were with The Times that night. This over-zealous policeman had already figured out in his own mind—Heaven only knows how—which were Marconi and his manager. He put his hand against Bottomley's chest and with evident relish thrust him deep into the crowd. Marconi and Speers stood in the clear, on the dock. They were escorted up the gangplank to the wireless room.

Dark-haired Harold Bride was still working the key. Blue flame spurted from under his tired fingers. His eyes were hollows in his head, from exhaustion. "His face was spiritual, something you might expect in a painting," the reporter said later. He did not recognize Marconi immediately; the cabin was ill-lighted. Then his eyes flared. He extended a heavy hand and the inventor grasped it warmly. Bride said: "Mr. Marconi, Phillips is dead. He's gone." He told how Phillips had calmly sent the first message to the Carpathia:

"Come at once. We've struck a berg. It's CQD, old man." Then later, "Come at once, our engine room is flooded to the boilers."

That was why the Titanic had fallen so tragically silent. The seas had drowned her batteries.

Harold Bride, at Marconi's request, told his version of the Titanic's sinking to Speers, who took it verbatim. It was to run five columns wide on the front page next morning, one of the most gripping sea stories in history. Innocent of literary pretense, it was to cause weeping from one end of the world to the other. There was a copyright line on Bride's story, and on Coltani's rescue account, which ran five columns wide on Page 2. No other newspaper had either of them.

Between 9:30 P.M. and 12:30 A.M. the Tower's upper floors hummed with activity. Van Anda was in his element. Marconi came in to watch in fascination as the story took shape. This was Van Anda's greatest journalistic achievement. Top men in the profession everywhere conceded that. No other great news story anywhere had been nearly so well organized.

Fifteen of Friday morning's twenty-four pages were devoted to the Titanic disaster. The front-page eight-column headline read:

745 SAW TITANIC SINK WITH 1,595, HER BAND PLAYING;
HIT ICEBERG AT 21 KNOTS AND TORE HER BOTTOM OUT;
'I'LL FOLLOW THE SHIP,' LAST WORDS OF CAPTAIN SMITH;
MANY WOMEN STAYED TO PERISH WITH THEIR HUSBANDS

From the staggering flow of survivor accounts, Endicott Rich, top Times rewrite man, had written a quiet lead for the main story:

"In a clear starlit night that showed a clear deep blue sea for miles and miles, the Titanic, an hour after she had struck a submerged iceberg at full speed, head-on, sank slowly to her ocean grave.

"Her band, lined on deck, was playing pleasant music as she sank in full view of the boatloads of her wretched survivors, and those left of her passengers and crew—fully two-thirds—stood quietly resigned on deck, awaiting the final plunge."

These subdued lines had incredible emotional impact, and most of the other stories were pitched in the same low key. Stark fact, simply told, was more powerful than any purple writing.

Estimates of the drowned and of survivors, as published in The Times, were somewhat off, as they were in newspapers everywhere, because the facts and figures were gathered in extreme haste to make deadlines. Subsequent investigation by a Senate Committee established that the Titanic had carried a total of 2,223 souls when she sailed from Britain. Of these 1,517 were drowned and 706 were saved.

That edition of The Times with the round-up of the Titanic story became a collector's item. Trade journals warmly praised it, here and abroad. Long afterward, when Carr Van Anda, visiting in London, called at Lord Northcliffe's Daily Mail, Northcliffe's editor opened a desk drawer at his right hand. In it lay The New York Times of April 19, 1912.

He said: "We keep this as an example of the greatest accomplishment in news reporting."

C H A P T E R
19

W<small>HEN</small> the Kaiser threw the fat in the fire with his ultimatum to
Czar Nicholas in the summer of 1914, The Times was already
firmly established as a newspaper of record.

The end of an era was approaching then, and the changes showed
in The Times day by day. The world of 1914 was a simpler world
than that we know now. It was a place where a man could buy an
imported overcoat for $15 or a Ford runabout for $440; in which a
Times Sunday real estate supplement of twenty pages was
crammed with pleas by landlords to New Yorkers to rent "seven,
large, sunny rooms" for $52 a month "with big concessions." A man,
then, could eat his fill at Maxim's in West Thirty-eighth Street for
60 cents, and the waiter's eyes would be misty with gratitude for
the dime tip. Reisenweber's on Columbus Circle gave a full dinner
with frogs' legs for $1.25, and served less exotic fare for $1.

The World War was to end all that. It was to halt experiments
toward speedier transportation and communication for peaceful
uses. A month before Europe trembled to the clump of German
boots, The Times carried long stories on Glenn Curtiss' experiments
at Hammondsport, N.Y., with a hydroplane in which Lieut. John
C. Porte was to try to conquer the Atlantic. It front-paged details
of a meeting in London at which Godfrey Isaacs, a Marconi representative, told of experiments with trans-Atlantic wireless telephone. The Britons at this meeting could not quite believe such a
miracle possible.

Even Sir Rider Haggard, creator of such fantastic stories as

"She," "Ayesha" and "King Solomon's Mines," who was on the committee, was inclined to be incredulous. He asked the Marconi man: "You really expect the time when a subscriber can have a telephone in his house by which he can telephone all over the world?" Isaacs assured him it not only was possible but might even be achieved within the next ninety days. Experimental equipment was under construction for tests between Carnarvon, Wales, and New York.

But the Curtiss plane did not risk the Atlantic and Marconi's tests did not come off—not then. Ominous little clouds in the shape of cabled dispatches from Central Europe showed up in The Times in late July, 1914. These were to swell, blacken and obscure all peaceful progress.

Early in 1908 William C. Reick, general manager, who was a news executive, among other things, had assigned William Bayard Hale, a former Episcopalian minister who had exchanged his pastorate in Middleboro, Mass., for journalism, to write a series on President Theodore Roosevelt.

Reick liked the stories so well that he sent Hale abroad to try for a similar series on Kaiser Wilhelm II. The German ruler was not inclined to permit a pen portrait in the manner of the Roosevelt stories, but agreed to grant an interview.

On June 19, 1908, he spoke blisteringly for two hours on the deck of the imperial yacht Hohenzollern off Bergen, Norway, while Hale just listened, completely fascinated but hiding his shock at the German ruler's intemperate utterances.

The Kaiser railed against Britain and her "ninny" rulers. He called her a "traitor to the white man's cause" in her dealings with Japan, and blasted loud and long at the "Yellow menace." He said flatly that he expected to go to war against Britain.

Then he inveighed against the Roman Catholic Church. He argued that the future belonged, as he put it, to the blond man, the Anglo-Teuton of Northern Europe, and that only Protestantism could save the future.

"The Bible," he told Hale, "is full of good fighting—jolly good fights . . . It is a mistaken idea that Christianity has no countenance for war. We are Christians by reason of forcible conversion."

When Hale got ashore he committed the Emperor's remarks to

paper at once and ended up with a 5,000-word memorandum.

He did not dare put even a summary of the interview on the cables. Instead he notified Reick, "Just had two hours' audience with Emperor. Result so startling that I hesitate to report it without censorship of Berlin."

"Impossible advise," Reick cabled back to Hale, "except anxious avoid even appearance betrayed confidence. Consult Lowenfeld or Hill."

Hill was United States Ambassador to Germany. Lowenfeld was in the German Foreign Office.

With this message on its way, Reick sent Hale's cablegram to Ochs.

Hale, meanwhile, had completed his lengthy memorandum, all from memory. He had not taken a note during the interview for fear that sight of pad and pencil might stop the Emperor's flow.

When the memorandum was complete he wrote a letter to Reick quoting extensively from it. It was dynamite, almost every line of it; enough dynamite to shake the civilized world.

On June 23 Hale wrote again from Berlin. He had seen Ambassador Hill and had talked with the heads of the German Foreign Office. They were horrified. They pleaded with Hale to suppress the story entirely.

Hale came home, and after Ochs, Reick, Van Anda and Miller had discussed the memorandum at length, they sent Hale to Washington with it so that the President could look it over.

The Kaiser had praised Roosevelt highly during the interview and had expressed warm friendship for the United States, but the President, like the others, was startled by the violent language Kaiser Wilhelm had used about Britain, Japan and other nations.

"Astonishing stuff," the President called it, and said: "I don't believe the Emperor wanted this stuff published. If he did, he's a goose. Yet I know he's very impulsive."

The President said that the interview should never be published. He had no power to prevent its publication, but he thought The Times would save mankind great agony by killing the story. Ochs thought so, too. He filed the memorandum and all correspondence concerning it in his private safe.

Hale put comparatively harmless portions of the interview—

mostly on religion—together for publication in the December issue of Century Magazine, then still run by Richard Watson Gilder, the man who had been judge in the "All the News That's Fit to Print" contest.

Even this, though, greatly worried the Kaiser's Cabinet. They got in touch with Hale again, and on his plea the thinned-down interview was withdrawn from the magazine, after the Century for December had gone to press. Two fiction pieces were fitted into the space the article had occupied and the interview type and all the printed copies were set aside.

A German cruiser came all the way from the homeland to take the type and the printed pages aboard. Both went into the ship's furnace, at sea.

The World and The New York American subsequently got wind of Hale's terrifying interview, and of the killing of the Century article. They ran pieces about them, but they never got Hale's text. Eventually the danger blew over.

Hale's story was to lie in Ochs' safe for more than three decades, hidden even from the publisher's own family. It was not to become public until after Ochs' death, when small bits of it ran in an article in The Times Magazine on July 16, 1939. At that time Adolf Hitler was publicly uttering much the same sort of stuff.

On Page 4 of The New York Times on July 22, 1914, a brief piece out of Berlin carried the headline: "European War Spectre Revived." The bank added: "Austrian-Servian Situation Fraught with Ominous Possibilities."

Four days later appeared the four-column headline:

> AUSTRIA BREAKS WITH SERVIA;
> KING PETER MOVES HIS CAPITAL;
> RUSSIA IS MOBILIZING HER ARMY;
> BERLIN AND PARIS MOBS FOR WAR

Frederic W. Wile, The Times man in Germany, sent a story from Berlin for the July 26 edition telling that, "This capital is afire tonight with war fever," and how Berliners swarmed through the streets shouting, "War!" "War!"

From The Times bureau in Paris came the story, "Tonight crowds on the Boulevards are shouting, 'To Berlin!' 'To Berlin!'" Then came the rumble and thunder of battles, and The Times sent all its European staff to watch them, and report them.

Van Anda could never get too much on the war. As great armies shifted and maneuvered, his men shifted and maneuvered with them. Ochs had worked out a news exchange with The London Chronicle and was able to give the United States superlative war coverage.

Wile was arrested as a spy and expelled from Germany, but Cyril Brown took his place and did a magnificent job of covering the German armies until America entered the war in 1917, when he had to pull out. Garet Garrett got to Berlin in 1915 and later Oscar King Davis, who had obtained the Republican platform beat for Van Anda in 1908, did a revelatory series on Germany's economic situation and wartime morale. Wythe Williams sent colorful descriptions of battle scenes, and George Le Hir's dispatches from the French front were war classics.

On Sunday, Aug. 23, 1914, The New York Times ran six tight, full pages on "The Complete Correspondence That Led Up To England's Declaration of War Against Germany." It was the so-called British White Paper, made up of 159 items of diplomatic correspondence between the British Foreign Office and the Central Powers. Beside it, for Times readers' guidance, was a sort of cast of characters so the reader could identify all the diplomats involved.

The White Paper had been brought to the United States by a minister, the Rev. Dr. Frederick Lynch, who had got it from a friend in the Foreign Office. He had turned it over to a Times ship-news man. No other copies of it had reached this country at the time; not even official Washington had them. The correspondence gave Times readers the full picture of British negotiations up to the moment that Austria and Germany sent their armed hosts against their neighbors.

On Monday, Aug. 24, The Times was able to give Germany's version of events leading to her war declaration. It had been brought home by Wile, fresh from Berlin. It was run exactly as the Kaiser's diplomatic aides had written it, without alteration, as the British White Paper had been. It was another clear Times beat. No other copy of this text had been sent to the United States. Wile reached

The Times Annex with it while Britain's White Paper was still thundering from The Times presses. The foreign desk went to work on it immediately and it was in type Sunday afternoon.

In Europe, meanwhile, as the Kaiser's armies overran Belgium, The Times carried lengthy accounts of battles and bombardments in Lille, Liége, Namur. Wherever it was possible, it carried the versions of both sides. The Sunday rotogravure sections, freshly introduced by The Times from Germany, carried page after page of excellent war photographs, clearer and better than anything previously seen in this country. Ochs had bought the rotogravure presses in April, 1914, after Van Anda, on a trip abroad, had investigated them and seen their great journalistic value.

On Aug. 26, 1914, The Times front-paged a story under the headline: "Zeppelin Bombs Fall In Antwerp." It told how, on the day before, "for the first time in history a great civilized community had been bombarded from the sky." Every line of the story indicated the extreme shock and horror such warfare had brought.

A Times editorial next day naïvely said: "It is not conceivable that the officers of the German Army would permit themselves to carry on war in such a manner," and in later issues military experts predicted that the Kaiser's airships would never attempt to bomb such great cities as London and Paris. It was wishful thinking. The subsequent bitter history of aerial warfare proves how wrong they were.

The Times became an open forum on war issues. Editorially it placed the blame for the war on Austria and Germany, holding that if Kaiser Wilhelm had not willed it, there would have been no conflict. It ran impartially, however, every word of evidence presented in the White Papers, Blue Books, Orange Papers, Yellow Books, printed by all the warring nations. In each case it gave these official documents in full, which no other publication did. The American reader then had a chance to fix in his own mind where he thought the blame for the war should be placed. College groups and high schools eagerly sought the official papers. The demand for them became so great that The Times put them out as pamphlets that it sold at cost. They were used in classroom discussions and in debates.

In the pro-German hue and cry the accusation most often hurled at Ochs and his newspaper was that they were controlled by British interests, and that Lord Northcliffe of The Times of London had a hand in Ochs' policy. Actually when war came in 1914, Ochs and Lord Northcliffe were not friends. In negotiations for an exchange of news service—and their relationship never got beyond that in the fifteen years they knew each other—there was a bitter split, just before World War I. Ochs then worked out an exchange with The London Chronicle, instead, that gave him the services of such men as Philip Gibbs. That was the full extent of British interest in The New York Times.

Curiously enough, The Times was also attacked during World War I by pro-Allies readers. Their anger stemmed from The Times' attempts, before the United States entered the conflict, to present to readers the arguments put forward by the Germans as well as those put forward by the Allies. It was Ochs' conviction that even during a war it was his journal's function to give "ALL the news . . ." Anyone with half an eye, though, could not have misunderstood the newspaper's editorial opinion as distinct from its news. On Dec. 15, 1914, Charles Miller's lead piece, "For the German People, Peace With Freedom," gave clear evidence of The Times' attitude.

". . . The headstrong, misguided, and dangerous rulers of Germany," it said, "are going to be called to stern account and the reckoning will be paid by the German people in just the proportion that they make common cause with the blindly arrogant ruling class."

It was to be the same in later years. Whenever The Times gave both sides of any controversy, it was attacked simultaneously by readers whose sympathies were with one side or the other.

But abuse did not change Times policy. The newspaper gave both sides of the war just as long as it was possible to do it.

In March, 1915, two Times executives were haled before a Senatorial Committee to explain the newspaper's editorial opposition to the Administration's measure proposing the purchase of interned shipping. Both Carr Van Anda and Charles Miller were sharply cross-examined by Senator Tom Walsh of Montana, the committee chairman. It developed that one motive for the hearing was a letter insinuating that British interests—again the British interests—had spurred The New York Times into action against the Administration's ship-purchase bill.

Van Anda was the first witness. It might be well to explain, at this point, that almost as soon as the war started, The Times, The World and The Tribune had pooled some of their war news because there were insufficient communications facilities for the sudden flood of war stories from Europe.

On Sept. 8, 1914, all three newspapers had carried a pooled London dispatch telling that British steamship lines were charging United States refugees excessive rates for transportation home from war zones. Senator Walsh pointed out that while The Tribune and The World dispatches were similar, The Times had made certain deletions. He wanted to know why.

"The action of certain steamship companies in taking what is considered a disgraceful and unfair advantage of Americans forced to return home, by raising rates, will shortly be made the subject of an official report and complaint to the State Department," both The World and The Tribune dispatches had stated.

". . . The situation illustrates what would be at least one advantage of Government-owned passenger steamers. If they were available now, they could afford to create competition which would compel the English lines to keep their rates normal."

Van Anda conceded that all three newspapers had received the dispatch in the same form.

"I observe," said the Senator, "that the adjective 'disgraceful' in the passage 'what is considered a disgraceful and unfair advantage of Americans forced to return home' and so on, appears in both The Tribune and The World printing. It is omitted in The Times. Can you tell us whether the adjective was in the dispatch as it came to The Times?"

The managing editor could not recall that particular word, but, he said, The Times did not allow reporters or correspondents to express opinions in news stories.

"You allowed them to say it was 'unfair,' " Senator Walsh insisted, and he read from the dispatch: "The action of certain steamship companies in taking what is considered an unfair advantage"?

"What is considered unfair." [Van Anda emphasized the word "considered."] "The word 'unfair' is referred to the other people who hold that opinion. The correspondent is not allowed to express his opinion that it is unfair.' "

Why, then, demanded the Senator, did The Times allow the use of the word 'unfair' and strike out the word 'disgraceful' which was used in the same sentence?

"I think," the managing editor answered, "that perhaps our editor took the view that the writer was using rather too many adjectives and very wisely omitted one of them."

Senator Walsh wanted to know why The Times had deleted the last part of the dispatch.

Van Anda said: "That was done for the very good and sufficient reason that it was an expression of opinion by the writer. It is propagating one side of a case, which is a privilege we do not permit to correspondents and reporters. They may state the facts, but inferences are to be left to the editorial page, or to the understanding of the reader. That paragraph is very distinctly in advocacy of one side of the case, and it was stricken out according to an established rule."

Senator Walsh got around to the amount of ship advertising carried in The Times. The managing editor gave the linage figures. Ship advertising brought The Times at that period around $50,000 a year.

"Do you care to say anything about the question of whether or not the payment of that sum of money to The Times would influence its attitude or policy toward the shipping bill?" the Senator asked.

Ochs' news chief bristled. His answer came in sharp, clipped phrases:

"I have not the slightest hesitation in saying that the payment of that or any other sum of money by shipping interests, or any other interests, would have not one iota's influence upon the conduct of The Times."

He fixed the Senator with a cold stare.

The committee chairman still pressed the point:

"The attitude of opposition to the ship-purchase bill on the part of The Times would have been the same if that newspaper were not getting paid for advertising from that interest?"

Again Van Anda bristled. He said: "It would have been the same, unquestionably. If the committee means to imply that The New York Times can be purchased for $50,000 or for any other sum, The New York Times, I feel quite warranted in saying, very much resents any such imputation of any form of question designed to carry before the public on the record of this committee any such insinuation." He paused, and added: "That could be attributed only to malice or credulity."

"So that the rule that the counting house controls the editorial page is one to which you do not give credence?" the Senator asked.

Van Anda became even more emphatic. He said, "As far as our newspaper goes, the idea that the counting house should have anything to do with it is absurd."

Senator Walsh asked for a list of Times stockholders and Van Anda produced them:

"We have no hesitancy whatever in supplying any information about The New York Times," he said by way of preface. "We might perhaps question the right of anybody to ask it, but if the question of giving it were raised we would not hesitate to supply it."

He read the list: "There are forty-three stockholders of The Times, I believe. There are 10,000 shares of stock of the par value of $100 each, making $1,000,000 capital. Of these forty-three stockholders, seven who are employed daily in the production of The New York Times and none of whom has any other occupation, own 8,834 shares, a trifle over 83 per cent. There are five other stockholders, some of whom have been employed by The Times and some of whom are the heirs of deceased employes of The Times whose total holdings amount to 526 shares . . . Mr. Ochs is the president and the publisher of the newspaper, and he is actively engaged in that business and no other. He i there daily."

Miller followed the managing editor on the witness stand. He was as outspoken in his answers as Van Anda had been. He then owned 14 per cent of the New York Times stock, Adolph Ochs 62 per cent.

But the legend of British gold behind The New York Times died hard, even before the committee. Senator Walsh asked the editor in chief about an editorial printed in The Times on Jan. 20, 1915, in which he had written: "Those who have our moral approval or their contentions are in control of the seas and can get all the contraband they need."

"Who was meant," the Senator wanted to know, "by the expression, 'those who have our moral approval'?"

"The Allies," said Miller.

"And the pronoun 'our' refers to whom?"

"The American people."

"That was intended as a declaration that the cause of the Allies had the general moral approval of the American people?"

"We have often said that."

"That is the position which The Times has taken?"

"Repeatedly."

Miller was at his New England best, not wasting words. Then the Senator came up with the question based on "information" in the letter suggesting that Britons controlled The New York Times:

"Has The Times any business connections of any character in England?"

"None whatever, except that we maintain an office there and have our own employes there; our own correspondents. There is no business connection with anybody in England."

"Mr. Ochs appears to be the largest stockholder of The New York Times, according to Mr. Van Anda?"

"Yes."

"Are you able to tell us whether he has any financial support of any kind in England?"

"I can tell you that he has none. So far as any one man who is in daily association with another, in confidential relations with him, knows his business affairs, I can tell you positively that he has not."

"I asked," Senator Walsh explained, "because I was informed that that was the case."

"He has none whatever. I suppose I know the rumor to which you allude. It is absolutely false."

"What is the rumor?"

"It is one that has been circulated by persons who are not in sympathy with our course, that The London Times has some relation with us. It has none whatever."

Senator Walsh assured Miller at one point that the committee did not desire to restrain the liberty of the press.

"My feeling," the editor said, "is this, if you will permit me. We appear before the jury every day. We appear before a grand inquisition, one of the largest courts in the country. We are judged at breakfast time. If the judgment were adverse, the criminal would be dispatched to execution before a great while."

Senator Walsh said, "I think you can very safely trust to the rectitude of the great jury of which you speak."

Van Anda was interested in Senator Walsh's statement at the inquiry that he "was informed" that Britons controlled The New York Times. The Senator turned over to him the letter he had received before the hearing started that contained the statement on British control. The letter writer said he had heard at the Junior Constitutional Club in London that "a well-known Englishman has been backing Mr. Ochs with money to get control of The New York Times"; further, that, "I understand that Mr. Miller is also mixed up in some way with this Englishman," and that "the name of Lord Northcliffe was mentioned." The signature to the letter was difficult to decipher, but it looked like "Arthur M. Abbey." Inquiry in London established that no such person was known at the Junior Constitutional Club. Senator Walsh had no idea who "Arthur M. Abbey" might be. The signature resembled those affixed to a series of scurrilous letters that had been sent to The Times over the name of "G. M. Hubbell" and "A. A. Abbey." The writer was never identified. He never came forward to support his own statements.

Shortly after the Senate hearing the Lusitania was sunk by a German submarine off the Irish Coast on the afternoon of May 7, 1915, and Van Anda put out a pre-dawn extra that surpassed anything of its kind in the United States. He gave the whole front page to it, but he was almost clinical in his handling of even this story. While some other newspapers got violently emotional over the incident, even in their news columns, The Times reported the facts as it had received them, free from editorial opinion. The headline over the story was a model of strictly factual statement!

LUSITANIA SUNK BY A SUBMARINE, PROBABLY 1,260 DEAD; TWICE TORPEDOED OFF IRISH COAST; SINKS IN 15 MINUTES; CAPT. TURNER SAVED, FROHMAN AND VANDERBILT MISSING; WASHINGTON BELIEVES THAT A GRAVE CRISIS IS AT HAND

The fourth line was based on a story out of Washington that said: "Although they are profoundly reticent, officials realize that the tragedy, involving the lives of American citizens, is likely to bring about a crisis in the international relations of the United States."

In the summer of 1916 while some seventeen to twenty Times men covered the war fronts and sent stories on what was going on behind the lines, Van Anda outstripped other managing editors. He followed late war copy to the composing room and wrote banner heads for it then and there to save precious time at deadline. This short cut enabled The Times again and again to beat its competition where the race was measured in minutes.

The staff's attitude toward Van Anda was difficult to define. The men had a kind of reverence for his extreme efficiency, and his professional enthusiasm on a big story was apt to infect a reporter and be mistaken for warmth. It was never that. On the news room floor and in the composing room he seemed to have no more warmth than a deep-sea fish. At Shanley's, at the old Hermitage bar, or in front of Parrish's King Cole paintings at the Knickerbocker, and sometimes at office dinners, he seemed to thaw, but not like other men. But some feared Van Anda and swore he was nothing more than a humorless news-producing machine in man's dress. On the other hand they told about the day he wandered back to the sports department to ask who had written a certain race-horse story—a rather inept job—the paper had carried that morning. Van Anda studied the past performances of race horses with the same intensity that he dug into sea charts, battle formations and astronomical formulas, and there was one horse he favored above all others. It was the horse in this story. The editor told him the writer's name, and Van Anda turned away. But the sports editor was curious.

"Any special reason you wanted to know who had written that piece, Boss?" he asked.

Van Anda looked back over his shoulder. "Just wanted to be sure," he said. "I thought it was the horse wrote it."

It was almost twenty years now since Ochs had taken over The Times. In those two decades the staff had repeatedly had reason to thank its stars that the new publisher never backed down when he knew he was right, and that he just as fiercely defended the men who worked for him, when they were right. That went in advertising, as it did on the news side. It had become The Times man's boast that "the Boss will back you up in a fight," which he would, if his man's hands were clean.

This was reaffirmed when Alexander Woollcott, then six years on the paper and acting as its drama critic, got into a brush with the brothers Shubert, the theatrical producers. On Wednesday night, March 17, 1915—a perfect day for a shindy—they opened "Taking Chances," a bedroom bit with bastard French accent. Woollcott found it "not vastly amusing," even with Lou Tellegen doing well in his part, and tartly wrapped up his sentiments with the statement, "The complaint here is not that it is vulgar, but that it is quite tedious."

The Shuberts did not approve. They pointedly mailed a set of tickets for their next offering to Van Anda, and the note from Charles Dillingham that was wrapped around the tickets suggested that they would not be honored if Woollcott presented them, that the Times would have to assign another critic to the opening.

When Ochs heard this, he ordered Woollcott to buy his own ticket, which he did; but Jake Shubert and the doorman barred the theatre door against him. The publisher thought only a moment about his next step. He ordered his attorneys to obtain an injunction to restrain the Shuberts from barring his critic, and told his advertising department to throw out all Shubert advertising.

Barrooms and restaurants around Times Square—and down in Printing House Square, too—tingled to this combat. The unique vision of a publisher not only backing up his reporter, but also throwing out the offending customer's advertising, heartened the entire Fourth Estate. The Times won its injunction, and devoted many columns of space to stories on the litigation. Woollcott's Sunday drama column, "Second Thoughts on First Nights," was filled with controversial letters on the subject. Newspapers and magazines all over the country took it up.

Safely wrapped in the injunction, Woollcott reviewed "Trilby" when the Shuberts staged it at their theatre on Saturday night,

April 4, 1915. He liked the performance, and said so with warmth and enthusiasm. Van Anda put a Woollcott byline (the first, and for years, his only one) over it. It was only a gesture, but everyone seemed to understand.

Months later, the Shuberts had their day; the Appellate Division reversed the original decision. It unanimously held that a theatre owner could not, under law, bar a prospective patron because of the patron's race, creed or because of any class distinction; but that the owner had the right to bar a person from a theatre for any other private reason.

The Shubert-Times feud lasted, altogether, about twelve months. At the end of that time, the Shuberts realized that they needed Times advertising space. Ochs' paper had just added more than 38,500 subscribers and was well past the 305,000 mark—a greater gain than was shown by all other morning newspapers combined—and the Shuberts sensibly figured that the Ochs ban on their advertising was affecting the box office.

They yielded, with the understanding that they were to admit to their theatres any critic designated by the editor of The Times. Woollcott triumphantly eased himself back into his seat in critics' row. The Shuberts even sent him a box of cigars for Christmas, 1916, and as Samuel Hopkins Adams related in his Woollcott biography years afterward, the critic delighted in telling friends, "The whole thing went up in smoke."

Late in November, 1916, Van Anda was puzzled by a cryptic cablegram from Wythe Williams, head Times man in Paris. It suggested he read a piece but recently done for Collier's Weekly by Alden Brooks, a free-lance writer who occasionally wrote for The Times, too. Van Anda got the magazine. It was an article on the career of the French general Pétain. The managing editor sensed that Williams' cable was a bid for him to use Brooks' article as a code. He tried a tentative message to Paris:

"Does Brooks' man," he asked, "want a job with us?"

"Yes," Williams shot back. "We are dickering for him now."

Van Anda began to see the picture. General Pétain was involved in a change of command.

"Is Brooks' man," he cabled on Nov. 29, "to have only the French branch house or the entire firm? In any case, will the present local manager be provided with another place, possibly administrative?"

Williams replied, "He wants both offices."

The censor did not divine the portent of this exchange. It looked as if The Times was merely dickering for the services of a writer.

A second Williams message came through on the heels of the previous one:

"Think Brooks' man demands too much. Cannot give it to him."

The meaning was clear. Pétain not only wanted the French High Command; he wanted to head all the French, British and Belgian forces on the Western Front.

Van Anda cabled: "See if Brooks' man will accept Paris [French High Command] only."

Williams' answer was: "Brooks' man wants too much. Think it best to consider his assistant." A few hours later another Williams cable was put on the managing editor's desk. It said: "Assistant accepts."

Van Anda did some fierce hand-rubbing. Here was an exclusive story that would shake competition. On Dec. 7, 1916, The Times carried a long front-page story built around the information hidden in Williams' wires: "Joffre's Retirement Considered; French Army Chief May Go." The banks said: "Nivelle, Now Commander at Verdun, Suggested to Succeed Him. Pétain First Proposed. But Is Said To Have Demanded Larger Control Than France Alone Could Grant. Crisis Before Deputies. Washington Hears Secret Sessions in Paris are the Scene of a Momentous Debate."

The Times story bore a Washington dateline to protect the Paris source. It told that General Joffre was about to retire from active service, and that his post had been offered to General Pétain, the hero of Verdun. "Difficulties arose, however," said the story, "over accomplishing the contemplated change . . . Enough is known to indicate that Pétain's declination was due to a belief on his part that in order to achieve victory, he must be invested with greater authority than it was proposed to give him . . . Pétain, however, is credited with the suggestion that General Nivelle, who succeeded him in command of the forces at Verdun and who is his junior in rank, be placed in command of all the forces in France."

Van Anda ran pictures of both Pétain and Nivelle with the story, and sketches of their military careers. It nad been simple enough to guess that the "assistant" mentioned in the Williams cable was General Nivelle.

The story kicked up diplomatic and journalistic surf. Paris denied it. London scoffed at it. The Times held firm, and, on Dec. 12, 1916, Paris officially announced General Nivelle's succession to General Joffre's post.

On April 16, 1917, Williams revived his "Brooks' man" cables. His message to Van Anda was: "Brooks' man coming to fore again." This followed:

"Brooks' man's assistant unsatisfactory. Considering new man for his position."

On April 27, Van Anda cabled back:

"Both offers received here. Does Brooks' man want same place and terms as before?"

"Paris post again offered to Brooks' man," came the answer. Then: "Brooks' man accepts."

Away went Van Anda again in high glee. The Times, on April 29, had a clean beat on the story of General Pétain's elevation: "Command of Entire Front in France Offered to Pétain."

Marshal Joffre happened to be in the United States as head of a French Commission at the time. Van Anda made it clear that The Times exclusive did not come from him. The story said flatly:

"It must be stated that this information did not come from the French Commission now in Washington whose members profess ignorance of the contemplated change."

There was less hullabaloo about this story. Times competition was just about weary of trying to discount exclusives that were appearing with such monotonous regularity in Ochs' newspaper. And just as well, too. On May 15, the whole world had the Pétain story from official sources: "Pétain Placed in Command of French Armies."

The war was well over before Van Anda disclosed how these beats were obtained.

In the meantime, the situation had become darker and graver. The Times of April 3 had carried as a front-page eight-column banner the stark announcement:

PRESIDENT CALLS FOR WAR DECLARATION

CHAPTER
20

D RUM BEAT and bugle call in New York streets spread war fever through The Times plant. Young men left their desks and their machines for the services until 189 had gone. Older men joined reserve units to march and drill with extreme gravity and gusto but fortunately were not called. Sgt. Alexander Woollcott went overseas, and eventually onto the Army newspaper Stars and Stripes; Joyce Kilmer of the Sunday department became a sergeant in the Fighting Sixty-ninth; Julius Ochs Adler, the publisher's nephew, a reserve officer, went overseas as a company commander in the Seventy-seventh Division. Five Times men, Sergeant Kilmer among them, were to die in service.

With the United States in the war, cable costs swelled to $15,000 a week, more than $750,000 a year. Some of the executives were concerned, but not Ochs. When it came to the cost of news the sky was the limit. Cable charges on battle coverage, full-length war papers and important speeches in Europe cost more in a week than foreign news for Henry Raymond's Times cost in a year, but advertising and circulation leaped. The Times was compelled to leave out sixty to seventy columns of advertising a day so that there would be ample space for vital news. The linage omitted would have filled Raymond's newspaper twice over without allowing an inch for news.

Charles Grasty, a Baltimore newspaperman, who was with Ochs

in New York the night the publisher's daughter was born, sailed for France with Gen. John J. Pershing, but was diverted to the Paris bureau where news was piling up faster than the staff there could handle it. In February, 1918, Carr Van Anda carefully pondered a choice for his American Expeditionary Force correspondent. He picked Edwin L. James, a Virginian, then 28 years old, who had served brilliantly on the city staff and at the State Capitol in Albany. James, outfitted at Stern's and at Herbert and Taylor in Fifth Avenue, drew envious banter when he showed up in the city room in whipcords and trench coat, ready to sail.

He left in late February. By mid-March he was billeted at American General Staff Headquarters in France, learning what it was to leap from a cot in the dark, cold dawn and to shave in icy water before going in to lukewarm cereal and coffee. Walter Duranty, a Briton with warm literary talent and a rare eye for color and human interest, was with the hard-pressed French. Philip Gibbs was sending steadily from the British front in Belgium, and Wythe Williams was on the line with Yank units scattered among both French and British troops. He was recalled as soon as James had made his contacts and had learned the correspondent routine.

At home Van Anda concentrated fiercely on the newest war maps from London, Paris and from Washington. He knew that soon, somewhere on Europe's spring-sodden chessboard, decisive action was due. He sensed that the German High Command had to risk a last gamble before the A.E.F. was battle-hardened and sufficiently large to tip the scales for the Allies.

When Ludendorff launched a major offensive March 21, 1918, Van Anda gave the story banner headlines. He said: "This is it." He cabled to Paris, London and to the listening post at Berne commanding that after March 21 all dispatches be sent at "double urgent" rate (75 cents a word) to insure immediate delivery. Van Anda kept the cables hot with messages.

"Fine dispatches Monday as throughout battle which began March 21," he told Duranty. "Times the only American newspaper printing dispatches of current date from battlefront." A few days later he asked Charles Selden in Paris to forward to James the message: "Job of our men is to beat everybody on American fighting. Send full rate double urgent." In April, as the Germans were hurled back he flashed, "Thanks to men London, Paris and front overwhelmingly beaten everybody since big battle began."

James wrote a moving piece on the death of Colonel Griffiths, an American hero, describing his burial under screaming shells in the rain while enemy planes strafed. When the story was finished James rode through a downpour on horseback to press headquarters to make certain of immediate transmission. He learned with some bitterness, later, that this story had been cut to bare detail by American censors. Van Anda, quick to back up his staff, got after George Creel of the censorship staff. He won mild censorship reforms.

In June, James was in the fighting at Château-Thierry, sending action stuff every day. His battle descriptions early in that month were a clean thirty-six hours ahead of competition.

So it went, without letdown, into early fall. Toll charges at "double urgent" unbalanced the office war budget, but the beats piled up consistently to the embarrassment of other newspapers. The Times was serving history red hot, and more of it than any newspaper in the world.

There was some talk in August of sending Times proofs to Europe by troopship each week for an overseas version of The New York Times, to be printed in Paris, but on Aug. 28 the idea was abandoned. On that date the managing editor cabled to Charles Selden: "Ochs says proposition has attractions but does not wish at present to embark on any new enterprises." It was just as well, perhaps. The staff was already straining fiercely to keep up with the news flow.

By mid-September the Germans were in full rout and again Van Anda applied the spurs to his correspondents by cable.

Austria, exhausted, put out a peace bid. It reached the home office on a Sunday, Sept. 15, when Ochs was in his summer home at Lake George. Van Anda read details of the Austrian proposal over the telephone to Charles Miller at his home in Great Neck, Long Island, and to Ochs in the Adirondacks. The managing editor was jubilant. He told both, "This is the Beginning of the End." Miller, apparently inspired by Van Anda's enthusiasm, wrote an editorial on the subject. When it was finished he dictated it by telephone to the office, and it went into the paper that night. It was written in utter good faith by a patriotic American whose previous war editorials had won praise and approval everywhere but in enemy countries. This one, though, almost stopped The New York Times in its tracks.

The editorial advocated that the Austrian bid for a "non-binding" discussion be considered. It said: "Reason and humanity demand that the Austrian invitation be accepted. The case for conference is presented with extraordinary eloquence and force, a convincing argument is made for an exchange of views that may remove old and recent misunderstandings . . . We cannot imagine that the invitation will be declined . . . When we consider the deluge of blood that has been poured out in this war, the incalculable waste of treasure, the ruin it has wrought, the grief that wrings millions of hearts because of it, we must conclude that only the madness or the soulless depravity of someone of the belligerent powers could obstruct or defeat the purpose of the conference."

Angry protest rolled in upon The Times from almost every corner of the earth—from New York, Washington, London, Paris, Rome and Belgium. Denunciatory letters and telegrams came from groups and wrathful individuals. Searing editorials appeared in contemporary dailies. The Times was accused of "running up the white flag." Even in its own city room staff members muttered against accepting anything but outright, abject surrender from a foe already on his knees.

The Union League Club of New York scheduled a meeting for Sept. 26, 1918, to consider public denunciation of The Times for the editorial. Nothing dismayed Ochs more than this; the Union League members were the most prominent and most influential men in New York.

Ochs did not know it at the time, but some of the foremost Union Leaguers flatly refused to attend the meeting. Chauncey M. Depew of The New York Central Railroad, one of the greatest orators of the period, wrote to Henry C. Quinby, the club secretary:

"I heard today that there is to be a meeting tomorrow evening to take action on a recent editorial in The New York Times. The editorial was unfortunate, but it is the first and only offense of a great journal whose opportunities to make mistakes occur on every one of the three hundred and sixty-five days of the year. The editorial was written late at night and the writer was in the country meeting a situation as it had been represented to him.

"No newspaper in the United States has done during the four years of the war better service, or is doing better, for the vigorous prosecution of the war, day by day, than The New York Times.

"The question has really become, what can rival newspapers make for their own benefit, and out of The Times, because of this slip of the pen? I do not think, in view of all the circumstances, the matter justifies any action by such a distinguished and important organization as ours."

The great jurist Elihu Root wired to the club secretary from Clinton, N.Y.:

"Regret cannot attend proposed meeting of club. In view of immense service rendered by The Times and its unquestionable loyalty, I think its temporary aberration regarding the Austrian note should not be made occasion for attack and I see no real occasion for special meeting of the club."

In a message to Louis Wiley later, Mr. Root confided that while he could not agree with Miller's viewpoint he could appreciate the argument upon which it was based. He wrote: "I wanted to make the club feel that granting their premises nothing could be more foolish than starting a quarrel among the defenders of the faith. I am glad to see that they cooled down and passed a temperate, innocuous and patriotic resolution."

Frank W. Woolworth of the five-and-ten-cent store chain refused to attend the meeting, too. He telegraphed that he thought the idea "unnecessary and undignified."

"There is no more loyal newspaper in the United States than The New York Times," he wrote to the club secretary. "Nothing should be done to impair the influence of The New York Times, which is foremost in its devotion to the welfare of the United States."

Ochs was utterly bewildered under the bludgeoning. Much of it was directed at him personally as publisher, though he had not seen the editorial before it appeared in print. Friends cut him dead. He sat, with the mail piled around him, like a man dazed by a head blow. He felt, in that hour, as if all he had struggled to build was about to be washed away in this surge of unreasonable anger. The experience all but broke the publisher, who was intensely patriotic.

Nothing, even in the darkest Chattanooga days, even approached the harm this wrought.

The moment dispatches told of the Austrian peace bid, Van Anda had cabled to his men in London, Paris and Berne for reactions to it. "Make good showing on Austrian peace proposal," he had ordered. "Get brief interviews important people—statesmen, journalists, asking morning papers for advance proofs for editorial comments. Send full rate." The Miller editorial had not been written when this cable left. Van Anda's orders were for routine coverage. He sent such messages on all vital stories.

Then the reverberations came. Ernest Marshall, London bureau chief for The New York Times, cabled back that the Washington correspondent of Lord Northcliffe's Times had sent a bitter piece about the Miller editorial. "New York Times unrepresentative of American opinion," Marshall cabled, paraphrasing the British correspondent. "Vigor with which its views are almost everywhere repudiated proves this to be the case. Even New York Times recognizes this today. It attempts to explain yesterday's faux pas by arguing that the conference would be the best way to get Central Powers to accept inevitable. This is not national, or official, view."

Marshall added his own observation that "New York Times Monday editorial caused flurry here and was subject much anxious speculation."

Ordinarily, Miller would have read his editorial in proof before passing it for publication which was traditional practice. A rereading might have led him to rephrase it, but since he was at Great Neck and not in his office that Sunday he got no proofs. As the fat crackled in the journalistic pan, Miller himself was bewildered.

He asked friends, among them President Eliot of Harvard, for their opinions. Dr. Eliot agreed with Miller's reasoning in the editorial, but indicated he thought some of the phrasing indiscreet. He did write, though, to say: "On the whole I see nothing wrong with it."

Ochs was pressed to publish some statement to let the world know that he had not seen the editorial before it went into print and that he did not approve of it. He said: "I could not do such a thing. I have always accepted public praise and public approval of the many great editorials Mr. Miller has written for The Times. When there is blame instead of praise I must share that, too."

Ochs was perhaps most deeply perturbed when he learned that President Wilson had openly stormed in the White House after reading Miller's editorial, and that the President had asked his aides to find out whether it had been cabled to Europe.

On Ochs' plea Henry Morgenthau Sr. arranged a private meeting between the publisher and Col. Edward M. House, the President's chief confidant. Ochs poured his heart out to House, explaining how the piece had gone into print without his knowledge. He pointed out that The Times had been consistently pro-Ally and fervently American.

But criticism kept pouring in on him, and on the paper, and he suggested to friends the idea of retiring from active interest in The Times; of possibly putting it into the hands of publicly chosen trustees who had no financial interest in it. He was talked out of that.

The crisis pointed up Ochs' attitude toward the journal he had rewrought. He thought of it then, and to his death, as a kind of public institution of which he had only temporary charge. He was fiercely determined that no individual, no favored group, was ever to use it for self-glorification or for selfish advantage.

The only important editorial voice raised in The Times' defense in this crisis was Frank Munsey's. That strange man, whom newspapermen generally regarded as bloodlessly cold, ran an editorial in The Sun that said, in effect, that the Miller editorial was sincere, honest and not unpatriotic. Ochs always remembered this kindness, virtually the only warm light in the sudden darkness. He was touchingly grateful to Munsey.

By and by anger's tide washed back, and the publisher could breathe again. Austria surrendered unconditionally. The war rushed toward a climax. There were recurring rumors that the Germans, stubbornly yielding ground to British, French and Yank armies, could not hold out much longer. On Thursday, Nov. 7, 1918, The Times carried a front-page box from Duranty at Marshal Foch's headquarters telling that the German rout was already on; that the Kaiser's hordes were retreating pell-mell toward home borders.

"For the first time," Duranty wrote for that morning's paper, "I can affirm with confidence that the end is in sight."

At the same moment, Edwin James was pushing forward with the Americans who were driving the Germans before them in panicky masses, while Gibbs' dispatches clearly showed that Generals Haig and Pétain had the Germans in full retreat from the Meuse to the Scheldt.

On Nov. 7 at noon in New York the United Press released a bulletin from Paris. It said: "Urgent. Armistice Allies-Germany signed eleven this morning. Hostilities ceased two this afternoon. Sedan taken by Americans." No such word had reached The Times. Van Anda was stunned. Cables went hot with his messages to London and Paris. It developed that Roy Howard of the United Press had picked up the armistice rumor in Brest, though it had originated at an American Club luncheon in Paris. Howard filed at Brest for transmission to New York one hour before Marshal Foch was to meet the German delegation for opening negotiations.

Premature or not, the bulletin plunged this country and Canada into an unparalleled celebration orgy. Streets filled with shrill women and hoarse men using their lungs until they gave out. Factory whistles were tied down. River craft let go in chorus and kept it up for hours.

James Gibbons Huneker, Times music critic, watched the delirious demonstration in Times Square on his way to the office, and then tapped out a piece somewhat out of his ordinary line.

He covered the Big Noise as he would a concert, wrote learnedly of "diapasonic profundities" and told how "rumor, the invisible conductor, waved his wand and every man, woman and child began playing on the instrument nearest at hand, from toothcomb to cannon." He saw the great mob of uninhibited demonstrators as "a many-throated monster" and decided that "only TNT could have outdone this symphony."

Though Van Anda had covered every news angle of the unprecedented celebration, he coldly relegated it to the last line of a banner. His headline was a dignified "German Delegates on Way to Meet Foch; False Peace Report Rouses All America."

While the city writhed and roared outside his office windows, the managing editor alerted his European staff for the true armistice story. He cabled Duranty: "Assume you are watching for armistice meeting. Flash bulletins French Cable double rates. Be very careful facts. False U. P. report of armistice stopped business, set America wild this afternoon."

On Nov. 9, Selden flashed word to Van Anda that Duranty had not been able to establish proper contacts at Marshal Foch's Headquarters. The Marshal had been angered by the U. P.'s premature armistice story. It had robbed the Marshal's pending announcement of its dramatic effect.

"Poor Duranty is in Paris today, brokenhearted," Selden told the managing editor by cable. "I had imagined him hovering about Foch's Headquarters for the Armistice, getting one of the great stories of this war, but Foch has ordered all correspondents to be kept miles away, has shut down on all armistice news from the front to send it only through channels to the Government in Paris."

On Saturday night, Nov. 9, 1918, The Times Annex was at high boil. Dramatic dispatches from every front in Europe, from Paris, London, Copenhagen, Switzerland, and from Washington, cascaded into The Times from its correspondents:

LONDON, Nov. 9, 4:40 P.M.—Emperor William of Germany has abdicated.

COPENHAGEN, Nov. 9—German sailors have rebelled and have compelled their officers to leave the warships.

PARIS, Nov. 9—If the German answer is in the affirmative an armistice will be signed at Senlis, headquarters of the Allied Generalissimo.

LONDON, Nov. 9—All the Allied armies on the British front are advancing.

PARIS, Nov. 9—French cavalry has crossed the Belgian border, north and east of Hirson.

WITH THE AMERICAN ARMY IN FRANCE, Nov. 9, 9 P.M.—The message that the Kaiser has decided to abdicate reached the American front this afternoon. East of the Meuse Americans are advancing on Montmedy. We have just cleaned out Bois de Remoisville.

A front-page, two-column box gave the exact wording of the decree announcing the Kaiser's abdication. The heavy-type four-line head, bannered across the page, summed up the whole triumphant picture:

KAISER AND CROWN PRINCE ABDICATE;
NATION TO CHOOSE NEW GOVERNMENT.
MAX IS REGENT; ARMISTICE IS DELAYED;
REVOLT SPREADS ON LAND AND SEA

The third page on Sunday morning carried a Hy Mayer cartoon, a rare departure for the news section. It showed the Kaiser at a railroad ticket window. It was captioned: "Citizen Hohenzollern— Where Do We Go From Here?"

The armistice bulletin came into The Times office just before 3 o'clock Monday morning. It flashed first out of Washington on The Associated Press wire:

WASHINGTON, Monday, Nov. 11, 2:48 A.M.—The armistice between Germany on the one hand and the Allied Governments and the United States on the other, has been signed.

The World War will end this morning at 6 o'clock, Washington time, 11 o'clock Paris time.

Van Anda's eyes danced and sparkled. He mounted briskly to the composing room, and, in the characteristic din, with subordinates clustered eagerly around him, scrawled the historic front-page banners:

ARMISTICE SIGNED, END OF THE WAR!
BERLIN SEIZED BY REVOLUTIONISTS;
NEW CHANCELLOR BEGS FOR ORDER;
OUSTED KAISER FLEES TO HOLLAND

The managing editor ordinarily frowned on exclamation points, but even he could not resist one for this top line. He had the Washington story heavily leaded to get more white space between lines, and the type in this piece was larger than that ordinarily used. It amounted almost to screaming Times style, yet the page maintained its typographical dignity.

The armistice bulletins were posted in Times Tower windows. Electricians climbed to the turret, switched current into the great searchlights used only on election nights, and swept Manhattan's skies with darting broad-beamed rays in token of victory. River craft took up the signal, and awakened householders with their hoarse exultation. Times Square magically filled with shouting, singing men and women just out of restaurants and night clubs. Broadway scavengers stopped their garbage trucks around The Times. An English girl leaped to the Liberty Hall bond-sales platform in the Square, and the crowd stilled as she sang a doxology. Sleepers in the Cadillac, Astor and Claridge Hotels awakened in the dark to peer down at bareheaded men and ecstatic women singing, "The Star-Spangled Banner," "The Marseillaise" and, finally, "God Save the King." When the armistice extra came from The Times presses the crowds eagerly bought it, and the celebration had a second beginning. It kept up through break of day.

Not all Armistice Day dispatches got through to The Times that night. Special stories sent by James, Duranty and Gibbs from the different fronts were held up. They ran on Nov. 14, and were packed with throat-tightening drama.

From Verdun came:

BY EDWIN L. JAMES
Special to The New York Times

WITH THE AMERICAN ARMY IN FRANCE, Nov. 11—They stopped fighting at 11 o'clock this morning. In a twinkling, four years of killing and massacre stopped as if God had swept His omnipotent finger across the scene of world carnage and had cried "Enough."

The main story told how the "cease fire" order had been called, and then how the Germans climbed into the open from their trenches:

"Through the fog across the ravine the Yanks saw the Boches spring from their positions and shout, and sing with joy. They saw white flags in the cold wind, and they saw the Boches waving their hands in invitation to come over."

From the British front:

BY PHILIP GIBBS
Special to The New York Times

WITH THE BRITISH ARMIES IN FRANCE, Nov. 11—Last night, for the first time since August in the first year of the war, there was no light of gunfire in the sky, no sudden stabs of flame through darkness, no spreading glow above black trees where for four years of nights human beings were smashed to death. The Fires of Hell had been put out.

Walter Duranty with the French—he had returned to the trenches after Marshal Foch had closed armistice negotiations to reporters—wrote soberly. He told what was in the tired poilus' minds. His story held prophecy that was to prove too bitterly true:

"It is a strange and troublous situation that confronts Europe to-day. Russia agonizes in the throes of anarchy, and Germany bids fair to follow suit."

Red flags were at mast tops on the German fleet, and red flags and banners flowered everywhere in crushed Berlin. Somewhere in the enemy ranks tasting the gall-bitter humiliation of crushing defeat was a little Austrian corporal who would one day set the globe aflame trying to wipe out the memory of this humiliation. No one could have guessed it then. At least, no one did.

A fortnight after Armistice Day, President Wilson prepared to go to Europe for the Peace Conference. No American President before him had attempted such a mission. Many Americans were against it. The Times opposed it and made it the subject of several editorials. Wilson was adamant. He saw it as his duty, precedent or no precedent. On the night of Nov. 26, 1918, at a Foreign Policy Association dinner in the Hotel Astor, George W. Wickersham, an authority on international law, took up the issue. He suggested in this talk that Vice President Thomas Marshall might be compelled, under Article II, Section I, of the Constitution, to take the oath of President once Wilson had sailed beyond the three-mile limit on his way to Versailles.

Van Anda leaped on this point. He ordered Edward Klauber, a rewrite man, later night city editor, to phone the Vice President, who was in Boston, to put the question directly to him: would he assume the Presidency, or would he not? The reporter hesitated. He ventured that it might be something less than proper to try for such an interview by telephone. The managing editor froze. "Call Mr. Marshall at his hotel," he ordered coldly. "This is important." He turned back to his desk work. The reporter went out to the city room. He read and reread the Wickersham speech, then put through his call.

The Vice President came on the wire. The reporter read pertinent portions of the Wickersham speech, and then, but without too much hope, politely put the question. The Vice President said, "I cannot discuss such matters on a telephone."

The reporter parried for time, but the Vice President held firm. When it seemed apparent that Marshall was actually ready to put up the receiver, Klauber made a last desperate stab. He said, "Mr. Vice President, I do not mean to be disrespectful, but The New York Times thinks the people of the United States have a right to know what you will do in this situation."

It worked. The Vice President warmly denied that he wanted to keep anything from the American people and went on the defensive. He explained that he was reluctant to make a statement because he had not had a chance to give the matter mature consideration. Klauber, booth-pent and hot, furiously took notes, and kept murmuring agreement.

Marshall was assured that the story would emphasize that he had spoken informally and that he intended to get legal opinion on what course to take. Finally, Klauber had enough material for a two-column story. When he came from the booth and reported, the night editor whistled his astonishment. He ordered Klauber to set down every word.

Van Anda hurried from the news executives' enclosure. His eyes snatched each word run off under the reporter's nimble fingers. He himself read copy on the piece. Next morning's Times carried three front-page stories on the situation—the Wickersham speech, the Marshall interview and a story from Washington on President Wilson's pending departure. They tied in neatly.

The headline spread across the page said:

DISCUSSING THE PRESIDENCY, VICE PRESIDENT MARSHALL
SAYS HE WOULD TAKE IT ONLY ON ORDER OF A COMPETENT COURT,
DURING THE ABSENCE OF MR. WILSON, WHO SAILS NEXT WEEK

The interview took a full two-column front-page box headed: "Vice President Marshall on His Relationship to The President." To make clear to readers that the story had been obtained by telephone, the managing editor had a few lines to that effect written into the lead:

"Vice President Marshall was interviewed last night over long distance telephone at the Copley-Plaza Hotel in Boston with regard to George Wickersham's opinion, expressed in a speech in New York, that, should President Wilson by going to Europe to attend the Peace Conference put himself in a position where he could not exercise any of his duties, his powers and duties under the Constitution would devolve upon the Vice President."

The story made it clear that Marshall had emphasized that the Wickersham idea was new to him; that he was talking informally, and without mature consideration.

"Nevertheless," the story continued, "he was quite frank as to his attitude toward the contemplated departure of President Wilson, and as to his own course during the President's absence."

Some newspapermen argued that Van Anda was something of a gambler on a big story. They thought, for example, that he took dangerous chances on the Titanic sinking, on the Ludendorff eleventh-hour bid for military victory and on the Marshall story. They were wrong. In each case The Times managing editor turned over every available detail in his mind, and found that the sum added up to certainty.

He double-checked the Marshall interview. First he cross-examined Klauber intently. Was the reporter certain that the Marshall he had spoken to at the Copley-Plaza was the Vice President? Had he ever heard the Vice President's voice before? The answer was "Yes" in each case and supported with a detailed explanation.

"You understand, of course," the managing editor said, "that The Times could not afford to have this interview denied?" The reporter nodded. For a second check, the managing editor wired a copy of the interview to The Times man at Boston and had him show it to Marshall at the Copley-Plaza. The Vice President scanned the story carefully and approved it. Only then was Van Anda satisfied.

The Marshall beat stirred up the journalistic zoo. Roars and reverberations sounded across the land and echoed in European capitals. Finally the matter was worked out so that President Wilson was able to depart for Versailles, assured that he would not lose his powers as Chief Executive.

Van Anda did not slacken his European lines even after the war. On the afternoon of Nov. 11, 1918, he crisply ordered Duranty: "Follow French Army into occupied parts of Germany," and sent James toward the Rhine with the Americans. He not only put his men to dogging the heels of the Kaiser's vanquished legions, but even that day prepared for coverage of the coming peace negotiations, though they were not to start for months. He chose Grasty, Selden, James, Duranty and Marshall to work under Richard V. Oulahan, and hired Gertrude Atherton to do special side stories. His conference coverage was airtight. The Times' immediate presentation of official documents on the drawn-out negotiations exceeded anything printed elsewhere. The Times was a popular international textbook on contemporary history during this period, as during the conflict. It still is.

On June 9, James flashed from Germany, "Want full peace treaty terms? Can probably get access through German sources." Back flashed the answer, "We have treaty."

A reporter for The Chicago Tribune had brought an advance copy of the treaty to Washington and had turned it over to Senator Borah. On the very day that James cabled from Germany that he could get a copy, the Senator turned his copy over to the Congressional Record. Men from The Times Washington bureau worked in relays that night, getting wet proofs from the Government Printing Office. Van Anda had opened a total of twenty-four telephone and telegraph lines in New York to receive the document, and next morning's paper, the issue of June 10, 1919, carried the text. It ran to sixty-two columns and came to one-sixth of the entire forty-eight page issue. No other newspaper had it.

James stayed with the Army of Occupation in Germany until September. Then he was ordered to take charge in Paris while Selden returned to the United States for a visit with his family. Arranging for Selden's return, Van Anda worked in a slight chore; he fixed it so that Selden took passage on the steamship Albert Ballin on which King Albert of Belgium was traveling to the United States. All through the voyage Selden sent stories about the King by wireless. This showed Van Anda's frugal side; no waste. During vacation, when Selden decided not to return to Europe, James was offered the Paris job, and accepted.

The Times staff dug many exclusive stories out of the meetings at Versailles. One that stood out above the rest was based on Woodrow Wilson's threat, when proceedings waxed hot and angry, that he might leave the meeting and return to the United States. Peace table atmosphere was, incongruously, anything but peaceful. Old Tiger Clemenceau had no love for the idealistic American schoolmaster, but he had to suppress his dislike. There were intrigues within intrigues, and the maneuvering had to be carefully watched.

There were some readers who felt that perhaps The Times supplied too much detail on the negotiations, but Ochs and his managing editor were firmly agreed that the conference deserved full documentation and comprehensive reporting so that the peoples of the world might know the direction of their destinies. The human-interest side of the conference was covered, too. The Times provided portraits of the statesmen involved and descriptions of the diplomatic shadow-boxing.

The Times wholeheartedly believed in the League of Nations born at the postwar meetings. It gave the League earnest support in its editorial columns. Its news space, however, presented the arguments both for and against it. It became apparent within a few years that the League could not perform its avowed function without sturdy United States backing. As it paled and weakened, The Times portrayed its failure, though still editorially holding that it seemed to be the only body, properly nourished, that might prevent a second World War.

On Oct. 16, 1925, James was in lovely Locarno, to watch French and German statesmen set the official seal on the Rhineland security pact. He recalled then how he had stood in Verdun's rubble heaps on Armistice Day, seven years before, awed by the sudden stillness; how soldiers had talked of their governments mopping up behind them, and working out a way to end wars. He remembered the pathetic ranks of little crosses in France and Belgium where soldier dead had slept the years through—and still no true peace.

"At the end of a perfect day, just as nightfall descended rapidly from the surrounding mountains," he wrote that night for next day's Times, "Two middle-aged figures, both stoop-shouldered, one with flowing hair, the other as bald as can be, stood arm in arm framed in a brightly lighted window and looked out together on the lengthening shadows fast reaching across Lake Maggiore.

"They were Aristide Briand, Foreign Minister of France, and Hans Luther, Chancellor of the German Republic. Behind their backs, secretaries were blotting the ink on the signatures of a treaty by which their two countries promised never to fight one another again. Seven years after the end of the war, France and Germany had at last made peace."

Not long afterward he saw the League of Nations utterly enfeebled, a wraithlike thing that had never measured up to the hopes of men who had dreamed that it might end mass violence forever. He reflected then, how Woodrow Wilson's defeat of the nationalist spirit at Versailles in 1919 had been canceled when his own country coldly turned its back on the League.

"I recall," he wrote for The Times, "the first meeting of the Council of the League when it launched on its unhappy career. It took place in the Salle des Horloges of the Quai d'Orsay. Old Clemenceau, who presided, left an empty chair on the right. It was for the United States. It was a high-backed chair.

"As the afternoon wore on, the sun which streamed across the Seine through the windows cast a shadow of the empty chair across the table. The shadow lengthened that day, and in the days that followed, until the League died."

As the peace negotiations proceeded, men turned again to pursuits that had been stopped by the war. A United States Navy expedition negotiated the Atlantic in seaplanes between May 16 and May 27, 1919. They stopped along the way at the Azores and Lisbon. Meanwhile, at St. John's in Newfoundland, two planes were poised for a non-stop attempt to cross the ocean. They were after a $50,000 prize that had been put up in 1913 by Lord Northcliffe's Daily Mail.

Carr Van Anda sent Edward Klauber to cover the take-offs. Major H. G. Brackley primed a four-motored Handley-Page bomber for the attempt. Captain John Alcock and Lieut. Arthur Whitton Brown, who were later knighted, nursed a single-motored Vimy-Vickers. The Times man spent his days and nights with these Britons. Other American newspapers had men at St. John's, but one by one, as continued reports of poor weather came through, they were recalled until Ochs' representative was pretty much alone, except for local talent.

Alcock and Brown took off at 12:10 P.M. on June 14, 1919, and Klauber sent the story. Then the hours ticked off with no word from the fliers. Harry G. Hawker and Lieut. Comdr. Mackenzie Grieve, two other Britons, had started out over the ocean from St. John's on May 19, 1919, and had come down halfway over. For a week they had been mourned as gone, but had turned up in Ireland on a small fishing craft that had saved them at sea. Now it looked as if Alcock and Brown had vanished in the thick fogs reported from mid-Atlantic by surface craft. No one had seen them.

Sixteen hours and twelve minutes after take-off they landed with a splintering crash in a great bog on the Galway Coast in Ireland. They crawled out unhurt, were borne to a nearby village, and got news of their arrival through to The London Daily Mail. Lord Northcliffe and The New York Times had made up since their wartime tiff, and Ochs' journal had bought American rights to the Alcock-Brown narrative. It was bannered on the front page.

"We have had a terrible journey," the captain's story began. "The wonder is that we are here at all. We scarcely saw the sun or the moon, or the stars. For hours we saw none of them."

This account told how the two men had flown wrongside up for hours without knowing it. Hidden in the fog, they had no sight on the horizon to keep them level. They had flown light, had even dropped their wheels en route to conserve fuel. They carried one little parcel of mail. In the pouch was a letter written by Klauber to The New York Times London bureau. It was marked "Trans-atlantic Air Post 1919," and is probably a rare philatelic item

Lord Northcliffe's message to Alcock and Brown was boxed prominently on The New York Times front page beside the main story. Northcliffe had turned prophet. The message said: "I look forward to the time when London morning newspapers will be selling in New York in the evening, allowing for the difference between British and American time, and vice versa in regard to New York journals selling in London the next day." All this was to come to pass, but neither he nor Ochs would live to see it.

Two passengers aboard the British dirigible R-34 on her 108-hour flight from Edinburgh to Roosevelt Field at Mineola, L. I., the first week in July, 1919, helped give The Times the most complete coverage of that historic passage that ran in any newspaper.

One of the writers was Lieut. Comdr. Zachary Lansdowne, aboard as an official United States Navy observer and later skipper of the United States dirigible Shenandoah. The other was Brig. Gen. E. M. Maitland of the British Air Ministry, who supplied the entire log of the journey.

The Times ran a total of ten pages on the R-34's flight because it was man's first westward non-stop crossing of the Atlantic by air.

When the R-34 took off for Scotland again, at 11:50 P.M. Wednesday, July 9, it carried the first trans-Atlantic air-mail copies of The New York Times. These were addressed to King George, at Buckingham Palace, to Prime Minister Lloyd George, Lord Reading, to John W. Davis, United States Ambassador to the Court of St. James, to the editor of The London Chronicle and to Ernest Marshall, head of The New York Times London bureau.

An hour and twenty minutes after the R-34 rose from Mineola on its homeward crossing, it passed directly over Times Tower. Ochs and Van Anda had arranged this. The great ship, flying at 1,200 feet, had no difficulty finding the Tower, which was lighted from street floor to uttermost turret—every last window.

The Square and the roof tops around it were thick with human beings assembled for the sight. They cheered the R-34 as it pivoted over the Tower and headed eastward to the sea. Van Anda had a wire ready for the occasion:

"Thanks from The Times and from the thousands whom the spectacle thrilled," it said. "Wish you good luck . . . The New

York Times." "Thanks," said the R-34, and then its twinkling lights vanished.

The dirigible got safely to Pulham on Sunday morning, July 13. The air-mail copies of The Times, including a Sunday Magazine bearing the same date, July 13, became precious souvenirs. Marshall cabled a story telling how Col. Clive Wigram, the King's chief equerry, delivered the edition to the Monarch. British newspapermen marveled at the ten pages devoted to the dirigible's arrival in the United States. Their own stories on that event were puny beside this coverage.

After the war, world communications became hopelessly sclerotic. The cables were unable to carry the heavy press load in addition to the tremendous flow of official Government messages. The German cables were dead, cut by the British during the war.

The United States Navy operated a receiver at Bar Harbor, Me., and picked up a certain amount of press copy, but frequently messages would be delayed another full day getting to The Times by overland lines.

Ochs and Van Anda pondered this a while, then decided that The Times could vastly improve its handling of European news with its own trans-Atlantic wireless receivers. One was built into the Times Tower, overlooking the Square, the first of its kind owned by an American newspaper.

Five years passed before The Times installed its own transmitter, which became famous on the air lanes under the call letters 2-UO.

The receiving station got nightly press dispatches from Nauen and Eilvese in Germany, from Bordeaux and St. Assise in France, from Carnarvon in Wales and from a transmitter in Leafields in Britain. Twin dictaphones automatically recorded stories at better than 100 words a minute. A crude short-wave receiver picked up messages from ships at sea.

On the night of March 15, 1921, a Times radio man picked up an SOS from the United States Army transport Madawaska after it had been in collision at 9:37 o'clock with the United States Shipping Board's freighter Invincible, twenty miles northeast of Atlantic City. The calls of distress snatched from the air, coupled with information obtained by telephone calls to the Coast Guard Station at Cape May, N. J., gave The Times a first-edition exclusive.

Again, just after 5 o'clock on the night of Dec. 15, in the same year, The Times wireless station, which had been transferred from the Tower to the Annex to save the brief delay in running copy between the two buildings, picked up another SOS from off the New Jersey shore. The Panama had rammed the United States Navy destroyer Graham in heavy seas off Sea Girt. Van Anda rushed Merian C. Cooper, a staff man, to Sea Girt by special motor car with orders to hire a fisherman to take him out to the damaged craft. The two vessels had interlocked and were holding.

Cooper clambered aboard the Graham, got his story and went to the radio room to send it to The Times. By then, to his dismay, both the Graham's and the Panama's transmitters were out of commission because of flooding.

At midnight Cooper persuaded the Graham's skipper to put a boat over the side in the angrily tossing waves, to take him to the Merritt-Chapman tugboat Willett, which was standing by. She had a working transmitter and Cooper, drenched, with a fistful of sodden copy, sent The Times the most detailed account of the collision available to any newspaper.

Late in 1921 Reginald Iversen, a radio engineer fresh out of the Navy, was sent by The Times to work with engineers from The Chicago Tribune and The Philadelphia Public Ledger to build a strong relay radio receiver at Halifax for their combined benefit. The first equipment was rigged up in a coal shed, but later was moved. Out of this venture grew Press Wireless, which today handles press matter for hundreds of newspapers, including The Times.

FOUR WAR YEARS had changed the world. The same fierce fires that had reduced parts of Europe to embered ruin had shrunk the globe. War-spurred inventive genius had improved communications and transportation systems so that they laced the nations more closely together. Large newspapers in the United States had changed complexion; had whittled domestic news to make more space for the world picture. The New York Times' reputation for international coverage exceeded anything known up to that time. Its circulation lists read like an international Who's Who. Diplomats, scholars, financiers, merchants, scientists, industrialists and leaders in aviation and modern exploration had come to look upon it as the best daily medium of current history.

When Ochs took reminiscent stock in 1921 even he found it difficult to believe the changes he had wrought. The sorry wreck he had taken over in 1896 had become a model newspaper. It was, in the United States, at least, the newspaperman's newspaper. The Times had taken in more than $100,000,000 in the twenty-five years since Ochs had lifted the torch from Charles Miller's hand. Only 4 per cent, or a little less, of those earnings, had been paid out in dividends. Most of those millions had been plowed back into The Times for better equipment, for greater news coverage and for new buildings. Meanwhile, salaries had been raised, and social benefits had been established for the employes.

The circulation had gone from a feeble 9,000 to 323,000 daily, and advertising linage from 2,227,000 to 23,447,000 lines yearly. The increase in advertising would have been far greater if Ochs had been willing to sacrifice news space for paying linage, but he never even considered that.

At this point, the Southerner might well have called it a day. He had proved that a newspaper that existed primarily to give news was bound to win wide and profitable favor and he had grown rich during the demonstration. He had seen six other New York newspapers—The (Morning) Sun, The Herald, The News, The Mercury, The Press and The Advertiser—fade and die, or become mere epitaph lost in the masthead titles of journals that had absorbed them.

He was a different Ochs. The small-town publisher who had made his audacious bid for Henry Raymond's once great newspaper had taken on the coloring of his own creation. He was a world figure. His voice at The Associated Press council table, and at public meetings—though he spoke but seldom publicly—was heard in reverent silence. He was a dignified man who could and did walk with presidents and kings. He had attained to all these things in a brief twenty-five years—though at a price. At 63 snow was in his hair and time had run its graving finger down his face. He was sensitive about this. He established a Times rule that reporters were not to call men and women "old" who were in their late sixties and seventies.

At noon on July 18, 1922, Charles Miller died. Next day The Times ran his obituary between turned rules. It took the whole editorial page. The office was flooded with messages of regret. Ochs was glad then that he had persuaded Miller, not long before the end, to pose for a portrait by Haskell Coffin, which still hangs in the publisher's office.

Good Dr. Finley wrote a little verse about the chief's passing, based on the line, "He is mourned at the mill, he is mourned at the mess," from Alcman of Sparta:

> He is mourned at the mill, he is mourned at the mess,
> The greatest of millers, whose mill was the press;
> The grist it is grinding makes bitter our bread
> For the grist is the news that our Miller is dead.

Ochs, The Times editorial board and a host of prominent men who had known Miller, followed the editor's body to Woodlawn

Cemetery. They agreed that he had lived the good life and that he had managed, after long years, to rid himself of the heavy debts he had incurred when the old Times Publishing Company had crumbled. He left substantial Times holdings to his two children. Rollo Ogden, formerly of The New York Post, succeeded him as editor in chief.

Iphigene had finished at Barnard College in 1914, the year that Julius Ochs Adler, her cousin, finished at Princeton and came to The Times. She had majored in history and for a while thought she might make teaching her career. She knew The Times thoroughly, and would have preferred journalism, but her father discouraged it. He loved to take her through the plant and have her meet his journalistic aides, but he had rather Victorian notions about women in a newspaper office. He was overprotective of the women of his family; this made life difficult for them at times.

All through Iphigene's childhood, her romantic mother had fired her imagination with classic stories of great rulers and of stirring episodes in American history. Before Iphigene could read she could recite from memory the succession of English monarchs and could name in order the French kings and United States Presidents. Her exceptional memory was one of her father's great delights and, modest as he was in almost all other matters, he gave in to parental pride in exhibiting Iphigene's precocious historical knowledge.

The girl had developed into a dark-haired, dignified young woman, sombre-eyed and keenly aware of the poverty she saw all about her in European capitals and in New York's slums. The missionary zeal came upon her, and she yearned to do something to bring about social reform.

Though Ochs protected the distaff side of his family from commercial and worldly contact and believed that woman's place was in the home, he never tried to stifle Iphigene's independence. He did try to direct her life pattern. When her earnest desire to do something for the poor shook her emotionally, she was apt to engage in tense argument on the subject. She had thrown in, more or less, with other idealistic girls at Barnard who saw the need for a better welfare program in New York, and the subject became a major interest. She worked at the Henry Street Settlement and with the Big Sisters group.

Ochs admired his daughter's idealism and her humane instincts, but was startled, sometimes, by her earnestness. He told her: "Iphigene, I do not deny your right to speak what is on your mind on this or any other subject. I do quarrel with the arbitrary stand you take, and with the vehemence with which you present your views." On Page 95 of the family's copy of Benjamin Franklin's autobiography was a passage in which Poor Richard related how he had learned from Quaker friends that it was unwise to try to override opponents in debate by sheer dogmatic force.

"I made it a rule," Franklin said, "to forbear all direct contradiction to the sentiments of others and all positive assertion of my own. I even forbid myself . . . the use of every word or expression in the language that imported a fix'd opinion, such as *certainly, undoubtedly,* etc., and I adopted instead of them, *I conceive, I apprehend* or *I imagine* a thing to be so and so; or *it appears to me at present* . . . And this mode, which I at first put on with some violence to natural inclination, became at length so easy, and so habitual to me, that perhaps for these fifty years past no one has ever heard a dogmatical expression escape me."

The publisher gently insisted that Iphigene commit this passage to memory and keep it in mind when she felt herself about to give way to unqualified assertiveness in discussing a subject. The girl obeyed, and always, at her father's quiet reminder, "Page 95, Iphigene," would wait for emotional tides to recede before she renewed a discussion. The lesson stayed with her and governed her adult conversation.

Julius Adler had not been at The Times many months before the European war broke. He went to the first and second Plattsburg businessmen's camps and rose from private to sergeant. When President Wilson called for war with Germany the publisher's nephew was commissioned a second lieutenant of cavalry, and returned to Plattsburg for the first officers' training camp in May, 1917. He met a number of friends there, all of them eager for service in France. Among them was Arthur Hays Sulzberger, who was training for a commission in artillery.

Young Sulzberger was the son of Cyrus L. Sulzberger, a cotton merchant. His mother was Rachel Peixotto Hays, a former teacher at Hunter College. Her lineage traced back to the Hays family of

Spain, Portugal and the Netherlands that had first come to the United States in 1700. A relative was the extraordinary Jacob Hays, two-fisted first chief of the constabulary in New York. Chief Constable Hays had charge of city policemen who guarded George Washington as he took the first Presidential oath at the sub-Treasury Building, then Federal Hall. The family were Westchester farmers in the Colonial period, and during and after the Revolution. Jacob Hays' portrait still hangs in New York's City Hall.

Arthur Sulzberger had attended public schools in New York. He was born in an old red brick house opposite Mount Morris Park. He was graduated from Public School 166 in Eighty-ninth Street between Columbus and Amsterdam Avenues, where teachers were inclined to pamper him. One even used him as Cupid's messenger. He recalled with amusement in later years that he carried notes between his amorous teacher and a pretty lady who had a class down the hall. His reward at the end of the month was an unbroken row of A's on his report card, the highest academic rating he had ever achieved. The impact at home was gratifying. Mr. Sulzberger rewarded the boy with $1 for each A, and promised $5 for each A if Arthur could duplicate the perfect score. He never did.

In 1909 Sulzberger entered Columbia University with the idea of eventually trying his hand at sanitary engineering. His father liked to explain to friends that a sanitary engineer, as he understood it, was the man who held the candle while the plumber fixed the leak. This was the favorite parental jest. At Columbia, Sulzberger made the swimming team, was a chorus "girl" in the college show because he had a neatly turned calf, but did not particularly distinguish himself in his studies. Not until four years later when he went to school in the army did he apply himself to genuine study.

He had met Iphigene Ochs while both were students at Columbia, but, through Julius Adler, came to know her better in 1915. Good to look upon and excellent company, she was much courted. Wide travel had developed the social graces in her. As a grave-eyed child she had absorbed better than ordinary manners from contact with important men and women. She still had not fixed on a career, except that she still thought she might teach history. She was aiming at a professorship while at Columbia in 1916-1917.

Ochs had always hoped that Iphigene might marry a newspaperman. He never quite put that into words, but, since he thought chiefly of The Times, and of what might become of it after he had gone, his daughter was aware of it. When she told him in 1917 she intended to marry Sulzberger, he was unhappy. The officer suitor was clean-cut and alert, but the publisher could not overlook the fact that Sulzberger was not of inky tradition and that his father, for all his excellent business and civic reputation, was a cotton merchant and not of the Fourth Estate.

Once he was satisfied, though, that his daughter was fixed on her choice, he gave his consent, and on Nov. 17, 1917, Iphigene Bertha Ochs became Iphigene Ochs Sulzberger. Capt. Julius Ochs Adler, her cousin, was best man at the wedding held in the Ochs home at 308 West Seventy-fifth Street. Lieutenant Sulzberger and the bride entrained for Camp Wadsworth in Spartanburg, N. C. There he was with an artillery regiment momentarily expecting—and eagerly hoping—to be on his way overseas. Captain Adler was at Camp Upton on Long Island, awaiting sailing orders, too.

It worked out that Captain Adler eventually went to France in command of Company H of the 306th Infantry of the Seventy-seventh (New York) Division, while Lieutenant Sulzberger was transferred first to Chillicothe in Ohio and then to other artillery units, in the United States, condemned to close his military career without a sniff of battle smoke.

Adler, meanwhile, achieved an excellent combat record. He fought his way across France in command of his infantry unit and won a reputation for extraordinary courage under fire. On Oct. 14, 1918, his command was held up by enemy resistance at St. Juvin in the Argonne Forest. Captain Adler and another officer undertook to open the way for a breakthrough. Pistols in hand, they advanced toward a nest of some 150 Germans, firing as they ran, calling on the enemy to surrender. Fifty Germans threw down their rifles and gave up. The rest fled. Company H broke through behind the skipper. His lieutenant sent the prisoners to the rear under guard, while the company continued to advance. Maj. Gen. Robert Alexander, Seventy-seventh Division commander, cited Adler in general orders and recommended him for the Distinguished Service Cross.

Adler was gassed in the St. Juvin engagement and was sent to a hospital for treatment. The Distinguished Service Cross came through, and eventually the Order of the Purple Heart, the Silver Star with two oakleaf clusters, the French Legion of Honor, the French Croix de Guerre with palm, the Italian Croce de Guerra and his home state's Conspicuous Service Cross. When he got out of the hospital he was made a major and took over the First Battalion of the 306th Infantry. He returned to The Times when the war ended.

On Dec. 7, 1918, Sulzberger came to The Times. Newspaper work was all new to him, and Ochs was not inclined to have him learn it the easy way. Young Sulzberger was eager to try his hand in the news field and thought he might first learn something about writing, but Ochs would not hear of it.

The publisher turned his son-in-law over to George McAneny, a learned gentleman who had resigned as President of the New York Board of Aldermen early in 1916 to become The Times' executive manager. McAneny saw to it that the neophyte got an office and a secretary, and suggested that he turn his hand to anything that came his way. The annual Hundred Neediest Cases appeal was running in The Times that month. Sulzberger dug into that. He put in long hours, checking contributions as they mounted, day by day; when that was ended he found new tasks for himself. He wandered, rather lonely, in the plant, affable and pleasant, but with no fixed duties, a minister without portfolio.

Young Sulzberger's first major job was finding an adequate newsprint supply for The Times, a problem that had long concerned Ochs. The publisher told his son-in-law to familiarize himself with that phase of the newspaper's operation and suggested he start at the Tidewater Paper Mill in Bush Terminal on the South Brooklyn waterfront. Tidewater, which The Times owned, processed but did not produce wood pulp.

Sulzberger began an intensive survey of all phases of newsprint production, roving Canada and the Scandinavian countries. He added to Tidewater's output of 100 tons a day from the Laurentide Paper Company, north of Three Rivers in Quebec, and lined up other sources. He became a newsprint expert.

Some Times men watched the progress of Adler and of Sulzberger with cynical eye, but both independently won their journalistic spurs. Both sat in news-policy and editorial conferences—and still do.

Before time lifted Ochs' tired fingers from Times control, some fifteen years later, the division of responsibility was sharp and clear. Major General Adler—he was to win that rank eventually— explained at a Times labor hearing, when the question came up, how jurisdictional separation was arrived at. He said, first, that he and Sulzberger were both trustees of the Times-controlled stock.

"Mr. Sulzberger," he continued, "is senior officer of The New York Times, and is president of the company. I am vice president. He is first in command and I am second in command of the corporate structure. Mr. Sulzberger is publisher, which means that he is in direct charge of all operations. Actually, he gives his more direct attention to the news and editorial departments. My title of manager gives me supervision of the business, circulation, promotion, production, and mechanical departments.

"We confer on all matters of paramount policy, on both sides of the business. Naturally, if Mr. Sulzberger's views would differ from mine, his judgment would prevail."

The road to the future, just after World War I, was a little dim to both Sulzberger and Adler. Ochs had plunged into melancholy depths. The shock induced by public reaction to the Miller editorial, the crushing burden of publisher responsibilities and worry over the war—all these had made deep inroads. Ochs went into decline. The brilliant mind temporarily clouded. The Times flourished in the warmth of public and advertiser approval, and the Chattanoogan should have had no fears, no shadows, across his path, but it was in his nature to be crushed, for no apparent reason, when his prospects were brightest. This was one of those periods.

Early in May, 1921, before his melancholia, Ochs journeyed by train to Knoxville, to help celebrate Capt. William Rule's eighty-second birthday. Henry Clay Collins, his boyhood composing room foreman, met him at the station.

The next day, with Collins beside him, the owner of The New York Times walked down to the Chronicle office off Atkins Alley. He found Captain Rule was at work at his rolltop desk.

Ochs pretended that he did not notice, but his heart beat faster when he saw the two photographs framed above the captain's desk.

One was of fiery Marse Henry Watterson, the famous Southern editor; the other was of Ochs.

Captain Rule was bent with years. His hair was snow white, his cheeks were withered, and his black bow-string tie was hidden by a white goatee. The man who had hired Ochs as a wide-eyed boy a half-century before, had been a young, dark-haired gallant of 32.

At the Chamber of Commerce luncheon next day, Ochs modestly tried to keep out of the limelight. This was the captain's party and he had no wish to encroach on it.

"Should I assist in an effort to make a lion of an Ochs," he said when called upon to speak, "I fear I might display myself as an ass." He continued: "I have come here tonight because I love Captain Rule. As office boy I trimmed the lamps in his office. I always tried to keep them bright and burning, and I'm glad to say that Captain Rule has kept them bright through all the years that have passed."

When the luncheon broke up Ochs and Collins set out together to cover Ochs' boyhood newspaper route. The streets had changed in fifty years. Porches where he had dropped The Chronicle for sleeping families were gone. Newer and brighter homes had taken their place. Empty lots were filled.

With Collins at his side, he looked again on old University Hill and upon the eminence that had been Fort Sanders. New buildings graced the University knoll and were lovely in the light of the setting sun. Brambly Fort Sanders, where he had wandered with his brothers in blackberry-time, was covered with a housing development.

They moved past the old house in Clinch Street where his grandmother had died, rambled in and out of little side streets where he had hurried barefoot with his papers before the town was awake. He eagerly remembered Dr. Ramsey's house, the eastern limit of his route; the old Brownlow house, where he had dropped The Chronicle on the dawn-lit porch. If ever man went on a sentimental journey, Ochs did on this tour. Knoxville had changed, but his memory repeopled it with friendly faces of his childhood and with warm heart-tugging memories. He loved Knoxville.

He tore himself away, at last. Friends came down to the station with him. Henry Clay Collins was the last to shake his hand. Adolph

Ochs wondered then if he would ever look again upon this kindly printer's face. It turned out he would, but not for years.

After he had gone Collins wrote to Effie Ochs:

"Your dear companion fell into hands that dotingly fondled him like a tender child. His friends were reluctant to allow him to depart."

At the end of 1921, the publisher was himself again. On Jan. 7, 1922, he sailed from New York on the Adriatic with Effie, Fanny Van Dyke Ochs, his brother Milton's wife, and their daughter Margaret, for a tour of the Near East and the Continent. Sea air restored the sparkle to his eye and the spring to his step.

Wherever he traveled, doors eagerly opened for him—on board ship, at great hotels, at embassies, in palaces and castles. He took a childish pleasure in reporting in his letters the deference he encountered everywhere.

He wrote repeatedly: "Strangers say my face resembles that of G. W. I mean the Father of My Country. I am naturally quite flattered." It was not mere flattery. The publisher's white hair inclined to puff out around his ears, so that it looked like a colonial wig, and his features did resemble Washington's. He cultivated this look out of sheer vanity. All his portraits from this period to the end of his life emphasize the powdered-wig look.

In Paris Ochs had a series of talks with Edwin James on what it might cost The New York Times to improve its staff all over Europe to a point where it could say, without fear of dispute, that it had the widest and most comprehensive newspaper coverage in the world. The Paris news chief did some figuring, and finally decided the cost would run to around $500,000 a year. The publisher told James to draw up a plan for this superstaff. James did, and it was approved.

On his return from his sojourn abroad Ochs was fit to take the Times helm again. His newspaper was sailing smoothly at top speed, queen ship in the journalistic sea. There were no storms in sight.

CHAPTER

22

WHEN The Times was young it gave more space to news of science than any other New York newspaper, and John Swinton, a Times editorial writer, handled most of it. For example, in the summer of 1860 he wrote, and The Times used, three to four columns a day on the meeting of the American Scientists Association at Newport, R. I., and he contributed editorials on science on the side.

In March, 1860, when D. Appleton & Co., New York publishers, reprinted in the United States Charles Darwin's "The Origin of Species," The Times of March 28, 1860, ran a story three and a half columns long on the work.

"Mr. Darwin," this piece said, "as the fruit of a quarter century of patient observation and experiment, throws out, in a book whose title at least by this time has become familiar to the reading public, a series of arguments and inferences so revolutionary as, if established, to necessitate a radical reconstruction of the fundamental doctrines of natural history."

The same story recognized the potential influence of "The Origin of Species," saying: "It is clear that here is one of the most important contributions ever made to philosophic science; and it is behooving on the scientists, in the light of accumulation of evidence which the author has summoned in support of his theory, to reconsider the grounds on which their present doctrine of the origin of species is based."

That week, while the scientists' congress still sat at Newport,

The Times ran an editorial rebuking both the American savants and the members of the British Association for the Advancement of Science for ignoring Darwin's work. The writer assumed that they had, as he put it, "been stifled" by a ringing blast against "The Origin of Species" uttered by Bishop Samuel Wilberforce of the Church of England. The prelate had branded it as "heretical" which William Jennings Bryan was to do at the famous Scopes Trial many years later.

John Swinton left The Times after Raymond died, and science news in the paper fell off. It languished for a half century, more or less, so far as The Times was concerned. Other newspapers gave it even less attention.

Van Anda and E. W. Scripps of the Scripps-Howard newspaper chain were the first modern editors to recognize the value of science news, and were the first to give it any considerable newspaper space. Before they put qualified reporters on the science beat, the man in the laboratory shied away from the daily journal. Scientists had been hurt too often by clownish reporters who sought to amuse readers by treating scientific discoveries lightly, when they noticed them at all.

Although Van Anda had never hired specialists to cover meetings of learned scientific bodies, he had always handled the subject seriously. A mathematician with a zest for astronomy and physics, he leaped eagerly on the Einstein story when it came up in 1919. How much time might have passed before the subject excited the world if Van Anda had not gone after it as he did, no one will know, but Ochs' managing editor sensed its significance at once.

Einstein himself was then known to only a handful of learned Europeans, aside from the staff of the Kaiser Wilhelm Institute and his classes at Berlin University. His pioneering equations were understood by only a few other physicists. Even they could not readily translate his mathematical formulas into terms that laymen might grasp. But early in 1919, when Van Anda learned that the Royal Astronomical Society was setting up equipment in Sobral in northern Brazil and on the Isle of Principe off Africa's West Coast to test Einstein's theories, he kept sharp watch.

Henry Charles Crouch, an amiable Times man, whose forte was golf reporting, drew the assignment in the London bureau. He assumed that The Times of London would give ample coverage to the meeting and figured he might safely get it from that source, but learned early in the evening that it intended, instead, to give it short shrift because the whole subject was too difficult for the average reader.

Crouch called Arthur (later Sir Arthur) Stanley Eddington on the telephone in London for the details, but was unable to follow them. He finally pleaded with the scientist to dictate a story in such terms as a newspaper reader might be able to grasp, and Eddington obliged. Crouch filed it, not at all sure that it had much meaning. He was relieved and delighted when Van Anda cabled congratulations on the coverage, and copyrighted the piece.

On Nov. 8, 1919, the British astronomers met in London to discuss what they had discovered at Sobral and on Principe during a total eclipse of the sun on May 29, 1919. The story, which The Times copyrighted, appeared in the first column of Page 6 on Nov. 9, 1919. The astronomers had by then examined photographs of stars taken at the moment of eclipse totality. These proved, they reported, that Einstein's theory was decisively established. Light from these distant stars did not travel to the earth undeviatingly or in a straight line. Passing the sun, it was deflected or bent. This upheld the Einstein contention that stars actually were a measurable distance from positions they seemed to occupy. On the basis of the findings at Sobral and on Principe, the Newtonian theory of gravitation would have to be revised.

The story gave Americans their first brief introduction to the genius who had worked out the theory. It described the mathematician as "a Swiss citizen about 50 years of age who has been living in Berlin about six years." Within a year the name loomed large in men's consciousness everywhere. Albert Einstein, publicly introduced in The Times pages, was to lead the great thinkers of our period across the threshold of the Atomic Age.

Other newspapers took up the Einstein theory a little uneasily, as Van Anda had known they would. Little by little the physicist's aims became vaguely understandable to even the man in the street. When Einstein came to the United States to lecture at Princeton University a few years later even children had some idea of who, and what, he was.

Russell Owen, a Times man, was sent to Princeton to interview Dr. L. P. Eisenhart. Van Anda desired an explanation of Einstein's definition of the finite universe.

Owen was a great reporter but this assignment left him a little weak at the knees. The Princeton man was patient and kindly, though, and after some hours Owen thought he had his facts and figures straight. One of the subjects discussed was the diameter of the universe in terms of light years. Van Anda, after some figuring of his own, saw that Dr. Eisenhart had miscalculated; that instead of giving the diameter of the universe, he had given its radius. Dr. Eisenhart humbly conceded that he had made a slip.

Later, a translation of one of Dr. Einstein's extraordinarily complicated lectures at Princeton reached the managing editor. Dean Christian Gauss of Princeton always liked to recall what happened after Van Anda had gone through this paper.

"It came at a time," Dr. Gauss related, "when relativity was only understood by Dr. Einstein and by the Deity. When we sent up the translation Dr. Einstein had already lost even the professorial mathematicians who were here to hear him, but The Times called me before going to press to ask whether there was not some mistake in the figures.

"I called up Professor Adams. He had translated the lectures for us and had made abstracts for the newspapers. I told him that Mr. Van Anda thought one of the equations was wrong. Adams searched his notes and said, 'No, that is what Einstein said.'

"I told Mr. Adams that I took Mr. Van Anda very seriously, so he worked a while longer on his notes. Finally he called me back. He said, 'I am going to call Dr. Einstein.' When Einstein was consulted he was astonished. He scanned the notes and nodded. He said, 'Yes, Mr. Van Anda is right. I made a mistake in transcribing the equation on the blackboard.'"

Probably no other newspaper editor in the world could truthfully claim to have caught Einstein in a mistake. This instance was added to Van Anda legend.

In 1922 The New York Times raced away from the whole newspaper pack in science reporting. This was the year when Van Anda went feverish over an Egyptian King who had slept some 3,500 years, and restored him and his times with great fidelity and journalistic art. It all started on Nov. 29, 1922, when The Associated Press reported from London that Howard Carter, an archaeologist associated with Lord Carnarvon, had, after seven years' digging, come upon the tomb of Tut-ankh-Amen in the Valley of the Kings at Luxor in Egypt on the site of ancient Thebes. It was a rather modest news item of about 250 words, but it inflamed the peculiar Van Anda imagination. The Associated Press had picked it up from Lord Northcliffe's Times.

The cables to London vibrated with the managing editor's messages that night. He had his London bureau arrange a contract with the Northcliffe paper whereby The New York Times might have sole rights to all future Tut-ankh-Amen stories in New York, and offered to sell rights for The Times of London in all other North American cities where there might be purchasers. He made arrangements at the same time for New York rights to any pictures from the tomb at Luxor. No one in the office seemed to know it at the time, but the managing editor could read hieroglyphics.

On Dec. 21 Sir Harry Perry-Robinson of The Times of London entered the tomb for a story on what it looked like after thirty centuries as a dwelling for royal mummies. He came out, a few hours later, trembling with excitement over the wonders he had beheld. Van Anda put the story on Page 1, with a three-column run-over on Page 2. It was more thrilling than anything Rider Haggard might have conceived.

It told of the majestic figures of the Egyptian Monarch and his Queen still erect after 3,000 years, of their gold sandals and rich jewels, of magnificent royal couches and royal robes, and mysterious chests filled with ancient treasures. The reporter was awed by the royal couple's rare beauty, still intact in the time-defying masks that covered their mummified features. He described the throne as he had come upon it in wavering candlelight, as "incomparably magnificent and wondrously beautiful," encrusted with precious jewels. It was a powerful piece. Times readers lapped it up.

Subsequent stories and pictures, with rich spreads in The Times rotogravure section on Sundays, made all North America King Tut conscious.

The Times was flooded with queries from United States, Canadian and South American journals and from weekly and monthly magazines eager to spread the stories before their readers. Schools, museums and colleges wrote in for lantern slides. Designers and merchants pleaded for photographs on which to base Tut-ankh-Amen creations. The Times had never had anything quite like it. The average American came to know Tut-ankh-Amen, his Queen, their country and their times almost as well as he knew baseball scores and batting averages.

The Times managing editor often stayed at the office through daybreak studying photographs of objects taken from the death chamber for clues to something new about the Tut-ankh-Amen reign. He sent Russell Owen to Princeton one day for a photograph of a stele, and long after he had put The Times to bed that night associates passing his office saw him bent over the 4,000-year-old inscriptions with a magnifying glass, consulting his Breasted's Dictionary, rapidly scribbling in the characteristic tight Van Anda script on sheets of copy paper. He wore the zealot's look.

The managing editor, it later developed, had stumbled on a 4,-000-year-old forgery. He deduced from the hieroglyphics that one of young Tut-ankh-Amen's military chiefs, Horemheb, had erased —or had ordered someone to erase—the Monarch's signature and had his own put in, instead. Van Anda figured that Horemheb had killed the young Pharoah, since assassination was fairly routine with would-be throne-usurpers at that period. When Van Anda's deductions were laid before Prof. Philip K. Hitti, an Egyptologist at Princeton, he confirmed them. It developed that Dr. Le Grain, a French Egyptologist, had suspected the Horemheb forgery, but had never developed it. Dr. Hitti was impressed. He called the managing editor's discovery "a most remarkable example of scholarly intuition and acumen."

Three weeks after The Times reporter visited Tut-ankh-Amen's Tomb, Dr. D. T. MacDougal, general secretary for the American Association for the Advancement of Science, had his friend, John W. (Deacon) Harding of The Times news staff introduce him to Van Anda. Dr. MacDougal explained that some important and highly interesting papers were to be discussed at the association's three-day meeting at Cambridge, Mass., on Dec. 27-29. He wondered if Van Anda could spare a good man to cover the sessions.

It might have been that the stars were just right for The Times to take the lead in regular coverage of scientific meetings. Anyway, when Van Anda looked around the city room his eyes fell upon Alva Johnston, a brilliant reporter who had covered some science stories. Johnston had labored over Thomas A. Edison's famed questionnaire the year before, had found himself deficient in scientific knowledge and had doggedly studied to close the gap.

The managing editor took Johnston off the Hundred Neediest Cases on which he was then working, and assigned him to the Cambridge meetings.

When Johnston reached Cambridge on Dec. 27, the only other reporter there was David Dietz, sent by E. W. Scripps. For three days Johnston scurried from one group session to another, ferreting out papers most likely to have popular appeal, stripping them of awkward technical verbiage and boiling them down to newspaper-story size. He wisely figured that the anthropology division would yield the best human interest material and concentrated chiefly on that, but pounced on anything else that could be served up so the layman might easily understand it. He was a little shy at first, for fear of sending more than The Times would use, but when he saw that Van Anda was running every line, he multiplied his output.

On the first day Johnston was inclined to overcondense. When Dr. E. H. Moore, the association's retiring president, offered his own paper, a complicated screed on mathematics, Johnston politely suggested that the subject might be a bit too deep for the average reader. Dr. Moore did not agree. "If you send it in full," he told the reporter, "I think The Times will print it." Johnston sent a modified version and, to his astonishment, Van Anda ran it, along with livelier items on Page 1 next day. The main story carried the headline, "Scientists Uphold Evolution Theory." William Jennings Bryan, Dr. John Roach Straton and the fundamentalists generally were then in full cry against the scientists' theories of evolution, and the story stirred animated discussion.

The last paragraph of that first day's story indicated in general what the program was to cover. The world was still blissfully innocent of the tremendous forces the scientists were trying to release. Johnston wrote, "There will be laid before the convention the results of the latest investigations of the arrangements of electrons in atoms, of the artificial breakdown of atoms, of the Einstein and quantum theories of the colloid and crystal states of matter, and other deep subjects which today interest the scientists but are practically a sealed book to the general public."

Next day The Times presented the first newspaper story explaining in some detail what atomic energy researchers were up to. The headlines proclaimed, "Scientists Witness Smash-Up of Atoms." The story carried words completely new to most readers—"isotopes," "alpha particles"—terms that were to take on frightening importance with the passing years. Times subscribers got their kindergarten course in atomic energy from the Johnston stories out of Cambridge.

Reader response to the Cambridge series was astonishing. Times subscribers loved the stuff. Though more than a half page was devoted to the final session at Cambridge no one seemed to think that was too much. Among the letters that poured in from readers were many from scientists applauding the coverage. On the basis of their warm commendation Alva Johnston won the Pulitzer Prize for the best example of a reporter's work in 1922. The annual meetings of the American Association for the Advancement of Science have always been fully covered ever since by all great newspapers and news services.

Ordinarily, The Times devoted a minimum of space to run-of-the-mill crime news. While sensational newspapers served up gory detail on almost any murder, or dredged deeply for scandal, Times editors ignored the outright sordid and the inky tidbits about showgirls, playboys and wealthy exhibitionists who wove gaily in and out of the courts and local pokeys.

There were times, though, when Ochs' newspaper outdid all competition, sensational and conservative, on crime stories and, on rare occasions, on domestic tiffs. Mostly, though, it gave major space allotments in cases where it figured there had been great injustice, or where the personalities involved were social or public figures too important to be ignored.

Even when it devoted full pages to crime stories or to divorce actions, as it sometimes did, the writing was apt to be much more restrained than in most newspapers. Ochs was once asked about these rare instances of lapse from general Times policy on crime news, and his answer was, "The yellows see such stories only as opportunities for sensationalism. When The Times gives a great amount of space to such stories it turns out authentic sociological documents."

The Times gave extensive coverage to the shooting of Stanford White by Harry K. Thaw in 1906 and to the subsequent trial. Ochs justified this on the ground that White was a famous architect and Thaw a representative of one of Pittsburgh's leading families; that both were therefore unusual subjects for "sociological documents." He was chided, in this instance, by his friend W. Moberly Bell of The Times of London who pointed out that conservative British journals did not print so much crime detail that the Crown had difficulty finding unbiased jurors when cases came to trial.

An early example of broad crime coverage by The Times being motivated by the feeling that a great injustice had been committed was the Leo Frank case in 1915. Frank, a pencil factory manager, was convicted of the rape of a 14-year-old girl, on Confederate Memorial Day, April 26, 1913, in Atlanta, Georgia. On the night of Aug. 16, 1915, a band of men took Frank from the State Prison at Milledgeville, Ga., drove him 125 miles to the scene of the crime and hanged him from a tree.

The Times sent Charles Willis Thompson, one of its most brilliant reporters, to investigate the lynching. His series on the case was a model of objective reporting. He delved deeply into the lynchers' motives and into the regional viewpoint and stuck to fact. Other reporters handled the story with less restraint. Editorially, The Times denounced the lynchers, but the news columns never strayed from the facts as Thompson found and presented them. That has remained general Times policy.

There were later examples of The Times blanketing contemporaries in crime coverage—the still-unsolved murder of the Rev. Edward H. Hall and his choir leader, Mrs. Eleanor R. Mills, under a crabapple tree outside New Brunswick, N. J., in 1922; the trial of nine Negroes on a rape charge in northern Alabama in 1931; the Lindbergh kidnapping case in 1932; the public hearings on organized crime by a Senate Committee in 1951. All these came within the "sociological document" definition without leading The

Times into the fairly common newspaper practice of cramming readers with murder as daily breakfast diet.

In 1949 Russell Porter, a veteran on the news staff, spent 158 court days, without relief, reporting the trial in Federal Court in New York of twelve Communists indicted for conspiracy to teach overthrow of the United States Government. Testimony in this case came to around 5,000,000 words and filled 15,000 pages of transcript. Porter's stories totalled 175,000 words. He had help only on the day the defendants were convicted, when the city desk sent thirteen more reporters to do side-bar stories and to poll the jury. Porter's work on this assignment set a Times record.

This might be the proper point, too, to bring out the fact that although The Times does not use the news columns for crusading, it does on occasion send reporters to survey areas bedevilled by physical and economic misery. There has been more of this since Ochs' time than before.

Raymond Daniell, an utterly fearless reporter, entered northeastern Arkansas in early spring of 1935, for example, to get material for a series of six articles on the unhappy plight of the cotton sharecroppers. The district was then under the domination of planters' night-riders who wanted no surveys. They were trying to choke off unionization of the sharecroppers and were not the type to brook outside interference, but Daniell got the facts and presented them.

This excursion into crime coverage and sociological surveys has carried us a bit precipitatedly beyond chronological narrative. So we must backtrack.

In his twenty-seven years' stewardship at The Times Ochs had kept on friendly terms with his help. There had been no major labor trouble. The Times had come out every day, including Sundays and holidays, without missing a single issue.

When The Times first started in 1851 it had no Sunday paper. The first Sunday run was printed on April 21, 1861, when the public clamored for Civil War news seven days a week. For three weeks the Sunday paper sold for 2 cents, then went to 3 cents. It found eager buyers.

From that time on, except on New Year's day—a high holiday

during the Raymond period—publication was uninterrupted. The only other exception was on its seventy-second anniversary, Sept. 18, 1923.

A sudden strike of pressmen, general throughout the city, made it impossible to print on that day. From Sept. 18 through Sept. 26, The Times came out, as all other New York publications did, under the mass title: "The Combined New York Morning Newspapers." Set above this were the individual title lines of the various newspapers. Each day while the strike lasted volunteer pressmen, including many white-collar men, put out this combined sheet. For the first few days it ran to eight pages, then to sixteen. The combined journal had no editorials. News was condensed into brief paragraphs.

Two weeks after the strike had ended The Times ran off several thousand copies of the issue it had prepared for Sept. 18, 1923. It used some for its official news files and for morgue clipping purposes, and sent the rest to private and public libraries all over the world. Actually, though, it was a sort of ghost edition. General Times subscribers never saw it.

CHAPTER
23

O NE NIGHT in late July, 1923, President Warren G. Harding, who
had fallen gravely ill on the West Coast, took a sudden turn for
the worse after a brief rally. Van Anda sensed that the President
might die, and wanted a reporter in Plymouth, Vt., should Vice
President Calvin Coolidge have to take the presidential oath there.
He had The Times operator put through a telephone call for James
A. Hagerty, political reporter who was to leave New York that
night on summer vacation, but the switchboard in Hagerty's uptown apartment house had shut down for the night, and there was
no answer.

At midnight Jim Hagerty, packing the family luggage, was startled by pounding at the apartment door. He threw the door open
and faced Mike Haggerty, another Times man. "Van Anda sent
me," Haggerty explained. "Harding's dying. The boss wants you
to get up to Vermont right away to cover Coolidge." He said Van
Anda had found that the only train available at that hour was a
local on the West Shore. Jim would just about have time to make
it. Jim Hagerty bade his wife a hasty good-by, seized a packed bag
and followed his associate downstairs. A rumbling thunderstorm
lashed the city, but Mike Haggerty had held the cab that had
brought him from Times Square.

The pavement in front of The Times Annex was like polished
onyx in the rain when the cab skidded down the block. Before the
reporters could climb out, they saw the managing editor in the

261

middle of the street with a staff man holding an umbrella to shield him. He said to Jim: "You have just time enough to make the ferry and that West Shore train. Here's all the cash I could scrape up from the staff." He thrust a wad of small bank notes through the cab window, and unloaded silver coin from his pocket. It came to about $200.

He told Hagerty: "The train will stop at Kingston long enough for you to grab a cup of coffee. When you get to Albany, our circulation man there will be waiting for you with his car. He'll drive you to Plymouth. That's all arranged. Keep in touch."

He waved the cab away; watched it tear westward toward Weehawken Ferry.

Hagerty got into Plymouth at 8 o'clock next morning. He had been up all night because the slow-dragging West Shore local had no sleeper. He got neighborly greetings at the old Coolidge farmhouse. He had met the Vice President on assignment, and Mrs. Coolidge had been a family friend for years. When he was a cub reporter in Plattsburg, N. Y., she lived across the border, in Vermont. He explained his assignment, and on the Coolidges' advice took a room in the nearest hotel, the Okema, in Ludlow, ten miles away.

Only a few other reporters had come up—Roy Atkinson of The Boston Post, Paul Mallon of The United Press, an Associated Press man, and a man from The New York American. Each day as President Harding wavered between life and death they drove down to the Coolidge homestead for a quiet chat. Mrs. Coolidge would sit on the cool porch over knitting. The Vice President might say a word or two, but was characteristically taciturn. On Aug. 1, when reporters found him in D. P. Brown's hayfield, down the road, running Brown's horse-drawn hay rake, they did a piece about that. Mostly they just sat around the hotel porch after dark, and tried to talk above the crickets' strident chorus.

A few minutes after 11:30 o'clock New York time on the night of Aug. 2 the Associated Press machine in The Times telegraph room came violently alive with bulletin bells and the capitalized warning "EOS! EOS!" the signal for "extraordinary service." The teletype hysterically chattered: "San Francisco, Aug. 2—President Harding died at 7:30 o'clock tonight of a stroke of apoplexy . . ."

A copy boy tore the bulletin from the machine and raced to the telegraph desk with it. The editor there leaped up and hurried across the floor to the managing editor's office—and the smoothly geared Ochs news machine went into top speed.

Van Anda ordered column rules turned on all thirty pages that morning to make the traditional black borders. He sent directly to the Coolidge home at Plymouth Notch a wire that said: "Regret to advise you President Harding died at 11:35 New York time tonight. We would appreciate any statement you might care to have us publish." A copy of the Harding death bulletin with additional details assembled in the office was posted in Times Tower street-level windows for the passing throngs.

The moment the bulletin came through Van Anda had Lauren D. Lyman, on the city desk, call the hotel in Ludlow to pass the news to Hagerty, with orders to Hagerty to get to the Coolidge cottage at once for any statement that might be made by the Vice President, and to pick up reaction and color. The telephone service into Ludlow was poor in those days. Lyman (called "Deak") had difficulty putting the call through.

The reporters at Ludlow on the Coolidge assignment had sat around all night, with no word about Harding. Just as the old grandfather clock in the hotel lobby was tolling midnight Hagerty started up the carpeted stairs to his room. Before the last clock note died, the hotel telephone buzzed. It was The Boston Post calling Roy Atkinson. "Harding's dead," his desk told him crisply. "Get over to the Coolidge house."

Hagerty had paused on the staircase. Atkinson turned to echo the message, "Harding's dead"—and the whole group leaped to action. The reporters had hired a Ludlow car with a local driver to be prepared to rush them over the rutty mountain road—a rough highway at best, and then under repair—to the Coolidge place. They scrambled for the car, and tore away from the Okema in enfolding summer dark, with the horn mutilating the rural silence. Farm windows came alight and throughout the area telephone party lines spread word of Harding's death.

When the reporters sprang from their car on the Coolidge lawn they learned that Van Anda's wire and a telegram sent by President Harding's secretary had been delivered five minutes before by

Western Union messenger who had driven in from Bridgewater, Vt. The reporters asked for a statement. Coolidge asked them to make themselves comfortable and retired to a little chamber off the parlor to prepare it.

With characteristic caution he dictated it slowly, with many revisions, to Erwin C. Geisser, his stenographer. This took a half-hour. While he worked over it, neighbors awakened from deep slumber assembled outside in whispering clumps. Their murmuring came through the open windows. The news that Neighbor Calvin was to be thirtieth President of the United States was awesome.

Finally, Coolidge was ready with the statement. It was simple, as the reporters had known it would be. They read it rapidly, spoke thanks, withdrew with dignity, brushed past the assembled villagers, hopped back into the car, and, again with horn blasting and echoing through the mountains, raced back to Ludlow. There was no place in Plymouth Notch from which to telephone. The Coolidges had no telephone in their own home. Miss Florence Cilley had one in her general store, but the store was not open. Besides, that wire would have to be kept clear for Government use. Attorney General Harry Daugherty had warned Coolidge to be prepared to take the oath as soon as he learned of President Harding's death. It was the tradition that the United States was not to be without a Chief Executive, even for a few hours.

Back in The Times city room in Forty-third Street, meanwhile, Van Anda had stepped up office tempo. When Lyman finally got the clerk in the hotel at Ludlow and learned that Hagerty was on his way over the mountains, Van Anda ordered him to keep the wire open. The managing editor then had another desk assistant put in a second call to the central telephone office at Ludlow to open a reserve line, should the hotel link fail. These two calls, although Van Anda was not aware of it, blocked all other newspapers. The Times had a monopoly on service into Ludlow.

At 1:15 A.M. the car full of reporters came to a tearing stop in front of the hotel. The reporters stampeded into the red-carpeted lobby. It was filled with half-dressed farmers huddled around the clerk's single telephone. Deak Lyman was reading the news from early editions of the Harding extra, including baseball scores, and the clerk was passing the stuff along, as in a relayed broadcast.

Hagerty took over. He dictated the Vice President's simple statement to Edward Klauber who was on the rewrite desk:

"Reports have reached me, which I fear are correct, that President Harding is gone. The world has lost a great and good man. He was my chief and my friend . . ."

It ran on for 200 words more.

When Hagerty finished sending, The Times released the wires into Ludlow. The girl operator in the tiny central office still had trouble, though. Incoming calls had dammed up, and when the other reporters at the Okema tried to get through to their offices, the snarl was difficult to unravel. Some eventually got their stuff through, some did not. The men jumped back into their hired car and again bumped and jolted across the rutted highway toward Plymouth Notch to see Calvin Coolidge take the presidential oath.

Good fortune blessed The Times that night. After the Coolidge statement had been written in the office, Klauber called the hotel in Ludlow again, hoping to get Jim Hagerty. By freakish cross-connection, the call by-passed Ludlow and rang the telephone that linemen from Rutland had just hooked up in the Coolidge parlor. When Erwin Geisser answered the ring, Klauber assumed he had the Okema clerk. He asked for Jim Hagerty. Geisser said Hagerty had been and gone. He wondered if he could help The Times.

Klauber asked, "Has Mr. Coolidge taken the oath as President of the United States?"

Geisser said he had. He described the swearing-in by lamp light in the old parlor. He answered questions freely, and Klauber got a detailed picture of the ceremony. He thanked Geisser, hung up, and turned to the managing editor. Van Anda was delighted. His nervous hands went into the washing act. He hovered over the typewriter as Klauber pounded out the oath-taking scene:

Special to The New York Times

PLYMOUTH, Vt., Friday, AUG. 3—Calvin Coolidge took the oath of office as President of the United States at 2:47 Eastern Standard Time this morning (3:47 New York Time).

The oath was administered by his father, John C. Coolidge, who found the text in a book in the library, after having expected to wait until it was received from Washington.

The taking of the oath was a simple and a solemn scene. Those who were gathered in the living room of the Coolidge home at Plymouth Notch, besides the President and his father, were Mrs. Coolidge, L. L. Lane, president of the Railway Mail Association of New England; Congressman Porter H. Dale of Vermont; Joseph H. Fountain, editor of The Springfield (Vt.) Reporter; Erwin C. Geisser, Mr. Coolidge's assistant secretary.

As the elder Mr. Coolidge read the oath, Mrs. Coolidge looked on with wet eyes. When the end was reached, President Coolidge, raising his right hand, said in a low, clear voice: "I do, so help me God."

A moment later the group dissolved and the President and Mrs. Coolidge retired.

When the carload of reporters returned to the Coolidge house, the President and Mrs. Coolidge had already gone to bed, but the President's father was on the porch. He told the newspapermen that they were too late for the oath-taking ceremony, but filled them in on details. He told how the neighbors had leaned on the window sills to watch as Calvin Coolidge received the oath. By this time more telephone linemen had come. They had put telephones on trees outside Miss Cilley's general store and had laced in a few extra wires for Western Union. The reporters dashed for these instruments.

They were all a little too late. By that time The Times was on the street with the full story with exclusive features. An eight-column headline said:

PRESIDENT HARDING DIES SUDDENLY;
STROKE OF APOPLEXY AT 7:30 P.M.;
CALVIN COOLIDGE IS PRESIDENT

In the center of the page, under the banner, were large cuts of the dead President and of his successor. The Coolidge statement, and the story of the ceremony in the Coolidge parlor, were boxed in two columns at the left. The story on Harding's death had two columns at the right. A full six pages covered the lives of both men, with ample photographic illustration. It was superb coverage. No other newspaper in the country had anywhere near as much fact. The tied-up telephone wires and the freakish crossed wire had given The Times overwhelming advantage. Van Anda's thorough preparation had coppered it. Praise poured in from newspaper owners and editors here and abroad.

The Harding extra was Carr Van Anda's final major achievement as Ochs' managing editor. He was only 59 when he put out that edition, but several spells of illness had drained his strength and he wisely figured it was time to yield the reins. He turned them over to Frederick T. Birchall who had been his assistant, and who had the same keen news sense as Van Anda, but a warmer personality.

The week before Van Anda retired he plotted one more big assignment—coverage of the solar eclipse that was due on Saturday morning, Jan. 24, 1925. He hired Dr. W. J. Luyten of Harvard University Observatory to do one of the lead stories from a military plane flying at 15,000 feet; got experts aboard the United States Navy dirigible Los Angeles, which was to fly toward the sun; arranged for complete city coverage, and alerted Times correspondents along the track of totality not only to report the event but even to watch the behavior of livestock—cows, birds, barnyard fowl, zoo inhabitants—to study their reaction to the world's plunge into prenoon darkness. No angle was left open.

Though he was anything but sentimental, Van Anda moved among the city room desks the day before the eclipse, saying goodby to the men who had worked with him, in some cases, the full twenty-one years he had spent with The Times. The impersonal glare that Alva Johnston had described as the "Van Anda death ray" was softened as he made these rounds. One of the desks Van Anda stopped at was that of Orrin Dunlap Jr. Orrin Dunlap Sr. had been Times correspondent at Niagara Falls since the Eighties. His son had come on as The Times' first radio editor in 1922. Young Dunlap looked up. "R.C.A. engineers in Van Cortlandt Park are going to study the effects of totality on both short and long radio waves," he explained. "I'm figuring out some questions to ask. That's my eclipse assignment."

The managing editor knew. He had included that angle in his mapping. He offered his hand. He said, "Just stopped to say goodby, Mr. Dunlap. I'm retiring tomorrow. Going into eclipse myself." He moved along before the reporter could answer.

It was a magnificent eclipse at that. On Sunday morning The

Times had five solid pages on what had happened when the sun blacked out. No other newspaper in the world had an account so full or so thorough.

No one could suspect that Carr Van Anda had deliberately chosen this moment for exit, but it was perfect timing. He moved into the wings at the very moment that Heaven's spotlight went dark and dripped fiery beads from its perimeter.

Exit, The Master.

Long after he had left, on nights when news was slow, reporters who had worked for Van Anda would sit around and swap legends about him. They recalled a new Times man, Alan Johnson, but freshly come from The World, who was sent one night to cover a big hotel fire near Tannersville, N. Y.

Johnson got talking to a thin, pipe-smoking man with a cap down over his eyes, who seemed to know more details about the hotel's history, and about the fire, than any official in the community. The stranger all but filled Johnson's copy paper with pertinent details.

Johnson was extremely grateful.

He said, "You know, Mister, you would have made one hell of a good newspaperman."

The gaunt pipe-smoker nodded, and his thin lips sealed just a bit tighter in a suppressed grin. He was Carr V. Van Anda.

CHAPTER

24

THE CHANGING of the guard on the news room floor did not affect news handling at The Times. Birchall and Van Anda had worked together so long that the only noticeable difference in the newspaper was in improved literary style. Van Anda had cared little for good writing so long as he had all the facts. Birchall went after fact with the same fierce intensity, and jacked up the style, too. When a piece was particularly good he would come to the reporter's desk and his high-pitched, penetrating voice would cry out, "Well done, Laddie." He was a lively little man, who squinted at the world through lenses thick as plate glass. In deep thought his head bowed to his chest and his right hand worked at his goatee as if the gesture helped to pluck ideas from his mind.

The news machine that he took over was in excellent shape. So was the paper generally.

During the unhappy year and a half when Ochs groped in melancholia's thick gloom, and during the time he took to brush aside completely the darkening curtain, organizational momentum kept the great ship steady. Its gross income in 1924 exceeded $20,000,-000, bringing the twenty-five year total to $150,000,000, and still a major portion of its profits were going back into greater development. The Times' news coverage had greatly expanded. Its Wide World photographic service, started in 1919, counted 100 staff men and clerical assistants in every quarter of the globe by 1925. Its communications system, the most modern in journalism, showed the way to the field. In 1924 Fred E. Meinholtz, Times communications chief, built a super-heterodyne receiver in the Forty-third Street Annex for direct reception of press dispatches from Britain, France, Germany, Italy and Switzerland. The following year reception range was extended to include Japan, China and the Dutch West Indies. No other newspaper had such service.

The Times' enterprise in getting exclusive story rights from explorers, scientists, and pioneering fliers surpassed anything in journalistic history. It gave the world the most gripping adventure series ever published in a newspaper—William Beebe from the floor of tropical seas; Auguste Piccard from the stratosphere; stories from scientific expeditions in jungles or polar regions; from men and women scaling glacial peaks where no other human had trod. It was Jules Verne stuff—but true—and the new wireless set-up helped to serve it hot.

By the end of 1924 The Times' daily circulation was up to 351,000. Its advertising linage that year exceeded 26,000,000. This was greater by 2,000,000 lines than the 1923 total and was 8,000,000 lines beyond the nearest competitor. The Sunday paper, with its special features now following a crisp news line rather than rambling into the vague hearts-and-flowers field of Sabbath journalism, had reached 580,000 circulation. Lester Markel, the new Sunday editor, who succeeded Ralph Graves, was as fanatically insistent on the news peg for his material as Van Anda and Birchall on the daily paper were, and the jumps in circulation testified to his wisdom.

Ochs celebrated the great upsurge at a dinner in The Times restaurant on Dec. 12, 1924. With his assistants grouped around him, he analyzed the reasons for the newspaper's incredible growth. He recalled the early days of his ownership, when he humbly stood in prospective advertisers' reception rooms waiting a chance to plead The Times' worth as a medium for selling their merchandise. He said: "I remember how humiliating that was. How I would have welcomed the position in which I could have appeared and represented a newspaper of which I could say: 'I'm not soliciting advertising. I don't want yours unless it would be creditable to my newspaper and profitable to you.' If I could have assumed that position I would have been as proud as Lucifer." Actually, he had reached that position, and privately he was as proud as Lucifer.

He told how The Times had tightened advertising censorship to keep out questionable or misleading offerings; how it screened and sifted material sent in for its Business Opportunities ads and for its Shoppers' Column so that readers could depend on the reliability of statements made by advertisers. He recalled his pioneering in advertising censorship, how he compelled prospective advertisers to submit character, bank and business references for checking. He dwelt at some length on the need for making advertising matter interesting and seeing that it was consistent with general Times make-up and news content. He had set a new standard of good taste in advertising typography. He knew, and loved, type, and allowed no advertiser to use crude, messy blobs of ink to attract attention. He educated his clients to the drawing power of artistic printing and carefully made cuts.

The publisher spoke with unhidden pride, at the same meeting, of the tremendous success of his "Hundred Neediest Cases," the Christmas-season appeal for funds for exceptionally deserving persons among the city's poor that he had started in December, 1912.

"Today," he told his aides, "we passed over the total of $1,000,000 in cash to the Hundred Neediest Cases, growing from the $3,000 of twelve years ago to $175,000 last year, and with a prospect of $200,000 this year. That is a record never equalled by any other newspaper in the world. No direct appeal, no mail announcements, no canvassers, no soliciting, but wholly left to the drawing qualities of the columns of The New York Times."

It was understandable pride, but in the years ahead during and beyond Ochs' time, the fund was to climb to greater peaks. It reached a high of $400,121 in 1946, and by the end of 1950 the total raised by the appeal from its inception in 1912 had come to $8,933,613, the gift of 351,108 contributors.

The Hundred Neediest had justified Ochs' original stand. Soon after he initiated the project, a reader had offered to endow it with $1,000,000, the interest to be spent solely on cases investigated by The Times itself, rather than by charitable organizations. Another stipulation was that The Times administer the funds.

Ochs refused the endowment, gently explaining that The Times was a newspaper and not a charitable society. He pointed out that

one of his prime motives in establishing the appeal was to educate
the public on the plight of the city's unfortunate. In later years,
there were other offers of large endowments, some in the final
testaments of kindly and well-meaning men and women, but whenever they carried strings or stipulations that would have meant a
deviation from the original Ochs policy, they were refused.

It came to pass that in some cases beneficiaries of the Hundred
Neediest fund eventually became contributors. A number of or-
phans named in early appeals were adopted by Times readers. The
novelist Robert W. Chambers even had one of his fictional orphan
heroines marry the wealthy man who had helped her as one of The
Times neediest.

Yale University had conferred an honorary Master of Arts degree
on Ochs in June, 1922. At the ceremony Dr. Angell, Yale's president, praised Ochs' service to the nation by what he called "great
journalism which strives to print the truth and to discuss it with
insight, intelligence and impartiality." Two years later Dr. Nicholas Murray Butler, president of Columbia University, conferred
an honorary LL.D. on the publisher, called him "The master mind
of journalism in any land" and lauded The Times as "a great organ
of public education and public opinion which now has no equal in
influence, which sets the standard of excellence for newspaper
service and the fair and adequate treatment of the world's news,
and which faithfully represents the United States to the World and
the World to the United States."

These honors seemed to embarrass the publisher a little. He felt
keenly his own lack of formal schooling, and when educators and
statesmen extolled him and his works he could not get over the
feeling that he was an actor in a dream masquerade. This reaction
could not stop the flow of scholastic honors. On Oct. 15, 1925, the
University of Chattanooga gave him the Doctor of Letters degree,
and in June, 1926, New York University bestowed the same degree
on him. The curly-haired barefoot boy, who had dropped Chronicles on dawn-lit porches in Knoxville while contemporaries slum-
bered, had come a long, long way.

He was thrice a grandfather, now: Marian Effie Sulzberger had
been born on Dec. 31, 1918; Ruth Rachel Sulzberger on March 12,
1921; Judith Peixotto Sulzberger on Dec. 27, 1923; Arthur Ochs

(Punch) Sulzberger was to be born on Feb. 5, 1926. These four were to own The Times eventually, they and their children. Marian became Mrs. Orvil E. Dryfoos on July 8, 1941, and her husband later became assistant to Sulzberger. They have three children: Jacqueline Hays Dryfoos, born May 8, 1943; Robert Ochs Dryfoos, born Nov. 4, 1944, and Susan Warms Dryfoos, born Nov. 5, 1946. Ruth became Mrs. Ben Hale Golden on June 1, 1946, and the mother of Stephen Arthur Ochs Golden, born March 10, 1947, and Michael Davis Golden, born July 15, 1949. The Goldens devote their time to The Chattanooga Times. Judith Sulzberger married Matthew Rosenschein Jr. on Dec. 22, 1946, and both she and her husband are medical doctors. Punch married Barbara Grant at her home in White Plains on July 2, 1948. The other grandchildren were married at Hillandale, the 57-acre Ochs' estate in Westchester, but Ochs did not live to see the ceremonies. Hillandale itself was later to pass out of the Sulzbergers' hands. They sold it in June, 1949, and, preserving the name, took a much smaller home in Stamford, Conn.

On Jan. 13, 1925, Ochs talked to the students of the Joseph Pulitzer School of Journalism at Columbia. He told how the world had changed in his fifty years on newspapers; how he had seen the advent of newsprint made from wood, of the web press, the typewriter, the linotype, the telephone, the roll-film camera, the wireless, the electric motor, the automobile, the plane and radio broadcasting—among other great inventions. He dwelt a while on the wonders that the next half century might yield, and then he talked of conscientiousness as vital equipment for the newspaperman.

"A reporter," he told the group, "is assigned to a task; he arrives too late, or not at all, accepts from another reporter what occurred and writes it as his own observations. Deserving the same censure is another who does not take the trouble to confirm his facts; one who gets his own views tangled with the views of the person interviewed; one who fails to give the person affected by his story the benefit of the doubt; still another who needlessly gives pain and disregards, or is perhaps oblivious to, the sensitiveness that persons have about their personal affairs; one who, to appear smart and witty, misrepresents or exaggerates; one who is indifferent to the responsibility of his newspaper, who is careless with its reputation for truth and accuracy; one who plagiarizes, one who is cynical, offensive, discourteous, vulgar or impertinent; one who regards himself as an editor when he should be a reporter. No one can conscientiously represent a decent newspaper and be guilty of any of these offenses against the ethics of the profession, and what is expected of a gentleman."

All through his newspaper career Ochs had resented the too-common feeling in city rooms that reporting and editing were the most honorable callings in the profession, and this day he expressed his resentment.

"Now," he said, and the tufted white eyebrows perceptibly lifted, "we come to so-called commercial journalism—advertising. Why is advertising called commercial in contradistinction to news and editorial writing? Is it not a distinction without a difference? Why is not a doctor or a lawyer commercial when he accepts a fee for his services?

"Advertising in its final analysis should be news. If it is not news it is worthless. In its proper use the highest order of journalistic ability may be exercised, and through it a distinct public service may be performed. In advertising truth should abide and be controlling. In advertising the science and art of journalism may be more readily prostituted, for it is here that the devil of journalism plays his most alluring tunes to catch the credulous and the unwary. An honest man must make an honest appearance, and in promoting a righteous cause he should wear attractive clothes to compete with the devil's advocate. To do this successfully takes a high order of intelligence and of courage. Here is the zest of a fight. Here is to be found the thrill of victory . . . The better the class of advertising, the better the newspaper. You can more readily judge the character of a newspaper by its advertising columns than by any other outward appearance. Good advertising is of prime importance. It calls for the best talents—the same talents essential to the making of good editors, copy readers, headline artists, and all others engaged in gathering and presenting news, or expressing opinion."

With characteristic modesty, he did not dwell long on The Times itself except to say:

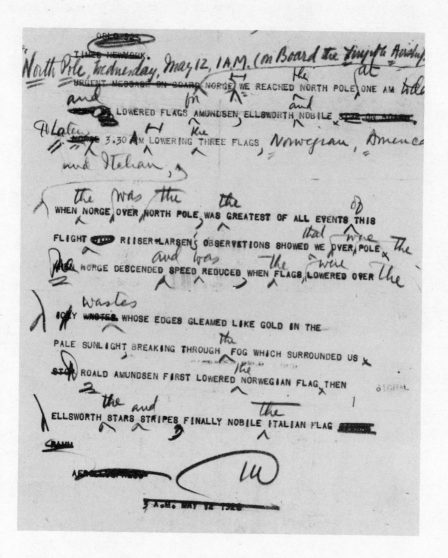

*The Top of the World Becomes a Dateline: The historic message
from the Norge.*

"Our greatest pride is that we have vindicated the newspaper reading public; that we have demonstrated that there is a reward for honest, decent, dignified journalism."

The New York Times' interest in the lost, the forgotten and un-penetrated places on earth dates back to 1886 when it gave its readers long-delayed accounts of Lieut. Frederick Schwatka's jour-ney up the frozen, barely known western shore of Alaska. Its report-ing of latter-day expeditions to unexplored places reached peak between 1923 and 1949. There was barely a season during this period, except in the second World War years, when its pages were without some first-hand account of man's thrilling air, sea and land conquests; of expeditions to Tibet, to the lost Incan and Mayan cities, to the jungles of Africa, South America, Asia and Central America. It bought exclusive rights to the stories, and equipped the expedition leaders with wireless sets for quick transmission of discoveries.

One of Ochs' reporters once described the publisher's approach to science news as a "romantic interest" in the subject. Van Anda approached it down calm avenues of thought, with cold, measured pace; Ochs went at it with wide-eyed wonder, with something bordering on emotionalism.

We must edge a little into the future, here, to illustrate this point. Ochs had enormous respect for Yankee ingenuity as exemplified in the Morse-Bell school of inventors. He thought of such men as scientists, but knew no more than any other layman, for example, of a man like Josiah Willard Gibbs of Yale and his research into the mysteries of thermodynamics.

In 1927 Ochs hired Waldemar Kaempffert, an engineer, to write editorials on science. Kaempffert was probably the first man on any newspaper editorial board anywhere to devote himself exclu-sively to this subject. He also did a weekly Sunday piece and occa-sional magazine features on the latest developments in science.

One day in 1927 Ochs eagerly took Kaempffert down to the Bell Laboratories to see one of the first experimental television ma-chines. He had just witnessed the workings of the crude television scanner and its possibilities had left him enraptured.

Kaempffert gravely studied the device, asked technical questions about it, and promised to do an editorial on the machine. On the way back to The Times the publisher talked in high glow about the wonder of television, and enthusiastically predicted that within a few months or a year almost every American home would have its own television set.

Kaempffert curbed Ochs' enthusiasm. He said: "I am afraid, Mr. Ochs, that at least another ten years, or more, will pass before we have commercial television, if then. These men are barely taking the first steps in its development."

That seemed to make the publisher a little unhappy, but his editorial writer had made a pretty good guess. The Times of Feb. 9, 1928, carried the thrilling headline:

PERSONS IN BRITAIN SEEN HERE BY TELEVISION
AS THEY POSE BEFORE BAIRD'S ELECTRIC EYE

But John L. Baird's images were extremely blurry and it took some imagination to recognize the shuddering shadowgraphs as the pictures of human beings. Another eleven years went by before commercial television was first shown publicly at the R.C.A. exhibit at the World's Fair on Flushing Meadow in New York in 1939, and large-scale television set production was held up by World War II.

But Ochs' hiring of Kaempffert, coupled three years later with the employment of William L. Laurence as the first newspaper reporter assigned exclusively to daily science coverage, marked an important step in the newspaper's history.

Laurence, on the news end, and Kaempffert, devoting himself to science editorials and interpretation of science news, gave The Times a headstart in this field that has never been overtaken. These two provided Times readers with the step-by-step story of breathtaking advancements in medicine, astronomy, chemistry and kindred fields. They were frequently first with the news of such discoveries as the sulfa drugs, penicillin, ACTH and cortisone. They told of the gradual development of hormones, of the Selye theory of bodily alarm reaction, of the new conception of matter in nuclear physics and of the expanding knowledge of relativity.

The Times devoted more space than any other daily journal in the world to keeping track of man's ever-increasing knowledge of the universe and of the nature of man. No one could have foretold it in the Twenties, but in the not-too-distant future a Times reporter was to be singled out to play literary midwife at the birth of the Atomic Age.

The extent to which The Times has followed scientists' groping into previously uninvaded realms was graphically illustrated in August, 1932. It was curious that members of two widely separated scientific expeditions, within a few days of each other, explained the eerie sensation of entering zones that men had never before penetrated.

On Aug. 18, 1932, after a twelve-hour ascent into the stratosphere with Max Cosyns, Auguste Piccard described the unprecedented thrill of floating through brilliantly lighted outer space, almost eleven miles above the earth.

"My greatest regret," he said, "was that I had to concentrate on my experiments in connection with the cosmic rays instead of devoting myself to admiring the grandeur of nature awakening at dawn." He described the sensation of lifting silently in a sealed gondola into "the kingdom of the stratosphere, a world apart, delightful beyond description" where, far below, the human eye could actually see both sunlight and moonlight transforming countless miles of cloud into overwhelming pearly beauty, such a vista as no human had ever beheld.

On Aug. 31, 1932, Beebe, in his bathysphere, beheld fresh wonders a half-mile below the ocean's surface off Bermuda by penetrating watery blackness with powerful new lights. On his return to the surface he wrote of the "complete and utter loneliness and isolation, a feeling wholly unlike the isolation felt when removed from fellow-men by mere distance."

Such coverage was part of the new journalism that Ochs and Van Anda had fostered and that Sulzberger and Birchall were to extend to ever-increasing limits.

Van Anda never really gave up his connection with The Times. Sometimes he wrote on vital subjects in letters to the editor and every now and then turned up with a science story tip that gave The Times a lead over its competitors. In his newly found leisure, he finished a learned paper on "The Unsolved Riddle of the Solar System," which put astronomers into high buzz. The paper refuted theories on the origin of the solar system previously presented by Sir James Jeans and by Dr. Harold Jeffreys of Cambridge University.

In the fall of 1928 Van Anda came to the office with a tidbit he had picked up in a British science magazine. It told how Jorgens Hals, a Scandinavian radio expert, had detected puzzling radio echoes that seemed to come from somewhere behind the moon. Prof. Carl Stormer of Oslo University had read a paper on the subject before colleagues at the Oslo Academy of Science and had confirmed Hals' theories. Van Anda dropped the item on Orrin Dunlap's desk and quietly suggested he might ask American scientists their views on the subject. Van Anda sensed that the Scandinavian was right, and that signals could be bounced off the moon, possibly from heavenly bodies remotely beyond it.

Dunlap wrote a long article on the Scandinavian's findings for the Sunday radio section of Dec. 2, 1928, (it was Dunlap, incidentally, who got out the Times' first full radio section on Sept. 13, 1925) and put an eight-column banner above it:

NORWAY HEARS ECHO FROM BEYOND THE MOON

A week later Dunlap ran the answers American radio men had sent him. Dr. Lee De Forest, obviously in a state of high intellectual excitement, had guessed, after some figuring, that if a radio beam could penetrate the Heaviside layer (which no one had actually established before Hals postulated it), an echo should return to earth about 2.7 seconds later.

" 'There are more things in heaven and earth, Horatio,' " he quoted in his statement, " 'than are dreamt of in your philosophy.' "

Dr. J. Barton Hoag of the University of Chicago and E. O. Hulbert and Dr. A. Hoyt Taylor, both of the United States Naval Research Laboratory, wrote along the same lines. Dr. Hoag thought the echoes might explain television ghost pictures and other distortion phenomena. No one used the term "radar" in connection with the echoes, but something like radar was what Van Anda had in mind when he tossed the morsel to Dunlap.

He was a mere eighteen years ahead of his time on that one. The Dunlap series had long been forgotten on Jan. 10, 1946, when

United States Army Signal Corps radar experts at Belmar, N. J.,
shot radio signals at the moon and caught the echoes. They kept
their secret for two weeks and then announced the results. Jack
Gould, then radio editor for The Times, wrote a front-page story
on it. It took the headline:

CONTACT WITH MOON
ACHIEVED BY RADAR
IN TEST BY THE ARMY

Gould's story said, "The first man-made contact with the moon
was achieved on Jan. 10 when the Army Signal Corps beamed a
radio signal on it and 2.4 seconds later received an echo reflected by
the celestial body."

No one in the office that night recalled Dunlap's stories and De
Forest's guess. De Forest had been off only a little—three-tenths of
a second.

Most readers were awed by the potentialities of man's first veri-
fied contact with a body in outer space, and a spate of philosophical
discussion followed the story. Ruth Sulzberger, daughter of the
publisher, worked up a bit of verse on it for The Times Magazine
section of Feb. 17, 1946:

> Diana, huntress, lovely maiden,
> Sometime symbol of the moon,
> Was it wise to break your silence
> Just to voice a high-pitched croon?
>
> Be the huntress, not the hunted.
> Let them find out nothing more.
> Speak not when you're spoken to.
> Don't assist the Signal Corps!

CHAPTER
25

WHEN SPRING of 1926 blew in, men were ready to approach the polar regions from the air. Space annihilation was becoming more than a dream—and The Times, in what was now an established tradition, was to lead the world in reporting the achievement through its own specialists and through first-hand accounts from the aerial pioneers.

Roald Amundsen, Lincoln Ellsworth and Umberto Nobile planned to fly across the North Pole from Spitzbergen to Alaska in the dirigible Norge in the spring of 1926. Lieut. Comdr. (later Rear Admiral) Richard Evelyn Byrd of the United States Navy meant, at the same time, to try for the Pole in the three-motored Fokker plane Josephine Ford, with Floyd Bennett as pilot.

Dr. John H. Finley, learned associate editor of The Times in this period, was thrilled by explorer contacts, too. The globe atlas in his office was autographed by visiting fliers and scientists across the places they had traversed and written about for The Times.

Until the Byrd and Norge expeditions set out, The Times had relied on long-wave radio to bring wireless press dispatches into the news room. It planned to get the polar flight stories by long-wave relay from Spitzbergen, to Norway, to Halifax, to New York. When Commander Byrd started North, though, with his plane on the Chantier's deck, a stowaway was found. He was Malcolm Hanson, a young radio engineer. He offered to work out his passage to the Arctic by building and operating a short-wave set. Byrd liked the idea.

Soon The Times wireless room began getting communications from the Chantier relayed through radio amateurs who had tuned in the Byrd ship. Meinholtz, The Times radio chief, immediately saw the possibilities of short-wave transmission for press dispatches and hastily had his staff rig a transmitter. He already had a short-wave receiver. In those days, almost all radio communication was by long-wave and an SOS from a vessel would force all broadcasting stations into sudden silence to clear the air until the emergency had passed.

Initial tests with the new short-wave outfit at The Times brought astonishing results. Meinholtz easily exchanged messages round the world with it. He decided to work his short-wave rig on the Byrd story.

Out of this, incidentally, grew The Times' free wireless news service to remote military and missionary outposts all over the world, and to ships at sea. The first regular recipient of these newscasts was the Byrd expedition in 1926. They were so successful and so much appreciated that they became—and still are—a boon to ships everywhere and to settlements hopelessly beyond newspaper routes.

Both the Norge and the Fokker attempts were scheduled for early May, 1926. The Times assigned two men, Russell Owen and William Bird, to cover the rival groups. The Times had arranged with Norwegian and United States radio stations in the Far North to listen for messages from the two expeditions, but to make doubly certain of getting the stories the moment either ship made the North Pole. It sent its own radio crew into the Arctic. William C. Lyon, a Times part-time correspondent who worked out of Seattle, got this assignment. He and Sgt. Leo W. Bundy of the United States Army Signal Corps left Nenana, Alaska, on March 13, with a twelve-dog team and sled, carrying a 200-pound portable radio station that they were to set up at Point Barrow, the northernmost tip of Alaska, there to intercept messages from the Norge. Byrd carried no wireless equipment in his plane.

The radio expedition had 1,220 miles to go, some of it over icy mountains, with Eskimo settlements few and far between. For four weeks Lyon sent back stories of the heartbreaking conditions he and Bundy had encountered. The last word The Times had from

Lyon came on April 13 from Kotzebue, just inside the Arctic circle, when he still had 700 miles to cover.

At Kings Bay, meanwhile, Bird, the reporter, hung around the camp set up by the Commander and Floyd Bennett. He sent his stories by short-wave directly to The Times on the Chantier transmitter. He had little difficulty. Owen, assigned to the Norge group, had to use an old-fashioned spark wireless rig at Kings Bay. His dispatches traveled long-wave to Norway and from there were usually sent by cable to The Times. Bird had to skip from ice cake to ice cake to cross the Bay from the Chantier to the Fokker hangar. Owen had to flounder between the Norge hangar and the ramshackle wireless station on skis—and he had never used skis before.

Neither camp would say so publicly, but each was eager for first crack at the pole. The Times correspondents at Kings Bay kept readers up to the minute on preparations, and it was evident that a race was on. Bird's dispatches came through in good time, but Owen found the Norwegian radio operators irritatingly resistant to haste. When night fell they closed the station, and only by marking his stories "urgent" could Owen persuade them to reopen for later material. On the "urgent" basis, The Times had to pay triple the normal sending rate. Some of Owen's longer pieces cost as much as $1,000.

The Josephine Ford got away for the pole first, on Sunday, May 9, 1926. Birchall crammed the story into the Sunday edition with eight-column banners that proclaimed:

BYRD HOPS OFF FOR NORTH POLE; SHIFTS PLANS, MAKES DIRECT DASH AND HOPES TO BE BACK IN 24 HOURS

The story carried the proud byline "By William Bird, The New York Times Correspondent with the Byrd Expedition." It said:

KINGS BAY, Spitzbergen, Sunday, May 9—The Byrd Polar Expedition's three-engine airplane the Josephine Ford flew toward the North Pole from its base here at 1:50 o'clock this morning [9:50 P.M. Saturday, New York Time.] The airplane is expected back in sixteen to twenty-four hours.

The thought of two mortals venturing by air into uncharted frozen wilderness where no man had ever risked wings before had kept hundreds of thousands of Americans—Europeans, too—awake on Saturday night. The New York Times switchboard was clogged with anxious queries as to whether any further word had come through after take-off. None had.

An hour or so after the Fokker's motors bored into the polar regions to previously uninvaded silences, New York theatres emitted their Saturday night crowds, and there was a rush for The Times Byrd extras. The edition was gobbled by crowds that poured out of "Abie's Irish Rose," "The Garrick Gaieties" and Marilyn Miller's "Sunny." The names on movie houses' marquees in Times Square that mild May evening were Dolores Costello, Pola Negri, Rene Adoree, Lillian Gish, Thomas Meighan and John Gilbert. Charlie Chaplin's "The Rookie" was a screen hit of the day.

On Monday morning The Times had a complete and exclusive account of the Josephine Ford's spectacular dash:

BYRD FLIES TO NORTH POLE AND BACK;
 ROUND TRIP FROM KINGS BAY IN 15 HRS. 51 MIN.;
 CIRCLES TOP OF THE WORLD THREE TIMES

The reason for Commander Byrd's anxiety to get away before the dirigible Norge started with her combined Norwegian-American-Italian crew was apparent in William Bird's dispatch that morning:

KINGS BAY, Spitzbergen, May 9—America's claim to the North Pole was cinched tonight when, after a flight of fifteen hours and fifty-one minutes, Commander Richard E. Byrd and Floyd Bennett, his pilot, returned to announce that they had flown to the pole, circling it several times, and verifying Admiral Peary's observations completely.

It was not just the man in the street who strained for news of the Josephine Ford in the agonizing hours when she remained wrapped in Arctic mystery; many men in high places kept anxiously asking for the latest word. When Byrd's flash on the Fokker's return came into The Times wire room on Sunday it was immediately relayed to President Coolidge. He was spending that week-end on the presidential yacht Mayflower on the placid Potomac, and he asked his aides, through Richard V. Oulahan, The Times Washington Bureau chief, for any fresh word of the Byrd expedition. The President's congratulations to Byrd and Bennett were transmitted through The Times.

The whole Times news staff sent congratulations, too, to the Chantier. This was, in a way, a rather extraordinary phenomenon. Newspapermen are traditionally supposed to accept even the most startling events and achievements without emotional overflow. The message said: "Commander Byrd, this is a little group of your friends who wish you to hear their voices raised in gleeful appreciation of your great achievement on Sunday. Hearty congratulations to you and to your brave comrades, particularly Pilot Bennett, who was your right hand man."

Commander Byrd wrote a series on his flight that ran in The Times for the next ten days. Readers everywhere thrilled to it. Byrd had circled the pole at 2,000 feet. He had seen no land, no birds, no bears, no seals, no other sign of life.

The Times syndicated the story widely and gave the proceeds in full to Byrd and to Bennett. The sum was substantial.

Times readers were devouring Byrd's first-person accounts of the Fokker's polar dash when they were plunged into another story that had even more powerful suspense elements. The Norge had left Kings Bay to cross the pole to Alaska. Arctic exploration history was popping at a rate that would have made Peary gasp.

On May 11 Russell Owen flashed the story of the dirigible's take-off:

KINGS BAY, Spitzbergen, May 11—At 9 o'clock this morning, Greenwich Time [5 A.M. New York Time] the Norge of the Amundsen-Ellsworth-Nobile Expedition started for Point Barrow, Alaska.

Straight into the morning sun a tiny speck soon lost in the golden glow of the North, the dirigible disappeared on her journey across the pole and into the unknown wilderness of the Arctic.

The New York Times man aboard the Norge, Fredrik Ramm, an amiable Norwegian giant, was sailing into journalistic legend. He kept sending terse, colorful bulletins from the Norge throughout the flight, and the unprecedented datelines they carried caused heart thumps, especially among newspapermen.

As the bulletins came in Frederick Birchall's little goatee quivered. His pink cheeks were flushed with excitement. He held each fresh bulletin within three or four inches of his thick-lensed pince-nez, and his lips mumbled Ramm's meaty progress notes. The whole Times news room was caught up in the significance and tension of this running adventure story. Only Joseph Tebeau, night managing editor, who had come to The Times from The Sun with Birchall and Van Anda, seemed calm. His white thatch bent briefly over the bulletins and his crisp notes for their handling were hurried to the foreign desk. Tebeau was one of the newspaper greats, always at his calmest when exciting news was delivered into his competent hands.

At 3 o'clock in the morning of May 12, after three editions had been run off, the door of The Times wireless room flew open and a breathless copy boy raced across the floor. He dropped duplicates of a new bulletin at different editors' desks. Birchall again charged onto the floor and orders crackled. The slower-moving Tebeau strode from desk to desk, checking headlines. Composing room and other mechanical forces, standing tensely by, sprang into action, and within a half-hour the fourth edition carried the sprawling three-line headline into Times Square, and across the world:

THE NORGE FLIES OVER NORTH POLE AT 1 A.M.;
REPORTS HER FEAT TO TIMES BY WIRELESS;
GOING ON OVER ARCTIC WASTES TO ALASKA

In the center of the page, four columns wide in bold face type and boxed for better display, was Ramm's epochal bulletin under the headline: "First Message Ever Received From the North Pole."

BY FREDRICK RAMM
New York Times Correspondent Aboard the Norge
By Wireless to The New York Times

NORTH POLE, Wednesday, May 12, 1 A.M. (On Board the Dirigible Airship Norge)—We reached the North Pole at 1 A.M. today, and lowered flags for Amundsen, Ellsworth and Nobile.

The first dateline of its kind in human annals did strange things to newspapermen's emotions, as it did to all Times readers. Man had spoken out of the Ice Age to man in turreted New York. He had launched a thin whisper out of the skies over the glacier that had grimly locked man out of its frozen fastness for aeons, and a bit of wire in Ochs' newspaper had caught it, thousands of miles away, and had made it into living words.

A pale spring dawn lay on the Times Tower and in Times Square when the last edition was put to bed with the historic news. One hundred and fifty thousand extra papers were run off and trucks roared west in Forty-third Street with them to make trains, ferries and planes. The Times air-mail editions had become quite popular by this time, and mail planes carried them swiftly all over the continent. Times air-mail service to Texas had started the night before.

The Times had waited 153 days for Peary's message that he had gained the North Pole. Ramm's message, relayed from the Norge, was seven hours spanning the distance.

But the Norge had still a long way to go over terrain never seen by human eye. The Times of Thursday, May 13, carried a Ramm dispatch that bore the mystery-filled dateline: "BEYOND THE NORTH POLE, May 12, Aboard the Dirigible Norge, 3:30 A.M. Norwegian Time (2:30 Greenwich Time, 10:30 P.M. Tuesday, New York Time)." The Norge was slipping through virgin air over limitless frozen desert converted into a dreamland El Dorado by the watery polar sun, and No Man's land was No Man's land no more.

"The three flags, that of Norway, America and Italy, which we lowered when the Norge was over the North Pole at 1 A.M. are so fastened," this dispatch said, "that they are upright in the ice and the flowing wind. The strong bright colors are lighting up the fog. . . .

"What, up to now, we have seen of this region is the same sort of ice as on the other side of the pole. The ice is thick, a few lanes being covered with new ice and ice walls. Our speed is 80 kilometers (49 miles) an hour."

On that same Thursday morning The Times editorial page carried a long piece about the Ramm North Pole datelines and how these had stirred the world.

"What an experience for mortals it was!" this piece said, in a newspaper that ordinarily frowned on exclamation points. "We read all about it at the breakfast table."

But the Norge chapter wasn't ended—nowhere near. After that Thursday message there was only silence. The hours ticked away in Forty-third Street. Birchall paced the news room floor. The staff discussed all possibilities, even the more fantastic. Some thought the Norge might have run into some invisible wall beyond the pole that prevented radio waves from coming through. Some thought all scientific calculation might have overlooked the effect of magnetic force in the dark wilderness on the far side of polar vastness. What everyone really thought was that the Norge had probably wrecked in the unknown, beyond reach of human aid.

Birchall and the Aero Club of Norway had worked out a complicated code for Ramm to use, just as William Bird had used code from the Chantier to prevent news piracy of the Fokker stories.

The great fear in The Times when the great silence closed in on the Norge and her passengers was that if any word pierced the Arctic veil it might be *driny*, which would mean "We are in danger of destruction"; or *drobs*, "Send relief expedition," or *dreft*, "We continue on foot."

But nothing came. Norwegian, Alaskan and Spitzbergen radio stations sent message after message into the Far North in vain.

Birchall was in a dilemma. No word from the Norge, no word from Lyon and Bundy. He wired the editor of The Nome Nugget to ask for a man to represent The Times at Point Barrow, and the editor assigned Antonio Polet.

On May 13, the Thirteenth Naval District in Puget Sound, State of Washington, reported to The Times that three of its Far North stations thought they had heard the Norge's radio flash "Quite terrific gale northeast. Drifting. Probable Latitude 80. Ten One Sixty Zero Zero. Roger Dog George." The Government stations reported the message broken and not quite steady; that the Norge was probably saying she was caught in a wicked Arctic storm, and that she was 80 degrees 10 minutes north, 160 degrees west. Birchall and The Times wireless staff finally figured out that "Roger Dog George" stood for the Siberian code station RDG at Yakutsk.

Birchall sent a wireless message to Walter Duranty in Russia:

ALASKA THOUGHT THEY HEARD AIRSHIP CALLING STATION RDG AT SREDNEKOLYNSK, GOVERNMENT OF YAKUTSK. PLEASE INVESTIGATE.

Meanwhile, Nome sent word to Birchall that the barometer was plummeting, and that a great storm was brewing over the Norge's predesignated landing place there. Duranty came through with word from Leningrad that the Soviet Government had no news of the Norge. It looked blacker and blacker for the dirigible's pole pioneers. One bright spot broke through the gloom, though, at 2:18 P.M. on May 14. The Simpson Radio Corporation in Seattle told Birchall by wireless: "U.S. Army Signal Corps reports safe arrival Lyon and Bundy at Barrow."

The Times went to press that night with no official confirmation as to the Norge's whereabouts. It printed fragmentary reports of messages purporting to have come from it, but The Times of Friday, May 14, carried the headline:

THINK NORGE WAS HEARD WEDNESDAY NIGHT; EFFORTS TO REACH HER SINCE HAVE FAILED

On Friday night, after a confusing day of conflicting rumor about the Norge's appearance over Alaska, the Simpson Radio Corporation in Seattle flashed word to The Times that:

Lyon and Bundy arrived Barrow yesterday. Norge passed over them thirty-five miles south of Barrow at elevation five hundred feet, shut off engines for moment, then proceeded direction of Nome. They could plainly see lettering and cabins of Norge. Signal Corps Station at Fairbanks, Alaska, relays for Barrow. No direct message from Lyon.

This message came to The Times at 7:13 P.M. Birchall, harassed by whispers and counter-whispers reaching him through the air, still held firmly to Times tradition. He would not report the Norge safe until he had complete confirmation. Saturday's Times came out with the headline:

NO WORD FROM NORGE, MISSING TWO DAYS; MAY BE ADRIFT IN POLAR STORM OFF ALASKA; BYRD PREPARES FOR A SEARCH BY AIRPLANE

Before Byrd could take to the air, though, on Saturday morning, delayed word came out of the North that the Norge had landed with all its passengers. Sunday morning's Times splashed the story all over the front page. It led with a message from Lincoln Ellsworth and gave six columns to Ramm's quietly worded but hairlifting account of a thrill-packed seventy-one hour voyage, of extraordinary phenomena seen from the Norge's gondola as it slid across the roof of the world. It told how the dirigible had been buffeted, kicked and slapped by Arctic gales and how it had been tossed, its skin ripped and open, as it groped through Arctic fog for a landing. It had been compelled, at last, to land at Teller on the Alaska Coast, ninety-one miles west of Nome.

There was a struggle to pack all this dramatic material into the early Sunday edition. That edition was another historic Times triumph. The detailed stories by Ellsworth, Amundsen and Ramm were one of the great journalistic beats.

It was not until June 7, that The Times printed William Lyon's story of his great frustration. It was dated May 29, at Point Barrow, but had to go by dog-sled to Kotzebue and by radio from there to Seattle, before it got to the office.

"This," Lyon wrote, "is a story of bitter disappointment and of at least partial failure from a land which perhaps has seen more and knows more of both than any other on the face of the earth."

He told how he and Sergeant Bundy had run into one bitter storm and blizzard after another on the 1,200-mile trail to Point Barrow, only to find when they arrived that the power plant they had expected to use there was out of order. Spare parts for it could not be mushed in for many months.

On the evening of May 12 he sighted the dirigible and ran out on the ice field. He waved his red bandana. The silvery ship slowed and nosed down. Lyon had discussed with Captain Amundsen, back in the States, the possibility of the Norge's taking him off the ice with a rope. His heart beat high. He thought the Captain really meant to attempt it.

He stood there, a pitifully tiny mortal in the limitless icy waste, frantically wigwagging.

"The ship came steadily toward me. I could plainly hear the

steady purr of her engine . . . She seemed to be swinging in my direction . . . some few hundred yards to my right."

But the Norge, wounded, was seeking a haven, and this was not it. Her nose came up again, the ship sailed on, and vanished. Bill Lyon trudged toward his Eskimo igloo, burningly bitter. He was a reporter with a great story to tell—and no way to tell it.

William Clyde Lyon died in Seattle on March 26, 1932, six years later, in his forty-seventh year.

Fredrik Ramm died in Norway after World War II, a victim of a German concentration camp, though the direct cause of death was tuberculosis. He left behind him a legend of good works, and probably the most everlasting of these will be the dispatch he wrote datelined: "NORTH POLE, Wednesday, May 12, 1 A.M. (On Board the Dirigible Airship Norge.)—We reached the North Pole at 1 A.M. today."

CHAPTER
26

S UNDAY MORNING, April 10, 1927, was pleasantly mild in New
York. In Manhattan apartment houses after church services,
and in the sun-bathed stretches of the Bronx, Queens and greening
Flatbush, Times readers, with vernal fever upon them, scanned the
paper a little sleepily. A story at the left side of the front page told
of plans for trans-Atlantic flights. There had been much of similar
plans before. Men had died in abortive take-offs on Long Island.
Nungesser and Coli were about to attempt a crossing from France.
The Times, now more than ever, was the modern explorer's day
book, the diary of the aviation pioneer.

On this Sunday morning, The Times gave front-page center to
a piece about the strutting man with the outthrust jaw who had
taken over in Rome. The lead story on the front page told of the
sentencing of Sacco and Vanzetti at Dedham, Mass., after seven
years of bitter litigation. It carried the full transcript of that day's
court session, including Judge Thayer's words to the condemned,
and their emotional reaction. Allen Raymond, one of Birchall's
bright, young men, did the story with rare literary skill so that it
had color, breadth, depth and throat-seizing qualities. It belongs
with the newspaper classics.

The front-page aviation story that Sunday proclaimed:

TWO FAMOUS NAVY FLIERS PREPARING
FOR DASHES ACROSS ATLANTIC NEXT MONTH;
BOTH TO REPORT BY WIRELESS TO THE TIMES

It ran over onto the twenty-fourth page and overflowed to the twenty-fifth, with pictures of the Navy fliers, Commander Richard E. Byrd and Lieut. Comdr. Noel Davis, and their planes, and with maps of the courses they meant to follow across the big water to Paris, to try for the $25,000 prize offered by Raymond Orteig of that city.

Hardly anybody glanced at a small news box squeezed into the upper right-hand corner on Page 24 that morning, a tiny item out of St. Louis, Mo., dated April 9. The little headline said: "Third Attempt to Fly Ocean to Be That of Air Mail Pilot." It was an off-hand bit, for the record, about a young unknown who was tuning a little Ryan monoplane in San Diego, Calif., for a test flight to St. Louis, where his backers lived, in preparation for a crack at the Orteig prize. It was the first time this pilot had been mentioned in The Times.

He was Charles Augustus Lindbergh. The Times had heard about him from E. Lansing Ray, publisher of The St. Louis Globe-Democrat, fellow-member with Ochs on the Board of Directors of The Associated Press. Ray had enthusiastically assured Ochs and other newspaper executives at the annual Board luncheon that Lindbergh was an extraordinary flier. He said that Harry Knight, President of the Aero Club of St. Louis, would handle any contracts for Lindbergh ocean-flight stories.

No one bothered to follow up this lead because all eyes were on Byrd and Chamberlin. But the name of Lindbergh grew.

He flew from San Diego to St. Louis in 14 hours 5 minutes, setting a record for a non-stop solo flight. He flashed from St. Louis to Curtiss Field in 7 hours 5 minutes, to set a solo record of 21 hours 10 minutes from coast to coast. He flew in a blind cockpit, and his only view straight ahead was through a periscope, but the flights were arrow-true. His landings compelled admiration.

Russell Owen and Deak Lyman, covering aviation for The Times, cottoned to this Johnny-come-lately in the trans-Atlantic race. They told Birchall that something about him, despite his shyness, taciturnity and extraordinary modesty, compelled utter faith in his flying ability.

On May 10, 1927, The Times carried long accounts about the different expeditions that were tuning for the Atlantic attempt.

Byrd's huge America, and Clarence Chamberlin's Bellanca, the Columbia, got most of the attention. These ships were larger and much sturdier than the dragon-fly job that Lindbergh was carefully nursing.

Meanwhile, the White Bird in which Nungesser and Coli had flown from France, had borne them into oblivion. Searching expeditions looked for them in vain.

At 5 P.M. on Friday, May 13, 1927, when Sulzberger came down to the city room to speak with Birchall on some routine matter he found Birchall having a little difficulty understanding Knight, a Lindbergh sponsor, whom he had reached by telephone. Sulzberger took over the conversation. It was crisp and brief. Sulzberger extemporaneously dictated a contract for the venture and Knight accepted for Lindbergh. Then Sulzberger dictated this memorandum to Miss Florence Williams, Birchall's secretary:

"The New York Times agrees to pay $1,000 to bind the contract, with a further payment of $4,000, making a total of $5,000, in the event of a successful flight to Paris, this payment to cover world rights to the story.

"Should the flight not be successful, it is agreed that we are to have an option on the story for the payment of an additional $1,000 to the $1,000 already paid.

"Should the flight actually not start, Mr. Knight agrees to return to us the $1,000 binder money."

It was worked out that the term "successful flight" meant a landing anywhere within fifty miles of the European shore, and that The St. Louis Globe-Democrat, which had already advanced $1,-000 to Lindbergh on its own, was to have story rights for its own circulation area. Later that evening, Birchall dictated a cable to Edwin James in Paris:

"Have just purchased world news rights to Lindbergh flight, which probably starts tonight. Lindbergh instructed silence except to Times correspondent bearing your credentials. Prepare to isolate him if he's successful. In event of failure and rescue ne communicates with us by whatever means possible."

But Lindbergh did not start that night, nor the next. Ocean weather was violent. On May 17, he came to The Times studio to be photograpned.

A wet spring dawn, heavy-misted, brought in Friday, May 20. At 5 o'clock that morning, as the sun tried to push through scud and mist, Lindbergh's plane was rolled from the hangar at Roosevelt Field. Owen and Lyman, with other Times men, formed the journalistic equivalent of a fire-bucket brigade between the plane and a special telephone set up in the hangar, to relay preparation details and the take-off. Rewrite men at The Times office wrote a running story from these forward-passed fragments. At 5 A.M., Tebeau decided the extra could be held no longer. Take-off might not be until 7 A.M. or later. He rushed the edition to press. It carried a modest two-column headline saying that Lindbergh was set to fly at daylight if weather conditions permitted.

Chamberlin and Byrd kept their ships grounded that morning. The America needed further motor adjustments and Charles Levine, who owned the Columbia, was tiffing with Lloyd Bertaud, who was to have been Chamberlin's co-pilot.

Two hours after Friday's edition went to press Lindbergh was on his way. The slender mail pilot, who had achieved only a two-paragraph box ten days before, was suddenly a world news figure. Owen rapped out a story that made ten columns of type for the Saturday paper. Above it ran a three-line, eight-column headline:

LINDBERGH SPEEDS ACROSS NORTH ATLANTIC,
KEEPING TO SCHEDULE OF 100 MILES AN HOUR;
SIGHTED PASSING ST. JOHN'S, N.F., AT 7:15 P.M.

A boxed front-page notice under a two-column picture of Lindbergh proudly announced: "When next heard from, Lindbergh will write the story of a great exploit for readers of The New York Times and associated newspapers. It will appear exclusively in New York in The Times."

Down two columns at the extreme right that morning ran the wireless dispatches sent from various points along the Spirit of St. Louis' path of flight. The silver ship had last been seen at twilight, steadily boring seaward, through a gap in the coastal hills at Main-à-Dieu, Cape Breton.

The whole world followed Lindbergh's course through the lonely ocean skies. Probably never in human annals had so many millions put their prayers behind one man's venture. It was a curious emotionalism, based in earth-bound man's age-old dream of solitary ascent into air's limitless realms, and no one followed the flight more anxiously than The Times staff. Birchall, busier than a bone-hiding pup, tore off reams of messages filled with orders for handling the story. He tapped all possible sources for news of Lindbergh's whereabouts in the ocean void.

He got off another long directive screed to James in Paris. He wirelessed ocean liners to ask that they watch for the Spirit of St. Louis.

"Airman Lindbergh flying Great Circle course Paris," the plea said. "Left New York 6:52 American standard time. Overpassed Cape Breton Island 4:05 Atlantic Time afternoon. Speed hundred miles hourly. Will greatly appreciate any dispatch giving time, latitude, longitude, weather conditions should you sight him, or anything heard from other ships. RCA agrees accept collect."

The message was sparked to the masters of the Carmania, the Stuttgart, the Belgenland, the Transylvania, the Drottningholm, the Corinthia and the Auronia.

Meanwhile, in Paris, James deployed his staff in and around Le Bourget airdrome. It never occurred to him that there might be any difficulty in complying with Birchall's "isolate-Lindbergh" order. Lindbergh was under contract to The Times. He had been briefed on talking to no one but a Times man. It sounded simple.

Every inch of the first five pages of The Times for Sunday, May 22, 1927, including the front page, was devoted to Lindbergh. The headline, a little off traditional conservative style, proclaimed:

LINDBERGH DOES IT! TO PARIS IN 33½ HOURS;
FLIES 1,000 MILES THROUGH SNOW AND SLEET;
CHEERING FRENCH CARRY HIM OFF FIELD

Edwin James's lead piece on the Spirit of St. Louis' landing, dated Paris, May 21, was a slick professional job.

"Lindbergh did it," it said bluntly. "Twenty minutes after 10 o'clock tonight, suddenly and softly there slipped out of the darkness a gray-white airplane as 25,000 pairs of eyes strained toward it. At 10:24 the Spirit of St. Louis landed and lines of soldiers, ranks of policemen and stout steel fences went down before a mad rush as irresistible as the tides of the ocean."

The James story and Carlyle MacDonald's interview story (which did not become available until 2:30 A.M.) were deceptively smooth. No reader could have begun to imagine the sweat and strain that went into getting them. The "isolate-Lindbergh" order had gone up the flue along with all other carefully pre-arranged planning. James had not counted on impulsive Gaelic temperament. When the French broke the barriers at Le Bourget that night, James and all his aides were swept aside like insignificant chips in full-spate flood.

Five days after the Lindbergh landing, James wrote for The Times of May 27 a story that told in intimate detail what had happened when he and his Paris bureau staff attempted to carry out Birchall's "isolate-Lindbergh" command. The story is unique in Times annals. It has been reprinted in many anthologies:

BY EDWIN L. JAMES
Special to The New York Times

PARIS, May 26—There come moments in every newspaperman's life when he is all but overwhelmed by a feeling of insufficiency to tell what he has seen—when superlatives seem mere inadequacies.

That happened to this writer once on Armistice Night in the martyred city of Verdun. It happened again the other night when Captain Charles A. Lindbergh landed his plane on the airfield in Le Bourget to be welcomed by a reception committee of 150,000 people gone suddenly insane with joy. Four days later I still retain bruises, which are passing, but memories which will never pass.

When people talk this week about Captain Lindbergh's flight one hears, over and over, the question, "But you were at Le Bourget?" It is considered the mark of an extra privilege to have witnessed one of history's greatest mob scenes.

Official programs, formal reception committees, a regiment of soldiers, stout steel fences—all were enveloped and swept under a human sea when all those present, in one swift instant, took it into their collective heads to help welcome the aviator who became great that night.

The reporters assigned to cover Captain Lindbergh's arrival will not forget that night. And neither will they forget one of the toughest mobs they ever tackled. The Battle of the Argonne was a simple matter compared to it.

Preparations for the Arrival.

The Paris bureau of The New York Times had made elaborate preparations to cover the event. The preparations were so elaborate that they almost—perilously almost, as will be shown here—left the editors back in Manhattan in the lurch.

We had arranged complicated telephonic communications. We had made handsome relay plans to rush parts of the story to Paris, over six miles from Le Bourget. We had a fine automobile ready to bring the aviator back to the capital to give his own story, for which The New York Times had made a contract. We had stenographers ready to take it down. We had photographers with a battery of cameras and many plates on the spot.

Oh, it was a wonderful plan! Only when the story broke it was not worth one paper franc. Not even complete official documents for entrance to the field were worthwhile, for an ordinary police card was enough to begin with.

With everything set as described, Percy Philip, Carlyle MacDonald, Harold Callender and myself, plus our office clerk, named Maloussey, went out to the scene of the conquest at 6 o'clock.

We had planned to be smart and have dinner at the Airport restaurant so as to be free and fed before 7:30 o'clock, the earliest hour at which Captain Lindbergh was expected. The restaurant will hold about fifty people and 5,000 had the same brilliant idea we had.

All Set at the Field.

When we were through with dinner, Philip took his job at the elbow of the man representing the Commercial Cable Company, which had its own wire into Paris—only it did not stay open. There was Philip, all set and not to be moved, ready to choke the poor operator if any one else's bulletin of the aviator's arrival got out ahead of ours. Maloussey was to signal him from the corner of a building when the plane touched the ground. Great headwork that! MacDonald, Callender and myself went out on the field, ready to escort Lindbergh to the waiting automobile in triumph—mostly in triumph—before the eyes of several hundred envious confreres.

Honestly, that was our plan, and it looked all right at 7 o'clock—and, anyhow, those were our orders from New York. The editor said, "Isolate" Captain Lindbergh, and we were ready.

Now, Le Bourget airfield is in the shape of a triangle about three-quarters of a mile across, and with each side about a mile and a half long. On one leg of the triangle are ranged the hangars of the Thirty-fourth Aviation Regiment. On the near leg, that is the leg running along the Paris road, there is the civil airport from which planes go to all parts of Europe.

There are a small Customs House, a number of offices and a two-story restaurant and bar as well as a mile of giant hangars. Near the entrance stands the aviators' club-house and almost in front of this the great square concrete flooring from which passenger planes take off.

The Crowd Begins to Grow.

On one side of this nice, pretty square, beautifully decorated flags and colored lights had been arranged. Specially strong flare lights had been fixed in the corners of the field and for hours soldiers had practiced with flares which, when the aviator arrived, were to light up the field like noonday.

In order to make entirely sure of keeping the grounds and the crowd in order, a regiment of soldiers with rifles and bayonets and 700 Paris policemen supplemented the usual staff. Yes, the authorities had made great preparations, just as we had.

Along about 8 o'clock the crowd began to grow. MacDonald took a look around and estimated that 10,000 people were round about, standing alongside the airfield.

There was—note that I say there was—the very strongest fence, some seven feet high, with spikes on the top, which up to that night had kept out every one who ought not to enter. The gate was guarded by twenty policemen who let pass those who had credentials; which meant any card that had your picture on it.

By 8:30 some thousands of people had got into the field and were kept in orderly line along the edge of the big concrete landing floor. The policemen, in a solid bank, kept that line straight; and out beyond them were the soldiers, spick and span, showing that no foolishness would be tolerated.

Also Planning "Isolation."

In front of the soldiers stood a row of some fifty cameras and motion picture machines which were aligned under the direction of a precise and pompous colonel. And off to one side was the official Reception Committee, engaged in deciding at what hotel they were going to put the evening's hero. They also were deeply planning to "isolate" him and to see that those New York Times reporters did not do any "isolating." Well, if we did not, they did not. If there was one real tragedy of the evening it was that of the official Reception Committee. Some of them have not seen Captain Lindbergh yet.

Now, that was the scene as the sun went down about 8:30 o'clock and a chill wind began to blow.

"Go home?" echoed a young thing in an afternoon silk frock; "why you poor thing, I shall stay all night. Haven't you got any blood?"

And her escort stamped his feet and wished Captain Lindbergh would hurry.

There had been published in Paris a report that Captain Lindbergh had been seen over Plymouth. People were beginning to get free for the evening and the crowd started growing. By 9 o'clock there were 50,000 or 60,000.

The Paris road was jammed with cars and people arrived by the thousands from cars parked as far as several miles away. They kept on coming. The police estimate 9,000 automobiles reached Le Bourget and its vicinity and thousands more did not.

Spell of Gloom in the Crowd.

It got dark—and the stars came out, but it was one of those nights that stay kind of dark despite a million stars; or maybe it was the bright lights that made it seem so.

People kept coming, and as more kept getting through the gate onto the field, more soldiers were put in the line. The crowd kept growing and then about 9:30, by a strange freak of mob psychology, thousands got gloomy. They seemed to think all the reports about Lindbergh's being on the way were like the sad news about Nungesser and Coli. Expressions of sorrow went the rounds and sincere regrets for the fate of such a brave lad.

And the crowd kept growing! Then the police began getting rougher.

Callender and I figured at this stage that if we wanted to get there to isolate Lindbergh we ought to get from behind those troops. We walked with Mac and walked until the line was thin and there were not many policemen and there were not many lights.

Then we walked behind one big flare where it was dark behind the blinding rays. We made ourselves small and waited.

And the crowd kept on growing until all the houses around looked like a sugar barrel in August when a lot of flies are loose. It was cold.

Ten o'clock struck. A sort of shiver went through the crowd and we were thinking of the tears which were going to be shed, when all of a sudden the thousands were electrified by the sound of a motor. There was a plane up above us somewhere. The landing lights went up. Everyone thought it was Captain Lindbergh and a vast silence swept over and through as more than 100,000 pairs of eyes strained. And then the sound of the motor died out and the lights went down.

It was Lindbergh, as was shown by his story later. He had mistaken the location of Le Bourget and gone elsewhere looking for it.

But the crowd did not know that. Their hopes died down and they settled for the inevitable wait until there was no more hope.

Out of the Darkness.

Then there was that whirring again. Callender strained his eyes and shouted: "My God, look!".

There, 500 meters above us, was a gray-white monoplane, right over our head. Then it faded and the noise of the motor stopped.

We thought it a hallucination, and a glance at the crowd showed that very few had seen it. Certainly the officer in charge had not, for the lights did not go on.

Then in a moment, cold forgotten, the glares went on, and turning we saw, just as if thrown on a silver screen, a white-gray monoplane, twenty feet from the ground and softly settling.

Mac got off first. I was second, with Callender alongside. We raced as hard as we could toward the plane, which landed perhaps 500 yards from where we stood. Suddenly we found ourselves confronting the whirring propeller bearing straight at us.

We tried to halt. Good Lord! That crowd hit us like a shot out of a cannon. The propeller stopped turning when MacDonald was six feet from it.

The men from the military side of the field had now reached Captain Lindbergh and were pulling him from the plane. We could see he was struggling. He fell to the ground once and then was on the shoulders of a dozen men.

By this time we were jammed up against the plane, with a mighty roar behind us. Ducking, we went under the Spirit of St. Louis and then out under the tail.

Onrush of 100,000 People.

And then we turned to look and saw a sight words cannot paint. One hundred thousand men and women, with policemen and soldiers mixed among them, were sweeping down toward Captain Lindbergh and his plane.

That sight of those countless bobbing heads between us and the flares can never be forgotten. Fences, line soldiers, reception committees—all had been swallowed up.

And then we saw Captain Lindbergh with several French aviators trying to fight their way out.

Throwing away their rifles, soldiers formed a ring around him, only to be swept away. One man swung his cane to free a path for Lindbergh— and hit the aviator on the head.

And suddenly we saw that we had lost Lindbergh. We knew later that one of the French officers had put his coat above him, shoved him into the human mass and then wormed out with him into a little side building, where the lights were turned out and the aviator was kept for two hours in darkness rather than have his protectors take the risk of having him mobbed.

"Say," remarked MacDonald, "I wish the editor who sent that message had been here to isolate him. That's what I wish."

Hunt for the Missing Lindbergh.

Skirting the crowd, we tried to get back to see what happened to Philip.

All at once the crowd turned and started toward the aviators' club-house, where Ambassador Herrick had been waiting. Some one had turned on lights in the second story, and mob psychology told the crowd that Lindbergh was there. He was not there, but tens of thousands waited until 1 o'clock in the morning to try to catch a sight of him.

Maloussey had been swallowed up in the crowd, but Philip had got off his flash and then a series of bulletins giving the first news of the aviator's arrival.

"Well, boys," I said, "it's Saturday night and now it is nearly 11 o'clock. That one phone line isn't much good. The other lines don't work. Let's go back to Paris and send a piece to New York."

That sounded *so* logical!

Of course, having come so early we did not know what had happened on the road.

This was what happened. When the news of Lindbergh's arrival was flashed to Paris every one in the capital who had a car or could get one conceived the bright idea of going straight out to Le Bourget and shake hands with this altogether admirable young man.

Some five or six thousand cars started. About the same time a large part of the crowd at Le Bourget decided to go home and read about it in the morning papers. About five or six thousand cars started back to Paris.

Those coming out and those going in met about a mile below Le Bourget. Enough said!

For about twenty minutes we could not find our chauffeur. It took him that long to get out of the crowd. Then we were ready.

To make a long story short, we got into the traffic jam and stayed there two hours. Our profanity was no better, no worse, than that of thousands of others. Thoughtless people laughed about it, but we reporters suffered the tortures of the damned.

Saturday night—the world's biggest story in hand, and New York 3,000 miles away, with us stuck in a traffic jam!

Philip had gone off over plowed fields in a tree-climbing six-horse Citroen of his own. He went ten miles through trees and fields to another road, but Callender, Mac and I were stuck.

An Idea That Did Not Work.

Then Mac got an idea.

"Let's go over to that bistro and telephone to Warren," he said.

Warren was the night man back in Paris. We cheered Mac—until we found the country phone was cut off at 11 o'clock, and then we cursed him.

Every twenty minutes we moved two feet and then we stopped and sweated and cursed.

"Say, James," said Mac, "do you think we will get fired for this? If so, that makes it a tragedy."

Thank the Lord I work for the Sunday department," said Callender, "and we can get it by then."

Then he offered to buy our story for Sunday two weeks hence.

It was heartrending.

And then it dawned on us that the other reporters were caught there, too. We walked up and down the line and found half a hundred, and later we discovered that we had made the evening's second hero out of a young reporter whom we taunted about his paper going to press within an hour. That boy, when our backs were turned, leaped out of his car and ran five miles to Porte Villette, where he got into a taxi. His story was one of the best written that night.

A Side Road—and Victory.

Moving along like snails, we saw suddenly a little side road, more of a path than anything else. We took one look and turned.

We found ourselves in what seemed to be a cross between a plowed field and a sandpit. We were in the midst of excavations for a new city suburb.

We struggled on until we hit a hard field, on the other side of which glowed the lights of a village. There we arrived with only two broken springs and got on a fair road which led us back to the main Paris road. But in that struggle we had passed the traffic jam and at the corner found three policemen keeping things moving.

At 1:45 o'clock we reached our office, having taken three hours to do twelve miles. Philip had beaten us by ten minutes.

We started in getting the story together. Then we remembered we had not got Captain Lindbergh.

Where was he?

We knew where the Reception Committee intended to take him, but he was not there, as we found out by telephone. We called the chairman of the committee.

"Hell," he said, "I haven't laid eyes on him."

"Ambassador Herrick is a good fellow," someone said, "he will tell."

Off Mac went and found Captain Lindbergh sitting on the edge of a bed in the Embassy drinking a glass of milk.

When Mac told him we had intended to isolate him, he answered:

"There seem to have been a million other people with the same idea."

Captain Lindbergh gave a brief sketch of his flight and invited us to see him after he had had some sleep.

Mac came back, all proud of himself. We all wrote until about 4 o'clock Sunday morning.

Next day we got a cable saying that we had done good work and it all got there in time.

Next time Lindbergh does it, if France will mobilize her army to keep Le Bourget clear, we shall try to isolate Lindbergh.

By the end of June, Lindbergh was a household name in the world's farthest corners. The New York Times Index at that time contained four solid pages of one-line Lindbergh references to cover the encyclopedic amount of stuff that had been printed about him. His New York reception alone covered sixteen full pages in The Times of Tuesday, June 14.

Still the Lindbergh adoration mounted. He bore up under countless parades and dinners and a whole staff of men and women had all they could do to handle offers of one kind or another that poured in through the mails, telegraph and cable. Hollywood offered a cool $1,000,000 for Lindbergh films; a group of promoters offered $2,500,000 for a Lindbergh world air tour.

Lindbergh could have been rich beyond any mortal dream, but he quietly and politely turned down all the offers. When Mme. de la Meurthe donated 150,000 francs for an Aero Club Cup for him he turned the money over to the families of French airmen who had lost their lives in aviation pioneering. News syndicates made large offers, too, but he signed a new Times contract in Paris after the original one ran out and kept on writing only for The Times.

Ochs was in London when Lindbergh flew the Atlantic. In New York it was decided that all the money piling up from world syndication of the Lindbergh stories should go to the flier, although the contract originally dictated by telephone to Knight limited the return to Lindbergh of a flat $5,000.

This decision was cabled to the publisher, who had crossed over to Paris.

"I heartily approve all net revenue to Lindbergh," Ochs cabled back, "plus generous Times payment."

When this confirmation came through Birchall wired James:

"Inform Lindbergh we have paid his backers as per contract but feel nevertheless we do not desire to share financially in the receipts of his great exploit. Therefore we are turning over to him personally the entire sum realized from our sale of his story. Make funds available to him as he needs them. We will account finally on his return."

On June 27, with Lindbergh stories still running, and with prospect of fresh series on his flights to Mexico and South America, The Times had turned over to Lindbergh $42,000. A receipt for that amount, in the flier's boyish handwriting, is still in Times files:

"I wish to acknowledge herewith receipt of your check for $42,-000 as payment per account rendered therewith against my personal stories of the flight sold you."

Before the entire contract ran out Lindbergh's return on syndication of his Times writings was in excess of $60,000.

In full dawn on Saturday, June 4, a fortnight after Lindbergh had left New York, Chamberlin's yellow-winged Columbia leaped from Curtiss Field runway. Charles Levine, hatless but wearing a leather windbreaker, had jumped into the co-pilot's seat when the chocks were pulled.

It was a startling maneuver. The scrap-metal buyer had never flown a plane in his life and knew nothing about navigation; he was just going along for the ride. He owned the plane, though, and, if that was the way he wanted it, the quiet Chamberlin was not the man to try to talk him out of it.

The Columbia had no fixed destination at take-off. Chamberlin thought he would stay in the air as long as he had fuel margin. He took five copies of that morning's fourth edition of The Times aboard, one marked for President Gaston Doumergue, one for President Paul von Hindenburg, one for Premier Benito Mussolini.

At 3 o'clock next afternoon the Columbia dropped out of the clouds to circle the west-bound liner Mauretania, about 340 miles from Land's End. Crew and passengers thought Chamberlin might be in trouble.

He was, but only because his earth-induction compass had developed spasms. It turned out later he had used the Mauretania to get his bearings. When he was sure of her identity, he opened a copy of The Times of Saturday to the shipping page and noted when the liner had left Southampton. He roughly estimated her speed and knew just about where he was.

As the Columbia headed eastward into the clouds the Mauretania's wireless man flashed word to The Times that the plane had been sighted. On the same day Chamberlin passed the cruiser Memphis carrying Lindbergh back to the States.

On Monday morning, June 6, Birchall got out a 6 o'clock extra:

BERLIN, Monday, June 6—The Bellanca plane Columbia made a forced landing at 9:30 this morning [4:30 New York Time] at Eisleben, about 110 miles southwest of Berlin. The machine was in perfect order.

Lincoln Eyre of The Times Berlin bureau hired a car to burn off the miles to the landing spot. He wrote a complete story for Tuesday's Times telling how the Columbia had covered 3,905 miles, all told, in 48½ hours.

Chamberlin delivered Saturday's fourth edition to President von Hindenburg. His series on the flight started in The Times on June 9.

The Lindbergh flight acted like a stone cast onto some coastal rock where gulls nest. Men rose from America's shores, east and west, to fly the oceans.

On the morning of June 29, 1927, a Wednesday, Commander Byrd's America took off for Paris in a light rain. It carried copies of The New York Times for King George, the Prince of Wales, Ambassador Herrick, President Doumergue, Premier Raymond Poincaré, Lady Astor, Viscount Rothermere, Lord Beaverbrook, Lord Riddell and Sir Austen Chamberlain.

As Byrd's ship took to the skies, another Fokker, with Lieuts. Lester J. Maitland and Albert F. Hegenberger, was in the air on its way from Oakland, Calif., to Hawaii. It had taken off at 7:09 A.M., the day before. Both flight stories were to run exclusively in The

Times. Maitland and Hegenberger got to Hawaii in twenty-six hours, completing the first successful Pacific flight from the American mainland.

The morning after Byrd's take-off, The Times got a wireless message from him through R.C.A., at Chatham, Mass. It was dated 2:30 A.M., June 30. It said, "We have seen neither land nor water since yesterday on account of dense fog and low clouds covering an enormous area." This provided the lead for Thursday's paper. There were no other reports when the last edition went to bed at 5 A.M.

With the Lindbergh incident fresh in mind, James took extraordinary precautions for Byrd's arrival in Paris. He assigned Lansing Warren of the Paris bureau and Albert Travers, an expert stenographer, to await Byrd at the Hotel Continental. These two were to get Byrd's personal narrative and were to flash it to The Times in New York. James himself intended to cover at Le Bourget. With him were Percy Philip, who had slept most of the day to be prepared for a possible all-night vigil; Louis B. Kornfield, who was taking Carlyle MacDonald's place; Maloussey, the bureau clerk, and Harold Callender. James Graham, another reporter, stayed at the office to intercept any messages from New York.

Jean, the chauffeur, parked the office car outside Le Bourget gate, on the theory that getaway would be simpler there. The gasoline tank was kept full against the possibility that the America might come down some distance from Le Bourget, and that James' whole crew might have to dash to the scene of a forced landing. Samuel Zolotow, who worked for the drama department in New York, happened to be in Paris on vacation at the time. He offered his services, too. James felt he had his men properly placed for any eventuality. If anything, he was overstaffed, but he preferred it that way.

Late Thursday afternoon Paris lay under grumbling black rain clouds. Darkness fell early. When word came to the office at 6 o'clock that Byrd had been seen off Plymouth, England, James gave final orders and posted his staff. Jean took James, Kornfield, Philip, Callender and Maloussey to the airdrome. Thunderheads piled more massively over the Eiffel Tower as they neared the field, and fat raindrops splashed on the car windows.

At 8:30 P.M. the storm broke. Rain poured down. Dense cloud and denser fog hid the roof tops. James and Philip sat at a table overlooking the field and the other members of the staff perched disconsolately on packing cases in the freight hangar. Wireless rumors about the Byrd ship were confusing. The plane was simultaneously reported from widely separated places—over Brittany, over Brest, over Rennes, over the Channel. For eighty minutes there was no word at all.

It was certain around midnight that Byrd could not hope to find Paris in the deluge. Rain and fog cobwebs curtained the city lights from sight, even at street level. James left Philip at Le Bourget with the rest of his men, and rode to The Times office. Warren and Travers were at a nearby bar. James agreed that that was a more sensible place than the Continental. He taxied to Le Matin. As he came through the door at 1:30 A.M. an SOS report reached Le Matin's city desk. Byrd had had trouble with his wireless. It was repaired now and he flashed word out on the lashing rain that he had enough gas for about three more hours of flying. He could find no cloud opening anywhere through which to see France.

James sat down in Le Matin's office and started hammering out a first-edition story. He had been at it only a few minutes when Le Matin got a Havas report that a plane had wrecked itself in an attempted landing at Issy-les-Moulineaux, outside Versailles. Four Matin reporters joined him in a race for a cab. It tore down narrow roads, through fog and hammering rain, toward Versailles, at seventy miles an hour.

"Blow your horn, driver," a Matin man tensely told the cabby. The man kept staring ahead through the gelid stream on the windshield. "It would be useless, Monsieur," he said tightly. "If we meet anyone on this road we are gone."

They were at Issy-les-Moulineaux airdrome within an hour. The field was under several inches of water. The guard assured them there had been no wreck of any kind. He had heard nothing of the American fliers. The cab driver was too exhausted to return to Paris. "I am dead, Monsieurs," he kept repeating, "but completely dead." They thrust a wad of wet francs at him, found another old wreck of a cab at the airdrome gate, and splashed back to Paris, as fast as they had come out of it.

James got out at the Continental. Kornfield, it turned out, had cabled the false crack-up rumor to New York. At 4:35 A.M., James wrote a new lead, telling of the damp vigil, and how the crowds had been driven off by the storm.

At 6 o'clock Philip and James, both exhausted, walked the Boulevard des Capucines searching for some spot where they might get hot coffee, but Paris slept under the drumming rain. No coffee was to be had. Philip, with the advantage of extra sleep the day before, suggested that James go to bed, and James did. Philip walked to the Continental Hotel to see if Dr. Herbert Adams Gibbons, Byrd's representative in Paris, had heard anything. He was with Dr. Gibbons at 8 o'clock when word came through that Byrd and his men had landed their ship off Ver-sur-Mer, a fishing village near Caen.

James got out of bed again. He sent a new lead to The Times. It made the office in time for a 4:30 A.M. extra that carried the headline:

BYRD DROPS IN SEA 120 MILES FROM PARIS;
AVIATORS SAFE; PLANE REPORTED SMASHED;
LOST IN FOG ALL NIGHT; 43 HOURS IN THE AIR

As James worked over the final lead with the rain slapping at the windows, Philip, Kornfield and Harold Hinton, head of the Wide World photo service, started for Ver-sur-Mer over dangerous roads to get Byrd's personal story, and the stories of the fisher folk who had heard the America's descent out of the storm. Walter Gillet, a Wide World photographer, was hurt when the car screamed around a bend in a narrow road and threw him against the windshield, but The Times crew was lucky at that. Another automobile, carrying French reporters to Ver-sur-Mer, overturned. The reporters never got to the Byrd plane. They went to a local hospital.

Philip interviewed Commander Byrd in a seaside villa at the landing point. Kornfield, Hinton and the photographers worked among the fisher folk and Byrd's crew—Bert Acosta, George Noville and Bernt Balchen. It was 8:30 P.M. when Philip had the Commander's story. The last train for Paris had left by that time, and neither he nor Kornfield could get transportation out of Caen. The photographers had already started back in the office car.

Philip dictated Byrd's 5,000-word narrative over a bad telephone connection. James used the whole office staff, in relays, to take it down. Kornfield's story came over the same line. Together they filled several pages and gave the first-hand account of the America's groping for a landing in the fog; told how simple French fisher folk and the local prefect had reacted to the abrupt visitation of the Americans who dropped out of the heavens. It was all exciting reading.

Commander Byrd fell a little short in his Times series on the flight when he predicted that great air liners flying at 40,000 feet would span the oceans on schedule within a decade. It took a little longer than that. James' story on "The Long, Wet Wait in Paris for Byrd," printed in The Times on July 4, 1927, good-humoredly recapitulated his staff's agonies during the America's stormy passage.

"There is one consolation about the business," he remarked. "These flights are now being heralded as leading toward the frequent arrival of air liners from New York at Paris, and probably will be of daily occurrence and accepted as a routine part of life. That gives rise to the hope that New York editors will no longer get excited about them and that the whole situation may be disposed of by assigning one airship-news reporter at Le Bourget, and letting it go at that. The cable companies will lose and the correspondents will win."

This sounded a bit on the dreamy side when it was written—when single-motor ships like Lindbergh's and clumsy craft like the America were blundering their way through cloud wrack, and keeping the world on edge with their daring—but it worked out as James figured it might. In the early years of World War II and immediately after the war, airports on both sides of the ocean had become routine newspaper "beats" with yawning passengers and bored reporters at La Guardia Field, Le Bourget and Croydon thinking no more of ocean hops than they did of surface vessel journeys.

The track of this evolution is as clear in The Times files as a trail left by clumping dinosaurs in fresh snow.

CHAPTER
27

ADOLPH OCHS approached his seventieth birthday in 1928 with astonishing vigor. His cup was full. The New York Times had outstripped all American competition, and was generally acknowledged the world's model newspaper. Revenues were piling up at a prodigious rate and again there was need for plant expansion. Another addition to the Forty-third Street Annex was started, and a Brooklyn plant was under way.

The Times steered easily in the hands of Arthur Sulzberger, Julius Adler, Louis Wiley and its editors, but Ochs never took his eyes or mind off the course the newspaper followed. Wherever he went he was informed of day-by-day advertising volume and of important events and trends. His correspondence, even from afar, bristled with ideas for improvements.

The Times had a gross income then of $27,000,000 a year. Sunday circulation was up to 700,000, daily to 418,000. The Times Wide World photo service had expanded to virtually every corner of the earth, and the total staff was the largest in the newspaper's history. The publisher spent $300,000 a year for employe social welfare, and The Times group insurance represented $5,000,000 coverage, with a maximum of $5,000 a person. Ochs had initiated the insurance plan on his sixtieth birthday and intended to increase it on his seventieth.

On Saturday, Jan. 28, the publisher boarded the California for a long cruise. Effie went with him, and Mrs. Fanny van Dyke Ochs, his brother Milton's wife. He took Jules, his valet, and Rose, his wife's maid.

The world, at this moment, was perhaps as stable as it had been since World War I ended. There were still many sore spots at home as well as abroad, but they seemed to be slowly healing. The Times carried news agency rumors out of Moscow that four Bolshevist regiments under General Tuchatschowski, a Trotsky adherent, had revolted against Joseph Stalin's horde and that their artillery was firing on the Kremlin. The Stalinists labeled this "sheer fiction" and that is what it turned out to be.

Lindbergh had begun his Latin America good-will tour, and wrote daily of his experiences for The Times. Times men had gone ahead to each of his scheduled landing places to report local re-action. The day after the Ochses left New York Lindbergh lifted the Spirit of St. Louis over treacherous Andean currents from Bogota, Colombia, to Maracay, Venezuela, in a daring eleven-hour flight. The Times man at Maracay, William Morris Gilbert, wrote glowingly of the feat, and of the Venezuelans' ecstatic reception for Lindbergh.

Harold Denny, another Times man, was deep in tropical Nica-ragua, with Government forces trying to track down the insur-rectionist Sandino. The newspaper's columns kept pace with the progress of Herbert Hoover and Alfred E. Smith in winning their respective parties' nominations for President. The entertainment pages were filled with stage and screen names that have since dif-fused into soft memories—George Arliss in "The Merchant of Ven-ice," George M. Cohan in "The Merry Malones," Al Jolson in "The Jazz Singer," Sir Harry Lauder, then on one of his last American tours.

The world seemed to be getting back on even keel and Ochs was enjoying life. He spent his seventieth birthday in the Hotel Roose-velt in New Orleans. Bellboys were breathless trying to keep up with the torrential flow of congratulatory letters, gifts, telegrams and cables.

A message from the White House said: "Please accept my hearty good wishes on your birthday anniversary. May the future hold for you many years of service." It was signed, "Calvin Coolidge." Viscount Rothermere's note from London particularly pleased the publisher, too. It said: "Newspapermen all over the world will today reflect with pride and admiration upon your distinguished career. You have nobly sustained the best standards of our profession. Your own character and that of your great newspaper are an inspiration to us all."

Birthday luncheon in New Orleans was a quiet family affair. Dinner that night was served in the home of a Mrs. Pfeifer, a friend. Old Southern newspaper friends dropped by with gifts of wine and books. Next day the publisher went to call on Tom Rapier, an associate of the old Southern Associated Press days. Rapier was in his eighties then, and blind, but he was warmed by memories of their early newspaper days, fifty years before. The hours slid away in dreamy shop talk.

"The old man is very feeble," the publisher wrote. "He can scarcely make himself heard, but he hears fairly well. We had many pleasant reminiscences. He wept when we recalled pleasant memories. He is a dying man, but he is surrounded by a devoted family, a married daughter, some children and there are grandchildren."

Col. James Ewing, an old newspaper acquaintance, arranged an Ochs dinner, and had all of New Orleans' famous newspaper folk there—Dorothy Dix and L. K. Nicholson of The New Orleans Times-Picayune, among others. The colonel's wine cellar yielded rich old vintages and the guests were merry. Ochs enjoyed seven different wines and several cocktails, dipped into the crayfish bisque and other creole dishes, and was none the worse for it. These were happy days.

A week after Ochs' birthday, The Times got a modest letter postmarked Fairbanks, Alaska, from Capt. George H. Wilkins, the British explorer. He had been under contract with The North American Newspaper Alliance and with a Middle West syndicate in early attempts to reach the North Pole by plane. Hard luck had bungled these courageous attempts. Now he was back in the Arctic, his letter explained, and he meant to try again for scientific data over territory that had not yet come within man's vision.

"It has been my aim, this year," he wrote, "to avoid preliminary publicity, but if we reach Spitzbergen [from Point Barrow, Alaska] we will probably have some information to broadcast. I will, in that event, telegraph you and ask if you will accept the story.

"From my knowledge of your business methods and integrity I am willing to have you be the sole judge of the value of the matter submitted. My past association with newspapers will, I think, enable me to decide whether there is anything of interest to forward . . . I do not expect any word from you on this subject unless I telegraph."

The general feeling around the office was that Commander Byrd and the Norge crew had pretty well covered the Arctic for the average newspaper reader, but Birchall replied to Wilkins by cable: "We are willing to syndicate your story, giving you total proceeds, adding as Times share double the amount of the largest single outside subscription. If this is satisfactory outline what you have, enabling us to proceed."

Captain Wilkins replied that he intended to discover whether there lay within 800 miles of Point Barrow any land mass that might serve as a permanent meteorological station from which to broadcast regular bulletins on the weather. Since the Arctic cradles major storms, it was an interesting project.

Captain Wilkins' proposed flight receded in Birchall's consciousness when the German Junkers plane Bremen lifted from Baldonnel Airport near Dublin in Ireland on April 12, 1928, headed for New York. At this time no plane had made the westward flight across the North Atlantic, and the world again was stirred.

Three men were aboard the Bremen—Capt. Hermann Koehl and Baron Gunther von Huenefeld, both Germans, and Capt. James E. Fitzmaurice, Irish Free State airman. The Times had contracted for the Irish flier's story. The World had signed the Germans.

When The Times went to press with its last edition at 5 o'clock Friday morning, April 13, it seemed that the Bremen might have failed, as so many others had.

Alongside the Bremen story that morning on The Times front page was a sinister item from Berlin. The Opel automotive plant in Russelheim, Bavaria, had successfully completed a rocket motor. The Opel engineer, Max Valier, predicted that within a year giant rockets would be shot into outer space with scientific instruments for various automatic readings. Here, though no one guessed it at the moment, was the spawning of terrible new destructive engines that would turn up as wartime V-bombs and as motive power for aircraft swifter than sound. The Times, incidentally, was the first American newspaper to point out the possibilities of the Bavarian rocket motor. It later carried lengthy articles on the subject by the experimenters and by Kaempffert.

On Saturday morning, April 14, 1928, The Times gave three-fourths of its front page and two inside pages to the forced landing of the Bremen on isolated Greenely Island, 400 miles north of St. John's in Newfoundland. The plane had run out of fuel in stormy passage, and had just about bellied into land.

Humankind had finally, though at sad price, conquered the sullen and treacherous North Atlantic air reaches in both directions. It was a significant event in man's invasion of ocean airways. After Nungesser and Coli had died in the first westward attempt, two others had given their lives in 1927 attempts to westward crossings —the Princess Anna Loewenstein-Wertheim, who flew with Capt. Leslie Hamilton and Col. Fred R. Minchin from Upavon in England in August, 1927; and the Hon. Elsie Mackay who had hopefully set out from Croydon airdrome just a month before the Bremen's flight, with Capt. Walter R. G. Hinchliffe.

The Bremen story was difficult to get at. The plane was deep in snowdrifts. There was no direct communication with the island. Even Canadian icebreakers were unable to get through. There was no landing place for planes.

Competitive bidding for news and photographs of the Bremen reached a high mark. Almost a full week after the landing, C. A. Schiller, a private pilot, finally flew to a spot near Greenely Island, took Fitzmaurice off, and brought him down to Murray Bay, where Harold Littledale of The Times and W. Benedict Nyson, acting for The Times and for The Montreal Gazette, had to claw him loose from the newspaper pack. The captain had written his first Times story on the backs of envelopes and scraps of paper. It ran in The Times on Thursday, April 19, under the headline: "Fitzmaurice Writes For The Times Story of Sea Flight." It was a hair-raiser. The plane had skimmed the ocean waves at barely fifty feet a great part of the way across the Atlantic, trying to get out of fog, sleet and snow.

On April 22, as The Times was taking the next Fitzmaurice story from the wires along with a secondary piece telling how Floyd Bennett, Commander Byrd's pilot, had fallen gravely ill at Murray Bay after he had flown in parts for the damaged Bremen, a message from the Arctic flashed into the wireless room:

SVALBARD, Spitzbergen, April 21, 12:30 A.M.—We have reached Spitzbergen after twenty-one and one-half hours' flying. We made one stop for five days on account of bad weather. (signed) George H. Wilkins.

Birchall erupted. He sent: "Urgent Wilkins" by way of Radio Corporation of America the message: "Send as much as you can."

A second message notified Wilkins that The Times correspondent at Kings Bay would help him prepare his story.

Wilkins' brief announcement to The Times and a few paragraphs out of Copenhagen explaining that the flier had been marooned for five days on the Island of Dead Mens Rock, near Green Harbor, by a blizzard, were all Birchall had to go on, but the story got a three-line, eight-column head. When Isaiah Bowman of the American Geographical Society and polar explorers learned of the flight, they said it was the most remarkable instance of plane navigation in history. The Times radio station was cluttered with congratulatory messages from men anxious to praise Wilkins for his achievement.

Sunday's last edition went to press with a four-column map of Wilkins' route, and with filler material that Birchall's men had scraped together from all parts of the world—comment, praise, Wilkins' biography. One of the first things Birchall had done when the Wilkins wire came through was to ask James in Paris to sell European rights to the story, in Wilkins' behalf. James found buyers in England, France, Germany, Italy and Scandinavia.

The explorer Vilhjalmur Stefansson had stayed late at The Times, too, explaining Wilkins' feat to Russell Owen.

Commander Byrd joined other explorers in calling the Wilkins achievement "the greatest airplane flight ever made in the North." Wilkins and Carl Ben Eielson, his pilot, had flown, in three-fourths of their daring 2,200-mile course, over Arctic regions never before seen by man. They had clear evidence that there was no land where Peary and other early explorers had thought there might be. This settled an old controversy.

Wilkins' tiny wooden monoplane had taken off on Sunday, April 15, from a runway slicked out by hand by Eskimos. Part of the flight was through clear weather with perfect visibility. The ship changed course twenty-two times, skirting fog, sleet, snow and ice in treacherous polar air, and was almost out of gas when it ran into the blizzard. Eielson made the Dead Mens Island landing on instinct alone, and for five days the two men lived in the cabin with the snow swirling and drifting about them. When the skies cleared, they patted a runway for the skis and on the take-off Eielson almost left his chief behind. On a fresh start, Eielson zoomed the Lockheed to 3,000 feet, and from that height easily made out the snow-hooded shacks at Green Harbor. They landed there, found the regular radio man ill, and with some difficulty got off their message to The Times.

There was some slight unpleasantness about pirating of the Wilkins story as there had been with Lindbergh's story. In this case Wilkins' account appeared on news syndicate wires in thinly disguised rewrite. Newspaper chains in the United States printed it, and European agencies used a stolen version. Birchall, irritated, threatened to make a legal issue of it, but when the excitement ebbed the matter was dropped.

Wilkins was snowed in for weeks at Green Harbor. Eventually he got to London, with the world's plaudits in his ears. The Times of London, aglow over the success of his flight series, doubled the amount it had originally agreed to pay. By and by word of this got to Ochs. When later Wilkins came to The New York Times as Ochs' guest, the publisher recalled The London Times bonus. Although Wilkins' return from world rights to stories and pictures had been substantial—they sold from sub-Arctic Canada to far-off Australia—Ochs told the explorer, "Since The Times in London saw fit to pay you double the sum we asked, we'll pay, as our own share, double the total sum paid by The Times of London." The flight, incidentally, won the Briton a title. He became Sir George Hubert Wilkins.

The opening chapter of pioneer aviation was drawing near its end. The Times had made it an important item in contemporary history, had devoted ten times as much space to it as any other journal. The fact that this leaf was ready for turning, showed in a front-page Times box on Monday morning, April 30, 1928. It was headed:

LINDBERGH FLIES TO MUSEUM
WITH SPIRIT OF ST. LOUIS TODAY

The story under a St. Louis dateline began:
"Col. Charles A. Lindbergh announced tonight that he would fly the Spirit of St. Louis to Washington tomorrow and place the ship in the Smithsonian Institution."

Ochs thought women were intended by God and by nature to govern the household and to be ornamental. He frowned on the idea of their invading male realms, such as flying. After Colonel Lindbergh had hopped the Atlantic, The Times got letters from women eager to be the first of their sex to duplicate his feat. Ochs would have none of this. He firmly told Birchall so. All the offers were politely, but coldly, rejected.

Miss Thea Rasche, a German, approached The Times early in 1928 through Bruno and Blythe, fliers' agents. Birchall dictated the typical reply:

"Regarding Fräulein Rasche, I respectfully decline to sign this German lady, or any other lady, for a trans-Atlantic flight in advance of her making it. In other words, I decline to aid and abet any lady to attempt a dangerous feat which may result in her death."

In mid-June, though, three women were poised for the eastward Atlantic passage. Amelia Earhart, a Boston welfare worker who looked like the female counterpart of Colonel Lindbergh, was prepared to fly with Wilmer Stultz, pilot, and Lou Gordon, aviation mechanic, in a tri-motored pontoon-equipped plane named the Friendship. Miss Mabel Boll, called "The Queen of Diamonds" because she had a weakness for jewels, and Fräulein Rasche were getting sizable amounts of newspaper space. Ruth Elder, an American, had tried the flight, and had been fished out of the ocean alive 325 miles north of the Azores. The Dawn, carrying Mrs.

Frances Grayson, another American, had been lost at sea late in 1927.

When Miss Earhart was ready to take off from Trepassey early in June, 1928, The Times was in something of a dilemma. The Ochs rule about women fliers was still sternly in force. On the other hand, George Palmer Putnam, whom Miss Earhart would eventually marry, was a friend of Arthur Sulzberger's. Putnam was eager to have The Times handle the story. Sulzberger could not officially accept.

Newspaper editors in the United States, Canada, South America, Australia and Europe did want the Earhart narrative, and looked to The Times for it. Birchall had to tell them that no contract had been made.

Meanwhile, James was having a bit of a headache in London. English, French, and German newspapers wondered whether The Times would distribute the story in Miss Earhart's behalf, and kept plaguing him about it.

"Do, or do we not, sell lady?" he asked Birchall by cable. "Interest here."

"If we get lady," the managing editor cautiously answered, "you can sell." No commitment there.

There was another problem. Miss Earhart was not inclined to tell her destination, and when James asked about it Birchall sent the code message:

"James replying confidential. Goal probably roads [Southampton] not naval base [Calshot on Thames]. Both men fliers upsewed for thirty days after arrival. Plane now Trepassey fully loaded delayed by unfavorable crosswind. Waiting it moderate. Take-off probably s'afternoon. Will flash."

Putnam kept Miss Earhart informed through The Times radio station on ocean weather predicted by Dr. H. H. Kimball, meteorologist of the United States Weather Bureau in New York. On June 6 Birchall flashed to James in London:

"Daylong crosswind Trepassey prevented Friendship rising. Start promised daybreak Thursday. Mabel [Boll] also threatening start. You'd better remain until story satisfactorily under way."

The last line in this message referred to James' inquiry as to what he should do about rumors that Capt. Hugo Eckener was ready to cross the ocean by Zeppelin, another project in which The Times was interested. Later in the day this order was changed. James started for Germany, and Allen Raymond of the London bureau was assigned to take the Friendship flight.

When the Friendship started from Trepassey on Sunday morning, June 17, through sullen mid-Atlantic weather, Birchall flashed the information to Raymond. Now Miss Earhart was committed. She had sent Putnam a last-minute code message: "Violet. Cheerio." "Violet" meant "We are hopping off." Birchall and The Times then threw off all wraps. Raymond was told to handle the sale of Miss Earhart's stories in Europe, though the only contract that existed was an exchange of nods in the city room between Sulzberger and Putnam, when the take-off flash came through. "Understand girl can write," the managing editor cabled to Raymond. "Nevertheless aid her without undue intrusion. Get her story on landing. We have bought her story."

All day Sunday The Times kept getting reports from ocean liners that had seen the Friendship bucking the skies toward Europe. The last Monday edition told about:

EARHART SOARING OVER THE ATLANTIC,
REPORTED NEARLY HALF WAY TO IRELAND
EIGHT HOURS AFTER LEAVING TREPASSEY

Tuesday morning's paper played up Miss Earhart's safe landing on Lougnor Estuary at Burry Port in Carmarthenshire, South Wales. Her personal account of the flight led the paper that morning beside Raymond's color piece telling of the fisherfolk's wonder over the American woman who had dropped from the sky. She talked freely and graciously with all newspapermen; so much so that Birchall was a little worried about it.

Putnam sat with Birchall in The Times office throughout the flight, reading Miss Earhart's own account of her adventure and scanning the rest of the flight material. Birchall, still around when the other New York newspapers came out, exploded. They had done extraordinarily well, considering that The Times had exclusive rights to the Friendship project.

"Mr. Sulzberger," he dictated to the night bull pen secretary,

"I think after looking over the other papers that Mr. Putnam should be told that his lady is talking her head off for everybody, and that we haven't anything exclusive yet. He had gone before I discovered it."

Raymond in England got a somewhat similar message, but he knew the explanation.

"Miss Earhart telling nothing outside necessary general interviews London press," he cabled back. "That's ended now. Stories you saw probably from London Times."

This situation illustrated the change in journalistic concept of property rights since Raymond's era. When The Times pilfered Bennett's Arctic wreck story in 1854 its editors could safely score such a theft on the credit side; that was acceptable in New York's shirt-sleeve era in newspaper production. Now, after lengthy litigation, particularly by The Associated Press, rules against piracy have been established.

Back in the Nineties, Marse Henry Watterson, Ochs' friend and associate of Chattanooga days, had tried for extension of the national copyright laws to protect property rights in news, but the result was feeble. In 1917, though, the Supreme Court of the United States upheld The Associated Press against the International News Service in an action growing out of alleged news piracy. The A. P. was the complainant.

"The contention that the news is abandoned to the public for all purposes when published in the first newspaper is untenable," said the majority opinion in this case. "Publication by each member [of the A. P.] must be deemed not by any means an abandonment of the news of the world for any and all purposes . . . not for the purpose of making merchandise of it as news, with the result of depriving complainant's other members of their reasonable opportunity to obtain just returns for their expenditures."

Clear as this seems, it did not end news piracy. Every now and again it became an issue and affected The Times adversely when it had some special news morsel that was tempting to contemporaries.

The Earhart series was of special interest because it stressed the woman's angle on flying, and did it quietly and sensibly. The Times had given the world the most complete story of man's aerial conquest of the ocean in 1927. The Earhart stories added the official slant on the growing distaff invasion.

There were other exciting stories of the same type at the same time—Umberto Nobile's crash in the Arctic, and his subsequent rescue; Roald Amundsen's flight to try to save the Nobile crew. The Times recorded these developments, and its readers thrilled to them. It also told, in sorrowful detail, of Floyd Bennett's death in Jeffrey Hospital in Quebec on April 25, 1928; how Lindbergh flew to Quebec through snow and ice in the Spirit of St. Louis, carrying serum that he hoped would save Bennett. The serum was too late.

Ochs, who met Floyd Bennett after the polar flight in 1927, was deeply touched by the flier's passing. "The world," he told Mrs. Bennett, "bows in sorrow and mourns with you in the death of your distinguished husband."

CHAPTER
28

Fame had found Adolph Ochs difficult to pin down. Through most of his life he had talked quietly from the wings while front men and aides took the bows and the plaudits. In 1928, when he was 70, he could no longer stem the eulogistic flood. It rushed through the dikes and swept over him.

On Friday night, June 29, the publisher, his wife, their family and a trainload of friends rolled out of New York for Chattanooga. The town had labored mightily to make Ochs' golden jubilee as a newspaper publisher the most impressive event that part of the world had ever seen.

From the moment the special train rumbled into Chattanooga on Saturday night, Ochs was forced to dine on ambrosial praise. The local Legion band blared and tootled down Market Street ahead of the publisher and his party of sixty. The Chattanooga Savings Bank Building suddenly broke out beacons that swept the sky.

Seventy-five Chattanoogans with Mayor E. A. Bass at their head rode with the Ochs party to the new Lookout Mountain Hotel. Next morning Bishop Thomas Gailor presided at a special jubilee Sabbath service, there was an Ochs luncheon at the Fairyland Club on Lookout and later an excursion down the Grand Canyon of the Tennessee.

On Monday morning Mayor Bass gave the publisher a golden key to the city and during the ceremony at City Hall officially declared him Citizen Emeritus of Chattanooga.

Ochs was moved. He said, "What greater glory can come to a man, what more beautiful crown than the love and affection of neighbors?"

The climax was the jubilee dinner that night at Lookout Mountain Hotel. Messages for Ochs came from President Coolidge, from governors, mayors, from senators, representatives, publishers and the reading public. They came by telegraph, by mail and by cable and wireless, more than a man could read in a single night.

Captain Rule, bent now and withered with ripe years, sat at the publisher's table. So did H. C. Collins, now 80, who had ridden in on the Knoxville bus. They nodded and smiled all through the oratorical flood that night.

Louis Wiley summarized Ochs' extraordinary progress from the day he took over The Chattanooga Times. One by one other men spoke in lush praise—Darwin Kingsley, head of the New York Life Insurance Company, Dr. John H. Finley, Grover Whalen who had come as New York's representative, David Houston, the Rev. Tom McCallie, a local minister and old friend. The list was long.

The editorial praise heaped on Ochs during the jubilee indicated the great change in journalistic temper since Henry Raymond's time. Raymond got no praise from competitors until he died and even then some of his foes in printer's ink could not quite bring themselves to blunt their pens.

It was different now. The World, The New York Herald Tribune, The New York Evening Post, journals everywhere—not only gave generous space to the jubilee as straight news, but also paid special tribute to Ochs the man.

The Post said, "Mr. Ochs has contributed to American journalism something for which not only the public but also his profession owes him much." The Herald Tribune editorial, written around the theme that character builds great newspapers, said: "Without high purpose, virile resolve and steadfast action can build only for the day. The Times is the great structure that it is today because it was erected by a great builder." A New York World editorial done in much the same vein held that "the methods and ideals formulated in Chattanooga have affected newspapers for the better wherever The New York Times is read."

General Webb, the older Bennett, Horace Greeley and Henry

Raymond might have gasped at anything so unthinkably mag-
nanimous from one New York newspaper to another. In their day
editors took their venom neat.

There was some pain, though, in the jubilee. Ochs realized that
an invisible figure silently stalked these feasts. Of the fifteen men
who had signed the gift copy of Hood's poems for Ochs, the boy
printer, when he left Knoxville in 1875, only two still lived. Most
of his childhood friends were gone. The few who were left walked
falteringly. The publisher was sharply aware of this. The scrap-
book he kept in 1928 and in the years just before was filled with
obituaries of old associates, who now fell like autumn leaves.

A week after the jubilee dinner old Captain Rule wrote a piece
about the office boy he had hired sixty years before. It was an editorial about the dinner, and about the distinguished men and
women who attended. It said:

"One of the number was the humble writer, who enjoys the distinction of having employed Mr. Ochs, then a mere lad, in a newspaper office, and has, as a matter of course, kept an eye upon him,
and seen him become the most prosperous newspaper publisher in
the whole world.

"His old friends remain his friends. Friendship is not weakened
by the lapse of time. *His* friendship has not, and when counsel is
sought he gives it and its soundness ungrudgingly.

"What is here said is said without his knowledge or consent. It
is a case of 'out of abundance of the heart the mouth (or pen)
speaketh.'"

But even heart's abundance one day runs out. A month after
Captain Rule's wavering hand had written this piece about his
former office boy, the pen at last fell from his tired fingers. Another
living link with Ochs' past had snapped. It hurt deeply.

Evening's shadows were softly but inexorably closing in.

Other clouds were ominously shaping, not only for the publisher
but for all mankind. Characteristically, they first showed in The
Times as minor items, so short as to be generally overlooked, but
they grew in ink and before men knew it they were angry thunderheads darkening civilization. The Times was more sensitive to such

phenomena than other newspapers because it had more correspondents to watch the quaverings of the global web. These registered locally before they were felt over great areas.

One was mention of "Professor Benito Mussolini." It had been
buried deeply on page 17, column 4, in The Times of Nov. 20, 1919.
It merely said:

MILAN, Nov. 19—Professor Benito Mussolini, Director of Popolo
d'Italia, a Socialist candidate for the Chamber [of Deputies] has been
arrested. He is charged with concealing explosives in his newspaper
office.

Three years later Cyril Brown, The Times man in Germany, sent
a piece out of Munich on Nov. 20:

"The Hitler movement is not of mere local origin or picturesque
interest. It is bound to bring Bavaria into a renewed clash with the
Berlin Government as long as the German Republic goes even
through the motion of trying to live up to the Versailles Treaty. For
it is certain that the Allies will take umbrage at the Hitler organization of the military clauses of the treaty."

Another name utterly without meaning for Americans had blossomed in print. On June 15, 1922, a Times story out of Berlin noted
that three Red Commissars were to govern at the Kremlin while
Nicolai Lenin took six months' vacation for his health:

TRIUMVIRATE TO RULE WHILE LENIN IS ILL;
KAMENEFF, STALIN AND RYKOFF ARE SELECTED

The second paragraph under this head introduced one of the
triumvirate to the American reading public.

"Mr. Stalin," it explained, "is a Georgian Bolshevist of Turkish
nationality, described as a strong man."

Probably not one in a hundred thousand readers gave the name
a second glance that morning, but within a few years hardly a child
but knew it, and the stark statement, "Mr. Stalin . . . is a strong
man," was a bitter truism.

"Professor Mussolini," the first of this group that was to put mankind through years of dread and terror, had been placed under the
journalistic microscope by Anne O'Hare McCormick of The Times.

In 1921, as a free lance, she had sent several articles to Carr Van Anda. Some ran in the daily, some in The Times Sunday sections. They were remarkably prophetic. In them she discovered Mussolini and the Fascist movement and interpreted them to the world in brook-clear prose that transcended any routine reporting from post-war Europe.

One of her first free-lance offerings from Italy, "The Revolt of Youth," published in The Times Magazine on June 5, 1921, had told the world that violent change was simmering in "the Boot."

"It is impossible to blink the fact," she wrote then, "that all over Europe there is growing up a generation tired of old men's wisdom, of the fumbling of Parliaments, of the cautious formulas of states-manship. That is what the Fascisti Movement in Italy really amounts to . . . It is a ruthless movement, as youth is ruthless. It substitutes swift and decisive action for the slow processes of legislation and experiment."

On June 21, 1921, Mrs. McCormick got a pass from Elizabeth Cortesi, daughter of Arnaldo Cortesi, Times correspondent in Rome who then represented The Associated Press, to sit in on that day's session of the Italian Chamber of Deputies where both King Victor Emmanuel III and the still obscure Mussolini were to speak.

"More interesting than the speech of the King," she recorded in The Times Magazine of July 24, 1921, after picturing the color and fanfare of the meeting, "was the sudden emergence of the new party of the Extreme Right—the small group of Fascisti.

"Benito Mussolini, founder and leader of the Fascisti was among the parliamentary 'debutants,' and in one of the best political speeches I have ever heard, a little swaggering but caustic, power-ful and telling."

She made the flat assertion that in this swashbuckling newcomer, Italy had probably found her master. This was prophecy.

Walter Duranty, who had won his Times spurs on the French Front in 1918, spotted the Red cloud for Ochs' newspaper.

He had written from Riga on Jan. 13, 1920—he was then and would be for many years The Times correspondent in Moscow—of the dark brew he saw bubbling in the great Soviet caldron:

"An interrogation of Red prisoners [the Reds were then warring

with the White Russians] in which The New York Times correspondent took part a couple of days ago, reveals the Bolshevist
system in its true light as one of the most damnable tyrannies in
history. It is a compound of force, terror and espionage, utterly
ruthless in conception and in execution."

These were the evil formations that were to darken world skies.
Adolph Ochs' newspaper posted the storm warnings as rapidly as
they developed and the publisher himself sensed with inner, hidden
horror, that the first World War had been a mere dip in the blood
bath compared with what was to come.

Though The New York Times stressed the factual story above
everything else, a historian turning its pages of a hundred years
will find them anything but dull.

Whenever there seemed occasion to present authentic color and
human interest in any situation in the news, The Times did it.
Duranty's reports from Russia not only gave the constantly shifting
economic and social changes, for example, but were richly threaded
with local color and thumbnail portraits to provide historians with
a living image of a violently troubled land.

Duranty had described on Nov. 13, 1922, a State session of the
Red hierarchy. The story gave the straight news of that day, then
went on to describe how:

"On the dais where imperial majesty sat in golden pomp crowned
with diamonds and robed in ermine, Lenin stood, a stocky little
man in a plain sack suit, fumbling at his papers on a lecturer's desk
before him—Lenin with an authority beyond that of the greatest
Czar, master and lord of new Russia, like a phoenix strong and
young from the ashes of the past."

A few weeks before, on Aug. 26, 1922, Duranty and Samuel
Spewack of The World had stood fascinated before the animated
fire of the Russian crown jewels. Duranty's account was something
Dumas might have written:

MOSCOW, Aug. 26—This is what two newspapermen saw today in
Russia, land of strange contrasts:

An Arabian Nights' vision of the Romanoff Treasure—the Imperial
crown jewels of Russia—diamonds big as walnuts, rubies, emeralds
bright blooded or vivid green, large as pigeon's eggs, pearls like nuts set

in row after perfectly matched row, platinum, gold and flashing diamonds shimmering like running water with rainbow colors of a fountain in the sunlight.

No dullness there. Duranty's keen eyes caught every item on display. He described the sceptre and the dazzling crown of Catherine the Great, and the peasants who were handling them. First, though, he told how one of the Russians had plopped Catherine's 32,800-karat State headpiece on Spewack's brow.

"Spewack's face flushed dark, then went ivory pale. For this was the symbol of the world's biggest white empire, the imperial crown of Catherine the Great."

Duranty, on feeling the crown's weight on his own head, told his own emotional reaction. Then he struck off another picture:

"There sat opposite me at the table one of the smock-clad workmen who fondled and polished the sceptre in his huge hands with long spatulate fingers and what chirologists call 'murderer's thumb.' His cranial development was akin to that of a gorilla, with a pointed skull, a prognathous jaw and outstanding ears. A novelist might have made a romance of revolution around this low physical type handling the sceptre of a great Empress with its jewel of destiny. But the man was not a Communist or revolutionary, just a simple workman taking the naïve delight of the Russian peasant in a beautiful object, with no lust or avarice, nothing but mild pleasure in his soft blue eyes."

The poisonous political brew distilling in Europe's caldron, and the swift falling away of Ochs' oldest associates formed only part of the picture on the darkening canvas. Times pages recorded that the United States was tipsy with false-bottomed prosperity. Few financial writers seemed to sense, while this gay jig was on, that the piper was to put in for his due at any moment, but Alexander Dana Noyes, financial editor for the paper, did and he kept shaking his head in print. He did a long magazine piece on the mad speculation in Wall Street, recalled the panic that followed the Mississippi and South Sea bubbles, and warned that the bull market had got completely out of hand. His words were ignored. But two years after the inevitable happened, even the great figures in finance conceded the soundness of Noyes' prediction.

Some men in Wall Street found Noyes' repeated warnings irritating. The week before Ochs left New York for the jubilee, one of the Harrimans of Wall Street wrote to the publisher that The Times stood to lose valuable advertising if such writing were not kept from its pages.

The publisher pondered this letter, then dictated a reply over the telephone to his office secretary, Mrs. Lillian K. Lang:

"I have your interesting letter, and am pleased that you give me an opportunity to remove some wrong impressions you seem to entertain about The New York Times.

"The financial editors, as is the case with all editors of The Times, give no thought to the effect their reports or comments may have on the advertising columns. If they did they would violate one of the most rigid rules of The Times—that no editor must be interested in or seek, or solicit advertisements.

"The Times' advertising columns are available to legitimate and trustworthy advertisers, subject to censorship for the protection of the reader; but the appearance or non-appearance of advertisements has no influence on the fair and honest presentation of news or its interpretation.

"The New York Times does not advise the use of its advertising columns except to those who think they can profitably use them to attract the attention and interest of several hundred thousand intelligent thinking people who are accustomed to reading The Times for the happenings and occurrences of the day throughout the world."

Thomas Lamont of J. P. Morgan & Co., at a public dinner on April 10, 1931, said of Noyes: "His has been as a voice crying in the wilderness. Our American community would have been better off today if it could have heeded that voice. He is a prophet to be heeded." But this was afterthought.

The speculative mania was only one trouble sign at home. Bigotry was erupting. Two weeks before the jubilee in Chattanooga, Senator Tom Heflin of Alabama came to upstate New York to campaign against Gov. Alfred E. Smith, then Democratic candidate for President.

The Governor had asked his own son-in-law, Maj. John A. Warner, head of the New York State Troopers, to assign extra men to make certain that the Heflin meetings, in reality Ku Klux Klan rallies, were not disturbed.

On Monday, June 18, The Times ran a front-page story of a meeting held the night before in Hurtsville, just south of Albany. There Senator Heflin had condemned the Catholic Church as a political machine, denounced Governor Smith as a Catholic and as a Tammany man, and had proclaimed him "unfit to be President."

Major Warner, The Times recorded, was in personal charge of the trooper detail during the Senator's two-hour harangue to the hooded. There was no disturbance.

On the same front page the second lead story—the lead story was on Miss Earhart's take-off for Wales—told that:

HOOVER AND FAMILY
WORSHIP IN SILENCE
AT QUAKER MEETING

Still another front-page story that day pointed up a name that was to fill endless space in The Times and newspapers in earth's farthest reaches:

SMITH'S SUPPORTERS
PUSH F. D. ROOSEVELT
FOR GOVERNORSHIP

Ochs' business sense told him that Noyes' warnings were sound even though they drew caustic comment, and he was sickened by Heflin's political vaporings. Still it never occurred to him to have his newspaper play them down. They made news, and the news had to be presented regardless of whom it offended, including himself. In this he was grimly undeviating.

Though earth's evils multiplied in print, The Times still found ample space for man's nobler adventures. Byrd was preparing an Antarctic expedition, with the idea of approaching the South Pole from the skies as he had the North Pole, but this time he was to be equipped to do more scientific work. He was to take two ships, a large ground contingent and the best available instruments for making scientific observations. Russell Owen of The Times was to go along as expedition scribe. The Times had exclusive rights to the story.

It also had exclusive rights to interesting stories coming out of Mount Evans in Greenland, where a meteorological expedition, headed by Prof. W. H. Hobbs of the University of Michigan, was stationed. The Times short-wave radio station, on the other hand, sent Professor Hobbs' group each night a summary of the news so that the men in the Far North knew the world's happenings quickly —even more quickly than the New Yorker who had to wait for them till breakfast. The same arrangement worked with parties of explorers in Asia and in South America.

This free Times service, an innovation in the history of exploring, gave the newspaper on Sunday night, Sept. 2, 1928, the quickest rescue beat on record. The plane Greater Rockford flown by Bert Hassell and Parker Cramer had vanished two weeks before, somewhere in the Arctic, on a flight from Rockford, Ill., to Stockholm. The Times, which shared the flight story rights with a Rockford newspaper, was desperately anxious for some word of what had overtaken the fliers. Search parties had ventured out over the Greater Rockford's route in vain. The Government had worked its wireless sets in and around Greenland, with no answer. It was generally believed that Hassell and Cramer had died on the ice.

Dick Hilferty, a Times radio operator, finished sending the news on Sunday night, Sept. 2, and was about to sign off, when the dot-and-dash from Professor Hobbs' short-wave transmitter excitedly flashed "Urgent, urgent 2UO." Hilferty ticked back acknowledgment. The Hobbs wireless man sent: "Hold on, old man. We've just got flashlight signals that Hassell and Cramer are well and safe."

Hilferty hurriedly wrote out a bulletin, called a boy, and had him race to the city desk with it. He stayed glued to his receiver. After a time it spoke again, and the story came out. A few hours before, the Hobbs party had seen smoke rising against the Arctic sky, about ten miles from Mount Evans. Elmer Estes and Duncan Stewart, two of Hobbs' men, had started down the fjord toward the smoke in the expedition's power boat. They had arranged to semaphore their findings by flashlight. When the desk got Hilferty's bulletin it ordered him to keep the Hobbs operator at his key until the rescued fliers got back to the station. Professor Hobbs himself had run down Mount Evans' steep walls to get the fliers' story as they walked back with his men.

Two minutes after the motorboat slid into the Hobbs camp, the expedition leader started his story to The Times. The Greater Rockford had made an emergency landing at Sukkertoppen on Aug. 19. The fliers had lived on reserve rations and on Arctic ptarmigan they had shot. Eskimos from Fiskerness had seen their fires and had started the men toward Hobbs' base. They had hurried because the Hobbs party was due to pull up stakes in mid-September. All details of the rescue, and how the fliers were gorging themselves on thick soup and caribou steaks, even as Hobbs wrote, went into the story.

The Times got out an extra. It shot the story to Rockford and when the rescue bulletin was flashed on a local theatre screen, Rockford staged an impromptu celebration. Out on The Times news floor, happiest of all who heard the rescue news was William Cramer, the co-pilot's younger brother. He happened to be at The Times, pleading with Birchall to ask the Government to intensify its search for the Greater Rockford and he had just sent a message to Hobbs through The Times radio and was waiting for an answer when Hilferty's flash came.

A fortnight after the Hassell-Cramer rescue, Ochs, Sulzberger, Wiley, Van Anda, Miss Nannie Ochs and more of the publisher's friends and kin journeyed to northern Ontario to study the great plant in the Canadian wilderness where new mills of the Spruce Falls Power and Paper Company at Kapuskasing were turning out Times newsprint. About $30,000,000 had gone into the venture. Bonds provided one-half of this sum. Of the remainder The Times had put up approximately half and the Kimberly-Clark Company of Wisconsin the rest. This was the company from which The Times had for many years purchased its rotogravure paper and Ochs had come to hold in high esteem its president, F. J. Sensenbrenner of Neenah, Wis.

The plant had to be cut out of primitive forest. It was to become a self-contained community of some 4,000 persons with every conceivable comfort at hand including schools, libraries, churches and recreation facilities, with paved streets, modern lighting and heating plants, and with its own hotel and hospital. Ochs had entered into the project to assure his newspaper of a good grade of newsprint. The first yield from the Kapuskasing mills had gone to Times

Square while the publisher was at the jubilee. For many years a great part of Times newsprint was to come out of Kapuskasing.

Ochs had steadfastly refused to put Times profits into non-newspaper investments though he had had chances from the very beginning to make fortunes in Wall Street and abroad. He sternly adhered to the idea that outside investments would leave the newspaper open to attacks by critics who might argue that The Times was favoring this or that corporation or editorially supporting the government of a country in which the publisher had financial interests. But the Kapuskasing venture was part of his newspaper enterprise and not vulnerable to such attack. It was merely a safeguard against recurrent newsprint shortages, which are a publisher's nightmare. Ochs was highly delighted with what he saw at Kapuskasing. He was specially interested in the welfare program for the mill's workers. He spent generously on it, believing it paid off in employe loyalty.

Ochs got back from Canada in time to preside at a staff dinner for Russell Owen. The feast was spread in the publisher's dining hall on the eleventh floor in the Forty-third Street Annex on Sunday night, Sept. 30, on the eve of Owen's take-off for Little America, which was to be Byrd's Antarctic Base. Birchall extolled the reporter's talents. Rollo Ogden and Dr. Finley spoke in scholarly vein of what might come from this extraordinary assignment, and Arthur Krock, then on the editorial staff, got off a poem about it:

> Long years have passed since bold Glendower
> Harried the Marches in his pride,
> And the Walsh broom has been in flower
> Hundreds of times since Owen died.
> Yet still the breed that roved the border
> Is lured by man's adventurous trails
> And so tonight we're called to order
> To speed a Welshman to The Bay of Whales
>
> But what his breed and where he's going—
> Although it be the grimmer Pole—
> Is not what sets the heartblood flowing
> And grips the fabric of the soul.
> We, youths and graybeards, desk and streetmen,

The whole newspaper category,
Thrill to our tasks and find them meet when
A Times man goes on a thundering story.

A few weeks after Owen left, the Byrd expedition was in icy waters nearing the Bay of Whales off Antarctica but in nightly wireless contact with The Times. Owen sent daily stories, and sometimes other members of the expedition filed scientific dispatches. They came from the other end of the world in split seconds, and frequently were on Times presses within a half hour of transmission.

On the night of Dec. 12, 1928, just before the expedition entered the crunching ice in the Bay of Whales, Meinholtz, The Times radio chief, sat in an upper room in his own home in Laurelton, Queens, listening in on the Byrd dispatches, just to check on how they were coming through. The radio staff knew this was his habit. Meinholtz sat absorbed as the words crackled into his room across 11,000 miles of ice, sea and earth. Suddenly he jumped up. There had been a brief interruption in transmission from the Byrd Ship Eleanor Bolling, and then this message:

MEINHOLTZ, HILFERTY AT THE TIMES WANTS YOU TO HANG UP YOUR TELEPHONE RECEIVER SO THAT HE CAN CALL YOU ON THE TELEPHONE.

Meinholtz raced downstairs to the living room. The telephone receiver there was off the hook. His infant son had dislodged it and Hilferty had been trying in vain to get through to him. The central telephone operator had, naturally, reported a steady busy signal.

Meinholtz jiggled the hook, got the operator and called The Times. When this talk was ended, Hilferty mentioned the incident in the city room. Birchall recognized instantly that an extraordinary thing had happened, and had a night rewrite man do a piece about it for next morning's paper. The story brought many letters. It was the only time in history that someone in New York had telephoned to someone else in New York by way of Antarctica. The call traveled more than 24,000 miles, all told, to cover points less than eighteen miles apart.

It was a night of surprises, anyway. Bernard Murphy, another Times office radio operator, was working the Eleanor Bolling from

Forty-third street a few minutes after the Meinholtz incident when, from somewhere in infinite ether, he heard personal greetings. It turned out the call was from two old radio associates, O'Cleary and Sullivan, operators working at that moment in Monrovia, Liberia, for the Radio Corporation of America. They wanted the night's hockey scores from Madison Square Garden. They got them.

On Nov. 6, 1928, The Times assembled the largest election night news staff in all its years and put out a book-length version—about 75,000 words—of the results assembled by telephone, telegraph and radio and by legmen. The same evening, The Times electric bulletin board, which came to be called The Times "zipper" because it girdles the Times Tower in the Square with its racing golden letters, went on for the first time. One of the first stories it flashed was of the devastating defeat of Al Smith by Herbert Hoover.

For a while the national picture took on ever rosier color and Noyes' melancholy writings did seem unjustified. The Times closed the year 1928 with a record total of 30,736,530 agate lines of advertising. Only one or two other newspapers in the world exceeded this figure, and their linage was cheaper.

No newspaper in this lush period was as exacting as The Times in its scrutiny of the advertising it accepted; none imposed the same strict censorship that Ochs' journal did, yet The Times figure was greater than that of its nearest New York competitor by more than 11,000,000 lines. Significantly, its total financial linage, 4,030,969 lines, was greater by almost 2,000,000 lines.

On April 6, 1929, from 11 P.M. to midnight, Ochs and Mayor Jimmy Walker spoke to Owen, Byrd and their whole group in a radio broadcast from The Times Annex clubroom. It was one of a series of similar programs that included instrumental and vocal music.

"Talking to you in this way," the publisher said, "is little less than a miracle. Never in the history of newspaper enterprise has there been anything to compare with these daily reports from a remote and inaccessible part of the world. It is journalism at its best. The civilized world is thus in touch with you. It watches your every movement with eager interest."

Lucrezia Bori sang for the homesick explorers as they lay sprawled in their bunks in dark little huts buried in ice on the edge of the Ross Sea, and Ethel Hayden sang, "Carry Me Back To Old Virginny," and "I Pass By Your Window."

Birchall talked with Owen. He said: "In the daily tale of world wonders we tell to the people everywhere, you provide the one thing that is really new." He recounted what was going into The Times that night—a Mexican revolution, a liner aground in New York Bay, deaths and violence in prohibition raids, Grover Whalen's announcement that New York had 32,000 speakeasies.

"News of a sort this all is," he said, "but the tale of your life in this twilight of Antarctic winter, its mishaps and thrills, the dugouts and the snow tunnels of mother-of-pearl and chrysoprase— that is a fresh wonder of men's achievement such as we have ever known before." Before he passed on greetings from The Times staff, Birchall quoted:

> Age reads and old dreams waken,
> Youth reads and vows anew.

Beside the broadcast story next morning ran Owen's piece from Little America telling how the men listened, dreamy-eyed and silent, as voices and music from home poured from the receiver. He described the setting: "The sun low and just about to drop over the Barrier edge, leaving behind a soft pastel red with the Western sky glorious . . . There are a few clicks in the box [the radio set] a warning buzz, and an instant silence in the room. Men sitting at the table, leaning on their elbows and clutching pipes, lying on bunks with their heads sticking over the ends, or standing in groups, cease their badinage. From that box came not merely sounds, but a whole lost life, tantalizing memory. Voices from home, voices that have come 11,000 miles over land and sea, over silent wastes of ice and desolate storm-tossed waters, and music that represents familiar things of a far-off civilization."

All through 1929 Times advertising kept climbing to new record heights, but the piper's footfalls were near the nation's door—and in the last week of October that year the piper's hand was out. The dance ended in shrieking dismay.

The speculative mania had swept so far beyond reason's outer borders that first warnings were laughed off, but on Monday, Oct. 21, when Thomas Edison was in Dearborn, Mich., celebrating the fiftieth anniversary of the making of the first incandescent lamp, major tremblings shook Wall Street.

The Times on Tuesday front-paged a story headed:

STOCKS SLUMP AGAIN,
BUT RALLY AT CLOSE
ON STRONG SUPPORT

The story told of declines of 1 to 10 points all along the line in confused trading. There was some hysteria on the Exchange floor, but nothing to what was to come in the weeks ahead. Next day stocks rose, but slipped again at closing. By Wednesday the tremors had become violent upheavals. The Times on Thursday put a two-column head on the story:

PRICES OF STOCKS CRASH
IN HEAVY LIQUIDATION;
TOTAL DROP OF BILLIONS

The Wall Street staff labored far into that night, getting in touch with the nation's foremost financiers, with Government officials, with great corporation heads in leading cities all over the country. Down in Wall Street's canyons office lights burned in every window. Pale, overworked brokers' clerks tried in vain to catch up on transactions. Telephones, cables, telegraph lines into Wall Street could not begin to carry all the calls from men and women who were being wiped out. The Times covered all these angles and more. It sent feature writers into Wall Street to report the color and human interest in this overwhelming national tragedy.

By Friday morning the story took the four lead columns on the front page:

WORST STOCK CRASH STEMMED BY BANKS;
12,894,650-SHARE DAY SWAMPS THE MARKET;
LEADERS CONFER, FIND CONDITIONS SOUND

Beside the main story a piece out of Chicago added the dark note:

BIG DROP IN WHEAT;
PIT IN A TURMOIL

And out of Washington the despairing, hopeless strain:

TREASURY OFFICIALS
BLAME SPECULATION

The second and third pages that morning were filled with details of the national disaster. Secondary stories with datelines from Boston, Philadelphia, Cincinnati, Cleveland, Baltimore, San Francisco, Los Angeles, London and Paris were mere echoes of a common anguish.

Noyes' Saturday morning piece on Oct. 26 was a terse summation of all the arguments he had put forward before. It was not editorial gloating. There was sadness in it.

"It will not be easy after this week's occurrences," he wrote, "to dismiss the teachings of past financial experiences. Wall Street itself will now be ready to confess that, however surrounding circumstances may change from one era to another, the great underlying influences which go to make sound or unsound finance, reasoned prosperity or inflation and subsequent disaster, are precisely the same today as in the all but forgotten pre-war period."

But the knockout punch had not yet hit Wall Street. That crashed through on Oct. 28 and 29, after the market had taken a bare breath or two in gasping attempt to get back on its feet. On Monday stock prices slumped $14,000,000,000.

No other newspaper in the world was equipped to handle the sickening final crash on Tuesday as The Times handled it. That day 16,410,030 shares were traded. The ticker could not keep up with such volume. The story on Wednesday, Oct. 30, covered five and one-half pages. The lead summed it up grimly:

"Stock prices virtually collapsed yesterday, swept downward with gigantic losses in the most disastrous trading day in the market's history. Billions of dollars in open market values were wiped out as prices tumbled and crumbled under the pressure of liquidation of securities which had to be sold at any price . . . Hysteria swept the country and stocks went overboard for just what they would bring at forced sale."

The Times' journalistic seismograph registered the shock outside New York: "Many Wiped Out in Toronto," "Big Losses at Boston,"

"Chicago Crash Continues," "Record Drop in Montreal," "London Disturbed by Continued Fall."

Great Wall Street barons tried in vain to end the hysteria, but headlines like "Rockefeller Buys To Allay Anxiety," "Time To Buy Stocks, Says Raskob," "U.S. Steel To Pay $1 Extra Dividend," "Leaders See Fear Waning," could not reduce the condition.

Black days lay ahead. The Times covered them as conscientiously as it had covered the upsurge. It pictured the desolation, unemployment, misery, despair, the wanderings of hopeless and homeless men from city to city, the march of pitiful "Bonus Armies"; the rising of "Hoover Cities" in which men lived primitively in mere caves, trenches and pits; the forming of public soup kitchens and of breadlines. This was the news and Ochs saw no sense in trying to hide it. He was not overwhelmed by fear as many others were.

A few years before the crash, a writer in The Atlantic Monthly had drawn a refreshingly frank portrait of Ochs. He had set down that the publisher was "palpably ingenuous," mentioned Ochs' almost childlike faith in the eternal verities, and used the Ochs quotation, "It took no genius to build The Times; just hard work, common sense, self-reliance and honesty."

The writer held that Ochs, the great newspaper builder, was "essentially the same simple boy who fifty-seven years ago ran a newspaper route in Knoxville." "All of this success," the article said, "was implicit in his mother's encouragement of the 'ordinary virtues.' To doubt this success is to doubt her. And to it he clings with childlike simplicity. In his ingenuousness are all the resources of his personality . . . Mr. Ochs cannot bear to have his simple recipe of life doubted, because that is all he believes in. And when he defends his deep-felt conviction that The Times is merely theological reward of simple integrity a childlike hurt steals into his luminous eyes which is irresistibly human."

This was over-simplification, but it was as good a characterization as anyone had drawn. The Wall Street crash emphasized it. Ochs was not personally affected by it. He held no interests except in his own properties, his own home and his own government. Because of this and his old-fashioned belief in the ordinary virtues and because his life had been sturdily patterned on maxim and precept,

Ochs was almost immune from fears that swept other men into panic. His "simple recipe of life" sustained him at this time, when lesser men who lacked his faith were broken. He kept telling interviewers in all sincerity that the country could weather the crisis. He went ahead with building plans in Brooklyn and in Forty-third Street.

Before the year ended The Times electrified its readers with news from the Byrd base in Antarctica. Thursday night, Nov. 28, 1929—Thanksgiving Day—was a bitter night, only 20 degrees above zero in Times Square, with a mean wind viciously snatching at skyscraper towers. As office clocks crept up on the 11 P.M. deadline for the first edition, Birchall was nervous. He popped in and out of the bull pen, fingering his goatee, now beginning to grow white. Owen had sent word that Byrd would take off almost any minute by plane for the South Pole. It was the expedition's climactic moment.

Just before 10:30 P.M., the managing editor scribbled a message to Owen. It was easier now to get a message to a Times man 11,000 miles away in glacial vastness than it was to get the Bronx district reporter.

"If we get this take-off story in next twenty minutes," the Birchall message said, "we can still make first edition."

Before The Times operator could send this note, Byrd's Antarctic station sparked the code for:

"Byrd takes off."

It was 10:29 P.M. in New York, 3:29 P.M. in Antarctica. The message had come through one-twentieth of a second after the plane's wheels had left the ice.

Owen had written columns of advance copy for this moment—on flight preparations, on flight objectives and what these aerial pioneers hoped to find in the first attempt by man to study the South Polar region from the air.

The story bore the distinctive dateline, "LITTLE AMERICA, Antarctica, Nov. 28." In the lead Owen told how:

"A huge gray plane slipped over the dappled Barrier at 3:29 o'clock this afternoon (10:29 P.M. New York time), the sun gleaming on its sides reflected in bright flashes from its metal wing and whirling propellers. With a smooth lifting movement it rose above the snow in a long, steady glide. . . .

"Once in the air, as if liberated from the clinging influence of earthly things, the great plane became suddenly like a true bird of the air. With its three motors roaring their deep song, it turned southward and was gone into the wilderness of space over a land of white desolation."

Birchall, Tebeau, the copy desk and the composing room staff were all geared for swift action. They sent the Owen copy to the composing room in short sections or "takes," tore down the original front page, reshuffled stories, and had the extra on the streets within forty-five minutes.

Bernt Balchen flew the plane, the Floyd Bennett. Harold I. June was its wireless operator and Capt. Ashley C. McKinley, photographer. June's flight reports were relayed from Little America as fast as they were received:

AIRPLANE FLOYD BENNETT, in flight toward the South Pole, 4 P.M. (11 P.M. New York time) Nov. 28—Flying well over the Geological Party's trail. Just passed Forty-Five Mile Depot.

With each fresh message from the plane on the unprecedented 1,600-mile outward flight, Birchall slapped out a new edition. He got out six in all, the last at 7 A.M. It was based on a 6:30 A.M. (New York time) message: "All is well with the Byrd plane." The stories, maps and photographs that morning covered twenty-one columns. The final lead was:

LITTLE AMERICA, Antarctica, Nov. 29—Byrd landed at Little America at 10:10 A.M. Antarctic time, 5:10 P.M. New York time.

A three-line, front-page banner above it related:

BYRD SAFELY FLIES TO SOUTH POLE AND BACK,
LOOKING OVER 'ALMOST LIMITLESS PLATEAU';
DROPS FOOD, LIGHTENS SHIP ON PERILOUS FLIGHT

Under it, in three columns of bold type in a front-page box, was The Times' second historic wireless message from a plane in flight over a polar waste. It carried the headline: "First Message Ever Sent from the South Pole."

ABOARD AIRPLANE FLOYD BENNETT, in flight, 1:55 P.M. Greenwich mean time (8:55 New York time) Friday, Nov. 29—My calculations indicate that we have reached the vicinity of the South Pole, flying high for a survey. The airplane is in good shape, crew all well. Will soon turn north. We can see an almost limitless plateau. Our departure from the pole was 1:25 P.M.

The Owen story told in detail of the plane's eighteen-hour passage between glassy ice walls of terrifyingly beautiful gorges, over glacial passes almost 12,000 feet high, of Balchen's skimming the ship at altitudes down to only 300 feet above the ice; of tearing through great fog patches and of the discovery of two new mountain ranges up to that moment never beheld by man.

"It was the most magnificent sight I have ever seen," Byrd had told Owen. "I never dreamed there were so many mountains in the world. They shone under the sun, wonderfully tinted, and in the southeast a cloud bank hung over the mountains, making a scene I will never forget."

Byrd's own written version of the flight and what had been learned from it ran for days, all of it stirring stuff, wonderful depression antidote.

When the revised Antarctica map appeared months later, there were some new names on it. Byrd found a gigantic formation in Marie Byrd Land that he called the Adolph S. Ochs Glacier. It lies about 76 degrees 30 minutes South, 145 degrees 35 minutes West. Off the northwest coast of Marie Byrd Land the commander discovered a bay more than 100 miles wide. He named that Arthur Sulzberger Bay. Mount Iphigene, named for Iphigene Ochs, is reflected in the bay. And still another mountain was called Marujupu —not an Indian name but a combination of the names of the four Sulzberger children—Marian, Ruth, Judith and Punch.

C H A P T E R

29

THE NATIONAL FEAR that numbed the United States after Wall Street temples fell became a form of creeping paralysis and The Times recorded its progress almost like a hospital chart.

Most Americans had some savings when the market walls came down and industry tried to keep its machinery humming, but little by little savings drained off and by and by industrial wheels slowed —came to a shuddering stop in some places, and fell frighteningly silent.

A new type of migrant evolved. A tremendous army of white collar destitutes—doctors, lawyers, artists, writers, clerks, architects and engineers—roamed the land in a state of numbed shock, legion upon legion of economic zombies. Family men took to the national highways and scattered to cities and farms far from their homes in a desperate but vain hunt for jobs. Hundreds of thousands ended up physical and spiritual wrecks, living like primitives on the margins of great cities, searching garbage cans, pawing discarded and decayed fruit and vegetable mounds in the city markets for anything edible.

This was the piper's ultimate price. This was President Hoover's heritage. Bitter social and economic outcasts wrongly placed the blame at his door. Left-wing experts in social husbandry thought this was the time to sow their little red seeds for a great harvest, and Times pages showed how they labored mightily at it on the bread lines and in the miserable shelters where homeless men huddled, hungry and wretched.

When 1929 ended The Times led the world's newspapers in advertising with 32,162,870 lines, 1,600,000 more than in 1928. Circulation reached a daily average of 431,931, and Sunday established a new high with an average of 728,909. Within another year, though, faint symptoms of the common paralysis nipped at these figures.

Ochs' courage showed strongly in this period. Other publishers, infected by spreading national panic, hastily cut expansion programs, pared payrolls, started epidemic fright among their staffs. Ochs, holding steady, kept his staff virtually intact and went ahead with pre-October plans. The Times continued to spend at the rate of $10,000 a week, or around $500,000 a year, on national and foreign press dispatches alone, exclusive of Associated Press expenses. Ochs firmly held to his cardinal business principle that the most precious product he had to sell was news. He would not skimp on getting the most, and the most accurate, in the shortest possible time.

He kept telling interviewers that dark as things seemed he knew hope's light would break through, because it always had.

"I suggest," he told the trade magazine Editor and Publisher, "that we [newspaper owners] avoid hysteria, that we keep cool and have abiding faith in the stability of our institutions. We must advise the people that the United States will come out of this temporary period of adversity chastened and on solid ground. We are but paying the penalty of the universal waste and extravagance of the great war and the attempt to preserve its inflated values."

This was no uncertain whistling past the graveyard. In his seventy-odd years Ochs had seen Americans struggle out of other depressions to a national greatness they had never dared to dream. He believed every word he uttered, believed it with patriotic fervor.

Still, Times pages early in 1930 were something less than gay reading. It was the tenth year of Prohibition, the era of the Capone, Dutch Schultz, Legs Diamond and Owney Madden bootlegging dynasties. The country had grown almost indifferent to chain-reaction gang murders growing out of frenzied competition between beer and booze running syndicates, and out of the lesser rackets that were secondary growth. The nations had not recovered from their World War I wounds. There was bitterness over war-debt payments. Delegates to the five-power Naval Disarmament Conference bickered endlessly. In the news background, slowly materializing like evil ectoplasm, Europe's dictators were increasing in political stature. They were spreading the fuel for a second World War on ground barely cooled after the fires of the first.

To counterbalance the dark side of the news Ochs kept investing substantially in off-the-trail types of news story. Times readers in 1930 followed a number of interesting flights and exploration expeditions—the Smythe-Dyhrenfurth attempt to climb fearsome Kanchenjunga, Dr. Herbert S. Dickey's groping in the Orinoco's green darkness, Captain Bartlett's findings around Greenland, the Gregory Mason expedition to long-buried Mayan haunts in Yucatan, Sir Douglas Mawson's adventures in the Antarctic. The Times had exclusive rights to several east-to-west flights from Europe, including the successful Coste-Bellonte venture, and had extraordinary coverage on lighter-than-air ocean crossings by the British dirigible R-100 and the German Graf Zeppelin.

Up to Jan. 11, 1930, the longest text The Times had ever received by wireless was Mussolini's speech before the Chamber of Deputies on May 26, 1927. This ran to 11,000 words.

On Jan. 11, 1930, Pope Pius XI issued a 12,000-word encyclical on education that was not due for translation into English for some time. The Times staff in Rome immediately hired translators and at 8 o'clock Wednesday night, Jan. 15, Times short-wave station operators began copying the message sent through Coltano radio station in Italy. They kept at it through 10:30 Thursday morning and it ran in full on Sunday, Jan. 19. No other newspaper except the Vatican's official publication had it. The encyclical was widely read and inspired extensive editorial comment.

A year later Arnaldo Cortesi, chief Rome correspondent, transmitted another papal encyclical, this time a 16,000-word document on divorce, trial marriage and birth control. The text took all of Pages 14 and 15 in The Times of Jan. 9, and ran over onto Page 16. Like the encyclical of the previous year, this came by wireless. Longer texts were to come in later years, but no other newspaper tried to adopt the pattern; it was too expensive.

This documentary presentation of news had become almost solely a Times institution. Few other papers had the space for verbatim reports and those that had were apt to have few readers interested in them.

In May, 1930, when the publisher was in London, the University of Missouri's first gold medal for outstanding newspaper service went to The Times. Sulzberger, accepting it, told the journalism students how Ochs had built The Times; quoted the Ochsian creed from the salutation to Times readers in 1896.

"The publication of a newspaper differs from most enterprises," Sulzberger said, "in that, as the day closes, it has emptied its shelves. Gone are the galleys of type, the presses have run their course, the record has been made—and nothing remains of the newspaper. Nothing, that is, save the character, enterprise and purpose of the organization that assembled it. This purpose shapes a journal's character."

He spoke of Ochs' work methods. He said: "Mr. Ochs is the perfect newspaperman. He possesses an evenness of spirit and a catholicity of interests. He is simple and direct, able to strip the most difficult problem of its complexities and put his finger on underlying and motivating facts. The news angle becomes apparent under his touch. He devours The Times. There is little in it that escapes his attention, in its news, in its editorial content, or in its physical make-up.

"His greatest delight is to find an insignificant paragraph which under his prodding develops a first-page story. He refuses to go with the herd and frequently in editorial council takes what he himself would later admit was an extreme position, solely for the purpose of bringing out in argument all the points that could be made on both sides.

"I have never seen him lose his temper nor heard him raise his voice. He is fair in his judgment and sound in his estimate of people. He made a success of The New York Times with the same people who had themselves made a failure of it. Into them he instilled a new and fresh spirit which made The Times a pleasant place to work . . . You have only to look back a few years to realize that it was Mr. Bennett's Herald and Mr. Pulitzer's World, but that The Times was just The Times. I know no person on The Times today who is working for Mr. Ochs. I know 3,500 who are working for The Times."

Sulzberger told how Ochs in 1898 had turned down Tammany's offer of a $150,000 monopoly of city advertising when The Times was trying to wobble to its feet under the new management. Ochs' civic conscience dictated that the advertising was a waste of city money. He attacked it editorially on that ground. "It took character last year," Sulzberger said, "to refuse another $350,000 of miscellaneous advertising which for various reasons was found unacceptable, and much of which was then accepted and printed elsewhere." He pointed out that while Times readers remained ignorant of such costly ad-screening, The Times staff knew of it and was heartened by Ochs' integrity. It made for greater staff pride and warmer staff loyalty.

Sulzberger dwelt a moment on criticism occasionally aimed by cynics at the Ochs slogan, "All the News That's Fit to Print."

He said: "There are many standards as to what is fit. The newspaperman knows at least that what is untrue is unfit and the motto stands as the silent monitor at the copy desk, no matter how the public may regard it." He took up the popular fallacy that a successful newspaper must of necessity be occasionally venal because it depends on advertising for profit.

"Apparently," he said, "these critics never take into consideration that a newspaper whose columns are filled with high-class advertising is not only presenting news in its advertising copy, but that the visible revenue derived from advertising at least removes the need of any hidden subsidy. On the assumption that the normal man would rather be honest than not, it is the prosperous 'commercial' newspaper—I quote the word 'commercial'—that is least apt to be serving an undisclosed cause."

Ochs' integrity had other facets. He never valued a news story, however important, above the public welfare. On at least two or three occasions he withheld Times exclusives because he thought they would do more public harm than good.

When banks were toppling in the winter of 1930 The Times financial staff learned that the Bank of United States, a New York institution, was shaky and might go under. The bank had sixty branch offices and deposits of more than $160,000,000.

On the evening of Dec. 10, 1930, a group of prominent New York financiers met in the Federal Reserve Bank to discuss the possibility of saving the Bank of United States. A little after midnight Martin Egan of J. P. Morgan & Co., who was in the meeting, called Elliott V. Bell of The Times financial staff at his home.

Egan told Bell: "It's all over. They can't agree on any plan. There is only one chance in a thousand that the bank will open tomorrow morning."

Bell called the office, and was ordered to come in and write the story, but after he had begun to write the night desk ordered a halt. Ochs decided that if there was still even a 1000-to-1 chance that the bank might survive, publication of the story would merely serve to hasten local panic. The Times ran instead a story by Frank Adams telling of a run on the Bank of United States Bronx branch, indirectly caused by the branch manager's refusing to buy some Bank of United States stock that a local merchant had tried to sell. A garbled version of this incident led to a rumor that the bank had refused to let the merchant withdraw his deposit and a run started. The branch had paid out $2,000,000 to 2,500 depositors before its doors closed for the day. This story ran on Page 5 in The Times of Dec. 11. This story was true as far as it went, but it did not disclose that the institution was tottering.

Next day the Bank of United States failed, and on Friday, Dec. 12, The Times ran more than a page on its closing, beginning with a front-page lead under the two-column headline:

BANK OF U. S. CLOSES DOORS; STATE TAKES OVER AFFAIRS; AID OFFERED TO DEPOSITORS

There was hell to pay that day. Burnt readers bitterly accused The Times of stupidity, assuming the newspaper had been caught napping, and that it had had no knowledge of the impending failure. The Times took this angry assault without disclosing that it had known the bank's condition. It did not disclose, even in justification, the fact that The Times itself had $17,000 in one of the bank's branches. It had made no attempt to withdraw those funds; just took its losses as all other depositors had.

Seven years later, in a talk before the Columbia University Alumni Association, Sulzberger revealed what The Times had done with the Bank of United States story.

"We were up against a conflict of responsibilities that morning," he explained, "and had come to the conclusion that our duty lay in doing our utmost to prevent financial panic and in protecting the deposits of many thousands of people rather than in giving the news, which, if the worst happened—as it did—would be bound to reach the community in any case and, consequently, was not being withheld from it improperly."

Ochs was stern about printing "all the news" even in cases where The Times itself was the target, as it sometimes was. There was a second instance, though, in which he withheld publication of a story because he thought it might harm the public welfare.

Not long after the Bank of United States incident, Paul Crowell, an extraordinarily sharp Times reporter, stumbled on the fact that New York was not keeping up on its payments for municipal supplies. It was something he had dug out of The City Record.

Further investigation established that the city was financially wobbly and that it was desperately trying to raise $60,000,000 to tide it over a bad period. When Ochs read Crowell's story, he was gravely concerned.

"Mr. Crowell," he said, "shouldn't we let Mayor Walker know we have these facts? If we just run the story without some comment from him, we will embarrass the City and damage its credit."

Crowell knew Jimmy Walker's charm. "I wouldn't talk to the Mayor," he told the publisher. "He'll talk us out of the story."

Ochs phoned the Mayor. Crowell was right; Walker talked The Times out of running the story on the ground that its publication would make it impossible for the city to borrow the $60,000,000. Three weeks later the story broke generally, and Crowell was made unhappy. He had been deprived of an important beat. Ochs still felt he had acted for the common good.

Two days before The Times won the University of Missouri gold medal, Joseph F. Tebeau, assistant managing editor, had left his desk in the night bull pen just before the last edition had gone to bed and had plodded to his West Side home. He died in his own hallway, his heart overtaxed. When his wife called the office, James MacDonald, on night rewrite, hastily did the Tebeau obituary for that morning's final press run. Then the staff sat around and reverently swapped Tebeau legends. There were many. Tall, white-haired Joe Tebeau was a gruff soul, blunt as a battering ram. He had been Van Anda's and Birchall's solid right arm. He had performed heroically as head man at the waterfront the night the Carpathia had pulled in with Titanic survivors, he had been cable and telegraph editor handling all Washington and battlefront dispatches from 1914 until the armistice, and had headed field staffs at national political conventions. Sorrowing colleagues followed his coffin to the grave and one of the men, who had worked under him and known his bellowing anger at deadline, anonymously wrote poetic tribute:

> The forms are closed. The final page
> Has gone up; man's last story told.
> Today is ended, joined the fold
> Of vanished stars from earth's old stage.
>
> The presses move. This night they lag.
> Distrait, where once a virile roar
> Told all the world a man, and more,
> Led this brigade, bore high its flag.

In the spring of 1930 Richard Evelyn Byrd, who had become a Rear Admiral, finished his Antarctic adventure and started home with his ships and planes. Russ Owen had sent more than 300,000 words by wireless in the two years the expedition had spent on the ice and was eager for a look at the office and at Times Square. He got home in mid-June.

About the time that the Byrd fleet left Antarctica, Ochs served up another series of stories to offset the dominating unhappy national economic theme and the steadily decaying international picture.

On March 9, a group of mountain climbers representing Germany, Italy, England, France and Switzerland—there was harmony among individuals from these countries, if not among their governments—landed in Bombay to prepare to climb brooding Mount Kanchenjunga, legendary home of the Buddhist gods, towering 28,146 feet in the Himalayas.

The Times man with the party was Frank S. Smythe, 29 years old, a former engineer and British newspaperman. He had been invalided out of the Royal Air Force in 1926 because he had—of all things—a weak heart. Daily he sent out his Kanchenjunga reports by native runner from the base camp to Darjeeling. From there they were transmitted by wireless and cable.

By late April the party had deeply penetrated the Himalayan wilderness. Smythe's stories were warmly colored with descriptions of native tribes and of Tibetan lamas the party met in mountain monasteries.

On April 21, Smythe's story bore the dateline: "JONGRI, Sikkim, April 15, via runner to Darjeeling, April 20."

"At last," this dispatch said, "we are at grips with things. We are on the way up Kang Pass, having come through Sikkim by way of the Pemayangtse Monastery, Tingling and Kachoperi Monastery and Yoksun and up the Rangit Valley to Jongri at the head of Jowgri Pass . . . I am writing this on April 15 in a tent pitched in a bed of dwarf rhododendrons. Outside there is a roaring mountain torrent with stern dark walls on either side. A few snowflakes are falling from a black sky tempered with fugitive glimpses of the sun over Kang La, our pass tomorrow. The air is pure, keen and invigorating with the snows, compensating for the days of trudging through the steamy tropical heat of the valleys.

"At Pemayangtse Monastery, perched on a broad ridge, the lamas gave a dance in our honor. The morning was perfect with the mighty mountains of Kabru and Kanchenjunga, above the purple depths of Rangit Valley, forming a fitting background . . . A New York audience would have howled down the lamas' music, but here amid giant mountains and valleys it was wonderfully appropriate. Long horns, the thunderous note of drums, crashing cymbals and a clarinetlike instrument wailing a dirge, carried one away from civilized life into the spirit of this weird and wonderful mountain land."

Ochs instinctively knew that the Smythe stories would have just that effect—would transport those mentally weary of the civilized world to the rarefied never-never land, to remote and mysterious Shangri-La, far across the world. It was good escape stuff and authentic news.

The Sunday Times, adhering to the principle that news magazine pieces must tread closely on the spot story's heels, carried Smythe's background material.

On May 24, 1930, The Times front page carried Smythe's account of how sullen Kanchenjunga had wreaked its wrath on the party as it toiled up the peak's higher reaches:

AVALANCHE ENGULFS PARTY
ON KANCHENJUNGA CLIMB;
PORTER IS KILLED, 2 HURT

On June 8, Smythe's story acknowledged the expedition's defeat. "Kanchenjunga," he wrote wearily, "has beaten us. Our last hope was the west ridge, but despite our best efforts it proved impossible."

Ice avalanches had stopped the party somewhere above the 20,000-foot mark on the west wall. Screaming blizzards had all but swept the climbers to their death, had snatched their tents into dark void, and had left them helplessly staring up at forbidding sheer ice walls at the top of the world.

All through the summer of 1930 The Times balanced the melancholy social, economic and international developments with exciting news features. They were sorely needed. In June the only ray of promise for the immediate future was the announcement by John D. Rockefeller Jr. that he intended to build a $200,000,000 radio and television center on $250,000,000 worth of Manhattan Island. All the frantic building of the speculation-mania period had stopped dead.

The Rockefeller announcement made The Times front page on June 16. It was just as well, perhaps, that an already overburdened and sick civilization did not quite understand the full import of two other stories that appeared on Times front pages that month. One, from Hallett Abend, correspondent in China, bore the headline:

CHINA IN WORST PERIL
IN LIFE OF REPUBLIC;
REDS A REAL THREAT

It said:

SHANGHAI, June 16—Shuddering with fear of Communist domination in the Yangtse Valley, and fighting on five distinct war fronts, China today is in the worst situation since the overthrow of the Manchu Dynasty.

Abend's story described in fine detail Stalin's way of swallowing a great neighbor state. It was the slow, digestive process of the snake, absorbing an oversize meal. As the Reds slithered in they destroyed titles, deeds and other records of victim communities.

On June 24, a week after the story from Shanghai, The Times carried a front-page story from Berlin that bore the headline:

EDDINGTON PREDICTS
SCIENCE WILL FREE
VAST ENERGY IN ATOM

"Harnessing of the limitless energy stored away in matter," this item calmly related, "was the prospect Sir Arthur Eddington, British astronomer, dangled before the World Power Conference today. The same inexhaustible power which heats the sun, Sir Arthur predicted, may one day be put to the use of mankind . . . For engineers, he admitted, it was still a Utopian dream, and for physicists a pleasant speculation, but for astronomers it was already a practical subject of investigation."

There it was, plainly spread on The Times news mirror—the rolling-in of the Red wave in Asia, the pea-sized beginning of the tremendous Hiroshima mushroom cloud—but apparently no earthly power could prevent their spreading.

CHAPTER
30

THREE YEARS had passed since Charles Lindbergh had flown non-stop from the American mainland to the European Continent. On Monday, June 23, 1930, The Times carried a two-column story on the birth of a son to Mrs. Lindbergh on her twenty-fourth birthday. Mrs. Lindbergh's parents, Ambassador and Mrs. Dwight W. Morrow, lived in Englewood, N. J.

Next morning, just before sun-up, Maj. Charles Kingsford-Smith, an Australian pilot, and three flight companions zoomed from Port Marnock on the Irish Coast for New York in the five-year-old Southern Cross. The Major had signed a contract to tell his story in The Times.

When the take-off, at 4:30 A.M. Irish time, was flashed Birchall ordered the radio room to establish contact with the Southern Cross and to try to maintain it.

Contact was easily made with the highly perfected Times short-wave equipment, and was maintained most of the way. Messages were cheerful at first and readers got an hour-by-hour account of the plane's westward progress.

Eventually, as seemed to happen in all ocean flights, even in early summer, headwinds cut the plane's fuel supply dangerously and cottony fog and dense cloud shut the world below from Major Kingsford-Smith's vision. The crew flew blind in a mist-shuttered ship.

Early Wednesday morning, June 25, the Southern Cross was still in the air, bucking the headwinds with rapidly emptying fuel tanks.

"In very bad fog," the major whispered by wireless, "and trouble has held us up quite a lot. Afraid will have to land at Newfoundland or Nova Scotia for petrol, after all. Sorry to have to do this but delay was enormous. Will advise which place later."

This message with the flight's signature came over The Times radio receiver at 3:45 A.M. Birchall waited until 5 o'clock that morning for further word. At that hour the plane had hardly any fuel left. Birchall got out a 5:30 flight extra.

"Kingsford-Smith Crosses the Atlantic Ocean," the headline said. "May Land in Newfoundland or Nova Scotia; Messages Direct To The Times Tell of Flight."

Even after the paper was on the street, Times wireless operators kept in touch with Canadian land stations to which the plane's long-wave set had shifted for landing guidance.

At 6:30 A.M., Major Kingsford-Smith called: "Louisburg. Louisburg. Louisburg. Please can you do something to guide us to the field? Can you send a machine up quickly above the fog? CQ CQ CQ (all stations). Please ring Harbor Grace and tell them to send machine up above fog. Please stand by."

Twenty-six minutes later morning sun burned a hole in the woolly fog and men on Harbor Grace field saw the Southern Cross. She nosed down in a relieved plunge, straightened, rolled to a smooth landing.

The Times next day carried all the plane's tense messages, all the details of those harrowing last flight hours and the Major's own account of the experience, the start of a series on the first successful Atlantic crossing from the European mainland to North America. The stories gave The Times another exclusive on aviation pioneering.

Leo Kieran of The Times aviation news staff had been sent to Portland, Me., in anticipation of a possible landing there by the Southern Cross. Riding in another plane he guided the Southern Cross to Roosevelt Field, where Deak Lyman, who had flown with Kingsford-Smith in 1928, was one of the first to greet the flier.

The Times of early September, 1930, contained many accounts of high adventure. On the first day of the month, Capt. Dieudonne

Coste and Maurice Bellonte, two Frenchmen, started from Paris for New York in the Question Mark, a big red biplane with one motor.

It was more than three years since The Times had first contracted with Captain Coste for his story of such a flight. The expedition had been planned as France's immediate answer to Lindbergh's New York-Paris success, but for one reason or another had been repeatedly put off.

Edwin James had cabled Joe Tebeau on the night of Aug. 18, 1927, that Coste and his companion, who had been snarled up with agents in the deal, were ready to sign, and Tebeau had cabled back: "Agree to $10,000 for Coste provided he is first European to land here on western flight."

Two days later James sent the message: "Coste and companion signed for $10,000 if arrive first. Will need French-speaking reporter write story. Three articles, 2,500 words each."

Now Coste was on his way, and again the world's eyes, through The Times, were fixed on still another plane trying to beat east-to-west ocean-flight hazards. The ocean winds, Atlantic fogs, biting snow and heavy ice bedeviled the Question Mark as they had the Southern Cross.

The Times on Sept. 2, headlined the fact that Coste was nearing the American coast through thick and dangerous weather, and carried Coste's own story of his flight preparations, sent from Paris after he had taken off.

Coste's take-off and the astonishing discovery of relics left by two long-lost bands of polar explorers led by Salomon August Andrée and Sir John Franklin did not complete the early September adventure stuff in The Times. On the morning that the newspaper ran the Coste take-off story, it started a sunken treasure series.

This was a first-hand account of an expedition that had lowered deep sea divers to the ocean bed off Cape Finisterre on the French Coast, trying to get at more than $5,000,000 in gold and silver that had gone down in the S. S. Egypt in May 1922.

The Egypt series had Captain Nemo flavor and the universal appeal that seems to cling to hunts for treasure trove. It was especially thrilling to readers in the depression era when men dreamed of riches to lift them out of extreme poverty.

On Wednesday, Sept. 3, The Times carried a three-line eight-column banner:

COSTE DOES IT IN 37 HOURS, 18½ MINUTES!
FIRST TO MAKE PARIS-NEW YORK FLIGHT;
HOOVER, LINDBERGH AND BYRD HAIL FEAT

Coste brought the Question Mark down on Curtiss Field in descending sun with more than 10,000 persons hoarsely cheering. American fliers carried the Frenchmen off the field on their backs and the throng noisily returned the welcome that Parisians had given Lindbergh when he set the Spirit of St. Louis' wheels down on that wild night at Le Bourget three years before.

The pilots were exhausted. They had come through ice, snow and sleet, even in mid-September. They had thought, at times, that their names might go down on the long list headed by their unfortunate countrymen, the pioneers Nungesser and Coli.

Grover Whalen's committee hustled the fliers to a mid-town hotel. John L. Eddy Jr. of The Times staff, who spoke French, had been assigned by Birchall to get their first-hand accounts. The fliers had all they could do to stay awake to complete the narrative, and translation presented another difficulty.

There was no time to rush the story to the office. Eddy telephoned it in after 10 o'clock and it made the first edition by a cat's whisker. It was worth it. No other newspaper had this personal account of the first flight across the Atlantic from one continental city to another.

Coste brought with him in the Question Mark a new dress model and more than twenty-one columns of advertising, the first ad copy ever flown westward across the Atlantic. One was a seven-column display for the new dress, designed by Callot of Paris, to be shown exclusively at Wanamaker's in New York. The French designer proclaimed the model in a seven-column ad on Page 14 of The Times, and Wanamaker took another seven-column ad on Page 15. The official French Tourist Bureau took almost a full page with copy from Paris, advertising France's lure for travelers.

On Friday, the night of Sept. 5, The Times city room was unusually lively. Front-page stuff was breaking in every compass corner, and copy streamed across the desks. Four thousand persons were dead in a hurricane that had flattened San Domingo and was headed for the North American mainland. Divers had wrestled a bulky treasure from the Egypt's watery hold. From Poona in India came the portentous item:

INDIANS ASK BRITISH
FOR RIGHT TO SECEDE

Scientists in Chicago were listening intently to a theory that cosmic radiation originated new stars, earthquakes and hurricanes. Henry Ford, leaving for Europe, had given out the reassuring (but overoptimistic) statement that the national depression might lift by October. The big local story was the great hunt for Supreme Court Justice Joseph Force Crater, who had vanished suddenly, just a month before, as if snatched into some invisible dimension. Crater, incidentally, never was found.

The biggest story that night was from The Times correspondent in Buenos Aires. It told of a revolution there in which rebels had deposed Argentinian President Hipolito Irigoyen and replaced him with Dr. Enrique Martinez. Details were scant.

On Saturday night, bucking the early deadline for the Sunday paper, the foreign desk's great problem was how to break through for a second-day story on the Argentine coup. The rebels had closed down radio and cable facilities. No news was getting out.

As Birchall pondered ways to break through, someone suggested that the rebel censor might have overlooked the new wireless telephone, which was comparatively little used, even for routine message relay because of the expense. Birchall's eyes lighted. He strode onto the city room floor, into the clatter of typewriters and pounding teletype batteries. He shouted, "Ho, Denny!" And Denny left the rewrite desk to answer the summons.

Birchall told Denny to try to get Buenos Aires on the telephone— anyone in Buenos Aires who might be a reliable news source. Denny thought a moment, then asked Mary Slear, a Times telephone operator, to put a call through to the Buenos Aires daily La Nacion. An hour later, at 6:06 P.M., Denny was in conversation with La Nacion, 5,300 miles away.

Congenitally gracious and aware of Latin regard for the social amenities, Denny exchanged brief pleasantries. Then he asked, "What is the latest news of the crisis?"

"They have just captured the Government House," La Nacion's panting editor told him.

"When?"

"Just a few minutes ago; I have just come from there," the editor said. "I am still a little breathless." He launched into detailed narrative of fresh events, gave an excellent color picture of the rebel coup he had just witnessed.

Denny's pencil flew over the copy paper, with some eight or ten reporters and editors clustered silently about him, or whispering excitedly over this extraordinary assignment. No other newspaper had ever used a telephone to cover a revolution while it was still hot on another continent.

Birchall's eyes gleamed happily behind the thick lenses. He patted Denny, arranged for swift handling of the coup story and for ample front-page space for it. As Denny's typewriter chattered out short takes, boys raced the stuff to the foreign desk to be edited and headlined. It was Sunday morning's lead:

REVOLUTION TRIUMPHS IN ARGENTINA; JUNTA ASSUMES POWER AS TROOPS OUST IRIGOYEN'S REGIME AND ARREST HIM

It carried the historic credit line:

From a Special Correspondent of The New York Times
By Wireless Telephone

BUENOS AIRES, Sept. 6—Argentina's smoldering revolution burst suddenly into full flame this evening, and the Government of Dr. Enrique Martinez, formed only twenty-four hours before, was forcibly driven out.

Tonight Gen. José Uriburu, idol of the army and leader of the opposition to the government, is in full control of the capital city, with the complete support of the Argentine Navy, commanded by Admiral Alberti Storni.

The story described the street fighting, the hoisting of a white flag on Government House, civilians joining the attack on the seat of executive power . . . "This evening the crisis seemed to have passed completely," Denny's piece said, in closing, "and the city was quiet."

After the paper had reached the street with this exclusive first-hand account of the revolution, Associated Press wires sent in a story from sources outside of Buenos Aires, placing the number of dead at more than 1,000. Denny's story had said there were ten dead and seventy wounded in a battle with the palace guards.

Birchall ordered Denny to call La Nacion again to check. The call, put through at 10 P.M., confirmed his original figures.

The Times used the wireless telephone to Buenos Aires nightly after that through Sept. 12, and every night got fresher and more accurate news than any other newspaper or agency.

After Denny had written a first-edition story the night of Sept. 8, rumor seeped through of further trouble in Buenos Aires. When The Times tried to get through by wireless telephone again, the service between Buenos Aires and New York had closed for the night, even as it had at a given hour in more peaceful periods.

Fortunately, Argentine cable censorship did not apply to messages coming into that country, so The Times persuaded the American Telephone and Telegraph Company to arrange by cable to bring its South American telephone technicians back to their stations, and to round up the United States crew, too.

It was 2:20 A.M. before all this was arranged, and Denny got through again. The story he wrote then justified the effort:

COUNTER-REVOLT IN BUENOS AIRES MARS
THE INAUGURATION OF GENERAL URIBURU;
IRIGOYEN AND HIS AIDES ARE ARRESTED

BUENOS AIRES, Sept. 9—Buenos Aires was torn tonight by a counter-revolt, attributed to partisans of the deposed President Hipolito Irigoyen, while the capital was in the midst of a wildly enthusiastic celebration of the swearing-in of General Uriburu as Provisional President.

The story was complete in fine detail; it told how shooting had started at 8:30 P.M. in the Plaza de Mayo and kept up until 2 A.M. Sept. 9, leaving twenty reported killed, 200 wounded.

There was glory enough in the series of beats on the Argentine revolution, but one question was still unanswered: Since President Irigoyen had been openly unfriendly to the United States, it was important to know the new President's attitude.

Denny got up a list of questions, and put through a call to the President himself on the night of Sept. 10. They spoke for a full half-hour. A column-and-a-half story in next morning's paper was headlined:

URIBURU TALKS TO TIMES
IN A WIRELESS INTERVIEW;
REQUESTS OUR FRIENDSHIP

Newspapers all over the world and newspaper trade papers conceded that The Times telephone revolution coverage, capped with the interview across 5,300 miles, was something new in journalism.

Four days after the Uriburu interview, The Times ran a story sent from Berlin by Guido Enderis, one of its correspondents there. Adolf Hitler had grown to great political proportions. Members of his National Socialist party now physically attacked German newspaper offices that dared print editorials or items detrimental to the movement.

The leading story on Sept. 15 was headlined:

FASCISTS MAKE BIG GAINS IN GERMANY;
COMMUNISTS ALSO INCREASE STRENGTH
AS MODERATES DROP IN REICH ELECTION

"Republicanism," the Enderis story said, "suffered a heavy blow and Chancellor Bruening's reform Cabinet a decisive defeat when 13,000,000 of 36,000,000 votes went into the balance against the young republic and its champions in yesterday's election in the new Reich.

"Fascism voiced its contempt for parliamentary government by rolling up a vote of 6,000,000 and will send 107 deputies to the Reichstag, increasing its representation there nearly ninefold.

"The sensational gain of Adolf Hitler's National Socialist Labor Party in yesterday's election constitutes one of the most upsetting developments of post-war German politics . . . Back of it all was the cry for a dictator who would lead Germany out of the slough of parliamentary despond."

The Times Paris bureau, the same morning, sent this story:

"The results of the German elections, so far as they were known here early this morning, have caused a certain anxiety in France. With two-thirds of the vote counted, dispatches to Paris newspapers indicate disquieting gains for the Hitlerites, or extreme nationalists, whose policy is looked upon as one of war and revenge."

On Nov. 24, 1930, The Times began on its editorial page the first of a series of six pieces on a visit to Russia by Edwin L. James. The first was headed, "Russia, the Enigma, a Study of Politico-Economic Conditions in That Country Which Are Affecting the Whole World." James said:

"One of these days, and it may not be long now, the Kremlin dictators must tell the people that they are toiling and struggling, not for a Five-Year Plan, but on a Twenty-five-Year Plan.

"For at least another decade the people of Russia must do the bidding of Communist dictators; they must eat poor food and wear poor clothes, they must submit to rule by threat of hunger, and they must work when and where they are told . . . The dictators must be successful in making them do that if the revolution is to go through."

In the second article, James pointed out:

"There are forty American corporations putting many millions of dollars into Russia under the industrial revolution. The leaders of those corporations must believe that the Kremlin has at least a fighting chance."

James' articles were straight, objective reports of what he had seen and heard. He was doing no crystal-ball gazing, and to make that clear to Times readers, he said in his concluding piece on Nov. 29:

"I hope the reader will find in no line of these articles any effort to predict what will happen in Russia."

In a letter to Birchall, accompanying the articles, and dated Nov. 11, 1930 (oddly enough, the twelfth anniversary of the Armistice), he wrote:

"I am sending you some stuff I have written about Russia. You may well say it is vague and otherwise indefinite, but the only figures available are certainly not trustworthy.

"What I saw of Russia was miserable. It was dirty and hungry, and the people seemed strictly out of luck. But, then, they always were. I do not believe anyone can say what is going to happen there. Certainly, I do not wish to pretend to.

"When I came back I had lunch with Owen Young. He is firmly convinced that the Kremlin dictators have a fighting chance of going on for some years. It is his theory that the success of the industrial revolution will kill communism. At any rate, it seems a pretty good guess that General Electric is not putting a million or more dollars into a proposition unless it thinks it is not due to bust next week or next month.

"God knows I don't want any communism in mine! The Russians can have it. I do not believe any people in the world expected the Russians would stand for what is being done, but they *have* been standing it for some years and may keep on doing it. Who knows? I don't.

"I asked Litvinov if they could sit on the Russians for ten years or more. He answered: 'I don't know; do you?'"

These pieces were James' last major contribution as chief correspondent for The Times in Europe. No one else held the title until April, 1932, when Birchall went to Berlin. During the intervening two years James was Birchall's assistant. When Birchall went overseas, James became managing editor.

Against the forbidding backdrop at the end of 1930—unrest in Germany, uneasiness in France, revolution in Argentina, growing murmur in India, Red threats in Asia and over Europe, the hopeless gasping of Wall Street, United States workers living miserably in "Hoover Cities" and scientists rapidly delving into fearsome atomic secrets— Ochs went on with his building. He still believed that the United States—the whole world—would slowly swing back to normal balance. He was wrong.

In 1930 Times advertising fell by almost 6,000,000 lines as compared with 1929. Average daily circulation was off by more than 2,000 copies, but the Sunday average went against the tide, rising 12,500 copies. Ochs still led all local competitors, and in most advertising categories was world leader. Newspapers everywhere were ill with depression sclerosis.

Ochs still refused to cut salaries or to curtail plant expansion. On Nov. 3, 1930, Marian Sulzberger, his daughter's first-born, then almost 12 years old, laid the cornerstone for the new $2,000,000 Times plant in Pacific Street in Brooklyn with the same silver trowel her mother had used in Times Square twenty-six years before.

"I dedicate this building," the child said, "to the uses of The New York Times, and repeat here the words my mother used when she laid the cornerstone of The Times Building in Times Square in 1904." She echoed her mother's dedicatory remarks.

As this dedication was uttered, Ochs was also completing a new fifteen-story west wing to the Annex on a seventy-five-foot front in Forty-third Street, on the site of a row of dusty brownstones that had been called the Yandis Court Apartments. That was ready a few months later. It was The Times' seventh structure, vast and handsome companion to the Tower and to the original Forty-third Street building. A spreading white monument had materialized from the grubby Nassau Street lofts where Henry Raymond had put out the first edition by candlelight.

On the morning of Dec. 3 soon after the day telegraph editor had reached his desk, a dispatch from Knoxville, Tenn., began to hammer in on a Western Union wire in The Times syndicate room. The editor scrawled: "For Mr. Ochs," and sent a copy upstairs to the publisher's office:

KNOXVILLE, Tenn. Dec. 3—Col. Henry Clay Collins, 83 years old, typographical mentor of Adolph S. Ochs, publisher of The New York Times, died in Knoxville at the home of a daughter this morning at 4 o'clock . . . It was Col. Collins, who, in the early seventies, when young Ochs was office boy for Captain William Rule, then editor of the Knoxville Chronicle, taught Mr. Ochs how to set type . . . Mr. Ochs is now the only one left of that great trio of Rule, Ochs and Collins . . .

The publisher's blue eyes misted. They fixed on middle distance through his high window overlooking the great city. Memories swarmed, the memories of sixty years; of homeward walks through the dark with Collins past the old Presbyterian cemetery after they left the inky Chronicle shop; of the news route covered by a bare-foot boy. He thought of the May day only the year before when he and Colonel Collins had stood, alone, by Captain Rule's grave.

Ochs called Peter Brown, his office boy. He said: "Peter, have Mrs. Lang wire Crouch, the Knoxville florist, to send a wreath to Mr. Collins' funeral on Friday."

His hand shook a little as he wrote:

"I am shocked to hear of the death of my old friend. I did not know he was ill. My deepest sympathy."

". . . Mr. Ochs is now the only one left of that great trio . . ."

No need to remind him. He knew.

CHAPTER
31

A GE LINES were deeper and heavier in Ochs' face now, and his steps were slower, but he knew intimately everything that went on at the newspaper. Clear, decisive memoranda spilled from his active mind. He kept a keen eye on production costs, followed each promotion scheme, was still awakened at any hour when important news broke. He took frequent vacations, but his editors and business department heads kept him up to the minute on fresh developments wherever he happened to be. When a situation warranted, he used the mails, cable or wireless to veto or approve.

He maintained to the end the strict formality of address to which he had been bred; every man on The Times was "Mister" to him, no matter how long he had known him or how humble or important the man's job.

Alexander Noyes recalled that when he first came to The Times after long service on The New York Evening Post, he learned with some uneasiness that Ochs attended the daily conference of editorial writers.

"'On The Evening Post of Godkin's time," Noyes wrote, "neither owner nor publisher was ever present at the conference which determined editorial policies; we of the editorial staff then believed that their absence was visible testimony to the nonexistence of any counting room pressure or control.

"But Ochs, and with him the genial business manager, Louis Wiley, almost invariably attended the daily editorial conference.

To those of us (we were four in number) who had come over from the old Evening Post's editorial staff, this seemed at first somewhat sinister. But all of us came to recognize the valid reason for it. There is always the possibility that an editorial attitude may be suddenly adopted, which, without involving any question of principle, might jeopardize the fortunes of the newspaper. The presence of the publisher at the conference would at all events keep him in touch with what was being written.

"Necessarily, much depended on the part taken by the publisher in such deliberations. With a man like the late Frank Munsey, for example, his presence might easily mean peremptory dictation of policies by the counting room. But with Ochs that never happened. Usually he participated in discussion of public events requiring comparison of views, yet with complete absence of mandatory attitude. Not infrequently he would outline with animation and at some length his own ideas but would listen to what the others had to say, often allowing his own judgment to be overruled. Many of his associates, even in department work, will remember how, after Ochs had set forth his impressions of what should be done, he would end by saying: 'Do as you think best; I was only thinking out loud.' This self-restraint in the matter of editorial policies was all the more remarkable for a man whose judgment and imagination in the effective conducting of other departments of The Times were most extraordinary."

All Times promotion copy went through the publisher's hands, and his comment on it was frequently blunt:

"Mr. Wiley: The attached enclosures are very good, but I think that typographically they are very unattractive. I suggest you confer with some art printers and see if they cannot be gotten up to look not only dignified, but artistic . . ."

"I am curious to know what expense is involved in the printing and distribution of the attached circular. I fear that any costly use of it will not justify the expenditure . . ."

"This is one of the best circulars I have ever seen issued from the Advertising Department. It is not overdone, and it is impressive. I think the second page has a little too much reading matter. I am suggesting some little alterations."

"It is my judgment that there should be no solicitation for Business Opportunities. A nicely prepared pamphlet on the subject that would set forth the merits of Times Business Opportunities and show examples of advertisers who have had good results might be mailed to prospects acceptable to The Times. It should not, in any form, be a solicitation and should state clearly that bank references are required of all advertisers using the Business Opportunities . . . I would rather see two columns of severely censored Business Opportunities than a page of the trash that appears in other newspapers that exceed us in space."

"The Fashion Advts. in the Suburban Roto Sections are quite ingenious and, I think, most effective. Whose thought?"

Ochs constantly peppered Wiley with these and similar notes, sometimes twenty to thirty a day. He dictated some, but still wrote many out in old-fashioned script, with the letters definitely wavering as advancing age made his fingers tremble. Another crack in the publisher's physique began to show. Deafness encroached and an internal condition affected his breathing. But his carriage remained erect. His hair formed a snowy periwig and the tufted white eyebrows were craggy over the still-sharp blue eyes.

One day in late August, 1930, Herbert Pulitzer of The World called Ochs by telephone to ask if they could meet at Ochs' home on an extremely urgent matter. He stressed that a conference at The Times or at The World might be awkward for him. The Ochs town house was closed, but Ochs offered to meet Pulitzer at any convenient place. Pulitzer engaged a Ritz-Carlton parlor suite and telephoned the room number.

At 5 o'clock that night Ochs found in the suite not only Pulitzer but the two chief Pulitzer aides, Florence D. White, general manager, and J. F. Bresnahan, business manager. Pulitzer went straight to the point. He had reached the conclusion, he said, that the New York field for morning and Sunday newspapers was overcrowded. He would like to sell.

There had been rumors that The World was shaky and some had got into print, but Ochs was momentarily flabbergasted. The great newspaper that had torn The Times' hide when Ochs took it over and had sneeringly listed it with other wobbly journalistic enterprises on what it had called "Poverty Row," was itself in trouble now.

"I believe," Pulitzer told Ochs, "that if I can dispose of The Morning World and Sunday World I can do better with The Evening World. I am prepared to sell you the morning and Sunday for consolidation with The New York Times."

Ochs conceded later that "this was a startling and totally unexpected proposition."

Pulitzer argued that The Times and The Herald Tribune completely controlled the field for conservative high-class newspapers, and that the tabloids and The New York American amply covered nonconservative wants. He was positive that The World could not profitably plow the middle field; that it was steadily losing ground. He figured that The Times would be likely to attract the great bulk of World readers; pointed up the happy wedding of The Tribune and The Herald.

White followed up with a picture of what a personal triumph Ochs might achieve by absorbing The World and The Sunday World. He predicted that Times Sunday circulation would probably leap at once to more than 1,000,000 and that Times daily circulation would come close to the same figure. He said, "It would put The Times in a class by itself, beyond competition, beyond contest of its supremacy."

Bresnahan added arguments along much the same lines, but Pulitzer did most of the talking. Without being asked, he suggested that the two publications might be had for around $10,000,000, but indicated that the price would be open to negotiation.

The meeting lasted about an hour. When The World men had talked themselves out, Pulitzer told Ochs they expected no immediate answer to the proposition. He suggested that Ochs consider it a while and discuss it further two days later.

After Ochs had talked the matter over with Sulzberger and with Adler, he decided that The Times stood to lose more than it could gain by absorbing the Pulitzer properties. At the same time he did not want The World to die; he always hated to see a newspaper die.

At the second meeting in the same parlor suite in the Ritz-Carlton, Ochs faced only Pulitzer and White. Bresnahan did not come.

"I have given the proposition very serious consideration," Ochs told The World men, "and though you may be astonished to hear me say it, I am not certain that I would accept the morning and Sunday World if you wished to present them to me as a gift. The proposition has many attractions, I will concede, but Mr. White's argument of the great pride I could have in the achievement does not appeal. It is a dangerous thing to go into a matter of this kind influenced by pride of achievement."

Ochs outlined other objections that had occurred to him.

"I doubt," he told Pulitzer, "whether The Times would gain a great deal in circulation from consolidation with The World. World readers have always had an opportunity to switch to The Times, but it wasn't the newspaper that appealed to them. The World has educated its readers for many years to believe that The Times is ultraconservative, under the influence of big interests and an apologist for Wall Street."

Ochs thought that Hearst's American would probably gain most of The World's circulation. He said that any newspaper that took over The World would have to increase production costs greatly and, to balance that, would have to seek commensurate increases in advertising rates.

"The times are not propitious for that," he said simply, and they knew that he was right.

"If The Times took over The World, that would greatly increase the existing gap between Times advertising rates and The Herald Tribune's rates. It would also widen the gap between The Times' advertising rate and the rate charged by the afternoon newspapers. Another factor is that a consolidation would throw hundreds of people out of employment. I give these objections. There are others. Together they have caused me to conclude that the proposition does not interest me."

Ochs was not coyly bidding for a bargain price on The World. His arguments were sincere. He pleaded with Pulitzer to try to reshape his publications.

He said: "You might try to put out a newspaper like the early Daily Mail of London—a newspaper of few pages with news greatly condensed, but not sensational. You could keep all the most attractive World features; make it a 'snappy' newspaper. I am confident such a publication would have a great demand. I make this suggestion though I think it may take some circulation from The Times."

The idea did not seem to appeal.

Then Ochs asked Pulitzer to consider organizing The World employes into a corporation and to sell, or lease, the publications to them.

"That would preserve The World," he said, hopefully.

Neither Pulitzer nor White seemed interested. White said that if Ochs did not want The World it would be offered to Ogden Reid for consolidation with The Herald Tribune. Such a merger, he repeated, might contest The Times' supremacy.

"That is possible," Ochs granted, "but The Herald Tribune, too, would face the problem of having to increase advertising rates at a time when such a move might be economically unsafe. In any case, I do not think it a wise thing for The New York Times to acquire the property."

The conference ended on that. Before Ochs left next day for his Lake George home, he instructed his son-in-law to try to convince White that the best plan would be to sell The World to its own employes. He authorized Sulzberger to tell White that he was so certain this would save The World that he would be willing to contribute substantially to financing the venture. He asked Sulzberger to stress the point, too, that preservation of The World was important to the industry and vital to the men and women who would be jobless otherwise.

Sulzberger conveyed all this to White, who seemed to like the idea. They went together to discuss it with Pulitzer, but he turned from it. Ochs never learned whether The World was offered to the Reids. Ochs himself confided later that he was prepared to raise $5,000,000 to help World employes continue the newspaper with some changes he could have suggested, but that when Pulitzer seemed cold to the proposition, he dropped it, too.

In February, 1931, Ochs toured the Pacific. He was in Honolulu when he got word from the office that the Scripps-Howard interests were contracting to buy The World. He cut his trip and hurried homeward—spent his seventy-third birthday on the train bearing him back to Times Square.

On Friday morning, Feb. 27, The World and Sunday World died. The Evening World was consolidated with the Scripps-Howard Telegram.

Ochs was shocked by the sale, though the initial effect sent Times advertising and circulation figures leaping sharply upward. On March 1, 1931, The Times printed 220,000 extra copies for a total of 1,021,848, the largest Sunday run in its eighty years' history.

Ochs got home on March 15, a fortnight later. At The Times editorial conference next day he recalled how he had tried to save The World. He told his editors that if he had been in New York during The World proceedings that he would have testified before the Surrogate that The World had tremendous value, and that it could have succeeded as an employe cooperative.

He was extraordinarily animated at the conference; went into details as to what could have been done to save the Pulitzer enterprise. He was certain he could have lopped off from $1,000,000 to $2,000,000 in operating expenses by cutting out—among other things—the many columns of financial news that both The Times and The Herald Tribune amply supplied, and by dropping the expensive Sunday magazine section. He expounded again the idea of a World converted to London Daily Mail format and generally sober content, with popular World features.

During his trip to Honolulu he had figured that he could easily have found competent management for a changed New York World right among that newspaper's own ranks as he had done on The Times in 1896; and that, with the capital he could have raised, World employes, by giving up about 25 per cent of their salary for stock, could have made the venture succeed.

"New York would have supported a newspaper along the lines I suggested," he told the editorial board. "The men on The World would have worked their heads off not only to get out a newspaper in which they had an interest, but they would have exerted strong and legitimate influence on advertisers. If I had been here to testify to these things the Surrogate would have had a different question before him."

But it was too late for all that. Now of all the great newspapers that had compelled Ochs' awe when he landed in New York, a young Southern greenhorn thirty-five years before, only The Times and Hearst's American remained alive or unchanged by merger, and The American had only a little way to go.

The Times persevered on its own chosen path. Its news formula continued to include man's efforts to know more about his planet.

An exploration series written from Arabia by the British explorer Bertram Thomas began in The New York Times and The Times of London in February, 1931, and ran the full month of May as a Sunday Magazine feature. Leading scientists in every corner of the earth found these stories the most moving on exploration in a hundred years, and wrote learnedly for The Times of their significance.

Thomas, a six-foot blond giant, had studied at Trinity. He spoke, dressed and lived like an Arab for fifteen years in preparation for the great quest of his career—penetration of the vast Ruba el-Khali, the fabulous desert of Southern Arabia.

For centuries white explorers and scientists had talked and dreamed of entering this "Empty Quarter," as it was called, but its 300,000 square miles were guarded by hawk-nosed, savage tribes whose history was old when Scripture was written.

No scientist, though, had laid plans so carefully or so patiently as Thomas had. He had served as Finance Minister and Wazir to the Sultan of Muscat and Oman, and he had won by infinite pains a promise of aid from Sheikh Sahail, a powerful Rashidi chieftain. He looked and spoke like an Arab.

Late in December, 1930, Thomas slipped out of Dhofar on the Arabian Sea, northward toward Dohah on the Persian Gulf, some 800 miles away. If the Arab legends were true he would move through regions that held Solomon's Mines, a buried Atlantis deep in the desert's heart, the singing sands where jinn as old as time guarded the fallen splendor of the realm in which great King Ad ibn Shaddad had dwelt in earthly paradise.

Captain Thomas set out with a caravan of tribesmen who had courage for everything except facing the anger of the jinn. They had joined up only after prodding by tribal leaders.

Days passed into weeks until almost two months had gone by. But no word came from the caravan. Thomas carried no wireless; he did not dare. His camera and most of his scientific apparatus were hidden from the superstitious nomads who knew nothing of such gadgetry and were likely to distrust it.

Then, on Feb. 23, 1931, this story appeared in The Times:

WHITE MAN CROSSES
THE ARABIAN DESERT
FOR THE FIRST TIME

BAHREIN, Persian Gulf, Feb. 22—Ruba-el-Khali, or the Great Southern Desert of Arabia, has at last yielded up its secrets. The news has been received here that Bertram Thomas, explorer and orientalist, who left Dhofar in December, has crossed what was one of the greatest unexplored sections of the world, to Dohah on El Katar Peninsula, which he reached yesterday.

No white man had previously crossed this "no man's land," which extends 650 miles from north to south and 850 miles from east to west, and it is doubtful whether any Arab has done so. Only a few white men have ever seen the fringes of this region.

On Feb. 26, The Times carried a two-column front-page story signed by Thomas under the headline:

THOMAS TELLS HIS STORY
OF ARABIAN DESERT TREK;
FOUND 7-MILE SALT LAKE

The explorer's narrative was almost painfully restrained:

"My camel journey of 900 miles across the great Ruba-el-Khali or Unknown Desert of Southern Arabia took fifty-eight days. On thirteen of these I halted and on forty-five I marched, averaging eight hours a day in the saddle.

"I traveled in Arab kit, but otherwise as an undisguised Christian. I carried a prismatic compass, sextant and navigation instruments for mapping purposes.

"My starting point was Dhofar on the central South Arabian Coast, with an escort of thirty Arabs and forty camels. I arrived at Dohah on the Persian Gulf with an escort of thirteen Arabs and eighteen camels, having progressively reduced my force as the early menace of Hadramaut raiders was left behind.

"My route lay north over the Qara Mountains, 3,000 feet in altitude, through the frankincense country of the Bible across the steppes I explored last winter, to Shisur, then westward into the unknown.

"In Lat. 19 degrees N. and Long. 52.30 E. I came upon numerous deeply cut caravan tracks in patches of the steppes running across our path, evidence of centuries of usage in bygone days. The Bedouins call it the road to Urbar, their legendary city of the prehistoric Addites.

"In the course of the ages the sands have encroached to the southward. Hereabouts Urbar, according to local tribesmen, lies buried beneath them—the Atlantis of the Ruba-el-Khali Desert. The country now is a borderland 100 miles from the sea and 1,000 feet in altitude, strewn with seashell fossils.

"Proceeding northwest, I encountered the phenomenon of singing sands, a deep sustained humming caused by wind action among the sand cliffs, resembling the noises of a ship's siren.

"I carried no tent, from considerations of weight, although night temperatures average 50 degrees, falling to 40 on occasion, and actually below that on Lat. 23.40 where I discovered a lake of salt water seven miles long.

"West of my line of march the sands were reported rising in altitude, and waterless. East of it the sands are falling and water extremely plentiful, a veritable subsurface lake so brackish in parts, however, that it was undrinkable by man and sometimes even by camels . . .

"The inhabitants of the sands are scant nomad sections of the Al Kathir and Al Murra tribes, subsisting exclusively on camel's milk. Of wild animal life, the raven is the most persistent bird, the bustard is widespread, and I collected eagles' eggs. Foxes, hares and lizards were common. Wolves, wildcats, rats and all mammals were of the light sand color of their environment in contrast to herds of black Murra camels.

"The expedition enabled the mapping of names and locations of sands and wells, and the collecting of geological and other natural history specimens and of meteorological data."

Thomas gave only the bare bones of his adventures in this story, but The Times found scientists in New York, London, Vienna and Paris wildly excited over even these details. They contributed enlightening comment and went splash overboard in praise of the

Briton's achievement. All this provided background material that enhanced the series.

T. E. Lawrence, the strange British scholar and adventurer known as "Lawrence of Arabia," agreed with other authorities that Thomas had lifted the veil from one of the largest blank areas on world maps. He ventured that there would be "no new worlds to explore until a new winged, or jet-projected generation lands on other planets."

Oddly enough, news stories indicating the beginnings of such a possibility were already creeping into The Times. Von Opel's 1929 rocket flight was one scientific finger pointing toward adventure in outer space. Another was now in the making.

Auguste Piccard, Swiss physicist, was ready to explore the stratosphere. He cut loose from Augsburg in the Bavarian Alps at 3:57 A.M. on May 27, 1931, with Charles Kipfer, another physicist, to study the effects of cosmic rays at heights never before visited by man.

Piccard figured that the flight should take no more than five or six hours, but morning and evening passed, and night took over the skies and no one reported having seen the balloon come down again from beyond the clouds.

At 10 P.M. on May 27 Piccard's balloon fell out of the night onto glacial rock in the Austrian Tyrol. It was several hours before this news was flashed to Berlin—too late for the next day's paper.

On Friday morning, May 29, The Times told of the safe landing. Under a Vienna dateline, this story related how a defective valve had kept the scientists above the earth eighteen hours instead of the expected five or six; how they had floated ten miles up, experiencing sensations no mortal had ever known. They had landed with instruments intact, in a hamlet quaintly called Ober-Gurgl.

Times photographers and G. E. R. Gedye, correspondent in Vienna, who was contributing distinguished dispatches on Central Europe to The Times' columns, were assigned to fly to Ober-Gurgl for pictures and for Professor Piccard's story. Their adventures almost matched his.

They left Aspern Airport outside Vienna at 1:15 P.M. in a small private plane, hoping to make Innsbruck in the Tyrolean Alps within three hours. They intended to fly over the glacier where the balloon had landed, photograph it from the air and get back to Innsbruck at 5:15 P.M. Gedye and one photographer were to ride to Ober-Gurgl by horse or on muleback, and Stephen K. Swift, Vienna Wide World photo manager, flew on to Munich to process the balloon negatives for transmission.

Their plane took such a buffeting over the mountains, that the pilot was barely able to set the ship down in Salzburg. The last part of the flight was through thunder, lightning and pelting downpour. In this the pilot trusted pretty much to homing instinct. Ten minutes later the storm cleared a bit and the ship zoomed up again. The plane bucked and plunged alarmingly in bad air pockets, robbing the passengers of breath. They landed at Inntal, far behind Innsbruck, at 7:45 P.M. Gedye was impatient and the photographers were afraid that the competition might somehow beat them to Piccard. Together they persuaded the flier to take them up again and in a second and fiercer storm they rocked and plunged through grumbling skies to Innsbruck.

They abandoned the plane, to race and skid dangerously by motor car over mountain roads to Zwieselstein. They got there an hour before midnight, awakened an astonished innkeeper who indignantly refused to rent mules or horses at that hour, and tackled on foot the steep roads to Ober-Gurgl. A hired guide led the way in the darkness beside a tumbling stream. It was fifteen minutes before 2 o'clock when they awakened Piccard in the farmhouse where he had found shelter.

The physicist came out, sleepy-eyed, in full-length old-fashioned nightshirt, gold-rimmed spectacles teetering on his nose, but he was amused at such enterprise. He was firm, though, on one point: he would not be photographed in a nightshirt. He politely excused himself and returned to his bedchamber to get unhurriedly into his flying suit, complete with absurdly shaped crash helmet, a bit of gear he had specially devised for the flight. He had breakfast, too. Other newspapermen had, by this time, come by various routes from Austria, Italy and from Switzerland. Piccard and Gedye left them clamoring at the farmhouse and quietly retreated into deep woods nearby. Seated on a tree stump, Piccard completed his narrative. He wrote out in longhand a capsule version of his ascent for transmission to The Times by radiophoto.

It was almost noon when The Times men got back to Innsbruck. Gedye, worn after a sleepless night and the mountain climb, sat at a typewriter to hammer out the stratosphere story. The Times photographer flew on to Munich to distribute Piccard telephotos all over Europe.

In The Times on Saturday, May 30, Professor Piccard's own narrative started on Page one under the two-column headline:

PICCARD TELLS HIS STORY
OF TRIP TO STRATOSPHERE;
ESCAPED DEATH NARROWLY

An italic note preceded it:

Herewith is the only authorized signed narrative of Professor Auguste Piccard, the first man to reach an altitude of approximately ten miles above the earth. In his own story the scientist gives for the first time his experience during his sensational ascent into the stratosphere.

The Professor's account adhered to cold scientific facts and figures, and pretty much minimized the hazards of his historic journey into space. Gedye's story, on Page 3 in the same issue, supplied the color.

Piccard refused to make outright claims until he had studied his sealed gauges and other instruments, but he told Gedye he was certain that he had succeeded in measuring the force of stratospheric cosmic rays, and that he had captured air samples, and had firmly sealed them.

"I have also given proof," he told Gedye, "that it is possible to fly in the stratosphere in a sealed cabin, a fact of peculiar value to airships, as it is possible to fly great distances in the stratosphere infinitely quicker than through earth's atmosphere. I called attention to such a possibility earlier. Only recently I learned that the Junkers works in Germany were experimenting with the construction of airplanes for such flights through the stratosphere."

Again The Times had given to scientists—and to other readers who gobbled the stories for their sheer novelty—a first-hand account of a major step in man's expanding quest for knowledge. The Piccard achievement forecast the opening of busy skyroads literally out of this world.

Swift advances in flying, early experiences with jet propulsion, penetration of the polar regions for meteorological and air bases, the pioneer adventure in the stratosphere and the imminent dawning of the atomic era were indications of earth crowding, signs of global claustrophobia.

How much tighter the world's seams were being laced was proved on July 1, 1931, when Wiley Post and Harold Gatty brought their creamy monoplane the Winnie Mae to a safe landing on Roosevelt Field, L. I., at the end of a global flight. They had written of each day's experience for Times readers on every step of their trail-blazing journey.

On the morning of July 2 seven pages in The Times recorded the achievement:

POST AND GATTY END THEIR RECORD WORLD FLIGHT; CIRCLED GLOBE IN 8 DAYS, 15 HOURS, 51 MINUTES; 10,000 IN WILD DEMONSTRATION AT FIELD HERE

Raymond Daniell wrote the lead:

ROOSEVELT FIELD, L.I., July 1—The fastest trip ever made by man around the earth on which he lives ended tonight at this airport 8 days 15 hours and 51 minutes after its start . . .

The swift-flying monoplane came out of the West with the speed of a meteor as the sinking sun turned the cloud-flecked blue of the sky to a brilliant pink backdrop. A white flash in the sky, it tore past slow-flying biplanes, monoplanes and flying boats in the air, banked steeply and circled the field twice . . .

The third time it swung back, flying low, and swooped down for a perfect three-point landing at break-neck speed against the wind . . . Post, cheeks hollowed with fatigue, his face an ashen gray, leaped to the ground when the plane roared to a stop, its propeller whirling menacingly at the clustering crowd.

A four-column front-page map—The Times maintained a large staff of news cartographers—showed the Winnie Mae's global track, the oceans it had spanned, the nations that had fled under its hurtling fuselage.

Above the map, as if heady with the wonder of the achievement, was the caption:

AROUND THE WORLD IN LESS THAN NINE DAYS!

The fliers' own version ran several thousand words and their log was printed in detail.

The Times Annex's new west wing was opened on Aug. 2, 1931. At 8 o'clock that morning Mary Ann Timmons, telephone supervisor, started service on the new switchboard with a call to Ochs who was then in his Lake George home. He was in excellent mood.

"Greetings to The New York Times telephone operators," he said cheerfully. "May they find their new quarters pleasant and comfortable."

Sixteen days later a brief notice on The Times editorial page said, "Today, Aug. 18, is the thirty-fifth anniversary of the present ownership and management of The New York Times." Ochs took no notice of the occasion beyond that. On Sunday, Sept. 13, though, all of Section 10 was devoted to the eightieth anniversary of the first printing under Raymond.

Ochs, then 73 years old, must have known as he peered into the future through the columns of his own anniversary number that he had only a little time left—barely enough for a brief peek into the antechamber giving on The Times' next eighty years.

This was grievously forced home on Oct. 26, 1931, when Ochs' brother, George Washington Ochs Oakes (he had changed the name during World War I because of the Germanic flavor of "Ochs"), who had walked Knoxville's streets with him in predawn quiet dropping Chronicles on neighbor's doorsteps, died in Presbyterian Medical Center in New York on the eve of his seventieth birthday. George had been editor of Current History, a literary by-product of The Times, and an officer and director of The New York Times Company. One of his sons, John, is an editorial writer on The Times.

Four days before his brother died, Adolph Ochs answered a questionnaire he had received from Will Durant, the writer, who was getting up a symposium on the major forces that compel men to carry on. Durant was to include the answers in his book, "On the

Meaning of Life." Ochs wrote his answer at Hillandale, a lovely fifty-seven acre estate at White Plains, in Westchester County. He had bought the estate on Oct. 14 and had moved with his family from his handsome city house at 308 West Seventy-fifth Street.

Hillandale was a pleasant mansion with great rooms, lovely white columns, surrounded by giant trees and extensive green lawns. From his paneled study Ochs could look out through a great picture window toward a little private lake. He brought with him the white marble busts of great artists and musicians that had been a prominent feature of the city house, and countless photographs of his immediate family and kin, of Iphigene through every stage of her development, and of his grandchildren. These pretty much told the story of the Ochses through several generations.

"You ask me," was Ochs' reply to the Durant questionnaire, "what meaning life has for me, what help—if any—religion gives me, and what keeps me going, what are the sources of my inspiration and my energy, what is the goal or motive force of my toil, where I find my consolation and my happiness, where in the last resort my treasure lies.

"To make myself clearly understood, if I were able to do so, would take more time and thought than I can give the matter now. Suffice it for me to say that I inherited good health and sound moral principles; I found pleasure in work that came to my hand and in doing it conscientiously; I found joy and satisfaction in being helpful to my parents and others, and in thus making my life worth while found happiness and consolation. My Jewish home life and religion gave me a spiritual uplift and a sense of responsibility to my subconscious better self, which I think is the God within me, the Unknowable, the Inexplicable. This makes me believe I am more than an animal, and that this life cannot be the end of our spiritual nature."

This document re-emphasized Ochs' adherence to ancient verities. In seventy-three years of living he had never, somehow, got beyond the range of his father's and mother's voices.

CHAPTER

32

W HEN a newspaperman speaks of a "dull night" at the office the outsider is apt to misunderstand him. It means that the run of that day's news—though it included tragedy, pathos, death, fire, murder, arson, rape, war, storm, misery and some humor—had followed an expected pattern. These are things reporters and editors take for granted, and unless the events are clothed in extraordinary circumstance, they do not excite the city room.

Tuesday, March 1, 1932, was such a night except that Japanese soldiers had entered Shanghai, driving Chiang Kai-shek's men like dry leaves in high wind. Their way was lighted by burning towns and villages. Their weapons left pitiful Chinese dead in Shanghai's streets and alleys.

Hallett Abend, Times man in Shanghai, walked the dark streets getting detail for the night's lead story:

JAPANESE ROUTING CHINESE
IN FIERCE SHANGHAI BATTLE;
DEATH TOLL EXCEEDS 2,000

The national news desk ground out routine stuff: "Sales Tax Accepted by Administration," "Senate Acts for Broad Inquiry on Short Selling," "145 in House Force Vote on Dry Law Test," "Roosevelt Urges Public Funds Law." Nothing extraordinary.

There were no important local stories either, and the suburbs slept as city room clock hands crept toward first-edition time. Rewrite men took a restaurant hold-up story by telephone from Philly Meagher, the West Side district man; a $200 payroll robbery from the New Rochelle correspondent; a fire story from the upper East Side district man. Ted Sweedy, in from a New York University dinner assignment at the Waldorf-Astoria, wrapped up his piece and called, "Boy!" without enthusiasm.

Lloyd Glabb, handling the telephones across the desk from Bob Garst, then acting night city editor, languidly answered a bell just before the edition was in. He was bored. His pale face showed it, and his blond forelock drooped into his eyes.

He listened a moment on the wire, then suddenly went rigid.

"Let's have that again," he said tensely. He pressed his left cheek against the transmitter to shut out city room hum and clack. His pencil raced over his note pad.

"Hold it a minute," he ordered. He cupped his palm over the telephone.

"It's Delker in Hammonton [New Jersey]," he told Garst breathlessly. "He's in the State police barracks down there. They just got a flash over the police teletype from Somerville. The Lindbergh baby's been kidnapped."

Garst, thin, esthetic-featured, a man with remarkable self-control, could not prevent his eyebrows from crawling upward. His blue eyes searched the large city room floor and fell on Warren Irvin, senior man on rewrite.

"Give the call to Irvin," he said. His eyes then roved to a far corner where Deak Lyman sat, getting out a feature for the Sunday aviation page. He knew that Deak and Lindbergh were friends.

"Tell Lyman to call Lindbergh," Garst ordered quietly. "This may be a wild one. Tell him we just want to check."

It was wise precaution, characteristic Times conservatism. Another newspaper might have flashed an extra on such thin information, but not Ochs' newspaper. Besides, the whole idea seemed fantastic. It was an era of kidnappings in the United States, a sideline developed from rum-running, but that anyone would dare kidnap the son of the most famous figure on earth—that was incredible.

Irvin took the teletype message from Delker while Lyman put a call through to Col. Henry Breckinridge, Lindbergh's attorney and close friend.

Irvin rushed his copy to the city desk. Garst scanned it, marked it for a front-page two-column box—all that could be squeezed in at the last minute before press time—and sent a duplicate to the night bull pen.

"Colonel Lindbergh's baby was kidnapped from Lindbergh home in Hopewell, N. J., sometime between 7:30 and 10 P.M. this date," the teletype message had said. "Baby is nineteen months old and a boy. Is dressed in sleeping suit. Request that all cars be investigated by police patrols."

Across the room, Lyman talked in low tones and with suppressed excitement, to Colonel Breckinridge. He put up the receiver and lumbered toward the city desk.

He shouted, "It's true! It's true!"

Garst nodded to the head of the copy desk and the front-page box was released. There was a hurried conference in the bull pen, and Bruce Rae, night city editor, who was doing a turn as assistant managing editor, took over the city desk. Garst took command of the copy desk. Rae's orders poured out in a stream.

"Lyman, you and Sweedy hire a special Carey Service car and get to Hopewell. Tell the driver to step on it. Call as soon as you get anything there." "Glabb, tell Delker to watch the teletype and to flash anything that comes through—anything."

He assigned one reporter to get all the clippings on the Lindbergh child and to write all he could on the child's brief history.

Rae ordered a story from Washington on the proposed new Federal law on kidnapping, sent for photographs of the baby alone, of the baby with his mother, grandmother and great-grandmother, for air shots of the Lindberghs' lonely home on a Sourland Mountains ridge. He snatched an automobile road map from Lyman's fingers and had a Times artist prepare a copy showing the Hopewell area.

Lyman raced back to his desk to ask The Times correspondent in Princeton to meet the Carey car at the Nassau Inn to guide him to Hopewell.

By this time the office's traditional night bridge game had dissolved, and reporters stood by for orders. They were scattered to work the telephones or to hunt in the morgue for pertinent Lindbergh material. Lyman, Sweedy and a Times photographer stood out in Forty-third Street until the Carey car came. They piled in and Lyman stressed the need for speed. The chauffeur, horrified at the kidnapping news, shot westward to Ninth Avenue, then south toward the Holland tunnel.

On Route 1, near Elizabeth, N. J., Lyman saw a policeman. He thought the baby might have been found by then. The car screamed to a stop. Lyman leaped out. He said: "We're from The Times. We're on our way to the Lindbergh home in Hopewell. Heard anything new about the kidnapping?"

The policeman had not even seen the alarm for the baby. He waved the car on its way. Lyman made mental note of the fact that on a main highway that the kidnapper might have used the alarm had not yet been spread. The car roared on into Princeton, arriving less than an hour after it had left Times Square. It pulled up at the inn, and Deak got directions to Hopewell from the Princeton man.

In the dark climb into the brooding Sourlands, the Carey car became part of a traffic stream headed for the Lindbergh home. Lyman wisely figuring that telephones in the Lindbergh home would be tied up, and that there would be no other communication nearby, stopped at two farmhouses within two to three miles of the Lindbergh estate and arranged to use the telephones there.

The Lindbergh home of whitewashed brick stood out in the dark. All the windows were bright with light and shadowed figures moved about the lawn under the baby's window. It was raw and windy. The Times crew was the first out of New York to get to the ridge, but Sam Blackman and Frank Jamieson of The Associated Press had arrived earlier from nearby Trenton. Lyman recognized Lindbergh among the figures on the lawn, and Lindbergh recognized him. There was time for only a few sentences, but Lindbergh confirmed the kidnapping and admitted Lyman to the house to use a telephone.

As Lyman waited for The Times to come in on the line, the flier told him he had just returned from a tour of the grounds with the state troopers. They had found a ladder near the house and ladder marks in the mud under the window of the baby's room. They had seen two sets of footprints at the ladder's base and had traced them to the highway. One set of prints under the window, a woman's, had been identified as Mrs. Lindbergh's. The others were probably those of the unidentified kidnapper.

The Associated Press had sent out the fact that a ransom note had been found. Irvin, taking the story from Lyman, wanted more detail about the note, but Lindbergh and the State police had asked that the contents be withheld. The kidnapper had threatened to harm the baby if the note were made public. The Times could mention that there were reports of a note, but no more than that.

Lyman went into the wind-swept yard again. The State police wanted reporters and cameramen put off the grounds but Colonel Lindbergh intervened and they stayed. Colonel Breckinridge served hot coffee made in the Lindbergh kitchen, then sent into Hopewell for more.

Both in the office and at Hopewell, the men were up all night, with no word or sign of the Lindbergh baby's whereabouts. Rae had ordered more reporters into New Jersey to cover the story—Lew Nichols, Leo Kieran, Frank Nugent, Craig Thompson, Albert J. Gordon, Harold Denny. The final edition of The Times on March 2 came out with thirteen columns on the kidnapping, including photographs and a description of the missing child. It was noon before Lyman left the Lindbergh estate to take a room in the Williamson House in Hopewell. There he had the telephone company draw a line to his bed and immediately called Breckinridge.

He said, "Colonel, if there is anything The New York Times can do to help the Lindberghs, you can get us here."

On March 2 Lindbergh came to The Times from Hopewell with special photographs of the missing baby—the most recent he had taken—and asked The Times to distribute them for him to newspapers all over the United States. He had come to The Times, he explained, because he had confidence in it. He asked that the photographs be withheld from certain newspapers which he disliked, and The Times followed his wishes.

Eventually Gov. A. Harry Moore released the kidnap ransom note contents to Jamieson of The Associated Press and it went out on the A.P. wires. Lyman told his office that if the baby were still alive and in the hands of a crank, the threat of harm to him might still be carried out. The Times decided against using the note.

William R. Hearst Jr. had come to Hopewell to work with the staff assigned to the case by his father's various newspapers and news agencies. He sent Charles Bayer, a Hearst man, to see Lyman at the Williamson House. Bayer said: "Deak, Bill Hearst wants to talk with you about the ransom note," and he brought Deak to the Hearst staff's headquarters in Hopewell.

Young Hearst was lying on a couch, using the telephone when Bayer introduced him to Lyman. Young Hearst said: "Deak, I've just been talking to the Old Man. He'd like to know if The Times is going to use the ransom note that the A.P. has sent out?"

Deak assured him that The Times had taken the stand that it would print nothing that might jeopardize the baby's life.

Young Hearst passed this on to his father in San Simeon. He said: "Pop, I don't think The New York Times will use this thing." He listened for a moment, and hung up. He told Deak: "Pop said we're not using it either. He said we aren't going to print anything that might interfere with the return of the baby." He thanked Deak.

Lyman called Breckinridge and told him that the Hearst papers had decided against printing the ransom note text. One New York newspaper, however, took the stand that since the text of the note had been spread by syndicate wire, some newspapers were bound to use it, and that it would leak sooner or later, anyway. The note was eventually used everywhere.

The Lindbergh kidnapping stayed on the front page for weeks and The Times used a large staff for coverage. It had men in Trenton, Hopewell and Somerville, and kept rushing staff men out to every spot where there were new developments. Endless man hours were spent by reporters tracking down "sure thing" tips that eventually evaporated.

On May 13 the Lindbergh baby was found dead on Mount Rose, not far from the Lindbergh home. He had been murdered a short time after he had been kidnapped.

More than three years later there was to be a sequel to this story that produced another remarkable page in Times history.

CHAPTER
33

WHEN Ben C. Franck, Ochs' first cousin and boyhood friend, died at his home in New York on April 6, 1932, in his seventy-fifth year, Ochs could not go to the funeral. Age's hand was heavy upon him and he was slowly failing. The snipping of another link with his past—Franck had been The Times' executive secretary for 36 years—did not improve his condition. Nor had his morale been improved by the necessity, with The Times down to less than forty pages daily because of the national doldrums, of cutting Times wages by 10 per cent. He had signed the reduction order on April 25, 1932, to take effect May 1. Other publishers had made this or bigger cuts long before, but he had stubbornly held out. He had, moreover, firmly resisted laying off any members of the news staff, which had also generally been done. The pay cut was the alternative.

"For more than a year," his notice said, "notwithstanding decreasing revenue, The Times has made an effort to maintain employment and sustain salaries. Due to unexpected continuance of the period of depression and in keeping with sound and prudent business management, The Times is compelled to reduce salaries as has been done generally throughout the newspaper industry.

"There arises, however, some consolation in this disagreeable decision from the thought that the deep regret with which we make it will be understood and appreciated, and that moreover the delay until now makes the hardship it must entail somewhat mitigated by the decided reduction which has taken place in living expenses."

But this was a blow to Ochs' pride. He had held out as long as he could. It was the only time in his ownership of The Times that he had been forced back so much as a single step. It was another deep hurt, and in his poor physical condition, not easy to bear.

He was so downcast at the necessity for the wage reduction that friends were deeply concerned. Lucien Franck, Ben's brother, in charge of building supplies for The Times, urged him to forget it.

"I can't, Lu," he answered unhappily. "This wage reduction has hurt me more deeply than anything I can remember in my newspaper career."

Early in June, 1932, Dr. J. Bentley Squier, Ochs' physician and close friend—though always "Dr. Squier" and never "Bentley"—determined by tests that a defective kidney was poisoning the publisher. Several consultants agreed that the condition called for surgery.

Ochs went into Harkness Pavilion in the Columbia Presbyterian Medical Center in New York on June 27, 1932. Mrs. Ochs visited him there that night and then went to stay with Mrs. Squier. Next day Dr. Squier performed the operation, a grave gamble with a 74-year-old patient, but it was successful.

Three months before Ochs entered the hospital, Vincenzo Miserendino, a noted Sicilian sculptor who had been one of Dr. Squier's patients, had pleaded with the surgeon to pose for a bust. Miserendino wanted to do the bust out of gratitude for Squier's kindnesses to him.

The surgeon had an idea that with Ochs about to celebrate his fiftieth wedding anniversary, a bust might be a fitting gift. He said he would rather have a bust of Ochs than one of himself, and the sculptor accepted the commission. But there were complications. "If we ask Mr. Ochs to pose," Dr. Squier explained, "he will most certainly refuse. He is an inordinately modest man. Can you do a bust from photographs, and from description?"

Miserendino thought he could, but he said such a work would be imperfect. He had done notable heads of Theodore Roosevelt, Eleanore Duse, Enrico Caruso, Rear Admiral Byrd and Irvin S. Cobb, but most of these subjects had sat for him.

The sculptor and the surgeon entered into an innocent plot.

Dr. Squier quietly arranged for Miserendino to study Ochs as he went to and from The Times building. For weeks thereafter a small gray-haired man with eyes bright behind gold spectacles, haunted the elevators in the Annex, catching occasional glimpses of the publisher, and translating them into little pencil sketches when Ochs had vanished from sight.

With these notes and with photographs Miserendino labored in his Bronx studio at the Ochs bust through March, April, May and most of June. He had a plaster likeness ready then, and wanted Dr. Squier to see it.

Ochs was still in the Harkness Pavilion and not yet out of danger. Mrs. Ochs was due at the Squier home at 8 East Sixty-eighth Street one day at noon when Miserendino showed up with the plaster likeness of her husband. Afraid that Mrs. Ochs, coming upon it without warning, might mistake the plaster head for a death mask of her husband, the surgeon's wife hurried the sculptor and his work out of the living room and hid him on another floor, where Mrs. Ochs was not likely to go.

The Squiers liked the bust. It was not perfect, but Miserendino had caught the Washingtonesque contours with astonishing fidelity and had captured the brooding quality of the deep-set blue eyes cast in the deep shadow of the jutting white eyebrows.

Two weeks after the operation, Ochs was recovering rapidly, and after he had had another fortnight's rest, on July 26 Effie came to take him back to Hillandale. They stopped in at the Squiers' on the way and the surgeon took the publisher to the fifth floor of the house. There Dr. Squier had set up the plaster bust and with Miserendino's help had softly lighted it.

Ochs saw it the moment Squier opened the door. He stared for a full minute, speechless. Then he turned to the surgeon.

He said, "Who is it—George Washington?" but it was evident that he had recognized it, and that he was delighted. He walked around it, as if a little awed. Mrs. Ochs liked it, too.

"This is the best we could do without the living model," Dr. Squier explained, as the plaster head still held the publisher's eyes. "We want it for your golden wedding." He paused. "Would you sit for Mr. Miserendino, Mr. Ochs? He wants to study you at your office work."

The publisher said it would be a new and strange experience for him, but he consented.

The day after Ochs left the hospital a front-page story from Berlin told how Lieut. Gen. Kurt von Schleicher, Minister of Defense, had boldly told the world in a broadcast that Germany intended to rearm in defiance of the terms of the Versailles Treaty. Companion pieces next day from Paris showed the impact this had had in France, and throughout Europe. Hitler's power was rising at frightening pace. The von Schleicher threat was only one of a thousand evidences of it.

Even more bitter reading broke on The Times' front page on July 29, 1932. For two months previous, homeless and penniless veterans of the World War, some with their wives and children, had converged on Washington to plead for a soldiers' bonus to help them through the financial depression. They called themselves the Bonus Expeditionary Force.

The group was led by conservative, sound Americans and its head, Walter W. Walters, was a quiet westerner, but hotheads and some radicals in its ranks were stirring for violence. The "Army" had set up shelters in abandoned Government buildings in lower Pennsylvania Avenue, and had obtained Army tents for a second colony on the banks of the Anacostia River. They picketed the White House daily.

District of Columbia policemen had been unable to move the bonus pleaders, who numbered from 10,000 to 15,000. The more resentful and hasty in the B.E.F. ranks laid their plight at President Hoover's door, despite the fact that he had sought legislation to help them. They refused to obey Government eviction orders, and finally, on July 28, the President ordered regular troops under Gen. Douglas MacArthur to enforce the order.

The result, distilled into The Times four-column headline on July 29, was:

TROOPS DRIVE VETERANS FROM CAPITAL;
FIRE CAMPS THERE AND AT ANACOSTIA;
1 KILLED, SCORES HURT IN DAY OF STRIFE

Ochs was still sick, and the turn of events all over the world made him sicker. There was war in the Chaco and war in Manchuria, and the shadows of Stalin, Hitler and Mussolini were lengthening across Europe. Americans were restless for new leadership, too, and awaited uneasily the day when Franklin D. Roosevelt, elected the previous November by carrying all but six States, would take over in Washington.

Ochs' unbending policy of keeping The New York Times and his close kin from any outside business enterprise or any political affiliation was sharply re-emphasized about this time.

On Nov. 22, 1932, his nephew Capt. (later Colonel) William Van Dyke Ochs, United States Army, his brother Milton's son, had obtained several endorsements for the post of military attaché at the White House.

"I have just been told," Ochs wrote to his nephew, then stationed at Fort Oglethorpe, Ga., "of your very laudable ambition to be a military attaché to the White House during the Roosevelt regime, and that you have obtained some powerful endorsements from Senator Hull and others.

"It is my wish that you cease all efforts in that direction because, not only could I not approve of it, but I would have to enter an absolute protest against it even in the doubtful contingency that you could obtain it.

"There are many reasons for this: First, while some advantages would accrue to you as a nephew of mine of whom I am very fond, this relationship might in some instance be a liability and crimp your style.

"Second, to have the matter placed before President-elect Roosevelt would, I am sure, cause him some embarrassment.

"Third, if you were to obtain the post, because of your relationship with me and, consequently, with The New York Times, any leakage of news from the White House that might appear in The Times would place you under suspicion.

"Fourth, in the remote possibility that you could get the appointment, your relationship to me would, I am sure, play no small part in the favor shown you. I have to lean far backwards to avoid personal obligations to public officials, high and low. Your father well knows my position, for at one time he had to decline an attractive and lucrative position offered him by President Harding.

"I hope there has been no approach to President-elect Roosevelt, for if so, I should feel it incumbent on me to advise him at once that I disapprove the application and any consideration of your name for such a position, to avoid embarrassment to him as well as to myself.

"I regret that I must send you this discouraging note, but I am sure your good sense will see the wisdom of my decision . . ."

Captain Ochs dropped the idea.

On Tuesday, Jan. 31, 1933, The Times carried a three-column head over a story from Guido Enderis in Berlin:

HITLER MADE CHANCELLOR OF GERMANY, BUT COALITION CABINET LIMITS POWER; CENTRISTS HOLD BALANCE IN REICHSTAG

The crackling of tinder about to set the world aflame became daily more audible.

It was now more than four years since President Hoover had told his countrymen in honest optimism in August, 1928: "We in America are nearer the final triumph over poverty than ever before in the history of any land." So it had seemed, but now blackness was universal. The market crack that had developed in October, 1929, had widened to an abysmal canyon, and the United States seemed doomed to fall into it.

By February, 1933, the national scene was so forbiddingly black that Americans had little thought for the rapid spread of Hitlerism and only vague concern for the horror Japan was wreaking in Manchuria.

Franklin D. Roosevelt was preparing to take the oath as the thirty-second President of the United States. He had picked a good part of his Cabinet and he and his "Brain Trust"—a term coined by James Kieran, a Times Albany correspondent, on seeing a group of young Columbia instructors leave the Roosevelt campaign headquarters—were about to take over in Washington.

Banks had been toppling all over the United States, and the situation was getting worse. Bank runs and hoarding were widespread. National paralysis was almost complete. The bread and soup lines had grown, the colonies of homeless were almost beyond control. Hunger and misery were prodding men and women to acts of desperation. The Communists watched their seed ripen.

The Times of March 4 carried the headline:

TWO-DAY HOLIDAY
FOR BANKS HERE
LEHMAN'S ORDER

A similar order, calling for a three-day bank holiday, had just been issued in Chicago.

The Times of Sunday, March 5, carried an eight-column headline on the inauguration:

ROOSEVELT INAUGURATED, ACTS TO END
THE NATIONAL BANKING CRISIS QUICKLY;
WILL ASK WAR-TIME POWERS IF NEEDED

The text of the new President's speech—"first of all let me assert my firm belief that the only thing we have to fear is fear itself"—was prominent in a two-column front-page box. Roosevelt said, "This great nation will endure as it has endured, will revive and will prosper." The words took root, and the people were cheered.

The story in the front-page left-hand column reviewed the bank situation: "The New York Clearing House Association prepared to print and issue certificates to be used by the public as substitute money. In every State of the nation including the District of Columbia, banking was wholly or partly suspended. In London, Paris and other European capitals, dollar transactions were suspended. Bankers from New York and other financial centers will confer with Secretary of the Treasury Woodin on remedial plans for presentation by the President of this afternoon's legislative conference."

The whole nation breathed just a little easier over the week-end, and on Monday morning The Times spread the headline:

ROOSEVELT ORDERS 4-DAY BANK HOLIDAY,
PUTS EMBARGO ON GOLD, CALLS CONGRESS

Three days later the President got Congressional authority placing all banks under government supervision. Banks in good condition were allowed to reopen; moves were planned to conserve and build up the assets of others.

Franklin D. Roosevelt had jammed on the brakes, and they seemed to be holding. His bold and decisive acts had powerful psychological effects. Hoarders began to return their money to the banks, relief work projects gave men a little cash and restored their self-respect. Little by little the migration of the hopeless and the helpless ended. The country's way back was long and hard, but this was a start. Times coverage of the swift and startling changes in the bank situation and of the economic picture generally was so superior during this period that it brought 50,000 new readers.

On March 5, Hitler's overwhelming power had been demonstrated in the elections for the Reichstag and the Prussian Diet. His party had garnered 17,300,000 votes, or 44 per cent of the total poll. Reporting this from Berlin, Birchall, who was now chief European correspondent, wrote:

"Just as two and two make four, so suppression and intimidation have produced a Nazi-Nationalist triumph. The rest of the world may now accept the fact of ultra-nationalist domination of the Reich and Prussia for a prolonged period with whatever results this may entail."

It took courage to write so bluntly in that period in Berlin, but Birchall had courage in abundance. He continued with equally forthright reporting as the Nazis laid about them with the iron fist. He was the first American correspondent to tell the world about Nazi concentration camps. Men who had worked for Birchall in the city room were a little uneasy lest he come to harm, but they said, "That's Birch, little gamecock," and praised and admired his work. They admired it all the more because he had eagerly returned to field work when in his sixties, a time of life at which many men, instead of seeking the thick of the fight, begin to look about them for their carpet slippers and the easy chair.

Ochs, his superior, was by many years his senior and he had not yet retreated to his easy chair either. On Feb. 28, 1933, the publisher and Effie celebrated their golden wedding anniversary in Palm Beach, Fla., and were buried in congratulatory messages. The following month Ochs reached his 75th birthday. On that morning, a Sunday, The Times front page told the world of an earthquake in Southern California that had taken more than 130

lives and injured 5,000 persons; of Roosevelt's plan to spend $500,-
000,000 on unemployment relief projects; of Hitler's using "the
iron broom" to sweep republican office holders out of their jobs in
Germany; of how the banks and the Stock Exchange, after forced
closing, were about to reopen. Out of Moscow, where purges were
now common, had come a story headlined, "Soviet Executes 35
for Sabotage."

Would-be interviewers besieged Ochs for comment on the state
of the nation. Finally, aware that his words would be carefully
weighed in that tense hour, he sat down and wrote a rather cheerful interview outline in his own hand.

"Adolph S. Ochs, controlling owner and publisher of The New
York Times, is 75 years old today," it said. "He was born at Cincinnati, Ohio, March 12, 1858. He is quietly celebrating the day here
with Mrs. Ochs and his only child, Mrs. Arthur Hays Sulzberger,
and her four children. One of the children, Ruth, also has a birthday today; she is 12.

"Mr. Ochs is in good health, active and alert. He is in touch with
the minutest details of The Chattanooga Times and of The New
York Times of which he has been the sole owner for thirty-seven
years. He is also fully advised of the affairs of The Associated
Press, of which for thirty-five years he has been a member of the
Board of Directors, and Executive Committee member.

"Mr. Ochs . . . expressed his confidence that the United States
was still up to par and would so continue. He said we would emerge
from the mess and confusion that the country was now in as we
have on many other occasions when the pessimists had their day
and were sure the country, and particularly our Government, was
doomed to destruction; that universal bankruptcy was certain."

Then he added for direct quotation:

"Never in its history was the United States so rich, so strong, so
powerful and with brighter prospects ahead than at present. We
have barely scraped the soil of our opportunities, our ultimate
resources, our industries, our inventive genius.

"We are, for the present, recovering from a wild debauch of
frenzied finance, crazy speculation, and insensate greed. Everybody seemed to have lost the sense of responsibility of wealth, and
a get-rich-quick epidemic swept the country, but I think the situa-

tion is now well understood and that we are sobering up and painfully getting our house in order. The tragic experience we are
having will result in educating the people that care, caution and
conservatism are as necessary in economics as in physical health,
and that the Ten Commandments and the Sermon on the Mount,
cannot be ignored, nor forgotten. They should continue to be our
guide to a philosophy of life. Spirituality and idealism, now so
frightfully dormant, will be awakened for the peace and comfort
of our children, and this will be full compensation for our tribu-
lations."

If Ochs was optimistic about the ultimate triumph of idealism
at home, there seemed little cause for such a view of the foreign
scene.

In The Times of May 11, 1933, Birchall told how Storm Troopers
and Hitler propaganda chiefs had presided over nation-wide burning of literary works that did not conform to their ideology. He
witnessed the burning at the University of Berlin in Opera Square:

BERLIN, May 10—In most of the German university towns tonight
enthusiastic students are ceremoniously burning the 'un-German spirit'
as exemplified in literature, pamphlet, correspondence and record. It is
all being done to the accompaniment of torchlight parades, martial
music and much patriotic speechifying—the British Guy Fawkes Day
intensified a thousandfold.

There followed a colorful description of the scene as Birchall
had watched it in Opera Square. As he walked from the great book
bonfire to his office, the flames still soared to the night sky.

"The bonfires are still burning as this is being written," his story
said, "and there is going up in their smoke more than college boy
prejudice and enthusiasm. A lot of the old German liberalism—if
any was left—was burned tonight."

Birchall's outstanding stories from Europe in this year won him
the Pulitzer award for foreign correspondence. Within seven years
of the allotted scriptural three-score and ten, he was a greater
reporter and a far better writer than most correspondents half his
age.

A few weeks before Birchall's first stories on the Nazi violence,

Ray Daniell had gone into Decatur in northern Alabama to cover the so-called Scottsboro Case, the second trial of nine Negroes accused of the rape of two white girls. Defense lawyers and northern newspapermen encountered hostility. Daniell recalled later that, "Threats to lynch not only the defendants but their lawyers and your correspondent were made openly and often." Daniell was not afraid. He wrote his stories day after day for weeks, giving both sides impartially. The Times continually gave the Scottsboro Case more ample coverage than any newspaper in the North, proving again that it continued to present the news "without fear or favor."

The Roosevelt Administration meanwhile worked under forced draft, putting through new national legislation to curb speculation, setting up bewildering alphabetic Federal agencies to provide work for the jobless and proceeding with bills and measures for social security that left Republican—and all other—conservatives, a little breathless. The Times printed verbatim virtually every important measure put through by the New Deal, and gave complete versions of every Roosevelt fireside radio chat. Except for the Congressional Record, no other publication carried in such detail the historic and socially significant changes that were taking place.

Ochs and his editorial writers approved of many of the changes, but the publisher felt that they were coming too rapidly and in such volume that some had not been fully thought out. By the end of 1933 the Republican National Committee uttered somewhat the same sentiment. This was the beginning of a period of increasing political bitterness with Republican outsiders pounding in vain against the New Deal political bastions. The Times Washington bureau was hard put, even with additions to its already large staff, to keep up with the unprecedented rush of events.

Ratification of repeal of the Eighteenth Amendment was achieved on Dec. 5, 1933. The Times that day ran a lead story out of Washington that said:

"National prohibition will pass into history as an unsuccessful experiment late tomorrow afternoon or evening—thirteen years, two months, eighteen days, a few hours after it was declared in effect.

"By that time the States of Pennsylvania, Ohio and Utah by duly authorized conventions, will have ratified the Twenty-first Amendment to the Constitution, which also will establish in history the first repeal of an amendment—the Eighteenth."

The Times of Dec. 6 carried a five-column headline on the ratification. It said:

PROHIBITION REPEAL IS RATIFIED AT 5:32 P.M.;
ROOSEVELT ASKS NATION TO BAR THE SALOON;
NEW YORK CELEBRATES WITH QUIET RESTRAINT

The stories told of the closing of speakeasies, how prices of drinks had dropped in some instance by half from bootleg prices—to 35 cents for cocktails, $8 for a bottle of champagne, $2.50 for still wines, and to $3.50 a quart for blended whiskies.

In Times Square, as in other entertainment centers in great cities, impromptu celebrations were staged. At midnight a hilarious crowd from the Hotel St. Moritz in New York drowned prohibition in effigy in Central Park lake. The Times had a round-up of repeal's effects from its correspondents in all large American cities and the reaction in London, Paris and Berlin. Editorially, the day before, Ochs' newspaper had pleaded for "Moderation in All Things," stressing "honest recognition of a new obligation of citizenship."

It was an important day in national history. It spelled the end of bloody rum-row aristocracy—the twilight of the Al Capones, Jack (Legs) Diamonds, Waxey Gordons and Dutch Schultzes. Repeal accomplished what the Coast Guard, Federal and municipal law enforcement agencies had tried in vain to do for more than thirteen years; it crushed the powerful booze and beer mobs.

The Times of Dec. 6 devoted ten of its forty-eight pages to the repeal story.

Toward the end of 1933 Ochs seldom appeared in public. He was now broken mentally as well as physically. The spread of intolerance, the ever more melancholy cast of the international situation, the country's slow and painful drag from the depression's pit were too great a burden for his years to cast off. The spread of Hitler's power became his nightmare.

He kept more and more to his paneled study at lovely Hillandale, and the blue eyes were filmed with sadness. There were periods when he saw no glimmer of hope—only gathering darkness ahead. He was apt, then, to look wistfully back over his shoulder toward his youth and his childhood. His talk was chiefly of these things, as if he sought retreat into the pleasant past, but could not find the way.

On Oct. 5, he entered the Neurological Institute at the Columbia Presbyterian Medical Center. He was now in the deep stony-floored valley of melancholy, in much the same condition as that into which he had fallen in the early Twenties when the Austrian peace editorial and readers' subsequent anger had buffeted and bewildered him. The brilliant mind went completely dull. Older now, Ochs was less able to withstand the battering than he had been thirteen years before.

Until this final assault, Ochs had loved to walk and to dance. He had liked to play mischievously with his grandchildren. He had never stayed away from The Times, and had avidly read every line of news, all editorials and letters, and all display advertising. He knew the paper day by day better than any executive who worked for him.

Now, even this was ended. When the paper was brought he stared at it with unseeing eyes. He might toy with it and finger it, but he no longer read it. Peter Brown, his secretarial aide, brought office mail to the house, but it remained unopened until Mrs. Lang, his secretary for many years, arrived to go through it.

Louis Wiley had called the publisher on the telephone every morning at 7:30 for years, but Ochs no longer answered.

It was all a sad visitation upon the genius who had built The New York Times. The world outside knew nothing of his increasing weakness. Sulzberger, Adler and their executives kept The Times on a steady course through troubled waters. Ochs had built The Times well. It handled easily.

Another blow now fell upon the aging publisher.

On March 6, 1935, Louis Wiley, then 65 years old, became ill. He was taken to the Columbia Presbyterian Medical Center. Two weeks later, after an operation, he was dead. The eager little man had trotted happily at Ochs' heels for thirty-nine years. He had never married. The Times had been his one great attachment.

Ochs had grown extremely fond of Wiley through the years. They had worked together as a team and Wiley had been a frequent guest in the publisher's home, a kind of uncle to Ochs' grand-children. Like Ochs, he would scramble on his knees to play with them and would lavish gifts on them.

They remembered in later years the day when, cavorting on a parlor rug with them, he had leaped up in play and had struck his head against a marble mantel. This had cut a deep gash and had momentarily stunned Wiley, but he did not want to frighten the staring children. He managed a grin while tenderly rubbing the spot. "I hit my mental piece on the mantelpiece," he said comically, and the children expressed relief in shrill laughter.

Wiley had been a reporter on The Fort Wayne Journal in Indiana when he was only 16 years old, and even as The Times business manager he was always calling in with news stories or tips for news stories. It was he who "discovered" Will Rogers at a public dinner and persuaded Ochs to run a daily Will Rogers box.

Now he was suddenly gone. The Times on March 21, 1935, ran the story of his death on the front page between turned rules that made black borders. On March 22, Ochs, Rollo Ogden, Sulzberger, James, Adler, a host of other Times men, and many of Wiley's friends outside The Times—Owen D. Young, Gen. Dennis E. Nolan, former Ambassador James W. Gerard, among others—followed the body to the grave in Kensico Cemetery.

About this time, curiously enough, Ochs suddenly emerged from engulfing darkness. Almost overnight he was suddenly brightly alert and eager. A few weeks earlier he had returned to The Times. He had tried to sit at the desk in his magnificent office, but had not quite brought himself to do that. He had looked in on Ogden and the genial Dr. Finley, and then had left the building.

Suddenly, now, he was boyishly eager to visit the scenes of his first newspaper triumph. It could have been some psychological door to escape and nothing more, but he justified it with business reasons.

On the day that he revisited The Times office—it was the first week in April, about ten days after Wiley's burial—he dropped into Adler's office and took a chair beside his nephew's desk. Adler was a little startled to see him. The family had been almost certain that he would never go back to Forty-third Street.

In January he had attended a party on his sister Nannie's birthday. But the gloom had not lifted then. On March 2, ten days before his seventy-seventh birthday, his daughter had attended the annual dinner of the New York Southern Society in his behalf, to accept a scroll of honor from that group in tribute to his achievements for the South.

But now, in Adler's office, he was crisp and almost chipper. He said: "I am going to Chattanooga, Julie. There are some things I want to do down there." He discussed some changes he had in mind for The Chattanooga Times.

His nephew said: "Let me go down and do them for you."

Ochs shook his head. He said: "No, some of it may be unpleasant. I must handle it myself. It's my duty, and I'm going." And he did.

On Saturday night, April 6, Ochs boarded a train in Pennsylvania station with Marian, his granddaughter, and with Miss Cunningham, his nurse. He was almost gay, if somewhat pale and nervous, but his clothes hung on his shrunken frame and his eyes were more deep-socketed than ever. He kissed his kin and Mrs. Squier, and went aboard.

In Chattanooga Sunday night, he went to the home of his sister, Mrs. Harry Clay Adler, chatted freely as in his best days and was astonishingly cheerful. He talked about his Knoxville and Chattanooga boyhood, but it was normal old man's talk and delighted the listeners.

He slept well, rose early, clear-minded and brisk. After breakfast he went to The Chattanooga Times. He moved from one department to another, sharply noticing all detail, talked with some of the older printers, then sat a while with Adolph Shelby Ochs, the newspaper's general manager, son of his brother Milton.

It was almost 1 o'clock before this talk ended. He stopped in the city room to invite R. E. Walker, the editor, to dine with him and with Milton Ochs. At the restaurant, a few blocks away, they chatted pleasantly. A waiter passed menu cards and the men studied them.

Milton Ochs turned to his brother.

He said, "What do you think you'll have, Adolph?"

He got no answer. Swiftly then he noticed unusual pallor in his brother's features. He called his name louder. Adolph Ochs was unconscious. He had had a cerebral hemorrhage. It was 1:45 P.M.

An ambulance took him to the Newell Sanitarium. His brother, his sister and her husband, Adolph Shelby Ochs and his granddaughter, waited anxiously at his bedside there, but Adolph Ochs never spoke again. Two hours and ten minutes after he had been stricken he was dead.

From all the civilized world, men wrote in tribute, President Roosevelt among the rest. He said, "I am deeply distressed to learn of the passing of my old friend. His great contribution to journalism and to good citizenship will always be remembered."

As Ochs was buried on Friday, April 12, in Temple Israel Cemetery in Mount Hope, New York, not far from Hillandale, Associated Press and other syndicate wires fell silent all over the world. Work stopped at The Times. New York City's flags were half-staffed.

Mrs. Ochs had been sharply shocked when her husband had died, but no stranger could have detected it at the service, nor at the grave. There were no tears. A light rain fell as the body was reverently placed in the tomb.

On May 18, 1950, President Truman was to accept in Washington a presentation copy of the first volume of the "Papers of Thomas Jefferson," the first of a series put out by Dr. Julian Boyd, Princeton University Librarian, and his staff. The series is "Dedicated to Adolph S. Ochs who by the example of a responsible press enlarged and fortified the Jeffersonian concept of a free press." The New York Times Company advanced $200,000, in December, 1943, to cover the estimated editorial costs.

This was the second great literary memorial with which the untutored Tennessee newsboy's name was prominently associated. He had helped launch the American Council of Learned Societies' Dictionary of American Biography. He and The New York Times Company had put a total of $532,000 into the venture. The Dictionary was edited by Allen Johnson and by Thomas Dumas Malone. It was entirely consistent with Ochs' tendency toward understatement that his sketch in the Dictionary was much less than a man of his public stature might honestly have expected.

CHAPTER
34

THE CHANGE in publishers at The Times came in a stormy period in world history. Mankind was moving swiftly down the road toward the most violent of all wars. Mussolini was about ready to use his boot on Ethiopia, Hitler was creating the most powerful military organization in history, Spain inwardly boiled with the makings of civil war, Japan was devouring huge, helpless China and Russia's propaganda kept up incessantly. At home the New Deal fussed with recovery and social reform but was running into political headwinds. The depression was far from over and The Times was down to roughly two-thirds its lush 1929 volume.

Sulzberger, now 44 years old, and Adler, one year younger, had trained for top-management jobs for almost eighteen years and had carried a major share of The Times administrative load from the moment Ochs, in his last illness, had let go the wheel. Sulzberger had been The Times' voice in public for a good three years and in talks before newspapermen and other groups had fervently stressed the point that there could be no real human freedom without freedom of the press. He had indicated in these talks that he did not intend to swerve The Times from the steady course Ochs had set for it. He had ideas for some changes but none that would alter basic Ochsian journalistic concepts.

On May 7, 1935, the Board of Directors elected Sulzberger president and publisher of The New York Times Company and created the new post of general manager for Adler. Adler retained his vice presidency and also remained as treasurer. Godfrey N. Nelson, secretary of the company, was named a director in Ochs' place. The other directors were Hoyt Miller, son of Ochs' first editor in chief, Mrs. Sulzberger and Adler.

On May 8 The Times editorial page carried the new publisher's statement of policy:

"Custom among newspapers requires a new publisher to announce his policies and to them pledge adherence.

"For eighteen years I have been close to Mr. Ochs. I have seen him in his office and in his home. I have watched him in the period of his full vigor and during the time when ill health had diminished his active participation in the affairs of this newspaper. I have studied him, admired him, and now that the responsibilities that he bore fall upon my shoulders, I pray that some of the qualities of heart and mind which he possessed in such amazing strength may be vouchsafed to me, and that I may never depart from the principles of honest and impersonal journalism which he, with such force and courage, impressed upon our land.

"I pledge myself, in the words of his salutatory of Aug. 19, 1896, 'to give the news impartially, without fear or favor,' and I join with the men and women who daily make The New York Times in rededicating themselves to the fundamental principles of our democracy and the high dreams of our nation's builders.

"Reverently we close our ranks and continue toward our objective . . ."

Ochs' personal fortune was not as great as many persons had imagined, because up to the time of his death he had put two-thirds of The Times earnings back into the newspaper. His will left controlling interest in The Times in trust to his four grandchildren—the Sulzbergers' son and three daughters. Their parents and Adler were the trustees. To preserve the controlling interest the Trustees caused The New York Times Company to offer to purchase its 8 per cent preferred stock which was then outstanding. The estate and a sprinkling of other stockholders took advantage of this offer. By this arrangement the Trustees were able to realize the $6,000,-000 needed to pay inheritance taxes, attorneys' fees, etc. In so doing they gave up an annual income of $480,000, but no other method could have preserved the integrity of the controlling common stock and the new publisher was strongly opposed to letting control of the property pass into the hands of bankers or any other outsiders. Under the terms of Ochs' will, his heirs also inherited The Chattanooga (Tenn.) Times, a separate corporation.

The day after Ochs' funeral Sulzberger called Charles M. Graves, his picture editor, to a meeting. "All those changes we have planned," he said, "were good, but I want you to put them away now. There will be no radical change for at least one year. We don't want people saying we were waiting for Mr. Ochs to die. Let's just go along on existing lines for a year. We'll take up changes then."

The new publisher had plans for reducing operating costs without damaging The Times' efficiency as a news purveyor. Broadly, these contemplated sale of The Annalist, Current History and Mid-Week Pictorial, by-product publications. He had started in Ochs' lifetime a project for merging the rotogravure section with the Sunday Magazine, and before Ochs' death had sat in on meetings at which he, Ochs and Markel had mapped out a new Sunday news feature: News of the Week in Review. He had plans for getting improved news-writing from his staff, and eventually he put these into effect. He was concerned, though, lest outsiders seeing swift changes might assume that The Times itself was to be fundamentally altered. He moved carefully.

Sulzberger had made three distinct contributions to The Times' development before he stood alone at the helm. He had assured The Times an adequate newsprint supply. He had, under Ochs, Birchall, Van Anda and James, helped establish The Times way out in front as the foremost exponent of aviation advancement. His third contribution was the development of wirephoto service.

In the fall of 1934 when illness first beset him, Ochs was hurt when he discovered that The Associated Press had contracted for a wirephoto transmission system from the American Telephone and Telegraph Company and guaranteed the venture by the underwriting of several large newspapers throughout the country. The Times was not included. Instead, New York City's $150,000 was taken care of by The Daily News, the picture newspaper.

This allocation was of course used only to start the venture. The Associated Press as a mutual organization was bound to offer this service to all its members. If a second newspaper in New York decided to subscribe it would pay $75,000 and reduce the payment of The Daily News by that amount. If three newspapers took the service each would pay $50,000.

But Ochs figured that he was not included in the original underwriting because he had his own picture syndicate, Wide World Photos, Inc., and in his depressed state the fact bit deeply. He was a director of The Associated Press and he had never heard the matter discussed. He forgot that his illness might have played a part, and attributed the slight to lack of trust in him as a competitor. Sulzberger knew the harmful effect the A.P. wirephoto deal had had on Ochs and was anxious to offset it. He pointed out that the A. T. & T. system had probably cost more than $3,000,000 to develop and that it was stiff and awkward; that service was restricted to the A. T. & T.'s own specially built wirephoto lines.

When Sulzberger realized the publisher's hurt, and had heard him repeatedly say, "This puts us out of the photographic business," he tried to buoy him up. He said, "This will not put the Wide World out of business. Let's go out and beat the A.P. wirephoto system."

Ochs said, "How? What do you mean?"

The situation called for fast thinking, for actually Sulzberger had no specific plan. He improvised. He suggested that The Times might be able to develop a portable machine for transmitting pictures over any telephone line, instead of using the expensive special wirephoto lines now leased by The Associated Press.

"Maybe," he said, musing aloud, "we could get up something that would make it possible for us to call up, say Chicago, and send pictures there instead of talking; and when we hung up we would merely pay the ordinary toll charge, and not be burdened with the heavy rental fee which the A.P. has to pay."

Ochs shook his white head, still discouraged. He said glumly, "You can't do that." But Sulzberger asked permission to try, and it was given.

The Times hired a young engineer who had worked with R.C.A. on similar projects, gave him work space in The Times Building, and hopefully awaited results. He failed. Orrin Dunlap, The Times radio editor, then recalled Austin G. Cooley, a young engineer whose work he had described some time before in The Times. Cooley had specialized in facsimile transmission at the Massachusetts Institute of Technology and had put in, all told, more than fifteen years on the problem. Sulzberger interviewed Cooley on Nov. 21, 1934.

Cooley's equipment at this stage was semi-portable. Sulzberger wondered if he could reduce it to a point where a man could carry it. Cooley thought he could, given enough money for helpers and parts. Sulzberger told him to go ahead, and to try to complete the transmitter and receiver within sixty days. Cooley headed back to his home in Rutherford, N. J., and fifty-nine days later, at the end of the third week in January, 1935, was ready to test his outfit over long distance wires. It had worked well on local circuits in Rutherford.

Sulzberger, meanwhile, had established that transmission over regular telephone wires would be legal, provided no part of the wirephoto transmitter was actually hooked into telephone company property. Cooley's machine was rigged both to send and to receive by induction, which made it unnecessary for him to tap any part of the telephone company's equipment; it worked by a sort of electrical osmosis.

A few weeks before Cooley was ready to begin his long distance tests Sulzberger and Walter Gifford, head of the A. T. & T., met at a public dinner.

"Does it make any difference to the telephone company," Sulzberger casually asked Gifford, "if a telephone user talks English or French?"

Gifford said the phones were open for all conversation except profane.

"Then a telephone user," Sulzberger pursued, "can talk French, or even Turkish, and that would be all right?"

Gifford was amused. He nodded.

"How about Turkish or gibberish, that still all right?"

The A. T. & T. man was puzzled.

He said, "Arthur, what are you getting at?"

"This," said Sulzberger, "since it doesn't matter what language goes over a telephone, it should make no difference to you if we take a picture and transform its light values into sound values, send them over ordinary telephone lines, and then re-translate them into light values at the other end of the line."

The A. T. & T. man pondered the question a while.

"No," he finally decided, "I don't think that would concern us at all."

Up to this point, so far as anyone at A. T. & T. knew, the only telephone system that would change light values into sound values, then change them back to light values as in picture transmission, was the wirephoto system that A. T. & T. had leased to The Associated Press. A Western Electric engineers' report released only a short time before had stated without qualification that no picture transmitter would work on any telephone circuit stretching more than 100 miles, except on the special wirephoto circuits the A. T. & T. had set up at such great expense.

Cooley, meanwhile, tested his equipment in The Times. He worked day and night on it, even slept in The Times' ninth floor photographic studio so that he would lose no time in travel. Mrs. Cooley sometimes stayed with him to make certain that he ate.

On Jan. 24, 1935, Garrett V. Dillenbach, a technician who had been working with Cooley, went to a remote farmhouse, the home of a friend, in Slingerlands, west of Albany, 150 miles north of New York, to make the first long-distance transmission test. He took some stock photos from the Wide World files to use in the experiment.

Dillenbach set the portable transmitter—small enough to fit into a valise 23 inches long, 13 inches wide and 8 inches deep—next to the farmhouse telephone, called The Times, and announced that he was ready. Sulzberger, Graves, Meinholtz and Cooley huddled around the receiver in the special seventeen-foot-square dark room set up for the experiments, and held their breath as the receiver drum hummed in its spinning. The pictures were almost perfect.

The second tests, after a few bugs in the set had been corrected, were made from the Chicago offices of Wide World Photos at 400 Madison Street on Feb. 6 and 7. Again reception was good. Pictures spoiled if telephone operators broke in on the line, but Dillenbach always warned the long-distance girls not to monitor the calls and they heeded. Sulzberger, Graves and Cooley were quietly jubilant. The pictures had better quality than any they had previously seen.

Then Cooley told Dillenbach to get out to San Francisco and to try to send across the continent. The transmitter was set up in the home of Lester Kerie, Wide World manager on the West Coast. The first tests were disappointing. A slight variation in synchronization between the transmitter and the receiver, traceable to infinitesimal lag in telephone company long-distance relays, caused figures in the pictures to tip drunkenly when they came in on the receiver at The Times. This was due to what Cooley called "drift" or "skew," but he worked out perfect synchronization, and the pictures were good again.

Just about the time these corrections were finished, on Feb. 12, the United States Navy dirigible Macon exploded in mid-air off the California coast. Survivors were brought to San Francisco Harbor next day, and Wide World photographers got good pictures of their landing. Up to then The Times experiments had been kept secret, and all tests had been made with old stock shots.

Graves figured that the Macon pictures offered a chance for a dramatic beginning for the new service. He ordered Dillenbach to transmit a half-dozen shots and assigned Jack Shildnecht, an operator, to stand by with Cooley to receive them. Bill Freese, The Times studio boss, stayed late to handle the picture processing to prevent news of the first coast-to-coast transmission from getting through the building before edition time.

The news room, six floors below, was rather high-keyed that night but for a different reason. Telegraph wires were open to Flemington, N. J., where a jury was weighing a verdict on Richard Bruno Hauptmann, a carpenter, who had been arrested on Sept. 19, 1934, for the kidnapping and murder of the Lindbergh baby.

It was almost 11 P.M. when the last of the Macon pictures materialized on the receiver drum in the dark studio chamber at The Times, but Graves and Raymond H. McCaw, night managing editor, had chosen two of the earliest to run—one marked for four-column width, another for three. They considered, for a moment, putting one of the pictures on the front page, but at 10:45 P.M., Russell Porter of The Times staff flashed from Flemington: "Hauptmann Guilty." His lead rapped right out on the heels of the flash:

FLEMINGTON, N.J., Feb. 13—Bruno Richard Hauptmann was convicted of murder in the first degree at 10:45 o'clock tonight for the killing of Charles A. Lindbergh Jr. at Hopewell on the night of March 1, 1932 . . . He was sentenced to die in the electric chair in the State prison at Trenton some time during the week of March 18.

The kidnapper's conviction was the big story that night, but to a few readers of The Times next morning the Macon pictures were somewhat more startling. Telephone company executives, publishers who had invested heavily in exclusive rights to A. P. wirephotos, and the A. P.'s own wirephoto crew could not quite fathom the puzzling credit line that ran under the Macon survivor cuts—"Copyright W.W.W. Photo." They had never seen such a credit line before and no news story explained it.

It took a moment's thinking, but finally they figured as the publisher had hoped they would, that it could stand for only one thing—"Wide World Wirephoto." Since they had no knowledge of The Times experiments they could not explain how the pictures had reached New York from the West Coast. So far as they knew only the special telephone company leased wires could transmit photographs.

Photo executives of the Scripps-Howard chain and of International News Photos and picture editors around town kept Graves' wire busy with eager questions. How had The Times managed to get spot news pictures across the United States, they wanted to know, and was the equipment or service available to other newspapers?

Theodore Miller and Edwin Carter, both telephone company vice presidents and engineers, also investigated. They had the Western Electric engineers' confident report that wirephotos could not be sent over ordinary telephone circuits for any considerable distance, yet The Times had used ordinary long-distance wires. The telephone company men listened to the details, stared at Cooley's dwarf equipment, thought of their own $3,000,000 special wirephoto circuits—and gave up. "Guess there's nothing we can do about it," they conceded.

The Times ran a modest editorial next day to answer the flood of inquiries about the pictures.

"The pictures of the Macon survivors which appeared in The New York Times of Feb. 14," the editorial said, "were transmitted from San Francisco to New York by a process with which The New York Times with Wide World, Inc., has been experimenting for the past few months. These particular pictures were but two of many which have been sent from various points in the United States. The method is not yet ready for service. Numerous problems have still to be adjusted, but the fact that reasonably good photographs can be transmitted by wire at no great cost is in process of being demonstrated."

The cost was measured in wire time. It cost no more to send a wire picture than it did to talk by wire.

The successful adventure in wirephoto development stimulated Sulzberger's interest in news photographs. He thought more and more in terms of pictures, which were becoming increasingly popular and, eventually, when he became publisher, this was reflected in a broader picture policy for The Times. It began to use more pictures on the front page and throughout the paper. Today, because of the size of The Times, the photo content frequently equals, and often exceeds, the space devoted to pictures in the smaller tabloids. This was all part of Times modernization that was taking place so subtly that many readers did not notice it.

CHAPTER
35

D EAK LYMAN lolled at his desk in the city room on Thursday, Dec. 19, 1935. He had finished his Sunday aviation page make-up, and looked forward to Friday and Saturday with his wife, Mabs, and the children at their Port Washington home. He had no night assignment.

Late in the afternoon Colonel Lindbergh called him. They had been friends eight years now. Lindbergh said, "Deak, when could you drop out to see me? I'm staying with the Morrows in Englewood and I've got something I want to talk about, but not on the telephone."

Deak had figured on driving out to Somerville, N.J., on Friday to pick up a Christmas bicycle for Phil, his son. He dropped in on Friday in wintry twilight on the way back. His wife, Mabs, talked with Anne Lindbergh and played with Jon, the Lindbergh baby. The flier took Deak into another room.

"Deak," he said, quietly, "I'm taking my family to England. I've got to get Anne and the baby away. Since the furor over the Hauptmann verdict, crank letters have started again. There have been threats against the family. I'm going to make England my home."

Kindly Deak, silver specs down a little too far on his nose, stared in disbelief. His lips parted, but he could not speak for a moment.

"Look, Slim," he finally said. "Why don't you give this to the news services too, and to Carl Allen [of The Herald Tribune]. I

414

don't think you know what impact this will have on the country."

Lindbergh said: "If I give the information to a half-dozen people there will be a half-dozen versions. I know if I give it to you it will be right. If it's in The Times first the others will pick it up."

Deak said, "Judas, Slim, don't you know this is one hell of a news story?"

Lindbergh said, "I don't know about that; it's up to you."

Finally they worked it out. The Lindberghs would board the American Importer at the foot of West Twentieth Street in New York at midnight Saturday. They wanted twenty-four hours' head start, no reporters—not even Deak—at the pier, and no photographers. The story was to be held for Monday morning's Times.

Lyman again offered to share the story with other newspapers. He said: "We're talking as friends, now, Slim; it isn't just a professional thing. I do want the story for The Times, of course, but I want you to be sure that's the way *you* want it."

"I want it in The Times first, Deak."

The Lymans drove home in winter darkness. When Deak told Mabs, she sucked in her breath. Deak said: "I don't think I'll go into the office tonight. I'm afraid if I tell anyone it might get around. I can't take that chance."

"Never drove as carefully as I did on the way home from Englewood that night," he recalled later. "I didn't want anything to happen until I had unloaded that story."

Deak told his wife how Lindbergh had asked that no pictures be run with the story, and that he would rather have The Times use the story on an inside page than out front. Because he had become newswise through the years, he finally agreed that it would probably have to be front-paged.

All day Saturday, Deak stayed close to his home phone. He studied old Lindbergh clippings though he knew the flier's biography by heart, and all the details of the kidnapping too. He was uneasy. Lindbergh called him late in the afternoon to say departure plans were unchanged. Then the flier said, "Good-by, Deak," and Deak said, "Good-by, Slim, and good luck."

At 6 o'clock on Saturday night, Deak took the Long Island Railroad into New York. After the first edition was in—it went early on Saturday because of Sunday morning volume—he asked City Editor Bruce Rae to leave the desk for a moment. They walked to Deak's own desk, where no one was within earshot, before Deak spoke.

He said: "Bruce, I've got the god-damndest story of the year. I don't dare keep it to myself. I've got to ask you to promise to keep it secret."

Bruce knew that Deak was not ordinarily excitable. "Let's have it," he said with characteristic curtness.

Deak said, "Lindbergh's leaving this country to seek safety in England."

The news-stalker gleam showed behind Rae's gold-rimmed spectacles.

When Deak finished the details, the city editor's jaw tightened. He said: "We can't hold this up. Someone else may break it," but Deak said: "We can't, Bruce. I promised Lindbergh we'd hold for Monday's paper. By that time he'll be twenty-four hours out."

McCaw was afraid, too, that the story might get out. To him, too, Deak said: "You've got to back me up, Boss. We can't break it."

Rae said, "Suppose Winchell gets it and puts it on the air tomorrow night?"

Lyman shook his shaggy head. "Lindbergh won't talk," he insisted. "I'll stick around tonight and watch the ship ticker. I promised I wouldn't go near the pier. He told me he would call me here at the office if fog, or anything else, happens to delay his get-away."

After midnight, in a dimly lighted city room corner away from all his associates, Lyman bent over the glass-domed ship-news ticker until the chattering little type wheel stammered out: "12:53 A.M. . . . American Importer . . . Passing Quarantine . . . Bound Out . . ."

There had been no phone call from Lindbergh. He was on the high seas with Mrs. Lindbergh and the baby. Deak left the office and rumbled back to Port Washington for restless sleep.

Sulzberger was at Hillandale for the week-end, but McCaw did not tell him what was coming up. He did not dare risk a telephone leak.

On Sunday afternoon Deak got into the office at 2 o'clock, the regular reporting hour. He asked Walter Fenton, day city editor on Sundays, to walk to an unoccupied corner of the city room for a

moment. There he outlined the Lindbergh story. Fenton, famous
for his poker face in moments of office excitement, quietly listened.
When Deak had finished he nodded. He said, "Get over to your
desk and write it."

Deak got Frank Walton, another Times man who did aviation, to
sit beside him as he wrote, to ward off gabbily inclined fellow staff
men. The story did not come easily. Lyman wanted to tell it as
simply and as carefully as he could.

He tried thirteen leads, hacked at one after another with his copy
pencil, then mutteringly threw them away. Walton saw to it that
none of these discards remained in readable form. He tore them
into bits and dropped the pieces into a waste basket that he kept
close to his leg.

Finally Deak had the formula: "Col. Charles A. Lindbergh has
given up residence in the United States and is on his way to establish his home in England. With him are his wife and 3-year-old son,
Jon.

"Threats of kidnapping and even of death to the little lad, recurring repeatedly since his birth, caused the father and the mother
to make the decision. These threats have increased both in number
and virulence recently.

"Although they do not plan to give up their American citizenship, they are prepared to live abroad permanently, if that should
be necessary. Where they will live in England when they get there
not even their closest friends know, and it is probable that neither
the colonel nor his wife knows. They have many friends there and
expect to visit at first until they can find a place that suits them."

At 6 o'clock Mrs. Lyman came in from Port Washington. She
sat with Deak a while as he hammered the keys and muttered.
Every reporter has some special writing quirk and Deak was a
mutterer.

Sensitive to her husband's little eccentricities, Mrs. Lyman got
up after a few minutes. She said: "I make you nervous. I think I'll
run along." She went to Abingdon Square on the edge of Greenwich Village, where Shepard Stone, another Times man, was holding an office party.

When Rae took over the night city desk a few minutes later,
Deak carried up his first three sheets and Rae carefully scanned

them. He nodded, locked them in his desk drawer, and said, "You're doing all right; let it run."

It was 9 o'clock when the story was finished. No copy boy had been allowed to handle any part of it and no copy editor knew about it. Rae took the story to the deserted day bull pen, made a few changes in it, and showed them to Deak. Then the copy went to the night bull pen.

McCaw read it, and wrote the headline:

LINDBERGH FAMILY SAILS FOR ENGLAND TO SEEK A SAFE, SECLUDED RESIDENCE; THREATS ON SON'S LIFE FORCED DECISION

McCaw called Tom Dillon, night foreman in the composing room. He told him to choose two printers who would not be likely to gossip, and to have them set the story and the head in type. He impressed on Dillon the need for utter secrecy.

"Don't let the galleys get into any other hands but yours and the printers'," McCaw emphasized. "Pull the proofs yourself, and lock the type in your own drawer. Bring the proofs to me yourself. Don't send them by boy."

McCaw purposely held the story out of the early editions to prevent competitors from lifting it. At 3:30 A.M. he gave Dillon the word to slip the head and the story into the Late City Edition as a postscript. Several hundred thousand copies of this edition were run off.

After the first proofs had come down, Rae advised Deak to join Mrs. Lyman at the Stone party. When he got there Hanson Baldwin sat down with him.

"What kept you?" he wanted to know.

"Had a pretty fair piece for the paper," Lyman said.

Deak told Baldwin about the story in a low whisper. Baldwin looked shocked. He said, "Get out of here. Get back to the office. If they keep passing these strong drinks they'll worm it out of you."

Deak mumbled something to Stone about having to go back to the shop and Stone was sympathetic. He gave Deak a gallon of the lusty punch, and Deak returned to The Times. He sat with Brooks Atkinson in the drama critic's little cubicle at the back of the almost deserted news room. They discussed the social implications of

A Great First: This picture, appearing in The Times the day after the rescue, 3,000 miles away, puzzled editors of other newspapers. It marked the beginning of transcontinental photo transmission by Times Facsimile.

Lindbergh's flight from the States, and little by little the punch tide receded in the jug.

When the paper came off the press, Deak grabbed a few copies and made the 4 A.M. local for Port Washington. When he unfolded a copy as the train neared Flushing, he was aware, somehow, of eager eyes focused on the story from the seat behind him.

Deak turned. The man who had stared over his shoulder seemed dimly familiar, but Deak could not fit him into any solid memory pattern. The man left the train at Flushing station.

By the time the train had crawled out of the station, Deak had figured out who the man was—he worked for The New York American. By curious coincidence only The New York American that morning managed to fudge a bare paragraph on the Lindbergh departure onto its front page in the last edition. No other newspaper had it.

That did not matter. The Times had put over one of the greatest exclusive news stories of the generation. The story won that year's Pulitzer prize for Deak. It was generally recognized that the story had come his way because of the character he had established as a trustworthy newspaperman.

Ten weeks before Lyman started work on the Lindbergh story another Times man had left Naples by Italian troopship, on a weird war assignment. Benito Mussolini, who had grown into a terrifying figure since Anne O'Hare McCormick had prophetically written about him fifteen years before, had flouted the League of Nations and the imposing British Mediterranean fleet, and had landed an army of Blackshirts in Eritrea, intent on annexing ancient Ethiopia to the expanding Italian Empire.

It was an assignment that few newspapermen would have relished. This war was to be fought in hellish country—in a nightmare land that swarmed with sticky flies and countless vermin, where the day's heat made men's tongues hang from dry lips, where there were only bad odors and no modern comforts, no fancy foods to supplement Italian army ration. Herbert L. Matthews of The Times, a tall, lean, solemn man, somehow liked that sort of thing. He experienced a strange exhilaration in moving across stark desert country with fighting men, in sitting by their camp fires, in writing his pieces for the paper in the dim light of storm lanterns, in watching the primitive natives—Danakils, Askaris, Somalis, Berbers and Gallas—men and women whose living habits and thinking had barely changed since their forebears had figured in Scripture.

Matthews sensed that this venture into a sleeping land so rudely awakened by clanking tanks, malodorous military motor transport, thundering planes and coughing machine guns, was mere rehearsal for greater wars in more modern countries. It was as if the romantic militarist of Rome had deliberately chosen a Biblical setting for the jump-off toward Armageddon.

Fussy Italian censors made it difficult for correspondents to catch up with the actual fighting. Cruel climate, meals out of sun-heated tins, bathless days and weeks, could have been borne a bit more easily if only there were ready access to good battle stories. But the Blackshirts were stubborn; they let only scraps of war news through, and that little was sometimes garbled in erratic wireless transmission across 10,000 miles.

By New Year's Day Matthews was sick of censor obstruction. "I am convinced," he cabled to James in Times Square, "that further sojourn here under present circumstances is a waste of my time and the newspaper's money. Unless situation changes soon, which nobody expects, suggest your recalling me. However, perfectly willing to continue if you think worthwhile."

The censor balked when he read this message, as Matthews had known he would. It would make a bad impression on the whole world if the correspondents, and especially if The Times, left the war unreported, the censor argued. He promised to see whether he could not have Matthews moved up to the fighting.

It took ten days for James' answer to come back across the globe. On Jan. 10, 1936, the jubilant censor handed Matthews the managing editor's curt reply. "Remain for present."

By that time, though, the Italians had paved the way for Matthews to see front-line action. He was to remain from the beginning to the end, the only American correspondent on the Italian side who did.

He was with Gen. Oreste Mariotti in the drive from Massawa to Azbi. He crossed the burning Danakil Desert, saw the fierce native allies of the Blackshirt Army in action, and was sickened by evidence of their expertness with mutilating knives. Eventually, he departed from Mariotti's camp to join Marshal Badoglio on the grinding march from Dessye to Addis Ababa, reporting along the way the results of the uneven war, graphically picturing the fighting in the mountain passes and on plains strewn with Italian and Ethiopian dead.

Finally, on Tuesday, May 5, 1936, Badoglio's columns—Eritreans, bedraggled men of the Bersaglieri, the San Marco Marines, the dark Alpini, the Italian Grenadiers—were within sight of the citadel of Haile Selassie, King of Kings, in Addis Ababa. The columns moved through pounding equatorial rains. Matthews rode in a tatterdemalion Fiat, clutching his precious typewriter, his damp copy paper. He was wracked with fever, but would not be denied the final spectacle of this weird military adventure. He was in the caravan behind the triumphant marshal when the Italian commander pressed into the public square in Addis Ababa.

Matthews had thought for months of how he would handle the dramatic story of this final hour, of the colorful background material he might put into it, but it didn't work out that way. The censor gave him a bare half hour to get his piece done. Unless it were ready by that time, the censor warned, it might not clear that night.

Matthews planted the typewriter on his long knees in the Fiat and, with the rain pounding the roof and running in rivulets at all the car seams, started a 500-word description of the great victory that Marshal Badoglio had won for Il Duce:

ADDIS ABABA, May 5—Ethiopia's era of independence, which had lasted since Biblical times, ended at 4 o'clock this afternoon (10 A.M. New York Time) when the Italian Army occupied Addis Ababa . . . The Marshal with his staff is standing at salute several yards away while the Italian flag is being hoisted on the former Italian legation . . .

CHAPTER
36

T HERE WAS to be no clear sailing for Sulzberger in his early
years as Times helmsman. Everywhere on earth's horizon
were portents of wars and great social changes. The whole human
pattern was reshaping under stress.

Sulzberger read the storm signals in The Times' own pages and
trimmed canvas without retarding forward speed. In 1936 he sold
both Current History and Mid-Week Pictorial, by-product publications controlled by The Times. He was persuaded that they had
served their purpose. Ochs had clung to them out of sentiment.

The Sunday Times sections under Markel's direction had made
Current History obsolete. It was a swifter medium for news interpretation and for presenting news background, giving news fill-in
weeks before Current History could publish. It breathed right on
the neck of spot news.

Mid-Week Pictorial had begun to retreat in value, too. From the
moment that wirephoto took hold, its material tended to be stable.
It ceased to exist as a Times by-product on Oct. 3, 1936.

The rotogravure section, which Ochs had introduced as a Sunday feature in 1914, was near the end of its run, too, doomed by
wirephoto and newsreels. It had been highly profitable and for a
long period had swelled Sunday circulation and Sunday advertising revenue, but by 1936 was outdated.

Markel had tried to persuade Ochs some years before his death that it might be a good idea to incorporate the roto section with the Sunday Magazine. He wanted roto converted into a twelve-page center picture spread in the magazine and had worked up convincing dummies. When Ochs finally seemed to have been more or less won over to the idea, a newsprint shortage and his illness held it up.

Sulzberger, though, made the change on Feb. 15, 1942. He poured a sizable fortune into the venture, but it paid. The magazine with roto and color attained a fat eighty-page maturity, outstripping everything in its field.

The Annalist, which had started as The Times Weekly Financial Review in January, 1913, was sold to the McGraw-Hill Publishing Company in October, 1940. Wide World Photos was sold to The Associated Press in August, 1941.

"There were times," Sulzberger conceded later, "when I was concerned as to whether I was moving too fast, or tightening things too much. I was anxious to perfect The Times' readability. I wanted the paper to move editorially out of the ivory tower. I saw the effect that radio commentators were having; it called for more news interpretation on our part because news was growing almost alarmingly complex. It was clear to me that it was time for change, but I feared that I might be ruining The Times. The changes had to be made without affecting the basic Ochs formula."

Perhaps the broadest step toward adding extra dimension to news presentation without altering Ochsian principle, was made with the start of The News of the Week in Review in the Sunday paper. Markel had proposed it to Ochs in the late Twenties, but the Chattanoogan then saw no need for it.

Ochs could justify this opposition in his own mind. He was accustomed to reading The Times religiously from masthead to the last item on the last page every morning—he read little else—and assumed that most Times readers did, too. He thought a Sunday review would be unnecessary duplication.

Illness finally brought Ochs around to the Markel idea. As his sight dimmed he found it more and more difficult to read painstakingly every line in the daily. Besides, he found the review dummies attractive. When the Review was launched on Jan. 27, 1935, it brought a substantial circulation rise.

Sulzberger's greatest fear had been editorial-page change. Ochs had favored the Miller-Ogden style, which had scholarly charm, but on only a few occasions got anywhere near the bare-knuckles attitude. Ochs had even toyed with the idea, when he first took over, of having no editorial page. He never actually tried it.

Only after long deliberation did Ochs give his consent to a signed Washington column on the editorial page. It was started by Arthur Krock, Washington bureau chief, on April 26, 1933. Though Ochs had conceded in this break with original principles that the spate of complex national news in Franklin D. Roosevelt's Administration called for such a column as Krock's, he held out against a similar column on international affairs.

Sulzberger, though, unhesitatingly instituted the international column and assigned the writing to Mrs. McCormick. He made her the first woman in Times history to hold a place on the editorial board, a move that his father-in-law would never have made.

"Your field," the new publisher told Mrs. McCormick, "will be the freedoms. It will be your job to guard against encroachments on them anywhere."

Her column, originally called "In Europe," later "Affairs in Europe" and eventually just "Abroad," began on Feb. 1, 1937, alternating with Krock's. Her crystal compositions, warmly touched with human understanding, won general reader approval. She became the most honored newspaperwoman in the world.

Mussolini's victory in Ethiopia had heady effects on his German counterpart. Stalin cagily watched both and the democracies, too, as the pieces shifted on the international chessboard.

On July 17, 1936, a garrison uprising in Spanish Morocco touched off the revolt against the Spanish Republic. William P. Carney, The Times man in Madrid, took over as correspondent with the forces of Gen. Francisco Franco, the rebel leader. Matthews, back in New York only a few weeks since the fall of Addis Ababa, pleaded with James to send him to Spain, but his start was delayed until November.

Frank Kluckhohn, another Times man, assigned to Spain, had been there less than a month when he made the startling discovery:

32 GERMAN, ITALIAN PLANES
REACH REBEL ARMY IN SPAIN

Only The Times had this news. Kluckhohn wrote it in Seville on Aug. 11 and got it by courier to Gibraltar. The German and Italian Governments were not eager, just then, for the world to know they were ready to test their fighting ships against the Loyalists. The story almost cost Kluckhohn his life. He had to flee Spain.

"Twenty heavy German Junker bombing planes and five German pursuit planes manned by German military pilots arrived at rebel headquarters in Seville today," the story said. "The airplanes had been landed from a ship at the rebel port of Cadiz and were then flown here.

"With these and seven Italian Caproni bombers, which arrived during the past few days piloted by Italians, the rebels are in a position to sweep the Madrid Leftist Government's planes from the air over the Guadarrama Mountain passes north of the capital and to bomb strategic points, the Loyalist fleet or anything else they wish to attack . . . The writer saw some of the new German planes. The German Consul here privately admits they were flown by German military aviators . . . The Italian and German aviators are living at the Hotel Cristina here. Neither group is in military uniforms."

The Times foreign desk sent an outline of Kluckhohn's story to its Berlin bureau for official comments there, but information was difficult to get. Under Kluckhohn's piece, which carried a four-column front-page head, The Times ran the only reply available:

BERLIN, Aug. 11—The report of the arrival of German bombing and pursuit planes for the Spanish rebels at Seville was characterized by the Propaganda Ministry tonight as "fantastic," but beyond that it was impossible to obtain confirmation or denial of the report.

Only the highest officials, it was said, were able to answer questions about such an important matter, and they were busy with Olympic receptions and could not be reached . . .

Kluckhohn's passport was canceled by the rebels some weeks later and he was recalled to the United States. He was assigned to the Washington bureau.

"This," Sulzberger subsequently told the Columbia Alumni Association in a talk on censorship, "is an excellent example of where the sending of a single story is worth the expulsion that may follow it. It was not until the dispatch was published that the full extent of Fascist aid to rebel Spain was comprehended."

It developed later that Russian pilots and mechanics with Russian equipment had come in on the Loyalist side and The Times carried that fact, too.

Matthews had been labeled "Fascist" when he marched with Il Duce's Blackshirts in Ethopia, and now was blindly tagged "Red" because he reported from the Spanish Loyalist front. He was neither, but just a truthful and discerning reporter obeying assignment.

Late in November, 1936, he summed up the truth of the Spanish situation in one sentence in The Times: "Officially it is just a civil war they are fighting in Spain, but people for whom realities count more than diplomatic amenities are starting to call it the Little World War."

He was right. The clump of military boots that had begun in Biblical setting in Haile Selassie's ancient empire was carrying across ancient Castile toward Europe's broader stage. Times stories recorded each terrifying tread. Sulzberger and his newspaper were under constant cross fire throughout the war in Spain, and after it had ended with the fall of Madrid on March 28, 1939. It did not seem to matter to some readers that The Times was only fulfilling its journalistic function in having reporters cover both sides of the war. One group protested against Carney's reports from the Franco side, and an equal number were angry against Matthews' pieces. The Times ran occasional letters from both sides, but even that did not always satisfy, and adherents of one side or the other muttered that The Times was biased. It was the penalty of impartial journalism.

In late November, 1936, gossip columns in the United States served their readers the richest hors d'oeuvre in the annals of backstair journalism—hints that King Edward would renounce his throne to marry Mrs. Wallis Simpson, American divorcée. There was no official indication that this was anything more than romantic speculation. The British press was stonily silent on the subject.

It developed later that Mrs. Simpson's attorneys were also counsel for the British Newspaper Proprietors Association, and that they had asked member papers to stand aloof from the story in the interest of the empire—and the papers had. British statesmen had suggested to the King that he ask the country's newspapers to disregard the situation between himself and Mrs. Simpson until it was officially settled. He had refused.

In London, meanwhile, Ferdinand Kuhn Jr., acting head of The New York Times bureau during the illness of the bureau chief, Charles Selden, had been sending cautious, guarded, news of the shaping crisis. The scurrying of important British officialdom—Prime Minister Stanley Baldwin, Foreign Secretary Anthony Eden, and fellow Cabinet members—had been reported in detail, but The Times had done no loose speculating.

A long dispatch from Kuhn that reached the bull pen about 8 o'clock one night set McCaw to pursing his lips. He held the copy in his left hand a moment and drummed on his desk with the fingers of his right—a McCaw mannerism that betrayed deep thought. He turned to his secretary and dictated a cable to Kuhn:

"This is pretty strong stuff. None of the agencies carry it. You sure it's okay?"

Kuhn's affirmative answer whisked back across the Atlantic before first-edition time and McCaw gave the story lead position, ordering a four-column head for it. It ran in The Times of Dec. 3:

EDWARD MAY ABDICATE THRONE TODAY, REFUSING TO BREAK WITH MRS. SIMPSON; BRITAIN IS ASTOUNDED BY THE CRISIS

A deep box preceded Kuhn's story. It told of a hasty meeting of the King's entourage, of royal dispatch riders roaring in and out of Fort Belvedere where the King had spent the night, of the Duke of York, the King's brother, arriving with his wife in London from Edinburgh.

The main story began:

LONDON, Dec. 2—The reign of King Edward VIII came perilously close to the breaking point tonight after a day of such fantastic happenings as the proud British monarchy has not had to experience for hundreds of years.

Upon the utterly astounded country there has burst a constitutional crisis involving the possible abdication of the King tomorrow and succession of the Duke of York to the throne. The crisis is no longer hidden; the conflict between the King and his Ministers has blazed up into open flame.

McCaw felt safe in running the story for a full three columns. It was evident, though no other responsible newspaper had the abdication angle, that Kuhn had gone to great pains to verify his facts. The story stood up, except as to abdication date. The King did not send his "final and irrevocable announcement" to the Ministers until Dec. 10.

Next day's Times carried Birchall's story on it under a three-line eight-column banner.

LONDON, Dec. 10—Some time Saturday morning, perhaps even as soon as tomorrow night, Edward VIII will cease to be a King and Emperor. He has made his choice between a woman and a throne, and the woman has won.

Another front-page story from Cannes told how Wallis Simpson, hearing the news over the radio, bowed her head to hide the tears that plunged down her cheeks.

On Dec. 11 Edward stood before a microphone and in quivering accents told the whole world his decision: "At long last I am able to say a few words . . . A few hours ago I discharged my last duty as King and Emperor . . . You must believe me when I tell you that I have found it impossible to carry the heavy burden of responsibility . . . as King . . . without the help and support of the woman I love."

The Times carried the full text of "Edward's Farewell" next day beside Birchall's account of the renunciation.

The tingle of this most romantic story in newspaper history was still upon the world when Kuhn cabled for publication in The Times of Christmas Eve 1936 a wireless dispatch that brought dreamers back to frigid reality:

LONDON, Dec. 23—As the holidays approach with their message of peace the British press and public are showing a sudden new anxiety to know just what war-like moves may be brewing across the North Sea.

The Christmas air is thick with rumors. There is a vague sense of uneasiness in the atmosphere and fear of the "explosion" which Dr. Hjalmar Schacht, Economics Minister, threatened the other day if Germany could not obtain satisfaction from the hostile world.

Strident demands from Berlin made harsh counterpoint to Yuletide bells. Hourly they grew more shrill, more insistent. It required a none too sensitive ear to hear the swelling obligato of military boots. It came on apace, with The Times chronicling every tread, each vital speech and document, in greater detail than any journal on earth.

When spring came 'round in 1938 even a blind man could have foreseen what was to be. Hitler's mechanized might, built under the very eyes of the complacent democracies, rolled into Austria on the night of March 11 that year, and embraced that weak country in steely Anschluss. Times presses roared at unprecedented pace to keep up with the story.

The Nazis turned on Czechoslovakia after Hitler's visit to Il Duce in early May. In August, as the Czech crisis set the world on edge der Fuehrer went on a significant tour of forts along the Czech border. Now he had grown shrill over the Sudeten question—so shrill and threatening that Prime Minister Neville Chamberlain flew from London to Berchtesgaden in mid-September, hoping through appeasement to prevent war.

Times coverage of those tense days was magnificent. Geared for printing texts and speeches in full from all the nations involved, and with more men in Europe to sound public and official opinion, it added to its prestige as a journal of record.

When France and Britain agreed to Hitler's demands on Czechoslovakia, Times men in Berlin, Prague, Paris and London laid the whole Munich plan before the world as no other newspaper did. They watched and reported the Nazi occupation of the Sudeten area on Oct. 1. It was a tense period full of complex happenings and readers turned to The Times not only for reports of the events themselves but also for interpretation of events.

CHAPTER

37

O N WASHINGTON'S BIRTHDAY in 1937 Rollo Ogden died. He had
been head of The Times editorial page since Miller's death in
May, 1920, and he had written and supervised the page pretty
much in the Miller tradition. He was a kindly old gentleman—81
when he died—and had measured up, mentally and to all outward
appearances, to the general conception of the ivory tower school of
editorial writers. On stately rounds of the building his tall, lean
figure was draped in frock coat, striped trousers and wing collar,
and even his kindly features bore the patina that somehow was
immediately associated with everything Victorian. He had even
served as prototype for a Rea Irvin cartoon in The New Yorker that
pictured The Times editorial room as a dusty holdover from the
journalistic past, which in a sense it was.

Ogden was succeeded by Dr. Finley, who belonged to the
same school in dress and in thought—steeped in the classics, with
much of the academic aura clinging closely to him, though he
was famous in Manhattan's streets as the hatless pedestrian with
the blue thistle in his lapel. Sulzberger placed Finley in Ogden's
former post on April 21, 1937. The good doctor, too, was past three-
score and ten at the time. His tenure was by agreement to last until
he was 75, but because of ill health he retired on Nov. 16, 1938,
with the title of editor emeritus, and Charles Merz, a much younger
man, took over. Finley died quietly in his sleep on the morning of
March 7, 1940, in his home at 1 Lexington Avenue, and the whole

city mourned him. Mayor LaGuardia, his close friend, ordered all flags at half-staff the day of the funeral.

The human crop that had been seeded in mid-nineteenth century was all but gathered in, now; only a few were left in the windrows, and time reached gently for them. On the morning of May 6, 1937, on the eve of her 77th birthday, death came to Effie Wise Ochs. She had a slight seizure in her sleep that morning. The doctor hastily telephoned to Mrs. Sulzberger, but before the family could reach the bedside the Tranquil Lady of Hillandale had drifted out of life.

Sulzberger, meanwhile, had been abroad and had talked with his European chiefs. He had heard their private fears and was deeply concerned. It was obvious that the Germans were mad-drunk with dreams of world conquest and that they looked upon the democracies as contemptibly soft.

Sulzberger knew that most Americans found Germany's bullying of smaller nations offensive, just as they did Japan's, but he had also realized that they could not relate the distant war rumblings to their own interests.

In editorial conference he discussed his findings with his aides. He felt that it was The Times' duty to drive home to Americans where they stood in the gathering global storm; that they could not hope to isolate themselves from it when it broke; that the Neutrality Act was an inadequate and defective shield against it; that their moral, if not their physical, support would have to be on the side of the democracies.

The result of these discussions was the grave editorial-page lead written by Merz for The Times of June 15, 1938. It was headed, "A Way of Life." *

While the hell brew came to bubbling pitch across the Atlantic, New York had built on a reclaimed meadow in Queens Borough a lovely set of buildings to house the World's Fair. Grover Whalen, the city's minister without portfolio, had dreamily named it "The World of Tomorrow."

It was a happy but hopeless theme. Sulzberger knew that because he comprehended the significance of the foreign news that was appearing daily. Still he gave generously of Times space and funds to promote it. A man could dream of peace. Whalen did.

* See Appendix for editorial.

"We convey to you," Whalen proclaimed to visitors from all over the world, "the picture of the interdependence of man on man, class on class, nation on nation. We tell you of the immediate necessity of enlightened and harmonious co-operation to preserve and save the best of our modern civilization. We seek to achieve orderly progress in a world of peace. . . ."

Britain's new King and Queen arrived on June 10, 1939, to look upon The World of Tomorrow. They were awed by its pastel beauty, by its soft colored lighting, by the promise it held for the world, if the world could retain its sanity.

They saw, as millions of others did, great nations and small dwelling in quiet neighborliness on New York's enchanted meadow. Even Japan, Italy and Russia raised proud edifices above the marshes to show their culture and the good things they could create in times of peace.

Only one great nation had turned its back on Whalen's World of Tomorrow. Only one country famed for its technicians and craftsmen held coldly aloof from this democratically conceived utopia. Germany was significantly absent.

CHAPTER
38

T HE REASON for Germany's absence from the meadow burst upon the world on Friday, Sept. 1, 1939, when a Times extra gave its whole front page and a great part of its inside content to the staggering news:

GERMAN ARMY ATTACKS POLAND;
CITIES BOMBED, PORT BLOCKADED;
DANZIG IS ACCEPTED INTO REICH

The lead story came out of Berlin. Otto D. Tolischus who wrote it had been sending pieces for many months about Hitler's extravagant rearmament and pretty soon he was to be forbidden to re-enter Germany. This day, though, he told the world in The Times:

BERLIN, Friday, Sept. 1—Charging that Germany had been attacked, Chancellor Hitler at 5:11 o'clock this morning issued a proclamation to the army declaring that from now on force will be met with force and calling on the armed forces to "fulfill their duty to the end!"

Jerzy Szapiro, The Times man in Poland, gave the picture from Warsaw:

"War began at 5 o'clock this morning with German planes attacking Gdynia, Cracow and Katowice." He gave details of the death rain from the skies and closed with:

"While this dispatch was being telephoned the air-raid sirens sounded again in Warsaw."

In London, Birchall described the initial exodus of the sick, the aged, and women and children from Britain's major coastal cities in anticipation of air attacks:

LONDON, Friday, Sept. 2—The greatest mass movement of population at short notice in the history of Great Britain is under way. It is an evacuation under government order, of little children, invalids, women and old men from congested areas.

From London, Birmingham, Manchester, Liverpool, Edinburgh, Glasgow and twenty-three other cities the great exodus is going on as this dispatch is being written. The numbers are stupendous. More than 3,000,000 of these helpless human beings are being taken out of danger of German bombs . . .

A special Times dispatch from Danzig related how Albert Forster, Nazi Gauleiter, had seized that city in Hitler's name and had proclaimed it part of the Reich.

In Paris, Edouard Daladier had hastily summoned the Cabinet. From Moscow another correspondent wrote of Soviet ratification of a non-aggression pact with Germany, first of a bewildering series of politically advantageous flip-flops. The pact was announced by Vyacheslav M. Molotov in a speech to the Supreme Soviet.

The Times radio room had monitored a world broadcast by Hitler in which the Nazi Chancellor used the brazen-lie technique; he accused the Poles of having shunned "neighborly relations" and of having "instead, appealed to weapons." He repeated his threat that "from now on bomb will be met by bomb," though the bombs had fallen on Warsaw, not on Berlin.

The Times city room that September night was a model news mill. Hundreds of thousands of words on the German plunge into war poured in by cable, wireless and telephone from Berlin and from neighboring capitals, and the foreign desk processed them for immediate printing. Sulzberger, Adler and James, grim-faced and conscious of what lay ahead, stayed up through the last extra at dawn.

Sunday's Times carried a top line in the space above the title, a

The Flaming End of the Dirigible Hindenburg.

device but rarely used. It said: "Chamberlain Announces Britain Is At War With Germany."

The three-line head across the front page trumpeted the breaking of the storm:

BRITAIN AND FRANCE IN WAR AT 6 A.M.;
HITLER WON'T HALT ATTACK ON POLES;
CHAMBERLAIN CALLS EMPIRE TO FIGHT

The heartbroken Chamberlain in a short-wave address to the world—global broadcasts were now part of men's wars—had said in part:

"You can imagine what a bitter blow it is to me that all my long struggle to win peace has failed . . . We have a clear conscience and the situation has become intolerable . . . May God bless you all and may He defend the right, for it is the evil things we shall be fighting . . . brute force, broken promises, bad faith. But I am certain that right shall prevail."

The Times ran the full text on the front page over a Sunday morning flash from its London bureau:

"Air raid sirens sounded an alarm in London today at 11:32 A.M. [5:32 A.M. New York E.S.T.].

"The whole city was sent to shelters by the wail of the alarm, but all-clear signals were sounded seventeen minutes later."

On the left-hand side of that morning's edition a special wireless dispatch to The Times told of a Moscow warning to Paris and London that the Russians would be, as the threat was diplomatically worded, "compelled to revise our Western borders."

Germany's male Pandora had finally done it. He had released on the world such plagues and misery as it had never known.

The Times had expressed horror on Aug. 26, 1914, when the Germans, over Antwerp, first introduced aerial warfare against civilians far behind battle lines. The Nazi air force, nurtured in secret while the democracies snored, now rained death on crowded cities in a highly developed refinement of that technique.

The little Austrian corporal who had fostered the hate canker in his own heart and in his fellows' had inspired German ingenuity to frenzied manufacture of secret weapons for human annihilation.

Actually, they should not have been secret. The Times and other great newspapers—The Times more than most—had carefully printed the news of the forerunners of these devices. It had given the pattern of Opel's rockets, it had told of the steps toward stratospheric flight, of the development of new engines—all potential "secret" weapons.

The democracies had ignored them, more or less, but Hitler had made them his own. Out of them he had fashioned the material for his military lightning—for what he proudly labeled "the blitz." Suddenly he was a mortal Jove gone mad, destroying everything about him with man-made bolts.

Times headlines recorded the results:

GERMANS OCCUPY DENMARK, ATTACK OSLO;
NORWAY THEN JOINS WAR AGAINST HITLER;
CAPITAL IS REPORTED BOMBED FROM AIR

NAZIS INVADE HOLLAND, BELGIUM, LUXEMBOURG
BY LAND AND AIR; DIKES OPENED; ALLIES RUSH AID

DUTCH END RESISTANCE EXCEPT IN ZEELAND;
NAZIS TAKE SEDAN, STRIKE AT FRENCH LINE

NAZIS PIERCE FRENCH LINES ON 62-MILE FRONT;
TAKE BRUSSELS, LOUVAIN, MALINES AND NAMUR

LEOPOLD ORDERS BELGIAN ARMY TO QUIT;
ALLIES FORCED BACK IN FLANDERS POCKET

It seemed then that no nations could halt the Germans. Everything fell before them. At the end of May, 1940, they had some 335,000 French and British troops (Harold Denny of The Times was with them) with their backs to the sea at Dunkerque with seemingly no chance of rescue. Nazi bombers rained death on them from the skies and poured death into their mass from a wide semicircle of artillery. And then—the miracle.

Under Winston Churchill, Prime Minister, former First Lord

of the Admiralty, the British organized a fleet of almost 1,000 small civilian craft manned chiefly by civilians that succeeded in taking the harried legions from the Dunkerque beaches. It was a heroic achievement.

Robert L. Duffus of The Times editorial staff was deeply moved by it, as, indeed, was most of the world. "I think," he told Merz on the last day of May, 1940, "that I would like to do a piece on the evacuation of Dunkerque." Merz nodded. "I think," he said, echoing the ideas of many that day, "that might be good. It is the one bright spot in the whole dark picture." Within an hour, Duffus wrote the editorial, "Britain Saves Her Army."

"So long as the English tongue survives," it said, "the word Dunkerque will be spoken with reverence. For in that harbor, in such a hell as never blazed on earth before, at the end of a lost battle, the rags and blemishes that have hidden the soul of democracy fell away. There, beaten but unconquered, in shining splendor, she faced the enemy.

"They sent away the wounded first. Men died so that others could escape. It was not so simple a thing as courage, which the Nazis had in plenty. It was not so simple a thing as discipline, which can be hammered into men by a drill sergeant. It was not the result of careful planning, for there could have been little. It was the common man of the free countries, rising in all his glory out of mill, office, factory, mine, farm and ship, applying to war the lessons he learned when he went down the shaft to bring out trapped comrades, when he hurled the lifeboat through the surf, when he endured poverty and hard work for his children's sake.

"This shining thing in the souls of free men Hitler cannot command, or attain, or conquer. He has crushed it, where he could, from German hearts.

"It is the great tradition of democracy. It is the future. It is victory."

Raymond Daniell, Times star, who had won international reputation for courageous reporting—among other stories, the Scottsboro case in Alabama, and on the doings of the Louisiana Kingfish, Huey Long—was now in charge in London. Birchall had been sent to Ottawa because, great reporter though he was, the job now called for younger men.

On June 4, 1940, Daniell reported Winston Churchill's great fighting speech in the House of Commons. It ran in The Times next day:

LONDON, June 4—In a moving and dramatic speech to the House of Commons this afternoon Prime Minister Winston Churchill declared that even if the motherland had to fight alone against the German military machine the British fleet and empire would fight on to the bitter end until in "God's good time" the New World came to the rescue of the old . . .

Before a hushed house, some of whose own members had fallen on the field of honor, Mr. Churchill delivered these words:

"We shall go on to the end. We shall fight in France; we shall fight on the seas and oceans; we shall fight with the growing confidence of strength in the air; we shall fight on beaches; we shall fight on landing grounds; we shall fight in fields, streets and hills. We shall never surrender and even if—which I do not for a moment believe—this island or a large part of it is subjugated and starving, then our empire beyond the seas, armed and guarded by the British fleet, will carry on the struggle until in God's good time the New World, with all its power and might, steps forth to the liberation and rescue of the old."

A week later Herbert Matthews flashed from Rome the news that Mussolini had joined forces with Hitler:

ROME, Tuesday, June 11—Italy declared war on Great Britain and France yesterday afternoon, to take effect at one minute past midnight . . . It is a war, as Premier Benito Mussolini announced from his balcony at the Palazzo Venezia at 6 in the evening, against the "plutocratic and reactionary democracies of the west."

That same day The Times reported the Nazis approaching Paris. Premier Reynaud had moved southward with the armies. P. J. Philip, bureau chief, and the staff had evacuated The Times Paris office, and shifted with them. They were to keep moving with waning French officialdom as the Germans pressed onward.

In Charlottesville, Va., when President Roosevelt heard of Italy's decision, he spoke bluntly:

"The hand that held the dagger," he told a college commencement group at the University of Virginia, "has struck it into the back of its neighbor." He pledged American aid to Great Britain and France, "opponents of force."

General Adler, who had been one of the nation's leading advocates of some form of compulsory military training for the United States ever since he had attended the first Professional Men's Military Training Camps at Plattsburg in 1915, had never seriously attempted to get The Times to back the movement editorially. He had worked for it independently outside The Times, with Maj. Gen. Leonard Wood, Theodore Roosevelt Jr., Elihu Root Jr., Grenville Clark and later with President John G. Hibben of Princeton University and with President Henry Drinker of Lehigh University.

The publisher did not go along with the compulsory military service idea. He had inclined to the pacifistic side, had even frowned on filling children's playrooms with tin soldiers and other toys that might breed militaristic spirit. Now, though, events were slowly changing his attitude. He watched the German's conquest of feeble, unprepared neighbor nations in Europe, and felt that the United States should make some move toward strengthening its armed forces. When he first suggested that he thought The Times might do an editorial urging universal military training, other members of the editorial council were against it. General Adler brought the same thought up at a later conference and got the same response.

By early June German fliers were reddening Paris with incendiary bombs, softening the city for converging Nazi armor and ground troops. The publisher told the editorial board, "Gentlemen, we have got to do more than we are doing. I cannot live with myself much longer unless we do." By June 5, as the situation in Europe became increasingly dark, Merz found that he had come to accept the need for compulsory military service. He said so at a conference and the publisher said, "Why don't you put a piece into type?"

Two days later Merz's editorial appeared in The Times, leading the page. It opened on the note:

"The time has come when, in the interest of self-protection, the American people should at once adopt a national system of universal compulsory military training. We say this as a newspaper which has never before believed in the wisdom of such a policy in time of peace. We say it because the logic of events drives us remorselessly to this conclusion."

Merz piled cold logic on cold fact to prove that "we have no possible alternative but to take advantage of such time as is given us to strengthen our defenses," and urged readers to "let Congress go to the American people and let it ask them whether they are not ready to defend against all possible risks and all possible challengers the only way of life which they believe to be worth living."

No other major newspaper had come out for a peacetime draft. Several Times contemporaries, somewhat astonished, wondered if The Old Lady (some called The Times that because of its former maiden-aunt softness) was not lifting her petticoats a little too high—and said so in print. They felt that war was still remote and that there was time enough to start training the country's youth.

President Roosevelt had read part of the editorial and had told reporters at a press conference that he liked it. That in itself was astonishing. The President's attitude toward The Times was not overfriendly. It had taken a firm stand against his Supreme Court packing and had opposed him on other major issues. It had supported him in 1936 because it was then convinced that he had saved the United States from revolution, or near revolt, during the black depression, but now The Times had come out against him in favor of Wendell L. Willkie, the Republican candidate for President.

German boots crunched into Paris on June 13 a week before Congress took up a bill proposing Selective Service. Two days after that the French surrendered in Compiègne Forest, and Hitler turned toward Britain.

From Aug. 8, 1940, onward for almost five years Daniell and others on The Times London staff knew no rest. The Nazi air force raided Britain for seventy-two consecutive days after Aug. 8 and each day's raid made one or more stories, many written while bombs still fell.

Daniell did not know the British temperament when he took over as London bureau chief. He told friends later it was like playing a part in a Noel Coward stage production.

Working with him were Robert P. Post of an old New York family, James (Scotty) Reston, Walter Leysmith, a Briton, Miss Tania Long, later to become Mrs. Daniell. From time to time, men were sent from New York or were picked up in the field—David Anderson, Drew Middleton, Hal Denny, James (Jamie) MacDonald, a lovable Scot who had been a reporter and rewrite man for The Times in New York. A loyal staff of Britons stuck through the long period of travail.

London time is five hours ahead of New York time, so the staff usually stayed up through dawn banging out copy while bombs shook the city and plaster rained on them. Most of them slept through the afternoons, raids or no raids, and were out again when fresh fires from Nazi incendiaries reddened the London night skies.

They were bombed out of their homes so many times that it became routine for them, as it had for all of London's populace. By Aug. 13, 1940, it was plain that Hitler meant to reduce Britain to powdered debris. The Times that morning carried a story from Bob Post headed:

NAZIS INTENSIFY AIR RAIDS ON BRITAIN
AS 500 PLANES POUND AT STRONGHOLDS;
BLITZKRIEG ON, LONDON PRESS WARNS

Next day the Germans sent 1,000 planes over. Leysmith's story told how they ranged from the south coast to Scotland, smashing homes and lives while British Spitfires and Hurricanes, outrageously outnumbered, tried to cut through them. Every day C. Brooks Peters, Times man in Berlin, serving under Guido Enderis, bureau head, gave the German version of the attack.

On Aug. 17 Scotty Reston took over the raid story. That morning The Times carried the headline:

LONDON AREA BOMBED IN RUSH HOUR, MANY DEAD;
NAZIS SEE WORSE TO COME, CLAIM AIR CONTROL;
BRITISH AIR FLEETS ATTACK 13 ENEMY CENTERS

Brooks Peters reported from Berlin that the Germans were exultant and that officials let it be known that "what has gone heretofore has been but child's play, and real pressure is about to be felt for the first time by the British."

Every night in the London office Times men worked on what were scheduled as "inraids" and "outraids"; the "inraids" were the Germans over Great Britain, the "outraids" were the R.A.F.'s answer. They struck at Berlin, at manufacturing centers, and at the French Coast, to stave off possible Nazi invasion by sea.

On Sept. 4 The Times carried a significant headline:

ROOSEVELT TRADES DESTROYERS FOR SEA BASES; TELLS CONGRESS HE ACTED ON OWN AUTHORITY; BRITAIN PLEDGES NEVER TO YIELD OR SINK FLEET

The story out of Washington gave details of the trade. Britain had yielded eight strategic island and continental bases to the United States in return for the destroyers, extending the United States defense line from Newfoundland to British Guiana, giving America control of possible enemy approaches to her own soil.

From London that day Daniell told of Britain's jubilation over the trade, and over Roosevelt's promise of "all aid short of war," and Scotty Reston, on the "inraids" began his story almost with a yawn:

LONDON, Wednesday, Sept. 4—German bombers started ringing that big London doorbell early yesterday morning. They rang it again in the afternoon while Prime Minister Churchill and his Ministers were commemorating the first anniversary of the war, and they kept ringing it right up until midnight.

When the staff members had finished their stories, they wandered the darkened London streets, watched panting fire wardens putting out incendiary-bomb fires, got accustomed to strolling through areas half hidden in acrid smoke and drifting flake ash. Jamie MacDonald would stand at the office windows with flame reflected in his kindly freckled face. He would mutter, "Bang, you bastards," as bombs fell and ack-ack shook the panes, or, "Get home, you Nazi swine."

Tania Long, a young and pretty newspaperwoman who had worked for The Herald Tribune in Berlin, was a kind of mother to the London staff. When men left on a harrowing job or just got back from one, she would bestow a light maternal kiss. She served them tea or stronger refreshment as they battered away at their typewriters all through the night and through the dawn behind the office blackout curtains, getting the news to sleeping, faraway, Times Square.

Tania was out with several of the staff during a raid one night, having dinner in a little restaurant that would have been solemn and quiet except for the bombs' roar. A nearby hit shook the restaurant and dropped ceiling plaster in her soup. Miss Long gently touched the waiter's arm as the dust sifted ghostlike across the room.

"Please," she told him, "no more croutons."

That was what Ray Daniell had meant; you lived with the Britons in this period of ever-impending death and unconsciously you adopted their attitude toward it. You felt like a character in something done by Noel Coward.

On Sept. 7, 1940, Daniell returned to his quarters at Lincoln's Inn to find them shattered, and all his furniture and his bedding covered with rubble and siftings. He shrugged, swept the debris from the bed covering and crawled between the sheets to sleep, after one swig of Scotch. The blast had mercifully spared his bottle.

Daniell and all the staff moved to the Savoy Hotel after this, discouraged at losing one dwelling after another (the Leysmiths had been partly buried in the rubble of their own home in East Sheen which had been his temporary office). The bureau operated in the Savoy, too.

Another time, David Anderson, who had reported to the London bureau after a journey across the Atlantic on one of the fifty destroyers the United States had traded for bases, was mildly grousing about his first late hitch when at 2 A.M. the Savoy shook and shuddered under the impact of an aerial bomb.

Daniell got up when hotel officials came to ask where Anderson and Jamie MacDonald were. Their fifth floor rooms had been all but torn to bits by the hit. When Daniell led Anderson to the chamber the newest bureau recruit paled. He returned to his typewriter. Just before he took up where he'd left off he turned to Daniell. He said, "Next time I crab about a late assignment, boss, you just give me a swift kick in the pants."

MacDonald, off for the night, stayed out until dawn lifting the wee cup with R.A.F. pilots. He had formed warm friendships with them, and they loved him, as did anyone who had ever worked with him.

MacDonald stared through convivial haze at the ruin that had been his sleeping chamber, then gravely shook the plaster and glass from the coverlet, crawled into bed and fell fast asleep. The door had been blown off its hinges, but he never noticed that.

When the morning shift of waiters came by and saw the Scot deep in slumber amid the plaster and glass they marveled.

"You were quite fortunate, sir," they told him, with awe.

They thought he had slept through the bombing.

On Nov. 16 The Times carried a vivid description by Daniell of the raid on Coventry.

That same night, President Roosevelt, who had been re-elected for a third term, made a historic address. Turner Catledge sent the story from Washington and The Times carried full text. The headline said:

ROOSEVELT CALLS FOR GREATER AID TO BRITAIN AS BEST WAY TO HALT DICTATORS AND AVERT WAR

It was the famous speech proposing that the United States become "the arsenal of democracy" in which the President said: "Our present efforts are not enough. We must send more ships, more guns, more planes—more of everything."

On the following night Senator Burton K. Wheeler of Montana, chief spokesman for isolation advocates, suggested in a radio address that restoration of her pre-1914 boundaries and her former colonies be offered Germany in return for release of the nations she had just overrun. The isolationist group still maintained there was a path to peace without United States entry into war.

The Times continued to support the President in his drive for aid to the nations opposed to the Axis but it urged in an editorial on Nov. 10, 1940, that he recognize in the huge minority vote polled by Willkie a sign of "healthy opposition to some of the methods and some of the objectives of the Administration."

As the year closed both Britain and Germany were stepping up their attacks. In the United States the armed forces had been strengthened, National Guardsmen were in training the length and breadth of the land and more than 16,000,000 men had registered for selective service.

Germany, though, seemed to be winning the battle of the Atlantic and her aerial and ground forces were successful almost everywhere except in Africa.

Grover Whalen's World of Tomorrow, meanwhile, had suffered the fate that had overtaken Europe. As one by one the victim nations darkened, so did the buildings on Flushing Meadow that represented them and their good works. Czechoslovakia, Poland, Holland, Belgium, Denmark, Norway, France—their lights went out, and little by little over the meadow in New York's geographical center the same brooding and melancholy spread.

In 1941 as throughout the war Times coverage of a world in torment was unequalled. Sulzberger spent unstintingly to get the news and sacrificed revenue-producing advertising space to make place for it, as Ochs had done in the first World War.

On March 27, 1941, The Times beat the world on a Yugoslav Air Corps coup that unseated the pro-Axis regime there. The story came from Ray Brock in Belgrade. He had telephoned his eyewitness account to Daniel Brigham in Berne, who in turn had relayed it by radiophone to New York.

At 1 o'clock that morning Brock heard heavy tanks and antiaircraft guns rumbling through Belgrade's streets. He got out and followed their course, moving between and around them as they blocked routes leading to the palace on Kralja Milana, the main thoroughfare.

An hour later he saw men of Air Force patrols hammering at the doors of homes where pro-Axis Cabinet Ministers lived, heard them politely but curtly order the ministers to dress, and saw the ministers moved off under armed guard. The story was packed with dramatic interest:

"Premier Dragisha Cvetkovich [pro-Axis headman in Yugoslavia] was aroused and a patrol of 'King's Men' rushed past the guards of the Premier's spacious hilltop home and knocked on the door. Another guard barred the way. Witnesses' reports said the guard declared:

" 'The President cannot be disturbed.'

" 'Nevertheless, disturb him,' commanded the officer.

" 'He must not be disturbed, and you cannot enter,' replied the guard.

" 'Stand aside!' " commanded the officer, whereupon the guard raised his rifle. The officer drew his pistol and pointed it at the guard's chest, and repeated, 'Stand aside!'

"The guard stood aside."

Between them that morning Brock and Brigham sent 17,000 words of color and exciting incident to The Times in New York by wireless telephone.

The Times headline on the story said:

ARMY OVERTHROWS PRO-AXIS YUGOSLAV REGIME;
  PETER IN POWER, PAUL SEIZED, 1,200,000 IN ARMS;
  NAZIS ASK EXPLANATION; U.S., BRITAIN, PLEDGE AID

It did not matter that the victory was short-lived, and that on April 6, 1941, the Germans invaded Yugoslavia and Greece. Brock got that story out, too, just before the Germans cut off the telephone exchange, and again Brigham at Berne relayed the account to New York. This was story-book journalism, and editors all over the country applauded The Times for it.

Memory of the war is only too bitterly fresh, now, in human minds, and this volume does not attempt to trace in detail how the conflict spread and how The Times scattered its men all over the globe to report it, but Sulzberger and James dispatched fresh men to new fronts as fast as those fronts developed. The correspondents moved with the Allied armed forces everywhere, on land and sea and in the sky, while others carefully watched world capitals for important breaks on diplomatic fronts.

They were at all major meetings of the heads of the United Nations, with orders to send freely of all important official action and text on official documents. Together with wordage from local and national correspondents and from men in the few far-off places where war had not yet touched, they deluged the copy desks. Their daily output, together with copy chattering in from nineteen news agencies and from wireless pick-ups of foreign government emissions, averaged more than 1,000,000 words a night, exclusive of tabular matter. The Times published more war news than any other newspaper on earth. Its editors managed to cram around 125,000 words into each day's paper not counting from ten to twelve columns of tables on the financial, business, radio and sports pages. The Sunday paper, not counting tables, averaged around 240,000 words, or 10,000 more than were used in the 900-page best-seller "Gone With The Wind."

Just after midnight, on Sunday morning, June 22, 1941, American short-wave radio stations picked up a statement brought to German microphones in Berlin by Propaganda Minister Joseph Goebbels in Hitler's name. Der Fuehrer had decided to move against Russia.

Times rewrite men hammered out a local lead for this astonishing turn of events in a world already mad, and made the late city editions with it. Readers awoke that Sabbath morning to find on their doorsteps the headline:

HITLER DECLARES WAR, MOVING ON RUSSIA;
ARMIES STAND FROM ARCTIC TO BLACK SEA;
DAMASCUS FALLS; U.S. OUSTS ROME CONSULS

Under it was the full text of the Reichsfuehrer's statement to the world.

"Germany," said the lead story, "last night declared war on Soviet Russia, according to an official Berlin radio broadcast heard by short-wave listening stations . . .

"The announcement was made in a statement by Adolf Hitler, read over the air by Propaganda Minister Joseph Goebbels. Hitler, viciously attacking the regime of his former associate in European diplomacy, Joseph Stalin, charged that the Soviet Union was acting in concert with the United States and Britain to 'throttle' the Reich."

After the Germans had moved on Russia The Times continued to get German versions of the fighting from its still-functioning Berlin bureau. Ralph Parker, an Englishman, sent the Russian version through Moscow. The Times, incidentally, never abandoned its policy of presenting all sides of a story when they were available. It printed all the war communiqués, both Allied and Axis, right through the war even when they conflicted outrageously, as they often did, and let the reader judge for himself which was true.

The news still ran black. The Russians stubbornly met the Nazis' northward blitz with a scorched-earth policy that made grim and gripping copy. They were giving ground in the Ukraine before combined Axis armies when President Roosevelt and Prime Minister Churchill, in mid-August, 1941, met aboard H. M. S. Prince of Wales and drafted the Atlantic Charter. The story was headlined on Aug. 15 thus:

ROOSEVELT, CHURCHILL DRAFT 8 PEACE AIMS,
PLEDGING DESTRUCTION OF NAZI TYRANNY;
JOINT STEPS BELIEVED CHARTED AT PARLEY

In September of that year the seemingly unstoppable Germans entered burning Kiev and Hitler announced, not too accurately, that "Russia is broken."

America keyed to unprecedented production. Nazi submarine attacks on American destroyers in the Atlantic brought from the President the pledge that the United States would do all in its power to "crush Hitler and his Nazi forces." History unreeled at frightening speed and even The Times with unequalled journalistic resources strained mightily to keep up with it.

By 1941 Hal Denny of The Times had seen as many wars, probably, as any living newspaperman. The Iowan had fought as a Rainbow Division sergeant in the first World War and between 1926 and 1939 had covered six foreign wars for The Times—in Morocco, in Nicaragua, in Cuba, in Ethiopia, in the Russo-Finnish fighting of 1939, and in France with the British Expeditionary Force to report the Dunkerque disaster.

In the winter of 1941 he was with the British Eighth Army covering the desert fighting around Tobruk in Libya. He moved across the desert with the Britons as they went out in American-made tanks to engage Field Marshal Erwin Rommel's Afrika Corps. His dispatches from the desert were magnificent.

Denny was 52 years old then, but his restlessness had not diminished. Something in his make-up urged him into battle smoke, but another instinct kept his copy objective and beautifully restrained. Whoop-and-holler correspondence pained him.

"It is not among the duties of the war correspondent of a serious newspaper or news-gathering agency," he wrote once, "to show how brave he is. My own feeling has been that a correspondent should not take risks for the sake of adventure, that he should go into concrete danger only if it is necessary to the procurement of worth-while news and if there is a good gambler's chance that he will get through . . . My own motto has always been, 'A dead correspondent sends no dispatches.'"

Denny sat under the desert sky at night, during halts, chatting with British officers and with British correspondents. Like Matthews, he found in camp life a kind of quiet brotherhood that men somehow held back in times of peace.

On the morning of Nov. 22, forty-five German Stukas dived on the British tank column and strafed it. Denny, along with the others, flung himself flat as machine-gun bullets sprayed and showered them with desert sand. A slug tore through Denny's trouser leg but did not hurt him. The German pilot who fired it struck the sand himself a moment later and his plane exploded.

The column moved on toward Tobruk.

Next morning, Rommel's tanks struck at dawn. The battle raged all day in the burning desert sun. Suddenly, as the fighting seesawed, with Denny and the other correspondents taking notes under machine-gun and cannon fire, the newspapermen found themselves trapped between the opposing lines.

Rommel all but destroyed the British column after fierce fighting. When the day ended, Denny and several British writers were in German hands.

A week passed before The Times heard of his capture, and it was not until June, 1942, after he had been repatriated, that he was able to tell the full story of his experiences.

"When something occurs as drastic as capture in battle," he wrote, "one cannot grasp it at first. It is one of those things that can happen to other persons, but never to oneself.

"We correspondents had all accepted the possibility of being killed or wounded, though the mathematical chance of being hit was small. But we had hardly thought of being captured."

Edward Ward, a B. B. C. correspondent, murmured to Denny as they trotted, arms up, ahead of their captors in the yielding sand: "I don't believe it. These things just don't happen. This is a dream."

It was no dream. Nazi soldiers with tommy guns barked at them as they were herded through the dusk. Six fresh British tanks roared down on the Germans, but they were blown to scrap metal and Denny and the other prisoners were hurried on again. They dropped, exhausted, hours later, to sleep in a huddle under the star-powdered sky. It was cold, and they wore desert shorts.

Rommel himself came to look over the prisoners next morning and to snap pictures of them. He was a camera addict. Suddenly he turned on the guards.

"Why are you wasting your time gaping at this little lot of English?" he roared. "These are only a sample of what we will get. Go on! Get about your business. Get all the schweinehunde. Alle! Alle!"

Denny and his fellow prisoners spent that night in a barbed-wire enclosure on the desert west of Tobruk. Italian soldiers took up the guard there.

"As we reached the pen in the darkness," Denny wrote later, "we were searched by Italian soldiers. One soldier took my pocketknife, watch, fountain pen and a cigarette lighter given me by my wife. I got mad at that and snatched back at them, getting the pen and the lighter before two other Italians prodded me with bayonets through the opening in the pen."

Italian troops herded the prisoners along the Libyan coast to Bengazi. British fliers bombed the convoy and killed two British soldiers. In Bengazi the prisoners were under British bombs again.

"It was full moonlight," Denny related, "and nightly British bombers raided. These were the most enjoyable air raids I have ever experienced. Only a few weeks before I had ridden over the city in a raiding British bomber and had sat at the apex of a cone of searchlights and anti-aircraft fire.

"It was fun to see this same anti-aircraft defense from the ground as we peeked through the door from time to time against the protests of the Italian sentries. As the bombs burst with shattering roars the British cheered."

Three days later Denny was aboard an Italian light cruiser for transportation to Brindisi, Italy, by way of Crete. Part of the journey was on an Italian luxury liner where the food was good and the treatment kindly.

Denny was eventually taken to the Calvary Barracks in Rome. There he heard that the Japanese had smashed most of the United States fleet at Pearl Harbor on Dec. 7. On Dec. 11 his Italian captors told him he could not hope for release. Italy and Germany were at war with the United States.

A week later the Gestapo came to take Denny across the Alps to Berlin. Berliners stared at him as he walked, in his correspondent's uniform, between the men of the Gestapo. He was the first United States prisoner of war brought into Germany. He was put in a cell in Gestapo Headquarters in the Prinz Albrechtstrasse.

"I wish," he wrote after his release the following May, "that I could tell a story of mistreatment and torture by the Gestapo, such as we know many other prisoners have suffered . . . but in honesty I cannot tell any such story of myself. I was placed under strict prison discipline, but it was intelligent discipline. I was never manhandled or abused, nor was I subjected to any indignities."

Before Denny was taken out of Italy into Germany, other Times men became Axis prisoners. Germany and Italy declared war on the United States on Dec. 11, 1941, and the American correspondents in Rome and in Berlin were immediately jailed.

Matthews knew what was coming that afternoon when he stood in the great Palazzo Venezia and heard Mussolini thunder from his balcony to a crowd of some 150,000: "The powers of the steel pact, Fascist Italy and National Socialist Germany, ever closely linked, participate from today on the side of heroic Japan against the United States of America."

Soon afterward Government police were at The Times Rome office. They were courteous. They took Matthews, whom they had once rewarded with a medal for heroism in Ethiopia, to the ancient Colli Euganei, and jailed Camille M. Cianfarra, his assistant, with him.

In Berlin Paul Schmidt, German Foreign Office press chief, summoned the American correspondents and told them, "It has become my duty to order you all to proceed to your homes immediately and to remain there."

In May, 1942, all these Times men, except Guido Enderis who was Swiss, and George Axelsson who was Swedish, were returned to the United States on the Drottningholm. Matthews and Cianfarra had been detained in Siena most of the time, and Denny had been sent from Berlin to Poppi in Italy. None had been hurt or abused. They met on the repatriation ship.

The Times was not shut off from news out of Italy and Germany. Brigham, stationed in Berne, got important stories from Swiss newspapers and from Axis radio broadcasts. Both German and Italian publications were to be freely had in Berne, too, and he watched them.

One other Times correspondent was less fortunate than the men held in Rome and in Berlin. Otto D. Tolischus, who had not been readmitted to Berlin after his stories on the Nazi invasion in Poland, had left Scandinavia when the Germans invaded there later and had been assigned to Tokyo.

His stories had been fearless. He had shown pretty much the course that Japan seemed to be following. Actually, his analyses of the growing tenseness between the United States and Japan as he sensed it in Tokyo were so perfect that they were to bring him pain and misery.

On Dec. 8, after the attack on Pearl Harbor, four Japanese policemen called at Tolischus' home and read him a paragraph from their National Defense Act. Tolischus, blunt and courageous, had anticipated the visit but brusquely asked how it applied to him.

"You sent political, diplomatic and economic information to foreign agents harmful to Japan," one of the Japanese said tensely. "That means penal servitude up to ten years."

Tolischus, never a word-mincer, showed his scorn of the charge.

"That's utter nonsense," he said. "I am here as a foreign correspondent with the full knowledge and approval of the Japanese Government, and everything I sent was censored."

There was further exchange, but the policemen made Tolischus pack. They took him to Tokyo Detention Prison. They fed him scantily, mostly bread, fruit and Japanese prison soup and kept breaking in upon him, in teams, for endless cross-examination. They wanted a "confession" and it did not seem to matter what it was.

They made Tolischus, a heavy man, sit back on his heels, native fashion, while they took him repeatedly over old ground and the burden of their accusations was "You have written bad things about

Japan." His interrogator straddled a chair and placed two of its legs upon Tolischus' knees while this was going on. They had taken his office files, and quoted from them endlessly, especially from his dispatches, in an attempt to force him to concede that he had engaged in espionage and that his intent was to present their country in an evil light.

"All correspondents are spies. You must sign a statement that you spied."

All through the winter months they harried Tolischus. His weight fell away. He was naturally tidy, but they withheld his toilet equipment, and he gradually fell into distasteful shabbiness. They knew that making him sit native fashion was torture, but they kept him at it for hours at a time.

To break the deadlock Tolischus finally signed a perfunctory statement. It cast no guilt on him; it was mere form to help his inquisitors save official face. It was all technical, a sop to the Japanese fondness for the formal.

At last on May 1, 1942, Tolischus, bearded and haggard, came before a rather kindly Japanese magistrate and was sentenced to one and a half years' penal servitude. This was technical, too; sentence was suspended.

On Aug. 25, 1942, the repatriation ship brought Tolischus back with other exchanged prisoners. He recalled later how they stood on dawn-washed decks that morning when they sighted the Statue of Liberty and how the tears rolled as spontaneously they broke into fervent chorus. They sang "The Star-Spangled Banner."

Sunday afternoon, Dec. 7, 1941, had been a rather mild winter Sabbath, especially along the Eastern Seaboard. Americans went quietly to church, returned for hearty dinners. Nowhere in the world, at this stage, were people so well fed or so comfortably housed. The depression had eased off. Men who had wandered in hopeless quest for work in the gloom after 1929, were, happily, mostly restored.

The Times city room was characteristically quiet that day. European and African war copy was piling up in the ticker rooms, but the machines' clatter was sealed off and the noise did not invade the city room. Walter Fenton, at the city desk, had handed the sermons to Joe Shaplen to be assembled for Monday morning's paper, and had sent some of his Sabbath-thin staff on sundry news quests. A few men on emergency schedule sat at their desks.

Suddenly the radio room operator sat upright. Boys on the news agency tickers tore off bulletins and rushed out with them. The Washington wire burst into excitable chattering.

The Japanese had struck.

There was no hysteria in The Times city room; there never is. The typical Hollywood version of what happens in a newspaper office when great stories break is sheer exaggeration, and The Times city room rarely gives outward sign of emotional reaction, even to staggering calamity. It is too smoothly geared for that.

Quick phone calls brought James, Merz and other Times executives to the office from their homes. The switchboard clogged with subscriber pleas for more details of the attack. Reporters off duty either came to the office or telephoned to offer their services. Sulzberger, in Pinehurst, N. C., when he heard the news, caught a plane in Raleigh and helped get out the first edition. He slept at The Times that night.

There was no office shrillness in putting out the attack edition. No observer standing in the great city room would have known that there was anything extraordinary about this Sunday afternoon.

Fenton on the city desk quietly worked out an emergency schedule. Foster Hailey of the city staff was assigned to get a story on F. B. I and Navy Intelligence activities, but an hour later his name was penciled out and another man took over the chore. Hailey went out of the building as if he were just going for a quick coffee across the street. Actually he was on his way to join the Pacific Fleet—or what was left of it.

On the way to the railroad station Hailey called in to give the office a few details of street-crowd reaction to the Pearl Harbor news, but Fenton already had men on the sidewalks all over the five boroughs getting public-reaction copy and pictures.

The work schedule had only a few items on it when the attack bulletins crashed through. Hailey had covered a Notre Dame communion breakfast, Murray Illson had attended a Newman Club meeting, Milton Bracker had been assigned to Harlem crime, Sidney Shalett and Jerry Smith to a murder, Abe Raskin to a coal conference, Al Gordon to a piece on Sunday beer, Walter Ruch to a C.I.O. convention.

Before the night staff came to work sixty assignments had been added, most of them on the war. Frank S. Adams had done a sketch on General MacArthur, Shalett had written histories of the bombed ships, Hanson W. Baldwin had turned in pieces on Manila and Pearl Harbor; the Wall Street man had a story on Japanese finance, Murray Schumach had done a shipping round-up, Bracker had covered the Japanese consulate, Hilton Railey had written a story on canceled Army leaves and recruiting, Manny Perlmutter had covered the Navy Yard in Brooklyn, George Mooney had covered Camp Upton, Gordon had gone to the Japanese newspapers, Rudy Stewart had done a radio war-news round-up, Smith had worked on police emergency precautions, Paul Crowell had covered Mayor LaGuardia's broadcast to the city.

The schedule had been expanded to cover bombardment protection, airport activities, Army and Navy mobilization, activity and reaction at Army camps.

The Washington bureau, meanwhile, had become a news mill grinding out copy at top speed, though ordinarily Washington Sundays were quiet. Frank Kluckhohn wrote the lead. C. F. Trussell did a front-page piece on President Roosevelt's plans. Bertram Hulen covered an interview at which Secretary of State Hull denounced the Japanese attack and gave out a full summary of the Government's attempts to work out a non-aggression pact with Japan. He also released the Japanese answer that he had just received that day from Admiral Kichisaburo Nomura, the Japanese Ambassador, and Saburo Kurusu, special envoy. It was insulting, and Hull, incensed, had just about terminated negotiations when the bombs rained on Pearl Harbor.

The foreign desk, under James' supervision, ordered European reaction stories, and within a few hours the copy was pouring in by cable, wireless and telephone from Berlin, Rome, London, Ottawa, Mexico City and other important capitals. South American correspondents had similar stories on the wire, and the telegraph, or national, desk was flooded with wire pictures and with story material from coast to coast.

The Times on Monday morning, Dec. 8, gave a clear picture in stories, maps, photographs and in the full text of the United States-Japanese negotiations, of what had happened the day before.

JAPAN WARS ON U.S. AND BRITAIN; MAKES SUDDEN ATTACK ON HAWAII; HEAVY FIGHTING AT SEA REPORTED

CONGRESS DECIDED

ROOSEVELT WILL ADDRESS IT TODAY AND FIND IT READY TO VOTE WAR

CONFERENCE IS HELD

LEGISLATIVE LEADERS AND CABINET IN SOBER WHITE HOUSE TALK

HULL DENOUNCES TOKYO 'INFAMY'

BRANDS JAPAN 'FRAUDULENT' IN PREPARING ATTACK WHILE CARRYING ON PARLEYS

JAPANESE FORCE LANDS IN MALAYA

FIRST ATTEMPT IS REPULSED— SINGAPORE IS BOMBED AND THAILAND INVADED

TOKYO BOMBERS STRIKE HARD AT OUR MAIN BASES ON OAHU

An Associated Press dispatch from Tokyo disclosed that Ambassador Grew did not get Japan's reply to Secretary Hull's note of Nov. 26 until after the bombs had been dropped.

The leading story summarized the situation:

WASHINGTON, Monday, Dec. 8—Sudden and unexpected attack on Pearl Harbor, Honolulu, and other United States possessions in the Pacific early yesterday by the Japanese air force and navy plunged the United States and Japan into active war.

The initial attack in Hawaii, apparently launched by torpedo-carrying bombers and submarines, caused widespread damage and death. It was quickly followed by others. There were unconfirmed reports that German raiders participated in the attacks.

Guam also was assaulted from the air, as were Davao on the Island of Mindanao and Camp John Hay in Northern Luzon, both in the Philippines. Lieut. Gen. Douglas MacArthur, commanding the United States Army of the Far East, reported there was little damage, however.

The story was two columns wide on the front page and ran over for considerable space inside, with large photographs of American installations that had come under Japanese bombs.

In Billings, Mont., Senator Wheeler, who had been assailing The Times as "interventionist," declared for immediate war on Japan. He grimly told an interviewer, "The only thing to do now is to lick the hell out of them."

Other members of the so-called "isolationist bloc," including Senator Nye and John Flynn of the America First group, held out for a day awaiting more detailed reports before commenting, but on Tuesday Arthur Krock wrote:

"The circumstances of the Japanese attack on Pearl Harbor were such that national unity was an instantaneous consequence. You could almost hear it click into place in Washington today."

There was no questioning the truth of this observation. Recruiting stations all over the country were overrun with volunteers. Interventionists and non-interventionists closed ranks. Political differences were cast aside.

The nation was united. It had to be. Tuesday's Times carried the first casualty list of World War II.

On Dec. 8, the city desk began to run two daily schedules, instead of one. One was captioned "War Schedule" and the other was for routine local assignments, which fell to a bare minimum. Every conceivable local war angle was covered.

On Dec. 9, there was a separate "Air Raid" Schedule. Rumors that enemy planes had been spotted approaching the East Coast begot public jitters. The rumors turned out after a brief period of local excitement to have been entirely false, as London's first air-raid alert had been.

The schedule, though, indicated how well prepared The Times was to handle any major wartime disaster. Five reporters were assigned to air fields and one man in the office was prepared to handle their calls. One man was detailed to the flight interceptor command and to civilian defense headquarters; one to the Navy yard, two to metropolitan area coast artillery and anti-aircraft stations; two to the police and fire departments; one to Wall Street and the Stock Exchange; three to cover the city schools, several to city hospitals, one to cover the Mayor's office and the local Disaster Control Board. All suburban correspondents along the coast were alerted and the radio editor was in constant touch with radio stations to describe the alarm-spreading system.

This was only the beginning. The city came to know the black-out, the dimout and the brownout. The Times' moving electric bulletin went dark, as did all of Times Square. The Times carried descriptive stories of all public drills and gave ample space to messages to the public on how to co-operate in event of air attack.

Manhattan's streets filled with G.I.'s and gobs. The Square was packed every night with boys, men and women wearing the uniforms of all the countries warring against the Axis. Broadway and Forty-second Street now was literally a dim-lit crossroads of the world.

By Jan. 26 the first American Expeditionary Force of World War II had landed in Ireland and Jamie MacDonald had flown from London to meet it. His story of the landing ran on page one with a four-column cablephoto under the caption: "At a Port in Northern Ireland: Again an A.E.F. Lands."

The whole world was aflame. The little flickerings that Anne O'Hare McCormick had spotted in Italy more than twenty years before and that Times men had reported from Germany, Ethiopia and Spain had spread clear around the globe, even to the polar regions.

The Pacific war presented new assignment problems. The Times had H. Ford Wilkins, its regular Philippines man, in Manila, F. Tillman Durdin in Singapore, and Hailey, out of main office, with the Pacific fleet, but these were not enough. On Feb. 9, 1942, Byron Darnton of the city staff was sent to join General MacArthur in Australia. In this hour gloom was thick as melted pitch. The Japanese were unchecked and the Germans and Italians still were triumphant in Europe and in Africa. At only one spot on the globe had the Axis forces been stopped. In Russia winter had iced them in.

Barney Darnton—he was never "Byron" either at home or in the office—was a genial and unusually competent newspaperman, as good on a desk as on the street, and with a genius for organization. He was from Adrian, Michigan. Most Times newsmen, incidentally, were non-New Yorkers—a good 85 per cent, at least. Darnton had done the preliminary work for The News of the Week in Review, and had helped set the writing pattern for it. He had also shaped the form for The Times' news broadcasts that first went out over radio station WMCA on Dec. 1, 1941, and, after July 1, 1946, over The Times' own station, WQXR, which Sulzberger had bought.

Darnton was 45 years old. He had two sons, Bob and John, and a cozy home in Westport, Conn., but after Pearl Harbor he had been restless, and eager for a war assignment. He felt strongly that the world's freedoms were at stake, and he believed fervently in the freedoms.

His copy out of the Pacific was what everyone expected—fresh, lively, filled with human interest. He wrote home almost every night and the letters were humorous, but nostalgic, too. One June morning in Australia, for example, he wrote to his wife, Eleanor:

"This morning, before the sun came over the hill, I stood in front of our headquarters, toothbrush in hand, and was amazed by what God had done . . . You would not like the birds, I'm sure of that. They shout insults at you . . . particularly when you are writing a piece. They perch in a tree above you and emit such things as, 'That's lousy; throw it away,' or, 'Wasting cable tolls. Wasting cable tolls' . . . You would not like the separation from home, and from you. You would be enthralled by what goes on in the sky now and again, and by the kids who do it. A high school loose in whining motors."

He started another letter on Oct. 15, 1942, from New Guinea. He said in it: "The correspondents have a jeep. We shall have a jeep when all this is over and I shall use it for getting to and from the station . . . Now it's Oct. 16, there having been an interruption . . . We near November and that'll be one for Johnnie. [Johnnie was born shortly before Darnton left.] It's going to be pretty nice under that apple tree with that Tom Collins . . . Good night, my dearest."

It was his last good night, across some 14,000 miles. The morning of Oct. 18 he left a jumping-off place in Wanigela in New Guinea, with fifty G.I.'s aboard an old Australian ferryboat, the King John, for the invasion of Buna. Lieut. Bruce Fahnestock was at the wheel. They shoved off at dawn. Tropical birds and monkeys woke the jungles with raucous outcry as the boat moved over rose-tinted waters to combat with the Japanese. It was to be an important story and Darnton wanted to be in on the beginning of it.

He took notes as they glided onward:

"6:30 A.M. Sighted planes. Think they're ours.

"8 A.M. Planes returned. Ours, or one of theirs?"

He had reason for the question mark. The plane circled and came in for a bombing run. It dropped two bombs some 400 to 500 yards from the old King John. That was strange; it looked like an American B-25.

A bomb fragment caught Lieutenant Fahnestock in the back, as he stood behind the machine gun at the King John's prow. He slumped to the deck. The G.I.'s had hit the deck, too, behind the battered wheelhouse, as fragments screamed and whined viciously overhead, or thudded into the boat's ancient planking.

Barney Darnton grabbed the wheel forward of the deck house. He zig-zagged the boat in an attempt to escape the bomber when it came in again, but this time another anti-personnel bomb hit the water just behind the King John. A fragment caught Barney back of the neck, just below the helmet. He fell away from the wheel.

It turned out, bitterly enough, that one of Barney's beloved "high school kids" had made a grievous error; he had mistaken the King John for a Japanese craft because it was so far forward of any previous American position on New Guinea.

The Times got a United Press dispatch on Oct. 21 from MacArthur's Headquarters. It said:

AT UNITED NATIONS HEADQUARTERS, Australia, Wednesday, Oct. 21—Byron Darnton of The New York Times was killed accidentally Sunday in an advanced operational area in New Guinea, it was announced today.

It ran in The Times beside Barney's obit, written by Frank Adams, and beside Barney's last story, which said:

SOMEWHERE IN NEW GUINEA, Oct. 7, Delayed—From the hill near the airdrome a man can see his countrymen building with blood, sweat and toil the firm resolution that their sons shall not die under bombs, but shall have peace, because they will know how to preserve peace—"

General MacArthur sent a message that was run as a news story:

SOMEWHERE IN AUSTRALIA, Wednesday, Oct. 21—It is my painful duty to inform you of the accidental death in New Guinea of Byron Darnton.

He served with gallantry and devotion at the front and fulfilled the important duties of war correspondent with distinction to himself and to The New York Times, and with value to his country.

I had but recently conferred with him at Port Moresby and had been gratified by his comprehensive grasp of the battle situation. I deeply regret his death. Please inform his family and convey to them my sincerest sympathy.

The Sulzbergers drove to the Darntons' cottage in Westport and talked quietly with Mrs. Darnton of Barney and of the love all men at The Times had had for him. Mrs. Darnton had been a newspaperwoman, and would be again. She was dry-eyed throughout their visit.

On Feb. 26, 1943, Bob Post of the London bureau flew out of an Eighth Air Force Base in Britain on a bombing mission over the heavily protected German city of Wilhelmshaven. The Air Force commander, a colonel, had tried in vain to talk him out of the flight.

Post was 32 years old. He had gone to Groton and to Harvard where his father, Kitty Post, poet and author, and his brother had gone before him. He had worked as messenger in the Washington bureau under Arthur Krock.

While he was junior man in the bureau he came to be something of a legend as the result of a White House interview a few years before the war. Word had got around then that President Roosevelt might try for a third term. Other correspondents had edged around the question, from time to time, and the President had always been able to fence them off.

Young Post, a fellow alumnus of the President—their families were friends—finally felt the time had come for someone to put the question more directly.

"Mr. President," he asked bluntly, "will you accept nomination for a third term?"

A hush fell on the room. The President's face reddened.

"Bob," he said shortly, "go over in the corner and put on your dunce cap."

Ray Daniell wrote of Bob Post's Wilhelmshaven flight for The Times on Feb. 28:

"Robert P. Post, member of the New York Times London bureau, accompanied the United States Air Force yesterday over Wilhelmshaven. He did not come back."

A month before Post flew to his death, Jamie MacDonald had gone on the first major bombing raid on which a newspaperman had been permitted to fly. The Times won a place on the flight because Ray Daniell had picked a winning number in an American Correspondents' Association lottery.

Daniell, sometimes known as Pete, decided to go on the mission, but MacDonald insisted that he make the trip. He said: "I'm not married, Pete. You've got Tania." Tania Long had become Mrs. Daniell by that time. She knew nothing of the mission.

The two men discussed the flight in the Hotel Savoy lobby and decided, finally, to match coins for it. MacDonald won, not once, but twice. He left the office secretly and by pre-arrangement with the British Air Ministry, rode to the R.A.F.'s Forty-seventh Bomber Squadron Base in Lincolnshire. He lived with the Squadron for ten days, drinking with the pilots at local pubs, sharing in their horseplay and laughter, eating at the squadron mess.

Up to this time, no one had mentioned the mission's target. Though MacDonald had hoisted glass with the fliers and had sat by their fire as the Lincolnshire wind howled over the slush and snow outside, he had no inkling of the destination.

After noon mess on the tenth day the fliers at last were summoned for briefing. They took MacDonald with them. The briefing officer, pointer in hand, stood before a wall screen until a lantern slide projector threw a colored map of Germany on it. He planted the pointer on Berlin, turned and grinned.

He said, "Well, you see it now; the target for tonight is the Big City."

Late in the afternoon on Saturday, Jan. 16, the Lancasters lifted from the field, one by one, into a muddy twilight, each with one blockbuster and two tons of incendiaries. Jamie MacDonald, muffled to the ears in winter flying outfit and plugged in on the inter-com, stretched on the plexiglass floor up in the ship's nose, and saw Lincolnshire fall away. He was fascinated by the crew's quiet chatter.

They rose to 20,000 feet in the murk, ever climbing, rode over the North Sea, then over Denmark. Snow flew at the windows and German anti-aircraft guns tried to find them in the darkness, but they droned on. Before they left the Danish coast, a Lancaster to starboard exploded in a brief flower of flame and vanished. The Germans had reached it with a direct hit.

The Lancaster with MacDonald in it dived out of range. It was moonlight, now, and though the windows were frosted The Times man could make out snowy peaks, four miles below.

"Turning the corner," the navigator droned, and they pivoted on swirling snow over Rostock on the North German coast. They headed south through the moonlight in the clear, with angry ack-ack exploding all around them all the way to a point some miles south of the Big City.

Berlin was a pattern in ghostly white in the moonglow. They approached it at 14,000 feet with searchlights fingering them and making their shadows race in the cabin. Ground fire was terrific. They could see it, but they could not hear it.

The bombardier said, "That's Unter den Linden," and MacDonald, staring through the frosty bay saw it plainly, with the streets on either side like bone-white vertebrae. The night now was sharp and clear as they rushed through the stars.

The first Lancaster groups dropped their flares and bombs. They swam through the fingering searchlights and MacDonald heard the bombardier's crisp orders.

MacDonald had been on the receiving end of Nazi raids for more than two years, but this was his first experience in a bomber. His heart beat wildly.

Their blockbuster fell. Released of its enormous weight, they shot upward. Then their incendiaries spilled on order, and over the earphones the bombardier called, "Bombs gone."

They had added destructive red blossoms to the white garden that was Berlin.

The Lancaster picked up speed. The pilot called cheerily to MacDonald, "Okay, Old Mac; they've had it," and dipped the Lancaster's enormous wing to give the reporter a better view of their grim handiwork. MacDonald's last view of Berlin, as the bomber droned westward, was of a city redly glowing like a blast furnace.

The pilot steadied the Lancaster in air lanes panting with con-cussion from Berlin's anti-aircraft guns. The crew broke out hot tea from thermos bottles and passed cake and oranges. Presently the sea was under their wings again.

There was one last breath-taking experience. A companion hom-ing bomber tore at them, in tactical error, as if it might cleave them in two, but MacDonald's pilot dived under it in the moonlight and leveled off for the final run to the hazy blur up ahead that was England.

MacDonald's story ran more than five columns in The Times on Monday, Jan. 18, under the headline:

R.A.F. BLASTS BERLIN WITH BIGGEST BOMBS

The story began:

AN R.A.F. BOMBER STATION, somewhere in England, Jan. 17— Royal Air Force bombers transformed a large area of Berlin into a particularly hot corner of hell on earth last night.

I know, because as a passenger aboard one of the planes making up the large force that battered the German capital I saw a great number of 4,000-pound high explosive bombs and thousands of incendiaries blasting buildings right and left and starting widespread fires reminiscent of some of the big German raids we have gone through in London.

MacDonald's flight story was one of the most exciting of the war, the first eyewitness account of its kind to get into print. The Times ran an editorial on it next day, and beside the editorial "Topics of The Times" saw in the bombing a kind of "fire music" for the final scene in the mad adventure on which Hitler had taken the German nation.

"We have passed the end of the beginning," the piece said. "The curtain is going up on the beginning of the end."

So it was. The Russians had broken back through Stalingrad and were slaughtering the frozen Germans. The Allies had landed in North Africa, and after a few bitter defeats, were driving the Germans and Italians before them. In the Pacific, where The Times had sent additional men as the fighting tempo picked up, the Americans, the British and the Australians were island-hopping, though at bitter cost, toward Tokyo.

In late January, 1943, President Roosevelt and Prime Minister Churchill met at Casablanca. Drew Middleton covered the meeting for The Times and on Wednesday, Jan. 27, the session yielded the headline:

ROOSEVELT, CHURCHILL MAP 1943 WAR STRATEGY AT TEN-DAY CONFERENCE HELD IN CASABLANCA; GIRAUD AND DE GAULLE, PRESENT, AGREE ON TERMS

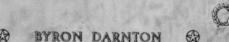

⊛ THIS TABLET IS ERECTED ⊛
TO THE HONOR OF THE AMERICAN CORRESPONDENTS
OF THE SECOND WORLD WAR
WHO BRAVED EVERY PERIL
WITH UNSURPASSED AND UNSPARING DEVOTION
AND WHO·BY THEIR WRITINGS·
HELPED TO FORGE THIS DEMOCRACY INTO
THE GREATEST WAR MACHINE OF ALL TIME

TO THIRTY-FOUR THIS WAS THE LAST ASSIGNMENT

TWO CORRESPONDENTS OF THE NEW YORK TIMES
WERE AMONG THIS HEROIC BAND:

⊛ BYRON DARNTON ⊛
WHO DIED ON A LANDING ON NEW GUINEA
⊛ OCTOBER 18ᵀᴴ 1942 ⊛
AND
⊛ ROBERT P·POST ⊛
WHO WAS LOST IN AN AIR BATTLE OVER GERMANY
⊛ FEBRUARY 26ᵀᴴ 1943 ⊛

DYING IN THE LINE OF DUTY·
THEY LEFT AN UNFORGETTABLE HERITAGE
OF LOYALTY AND VALOR

Last Assignments That Were Perpetuated in Bronze.

CASABLANCA, French Morocco, Jan. 24 (Delayed)—President Roosevelt and Prime Minister Churchill today concluded a momentous ten-day conference in which they planned Allied offensives of 1943 aimed at what the President called the "unconditional surrender" of the Axis powers.

The President flew 5,000 miles across the Atlantic with his Chiefs of Staff to confer with Mr. Churchill and British military, naval and air chieftains in a sun-splashed villa within sound of Atlantic breakers.

Every phase of the global war was discussed in conferences lasting from morning until midnight.

The curtain was indeed going up on the beginning of the end.

CHAPTER
40

IN THE spring of 1943 as United Nations forces rolled the Axis armies back across the Mediterranean and reduced German war plants and German submarine bases to rubble, Sulzberger undertook a 28,000-mile air journey to Moscow. Scotty Reston went with him.

The publisher first broached his idea for the trip in talks with Secretary of State Hull and Under Secretary Sumner Welles. He said, in effect, that Americans and Britons—and The New York Times as much as any other of their publications—had fallen into the habit of thinking of the war as solely an American-British crusade.

He told them: "I believe it is necessary, now, to find ways to get the Russians to understand that we are not trying to run an exclusive world club to which they are not admitted. I feel that I might make some small contribution to such an understanding if, as a publisher, I went to study conditions there myself."

The two Government officials warmly approved and mentioned the project to President Roosevelt. He had not been on friendly terms with The Times for some years, now, but he sent for Sulzberger and heard him out.

"Well," he finally said, "as you know, Arthur, we don't like to have publishers traveling around; they're so indiscreet."

Sulzberger smiled, but did not answer. The President pondered a moment. He said: "Let's see, now. When you went abroad last year for the Red Cross you didn't write anything, did you?"

The publisher said, "No, sir, and I won't write anything this time, not even a book."

The President chuckled. He approved the trip to Moscow. The State Department, on his authorization, urged American and Russian officials to extend all courtesy to Sulzberger. It was made clear to Moscow that the publisher was on a two-fold mission—to inspect Red Cross installations and to gather background information for The Times. He was also to inquire, on the side, into certain situations for the Rockefeller Foundation. Sulzberger was a member of the Governing board of the American Red Cross, and was a Rockefeller Foundation trustee.

Behind the practical purposes of the publisher's wartime travels was a subtler reason. Though he never put it into words he wanted to experience some share of the risks undertaken by the correspondents who covered the global war for The Times, and he felt that by visiting the zones where they worked he could better understand their problems. It helped in another way—gave him a far better idea of G.I. needs, and brought him into warm contact with the men who commanded them.

He had visited London by air in 1942 for the Red Cross and had experienced bomb raids during his stay. One night at the Hotel Savoy he would have slept through a raid, but Ray Daniell had him waked. The publisher came to The Times workroom in the hotel to chat while the building shook under ack-ack thunder, and watched his men sending the news through dawn.

The publisher and Reston left on the Russian trip before noon on June 10, 1943, from Washington Airport in the Apache, an A.T.C. stratoliner.

They touched at Miami, San Juan in Puerto Rico, Georgetown in British Guiana, Belem and Natal in Brazil, Ascension Island in the South Atlantic, and were in Accra on the African Gold Coast at 8 o'clock in the night of June 13. Then on to Maidugari in Nigeria, to Khartoum in the Sudan, to Cairo, to Habbaniya in Iraq and into Teheran in Iran before sundown on June 17.

Sulzberger was profoundly impressed by the weird backgrounds against which the war had set young Americans from farm, factory and office. He ate at their mess and sat with them under the stars to see American movies. He talked with them. In no other way could he have comprehended the almost miraculous spread of the United States war effort. There was not a spot on earth, it seemed, where it had not reached.

On June 20 as they sat with Gen. Donald H. Connolly in the Persian Gulf Service Command Headquarters in Teheran the talk turned to one of the publisher's chief concerns—service men's morale. Visiting the post at the time was Capt. Eddie Rickenbacker and Col. Theodore N. Osborne, Assistant Chief of Staff for Operations, among others.

Two summers before, Sulzberger told the group, he had sent Hilton Railey to study Army morale in military camps throughout the United States. The country was not at war then, and the publisher had heard increasing talk of the soldiers' inability to grasp why they had been snatched from their jobs and their homes.

Railey's report confirmed these rumors. He had visited ten camps and two maneuver areas, and morale was indeed low among National Guardsmen and selectees. As near as they could understand, it was Britain's war, and they saw no sense in their being called out to suffer for her mistakes.

At only one place—Camp Lee in Virginia—had Railey found morale high, and there the credit went to Maj. Gen. James E. Edmonds, a former managing editor of The New Orleans Times-Picayune, the commanding officer. He had made the whole international picture clear to his men, through briefing his officers. The enlisted personnel at Camp Lee understood they were in uniform because Axis madmen had set out to overrun the world.

Railey's survey reports impressed Gen. George C. Marshall and President Roosevelt and eventually resulted in establishment of the Army Information School. Sulzberger suggested at that time that a special newspaper for the armed forces overseas, giving world news and war background, would make for better understanding of the war issues, and Army Special Services eagerly went for it.

Special Services officers with Reston, who was then assistant to the publisher, and Lester Markel worked out the format for an overseas weekly tabloid for the armed forces. It was to give the news and some Times features, but would carry no editorials, and no advertising. The publication was to be, more or less, a condensed version of The Times' News of the Week in Review.

Then, Sulzberger explained to his audience in Teheran, Special Services suddenly balked. It realized that ill feeling might be created among other newspapers if a Times-planned soldier newspaper were distributed, even though The Times had undertaken to foot the bills.

It was curious that this idea, conceived in the United States only to die there because of political fear, should find renewed life in faraway Iran, but it did. Col. Edward F. Brown, aide to General Connolly, persuaded his chief that there was need for such a newspaper. There was no military rule forbidding the General to place a specific order with the Army Exchange Service for any commodity he wanted for his own troops.

Eventually Special Services gave up its original interest in The Times Overseas Weekly idea and Army Exchange Service, which ran the post exchanges, took it over. It ordered the weekly just as it ordered any other post exchange commodity. The first edition, in the form of plastic plates made up at The Times, was flown to Iran, arrived at the Persian Gulf Command on Aug. 22, 1943, and was printed there.

Sulzberger offered the same service to the Army, Navy and Marine Corps all over the globe, and in a matter of months Overseas Weekly plates were flown to all corners of the earth. Before the war ended the paper was available on sixteen war fronts. Other American newspapers adopted the same idea.

Sulzberger and Reston were in Moscow from June 21 to July 12. They discovered that State Department personnel in the Russian capital got most of their news from the British Broadcasting Company and only a trickle from American newspapers by Morse code from Washington. United States officials in Moscow were nowhere near as well informed as the British. Sulzberger thought Overseas Weekly might well help out in this situation, too.

The publisher found Russian officials polite, but extremely stand-offish. On a tour of the plant where Pravda, the official Communist newspaper, was published, he noticed that the linotype machines had come from the United States, the presses from England, the stereotype equipment from Germany—that almost everything in the plant was of foreign production. He looked in vain for a news-room. It occurred to him then that Pravda's chief native product, its party propaganda, was probably piped in from official sources, so that there was no need for a news-assembly point such as he had in Forty-third Street. This lack sharply pointed up the major difference between newspaper work in a country that had a free press and a nation where the press was state-controlled.

Early in July Sulzberger and Reston were allowed to visit the Russian front and to talk with Russian Red Cross officials. They visited Russian Army hospitals, saw how the wounded were handled and were entertained by pretty Russian nurses who sang and played the accordion for them. They inspected cities the Germans had destroyed.

On his return to Moscow, Sulzberger talked with Foreign Minister Molotov. He explained that one of his missions was an attempt to get a better understanding of Russia's problems, and a clearer grasp of the Russian viewpoint and post-war plans. The interview was unfruitful. Molotov was friendly, but managed to say nothing.

Sulzberger caught the charm of the average Russian and was fascinated, as other travelers had been, by the architectural beauty of Red Square in twilight, but he and Scotty came to the same sad conclusion: Russia did not want to be known. She preferred to remain, so far as the West was concerned, a dark mystery.

Ilya Ehrenburg, Soviet writer, told Sulzberger at luncheon one day that America's stock was depreciating in Russia for what he termed "four main reasons."

"In the market-places of the world," the Russian journalist said with some bitterness, "one American or British life is counted as equivalent to ten Russian lives.

"Americans place too much stress on food and material. You take a lot of time gathering too much food and equipment for your soldiers while Russian blood continues to flow.

"Americans and Britons do not use their manpower properly. You place too much emphasis on youth, while we Russians have proved that men of 45, with World War experience, are better soldiers.

"You just do not understand Russian psychology."

Sulzberger patiently pointed out that a nation's history and philosophy affected its action; that America's solicitude for proper food for her soldiers had developed out of unfortunate experience with poor food in the Spanish-American war; that in the United States the social pattern was based on the conception of the supreme importance of the individual whereas the Russian pattern placed the state above the individual. He contended, though, that even if their concepts differed, Russia, the United States and Britain would have to find among them some peace formula for the world.

The publisher and Scotty agreed that the Russians trusted their Allies no more than their Allies trusted them, and that the Soviet would in all likelihood stubbornly cling to a strictly nationalist policy.

Sulzberger and Reston journeyed back to the States by way of Iran, Cairo, Gibraltar, London, Prestwick, Iceland and Labrador. The publisher reported to the President and to the Red Cross and turned back to running the newspaper.

In 1941 Sulzberger had sold Wide World Photos, Inc., to The Associated Press, but had retained the facsimile equipment he had set up for his wirephoto system. He formed Times Facsimile Corporation as an independent unit, owned solely by The Times and placed it at the disposal of the armed forces. Orvil E. Dryfoos, the Dartmouth man who had married the publisher's oldest daughter, Marian, was installed as executive vice president.

Under the direction of Austin G. Cooley, Times Facsimile worked throughout the war turning out equipment for the armies and navies of the United Nations. Communications officers came and went as Cooley's men, working in utter secrecy on the seventh floor of The Times, improved sending and receiving sets that were becoming daily more and more necessary in directing artillery fire and in helping military aircraft through thick weather.

At the publisher's suggestion, in 1943, Mrs. Sulzberger, who knew the paper's policy, began a series of public service programs at Times Hall, formerly the Little Theatre, in Forty-fourth Street, back of The Times Building. She worked on this project for The Times promotion department.

The first series at Times Hall helped clarify civilian war problems. There were talks by experts on wartime nutrition, on civilian defense, defense savings, on care of children in wartime, on a program for getting children out of the city in event of possible air attack, on home factors in national morale, on books as weapons in the war of ideas, on victory gardens.

In a later series Times war correspondents, home for a breather, and other Times men explained to women's clubs and to school teachers where they thought new dangers and problems lay. Harold Denny, Hanson W. Baldwin, Herbert L. Matthews, Otto D. Tolischus and Cyrus L. Sulzberger, the publisher's nephew and chief foreign correspondent, addressed such groups.

In a talk before teachers in The Times Hall the publisher outlined the spirit and the principles that guided the newspaper under his administration. The staff called it his "We" speech because it described in detail how The Times functioned as a corporate body.

The publisher recalled the basic Ochs determination "to give all the news without fear or favor, regardless of any party, sect or interest involved" and said that that remained the newspaper's role in the community.

"What we are interested in today," he told the teachers, "is to see if we are performing our allotted task accurately, and without fear, and without favor.

"We recognize that there is no way to recapture the past with the printed word or in any other manner that will be satisfactory to all.

"We know that if each one of you were to report the same event there would be many different versions . . .

"We know that all men have their prejudices, their predilections, their special interests or biases and, accordingly, we would not put the writing and editing of the news into the hands of any single group—political, economic, religious or social.

"We would not knowingly employ any so-called Communist, or any other kind of totalitarian, in our news or editorial departments, for we have a deep-rooted prejudice for democracy and a deep-seated faith in our capacity to develop under system of law.

"On the other hand, we believe that trained and skilled newspapermen and women, such as you have seen here, who have no common denominator other than their Americanism, have the ability to write and evaluate a news story that will be acceptable to most of our readers as an accurate report of what transpired. I stress that this is for *our* readers—not for all; for every newspaper must decide upon the clientele it wishes to cultivate.

"For our part, we solicit the patronage of intelligent Americans who desire information rather than entertainment, who want the facts unadorned and who, in this critical period of our history [savage global conflict had spread the world over by that time] place first their country and the freedoms which it guarantees.

"We do not crusade in our news columns.

"We are anxious to see wrongs corrected, and we attempt to make our position very clear in such matters on our editorial page. But we believe that no matter how we view the world, our chief responsibility lies in reporting accurately that which happens.

"Whichever way the cat should jump, we should record it, and we should not allow our excitement about the direction which it takes, or plans to take, to interfere with our primary mission. We believe that you will look after the cat if we inform you promptly, fully and accurately about its movements.

"We have never had a single advertiser attempt to shape our editorial policy, although it is not uncommon for an occasional one to show disapproval of our policy by withdrawing his business. Every election year is apt to bring a flare-up of this manifestation, but, despite stupid and vicious remarks to the contrary, we take it in our stride and pursue our course.

"We are not afraid of advertisers, but maintain a normal, friendly business relationship with them.

"We maintain a committee of acceptability of advertising and subject copy to its scrutiny. In normal years we turn down many thousands of lines of business which does not comply with our standards and, in addition, require the advertiser to edit some of that which we use.

"We are financially independent.

"We have no investments except in our own business and in Government securities.

"We have no mortgages or bonds outstanding—no debts other than our monthly bills. The majority stock of The New York Times Company is held by three trustees, all of whom are employed on The Times. There is no outside interference.

"We have no temptation to be other than honest.

"We have no wish except to hold high the banner of responsible journalism raised by Mr. Ochs and held aloft by him until his death ten years ago."

The "We" speech gave full credit for The Times' success to the men and women who worked with, and for, Sulzberger.

"The control that the publisher of this paper exercises over its policies is anything but arbitrary," he told the teachers earnestly. "It lies primarily in picking his associates and working with them in harmony—talking things out and, on many occasions, being willing to give *way* rather than give *orders*.

"I do not wish to appear naïve or sentimental in this matter. I merely assure you, out of twenty-seven years' experience, that you could not have a newspaper as good as this one if what I have outlined were not so."

Late in November, 1942, the publisher had been in Ottawa to talk to Government officials and to address the local Rotary Club when he got a telephone call from Washington, asking him to serve on the Publishers Newsprint Committee. The newsprint supply situation was critical.

Sulzberger sat down that night to try to figure out what he might contribute to balancing the awkward newsprint muddle. His notes, it developed, added up to just about the same plan as was conceived independently by Fleming Newbold of The Washington Star, who was also anxious to clarify the newsprint situation. Their plan, with modifications suggested by other members of the Publishers Newsprint Committee, was finally resolved in what became Order L-240, the formula for national restriction of newsprint consumption. It kept all newspapers supplied without allowing advantage to those that owned their own mills, as The Times did. Allotment was fixed on the basis of each newspaper's 1941 newsprint consumption.

The restrictions imposed by L-240 were particularly hard on The Times, which printed more news than any other newspaper. Competing publications that printed less news gained correspondingly in advertising revenue.

CHAPTER
41

B Y MID-JULY, 1943, Allied pressure on the Axis gained intensity on all fronts. The Japanese were paying dearly for their attack on Pearl Harbor and the Germans and Italians were on the defensive. Only Rome, of all Axis capitals, had been free of Allied bombing raids.

Before noon on July 19 a swarm of heavily loaded Fortresses and some British heavies lumbered from runways in North Africa, bound on a mission that Allied leaders had long withheld. They wanted to be extraordinarily careful on this target.

They drilled the bomber crews for weeks, stressing and restressing the moral harm that might result if churches, cathedrals or any sacred ground were damaged. The bombing maps had been drawn with special care.

In one of the Fortresses that beetled heavily down a sun-baked airport runway east of Algiers, lean Herbert Matthews lay far up in the ship's nose. He knew Rome as he knew his right hand and he had hoped for this assignment. Five other newspapermen were scattered among other ships.

It was a dramatic daylight raid. The planes were to hit at freight yards in San Lorenzo outside the main railway station in Rome, at the Littoria yards on the northern edge and at Ciampino airfield, four miles southeast of Rome, all several miles from Vatican City.

Matthews' account of the mission covered five columns, and

Drew Middleton's summary of it, written at Allied headquarters in Algiers from official communiqués, covered one and a half columns more. Both ran under the headline:

ALLIED BOMBERS BLAST ROME MILITARY AREAS:
TIMES MAN FROM AIR SEES SHRINES SPARED

Matthews carefully explained in his story that the raid was dictated by military necessity. Mussolini and the Germans had established vital supply and air bases in and around the Holy City in the firm belief that the Allies would not dare risk attacking them.

There was a detailed account of the orders passed to the bomber crews by Col. Fay P. Upthegrove, an up-state New Yorker, in briefing on the African desert in the moonlight that morning. He warned them to take no chances, to be sure of each target.

Up in the nose of a formation-leading ship called the Sirocco, The Times correspondent looked like a man from Mars in his Mae West, oxygen mask and other cumbersome equipment. He found it difficult to take notes.

"A newspaperman," he wrote, "ought to have four hands, and eight eyes when he is covering a raid, for there are an amazing number of things to see in the briefest space of time. Not the least of his difficulties is keeping out of the way of the crew members."

He described the flight high above the Atlas Mountains and over the Italian coast, at around 18,000 feet. His was the second Fortress wave. He saw smoke rise from targets hit by the first formation.

"Our first wave had been over and done its job," he wrote. "Now it was for us to finish it. At 11:30, as we were exactly above a village on the road to Florence, we turned south on our target and opened our bomb-bay doors.

"As our navigator peered tensely into his bombsight, I glanced around in all directions at Rome below. There was the winding Tiber, and there the Mussolini Forum. St. Peter's stood out so clearly that it seemed to dominate the city. Not even a wisp of smoke had reached over there.

"I picked out landmark after landmark, all so famous, and wondered on seeing the Palazzo Venezia whether Premier Mussolini was in his office on the first floor or safely below in his air raid shelter.

"The house where my family lived when I was a correspondent in Rome was just down to the right as a reminder that not much more than a year ago I and other Americans of the diplomatic and journalistic corps had left somewhat ignominiously along those very railroad tracks we were now bombing."

Matthews described how the bombs fell, swift and true, smack on the targets in the brilliant sunlight. Like MacDonald over Berlin he knew the breath-taking leap of the bomber when its heavy load dropped away. The ship steadied, pivoted and headed home. The crew broke out cheese sandwiches and coffee.

"Back at our base, which we reached as scheduled about 3 o'clock, the pilot let the plane down gently, and the adventure was over. I thanked the crew. I said to them: 'You've made history in a very large way today.'

"It had not seemed to occur to any of them. It was just another raid against another military target. So far as they were concerned—another mission ended.

"And they were right in their way. It was a military mission, and an extremely important one. The political, and especially the religious, implications were incidental. History, like justice, is blind."

But the raid had powerful effect. It was one of the factors that broke Fascist resistance. Less than two months later, on Sept. 9, 1943, The Times said:

ITALY SURRENDERS, WILL RESIST GERMANS; ALLIED FORCES LAND IN THE NAPLES AREA

It took another eleven months of blood and toil, though, before the American Fifth Army's doughfeet pushed into the Holy City. On Monday, June 5, 1944, The Times announced:

ROME CAPTURED INTACT BY THE 5TH ARMY AFTER FIERCE BATTLE THROUGH SUBURBS

Matthews told under a Rome dateline how Germans still held grimly to some outer edges of the city south of Highway 6, then continued:

"But Rome has been reached—the goal of conquerors throughout the ages, though none was ever before able to make the almost-impossible south-north campaign. What Hannibal did not dare to do, the Allied generals accomplished but at such a cost in blood, material and time that it will probably never again be attempted."

Milton Bracker of The Times wrote an account datelined, "IN THE OUTSKIRTS OF ROME, June 4," in which he described grimy and battle-weary G.I.'s hugging road edges along Route 6 past wrecked Sherman tanks as they slowly advanced on the city.

The first Axis capital had fallen. That night on the radio the President grimly exulted. "One up," he told his listeners, "and two to go."

The Allies were due to strike, any moment now, at the European mainland. Even the Germans knew that, though they did not know where or when. The Times had been alerted by Daniell to expect "something big," though that "something" was never given specific name.

Sulzberger spent few nights away from the office in this watch period. He slept in his fourteenth-floor bedchamber high above Times Square.

Ted Bernstein, then foreign news editor, easily guessed that the anticipated "something big" would be an Allied blow, in tremendous mass, by air, by assault craft, parachutists and infantry. He knew that it might come a bare moment before edition time, and that he had to be prepared.

Early in April he assigned his experts and rewritemen to get up all possible advance copy. On the basis of analysis by Hanson Baldwin he explained to a Times artist what a coastal invasion would look like. And from that information, Luke Manditch made a realistic five-column wash drawing. Ben Dalgin, veteran art director, supervised this and other art layout details. A rewrite man did a brief history of the war up to invasion point.

Bernstein ordered a glossary of invasion terms, an outline of historic Normandy invasions, cuts of the points he figured the Germans would defend most fiercely and a piece on what the Allies had learned in their Dieppe raid on Aug. 19, 1942, a costly rehearsal for ultimate mass invasion. For all possible landing points maps were ready in metal into which numbers and arrows could be quickly inserted.

Night after night, for weeks, the news room held open through daylight but aside from the fall of Rome, which came in at an early hour, no earth-trembling story broke. The morning of Tuesday, June 6, started another dull vigil. It was humid and the dimmed streets were dismal under a heavy sky.

Bernstein pushed back his chair a little after midnight, got a "Good night" from McCaw in the bull pen, and took a cab home. His wife was waiting for him, with his customary highball.

A moment later the phone rang. It was Clarence Howell, an assistant night managing editor.

"You'd better come back, Ted," he said. "The German radio says the invasion's started."

Bernstein gulped his highball, ran for the elevator, hopped into a cab and was back in the office in ten minutes. The floor was tensely quiet. McCaw told him: "The Germans say the invasion's on. No word from Allied Headquarters on it."

Bernstein shucked his jacket, took over the foreign copy desk, and his men worked over copy written from the monitored German DNB broadcasts. There was only a moment's hesitation as to whether to run it on the basis of enemy reports alone or to wait.

McCaw figured the Germans would not broadcast an invasion unless they were certain the assault was actually under way; that they stood to gain nothing by such a tactic. He walked over to Bernstein's position.

"Okay," he said crisply, "we'll replate."

He ordered sixteen columns—a full two pages—of the material prepared in April thrown into the extra.

Invasion copy with headlines moved quietly and rapidly through Bernstein's and McCaw's hands, and was shot by carrier to the composing room on the fourth floor. The foreman there had been ordered to watch for it, and to clear decks for an extra.

At 1:30 A.M. The Times was on the darkened city streets with the news:

GERMANS REPORT INVASION IS ON
WITH ALLIES LANDING AT HAVRE
AND NAVAL BATTLE IN CHANNEL

The Times' first extra that morning was the earliest of any in New York to reach the street because other newspapers apparently hesitated to accept the enemy broadcast as authentic.

On word from McCaw, Times telephone operators waked other executives. Sulzberger was in Chattanooga, but the flash was sent to him, too. He made immediate arrangements to fly back to New York.

Dryfoos rushed down from his uptown home. James came in. The mechanical chiefs reported. They had rehearsed their staffs for D-Day, and edition after edition as official news began to filter through by broadcast and by wireless from Daniell in London roared from the presses.

When it became obvious at 2 o'clock, two hours after The Times restaurant had closed, that The Times would keep printing through dawn Dryfoos sent two copy boys out to buy $50 worth of sandwiches and coffee. They trundled a mailing room handcart into Eighth Avenue, shopping at all-night eating places along the way for snacks for all hands.

At 3:30 A.M. when General Eisenhower announced the invasion, The Times radio room picked it from the air. This message, under London dateline of June 6, led the paper above Daniell's story, which said:

SUPREME HEADQUARTERS ALLIED EXPEDITIONARY FORCES, Tuesday, June 6—The invasion of Europe from the West has begun.

In the gray light of a summer dawn Gen. Dwight D. Eisenhower threw his great Anglo-American force into action today for the liberation of the Continent. The spearhead of attack was an Army group commanded by Gen. Sir Bernard L. Montgomery and comprising troops of the United States, Britain and Canada.

General Eisenhower's first communiqué was terse and calculated to give little information to the enemy. It said merely that "Allied naval forces supported by strong air forces began landing Allied armies this morning on the northern coast of France."

After the first communiqué was released it was announced that the Allied landing was in Normandy.

Under this lead, The Times ran the text of the German broadcasts, which gave far more detail than General Eisenhower had seen fit to release.

Dictator's Path to Glory: The Times turned down $5,000 for exclusive shots of Mussolini's sorry ending, but permitted newspapers everywhere to use them free the next day.

The last edition that day, a 6 A.M. extra, carried the most complete invasion story of any morning newspaper in the world. It had the Times Square scene, with photographs of servicemen reading earlier Times editions, a full list of invasion commanders, pictures of the landing points, the five-column wash drawing showing planes and ships swarming toward and over the French coast, a four-column front-page invasion map, a description of the scene as broadcast by Wright Bryan of NBC flying with the Ninth Air Force, Hal Denny's description of American and British bombers leaving England in swarms for the attack.

It developed, later, that Times Facsimile had played a vital part in the D-Day invasion. Allied photographers in small spotter planes flew over enemy territory just ahead of the invaders, took pictures showing where the far-flung lines had been established and where Allied shells were falling. The photographs were developed within the hour in London and were sent by radio facsimile to field commanders in Normandy. They gave a clear picture of what lay ahead, and how better to direct the fire.

The Times poured correspondents into Normandy—David Anderson, Jamie MacDonald, Harold Denny, Gene Currivan, Fred Graham, Richard J. H. Johnston and Drew Middleton. Baldwin had watched the invasion from the flagship, the cruiser Augusta, and had landed on Normandy Beach with Gen. Omar Bradley. Daniell and his wife, Tania Long, left London to report from battle and liberated areas. Daniell knew the experience of hedge-hopping over Allied and German lines in a tiny spotter plane. Miss Long went into liberated towns and villages on the heels of the advancing armies to talk with French and German women, and to report their reaction to the turn the war had taken. All The Times copy was supplemented with special stories from British correspondents and from recorded broadcasts of battle scenes and with great volume of wordage from American, British and Canadian news agencies.

Photographic coverage exceeded anything seen before in the daily Times, which was in keeping with Sulzberger's gradual departure from Ochsian adherence to a minimum of story illustration in the daily. He had called for more and more photo coverage. It had become a picture age. The Times had to keep step with it.

The paper stayed open late every morning for weeks after the invasion because of the heady rush of battle events, in both Europe and in the Pacific, and Times headlines marked Allied advances:

AMERICANS IN ST. SAUVEUR, CUT CHERBOURG LINE;
  SECRET ROBOT PLANES HIT ENGLAND IN FORCE

U. S. TANKS SMASH GERMAN LINE IN NORMANDY;
  GAIN AS MUCH AS 5 MILES ON 25-MILE FRONT;
  RUSSIANS REACH THE VISTULA RIVER IN FORCE

DE GAULLE REPORTED LEADING SMASH INTO PARIS;
  DEEP ALLIED DRIVES TIGHTEN POCKET AT SEINE;
  RUSSIANS BATTER DISORDERED FOE IN RUMANIA

Three Times men were with the Allies at the liberation of Paris on Aug. 24, 1944. Denny with the American First Army, Currivan with the Third, Graham with LeClerc's Second French Army.

They entered the city while machine guns and grenades were still in action on the Esplanade and while French partisans and Germans still sniped at one another from house windows and from behind chimney pots.

Both Graham and Denny filed stories of the surrender only to learn later that their couriers had not been able to get through to the Press Wireless transmitter seventeen miles outside Paris. The stories had finally been flown, instead, to the London bureau, but there was delay in that, too, and a full week had passed before the copy came into Daniell's hands. Such things happened over and over again but they were to be expected. James understood, even when he scolded about delays. He had known similar experiences in the first World War.

Finally the three Times men met at the Hotel Scribe in Paris. They were gaunt, unshaved and in grimy gear. Graham had dumped his musette bag outside the city in his haste to catch up with Le Clerc as the French stormed the Paris gates.

Now the bag was beyond his reach. He wrote his story by lantern light in a little fourth-floor room, and got it to the censor. Then he was utterly bushed. Outside, Paris was shrilly and hoarsely hysterical over the liberation, and the din was great.

Graham tried to keep awake, but could not. He curled up on the bed, marching shoes and all, and sank into deep slumber.

Denny's story on the reopening of The Times Paris bureau, which had been gathering dust for three years, ran in the edition of Aug. 29.

"The Paris bureau of The New York Times was reopened today in its old quarters at 37 Rue Caumartin," it said, "for the first time since America entered the war.

"It began operations in a small way with three American correspondents, Frederick Graham, Gene Currivan and the writer. Princess Marie Scherbatoff, secretary of the Paris Bureau earlier in the war and for a time in charge of its news coverage after the Germans entered the city, was ready to resume her duties when the American troops entered. She looked us up soon after we had arrived.

"Together we hunted up what we could find of our old French staff. Of all the reunions that we have had with French friends since our entrance on Friday, none has been so touching as those with these people who worked together with us in this office in the days between two wars. To them it was the restoration of their bureau besides being the liberation of their country's capital. They have fared variously.

"Joseph Noel, the old concierge, greeted Mme. Scherbatoff and me at the door and embraced us. He had continued his loyalty to The Times even after Germany and the United States had gone to war. Just after Pearl Harbor, the Germans began a search of The Times offices. There were some documents relating to 'inside' stories that it would not have been well for the Germans to read.

"When M. Noel warned Mme. Scherbatoff she told him where these documents were. He went boldly back into the bureau and while the Germans were ransacking one room, he got the documents from another, slipped them under his coat and got them safely out.

"In their little bachelor flat out beyond the Bois de Vincennes, we found Gaston Humbert and his brother, Frederick. All who knew The Times Paris office well in all the years since the first World War knew and loved Gaston and many visitors in later years also knew his brothers, Emile and Frederick, who came to work for this bureau more recently as receptionists and messengers.

"Our old offices are in better condition than we expected, but they are surely changed. Different floors of the buildings have been re-let to various organizations and our furniture is scattered among them all. Some typewriters were still there; others, and the expensive telephone-transmission equipment, had been hidden in a safe place. Our newspaper files are intact.

"A French association is now occupying the premises, but we have mutually arranged to cramp The Times' activities into two rooms while the French tenants limit themselves to the rest until they find other quarters. 'The New York Times' sign has remained over the front of our offices all through the occupation and it is now heaped with American, French and British flags."

The headlines kept step as the Russians pressed unrelentingly from the east, the Yanks, the British and the French from the west:

RUSSIANS TAKE WARSAW, REPORTED IN CRACOW;
WIN A CITY 14 MILES FROM REICH IN 240-MILE GAIN;
BRITISH ADVANCE, AMERICANS CLOSE ON ST. VITH

FLEET PLANES RENEW POUNDING OF TOKYO;
SHIPS HIT IWO AGAIN; BATAAN RECAPTURED;
BRITISH GAIN IN WEST; RUSSIANS PRESS ON

U. S. 7TH IN MUNICH, BRITISH PUSH ON BALTIC;
RUSSIANS TIGHTEN RING ON BERLIN'S HEART;
MILAN AND VENICE WON; MUSSOLINI KILLED

The Allied nutcracker had begun to squeeze Germany to its final gasps just after the end of 1944. Now it was spring in 1945, and the steel rings tightened inexorably and Allied airmen kept pulverizing the last of the Axis strongholds.

On Sunday morning, April 29, 1945, Milton Bracker, who had moved into North Italy behind the American Fifth Army, with his wife, Virginia Lee Warren, another Times reporter, saw Milanese partisans tear Benito Mussolini with bullets and with bare hands in the Piazza Loretto.

"Benito Mussolini," Bracker wrote for The Times of April 30, "came back last night to the city where his fascism was born. He came back on the floor of a closed moving van, his dead body flung on the bodies of his mistress and twelve men shot with him."

Bracker saw partisans kick and slash at the dictator's corpse, watched G.I. cameramen prop the battered head with rifle-butts to turn it into the sun. The mob had hanged the Fascist leader from a gasoline station girder by his ankles and had dangled the body of Clara Petacci by hers.

An Italian photographer who knew Dan Brigham, The Times man in Berne, took pictures of the corpses. He offered by phone to get them to the Italian-Swiss border at Ponte Chiasso and to put them on a train destined for Berne. Brigham said he would meet the train and pick them up.

While the photographer thumbed his way from Milan to Ponte Chiasso—an exciting journey on highways blocked with bewildered countrymen and kept in ferment by roving partisan bands—Brigham arranged to wire the pictures to New York.

There were no more trains that night for Geneva, the only spot in Switzerland from which Press Wireless could send to The Times. Brigham had to beg gasoline for the trip and routed a military censor out of bed to get the pictures stamped for transmission.

Before he left Berne he called The Times by radio-telephone. He was highly excited when The Times radio room answered: "Oh, boy, have I got something special!" He described the pictures and asked John Dugan of photo department to arrange to have Press Wireless open its receiver in The Times Tower to record the photographs. Ordinarily, Press Wireless was closed on Sunday.

Then Brigham set out on a dangerous ride through Alpine passes to Geneva, 125 miles away. He headed into a mountain blizzard, careening and skidding over black precipices on the dark and narrow alpine roads. Half way to Geneva a tire split. Brigham changed it, with wind tearing at his garments and freezing his hands.

It was 11:30 P.M. when the radiophoto receiving drum in Press Wireless began to hum, picking up the print images as they came across the Atlantic. Dugan was fascinated as they took shape. They were sharp and clear in photographic detail. At 11:45 they were in The Times photo darkroom for printing.

One print showed Mussolini lying side by side with Clara Petacci at the feet of grim-visaged partisan riflemen. McCaw captioned it,

"Inglorious End Of A Dictator," and marked it for four columns on Page 1. Two others—one showing the pair dangling from the girder, the other depicting Lieut. Gen. Achille Starace being prodded toward the execution spot in the Piazza Loretto—ran on Page 3.

On McCaw's order Dugan locked the negatives and prints in the photo room safe, after the cuts had been made. The pictures had missed The Times' first edition, but made the second. The front-page photograph ran beside Bracker's dramatic account of the dictator's death.

When The Times reached the street with the Mussolini pictures, city desk telephones set up a continuous din. Picture agencies and individual newspapers bid frantically for copies. Dick Clark, managing editor of The New York Daily News, offered $5,000 for them.

Sulzberger had been notified when the pictures came through from Geneva. Now McCaw called him again to pass on the bids that had been made for them.

"Tell them," the publisher said, "that they are not for sale. Tell them that The Times will give them away, without charge, to any publication that wants them, after 8 A.M. today. I think it will be a public service to give them maximum circulation."

This offer was eagerly accepted. The pictures were reprinted all over the world.

As Times correspondents moved with the onrushing Allied armies in Europe, other Times men moved with the ground forces through the South and Central Pacific jungles or sailed with the United States Navy in tremendous sea engagements. Foster Hailey had been on Guadalcanal, had witnessed the battle of Midway, and covered the action in the Aleutians. Bob Trumbull, George Horne, George Jones, Lindesay Parrott, Kluckhohn, Clinton Green and Tillman Durdin had covered bloody Asia mainland fighting and Pacific Island landings. They were to be joined later by Bruce Rae, who had left his assistant managing editor's duties for a while to set up Times Headquarters on Guam. With him went Warren Moscow, a political reporter, and William H. Lawrence. Rae commanded all Times men in the Pacific and when big stories broke, turned his hand to reporting again. He had always been one of the best.

The Times man who looked least like a potential war correspondent was Justin Brooks Atkinson, the drama critic. He never weighed more than 130 pounds, even in a rainstorm, and was more apt to tip the scales at 115. He was—and still is—the tweedy, spectacled, pipe-smoking scholarly type.

Atkinson looked more at home in his specialties. He had been Book Review editor from 1922 to 1925, and drama critic since then, had quaffed deeply of classics at Harvard, and was steeped in Thoreau and Emerson. He was New England clear through.

In June, 1942, though, he had persuaded the publisher to loose him from Broadway. He was unhappy writing about the theatre when men were dying in a world war. The Times sent him through the South by bus and by day coach on a survey of war sentiment in that region.

The pieces were delightful and highly informative. Atkinson had a philosophical calm that moved rural folk, black and white, to pull up a chair for him under the chinaberry trees with the hound dogs panting at his feet.

The series disclosed that people in the hills and cotton patches off the beaten track were thoroughly loyal but apathetic about the war. They were confused by what little reading they did.

"What they say on one page," Tyler Edwards of Elmore County told Atkinson, "they take back on the next."

The series indicated clear need for getting the war message across to these people. When the tour ended, though, Atkinson was sent back to his old chore, and he was unhappy again.

On Nov. 25, 1942, Atkinson readers were startled to find in The Times a dispatch under his byline datelined "Somewhere in Africa." Only three days before they had seen a piece by him in the Sunday Drama Section about the new Thornton Wilder play.

Subsequent bylines relieved their bewilderment. The Times drama critic, now a full fledged war correspondent, was on his way to China by way of Africa, Cairo, Persia, India and the Hump. Within a week he was with Lieut. Gen. Joseph W. (Vinegar Joe) Stilwell's forces.

Atkinson found time, between excellent war stories in the China-Burma-India areas to keep his hand in at drama criticism, even at that distance. He reviewed a Chinese version of "Hamlet" in the Kuo T'ai Theatre in Chungking on Dec. 17. It made front page in

The Times next morning under Atkinson's customary theatre head, "The Play," and gravely followed conventional review form. Readers were delighted with it.

Even battle stuff was sometimes touched with the critic's viewpoint. Five days before the "Hamlet" piece, Atkinson flew with Maj. Gen. Claire L. Chennault's Flying Tigers on a bombing mission over the Japanese front lines at Tengyueh, west of the Salween River.

"As guest drama critic," he reported in The Times on Dec. 15, "this correspondent was invited to occupy an orchestra seat in the nose of the ship where the space was cramped but the view was excellent and there were opportunities for pipe-smoking. As far as our ship was concerned, the raid was as pleasant as a tennis match and seemed to bear no relation to a murderous errand."

The drama man flew, floated and flat-footed it through the entire China-Burma-India theatre. He went into seemingly inaccessible places to reach American, British and Chinese troops. He ascended the Himalayas and the lofty Kaoling, got into remote Yenan Province. He traveled two months by plane, broken-down Chinese truck and junks, to get to Chinese pirates who were smuggling stolen Japanese medical supplies into Foochow, the last Chinese-held port. It all made excellent copy.

Illness overtook Atkinson as everyone had predicted it would. His weight fell below 114 pounds under a jaundice assault and a hernia slowed him, but still he poked around Burma and China, coming up with good stories. There were occasional breathers in Chungking. Paulette Goddard, touring with a U.S.O. show, turned up during one of these and left two bottles of rye, a heavenly gift to a parched correspondent too long on mao-tai, the Chinese rice wine.

The Times drama man had just finished an exhausting journey to the Salween River for a series on the Chinese offensive there and was back in Chungking in October, 1944, when Vinegar Joe Stilwell, C.B.I. commander, sent for him. Jaundice and a hernia condition had pitifully reduced Atkinson, but he went promptly to the general's Chungking Headquarters. He admired Vinegar Joe.

The general poured into the correspondent's ears a long and bitter story. It boiled down to the fact that Stilwell and Generalissimo

Chiang Kai-shek had split on vital issues and that Chiang had insisted that Stilwell be removed. Chiang had had his way. Gen. George C. Marshall had ordered Stilwell home, and the C.B.I. theatre was to be split. Maj. Gen. Albert C. Wedemeyer was to assume command in China.

Atkinson was shocked, but knew that he could not send the story from China because Chiang's censors controlled all communication lines. The only way to get the story to The Times was to bring it home, over all the censors' heads. Atkinson decided to do it that way, and Stilwell arranged plane passage for him. They left Chungking together, Stilwell to stop off in Delhi to turn over his command, as ordered.

It developed that a few other reporters had some of the facts about the order relieving Vinegar Joe of command. This worried Atkinson, and when the plane stopped at Myitkynia in North Burma for a three-day lay-over mere worry grew to brooding.

He confided his fears to the general in an open field beyond the airport. He said, "I'm afraid, general, that this story may break before I get to New York with it."

Stilwell reassured him. He said, "Don't worry about it. I can see to it that it doesn't get out until you've made it."

"You're sure, general, that it will be fresh news when I get to New York?"

The general nodded.

Other correspondents at the Press Hotel in Chungking assumed, meanwhile, that The Times man had merely gone on some brief journey. He had left all his kit in his room except toothbrush and typewriter.

Atkinson started pounding out the story on his portable as the plane thundered over wild country from North Burma to Delhi. He said good-by to Vinegar Joe there, and flew on in an A.T.C. plane bound home by way of the Persian Gulf, Cairo and Casablanca.

At John Payne Field, the A.T.C. airport on the desert outside Cairo, a G.I. took Atkinson's briefcase. He explained that all papers had to be examined by the Air Base censor. The former critic paled under the jaundice tan, then suddenly recalled that the Stilwell story was in his jacket, not in the briefcase. After the G.I. had gone off with the briefcase, Atkinson passed the story to a State Department man who had ridden in with him from India. It went into the diplomatic pouch, with the Government man's promise that he would deliver it only to James, at The Times, if by any chance he and Atkinson were separated somewhere along the line. The pouch was immune to search.

At Casablanca Atkinson was held up one day, but the State Department man went on. He got the story to James a day before Atkinson landed in Washington. Army censors held the story for two days. It was too hot a political potato for them to handle.

James, irked by the delay, put pressure on in Washington. The matter went up to the President himself. He ordered the censors to pass the story. His comment, James learned later, was: "The facts in the story are true, and Atkinson's back in the United States. He could have written it here, anyway."

The story ran on the front page in The Times of Oct. 31, 1944. It was in the third line of an exciting war head:

ALLIES HERD 40,000 NAZIS TOWARD MEUSE;
3 JAPANESE CRUISERS BOMBED AT MANILA;
STILWELL RECALL BARES RIFT WITH CHIANG

James put an italic editorial note ahead of the story proper:
"The following account of the recall of Gen. Joseph W. Stilwell is by the Chungking correspondent of The New York Times who has just returned to this country. It was delayed and finally cleared by the War Department censorship in Washington."

It was Atkinson's last story out of Asia—and his most important. It started chain reaction editorials across the world. In Washington next day, White House correspondents swarmed to take the matter up with the President. He confirmed The Times story, but insisted the recall had been due to personal differences between Vinegar Joe and the Generalissimo Chiang. He said that the position of the Chinese Communists had not been a factor in the recall.

The battered Times drama critic, weak and underweight, went into the hospital. He had landed in Washington with a high fever and was physically exhausted. He was not through as correspondent, though. More of that lay ahead for him, and out of a series on Russia, his next assignment, was to come a Pulitzer prize.

CHAPTER
42

WHEN President Roosevelt ran for a fourth term in 1944—and was re-elected—Sulzberger had to face some grumbling and withdrawal of certain important advertisers who disliked The Times' support of the President's candidacy. But he held firmly to the decision. The climax of the greatest war in history lay near at hand, and in the judgment of The Times the decisive issue of the 1944 election was the conduct of the nation's foreign policy. On this issue The Times found the record of the Democrats more reassuring than that of the Republicans.

The Times had gradually shucked the "Independent Democrat" label affixed to it during Ochs' tenure; it was politically independent. It had backed Willkie in 1940 because it did not favor a third term for any United States President, but had put even this consideration aside when Roosevelt was renominated in 1944, because it thought he was better equipped to guide the nation to ultimate war victory than any new man might be.

By this time Sulzberger had expanded his staff into the largest in the world and had introduced some innovations that had worked out exceedingly well. The new Sunday Magazine had flourished, so had The News of the Week in Review, the Book Review and the changed drama section. They were perfect complements to the main, or news section, and performed the function Markel had outlined for them; they gave the background to the news, what the Sunday editor described as "the deeper sense of the news."

The daily column, News of Food, that had started on March 11, 1941, had evolved into a page devoted solely to news of particular interest to women—news of food, fashions, furnishings, child care, club activities and welfare work. The publisher defended this, against original criticism, as a natural evolution. He pointed out that he was putting nothing new into The Times by this move, but was merely assembling onto one page items that had always been news, but had been scattered through the daily paper.

There was some apprehensiveness in the editorial departments when he established an annual fashion show at Times Hall under the title "Fashions of The Times." Older men on the staff mumbled that Ochs never had tried such frippery, but they had forgotten that Ochs had run fashion contests in The Times in 1913, with cash awards for the best dress designs.

The idea for "Fashions of The Times" originated with Miss Virginia Pope, Times fashion editor. Between 1935 and 1940, under sponsorship of the promotion and circulation departments, she had given a series of small fashion shows before women's clubs in the New York metropolitan area, and desired to produce them on a larger scale because women had shown eager interest in them.

Around the same time a survey indicated that the textile trades in New York were gradually pulling out, a fact that worried the city fathers. When the war cut off Paris fashions the situation became acute and Miss Pope wisely figured a Times-sponsored fashion show might help anchor the industry—and help bring in more national apparel advertising.

The publisher had had a brief fling in the textile field in his youth and he knew of the concern over the slow dispersal of the city's garment plants. He approved the show idea and gave Miss Pope and the promotion department a free hand with it.

They worked up a dramatized style show, unlike any ever seen in New York—or in Paris, for that matter. It was done with Broadway theatre technique, under professional direction, with professional lighting, professional models, special sets, special music and with original designs of dresses, gowns, furs, millinery, shoes and all the accessories. The foremost men and women in the industry contributed to it. The first show was produced in October 1942.

Office wags had secretly dubbed the project "Sulzberger's Folly," but the show was a professional triumph. Even Mayor Fiorello H. LaGuardia, given to intermittent feuding with The Times, grumpily conceded that the production would be a powerful influence in halting the apparel trades' flight from the city, and in gaining world-wide recognition for the work of American designers.

It had that effect, and though The Times was eventually to put as much as $125,000 into productions of the show, the newspaper's national fashion advertising reflected substantial gains. It had stood at 97,865 lines in 1940. In 1950 it was up to 714,726 lines. No one could say that the show was not a major factor in this remarkable increase. Its popularity grew each year, so that by 1948 tickets that The Times sold for $1.65 were bringing $60 each and more from fashion agencies, department executives and men in the textile trades who were anxious to get extra seats.

It was a common Broadway comment that "Fashions of The Times" was the only hit show that consistently lost money. The publisher gave the proceeds of the earliest shows to charity, but in more recent years they have gone to the Fashion Institute of Technology where young people are trained for the industry.

On July 18, 1944, the Federal Communications Commission approved The Times' purchase of Radio Station WQXR and WQXR-FM. This step worried some executives, too, but worked out well. The station was an outlet for the hourly newscasts and served for facsimile short-wave experiments. It was kept as dignified as The Times' columns, and, like the fashions show, added to the newspaper's prestige.

Neither Ochs nor Sulzberger had ever made non-Times investments, because they wanted to keep clear of any entanglements that might embarrass The Times; the family's own investments were limited to their Times holdings and to Government bonds. Some outsiders could not reconcile that stand with the purchase of WQXR.

Sulzberger explained that the paper was not in the entertainment field. "We needed a vehicle for the broadcasts and for the experiments," he said, "and this was a practical way to get it. The Times was considered ivory tower, and somewhat aloof. We knew the station wouldn't change the tone of The Times, but felt it would show that we were modern, and keeping up to date."

A development that complicated every newspaper publisher's administrative load in the feverish Forties was the rise and spread of the Newspaper Guild, a unit of the C.I.O. Ochs had had to deal with the mechanical craft unions throughout his publishing career and had, on the whole, found them friendly and sound. The Times unit of Big Six, the printers' union, had frequently given him gifts in appreciation of his fair dealing and complete understanding of their needs and their problems. Their talks were smoothed by their knowledge that Ochs himself had once been a working printer.

Sulzberger, though, was confronted with something unique in Times history—a union embracing all workers other than the mechanical craftsmen. The mechanical unions maintained their original union status, independent of the Guild. In 1940 Sulzberger had been called to the witness stand by the National Labor Relations Board for examination as to whether he had discouraged Guild membership on The Times. He carried to the chair with him a scrap of paper on which he had written, "Keep calm, smile; don't be smart." He had prepared the memorandum as a reminder that he must not allow himself to be goaded to anger by any possible legal heckling. He needed it several times during the four days of the examination, but he lived up to it.

On April 21, 1941, The Times signed a Guild contract covering the newspaper's commercial departments—the business, circulation, promotion, advertising and kindred units, but "excluding all employes in the news and editorial departments, all employes who are members of, or eligible to, membership in existing craft unions with long bargaining histories." This contract fixed minimum salaries, for a five-day, 40-hour working week.

On May 1, 1942, The Times had signed a Guild contract covering the news and editorial departments. In these negotiations the publisher steadfastly refused to grant a union shop clause for those departments, a stand he maintained through all subsequent negotiations whenever the issue came up again. A contract signed on March 22, 1943, brought Times maintenance workers into Guild jurisdiction.

Sulzberger's stand against the union or Guild shop clause for news and editorial workers was clearly stated.

"Our position," he said during the negotiations in 1941, "has always been—and always will be—that those who are concerned with the handling of the news shall not be required to be members of any definite group, whether it be political or industrial or any other; a contrary position, we firmly believe, would militate against the complete impartiality that is the very essence of the news."

The publisher had discussed this point with President Roosevelt, when the two had met at the White House some time before, and even the President, stout champion of collective bargaining, and others had supported Sulzberger's stand. He, too, felt that it might be wise to permit men who wrote and handled the news to act as they saw fit about entering, or not entering, the Guild; that only in this way could complete impartiality in the handling of labor and political news be assured.

When the publisher entered into fresh exchange with Guild leaders on the issue in 1944, Sulzberger reasserted his belief and, incidentally, his whole attitude toward collective bargaining on The Times. He referred to the newspaper's history of friendly relationship with unions throughout Ochs' and his own administration. He pointed out that he had not fought the Guild in departments other than news and editorial.

"I recognize," he told the Guild in a written statement in 1944, "that varying backgrounds, temperaments and opportunities are responsible for divergent views. The latter, if within the framework of our national policy, not only have their place in a sound newspaper but are in effect an essential guarantee against any group's seizure and control of news channels . . . I am pleased to assure you . . . that an honest and accurate Guildsman will always be welcomed on The New York Times and since this . . . is to be posted as the final document in this correspondence, I can use it to give similar assurance to those of the staff who may not be sympathetic with the Guild or its management that honest and accurate non-Guildsmen will also always be welcomed on this newspaper. Only by preserving balance can we guard against the passions that result in error."

During the Dumbarton Oaks Conference in Washington the publisher had to make an extremely important decision on the newspaper's responsibility to its readers.

Scotty Reston had persuaded an official at the conference, whose identity he never divulged, that the outlines for a proposed world security organization as drawn by the chief participating nations—the United States, Britain and Russia—should be made public. There had been bitter editorials in many newspapers over the secrecy in which information about the security plans was bound, but official Washington had refused to release the substance of the discussions.

On Wednesday, Aug. 23, under the headline, "Three Powers Outline League Peace Plans," Reston gave the substance of the various outlines.

"An official communiqué disclosed," Reston's story said, "that the three plans had been discussed and that Mr. Stettinius had been selected as permanent chairman of the conversations, but it did not say anything about the questions asked after the reading of each plan.

"The New York Times, however, has obtained from an unimpeachable source the following digest of the three plans which were drafted by the Governments recently and exchanged by the Governments for study and comment."

The digests contained the first mention of the U.N. veto.

The Times story kicked up a furor. Correspondents for other newspapers and for the great news agencies set up angry clamor over the fact that one newspaper, and only one, had access to the draft outlines. Edward R. Stettinius Jr., then Under Secretary of State, complained directly to Sulzberger.

He argued somewhat forcefully that the Reston story endangered the success of the Dumbarton Oaks meeting. He held that if the Reston stories continued, the Soviet delegates, with limited experience in international relations, would feel that they could not trust their fellow-conferees to keep official discussions secret. It was at this meeting, incidentally, that the United Nations veto took shape. Reston was the first newspaperman to write about it.

Sulzberger quietly heard Stettinius out and then sat some moments in deep thought. Finally, he observed that the conference nations had had years in which to work secretly on the document and that there probably was no need for further debate on paramount issues.

"All the News That's Fit to Print"

The New York Times.

LATE CITY EDITION

VOL. XCIV..No. 31,869.   NEW YORK, THURSDAY, APRIL 26, 1945.   THREE CENTS

TRUMAN OPENS WORLD SECURITY PARLEY;
RUSSIANS ENCIRCLE BERLIN, CROSS ELBE;
3D NEAR AUSTRIA; BERCHTESGADEN BOMBED

VOL. XCIV..No. 31,870.   NEW YORK, FRIDAY, APRIL 27, 1945.   THREE CENTS

PARLEY IN DISPUTE OVER PERMANENT HEAD;
BRITISH WIN BREMEN, PATTON SWEEPS ON;
RUSSIANS SEIZE STETTIN, MOST OF BERLIN

MCGOLDRICK SWITCH | Fund for Red Cross | ODER FLANK TURNED | 2 REDOUBTS CRACK | THE AMERICANS CROSSING THE DANUBE RIVER | MOLOTOFF OBJECTS

VOL. XCIV..No. 31,871.   NEW YORK, SATURDAY, APRIL 28, 1945.   THREE CENTS

U. S. AND RED ARMIES JOIN, SPLIT GERMANY;
3D ARMY IN AUSTRIA; RUSSIANS IN POTSDAM;
PARLEY BARS LUBLIN, SOVIET GETS 3 VOTES

RUSSIAN ISSUES OUT | Parley Sessions | BERLIN NEAR FINISH | HANDS ACROSS THE ELBE: AMERICANS AND RUSSIANS MEET IN REICH | FIRM LINK FORMED

VOL. XCIV..No. 31,872.   NEW YORK, SUNDAY, APRIL 29, 1945.   TEN CENTS

ALLIES BAR PEACE PLEA THAT OMITS RUSSIA;
SURRENDER REPORT UNTRUE, TRUMAN SAYS;
MUNICH REVOLTS; HITLER SAID TO BE DYING

RUSSIANS DEMAND | Berlin's 'Fleet' Sails To Elbe to Surrender | REICH ARMY REBELS | BERLIN TOTTERING | RUSSIANS FIGHTING IN THE STREETS OF BERLIN | NAZIS' END NEAR

VOL. XCIV..No. 31,873.   NEW YORK, MONDAY, APRIL 30, 1945.   THREE CENTS

U. S. 7TH IN MUNICH, BRITISH PUSH ON BALTIC;
RUSSIANS TIGHTEN RING ON BERLIN'S HEART;
MILAN AND VENICE WON; MUSSOLINI KILLED

BIG POWERS SCAN | Moscow Blackout Ends for Big Day | SLAIN BY PARTISANS | THE INGLORIOUS END OF A DICTATOR | 3 DIVISIONS ENTER

VOL. XCIV..No. 31,874.   NEW YORK, TUESDAY, MAY 1, 1945.   THREE CENTS

RUSSIANS FLY VICTORY FLAG ON REICHSTAG;
U. S. 7TH WINS MUNICH, DRIVES FOR BRENNER;
FOE BROKEN IN ITALY; TITO MEN IN TRIESTE

BRADLEY 24 MILES | 54 War | CLARK SEES MARSHAL DE BRENNER CUT | SUICIDE PILOT COMES CLOSE TO U.S. WARSHIP | STALIN HAILS

VOL. XCIV..No. 31,875.   NEW YORK, WEDNESDAY, MAY 2, 1945.   THREE CENTS

HITLER DEAD IN CHANCELLERY, NAZIS SAY;
DOENITZ, SUCCESSOR, ORDERS WAR TO GO ON;
BERLIN ALMOST WON; U. S. ARMIES ADVANCE

Headline History of the Ending of World War II in Europe: The fourteen dramati

VOL. XCIV..No. 31,876. NEW YORK, THURSDAY, MAY 3, 1945. THREE CENTS

BERLIN FALLS TO RUSSIANS, 70,000 GIVE UP;
1,000,000 SURRENDER IN ITALY AND AUSTRIA;
DENMARK IS CUT OFF; HAMBURG GIVES UP

GERMANS AND ALLIES SIGNING UNCONDITIONAL SURRENDER IN ITALY EPIC SIEGE IS OVER

VOL. XCIV..No. 31,877. NEW YORK, FRIDAY, MAY 4, 1945. THREE CENTS

DOENITZ IN COPENHAGEN, PEACE TALK SEEN;
NORTH FRONT COLLAPSES, 150,000 CAPTURED;
PLANES RAKE FOE IN DANISH 'DUNKERQUE'

SOVIET OVERTURE | Date Set by British | BRITISH IN DENMARK | MARCH OF THE DEFEATED: NAZIS PASS THROUGH BRANDENBURG GATE | REICH SEAT MOVED

VOL. XCIV—No. 31,878. NEW YORK, SATURDAY, MAY 5, 1945. THREE CENTS

500,000 MORE SURRENDER TO MONTGOMERY;
YIELD IN HOLLAND, DENMARK, NORTH REICH;
U. S. AND SOVIET UNITS HACK CZECH POCKET

RUSSIANS DEMAND | Army Slash Will Be Slow | 7TH AND 5TH JOIN | THE SURRENDER OF HAMBURG TO THE BRITISH | WAR RACING TO END

VOL. XCIV—No. 31,879. NEW YORK, SUNDAY, MAY 6, 1945. TEN CENTS

NAZIS IN WEST AUSTRIA, BAVARIA GIVE UP;
END SEEMS NEAR IN NORWAY; CZECHS RISE;
16 POLISH LEADERS SEIZED, RUSSIA ADMITS

SOVIET ACTION HIT | Osmena Says Sons | DOENITZ IN APPEAL | THIS IS THE MOMENT: MONTGOMERY DICTATES GERMAN SURRENDER | TWO ARMIES GIVE UP

VOL. XCIV—No. 31,880. NEW YORK, MONDAY, MAY 7, 1945. THREE CENTS

NAZIS REPORTED READY FOR A FULL SURRENDER;
U. S. 3D ARMY CAPTURES PILSEN IN CZECH DRIVE;
PRAGUE PATRIOTS SAY HELP FROM ALLIES IS NEAR

Mayor Announces | BIG 4 IN 2 ACCORDS | ARMS CENTER WON | HORSE AND WAGON REPLACES BLITZKRIEG MACHINE | END LIKELY HOURLY

VOL. XCIV—No. 31,881. NEW YORK, TUESDAY, MAY 8, 1945. THREE CENTS

THE WAR IN EUROPE IS ENDED!
SURRENDER IS UNCONDITIONAL;
V-E WILL BE PROCLAIMED TODAY;
OUR TROOPS ON OKINAWA GAIN

VOL. XCIV—No. 31,882. NEW YORK, WEDNESDAY, MAY 9, 1945. THREE CENTS

FINAL SURRENDER SIGNED IN BERLIN RUINS;
SOVIET JOINS IN PROCLAIMING TRIUMPH;
TRUMAN WARNS VICTORY 'IS BUT HALF WON'

...ning with the encirclement of Berlin, through the death of Hitler, to final surrender.

He also told Stettinius that it was his opinion that if unity among the great powers was so feeble that it could be shaken by a few factual news stories, then it would not stand up, anyway.

He said: "I think, Mr. Stettinius, that The Times will feel compelled to continue Reston's series. The documents are authentic, and the people have a right to know what they contain. It is their interests that are at stake in this meeting."

Thomas E. Dewey used the information from Reston's Dumbarton Oaks stories throughout his presidential campaign. Out of this grew the United States' bipartisan policy in international issues, and President Truman's appointment of John Foster Dulles as Republican adviser on foreign policy.

The State Department, Reston later learned unofficially, had the F.B.I. try to trace the source from which he got the Dumbarton Oaks documents. Because Scotty had worked a long time in London and had been fairly close to Anthony Eden, the investigators were inclined to blame the Britons for the leak, but they were wrong. Anyway, they never found out how Reston got the charter drafts or from whom, and eventually the thing was dropped.

Reston kept the inside track at the conference and quoted liberally from the documents whenever a new story demanded it. The staff as a whole was delighted with the publisher's firm stand in the Dumbarton Oaks case, since it is any reporter's great fear that his managing editor or his publisher may not back him in an emergency though he has adhered to journalistic ethics.

The Dumbarton Oaks beat was only one of the series of Times exclusives on vital international pieces just before war's end, and in the post-war period. Most of these were obtained by the active Washington bureau. Three years after Dumbarton Oaks on Sept. 23, 1947, Reston got an advance copy of the Marshall European Plan Report when it was signed at the Paris Conference. Again, his source was never disclosed, and again men on other newspapers were chagrined at The Times' clear beat.

Delivery of the European Plan Report to Reston was more complicated than delivery of the world security charter outlines. Reston was in Washington when the delegate who had promised to send it delivered the document by trusted messenger to a cable company in Paris, with orders to send it collect to Reston personally.

The report ran to more than 25,000 words and Western Union was a little nervous about it. Cablegrams of that length were extraordinary. The company wanted to be certain the sender was not perpetrating an expensive hoax.

"Get it here fast as you can," Reston told the Western Union man curtly. "The Times will pay for it."

The report came into The Times over three lines—Press Wireless, Western Union and Commercial Cable. It started to flow into the Washington bureau at 10:30 A.M. on Sept. 23, but it flooded that office, so Meinholtz, communications chief, had it diverted to his Manhattan news room wires.

It took eight hours for the report to come through. As the wordage flowed in across the Atlantic, appropriate maps, charts and photographs to illustrate it were ordered by Bernstein of the foreign desk. The report cost more than $1,000 in cable and wireless tolls, not counting the man-hours that went into receiving it and setting it in type.

It filled thirty-two columns—four full pages—and was a world beat. The officially released version came to the United States in sealed State Department pouches after the cabled version was in Times type. Few other newspapers bothered to use it then, although it was one of the most important of all post-war documents. The Times had run it in full and everyone interested in it had already read it.

Such journalistic achievements more than justified Sulzberger's expansion of The Times specialist staff. From the moment the war began he had kept on adding good men as fast as he could find them, so that the paper's coverage at the battlefront, and behind it, was unequaled.

Soon Sulzberger was off on another of his trips to war fronts—this time a 27,000-mile flight in Pacific battle areas. He was again traveling to inspect Red Cross installations and to share the dangers of the fighting zones with his men.

Early Tuesday evening, Nov. 14, 1944, a Pan American Clipper bearing the publisher and Turner Catledge, then national correspondent and later executive managing editor, rose from San Francisco Bay, off Hamilton Field, as stewards drew blackout curtains in fast-descending darkness. The ship leveled off at 7,500 feet and thundered through the night. When the twenty-six passengers waked, it was almost dawn and two miles below lay Pearl Harbor, brilliantly floodlighted as civilian and military workers toiled at getting out the material that was pushing the war in the Pacific toward bloody and bitter end.

The flight took Sulzberger and Catledge to Johnson Island, Kwajalein, Guam, Tinian, Saipan, Peleliu, Leyte, Hollandia, Port Moresby, Townsville, Brisbane, Sydney, Melbourne, Ohakea in New Zealand, Pago Pago, back to Honolulu and home by way of El Paso and Washington. Wherever they ran into Times men the publisher got first-hand reports of their routines and of their difficulties.

Maj. Gen. Sanderford Jarman, commander at Saipan from Guam, was an enthusiastic host. "You're really in luck, you two," he told them. "Our B-29's took off at dawn this morning for their first major crack at Tokyo. They'll be dropping back tonight and we'll all go down to see them come in."

The newspapermen stood with Jarman in the dark control tower after 7 o'clock. They heard the returning pilots reporting as they came in for landing. Clinton Green, a new correspondent for The Times, was on the island, to do the story.

On Nov. 28 a Navy C-47 put Catledge and Sulzberger down on Peleliu. They had watched in awe as they roared over a United States Armada at Ulithi and had sailed high over ground fire from Yap, still Japanese-held.

Off Leyte they roared in over the great American fleet, with American fighters frisking on their flanks, just as the raid sirens sounded on the island air strip. They were barely out on the runway when lanky, dark-featured Kluckhohn came up. Parrott had been wounded in the chest by shrapnel during a Japanese air raid on Leyte a few days before, and had been evacuated to a base hospital at Hollandia. The publisher was relieved to hear that a large shrapnel fragment near a main artery that had endangered Parrott's heart had been successfully removed. The alert lasted through their brief conversation, and for some time after, before the jeep assigned to them by General MacArthur could roll out to them.

They rolled through thick mud to an improvised motor ferry and were taken to the General's Headquarters at Tacloban. The publisher sat between MacArthur and his chief of staff. They talked about Julius Ochs Adler, then a brigadier general, who had been flown from New Guinea to Walter Reed Hospital in Washington a few months before because of serious illness. Adler had been second in command of the Sixth Division in New Guinea but had been placed on the inactive list three days after Sulzberger had taken off from San Francisco on the Pacific flight. He was back at The Times in mufti, and broken-hearted about it. MacArthur had secretly told the publisher that he had intended to make Adler a major general but had withheld it when Adler fell ill.

The visitors spent three days with General MacArthur.

One morning the touring Times men went by jeep with General Krueger of MacArthur's staff to watch the Thirty-second Division on the far side of Leyte in action against the Japanese. "I ought to warn you," the general told them, "we may be bombed, and probably will be, but you can't know what this war's about until you see some of it. It's entirely up to you."

The publisher climbed into the jeep, and Catledge too. They slid and slithered through the viscous mud, following an M.P. car that held a few grim G.I.'s fingering tommy guns at the ready. At Carigara, some thirty miles from their take-off position, they boarded an amphibious craft to skirt the jungle shore to Pinamapoan Point, a toe of land jutting from the foot of a mountain ridge. They landed and Sulzberger rode up to the lines with the general, through a tropical downpour.

A few days later The Times men were aboard a C-54 transport with forty-two other passengers and an enormous amount of personal military gear, for the flight to Hollandia. The trip was uneventful. After Australia, New Zealand and some picturesque little islands gem-set in the sea, Sulzberger and Catledge started back. Donald Nelson, former War Production Board chairman, came through Melbourne in a special C-54, bound home from a mission in China for President Roosevelt. At a dinner for Sulzberger in the Athenaeum in Melbourne, all the Australians and New Zealanders were interested in a discussion about Russia between Nelson and the publisher. Nelson had just been wined and dined in Moscow, and was convinced that the Russians greatly admired American efficiency and industrial power.

Sulzberger questioned Nelson's conclusions. They did not square, he pointed out, with the impressions he himself had brought away after his visit to Moscow. He stressed that he had found no love for what he considered the most important American contribution to the world—a free press in a free society. Sulzberger's greatest passion was freedom of the press. He always spoke of it—still speaks of it—as one of the most vital heritages in modern civilization.

Nelson offered the publisher a lift all the way home in the special C-54. The plane left Wellington in New Zealand on Sunday, Dec. 11. At 9:20 P.M. on Thursday the silver ship let its flaps down and rolled to a smooth stop at National Airport in Washington. Sulzberger and Catledge then climbed into a special Army plane that had brought some radio men down to dinner with Secretary Forrestal. At midnight they skimmed Manhattan's skyscrapers, gliding down to LaGuardia Airport.

Just after the publisher got home the war news from Europe went briefly dark again as an American force was hemmed in at the Bastogne bulge created by a desperate German drive toward the sea that threatened vital Allied supply lines. This lifted late in January after bitter, bloody fighting, and the great last push to Berlin was resumed. In the Philippines, MacArthur was leading his forces in a tremendous effort that was to clear the islands of the enemy.

Early in February Roosevelt, Churchill and Stalin met at Yalta in the Crimea to discuss final battle plans, and division of control in Germany at war's end. They knew then the fighting had only a little while longer to go in Europe, and that the Japanese were at last definitely on the defensive. Times coverage at Yalta and in the battle zones continued more comprehensive than any other newspaper's, though not without price.

Richard J. H. Johnston, one of its younger correspondents, had been wounded on Sept. 2, 1944, in the American drive on the Harbor of Brest. On Dec. 27, Hal Denny was cut on the arms and face by aerial bomb fragments in a German attack on a small Belgian village. Jack Frankish of The United Press was killed by the same bomb. Jamie MacDonald had been hurt in a jeep accident as he moved against the Germans in the Netherlands with the British. During this period the daily casualty lists also carried the names of many Times men in the armed forces who had died in battle or had been wounded.

By the war's end in 1945, 910 men and women had left The Times to serve with the Army, Navy and Marine Corps, and nineteen of them had died in combat. One of the first names on the casualty lists had been Jimmy Hayes'. He had been a big, shy, untalkative kid carrying reporters' copy. He had volunteered for the paratroopers and just before he went overseas he had wandered into the city room one night for a characteristically quiet good-by. He had parachuted into Normandy on D-Day and had been killed in the first day's fighting. Little Tommy Kirk, a copy boy in sports, had gone into the Air Corps. He had been home on furlough when the D-Day story broke, and had voluntarily gone to the telephone room that morning to sit at The Times switchboard to help handle the flood of subscriber telephone calls. The publisher had heard about that, and had written him a warm letter of thanks. He said in it that Tommy had showed the stuff that real newspapermen are made of, but no one ever got to know how good a newspaperman Tommy might have made. He died a bombardier. His plane was destroyed in fighting on a dangerous mission over Yugoslavia.

There was another casualty about then—a casualty of time. On Monday morning, Jan. 29, 1945, John Becan, veteran in The Times news room morgue, made out a new red file card: "Van Anda, Carr 802331, managing editor New York Times 1904-1932. Died Jan. 28, 1945." In Times biographical files white cards are for living subjects, red cards for the dead. The front page on Monday had carried the story:

"Carr V. Van Anda, managing editor of The New York Times from 1904 to 1932, died at 10:50 o'clock last night of a heart attack in his apartment at 1170 Park Avenue. He was 80 years old." The heart attack had been induced by the shock of learning that Blanche Van Anda, his daughter, had died in her suite in the Hotel Fairfax at 116 East Fifty-sixth Street, at 8:45 P.M. the same night.

The Times ran a long editorial on its old news chief on Tuesday. It said, among other things:

"Carr V. Van Anda . . . was a legend in his lifetime, and will remain one . . . He and Mr. Ochs were among the first to realize the value of a fully documented newspaper . . . His coverage of the first World War made journalistic history . . . His signature is written large across The New York Times today."

Spring came, bright with hope for war's end. By the close of March the Yanks had captured or wiped out the Rhine-Moselle-Saar triangle. They had crossed the Rhine in force from the west and the Russians were bearing down in strength from the east. MacArthur held most of the Philippines and was invading Palawan, control point facing the Sulu and South China Seas. Tokyo was crumbling under constant B-29 bombardment in force. Japanese strength in the air, on the land and on the sea was rapidly diminishing.

In The Times office, as this news poured in and was processed and distributed around the world in the daily, Sunday and Overseas Weekly editions, preparations were under way for the mid-April San Francisco Conference of the United Nations. Neil Mac-Neil, assistant night managing editor, a kindly, giant Nova Scotian who had handled copy on many great Times stories including the Tut-ankh-Amen series and seven political conventions, was to be in charge. Krock, Reston and John Crider were assigned out of Washington for it; James, Mrs. McCormick and Russell Porter from New York. Lawrence E. Davies of the San Francisco Bureau was to work on it too.

Delegates to the United Nations Conference at San Francisco were mildly astonished when on the morning of April 25 there appeared at their appointed places a four-page wirephoto edition of The Times that had been set in type in New York, 3,000 miles across the continent, at 2 A.M. New York time. It bore the legend "2 A.M. Edition, Wednesday, April 25."

The delegates learned that they were beneficiaries of a Times experiment with facsimile, the first of its kind in journalistic history. The edition had been set in type in The Times composing room, and had been transmitted a half page at a time over Associated Press wirephoto facilities, to an A.P. receiver in the San Francisco Chronicle Building.

Prints made from the wirephoto negatives were processed at the

Richmond Independent publishing plant, fifteen miles from The Chonicle office. There photoengravers matched the half-pages, photographed the result, and from zinc engravings ran off at the rate of 2,000 copies a day on flat-bed presses.

The Times provided the United Nations delegates with this service without charge for the duration of the conference. It brought the newspaper an inpouring of grateful letters and excited comment on the potential effect such a method might have on journalism in the future.

Three years later, in February, 1948, The Times tried another facsimile experiment. Under the editorship of Robert Simpson, a copy reader, it put out six editions daily of a four-page newspaper —two pages of spot news, two pages of features—with an 8½ by 11 inch format, for simultaneous transmission by WQXR-FM to fourteen department stores in New York and the Columbia University School of Journalism. This experiment, conducted with the John V. L. Hogan equipment, ran a full month. The columns were set on varitype machines, and special photo cuts were made for this edition.

On Thursday afternoon, April 12, the run of news coming across the desk was consistently good. The foreign desk had prepared a top head:

NINTH CROSSES ELBE, NEARS BERLIN

Drew Middleton's story on which this was based had told that: "Thousands of tanks and a half million doughboys of the United States First, Third and Ninth Armies are racing through the heart of the Reich on a front of 150 miles, threatening Berlin, Leipzig and the last citadels of the Nazi power."

William H. Lawrence had just sent from The Times bureau on Guam an exciting account:

OUR OKINAWA GUNS
DOWN 118 PLANES

His story related: "Japanese attempting to halt the American march to Tokyo, have started desperate suicidal aerial attacks upon our ships and men in the Okinawa area, losing 118 planes on Thursday alone."

Nazi Propaganda Minister Goebbels had bitterly conceded in a broadcast from Germany that, "We have sunk very low . . . the war cannot last much longer."

Doughboy prisoners by the thousand had been freed by their on-rushing G.I. comrades, and some of these had already been flown home.

As the desk men handled all this copy and headlined it, a flash from Warm Springs, Ga., just before 6 P.M., rocked the office. The flash said: "President Roosevelt dead."

When the news came through, Sulzberger was still in his office and James, Merz and Markel were in theirs. They met at once in the managing editor's room, tense and grim, trying not to react like ordinary human beings, but like newspapermen.

David H. Joseph, then city editor, sent men scurrying into the Square and into local byways to get public reaction to the President's unexpected death. In Washington, Krock revised the whole day's schedule, and assigned himself to write the lead. His men scattered around the capital, and worked the telephones for details on the impending swearing-in of a new Commander in Chief. The telegraph desk wired its correspondents and stringers to send reaction stories from capitals across the nation. The foreign desk cabled for quick stories from Europe's capitals.

Sulzberger rarely attempted to dictate Times make-up, but this afternoon he took a hand. He sent for old Times files to see how Raymond had handled the death of another Commander in Chief eighty years before. Mourning borders edged every column on the front page that told of Lincoln's passing. Obviously that did not conform with Twentieth Century style or standards. The publisher recalled, then, the quiet, dignified front page that had been used when Ochs died. He got it out, studied it a while, and thought it would serve best. The same kind of black border was chosen for a four-column cut of the dead President. After quiet discussion the group decided not to turn all front-page rules for black borders for the type. Sulzberger and his aides compromised on turned slugs for black borders only for the beginning and the close of the Roosevelt editorial.

Next morning The Times, with perfectly balanced front page, proclaimed to the world:

PRESIDENT ROOSEVELT IS DEAD;
TRUMAN TO CONTINUE POLICIES;
9TH CROSSES ELBE; NEARS BERLIN

Krock's story led the paper next to another front-page spread from Washington that said:

TRUMAN IS SWORN
IN THE WHITE HOUSE

"Franklin Delano Roosevelt," said the Krock story, "War President of the United States, and the only Chief Executive in history who was chosen for more than two terms, died suddenly and unexpectedly at 4:35 P.M. at Warm Springs, Ga., and the White House announced his death at 5:48 o'clock. He was 63.

"The President, stricken by a cerebral hemorrhage, passed from unconsciousness to death on the eighty-third day of his fourth term and in an hour of triumph. The armies and fleets under his direction as Commander in Chief were at the gates of Berlin and the shores of Japan's home islands as Mr. Roosevelt died and the cause he represented and led was nearing the conclusive phase of success.

"Less than two hours after the official announcement, Harry S. Truman of Missouri, the Vice President, took the oath as the thirty-second President. The oath was administered by the Chief Justice of the United States in a one-minute ceremony at the White House."

It was as if the Divine Hand had led Franklin Roosevelt to the top of the hill from which he could see imminent victory, and then had gently turned him from it before final glory came in sight. A few weeks later, on Tuesday, May 8, 1945, The Times went to a rare four-line front-page display to note for hysterically joyful readers, and for posterity:

THE WAR IN EUROPE IS ENDED!
SURRENDER IS UNCONDITIONAL;
V-E WILL BE PROCLAIMED TODAY;
OUR TROOPS ON OKINAWA GAIN

The big surrender story was the controversial beat scored by Edward Kennedy of The Associated Press. The lead said:

REIMS, France, May 7—Germany surrendered unconditionally to the Western Allies and the Soviet Union at 2:41 A.M. French time today. [This was at 8:41 P.M. Eastern War-time Sunday] The surrender took place at a little red schoolhouse that is the headquarters of General Dwight D. Eisenhower.

Throngs filled Times Square and celebrants stopped traffic for hours. Ticker tape and textile fragments floated from skyscrapers and lofts. The Times flashed the official announcement by President Truman at 9 A.M. May 8. The lights burned brightly in New York that night and the long darkness slowly lifted everywhere but in the Pacific.

CHAPTER
43

E ARLY IN APRIL, 1945, William L. Laurence, science reporter for
The Times, suddenly vanished from the office. No one on the
staff knew where he had gone, though they did wonder at his
absence. James and Sulzberger had a fair idea of his assignment,
but they never discussed it.

Bill Laurence, a gentle, generous soul, was forever steeped in
his Times work, forever poring over medical journals and chemists'
reports or haunting scientists' conventions. He was inclined to dress
a little carelessly, and never got to the barber's until his graying
hair, in flat pompadour, washed over the top of his collar.

He had written for The Times of Jan. 31, 1939, a story headed:

VAST ENERGY FREED
BY URANIUM ATOM

The story said: "The splitting of a uranium atom into two parts,
each consisting of a gigantic 'cannon-ball' of the tremendous energy
of 100,000,000 electron-volts, the greatest amount of atomic energy
so far liberated on earth, was announced here yesterday by the
Columbia University Department of Physics."

Another Laurence story in The Times on May 5, 1940, disclosed
that the physicists at Columbia had proved that one pound of
U-235, a uranium derivative, yielded power equal to that released
by 5,000,000 pounds of coal, or by 3,000,000 pounds of gasoline.
The same account told how German physicists were working night

and day on converting this incredible power into offensive weapons.

These Laurence stories had, in a manner of speaking, been spawned a quarter-century before. Van Anda had foreseen them when he assigned Alva Johnston to the scientists' meeting in Cambridge in December, 1922. It was then that the brand-new terms associated with atomic power research had first appeared in The Times.

On May 30, 1940, another Laurence story had broken:

11,000 TIMES SPEEDIER WAY FOUND
TO OBTAIN ATOMIC POWER ELEMENT

The piece disclosed that U-235, the uranium element that yielded the fabulous energy reported in earlier stories, could now be produced 11,000 times faster than it had ever been.

Laurence had learned this from advance proofs of Nature, the British scientific weekly, which credited the new process to a Stockholm physicist, Prof. Wilhelm Krasny-Ergen. Former processes had yielded small amounts of U-235 only after years of labor. With the new formula a pound could be turned out in four days.

In September, 1940, a story by Laurence on U-235, titled "The Atom Gives Up" had appeared in The Saturday Evening Post. Soon afterward American military men got uneasy. They then knew they were in an atomic bomb race with Nazi Germany and that the first to produce the bomb would win the war. The F.B.I. garnered all copies of the Post story from public libraries, asked the Post to send no more out, and to let it know when anyone sent requests for copies.

Laurence had had the inside track on the atomic bomb story from the start, and had kept it. No other newspaperman knew quite as much about it. But the very scientists who had first mentioned U-235 to Laurence, now avoided him. He did not quite understand their growing aloofness at first, but slowly the truth dawned.

He guessed they were feverishly working on the bomb now and that their work was top secret. They could not discuss it. He never tried to pry into their experiments after that, nor did he discuss his conclusions with James or Sulzberger.

But all this explained his sudden disappearance from the city room in Forty-third Street. The Government had secretly asked James and Sulzberger to release Bill to them, under Government contract. The pay was to be less than his newspaper salary, but without inquiring into the nature of Bill's Government assignment, The Times undertook to make up the difference. Bill was to perform an important war service and they were proud that a Times man had been picked to do it.

Oak Ridge was unknown to the world at large at that time, but that was where Bill Laurence found himself after a secret meeting with Maj. Gen. Leslie R. Groves, head of the atomic bomb project, who had come to The Times to ask for him. Bill, he explained, was to be the project s historian. He was to watch developments and to write the whole story, which, when the proper time came, would be released to all newspapers. Bill was forbidden to communicate with anyone outside Oak Ridge.

It was a weird situation for a newspaperman. He was covering the greatest assignment in human history, but all his writings were going into a Government safe at Oak Ridge, not to the composing room. He was even told that he might not live to finish the story; that there was always an outside chance that at some stage of his reporting he and the physicists might be wiped out.

"It was Buck Rogers stuff," he liked to tell later. "I got a tremendous kick out of it."

"By July 12, 1945," Bill remembered, some months after, "I had been with the Manhattan District a little over two months. I had flown more than 35,000 miles, and had done a lot more mileage by motor car. I had been initiated in all the secret plants, which at that time no outsider knew by name—Oak Ridge, Hanford, Los Alamos and the Wellsian laboratories at Columbia, Chicago and California Universities.

"I had seen things no human eye had ever seen before—that no human mind before our time could have conceived possible. I had watched in constant fascination as men worked with heaps of uranium and plutonium great enough to blow major cities out of existence. I had prepared scores of reports on what I had observed, and I couldn't help but dream wistfully of what sensations they would have been in The Times. They never saw a copy desk. Each went into a strong safe marked 'Top Secret.' Some eventually got into print, but many have never been made public."

General Groves had asked Laurence after their first talks to draw up a list of tentative subjects to be covered. Bill's "Item 26" was: "Eyewitness account of initial bomb test in New Mexico (provided witness survives)." Item 60 was: "Eyewitness account of initial atom-bombing of Japan." On Thursday, July 12, Bill had cleaned up all preliminary copy explaining the story of the atomic bomb from its beginning. His last copy joined the stories already in the safe.

"The time had come," Bill told clusters of unashamedly wide-eyed associates in the city room, months later, "to shove off for Alamogordo in New Mexico and, God willing, for points beyond. The scientists didn't talk much about it, but in a professional way they wondered whether they would all survive the Alamogordo test to see the bomb dropped on Japan. You must remember that there was nothing romantic about such thinking; it was just that no one quite knew over what area destruction would spread. They had to guess, at that point."

The last piece Bill banged out on his typewriter before the trip to the testing ground was highly imaginative—it had to be that—to be used to explain matters in case the test bomb resulted in greater material damage than the physicists had figured on. Suppose it wiped out, among others, such world-famous scientists as Vannevar Bush, James Bryant Conant, J. Robert Oppenheimer, Enrico Fermi, James Chadwick and Ernest O. Lawrence? No fever-brained science-fictioneer could have conceived a more devastating yarn. Bill knew what *could* happen. The experimenters had told him.

Then another thought struck Bill—suppose the test bomb went completely wild, beyond even the worst extremity the physicists could figure on? Suppose some overlooked or unpredictable factor blasted such havoc that the phenomenon could not be kept secret? That gnawed at Bill. He felt, with strong newspaper instinct, that it was too great a story to be wasted. He knew that no one on earth could write it if he vanished with the men who had created this monstrous thing. He got an idea.

He wrote a confidential letter to James—a long letter that never mentioned the bomb nor even gave the faintest clue to what he had seen and heard. It went through channels.

"I have been in a constant state of bewilderment, now, for two months," it said. "The story is bigger than I could have imagined— fantastic, bizarre, fascinating and terrifying. It will be one of the big stories of our generation and it will run for some time. It will need twenty columns, at least, on the day it breaks. This may sound overenthusiastic, but I'm willing to wager right now that when the time comes you will agree that my estimate is on the conservative side . . .

"This is not just one big story. There are at least twenty-five individual page-one stories to be given out following the break of The Big News . . . The world will not be the same after the day of the Big Event. A new era in our civilization will have started, with enormous implications for the post-war period, both from military and industrial standpoints.

"I want you to know that I am not so conceited as to think that this opportunity was given to me as an individual. The honor of being the one selected to handle the story, I know full well, is due to the fact that I am a staff member of The Times. And I know that when the proper time comes, The Times will be the only news- paper to do the story justice, despite the fact that my services are not to be exclusive. I wish they could be.

"There is, however, consolation for my prolonged absence from the staff. After the story breaks I will be the only one with first- hand knowledge of it, which should give The Times considerable edge . . . My wife knows nothing about my . . . movements and it may come as a great shock to her when she finds out . . . I am looking forward to the time when I can see you again. My desk probably looks much too clean at present, and that must seem unnatural to you. As usual I am in need of a haircut . . ."

When the letter got to James, he digested it and sent it in a sealed envelope to Sulzberger with the memorandum: "I thought you would like to read this letter from Laurence. Of course, it is very confidential . . . E.L.J." The publisher read it, too, and sent it back, sealed, to go into the managing editor's safe. Across the memorandum he had scrawled:

"E.L.J.—Thank you. This looks like IT . . . A.H.S."

General Groves had discussed "IT" with James and with the publisher when he came to borrow Bill, but they knew the project only as "IT." They never pried into "IT."

At daybreak on July 16, 1945, clad in Army sun-tans, with dark glasses shielding narrowed eyes, Bill Laurence stood with bated breath in a control tower five miles from the steel bomb cage at Alamogordo in the New Mexico desert, awaiting the first atomic bomb blast.

All about him, hair-trigger tense, were General Groves, white-faced aides and physicists. One young scientist had broken under the suspense a few minutes before and had been led away. A sudden pounding downpour in pre-dawn desert dark, with lightning flashes and crashing thunder obbligato, had overstrained his nerves.

Dr. Samuel K. Allison of Chicago University called approach to zero in a tight monotone, his voice carrying by radio to observation points in the surrounding mountains. He called, "Minus twenty minutes," and after an excruciatingly long pause, "Minus fifteen minutes." All these men, utterly silent in the brooding desert dawn, knew they were vulnerable trespassers in a dangerous unknown.

Dr. Oppenheimer steadied himself at a control tower post.

"Now!" Allison shouted.

An incredibly weird and tremendous light almost blinded the goggled watchers. The earth rumbled. In the eerie, metallic glare of the bomb's brilliant flame, brighter than a thousand suns and somehow sharper, the devil's toadstool—the death flower of the atom bomb—rolled upward, and unfolded, building a boiling cloud tower into the desert sky.

Men slowly released their pent-up breath, Dr. Conant and Dr. Bush pumped the General's hands. Dr. George B. Kistiakowsky emotionally embraced Dr. Oppenheimer. For a moment all emotional flood gates were down.

Frightened and puzzled humans as distant as 450 miles away reported the unaccountable light, the rushing blast, the terrifying echoes. Men spoke of earthquakes, of heavenly signs and of meteors. Some thought they had seen a great plane explode in the sky. The sand at Alamogordo had turned jade green, and vitreous. No living thing was left in the whole area. Birds, rattlers and antelope withered in the atomic heat.

All these things Bill Laurence saw in human awe, and wrote about—but not for The Times. The greatest science story of the age, and he the only newspaperman to witness and understand it, yet compelled to silence. He choked with frustration. Noble leads and startling sentences leaped to mind, fond phrases about "the dawning of the new Atomic Age," about "elemental flame," "the first fire on earth that did not have its origin in the sun." Bill committed these to paper (as if he could ever forget), and saved them for The Times.

Ten minutes after the explosion Bill heard General Groves tell Maj. Gen. Thomas F. Farrell, "The war is over."

To all intents and purposes, it was.

General Groves thought Laurence should go home before the next step in his assignment—to witness and report the actual dropping of the first atomic bomb. He did not say when or where it was to be dropped. Not then.

He said: "Mrs. Laurence will want to know where you're going. Tell her you're going to London, but that you don't know what for. Clean out your desk first. Burn anything you have around." Bill knew that routine; his notes had been burned every night at Oak Ridge. When he got out of the plane in New York, a polite, nontalkative F.B.I. man picked him up and went to his home with him. He introduced his escort to Mrs. Laurence as a fellow-worker. She asked no questions. She was by then completely indoctrinated in secrecy.

Late in July when Laurence flew to Tinian Island in the Pacific, Japan was already on her knees. The glory-blinded little men who had bombed Pearl Harbor less than four years before were now under constant terrifying aerial bombardment themselves, seeing their tinderbox cities turned overnight to flaming waste and ruin, their production dropping drastically day after day. Their vaunted fleet was a wreck.

President Truman had called upon them to surrender. He had warned them, without giving the new weapon a name, that they were inviting horrors infinitely more terrible than any they had undergone or had inflicted. They ignored the warning. General Groves and the physicists prepared for the historic strike.

On Saturday, July 28, as the first atom bomb was prepared in extreme secrecy on Tinian, the United States Senate ratified the United Nations Charter by a vote of 89 to 2. That same morning Times men on Guam reported that B-29 Superforts had reduced six more Japanese cities and had wrought wide destruction on thinning enemy shipping. Admiral Nimitz's Headquarters had just announced that two enemy battleships and three cruisers had been crippled by carrier-borne planes.

Yet all these historic happenings that July Saturday paled in relative news value, if only briefly, beside a sensationally dramatic local disaster. At 9:45 A.M. mid-Manhattan was startled by a resounding crash. A B-25 twin-engined Army bomber, roaring through fog from Bedford, Mass., toward Newark Airport, shattered itself against the seventy-ninth floor of the Empire State Building, 915 feet above Thirty-fourth Street.

Times telephone operators leaped to their eleventh-floor south windows. They saw smoke and flame burst from the tower's side, dashed back to the board and passed the word to the city editor, David H. Joseph. He and Dick Burritt, his assistant, had been at their desks a bare forty-five minutes. Joseph hastily assigned men to the scene.

Because it was Saturday, with early deadline ahead for the big Sunday issue, the city editor knew he would need every man he could reach. He called Frank S. Adams, one of his top general reporters who was at home in Jackson Heights in Queens anticipating his day off, and assigned him to the lead-all, or first-position story. It was still well over an hour before normal reporting time for most of the staff, but within the hour, twenty-five Times men were at the scene, or working on phases away from it—airports, hospitals, police headquarters, the Mayor's office. The news photo department called extra men in, and instantly shot out William Eckenberg and Ernie Sisto, two of its veteran stars.

Sisto, a broad-shouldered man chronically ulcer-bedeviled, lugged his camera equipment to the eighty-first floor to get above the hole rent in the tower by the bomber. He removed the normal Speed Graphic lens, substituted a wide-angle lens, and with firemen clinging to his ankles straddled a window ledge. Almost 1,000 feet above Thirty-fourth Street, he hung, head down, for a series of exposures. One made a three-column cut on the front page.

In the Sunday paper the disaster story filled almost thirty columns, with more than a full page of photographs. All through the night, fresh information was inserted and changes were made in the lists of dead and injured. Bill Knox, night city editor, nervous but highly efficient, routed the flow of copy across the desk. The night bull pen scanned diagramed photographs and marked them for space. The Times could be magnificent on major disaster stories. It was that day.

The story carried a four-column headline on Sunday morning, with the first edition pre-dated and on the street by 9 o'clock Saturday night. With weightier and bulkier Sunday editions, that extra start was compulsory for complete distribution. The headline said:

BOMBER HITS EMPIRE STATE BUILDING;
SETTING IT AFIRE AT THE 79TH FLOOR;
13 DEAD, 26 HURT; WIDE AREA ROCKED

It had been a long time since a local story had moved the war out of the lead position in The Times, but this one did.

As July ended, President Truman, Prime Minister Clement R. Attlee and Premier Stalin met at Potsdam in broken, conquered Germany. Boatloads of battle-weary G.I.'s, some of whom had not seen home in four years, rode into New York's jubilantly sign-plastered harbor, thrilled by ten-foot "Welcome—Well Done!" greetings at pierheads and on waterfront walls. They dropped out of the skies in B-17's, B-25's and DC-4's in the greatest air migration in human annals.

Some were ticketed for swift transport across the country, after brief furlough, for the invasion of Japan. There was talk that the final enemy would hold out to the last man and of many months more of bloody conflict in Asia. The President had done his official best to persuade the Japanese that their doom impended if they did not yield, but The Times on July 30, 1945, published their response:

JAPAN OFFICIALLY TURNS DOWN
ALLIED SURRENDER ULTIMATUM

On sweltering Tinian on Aug. 5, Bill Laurence watched the

physicists put together the first atom bomb. They worked, with the perspiring B-29 crews, in a vest-pocket version of New York's Manhattan Island hastily set up by the miracle-passing Naval Sea-bees. The runways for the atomic bomb ships was on what had nostalgically been named "Upper Manhattan." The two main roads on Tinian bore street signs bravely marked "Broadway" and "Eighth Avenue." The physicists lived—and this delighted Bill Laurence—in a cluster of twenty-one sun-baked tents in "Times Square."

General Groves kept the President informed, in sealed reports flown to Potsdam, of the swift progress of preparations for the first atom bomb flight. Bill Laurence asked General Farrell where his spot would be on that flight.

"Filled up for this one," the General said. "You're going on the second flight."

Bill almost wept. His eyes blinked behind his thick lenses. He said, "There may not be another. This may do the trick."

"I hope," the General fervently said, "that it does."

At midnight, Bill's tender emotions almost overwhelmed him as the chaplain prayed with the first atom bomb crews:

"Almighty Father . . . We pray Thee be with those who brave the heights of Thy Heavens and who carry the battle to our ene-mies. Guard and protect them . . . May they know Thy strength and power and armed with Thy might . . . bring this war to a rapid end."

At 2:45 A.M. on Aug. 6, three B-29's lumbered down parallel runways, two flanking the bomb-bearing Enola Gay. Bill recalled later how everyone froze, mutely praying that the ships clear with-out fault.

"Almost at the last foot of runway," he wrote later, "the Enola Gay rose. It soared into the night, remained visible a little while, and vanished into the northern sky."

Washington, meanwhile, had prepared The Times for what was about to happen. James was away on summer holiday and Turner Catledge was sitting in as acting managing editor when a mysteri-ous telephone call asked The Times to send a man to a certain office in a certain Washington building. By coincidence, the Gov-ernment man who gave the message turned out to be an old school-mate of Catledge's whom he had not seen in many years. The man did not disclose his official position and Catledge didn't inquire into it. He knew, though, that his old classmate was an Army man.

When Sulzberger learned of the call he sensed at once what it might be. Catledge, who was not privy to the knowledge that General Groves had communicated to James and through James to the publisher, intended to assign someone from the Washington staff to keep the mysterious rendezvous. The publisher said: "No, don't do that. Go down yourself." And Catledge did.

Catledge arrived in Washington next morning on a Pennsylvania Railroad sleeper. General Groves introduced him to several other officers. The old school chum was not in sight, and Catledge has not seen or heard from him since.

The general went right to the point.

"You know what Bill Laurence has been doing for us, Mr. Catledge?"

"No, sir."

The general talked briefly about the test in the desert, but kept detail vague. He did not mention when or where the next phase of Laurence's work would take him.

He just said, "What we learned in this test we're about to apply somewhere, in a military operation."

Catledge nodded.

"We've called you down here," the general explained, "because we've taken your science man away, and this is strictly a science story. We feel a little under obligation to The Times, so I'm taking this way to give you a little edge. I just want to give your paper a fair break; get you alerted for an important story. You can pick your man to handle it here in Washington."

The general suggested Sidney Shalett, The Times War Department reporter for the assignment, and Catledge thought that would be all right. The general described what the probable effect of the secret "operation" would be, and Catledge was awed by the few meager details.

General Groves added: "We'll be in touch with Shalett. Just instruct your Washington bureau to keep him handy—always within call. We can't say when this operation will come off. You can tell Sulzberger as much as I've told you, and tell him I'm grateful for the loan of Laurence. Consider The Times alerted."

Sulzberger still spent his nights in the fourteenth-floor bed-chamber, except on quiet week-ends, but he had already gone to Hillandale when Catledge got back from Washington on Aug. 4. Catledge, invited out for Friday luncheon, found the Sulzbergers entertaining a few close friends. He took the publisher aside, while the guests were still at table, and told him, in low tones, what General Groves had divulged. Though the general had told no one Times man the whole story—no man, that is, but Bill Laurence—the publisher and James had a fair idea of what was coming up, and what earth-shaking consequences it might have.

The news plunged the publisher into deeply thoughtful mood. Mrs. Sulzberger noticed his unusual gravity and kept asking what had come up. Sulzberger could not tell her. "It's nothing," he insisted. "Put it down to the generally cockeyed state of the world. I guess it's gotten me down this week-end."

Waldemar Kaempffert was at Murray Bay in Canada on vacation at the time and the publisher thought he should be on hand to do a science editorial if, or when, the big news broke. He wired Kaempffert to return, and said in the message that though he was sorry to interfere with the writer's holiday, he was unable to explain at the moment why the interruption was necessary.

Catledge returned to the office. Before leaving Washington he had arranged to have Shalett put on emergency call without indicating the possible nature of the emergency; under his pledge he couldn't. Now he asked Clarence Howell, an assistant night managing editor, to keep the whole staff alerted for an important war story.

"We'll get the first flash on it out of Washington," he told Howell, "probably from the White House. The minute it comes let me know. I can't tell you any more about it than that."

Howell asked no questions.

On Monday morning, Aug. 6, the publisher dropped in to talk with Kaempffert, who had hurried home from Murray Bay. He said, "You must be wondering why I interrupted your vacation, and I want to say again I am sorry I felt compelled to do it. I can only repeat that I am confident that when you learn the reason for this recall you will agree that it was justified."

Sulzberger had barely returned to his own offices at 11 A.M.

when Catledge telephoned. He said, "They dropped it—on Hiro-shima."

The publisher called Kaempffert to his office and disclosed that the atom bomb had been dropped. Kaempffert hurried back to his book-lined chamber to write an editorial of almost two columns explaining the scientific discoveries that had led up to the dramatic event. It was headed "Science and the Bomb."

The Times of Aug. 7, 1945, told the horrifying story of the first atom bomb raid in history, in great detail:

FIRST ATOM BOMB DROPPED ON JAPAN; MISSILE IS EQUAL TO 20,000 TONS OF TNT; TRUMAN WARNS FOE OF A 'RAIN OF RUIN'

Shalett wrote the lead under the subheading:

NEW AGE USHERED

DAY OF ATOMIC ENERGY

HAILED BY PRESIDENT

REVEALING WEAPON

HIROSHIMA IS TARGET

IMPENETRABLE CLOUD OF DUST

HIDES CITY AFTER SINGLE

BOMB STRIKES

The Times devoted ten of its thirty-eight pages to the atom bomb story that Tuesday morning, and built its leading editorial on it. The major portion of the material in the news columns was a rewrite of the copy Bill Laurence had prepared for that hour, including outlines for the official atom bomb statements by the President, and by the Secretary of War. He had covered every possible phase of the agonizing development of this most horren-dous of all man's military devices.

That morning, for the first time, The Times staff learned along with the rest of the world through a modest story on Page 5 that Bill Laurence was the author of the atomic bomb's history. The head above the story said:

WAR DEPARTMENT CALLED TIMES REPORTER
TO EXPLAIN BOMB'S INTRICACIES TO PUBLIC

The Times had won another great distinction in journalism. One of its men had been sole reportorial witness and chronicler of the most dramatic news story since another reporter had written, for the ages to read: "In the beginning God created the heaven and the earth."

On Aug. 9 Laurence had a front seat in the Superfort the Great Artiste, which left Tinian at 3:50 A.M. At 12:01 P.M., less than eight hours later, the second atomic bomb fell, this one on Nagasaki. Its smoke boiled up to 17,000 feet, the Superfort's altitude, and kept climbing. Bill saw three separate cloud mushrooms venomously climb into the blue heavens. As the Great Artiste headed home by way of Okinawa, the refueling point, the evil mushrooms were still visible against the sky more than 200 miles away.

On that same morning, under date of Thursday, Aug. 9 (this was possible because of the time difference between New York and Nagasaki), The Times carried the story. Because by journalistic tradition any second report, even of a world-quivering event, always has less impact than the first, the Nagasaki bomb was subordinated in the headline:

SOVIET DECLARES WAR ON JAPAN;
ATTACKS MANCHURIA, TOKYO SAYS;
ATOM BOMB LOOSED ON NAGASAKI

It was to come about at The Times that Bill Laurence, the science reporter, was thereafter to be known as "Atomic Bill" and William H. Lawrence, the war correspondent, was to be "Non-Atomic Bill." Non-Atomic Bill wrote the Nagasaki atomic bomb story at Guam for that morning's Times.

Now the end was not far off. On August 14, a little more than three weeks after the first bomb had wrought its incredible destruction, Sulzberger was in Washington, a guest at the White House. President Truman saw him at noon, a little late. He told Sulzberger, "I'm doing what every other American is doing today; I'm waiting for the great news that the war is all over."

Sulzberger flew back to New York. It was reported that final word on the war's end would probably come through around 7 o'clock that night. In James' office the publisher himself wrote the bulletin for The Times electric sign in the Square.

He gave orders to Jim Torpey, who ran the sign, to prepare the message in sign type, but under no condition to release it until he had the word from Sulzberger himself or from James. Torpey prepared the letters and waited in quivering anticipation. He loved these dramatic moments. He had known many since the sign first went on. This was the most important.

The flash from the White House reached James at 7 P.M. It was telephoned to the sign operator. Torpey yelled with pent-up joy. Sulzberger went into Seventh Avenue, just off Forty-third Street in the Square. He saw the earlier news go suddenly dark, as Torpey threw the off-switch. The crowds stopped and stared. The lights flashed on and began their characteristic golden crawl around The Times Tower girdle:

* * * OFFICIAL * * * TRUMAN ANNOUNCES JAPANESE SURRENDER

The stars represented the three branches of the United States armed forces. Roar upon roar welled out of Times Square. Great volumes of confused, hysterical outcry in glad chorus, hoarse and shrill, rent the midtown sky. Servicemen were embraced. Strangers locked arms around one another. This was the hour free men had dreamed of, and for which they had strained and died.

CHAPTER

44

THE WAR and events that led to it had not altered Times news policy but the rapid and violent change in world affairs that came with the spread of dictatorship had altered Times editorial tone. The ivory tower atmosphere of the Ochs era had vanished. Editorials were still written with literary restraint, but now they carried more bite. The Times went on editorial crusade.

There were several influencing factors. Ochs, it will be recalled, always chose for his editorial chieftains men of classic scholarship. Neither Rollo Ogden nor John H. Finley was a newspaperman in the strict trade meaning of the term. Ogden had originally been a minister in the Case Avenue Presbyterian Church in Cleveland. He went to The New York Evening Post in the early Nineties, and in 1903 succeeded Lawrence Godkin as editor in chief there.

Ogden was 64 years old when Ochs asked him to take Miller's place on May 17, 1920. He still had literary fire and though he personally admired Alfred E. Smith and backed him in the editorial columns—with Ochs' full approval, for he too admired Smith—he was not taken in by the so-called "New Tammany." Like Ochs, he never compromised with that political group.

Ogden had courage. He fought hard for the League of Nations and the World Court. He saw through the thin substance of the "new economic philosophy" of the heady post-war boom years, and gave Noyes, who wrote the editorials on finance, a free hand in pointing out to readers that disaster lay ahead.

525

When the nation was on its knees with no eyes for the stars, Ogden wrote for The Times of Jan. 1, 1932, an editorial captioned "Lift Up Your Hearts," which was widely reprinted for its inspirational message: "Nothing to which the young men of America can look forward? There is everything . . . It will be a new world, and to those who dwell in it and shape it to their hearts' desire it will appear a fair world." It was unfortunate that time did not bear out the prophecy, but the editorial served at least a brief purpose in bolstering hope.

It was Ogden, speaking at a dinner for Edward A. Bradford who was completing a half century on the editorial staff in 1922, who had summed up The Times man's credo: "The newspaperman sinks his individuality in that of the institution for which he works. It is better so. In that way he adds his bit to the joint product and to the collective impress, which are greater and more important than any one man."

Rollo Ogden was 81 years old when death took his pen, and Dr. Finley, the kindly Presbyterian elder who moved into his place was already 74. Like Ogden, he was widely separated in years from the new publisher. He had never worked on a newspaper until he came to The Times in 1921.

Dr. Finley had been a rural schoolmaster in Illinois, where he was born during the Civil War. As a young man he had served as president of Knox College, later as Commissioner of Education of the State of New York and finally as president of City College. When he came to The Times, he wrote with an easily identified classic style. He was widely beloved for his smiling charm and he had made countless friends for The Times.

When Ogden died, Sulzberger appointed Finley as editor in chief to serve until he attained 75 years of age. When that time arrived Finley was gravely ill. On Nov. 16, 1938, a publisher's notice in The Times told its readers that there had been a change of editors. It said simply:

"After an absence of several months due to severe illness, Dr. John H. Finley, restored to health, returns to this page today as Editor Emeritus. Charles Merz becomes Editor, in charge of the editorial page."

The publisher's letter to Dr. Finley, printed with the notice, said:

"I am asking Charles Merz to assume the title of Editor, and know that as chief of the editorial page he will continue its tradition of balance and poise so firmly established and guarded by Charles R. Miller, Rollo Ogden and yourself.

"It is hoped that you will find opportunity to join the council of that small group of executives which, with Colonel Adler, consists of Edwin L. James, Lester Markel, Arthur Krock and Mr. Merz, and who by their counsel shape and direct the policy of this newspaper."

Time and events meanwhile had shaped a sharper editorial attitude. Time led the older editorial writers away and when Hitler, Stalin and Mussolini loosed universal plague and responsible newspapers had to face up to it, The Times had younger men ready to appraise the situation and put into forceful language the dangers that threatened.

Merz was 38 years old, two years younger than Sulzberger, when he came to The Times in 1931. Both had been Army lieutenants in 1918. Merz had worked for Harper's Weekly, for The New Republic, and had been a staff correspondent for The New York World in Europe and in the Far and Near East. He had served his editorial apprenticeship under Walter Lippmann of The World and was associate editor of that newspaper when it ceased publication in 1931.

There was no invisible wall between the new editorial chief and the new publisher when Merz replaced Dr. Finley, as there had been between Ochs and the men of his choice. Merz and Sulzberger spent a great deal of time together outside the office. They worked out crossword puzzles and double crostics together; even jointly fashioned one or two of their own for publication in The Times Magazine. They frequently spent holidays together.

More important, these two saw eye to eye on the great issues with which the country was now confronted, thought alike, worked together in complete confidence so that there was no chance of a breach in fundamental Times editorial principle, the liberal democratic tradition that had stood up through the long years.

Ochs, it has been pointed out, had followed a rather wary policy, editorially, and had even at one stage, wondered whether he might not try to run a newspaper without editorials. It had always been his fear that editorial crusading might inspire news reporters to slant stories to conform with the crusading. He had seen that happen on The World, on The Herald and in The American. He tended to shy away from any such influence on his own newspaper.

Ochs had, on extremely rare occasions, done a bit of mild crusading on the editorial page. An example was his newspaper's stand against encroachment by anyone on the city parks. When spring came in 1918 and a publicity man for the Fourth Liberty Loan tried to get the City Fathers to permit model trenches to be dug on Sheep Meadow in Central Park, Times editorials stood him off. The Times' attitude was that while the trenches might serve a patriotic purpose, they would set a precedent for other projects that might eventually wipe out the whole park system.

Merz and Sulzberger did not share Ochs' inhibitions about the strong editorial stand on vital issues. They felt certain that The Times was so thoroughly established as a *news* paper, first and above all else, that there was no longer reason to fear that editorial crusading would spill over into its news columns.

Ochs, a Southern Democrat, had clearly stated his political credo when he took over The Times. He was uncompromisingly a sound money man, an advocate of tariff reform, opposed to waste of public funds, favored the lowest tax consistent with good government, and wanted no more government than was absolutely necessary to protect society, maintain individual and vested rights and to assure free exercise of sound conscience. He was not party blind; he loathed Tammany methods and when the Democrats put up for office someone he could not in good conscience support he used Times editorials to make his position clear. Several such instances have been cited.

The new publisher followed the same general policies, but in his time it was more sharply established that The Times was completely independent, politically. He outlined the newspaper's stand in a Times Hall talk toward the end of World War II. He was explaining how The Times decided on support of any particular candidate, and specifically how it came to support Wendell L. Willkie when President Roosevelt (already dead when the talk was delivered) sought a third term in 1940.

"I would maintain that no other course could have been expected by those who read our editorial pages," Sulzberger said. "In times of peace a newspaper has few secrets. Its business is to tell what it knows and how it feels. And we had been telling quite consistently that we didn't like the effort to pack the Supreme Court; that we did not like the third term; that we did not like the President's expressed desire to send Congress home and run the country as a one-man show, without it.

"We believe that our record was entirely consistent and that our support of the great liberal, Wendell Willkie, should have been foreseen just as, conversely, our support in 1944 of Mr. Roosevelt should have been evident to a reader of our editorial page. During the war years he had gallantly upheld the position of our country in the world; and, after Mr. Willkie had been passed over by the Republicans, and Mr. Dewey in his speeches had failed to excoriate sufficiently the isolationists in his party, who had done their best to obstruct the passage of lend-lease, universal military service and other legislation in which we believed, the direction in which we were to throw our support should have been evident."

While The Times, restricted in size by wartime newsprint regulations, yielded revenue-producing space to give full war coverage, its editorial pages promoted all-out war effort in the sharpest crusading spirit the newspaper had ever shown.

This was most clearly evident on four vital points: the need to convince the United States of its significant international role and to stir the American people and the Congress to their responsibilities; the need for greatly buttressed defenses; the need for grim retention of fundamental government structure; the need for preservation of civil liberties to keep the democracy intact.

The Times editorial page said on April 11, 1932, after Hindenburg beat Hitler in the German election: "No event in modern German public life has equaled its importance not only for the German people but for the outside world . . . [but it cannot] be assumed that Hitler's defeat has obliterated the menace of his movement."

It guessed wrong in August of that year, when it thought Hitler had reached his "high-water mark" and again in 1933, after he became Chancellor, when it saw "no warrant for immediate alarm" though "Germany has entered upon a perilous political adventure."

In August, 1935, The Times strongly urged that the United States join Europe in imposing sanctions on Italy for her Ethiopian adventure. That October it ran an editorial every day for eight days, supporting the League of Nations and denouncing the Italian Government for its aggression. On Oct. 13, 1935, it contended: "The United States can find a way of doing on its own part of the work which the League is undertaking."

A short while before this, when the first of the American Neutrality Acts had been passed and an embargo had been placed on arms shipments to both belligerents The Times called the act "another ignoble chapter in American foreign policy." It spiritedly endorsed President Roosevelt's moves to prevent shipment of war materials to Mussolini and called for amendments to the Neutrality Act to give the President greater discretion in handling foreign relations. From that time on it consistently led the movement to free the Administration from the restrictions of mandatory neutrality legislation.

In May, 1936, when other newspapers had abandoned hope for the League, The Times kept pleading that we should "shoulder our responsibilities as a world power." It continued to uphold League principles. "It would be premature to conclude," an editorial said on May 5, 1936, after the Blackshirts had taken Addis Ababa, "that this victory incidentally marks the downfall of the League of Nations . . . The League is no stronger than the nations of the world are prepared to make it."

The most intensive editorial attack in Times history began on Feb. 6, 1937. It was aimed to prevent President Roosevelt from going through with his plan for enlarging the membership of the Supreme Court of the United States. Fifty separate editorials were done on this subject until the President abandoned his plan for good six months later.

The newspaper's motive for attack was plainly stated in the second editorial on Feb. 7, 1937, which argued that the court-packing plan, as it came to be called, would "disturb profoundly the balance of power on which American democracy has been founded."

The Times pointed out that four months earlier, when it had supported Roosevelt's 1936 campaign, he had not raised the court issue and that he had no mandate for attempting the reform.

Death Clouds of a New Age: The ghastly vapors in the heavens above Hiroshima.

A Great Crowd Picture: V-J Day in Times Square. The story of Japan's surrender is unfolding on The Times bulletin band.

"No other President in the history of the United States," said an editorial of March 1, "has even remotely had such powers. No President has ever had a better reason for referring directly to the electorate any proposed change in the Constitution or in the Court which is its guardian."

Late in July, when the plan had been conclusively beaten (and by which time the President had become heartily embittered against The Times) the newspaper breathed an editorial sigh. It said on July 23, "A great threat . . . has now been set aside." Its last word on the subject appeared next day:

"Mr. Roosevelt will not look in vain for adequate support of any genuinely progressive measure which is carefully prepared, properly debated and realistically founded in the tradition of this country."

But this bid for conciliation drew no friendly response from the White House. Roosevelt could not forget that The Times had said during its editorial attack that his court plan "would constitute an evil precedent," or that the newspaper had taken the view that the proposal "though not fashioned by the hand of a dictator, smacks of the dictator's method."

The Times got squarely behind Roosevelt's philosophy as outlined in his "quarantine speech" in October, 1937. It said: "It is largely because the peace-loving nations have permitted the defense of law and principle to go by default that parts of the world now suffer from a reign of terror . . . [The President has expressed] the deep moral indignation which is felt in this country against policies of ruthlessness and conquest."

In June, 1938, a powerful editorial appeared, titled "A Way of Life," embracing the major points for which The Times had forcefully pleaded and crusaded. "No remoteness," it said, "from the scene of a potential European conflict can isolate the United States from the consequences of a major war. No Neutrality Act can prevent the American people from favoring their natural allies. In any ultimate test of strength between democracy and dictatorship, the good will and the moral support—and in the long run more likely than not the physical power of the United States—will be found on the side of those nations defending a way of life which is our own way of life and the only way of life which Americans believe to be worth living." The ripples it set in motion washed across the globe.

When the Neutrality Act of 1939 was finally adopted in a world already plunged into open warfare The Times endorsed it because it at least gave Britain and France, facing power-hungry dictators, a chance to buy munitions in the United States.

"The fight along the ideological front is on now everywhere," The Times said on Oct. 8, 1939, "and will continue until there is a final victory for one side or the other. China and India, Chile and Nebraska, all are inside the firing lines . . . Democracy is that thing in men's minds and hearts that will not tolerate the gangster rule that goes by the name of dictatorship."

The Times in 1940 and 1941 applauded the move that provided Great Britain sorely needed destroyers, and the legislation that established lend-lease. "Passing the lend-lease bill has diminished the danger of our having to face the victorious dictators alone," it said, and, advocating American Navy convoy for supplies to Britain, it pointed out on May 7, 1941, that: "In all candor we are forced to recognize that if we use the American Navy to convoy merchant ships to Britain, Germany will not leave our escort vessels unmolested . . . [yet] the only question is whether we shall choose to fight under our own terms or under the terms and conditions set by Hitler."

Administration moves for the occupation of Iceland were stoutly supported, and when the Atlantic Charter shaped up it had The Times' hearty endorsement. An Aug. 15, 1941, editorial on the Charter said: "This is the end of isolation. It is the beginning of a new era in which the United States assumes the responsibilities which fall naturally to a great world power."

Two months before Pearl Harbor, on Sept. 1, 1941, The Times was still pleading for awareness of the mounting dangers: "Let us face the truth; in this coming year of the war we shall either turn the tide against Hitler, peaceably if we can, forcibly if we must. or in some subsequent year we shall have to meet him alone and unaided on a battlefield of his own choosing."

When battle sounds at last receded, The Times, which had consistently opposed communism's political and economic philosophy, nevertheless hoped that the United States and Russia might somehow get along in the post-war period. The newspaper put even more editorial support behind the United Nations idea than it had behind the League of Nations.

It said on March 2, 1945: "The old faith in American isolation is deader than the proverbial dodo" and two days later: "Once again, as twenty-five years ago, the United States must choose whether it wishes to co-operate with the rest of the world on the basis of compromises made in good faith and with the prospect of future betterment, or whether it proposes to insist 100 per cent on its own program even if the world goes to pot as a result."

Almost a year later, in January, 1946, when the first General Assembly of the United Nations met, The Times said: "It is a monument to man's eternal spirit which rises above doubt and despair and continues to search for peace along the only road it has yet discovered—the road that leads in the direction of 'the Parliament of Man, the Federation of the World' and if the U.N.O. is not quite either, it is at least an approach to them."

As Russian expansion gathered neighbor nations into the dark Communist closet, The Times' hope for United States-Russian agreement in the post-war world faded. The newspaper called editorially for strengthened Western frontiers. It stood whole-heartedly behind the Marshall Plan. It said of the Plan on June 14, 1947: "Born out of the hard logic of desperation, this project fires the imagination as nothing has since the end of the war . . . Our own future, and the world's, is at stake."

Times editorials lashed at Congress for unwillingness to vote funds for the European aid program. "That is playing politics with the country's safety" these articles said. "The men in the Kremlin do not sleep on their jobs, but Congress appears inclined to do so."

Long before the Western powers seemed headed for a North Atlantic Treaty, The Times urged some such coalition. It said on Jan. 16, 1949: "The interests of peace require that our European friends shall be in a position to defend themselves . . . There must be a real defensive union in Western Europe and a real undertaking on our part to come to their aid if they are attacked."

The Times approved the military aid program that grew out of the Atlantic pact. When the Korean crisis broke in the summer of 1950, Times editorials called for complete fulfillment of United States obligations to the South Koreans, and has maintained that attitude unwaveringly, as it has support of the United Nations.

The Times did its best to prevent hasty demobilization in 1945. It warned on Sept. 25, 1945: "The present pellmell rush out of Europe and Asia, under Congressional pressure, is nothing less than a new retreat into isolation." It kept up the demand for adoption of some form of universal military training. It hammered tirelessly in 1946, as the date for the end of Selective Service approached, at the House's "senseless weasel-worded measure that would make desperate the present army manpower crisis." On May 7, eight days before the Selective Service, in an editorial, "Eight Days to Chaos," it rebuked representatives who, in an election year "have taken the attitude that they would rather gamble with the country's security . . . than legislate courageously on a controversial issue." From that day until the act had been temporarily extended to July 1, The Times' editorial pounding did not let up. There were pieces successively labeled, "Seven Days to Chaos," "Six Days to Chaos" and so on, right down the line.

The publisher, Merz and his staff are champions of freedom of speech, freedom of the press, a fair trial and equality before the law, and The Times on April 30, 1949, praised President Truman's civil rights program, saying his insistence on it was "one of the most courageous acts of his Administration."

The newspaper backed Federal and state anti-discrimination laws, anti-lynching and anti-poll-tax legislation, and supported Negro rights. It attacked censorship at home and abroad, and was particularly outspoken when La Prensa in Buenos Aires was silenced. It urged ratification of the Child Labor Amendment, pleaded for an end of abuses of the American Indian, and has fought for fairness to aliens and for a liberal immigration policy. It has denounced Communist ideology without let-up, but it has warned of the inherent danger in extreme remedies. It said on Sept. 3, 1948: "We have to guard ourselves but we do not have to go into hysterics in the process." In August, 1949, when the Mundt bill to outlaw the Communist party was in debate, an editorial said: "In defending ourselves against the international threat of communism our country can ill afford to curtail its own precious and hard-won liberties."

Welcoming unequivocally the Supreme Court decision that

affirmed in late spring, 1951, the conviction of the Communist party leaders, The Times nevertheless warned:

"It is for us, the American people, to keep alive the habit of free and full discussion, to tolerate differences of opinion, no matter how distasteful they may be to the great majority, and to leave to the police and the courts the task of suppressing conspiracies intended to use liberty as a weapon for destroying liberty."

The publisher, incidentally, prevented ivory tower atmosphere from settling again on the editorial floor. He knew that men molder and go soft in editorial posts if they are not turned loose, at intervals, to explore the fields they cover. The Times sent its editorial writers to the Far East, the Near East, to other parts of the world for freshening on the subjects they handled. Mrs. McCormick spent months abroad every year. Krock, writing out of Washington for the editorial page, maintained live contact with officialdom. In addition, members of The Times staff in other departments were now encouraged to write editorials on subjects of which they had special knowledge—business, labor, art, theatre, music, etc. The editorial page today benefits from contributions of more than eighty such contributors a year.

"Letters To The Editor," an editorial page feature handled by Miss Louise Polk Huger, gets countless thousands of letters each year, from the humblest subscribers and from ambassadors, senators, representatives, college presidents, professors, authors, lawyers, clergymen, scientists and others eager to present their views on public questions. Letters are printed whether they agree or disagree with Times editorial opinion, but are carefully winnowed because of space limitations. On some days they come in such quantity that if all were used, they would fill a large part of the paper.

That, roughly, gives the current editorial attitude. The newspaper had cultivated a stronger editorial voice in the two decades before its centennial, without the effects that Ochs had feared. Its news columns were unchanged; they still gave both sides on all stories when such information was available, but news copy did not echo or mirror editorial opinion. There had been no spilling over. The Times remained primarily a *news* paper.

Although The Times used more document and speech text to

help readers better understand crucial developments in current history and followed up with dignified editorial comment and excellent supplemental and background material in the Sunday sections, it did not stop there. From the early Twenties it also went in, more extensively than any other contemporary, for important memoirs that shed brilliant light on historic events after the fact.

In December, 1921, it ran a series, "White House Looking Glass," written by Joseph P. Tumulty who had been President Wilson's Secretary from 1913 to 1921. Four years later it had Vice President Thomas R. Marshall's series on the Wilson Administration and in August, 1929, began Mabel Walker Willebrandt's "Inside of Prohibition." General Pershing's memoirs were serialized early in 1931, and in 1948 the newspaper began publication of memoirs from both Axis and Allied sources to supplement its coverage of the great global conflict. The memoirs of Cordell Hull, covering his twelve years as Secretary of State, ran in The Times from Jan. 26 to March 6, 1948, every day except Sundays; Walter Bedell Smith's "My Three Years in Moscow," the story of the cold war during his Ambassadorship in Russia, appeared daily from Nov. 6 to Dec. 2, 1949; and a 20,000-word autobiography of Joe Louis, the heavyweight champion, ran the week of Nov. 5–12, 1948. In March 1948 The Times carried extracts from Propaganda Minister Goebbels' Diaries, and in August, 1950, it ran extracts from, "Behind the Brown Curtain," by Paul Schmidt, chief Wilhelmstrasse interpreter during the Hitler regime. Important as these were they paled beside Prime Minister Churchill's "The Second World War," a monumental literary undertaking by the man who probably knew more than any other about that earth-shaking conflict.

General Adler, under direction from the publisher to "buy Churchill's story," handled the negotiations for The Times, which shared the memoirs jointly with Life, the Henry Luce publication. He went to England in April, 1947, and recalled with some delight later, his first meeting with Churchill at Chartwell.

The general had been invited for tea. Just before it was served Churchill came in from the grounds in rumpled dungarees, passed cheerful greetings and went upstairs to change. He overheard Mrs. Churchill some minutes later ask the general how he preferred his tea. The question had caught The Times man a little off balance. The general was no tea drinker.

Churchill sensed the situation. He called to Mrs. Churchill, "The general will have the same kind of tea that I have. Bring us both whisky and soda."

After tea, the host showed the general and other visitors a draft of the original Atlantic Charter, but had some difficulty getting it from the wall where it hung above a couch. Returning it was even more difficult, but Churchill, never stymied by major situations, solved this one in a way that astonished the guests. From the wall opposite the couch he took a running start and landed, Charter and all, *on* the couch. He was almost boyishly proud of this athletic achievement.

"How's that?" he said. He turned, grinning widely, then triumphantly hung the framed Charter from the hook from which he had removed it, and cigar and all jumped back to the carpet.

Adler merely discussed the general content and tone of Churchill's memoirs. Financial details were worked out with Lord Camrose of The London Daily Telegraph, as Churchill's agent. The original deal involved payment by The Times and Life of a total of $1,050,000 at the rate of $230,000 a volume. The Times and Life agreed to use no more than 40 per cent of the whole.

The first series of Churchill memoirs, "The Gathering Storm," started in The Times on April 16, 1948; "Their Finest Hour" began Feb. 4, 1949; "The Grand Alliance," Jan. 26, 1950; "The Hinge of Fate," Oct. 10, 1950. Each series ran about five weeks, all in advance of their appearance in book form. They made fascinating reading.

The general learned that Churchill used a corps of secretaries in preparing the memoirs, dictating the first draft then editing. A restless man, Churchill sometimes got out of bed at 1 or 2 or 3 o'clock in the morning, and the secretary who happened to be working that shift had to be prepared for dictation at those unholy hours.

One morning in late March, 1949, after Churchill had been a guest in the publisher's dining room at The Times, Adler visited him at the private residence in Manhattan that was his home during his stay. The general was astonished to see Churchill still abed at 10 A.M. working at papers on a bed-table. A lighted candle in a holder on the little table puzzled the general, for the chamber was brightly lighted by house current.

Churchill sensed that the visitor was too polite to ask about the candle. His round pink face creased in a mischievous grin. He said, "Perhaps, general, you wonder why I keep a lighted candle on this work desk?" The general acknowledged that he did. Churchill took a look at his cigar, which had gone out, put it between his lips, leaned over, and got a strong and fresh start at it with one deep draught at the candle's flame. When he talked it was with the cigar between his lips. He had frequent use for the candle.

CHAPTER
45

Approaching its centennial The Times prepared to throw off the wartime hobbles that had reduced its natural gait. As the last battle smoke lifted from global horizons, plans for over-all expansion went into immediate effect. They called for more building space, more presses, more newsprint and newsprint storage space, wider national and international news coverage and development of the overseas edition. The post-war push was on.

The large amount of advertising The Times had been compelled to omit because of newsprint restrictions and because of Spartan adherence to the policy of maintaining news columns, had substantially reduced its wide margin of pre-war advertising leadership. In the first nine months of 1944 it ran 3,000,000 more lines of news than any other publication and competition fattened commensurately on its advertising overflow.

The newspaper's prestige had never been higher, yet the management increased its budget for Times promotion activities. Today it spends at the rate of $1,500,000 a year on them under the supervision of Ivan Veit, promotion director. This puzzles some persons, but handling millions of dollars in advertising each year, the management knows the advantages accruing from that medium.

Though the owners were playing now with bigger chips than Ochs had ever tossed into the pot to back his "all-the-news" policy and were faced with mounting labor and production costs, their faith in Ochs' theory still held. On Aug. 30, 1945, The Times devoted a full fifteen pages to the 130,000-word Pearl Harbor Investigation Report.

This was the longest text The Times had run in all its ninety-five years. In ordinary book format it would have covered 400 pages. Its preparation for next morning's edition after a boy brought the report by taxi from a plane at LaGuardia Field at 5:45 p.m. Aug. 29 was the most prodigious copy-editing chore ever completed in so short a period. Probably no other newspaper was equipped, in terms of manpower and machinery, for such a task. At least, no other newspaper gave the report anywhere near the same space.

Wilson L. Fairbanks, a stern New Englander of the Van Anda breed who had been with The Times since 1912, for twenty-five years as head of the telegraph desk, supervised the job. He called extra copy editors from other desks and stayed through 3:30 a.m. Thursday to check for errors in late editions. This, incidentally, was Fairbanks' last major assignment on The Times. Nine months later he retired to his mountain farm in Vermont. He was 81 years old.

Soon after the Pearl Harbor story had evoked professional murmuring—the trade knew what advertising revenue had been sacrificed for its publication—Bill Laurence came home from the Pacific, still in rumpled G.I. sun-tans and with his long hair reduced to bristling Air Force crew cut. Every man in the vast shop from the publisher to the newest copy boy was fascinated by his atomic odyssey, and Bill, a notable reconteur, left out none of the drama or suspense.

When the war ended the Army gave Laurence permission to tell somewhat more, though by no means all, of the story of the development and use of the atomic bomb and of the potentialities of atomic energy for the future of humankind. Laurence wrote ten pieces on the subject that ran from Sept. 26 to Oct. 9 and were later reproduced by The Times as a pamphlet for use in schools and for the public generally. He stated flatly in this series—and the next five bitter years were to prove his writing sound—that:

"In the present state of world affairs atomic power for peacetime purposes must remain closely linked with its further development as a military weapon. The control of uranium and uranium ore is a major international problem facing the world."

New forces released by American physicists, Laurence disclosed, "are not promised for tomorrow. They are actualities . . . They could be of immense value in industry, medicine, chemistry, physics and biology." He told readers that with atomic energy man might even unravel the mystery of photosynthesis.

Through the Laurence series the outside world saw something of the secret work of the master physicists who had beaten Axis experts to completion of the first atomic bomb and who were to be the first, within a few years, to project the even more devastating hydrogen bomb.

General Adler, meanwhile, had been invalided home from New Guinea. He had undergone a major operation at Walter Reed Hospital and then had flown back to the Pacific to be in at the Japanese surrender as an unofficial observer aboard the U.S.S. Missouri. Now, returned to Forty-third Street, he was ready to handle his end of The Times expansion program—the mechanical details and anticipated increases in advertising and in circulation were normally under his supervision.

Cortland J. Strang, freshly retired from the United States Navy —he had held the rank of commander—closely watched each operation for The Times. He was the newspaper's mechanical superintendent, and an Annapolis graduate.

In mid-November, 1945, wreckers removed the old Forty-fourth Street Theatre. Blasters then moved in and for three months Sardi's on the western Times boundary and the Paramount Theatre to the east, shook and trembled. The rock blown out for the foundation is now strewn along Hudson River banks, as shore erosion barricade.

The new structure represented the eighth major change in expansion of Times working quarters since the night Henry Raymond and his hard-pressed crew had put out the first edition in the unfinished candle-lit loft in Nassau Street almost a century before. It was the ninth Times home.

In it the owners installed every available practical device for smoother operation and for employe comfort. Fresh presses, in addition to the great batteries already in use, were built into bedrock two floors below street level where their vibration was taken up by Mother Earth rather than by the building proper.

By February, 1948, the new building was merged with the old.

The joining was effected after the newspaper's greatly increased personnel—more than 4,000 men and women—had lived for two years and two months behind beaverboard barricades in contractors' dust and unceasing din of drills, hammers and blasting—but the change was worth it.

Lighting was improved throughout the whole plant. Air conditioning kept every foot of working space, from sub-surface press rooms to the top floor, in delightful comfort, even in extreme summer heat. The air-conditioning installation cost $1,800,000, and its maintenance cost is around $60,000 a year. Desks and lockers were refurbished. There were larger and more comfortable dining rooms. A liberal use of color gave more life to reception rooms and corridors.

In April, 1947, incidentally, The Times had put into effect a new annuity retirement plan at a cost of $603,000 a year. Four months later the trustees, H. H. Weinstock, Times auditor, and Louis M. Loeb, Times counsel, worked out a new group life insurance plan offering benefits up to a maximum of $20,000. Times employe security plans were to cost the newspaper $2,016,000 a year by 1950.

Employe clubrooms, circulating library, game room, restaurant, and shower facilities were expanded. Paintings and framed newspaper mats telling the history of The Times and of the scientific and exploring expeditions it had reported were blended into the decorative scheme. Provision was made for The Times radio stations WQXR and WQXR-FM, directed for The Times by Elliott Sanger. They moved into quarters on the ninth and tenth floors in April, 1950.

The new building, joined with the old, added 50 per cent to production capacity. The expansion was perfectly timed; there was urgent need for the added space and equipment. The Times had nowhere near approached its full growth as it swung toward the close of its first century.

Expansion gave the composing room a total of 40,000 square feet of work space, providing room for 106 line-casting type machines geared to turn out each day around 250,000 words of news, an additional 200,000 word-sized units in the complicated financial and business tables, 125,000 words of classified advertising and 1,100 display ads. This output is handled by 570 workers, 510 of them printers. Stereotyping capacity was greatly increased in the expansion program.

The Times Museum of the Recorded Word, established in 1938, traces the story of mankind's slow progress from awkward scratchings on clay and on cave walls toward perfection in writing and printing. For current examples of the printing art the museum carries, among other items, each new day's issue of The Times.

Today The Times has ninety-five press units that can turn out 400,000 forty-eight-page newspapers in one hour. On one Sunday they consumed 2,500 tons of newsprint and more than thirty-two tons of ink to run off an edition of 380-page papers that weighed more than four pounds each. Paper cost for that day came to $256,-300 and $2,635 worth of ink was used. Even with increased press capacity The Times had to exclude thirty pages of advertising. The presses had all they could handle.

General MacArthur's last day before the Senate Armed Services and Foreign Relations Committee, May 5, 1951, proved the value and efficiency of the new mechanical facilities that The Times had added after World War II. Beyond that it proved the value of a superbly trained staff. It was a Saturday, and the presses were crowded for the early Sunday paper run as the general answered senators' questions up to 7 P.M.

The press schedule was revised to run an extra section labeled "MacArthur Text," which gave that issue a total of eleven sections. Using four extra Western Union wires out of Washington The Times got the complete transcript into the office for editing five hours before The Associated Press had finished sending it to the rest of the nation.

The Times' first Sunday edition that day carried an eight-page MacArthur Text section that included some extra matter. The second edition carried a ten-page version. The Late City Edition went to fourteen pages, with a total of 80,000 words of the exchange between the general and the committee. This severely strained the mechanical crews, but the paper had lived up to its tradition of supplying complete available text on all vital issues. This Sunday issue ran to 346 pages.

The 380-page issue, published on Dec. 4, 1949, was larger than most Sunday runs, but the cost of an average Sunday issue is more than $500,000. Paper and ink account for about $200,000. The balance represents payroll and distribution. The current Times over-all payroll for its total personnel of more than 4,000 men and women comes close to $400,000 a week as against the $13,000 paid out by Raymond for services in the whole first year of The Times' existence. Raymond spent $40,000 for paper the first year, as against the more than $16,000,000 annual newsprint bill of The Times today.

The Times has 1,350 men and women on its 1951 editorial staff, clerical help included, and thirty-six men and women handling photography. It has correspondents in all major cities abroad and has considerably expanded its national staff in the last decade, a move ordered by Sulzberger. The national staff consists of regional representatives in the United States who cover for both daily and Sunday, and who are available for independent Times surveys. Seventy reporters, ten rewrite men and sixteen copy readers work on the city news staff. This does not include editors and reporters in specialized news departments such as foreign and national news, drama, radio, music, sports, the dance, education, ship news, financial, business news, aviation, motion pictures, radio, automotive news and motion pictures. Dr. Howard A. Rusk, a brigadier general of the Air Force, heads a department for physically handicapped ex-servicemen and civilians.

The Washington bureau, headed by the Washington correspondent, Arthur Krock, normally has seventeen men for capital coverage. During and immediately after the war it had twenty-two. When Lorenzo Crounse started the bureau on the second floor of a three-story frame dwelling at the southeast corner of F and Fourteenth Streets in 1863, he was the bureau, except for occasional help.

Almost every man on the capital staff today is a specialist of one kind or another—on military affairs, State Department, social security, agriculture, labor, economics, White House, Capitol Hill or Supreme Court coverage. The bureau's output of 12,000 to 25,000 words a day, not including texts, pours over special direct leased lines right to the home news room in Forty-third Street.

Twenty years after Crounse started the Washington bureau.

E. G. Dunnell was the capital correspondent. It was still a one-man assignment with most of the material assembled under the cover-all headline, "In Washington." News pick-up started at the century's turn, with fairly steady expansion, to reach truly heroic size when Franklin D. Roosevelt took over in 1933.

Capital news then washed in like storm-lashed ocean rollers, which in a sense they were. New Deal legislation and the bitter opposition it eventually encountered all but flooded the bureau. Documents came in sheaves, speeches multiplied and labor news took on vast, new proportion.

The newspaper had no labor expert until 1922, when it took on Guy Seems, a young man who had done some work in the field for The Associated Press. When Seems left in 1923, the assignment went to Louis Stark of the city staff. After Roosevelt went into the White House and labor and management issues called for more space, James told Stark to go to Washington for—as he put it—two or three weeks. The weeks stretched into months, then into years, and the assignment grew bigger and bigger. Stark is still there. The Times now uses three to four labor writers regularly. Other coverage went through pretty much the same evolution.

In 1925 Evans Clark, a friend of Sulzberger's who had taught government at Princeton University and had been for many years a director of labor publicity and economic adviser to labor unions, was hired to cover labor and economics for the Sunday Times. He held the post for three years.

Newspaper correspondents in Washington, as in all Government capitals, maintain close contact with the great and the near great who are major news sources. A few mingle socially with Government officials, and some of the best stories develop over after-dinner coffee and cigars.

On Feb. 13, 1950, Krock was guest at a dinner party in F Street arranged by Senator Brien McMahon. President Truman was there and Supreme Court Justice Vinson. Krock mentioned to Justice Vinson that he had conceived the idea of doing a study of the President to show that Truman was neither what his enemies nor what his friends pictured. Krock had just sent a formal request to the White House for an interview with the President. Up to that time the Chief Executive had never given a one-man press audience.

The President, aglow with the good dinner, strolled up to the Justice and The Times correspondent. He insisted that they remain seated while he stood. He said, with a nod at Krock, "I want to talk to the Brains Trust."

Justice Vinson said, "He has a few questions, Mr. President, that he would like to ask you."

The President said to Krock, "Just come and see me, and ask 'em."

Krock said, "I already have a request in the works, Mr. President."

The Chief Executive told him to forget the formal interview application. He said, "Just tell Charlie Ross I want to see you."

During the interview at the White House next day Krock took no notes—he rarely ever does, except an occasional date or a direct quotation—then hurried back to The Times bureau in the Albee Building to get the story on paper while the details were warm. The writing took several hours, and, on the way home at 3 A.M., Krock left a copy at the White House. It was returned to him that afternoon, with a few slight word changes, and ran in The Times of Feb. 15, 1950:

AN INTERVIEW WITH TRUMAN: HE SEES MAN'S BETTER NATURE BRINGING PEACE TO ILL WORLD

Krock had carefully avoided use of the word "interview" in his story, but the headline betrayed the story's origin. Other Washington correspondents stormed into Charlie Ross' office to protest against the President's granting audience to one newspaperman instead of to representatives of all newspapers, but the President ignored the protests.

Thirteen years earlier, Krock had had an exclusive interview with President Roosevelt. He got that by pointing out to Steve Early, the President's secretary, that the Administration's plans for Supreme Court changes and for over-all Government reorganization had raised a swelling murmur against what many called "dictatorship."

"I think," Krock suggested, "that this might be an opportune time for the President to answer some questions that would tell the people what he's striving for."

The interview was granted, and Krock realized at once that it was an important straight-news story rather than the Sunday Magazine feature he originally had in mind. When he told Early he would rather use it for the daily, he was asked to submit the headline that would go over it. He had the headline wired from Forty-third Street as soon as it was ready. The President passed it. It ran on Feb. 28, 1937:

THE PRESIDENT DISCUSSES
HIS POLITICAL PHILOSOPHY

The story, as in the Truman instance, brought other Washington correspondents in full cry. When Krock met President Roosevelt some time afterward, the Chief Executive grinned. He said: "My head was on the block after that story, and Steve's was, too. We'll never do it again." He never did. That was his last one-man newspaper interview.

Important exclusive stories are sometimes arrived at with extraordinary simplicity, as happened when Cordell Hull was appointed Secretary of State. Jim Hagerty got the first intimation of the appointment during a meeting at Warm Springs early in 1933, and a story that the appointment impended appeared in The Times as an unconfirmed report.

Soon afterward Hull innocently remarked at a meeting attended by Krock that he and Mrs. Hull had found a new apartment in the Hotel Carlton in Washington. On the basis of that remark alone, The Times coppered the appointment story.

Hull had obviously forgotten that some weeks before, in a talk with Krock, The Times man had pointed out that if Hull did become Secretary of State he and Mrs. Hull would have to give up their three-room suite at the Lafayette, where they had lived for years in homey comfort. "You know, Judge," Krock had said at the time, "if you do become Secretary of State you will need much larger quarters than you have now, because the post traditionally calls for elaborate entertainment of foreign representatives, and you wouldn't have the space for it in three rooms."

It was as simple as that.

It never became generally known that a Times man's intimate knowledge of Agriculture Department background helped save the Roosevelt farm program after the Supreme Court early in January, 1936, held that the basic principle of crop control as embodied in the Agricultural Adjustment Act was invalid. This spelled the end for A.A.A.

Felix Belair Jr. of the Washington Bureau wandered into the office of Chester C. Davis, Administrator of the Agricultural Adjustment Administration, just after the Court had announced its decision, and found that executive dismayed. It was vital that the all-important farm program continue without lapse.

Belair, who had started as a Times Bureau office boy, and had worked his way up, knew Agriculture Department background better than many officials who worked in it.

He said to the Administrator: "I don't see anything to worry about in this decision. No reason why you can't revive the Soil Conservation Act [of 1935] and by shift of emphasis make it cover current needs."

The Administrator's eyes brightened. He began pushing desk buttons, summoning his staff to act on Belair's suggestion. He said: "Thanks a hell of a lot, Felix. That'll do it. Now get out; I've got work to do."

Belair left the office with Russ Wiggins of The St. Paul Pioneer Press who had entered with him. Between them they had a sizzling beat. The Times of Jan. 16, 1936, led the story on Page 1 under a three-column head:

PLAN TO CONTINUE FARM AID
UNDER CONSERVATION LAWS

Almost every man on the staff in Washington has some similar anecdote to tell, particularly Louis Stark and Joseph Loftus on the labor beats and Scotty Reston on the State Department end, but the stories are too numerous to outline here.

Some newspaper readers and sometimes reporters for other journals assume that The Times gets important exclusive stories out of Washington because officials deliberately choose it as a public sounding board. In many cases that is the explanation, but exclusive stories now and then stem from official innocence.

Krock's beat on the news that President Roosevelt had decided on a gold-shipment embargo that ran in The Times on April 19, 1933, fits into that category. For days before the story ran, all Washington reporters—money markets all over the globe—were concerned as to what the Administration might do. There had been no decision as whether scrip might be used, whether the standard would change. In New York John Forrest, financial editor, was hot after the story, too.

Krock telephoned to an official who had sat in on the April 18 Treasury conference to ask him if he could confirm or deny the rumor that the scrip idea had been taken up at the session. When the official said it had not, Krock offered the opinion that continued use of currency was probably better, "even though there is to be no circulation of gold." (All domestic gold currency had been called in.)

The official agreed. He said, "But don't you think it's fine what the President has decided to do about gold?"

Krock had no idea what the President had decided to do about gold, but he didn't let on. He guessed.

"You mean the export embargo?"

The official, assuming that Krock already knew, said: "Certainly. Now we can breathe in peace while we repair our domestic situation. The Amsterdam traders were cleaning us out of our gold."

Krock murmured thanks, and sat back a moment. He had stumbled onto the story everyone was feverishly trying to get. But he knew that he could not rush into print with anything so important without further checking. The official with whom he had spoken was not a Treasury man.

Krock called William H. Woodin, the kindly Secretary of the Treasury, and put a question to him boldly:

"What date has been chosen, Mr. Secretary," he asked, "for official declaration of the export embargo of gold you have decided upon?"

Secretary Woodin said, "Don't you think you ought to wait until the President announces it officially?"

Krock countered that the newspapers had their obligation to the public, and that the embargo information was of vital interest. The official hesitated. Reluctantly he then said, "All right. The date will probably be Saturday."

When Krock put up the receiver and told Rodney Bean, another Times man, what he had, Bean seemed to pale. He thought it might be dangerous to release the story. Krock decided, though, that the story had been amply confirmed. When it broke as the leading story in The Times of Friday, April 19, it was eagerly picked up and relayed around the globe.

A recent example of The Times' sensitivity as a news machine, despite the size it had attained in almost 100 years' existence, was provided by the story on the dismissal of General of the Army Douglas MacArthur that broke the morning of April 11, 1951.

William H. Lawrence, White House correspondent at that time, was awakened at his home by Miss Louise Hackmeister, the Executive Mansion's chief telephone operator. She said: "Bill, get down here quick. There's to be an important statement at 1 A.M."

It was midnight. Half-dressed, Lawrence pushed his car hard and reached the White House in less than a half-hour. A few minutes later, George Tames, a Times photographer, joined him. There were some tense moments as the reporters guessed what the statement might be—MacArthur's removal? War? Some death in the Cabinet?

Lawrence found time to telephone to McCaw, night managing editor in New York. His own guess was that it would be a MacArthur story. McCaw figured from the time—it was 3 P.M. in Tokyo —that the President had probably timed his message to the Far East to delivery at that hour. He ordered Tames to keep the telephone wire open for Lawrence so that no time be lost in getting the news through, whatever it might be.

Bob Alden, on city rewrite in the main office, prepared a mound of "books"—copy paper backed with tissues and carbon for duplicates—and waited, his headphones on, his fingers resting on the typewriter keys. In the bull pen McCaw wrote tentative headlines, favoring, "Truman Relieves MacArthur of Command." He was fairly certain it would be that.

Lawrence burst from the conference chamber in the White House at 1:04 A.M., and, with official Government releases in his hands, rapidly began dictating to Alden. Copy boys snatched the story from the rewrite man's machine, paragraph by paragraph, and dropped them before the copy editors.

McCaw had warned Keenan McNally, night mechanical superintendent, that there would be a White House news break at any moment. The red "stop press" signal flashed eighty feet below Forty-third Street and the Late City Edition run, which had started nine minutes before, was halted. The massive machinery sighed as it slowed.

At 1:32 A.M. McCaw ordered a "bite"—the trade term for ending a story still coming in. There was enough material then to tell what had happened. Lawrence was still pouring in detail and giving official document texts, but the short version went to the composing room, with appropriate photographs.

Forty-two minutes after Lawrence had begun to dictate, the postscript edition was in Times Square and in Times trucks, roaring downstreet with the news that startled a nation. It was remarkable speed, but the new plant was geared for it. The last edition carried the complete MacArthur story, even though six columns of advertising had to be ripped out to make way for it. Some 300,000 copies of the Sunday Magazine had been run off on another set of presses when the removal flash came through. Markel ordered those presses stopped and substituted as cover illustration a striking photograph of Gen. Matthew B. Ridgway, MacArthur's successor. The Sunday editor kept that close to spot news.

On Thursday, April 19, as General MacArthur addressed Congress, calling the President's Far East policy "blind to reality," The Times covered the speech and general reaction to it at home and abroad. It ran the text, special articles by Arthur Krock and James Reston, sentiment at the United Nations by Thomas J. Hamilton, The Times United Nations bureau chief, and a piece by Jack Gould, radio and television editor, on how the nation followed the general's words on television and radio.

In The Times Washington Bureau in the Albee Building, men and women who were not assigned to that day's MacArthur coverage, watched the dramatic scene before Congress at a television receiver. In this group was Anthony Leviero who had preceded William Lawrence as White House correspondent. He had flown to Wake Island with President Truman the previous fall, for the

Truman-MacArthur conference, and it occurred to him as he listened that there had been agreement on almost all Far Eastern
policy at that session.

He turned to Luther Huston, the bureau's news chief. He said:
"I think the impact this speech has made indicates that the public
has forgotten there was a Wake Island conference. Maybe this
would be a good time to find out what really went on out there."

Huston agreed and Leviero went after the Wake Island story. He
tapped three Administration sources. He suggested that he thought
the time was ripe for letting the people of the United States know
what had really transpired on Wake Island. He said he would like
access to official reports of that meeting, and promised to be dis-
creet about disclosing how he had gained a glimpse at them.

The three men Leviero called would not promise he could see
the reports, but neither did they flatly deny his request. He went to
bed late that night, certain he had been turned down. At 11 o'clock
next morning, though, his wife called him at The Times office from
their new home in the capital. One of the three Administration
officials to whom he had appealed would see him at noon. The
name of this official and the meeting place were to be kept secret,
but the reports would be available.

Leviero hastily filled two fountain pens and hurried out of the
office. At the designated meeting place the Wake Island reports
were laid out before him. When he suggested that he could work
faster with a typewriter, the official was horrified. "You're just to
take as many notes as you need to give the sense of these reports,"
he said. "You may not quote any part directly."

Leviero, a tense, hair-triggered personality, wrote frantically for
more than two hours. He used up all the ink in one pen, and a good
part of the supply in the other. When he put the last paper aside he
had writer's cramp. He gobbled a hasty lunch, hurried back to the
Albee Building, and his typewriter gave off rapid-fire sounds for
hours. He wrote more than four columns for the next morning's
Times. "Wake Talks Bared" was the headline.

The story told how the general had assured the President of victory in Korea by Thanksgiving, that he did not think the Chinese
Communists would intervene in Korea and that he might be able to

release his Second Division—his best troops—to General of the Army Omar Bradley for service in Europe by January, 1951.

The explosive Leviero exclusive was copied all over the world. At the next White House press conference reporters for other newspapers and for the syndicates intimated that the Administration had "planted" the Wake Island report with The Times. Leviero knew from earlier experiences that this would be the general assumption, but never disclosed his sources. He only said: "In the three years that I covered the White House, no member of the President's staff ever volunteered to give me any kind of story. If I got exclusives, it was only by asking the right questions at the right time. I'm certain that any other newspaperman, known and trusted, could have had the story if he had figured out the prevailing mood of Administration sources that day, and had made the same approach as I did."

This important news break on an internationally vital issue proved again that where the discomfited saw mystery and intrigue behind a newspaper beat, there was only clear thinking and swift action. In most cases the answer was as simple as that.

CHAPTER
46

O N THE MORNING before General MacArthur's dismissal, the
staff of the Sunday department's News of the Week in Review
had held its usual Tuesday conference. A swarm of story ideas for
the April 15 Review had been reduced to a handful of domestic and
foreign items, and researchers were about to begin digging for
material for those stories.

The Truman-MacArthur controversy was bubbling then, but
there was no sign that the lid was about to blow. Reston had been
assigned to do a piece on the general with enough background
material to bring readers up to the minute on developments. Hanson Baldwin had been asked for a story on Chiang Kai-shek and his
Red China foes. Henry R. Lieberman in Hong Kong had been assigned to do a piece on Gen. Lin Pao. The rest of the schedule called
for foreign and domestic pieces needed for background on other
events or personalities figuring in current news stories.

The MacArthur dismissal changed the whole Review plan.
Markel, who has general supervision over the Review, the Magazine, the Book Review and the drama section (all parts of the Sunday newspaper that are independent of the daily operation), called
another Review conference. Most of the stories that had been
ordered on Tuesday were abruptly canceled or held up. The Review schedule was completely revised. Fresh messages were flashed
to Times correspondents in Washington, across the nation, and to
Times men in Tokyo, Korea and Europe.

Baldwin was asked to switch from the "Chiang vs. Communists" article to a piece on General Ridgway, MacArthur's successor, and Lieut. Gen. James A. Van Fleet, new commander of the Eighth Army. Reston was asked to switch from a straight MacArthur story to one sharply focussed on the dismissal. Correspondents in twelve major United States cities were asked to report on popular and editorial opinion in their regions. Lindesay Parrott in Tokyo was asked for reaction in Japan, and to assign one of his men on the Korean battlefront to G.I. reaction.

Cablegrams, memoranda, telegrams and telephone calls flowed from the Review office in a steady stream that Wednesday morning:

"Baldwin: In view of the MacArthur thing, we think this week's piece should be 1,400 words on the situation that confronts the new commanders Ridgway and Van Fleet. The piece should also discuss the qualifications of these two men to deal with the job."

"Parrott: Would like 1,200 words weekender on the reaction to MacArthur dismissal, reaction at headquarters and in military generally. Reaction in Japan politically, governmentally, etc. Going into question of how this will affect future course of events in Japan. Please acknowledge."

"Gilbert Bailey, London: In view MacArthur story lets kill British opinion of United States [previously ordered]. Lets substitute 1,000-word weekender on reaction to MacArthur matter. This should be a piece that pulls together editorial opinion on President's action and it is to run with companion piece pulling together editorial comment in United States."

Cabell Phillips, Sunday department man in Washington, was told: "Assume Krock will cover the domestic political effects of the MacArthur affair. From Reston we would like 1,600-word weekender on the policy dispute that lies behind it." This was followed by another message asking Phillips for material "on MacArthur drama—how Truman reached decision. Pressures on him for and against firing MacArthur. Description of meetings with aides on issue. Who attended? How much controversy was there? How did Secretary of the Army Pace's visit fit in with decision? Could this be in form of play-by-play description of what's happened since MacArthur's March 25 peace offer statement? Statement Administration policy on Korea. If Chinese hit do we hold and then offer peace again? Do we still say Formosa's future should be decided by international conference?"

Wires to regional correspondents at key points throughout the United States said:

"Would like 200-word memo on reaction in your section to MacArthur affair. Memo should be fair representation of both sides, if there are two sides, and should have quotes and editorial comment."

After consultation with Markel, the Review editors sent messages to Times men elsewhere. These asked for additional background material on important events in the Far East as far back as Pearl Harbor Day, to provide setting for the main controversy piece. There would be last-minute changes as the Review and the regular Sunday news sections raced to deadline that Saturday night, but on the following morning Times readers would have the latest angles against proper backdrop.

With Review plans set, six pages were ripped from the Magazine that had been tentatively laid out for the following week. A series of Truman-MacArthur stories was ordered instead. The Magazine does not keep as close to spot news as the Review does, but it is a news magazine, a vehicle for articles based on live ideas and live issues. It presents the long-term view.

From Wednesday through Friday the Magazine staff arrived at one story idea after another, discarding whatever seemed dated by each passing hour. By Friday, Markel felt safe in ordering: from Reston, a "Memo to General MacArthur" that would serve to tell the general—and Times Magazine readers—what had happened in Washington and throughout the United States in the fourteen years since the general had set foot on the mainland (this seemed the best literary device for getting the whole picture together); an article from Lawrence at the White House on how Truman arrived at important decisions; from Parrott in Tokyo who had covered MacArthur for five or six years, a portrait of the general; a piece on General Ridgway by Gertrude Samuels, just back from two months in Korea where she had watched Ridgway in action; an article by Herbert Feis, formerly of the State Department, on the basic issue in the Truman-MacArthur feud—should America concentrate her attention and main efforts on Asia or on Europe?

Awaiting these stories the staff assembled appropriate photographs and drawings so that the April 22 Magazine was ready by Tuesday night's deadline with five complete and sharply timed pieces intended to give readers a better understanding of one of the most exciting set-to's in modern American history.

The Magazine has attracted as contributors such authorities as John Foster Dulles; Senator Paul Douglas; James B. Conant, president of Harvard University; Chester Bowles, former Governor of Connecticut and head of O.P.A; Eric Johnston, former head of the United States Chamber of Commerce and Economic Stabilization Administrator; Raymond B. Fosdick, former president of the Rockefeller Foundation and consultant to the Secretary of State on Far Eastern Policy; Bertrand Russell, Nobel Prize winner; H. R. Trevor-Roper, history don at Oxford; Henry Steele Commager, history professor at Columbia University; Senator Henry Cabot Lodge Jr.

The list is almost endless—Sir Stafford Cripps, Senator Estes Kefauver, David E. Lilienthal, James V. Forrestal, Robert E. Sherwood, Thomas Mann, David Low, Robert M. La Follette Jr., Rebecca West, and on lighter stuff Tallulah Bankhead, Donald Culross Peattie, Richard Maney, George S. Kaufman, among hundreds of others. In most of these cases the bylines alone had news value. The reader was not apt to question the right of such authors to express opinion on matters in which they were recognized experts.

Markel was 29 years old, an assistant managing editor on The Tribune, when Ochs hired him as Sunday editor in March, 1923. The publisher had discussed the whole Sunday problem with him during a three-hour boardwalk rolling-chair ride at Atlantic City, and had liked his general ideas for reorganizing the Sunday supplements along strictly news lines.

Reorganization was planned on the theory that the disjointed manner in which a running daily news story reaches a reader leaves a vagueness in his mind that must be cleared away. The Sunday paper was to be reshaped by evolutionary process over a period of years to clear away that vagueness.

The ideal Sunday publication, it was eventually decided, should have three elements: first, the news of the day as given in the main news, business-and-financial, and sports sections; second, the background of the week's news to run in the Review; third, the broad picture, to be presented in the Magazine.

"Background" or "interpretation" was defined as the deeper sense of the news, placing a particular event in the larger flow of events, providing the color, the atmosphere, the human elements that give meaning and dimension to bare fact.

"Background, as we use the term in the Sunday department," the editor has explained, "is setting and significance. What General MacArthur said, for example, is news. To explain, or interpret what he said, is background. To remark or utter in print that you do, or do not, blame the general for what he said, is opinion, and opinion belongs only on the editorial page."

There were only five workers in the Sunday department when Markel took over—three editors, a secretary and an office boy. Today, the department employs eighty-four men and women including fifty-eight editors, desk men, and layout and picture crews, with special Sunday correspondents in London, Paris and Washington, and has access to the services of correspondents for the daily all over the world.

The Times tabloid Magazine had had a rather spotty history. Though it was acclaimed as something new in journalism when Ochs put out the first issue on Sept. 6, 1896, it had been discontinued in 1899. Increases in news volume and in advertising had strained the old presses at 41 Park Row and there was no money available then for new equipment to print the magazine. Ochs gave up the tabloid version and switched to standard size.

While it lasted, though, the first tabloid Magazine had achieved some notable beats. Its July 4, 1897, issue had run fifty photographs of Queen Victoria's Jubilee, purchased by Ochs from the official royal photographer for $5,000. No other American newspaper had them. They sent circulation zooming.

The Saturday Review of Books and Art, which Ochs had established on Oct. 10, 1896, had been more successful than the Magazine. It, too, was based on news formula—on the belief that books could be treated as news. It remained a Saturday feature in The Times until Jan. 21, 1911. When it came out as a Sunday supplement on Jan. 29, 1911, a front-page box told readers the change had been made in the belief that a Sabbath review would "have greater value for pleasure and instruction" and be read more carefully with subscribers "free from the cares and demands of the week-day vocations."

The Book Review's first editor, curiously enough, held the job longer than any of the men who succeeded him. He was Francis Whiting Halsey, an up-stater, born in the year when The Times was started. He became the newspaper's chief reviewer and foreign editor in 1880 and was its literary editor until 1902—almost a quarter century. His principal assistant during this period was Charles DeKay, who also wrote most of section's articles on art.

Edward A. Dithmar was Book Review editor from 1902 to 1907; after him, John Grant Dater, then Joseph B. Gilder, Louis Wetmore, George Buchanan Fife, Clifford Smyth who held the job from 1913 to 1922. Later editors were J. Brooks Atkinson, now drama critic, Lawrence Updegraff, J. Donald Adams, Robert Van Gelder, John Hutchens, and Francis Brown, who is now editor of the Book Review.

Little by little, as the years passed, the Book Review moved away from Ochs' original idea of keeping it a strictly news publication. More opinion crept into reviews. The Book Review today insists on sharp dating of reviews. And if there happens to be, say, a spate of books on President Roosevelt they are not only reviewed in time, but the Book Review editor assigns an authority to do a piece on the Roosevelt trend. As the book section was modernized, essays on general literary trends were added; so were tandem reviews on controversial works, and a column of informal notes on writers, books and publishers. Book Review illustration, done in rotogravure, was improved.

Almost all these changes had been discussed and had been generally approved in Ochs' last years, but most of the Sunday section revision came after Ochs died. The new publisher released ample funds for getting the new Magazine off to a good start and for improving all the other Sunday supplements. He realized that Sunday journalism had marked time too long. The investment, it was obvious after a few years, was fully justified.

Under Markel, the Sunday department's first major reform was the weekly feature section, which sometimes had carried articles pegged on fresh news, but ran mainly to pieces that were not directly related to current events. When the reform was complete the feature section had become The News of the Week in Review.

The theatre, music, art and radio got the fresh news-peg imprint, too. The Times had had some great music editors—William Henderson, James G. Huneker and Richard Aldrich before Olin Downes— and famous drama critics including Augustin Daly, Adolph Klauber, Alexander Woollcott, and John Corbin before Brooks Atkinson, but the new Sunday formula brightened the treatment of drama, music, art and radio. These fields were pulled together with television, photography, gardens, stamps, resorts and travel to form one Sunday section. Motion picture news and film reviews fill up to two pages in the drama section each week. This department is handled by Bosley Crowther, who also writes daily reviews. Science notes bearing directly on current news, which Waldemar Kaempffert had started writing for the Sunday paper in 1927, became a Sunday fixture on June 7, 1931. The education page, begun by Wilson Fairbanks in 1933, took fixed place in the Sunday paper in 1942. The camera and photography feature was started in January, 1938; a home furnishings section entered the Magazine in January, 1943, the stamp column in 1937.

The Review, it has been noted in an earlier chapter, was started on Jan. 25, 1935, in a period of crackling world tension and growing complexity. When Hitler began a series of week-end moves the first Review editors and writers were compelled repeatedly to jettison—as in the MacArthur case—material they had painstakingly prepared during the week. In each case the staff managed to assemble fresh comprehensive background and interpretive material before Saturday-night deadline to meet altered situations. It was good training; it honed the staff razor sharp.

The Magazine successfully introduced crossword puzzles into its dignified format with the issue of Feb. 15, 1942. Eight years more went by before the daily paper began printing crossword puzzles on the book page on Sept. 11, 1950. The Magazine, printed in black and white rotogravure with some advertising in color, frequently runs the press limit of eighty pages. Color for Magazine ads was first used in the issue of April 23, 1933. The Book Review averages around thirty-two pages and is carried on seasonal book tides as at Christmas or in the spring and fall to its limit, which is also eighty pages. The drama section fluctuates between twenty-four and forty standard size pages, Review of the Week from ten to fourteen. From time to time there are special editions of the travel section, or special fashion or home furnishing sections, that run to considerable size, sometimes in tabloid format, sometimes in standard pages.

The Sunday and the news departments get their material separately and by different work methods. Editors on the daily news end must winnow out of the 1,000,000 words that flow in spontaneously from all over the world each day what they think most newsworthy. They order some special articles, mostly features or surveys, but must deal with the news as fate unwinds it. The Sunday department orders everything, or almost everything. Ninety per cent or more of its material originates in the office, from assignments by Markel and his editors, and virtually all Sunday department picture spreads are home-spawned, so to speak. Unsolicited manuscripts reach the Sunday department at the rate of around 150 a week, but extremely few of these get into the paper.

"We hold firmly to the belief that the special Sunday sections, like the daily Times," Markel once explained, "are devoted essentially to news and its background, with our great source of inspiration the daily paper. But we differ in this: The daily's job is one of *selection* of news, and ours is one of *election;* we have to seek out our material."

Today the Sunday issue, all sections included, runs close to more than 300 pages a week. Its formula has been adopted in various parts of the United States and abroad, but no other newspaper gives as comprehensive a picture of a world in torment, and none provides news background with the same near-architectural dimension.

Sunday circulation passed the million mark in April 1946. In 1950 The Times' Magazine ranked third among all national consumer magazines in advertising linage, directly behind The Saturday Evening Post and Life. It is a unique journalistic institution.

Credit for bringing both Sunday and daily linage to record peak went to Harold Hall, business manager, and to Monroe Green, advertising director. The unprecedented circulation problem was supervised by Nathan W. Goldstein, who rose from Times office boy to circulation director, a major post, in less than twenty-five years.

CHAPTER
47

THE FOUR-PAGE hand-set sheet that The Times founders launched in Nineteenth-Century New York has grown to the stage where, on some days, its output is nine to ten times greater than the combined circulation of the fifteen newspapers published in the city when The Times was born.

When the paper was new, Raymond's editors and reporters were limited in their communications to shanks' mare, a few wabbly railroads, an uncertain telegraph system and the horse and buggy. Times editors today have Paris, London, Bombay and Tokyo literally at their elbows through use of transocean wireless telephone as well as by radio and cable. Times men clear across the world can dictate their stories to automatic recorders without a second's loss in transmission. Radio teletypes chatter between the New York communications room and Times bureaus in remote capitals.

Because The Times has won universal recognition as a newspaper of record, it is in demand in many forms—full size in bound newsprint, in rag paper for better preservation, on tiny microfilm where a full page is reduced to a little more than one inch. Libraries, parliaments, great business houses all over the world subscribe for it in these forms. The semi-monthly New York Times Index for quick reference to the newspaper's contents, and an annual index that runs to some 1,500 pages, are also available.

Raymond had only the infant railroads, handcarts and the horse and wagon to distribute his four-page issues. The Times today moves by mail, by hurtling special trains, by ship and by ocean-spanning plane at a cost to the newspaper's owners of more than $6,000,000 a year. It is in subscribers' hands, even in the most distant corners of the earth, before its contents can go stale. Storms, floods and reverberating human conflicts do not stay it on its rounds.

The Times International Air Edition, born of the overseas Weekly, is printed in Paris from stereotyped matrixes flown across the Atlantic in from seventeen to eighteen hours. Copies printed in the newspaper's own New York plant are on their way to Central America and to South America almost before the printers who put them together are in their beds in the city on the Hudson. They are at many of their destinations before the printers and pressmen are back in Forty-third Street to get out the next issue.

The newspaper's advertising linage has kept pace with the institution's physical growth and with its enhanced prestige. In 1950 its total advertising was the greatest in its history. The cost of maintenance and operation has swelled, too, so that the net profit is less than in Ochs' day, but this has not weakened the management's determination to hold firmly to basic policy—to keep printing "All the News That's Fit to Print."

Wherever men meet for peaceful purpose or in war, Times representatives stand by as observers, in greater numbers now than at any other period in the newspaper's century of public service. Two of its men, Burton Crane and Harold Faber, were wounded in Korea. As they were invalided home, other Times men flew out of New York and across the Pacific to replace them. So it goes, without end. The great news events of the last five years are too fresh in most minds to be recorded here, but The Times reported them in abundant detail—the global war that has not ended, the peace that receded before men could warm themselves a while in its glow, the struggle to perfect the United Nations organization, great social and economic change, awesome advances in science, the titantic conflict between two vastly different ways of life.

Through it all, Times men are still guided by the text that gleams from the walls of the new lobby in the plant west of Times Square, above the bronze bust of Adolph Ochs, softly spotlighted in a lobby recess:

"TO GIVE THE NEWS IMPARTIALLY,
WITHOUT FEAR OR FAVOR,
REGARDLESS OF ANY PARTY,
SECT OR INTEREST INVOLVED."

On a lobby wall, in other golden letters, Times men hurrying to and from assignments see the journalistic philosophy of Ochs' successor:

"EVERY DAY IS A FRESH BEGINNING—
EVERY MORN IS THE WORLD MADE NEW."

And somewhere in an inner chamber hangs one of the most recent tributes to a newspaper that has lived up to its public responsibility for a full one hundred years. It is a citation presented to The Times on May 14, 1951, by the Society of the Silurians which is made up of editors and reporters who have served on various journals in New York for twenty-five years, or more. It says:

To THE NEW YORK TIMES
a Great American Newspaper
1851–1951

Learned, but not pedantic; objective, but never indifferent; detailed and painstaking, but not dull; powerful, but never oppressive; devoted to truth, but not intolerant; forthright in politics, but rarely partisan; world-wide in vision, coverage and influence, but always American.

Respected, vigorous, steadily growing in usefulness; clear-eyed observer of social progress; advocate of alert citizenship and conscience in government.

Old enough to have recorded the election of Franklin Pierce; youthful enough to report with enterprise and clarity the arrival of the Atomic Age.

On your One Hundredth Anniversary we, veteran New York newspapermen, salute you for your Century of Achievement. May you continue for generations to come to maintain those standards which have made your name synonymous with accuracy, objectivity and character in the newspaper world.

APPENDIX
I

FOLLOWING is a list of Pulitzer awards won by The Times and members of its staff:

1918—The New York Times—its entire news staff—"for the most disinterested and meritorious public service rendered by an American newspaper"—complete and accurate coverage of the news of the war.

1923—Alva Johnston, for distinguished reporting of scientific news.

1926—Edward M. Kingsbury, for the most distinguished editorial of the year, on the Hundred Neediest Cases.

1930—Russell Owen, for graphic news dispatches from the Byrd Antarctic Expedition.

1932—Walter Duranty, for dispassionate, interpretative reporting of the news from Russia.

1934—Frederick T. Birchall, for unbiased reporting of the news from Germany.

1935—Arthur Krock, for impartial and analytical coverage of Washington news.

1936—Lauren D. Lyman, for a world beat on the departure of the Lindberghs for England.

1937—Anne O'Hare McCormick, for distinguished dispatches and special articles from Europe.

1937—William L. Laurence, for distinguished reporting of the Tercentenary Celebration at Harvard, shared with four other reporters.

1938—Arthur Krock, for distinguished Washington correspondence.

1940—Otto D. Tolischus, for articles from Berlin explaining the economic and ideological background of war-engaged Germany.

1941—The New York Times, special citation "for the public education value of its foreign news report, exemplified by its scope, by excellence of writing, presentation and supplementary background information, illustration, and interpretation."

1942—Louis Stark, for distinguished reporting of important labor stories.

1943—Hanson W. Baldwin, for a series of articles reporting a tour of the Pacific battle areas.

1944—The New York Times, for the most disinterested and meritorious service rendered by an American newspaper, a survey of the teaching of American history.

1945—James Reston, for news dispatches and interpretative articles on the Dumbarton Oaks Security Conference.

1946—Arnaldo Cortesi, for distinguished correspondence from Buenos Aires.

1946—William L. Laurence, for his eyewitness account of the atomic bombing of Nagasaki and articles on the atom bomb.

1947—Brooks Atkinson, for a distinguished series of articles on Russia.

1949—Charles P. Trussell, for consistent excellence in covering the national scene from Washington.

1950—Meyer Berger, for a distinguished example of local reporting.

1951—Special citations for Arthur Krock and for Cyrus L. Sulzberger: to Krock for an "outstanding instance of national reporting," the exclusive interview with President Truman; to Sulzberger for an exclusive interview with Archbishop Aloysius Stepinac. Both these were outside the regular Pulitzer awards.

Six times in the twenty years that the F. Wayland Ayer Cup for Typography has been offered The Times won first honors for a major newspaper—in 1933, 1935, 1940, 1942, 1949, 1950.

It won Honorable Mention in the Ayer Cup competitions in 1933, 1935, 1936, 1938, 1939, 1941, 1943, 1945, 1947.

APPENDIX
II

APPENDED are advertising and circulation tables covering The Times' past fifty-five years. Earlier tables were not available:

Average Net Paid Circulation and Total Advertising of
The New York Times
(1896–1949)

Year	CIRCULATION Weekdays	Sunday	ADVERTISING LINAGE Weekdays	Sunday	Total
1896	21,516 *	22,000			2,227,196
1897	22,456	28,071			2,408,247
1898	25,726	34,041			2,433,193
1899	76,260	40,210			3,378,750
1900	82,106	39,204			3,978,620
1901	102,472	38,743			4,957,205
1902	100,738	48,354			5,501,779
1903	101,559	46,681	4,214,157	993,807	5,207,964
1904	109,770	46,991	4,393,531	834,949	5,228,480
1905	116,629	54,795	4,825,538	1,132,784	5,958,322
1906	124,267	59,511	4,917,994	1,115,463	6,033,457
1907	133,067	71,330	4,853,682	1,450,616	6,304,298
1908	158,692	86,779	4,388,870	1,508,462	5,897,332
1909	171,653	100,278	5,185,767	2,008,936	7,194,703
1910	178,708	113,325	5,419,854	2,130,796	7,550,650
1911	187,018	128,085	5,522,914	2,607,511	8,130,425
1912	220,139	158,539	5,946,449	2,898,417	8,844,866
1913	242,624	180,143	5,973,099	3,354,270	9,327,369

* Though more than 21,000 papers were printed daily in early 1896, Ochs found, when he took over, that actual paid circulation came to only 9,000.

| Year | CIRCULATION | | ADVERTISING LINAGE | | Total |
	Weekdays	Sunday	Weekdays	Sunday	
1914	270,113	231,409	5,695,139	3,469,788	9,164,927
1915	313,391	344,015	6,003,803	3,678,759	9,682,562
1916	331,918	377,095	6,787,133	4,765,363	11,552,496
1917	344,585	414,202	7,467,376	5,042,211	12,509,587
1918	352,980	486,933	8,087,604	5,430,651	13,518,255
1919	341,559	510,311	12,188,974	7,493,588	19,682,562
1920	323,489	486,569	14,196,749	9,250,646	23,447,395
1921	330,802	511,731	13,161,937	8,490,676	21,652,613
1922	336,000	525,794	14,719,486	9,422,736	24,142,222
1923	337,427	546,497	14,617,646	9,483,580	24,101,226
1924	351,576	580,745	15,977,696	10,306,228	26,283,924
1925	352,655	588,699	16,914,730	11,285,714	28,200,444
1926	361,271	610,053	17,596,682	12,192,146	29,788,828
1927	391,497	666,235	17,783,297	11,927,309	29,710,606
1928	422,745	714,638	19,073,948	11,662,582	30,736,530
1929	431,931	728,909	20,198,004	11,964,866	32,162,870
1930	429,275	741,410	18,652,929	7,700,352	26,353,281
1931	461,884	754,914	17,084,058	7,318,854	24,402,912
1932	461,243	749,727	10,827,064	7,299,933	18,126,997
1933	466,708	729,493	9,877,707	7,421,586	17,299,293
1934	462,861	712,881	10,816,850	7,561,502	18,378,352
1935	465,078	713,259	11,126,209	8,294,760	19,420,969
1936	492,056	746,531	12,347,209	9,408,605	21,755,814
1937	526,978	769,482	12,256,212	9,808,153	22,064,365
1938	509,857	775,439	11,198,764	9,621,917	20,820,681
1939	485,036	812,142	11,336,071	9,726,525	21,062,596
1940	479,723	819,943	11,375,444	9,819,625	21,195,069
1941	459,346	809,163	11,113,383	10,230,498	21,343,881
1942	447,429	820,382	11,125,922	10,176,210	21,302,132
1943	423,912	823,442	12,842,736	10,844,935	23,687,671
1944	453,608	814,905	11,215,103	9,556,172	20,771,275
1945	525,317	844,711	11,122,563	8,504,053	19,626,616
1946	544,460	995,792	16,285,191	12,216,300	28,501,491
1947	548,281	1,114,571	17,882,862	15,173,348	33,056,210
1948	539,158	1,106,153	18,198,936	16,874,482	35,073,418
1949	546,021	1,134,460	18,018,080	18,071,656	36,089,736
1950	523,446	1,137,325	19,443,044	20,131,327	39,574,371

APPENDIX
III

A WAY OF LIFE*

THOUGH the United States has lived for two years under a Neutrality Act which expresses its wish to remain at peace, the American people are not neutral now in any situation which involves the risk of war, nor will they remain neutral in any future situation which threatens to disturb the balance of world power.

American opinion today is openly and overwhelmingly on the side of China as against Japan: so openly and so overwhelmingly, that it has winked at and approved a flagrant violation of the whole spirit of the Neutrality Act by the Roosevelt Administration and forced Congress itself to give tacit consent to the deliberate nullification of that law. American opinion was just as definitely aligned against the seizure of Austria by force of German arms. It is as nearly unanimous today as it has ever been, in any question of foreign policy, in applauding the determination of a small country in Central Europe—Czechoslovakia—to stand up for its rights as a sovereign nation and to fight for its independence, if need be, instead of tamely going under. It will be just as nearly unanimous tomorrow and the day after tomorrow, whenever and wherever something that comes home to the inbred American conception of liberty and democracy is at stake.

The truth is that no act of Congress can conscript the underlying loyalties of the American people. These loyalties have in the past prevailed and may prevail again even over our desire to remain at peace. Statesmen abroad who fail to reckon with this fact because they are

*Editorial in The New York Times, June 15, 1938.

571

impressed by what the Neutrality Act may say about cannon and high explosives and long-term loans and short-term loans, or because they think that the United States lies at too great a distance from the scenes of potential conflict in Europe to be interested in the points at issue, enormously miscalculate a well-established American habit of choosing sides the moment any issue basic to this country's faith is actually involved.

II

IN THE CASE of China's fight for self-existence against Japanese aggression, American sentiment is tapped by loyalties which come readily to the surface. We sympathize instinctively with the underdog. We cherish a special and long-standing friendship with the Chinese people. We resent the ruthlessness of Japan's attack. We are not ashamed of a frank commercial interest in desiring the continuation of the Open Door.

These considerations are responsible for the fact that American opinion has willingly supported Mr. Roosevelt in the maintenance of the elaborate fraud that no "war" exists today on the continent of Asia— since a finding that "war" is actually in progress would compel us to invoke sections of the Neutrality Act which would react to the disadvantage of China as against Japan.

This is the first consequence of American un-neutrality in the Far East. But something more decisive in the long run than nullification of the Neutrality Act is involved in our choice of sides in this dispute. We have cast our influence, in advance of an ultimate decision on the soil of China, against any possibility that Japan will profit from this adventure with our approval and support. We will not recognize as valid Japan's claim to one square foot of Chinese territory conquered by force of arms. We will not facilitate, through such recognition, the development of a new code of property rights which would encourage the investment of foreign capital. We will not permit our own capital to go to the aid of Japan in making her conquest a paying venture. The American banker or the American industrialist who dared to propose American participation in any plan to develop the resources of China under Japanese administration would find the opinion of this country overwhelmingly against him.

III

To THAT extent, at least, we have aligned ourselves with China in her present struggle. To that extent, and more, we are partisans in Europe; for in Europe we find not only the issue raised by imperialism running wild, but also the issue of dictatorship against our own democracy.

What is Czechoslovakia? For most Americans, a spot of color on a map of Central Europe, a toy country made of the broken bits of an old empire. But also, for most Americans, a country now revealed as a frontier on which men are prepared to fight for the traditions of democracy; for the right to think as they please and to vote as they please; for the right to worship in their own way; for the right to walk the streets as free men who are equals of those who sit in the seats of power; for the right to be secure against arbitrary power, against the verdict of the drumhead court and the dry rot of the concentration camp; for the right to live under a system of government deriving its just powers from the consent of the governed; for the right to follow, according to their own lights and without permission of a ruling clique, the pursuit of liberty as they have known it and of happiness as they have hoped to find it.

The average American may not define in words the loyalties he shares with certain other people. But in the democracies of Europe—in the little democracies in the danger zones; in the more fortunate democracies of France and Britain—the average American finds a way of life which he knows instinctively to be the way of life which he himself has chosen.

He knows that these democracies are the outposts of our own kind of civilization, of the democratic system, of the progress we have achieved through other methods of self-government and of the progress we still hope to make tomorrow. He knows that if these outposts are overrun by dictatorships of either Right or Left we shall find ourselves deprived of friends. He knows that, despite geographical remoteness and a traditional desire to avoid entanglement in other peoples' quarrels, we are inevitably the natural allies of the democracies of Europe.

IV

THE VAST power of the United States is not used effectively today in defense of international democracy because the American people do not wish to commit themselves in advance to any policy which involves even a potential risk of war. We have adopted a Neutrality Act not primarily because we are at heart a neutral people—our whole history belies that designation—but because we detest war, dread its human cost and fear the consequences it might have for our own democratic institutions. With the other democracies we have trapped ourselves in a paradoxical situation in which our desire for peace is so evident that the aggressor nations are encouraged to resort to acts which bring closer the very war we fear.

It is evident that some of the sponsors of the American Neutrality Act are themselves dissatisfied with the way that law has worked in practice. Criticism of it has been expressed on the floor of Congress at the present session. There is reason to believe that this criticism will increase, and that an effort to repeal the law will be undertaken and will succeed in reaching its objective when Congress reconvenes. Certainly that result is greatly to be desired, not only because it would liberate the foreign policy of the United States from the effects of a law which attempts to prescribe a fixed course of action in every possible emergency, regardless of when and where and how that emergency may arise and what its effect on our own interests may be, but also because repeal of the law would at least permit the material resources of the United States to count on the side of international law and order. Britain and France would be in a stronger position to resist aggression and to counsel peace in Central Europe if their hands were strengthened by the ability to purchase in this country, in the event of war, the materials to which they have access through their command of the Atlantic.

Beyond repeal of the Neutrality Act, however, no early change is likely in American policy. There is no reason to believe that the American people will agree at any time in the near future to be bound by commitments to help maintain world peace. Such commitments are not in the tradition of our foreign policy, and the tradition changes slowly. But the aggressor nations will make a mistake if they assume from our willingness to pledge ourselves to a specific course of action that it is safe to leave us out of their calculations. We shall be fully prepared, if war on a large scale envelops Europe, to choose the side of the democracies.

That will mean, at the very least, what it meant in the years from 1914 to 1916: an immense moral support which cannot be regarded as an unimportant factor in the winning of a modern war, and a deliberate policy of favoring our friends in the interpretation of laws which control our relations with other countries and of traditions which govern our policies on the high seas. At most it will mean, as it meant in 1917, a decision on the part of the United States to intervene.

On two occasions during our history as an independent nation a "world war" has been fought. We were drawn into both those wars, not because a small group of bankers and munitions-makers willed our participation, but because a point had been reached at which American interests were so deeply involved that it was no longer tolerable even for a peace-loving nation to remain at peace.

It is important that the statesmen of aggressor countries should realize that today, no less than in 1917, there are specific and vital American interests in all parts of the world which would almost certainly be affected by war on a large scale. It is important that they should realize the real depth of American loyalty to the whole set of principles and methods and traditions which goes by the name of democracy.

No remoteness from the scene of a potential European conflict can isolate the United States from the consequences of a major war. No Neutrality Act can prevent the American people from favoring their natural allies. In any ultimate test of strength between democracy and dictatorship, the good will and the moral support—and in the long run more likely than not the physical power of the United States—will be found on the side of those nations defending a way of life which is our own way of life and the only way of life which Americans believe to be worth living.

Index